INTERNATIONAL MARKETING

DANIEL W. BAACK | ERIC G. HARRIS | DONALD BAACK

INTERNATIONAL MARKETING

DANIEL W. BAACK | ERIC G. HARRIS | DONALD BAACK

PUT THE *i* IN YOUR *i*NTERNATIONAL MARKETING COURSE

*i*NTEGRATED

*i*NFORMATIVE

*i*NSPIRING QUOTES

*i*NNOVATIVE

*i*NDISPENSABLE

*i*NCREDIBLE VALUE

*i*NTEGRATED ILLUSTRATIONS & MAPS

Integrated illustrations demonstrate how five key international business factors interact with the 4 Ps.

Integrated maps expose students to global locations.

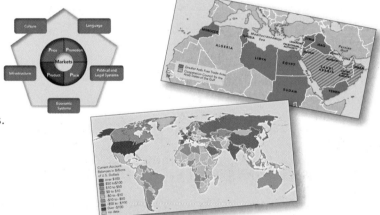

International Marketing in Daily Life

*i*NNOVATIVE REAL-WORLD APPLICATIONS

Innovative and thought-provoking **International Incident** features encourage critical thinking and class discussion.

International Marketing in Daily Life features help students apply marketing concepts to everyday life.

*i*NFORMATIVE CASES

Informative end-of-chapter **brief cases** cover key topics, including sustainability and bottom-of-the-pyramid issues. Six end-of-text **comprehensive cases** provide even more flexibility to your course.

CASE 10 ///

Microfinance and Bottom-of-the-Pyramid Consumers

For most consumers in developing countries, credit is an afterthought, an easily accessible component of making a purchase. Certainly credit scores are tracked and access to credit can be limited for individuals with a bankruptcy or foreclosure. Still, for the majority of consumers, the next loan is the swipe of a credit card away.

Photo 10.7: **Manual labor**
Obtaining credit is difficult for bottom-of-the-pyramid consumers in developing markets.

Women are more likely to repay loans, which makes them the target market for the majority of

¡NDISPENSABLE ONLINE RESOURCES

Indispensable online resources for the instructor

Password-protected resources at
www.sagepub.com/baack include:

- **Author-created** test bank available electronically and in Microsoft Word, with approximately 100 test questions for each chapter.
- **Author-created** PowerPoint® slides highlight essential content and features from the text
- Class assignments and answers to in-text questions
- Full-text SAGE journal articles, carefully selected for each chapter
- Video links with questions for discussion, sample syllabi, and country fact sheets

Interactive online engagement for students

See the inside back cover of this text for details and description of the free, open-access, interactive Student Study Site!

¡NSPIRING QUOTES

Reviewers say we are INTEGRATED, FRESH, REAL-WORLD, RELEVANT and GROUND-BREAKING

> ***"Who said that textbooks are boring?*** *This is one of the few textbooks written that is* **comprehensive,** *interesting, and* **ground-breaking."**

—John Hadjimarcou, University of Texas, El Paso

> *"The single most impressive aspect is a **fresh** approach! It is really nice to see the **integration** amongst topics."*

—Melissa Malabad, Mary Baldwin College

> *"This is not an international business text with marketing stuff in it. . . . It resembles the textbook that I have wanted to adopt but have not seen . . ."*

—Brent Smith, Saint Joseph's University

> *". . . there are more **real-world** examples in this text . . . **relevant** and **refreshing.**"*

—John Gironda, Florida Atlantic University

¡NCREDIBLE VALUE

What do your students pay for their current International Marketing text?

International Marketing by Daniel W. Baack, Eric G. Harris, and Donald Baack costs students a minimum of $100 less than any of the four best-selling International Marketing texts!

INTERNATIONAL MARKETING

I dedicate this book to my parents, my wife, and especially to my grandmother Pauline Burns. The support she has provided me the past thirty-five years has been invaluable. Thanks, Nana.

—Daniel W. Baack

I dedicate this book to my parents, my wife, and my kids. For all the love and support, thanks to you all.

—Eric G. Harris

My efforts on this book are dedicated to my brothers: Steve Kepford, who has been a constant source of inspiration, and Drew (Charles) and Landis Burns, who welcomed me as family from the beginning.

—Donald Baack

INTERNATIONAL MARKETING

DANIEL W. BAACK | **ERIC G. HARRIS** | **DONALD BAACK**

University of Denver | *Pittsburg State University* | *Pittsburg State University*

Los Angeles | London | New Delhi
Singapore | Washington DC

Los Angeles | London | New Delhi
Singapore | Washington DC

FOR INFORMATION:

SAGE Publications, Inc.
2455 Teller Road
Thousand Oaks, California 91320
E-mail: order@sagepub.com

SAGE Publications Ltd.
1 Oliver's Yard
55 City Road
London EC1Y 1SP
United Kingdom

SAGE Publications India Pvt. Ltd.
B 1/I 1 Mohan Cooperative Industrial Area
Mathura Road, New Delhi 110 044
India

SAGE Publications Asia-Pacific Pte. Ltd.
33 Pekin Street #02-01
Far East Square
Singapore 048763

Acquisitions Editor: Patricia Quinlin
Associate Editor: Maggie Stanley
Assistant Editor: Theresa Accomazzo
Editorial Assistant: Katie Guarino
Production Editor: Eric Garner
Copy Editor: Alison Hope
Typesetter: C&M Digitals (P) Ltd.
Proofreader: Theresa Kay
Indexer: Sheila Bodell
Cover Designer: Michael Dubowe
Marketing Manager: Michelle Rodgerson
Permissions Editor: Adele Hutchinson

Copyright © 2013 by SAGE Publications, Inc.

Printed in Canada

Library of Congress Cataloging-in-Publication Data

Baack, Daniel W.

International marketing / Daniel W. Baack, Eric G. Harris, Donald Baack.

p. cm.
Includes bibliographical references and index.

ISBN 978-1-4522-2635-4 (cloth)

1. Export marketing. I. Harris, Eric G. II. Baack, Donald. III. Title.

HF1416.B32 2013
658.8'4—dc23   2011049049

This book is printed on acid-free paper.

12 13 14 15 16 10 9 8 7 6 5 4 3 2 1

Brief Contents

Detailed Contents

Chapter 2. Country Selection and Entry Strategies   **36**

Chapter 3. Global Trade and Integration

PART II. INTERNATIONAL MARKETS AND MARKET RESEARCH   113

Chapter 4. Markets and Segmentation in an International Context   114

Chapter 5. International Positioning 156

Chapter 6. Market Research in the International Environment   190

PART III. INTERNATIONAL PRODUCT MARKETING

Chapter 8. International Product Standardization and Adaptation   **262**

PART IV. INTERNATIONAL PRICING AND FINANCE   297

Chapter 9. International Pricing   298

PART VI. INTERNATIONAL PROMOTION AND PERSONAL SELLING   439

Chapter 13. Globally Integrated Marketing Communications   440

Chapter 14. International Sales Promotions and Public Relations

Chapter 16. International Marketing Planning, Organization, and Control   548

Preface

"Marketing is marketing, no matter where you are. There is still a marketing mix. The focus continues to be on creating value for customers and building relationships with them. It just becomes a great deal more complicated when you operate on an international scale." This observation by a noted international marketing instructor succinctly summarizes the challenges international marketers face. Globalization, technological advances, economic upheaval, political shifts, and cultural trends are transforming society at an escalating rate. In this ever-changing global environment, the field of marketing must continually adapt to remain on the cutting edge.

Communicating the complexities and nuances of marketing on an international scale in a single course can be a daunting task for instructors. Students taking this course also face a unique set of obstacles. We believe many international marketing textbooks currently available complicate these challenges by focusing too much on international business in the first portion of the book and then introducing marketing topics later on. Instead of segregating the two topics, we concluded that a better approach would be to present marketing in an international context. We wrote this book out of our desire to help resolve some of the issues confronting both students and professors.

Market and Course

The textbook is for undergraduate courses in international marketing. It also can be used in undergraduate international business courses and in topical international marketing courses at the MBA level.

Instructor Challenges

The international marketing course is typically taught by either a marketing instructor or a business instructor. Marketing instructors, including Daniel Baack, the lead author on this book, often find the standard international marketing textbook to be fairly daunting, especially the opening chapters, which are typically packed with international business concepts. The pages are filled with charts, tables, and statistics that can overwhelm the reader. This group of instructors may be inclined to gloss over these topics and move quickly to the more standard marketing materials presented. When international business instructors teach the course, they may be more inclined to focus on international business concepts and are tempted to cover marketing material in less depth.

In essence, neither the needs of the marketing instructor nor the needs of the business instructor are met by the currently available textbooks. Our book utilizes an integrated framework designed to cover both the international business and the marketing concepts found in traditional international marketing textbooks in a new and integrated way, meeting the wants of both types of instructors.

Student Challenges

Students encounter several major challenges when taking an international marketing course. First, many students will have been exposed to only one of two topics areas. Some students may have already taken international business courses but have had little exposure to marketing. Other students may have backgrounds in marketing but an international marketing course might be their first and only exposure to international business. In essence, students taking this course may have little experience in marketing, international business, or both. We have endeavored to present the material in a manner that engages and reaches all three groups of students.

To assist students in learning the concepts, each chapter opens with a figure that integrates five key international business elements with the main elements in marketing. The figure provides students with a visual illustration of the connections between the marketing elements presented in the chapter with the most closely associated international business issues.

Some students may struggle when trying to integrate marketing concepts with international business concepts. The textbooks that begin with an overview of international business and then discuss marketing may worsen this problem by segregating the two topics and diluting the marketing focus. To help overcome this obstacle to learning, we outline the differences and similarities in domestic and foreign markets while maintaining a strong focus on core marketing concepts. This assists in understanding how to conceptualize the international marketing process.

The third complication some students face can be either ethnocentrism or a degree of naïveté. We try to overcome these impediments to learning with careful attention to the nature of culture and the cultural nuances of countries around the world. Our goal is to expand student awareness and understanding along with acceptance and appreciation of business practices in other parts of the world. We have created features and selected photographs designed to help students engage more deeply with the chapter materials. The International Incident boxes challenge students to make ethical or cultural decisions in international situations. The International Marketing in Daily Life boxes reveal how products they use in their everyday lives are impacted by global marketing.

Our Approach

We have backgrounds in marketing, international business, brand management, consumer behavior, market research, management, and marketing communications. We hope our academic and professional experiences and areas of expertise helped us to design a textbook that provides an important and fresh contribution to the field of international marketing. There are several primary differences and advantages between our book and the books currently available: core marketing concepts are integrated with international business principles, an emphasis on bottom-of-the-pyramid markets, and the incorporation of sustainability concepts.

INTEGRATED APPROACH

As noted, in this book we utilize an integrated framework that combines marketing concepts and international business concepts. This integrated approach was designed to ameliorate the challenges that students and instructors face. To do so, five key international business principles are defined in the opening chapter of the text:

- cultural differences
- language differences
- political and legal differences
- economic differences
- technological/operational differences

These concepts are placed into a figure along with the five key marketing elements: markets, products, prices, distribution (place), and promotion. The figure reappears in each chapter, noting when each will be given special emphasis as the topics are presented. Next the text moves directly into the primary marketing areas (markets and the 4 Ps) and concludes with operational, organizational, and managerial issues. International business concepts are presented in depth at points in which they have the greatest value in demonstrating international marketing concepts.

BOTTOM-OF-THE-PYRAMID

One major international target market consists of individuals who earn less than $2 per day. The bottom-of-the-pyramid segment is large and increasingly relevant to international marketing scholars and practitioners. The relatively untapped nature of the market appeals to many international companies. We argue that targeting this group of 4 billion people is viable and could lead to more efficient processing and innovations. We have incorporated issues associated with reaching this group in each chapter throughout the book.

SUSTAINABILITY

Sustainable business practices are of growing significance. Many students express strong interests in the topic. Sustainability issues are noted in the text, in various chapter-opening vignettes, and in end-of-chapter cases. We also link sustainability to bottom-of-the-pyramid marketing because these two crucial forces have generated a dramatic impact on globalization and international marketing programs. Successfully targeting the bottom-of-the-pyramid segment often necessitates the incorporation of business practices that emphasize sustainability. The synthesis of these themes provides a rich context for the exploration of international marketing concepts.

Features

To help students think critically about the concepts and principles provided throughout the text, we developed a series of features designed to reinforce learning and help maintain reader interest.

OPENING VIGNETTES

The chapters begin with presentations about companies with an international marketing presence or about widely-used products such as aspirin and fruit. Each vignette effectively sets the stage for the chapter material. Three questions then are posed to help students reflect on the company and prepare them to read about and discuss the issues that follow in the chapter materials.

INTERNATIONAL INCIDENTS

Each chapter contains brief boxes that describe an unusual event or challenge that arises in a specific international setting. Each hypothetical scenario is accompanied by discussion questions in a "What would you do?" type of approach. This helps foster critical thinking and prepares students for situations that will come up as they work in a global economy.

INTERNATIONAL MARKETING IN DAILY LIFE

Throughout the text, we note that many international marketing efforts deal with products that are not "sexy" or high-tech. In fact, items as mundane as toothbrushes, headache remedies, and toilets represent approachable markets for international companies. The incorporation of these products as illustrations helps explain how marketing works on a global scale when seeking to sell everyday life products, recognizing that the same concepts often apply to more glamorous and sophisticated items.

STRATEGIC, TACTICAL, AND OPERATIONAL IMPLICATIONS

This book does not provide the standard summary section at the end of each chapter. Instead, each chapter's materials will be reviewed under three headings: Strategic Implications, Tactical Implications, and Operational Implications. Strategic implications allow students to a integrate materials at the conceptual level, typically at the level of decision making directed by a company's CEO and top management teams. Tactical implications link strategic concepts to the various marketing functions, such as advertising, personal selling, and creating promotions. Operational implications explain the practical implementation of the various international marketing tools at the individual level, such as how a program might affect an individual salesperson in a retail store. This approach not only summarizes the materials but also integrates analytical thinking with actual marketing practices.

END-OF-CHAPTER RESOURCES

We created end-of-chapter resources for several reasons. We wanted to give students the opportunity to assess their understanding of the chapter, apply ideas and concepts in various settings, use mathematical and statistical methods when applicable, generate discussion, and analyze a case. Each chapter concludes with the following:

Terms. Each bolded key term defined in the text is presented in the same order each appears in the chapter to help students both review the chapter and reexamine the terms to make sure they understand them.

Review Questions. Brief questions were written for each chapter to help students quickly summarize and test their comprehension of what they have read in the chapter. These questions appear in the order that chapter concepts have been presented and are designed to highlight and test the primary points, concepts, and definitions addressed in the chapter.

Discussion Questions. These items can be used for individual analyses of marketing management concepts or to guide in-class conversations. Some of the questions require students to apply the mathematical and statistical models and formulas they have learned about in the chapters.

Analytical and Internet Exercises. Completing these exercises provides students with the opportunity to apply what they have learned in the chapter. The items are often web-based assignments that challenge students to use their analytical skills.

Cases. Each chapter concludes with a brief case designed to illustrate the major concepts in the chapter. Case questions can be used for class discussion or completed as an assignment.

Comprehensive Cases. Six comprehensive cases provided at the end of the book spotlight various international companies. The cases are designed to challenge students' abilities. They require an in-depth analysis and synthesis of the case material with textbook material. The cases are also accompanied by questions that lead students to apply knowledge across multiple chapters.

BOOK DESIGN

We hope you agree that this book is visually exciting. Our thanks to Ryan Kuo from clearspace.tw for his willingness to share pictures from his many global travels. By incorporating photographs and advertisements from around the world, we believe the text comes alive. We hope the colorful and meaningful graphs, tables, and photos will appeal to the visual learner.

Ancillaries

FOR THE INSTRUCTOR

The password-protected **Instructor Teaching Site** available at **www.sagepub.com/baack** gives instructors access to a full complement of resources to support and enhance their course. The following assets are available on this site:

- An author-created **Test Bank** contains multiple-choice, true/false, short-answer, and essay questions for each chapter. The test bank is provided on the website in Word format as well as in an electronic format that can be exported into popular course management systems such as Blackboard or WebCT.

- The book's authors also developed **PowerPoint** slides for each chapter. They can be used for lecture and review. Slides are integrated with the book's distinctive features and incorporate key tables, figures, and photos.

- **Video Resources** vividly illustrate key information in each chapter. Video icons are strategically placed within the textbook to indicate where a video resource is available on the companion site. These links allow both instructors and students to access videos directly related to the content.

- Full-text **SAGE Journal Articles** accompany each chapter, providing extra commentary and analysis on important topics from SAGE's marketing journals.

- **Answers to End-of-Chapter and Discussion Questions** provide valuable tools for facilitating classroom discussions.

- Suggested **Class Assignments** offer instructors a wide range of group and individual activities designed to enhance student learning.

- **Learning Objectives and Chapter Outlines** from the book provide an essential teaching and reference tool.

- Sample **Course Syllabi** for quarter and semester systems include suggestions for structuring an international marketing course.

- **Country Fact Sheets** provide detailed information and unique facts about various countries highlighted in the text.

FOR THE STUDENT

The open-access **Student Study Site** available at **www.sagepub.com/baack** is designed to maximize student comprehension of international marketing and to promote critical thinking and application. The following resources and study tools are available on the student portion of this book's website:

- **Flashcards** reiterate key chapter terms and concepts.
- **Self-quizzes** include multiple-choice and true/false questions, allowing students to test their knowledge of each chapter.
- **Learning Objectives and Chapter Outlines** from the book provide an essential study tool.
- **Video Resources** vividly illustrate key information in each chapter. Video icons are strategically placed within the textbook to indicate where a video resource is available on the companion site. These links allow both instructor and student to access videos directly related to the content.
- Full-text **SAGE Journal Articles** accompany each chapter, providing extra commentary and analysis on important topics from SAGE's marketing journals.
- **Interactive Maps** allow students to increase their knowledge of geography and engage with course content in a dynamic and meaningful way.
- **Country Fact Sheets** provide detailed information and unique facts about various countries highlighted in the text.
- Guidelines for **Developing an International Marketing Plan** are included.

Acknowledgments

There are many persons who have assisted us in the development of this book. We would first like to acknowledge our executive editor Lisa Shaw for her tremendous support and enthusiasm. We are very grateful to Deya Saoud Jacob for her initial interest in signing this project and for her later editorial work. A special word of appreciation goes to Maggie Stanley for her assistance, as well as to Theresa Accomazzo. We would also like to thank Eric Garner and Pat Quinlan for their tremendous assistance in finalizing the book. We would also like to note the work of Helen Salmon with regard to marketing the book.

We would like to thank the following individuals who assisted in the preparation of the manuscript through their careful and thoughtful reviews:

Mark Young, Winona State University

Ruth Lesher Taylor, Texas State University

Yun Chu, Robert Morris University

Laurie Babin, University of Louisiana at Monroe

Brent Smith, Erivan Haub School of Business, St. Joseph's University

Douglas Hausknecht, University of Akron

John Gironda, Florida Atlantic University at Boca Raton

William Lesch, University of North Dakota

Eric C. Wittine, John Carroll University

Xueming Luo, University of Texas at Arlington

Nicholas Didow, University of North Carolina at Chapel Hill

Mark Burgess, Rider University

David Crain, Whittier College

Catherine E. N. Giunta, Seton Hill University

John Hadjimarcou, University of Texas at El Paso

Ron Lennon, University of South Florida at Tampa

Melissa Huffman Malabad, Mary Baldwin College

Mary Lee Stansifer, University of Colorado at Denver

Loy Watley, Nebraska Wesleyan University

Fekkri Meziou, Augsburg College

Ken Fairweather, Letourneau University

Finola Kerrigan, King's College, London

Robert A. Lupton, Central Washington University

Mark Mitchell, Coastal Carolina University

Ben Oumlil, Western Connecticut State University

Al Rosenbloom, Dominican University

Mee-Shew Cheung, Xavier University

Andrew C. Gross, Cleveland State University

Donald Hsu, Dominican College

George V. Priovolos, Hagan School of Business, Iona College

Finally, Daniel Baack would like to thank his father Donald for inviting him to work on this project. It has been memorable and enjoyable, and has led to much learning about writing. He will always be grateful for the opportunity to publish a book with his dad; it was a once-in-a-lifetime experience. Thanks also to Eric G. Harris for making this such an enjoyable process. Daniel would also like to thank his mother and grandmother for their support, as well as his three great kids, Andy, Emilee, and Jason. His close friends Jason, Dan, Ben, and Ed, and his brother David provided a valuable stress release throughout the process. His talented brother-in-law, Ryan (Chih-Kuo) Kuo, provided many of the wonderful pictures used in the book. Thanks to him, and Daniel's wife's family, for their support. The support of individuals at the University of Denver has also been invaluable, including Carol Johnson, Donald Bacon, and, of course, Gloria Valdez. His graduate assistant, Julia Mariano, provided key last minute contributions.

Eric G. Harris would like to thank both co-authors, Donald Baack and Daniel Baack, for their cooperation and for including him on this project. He would like to thank his two children, Christian and Sydney, for their patience and support. He would also like to thank Paula Palmer, administrative specialist, for her assistance with his many work assignments. Finally, he would like to thank his mentor, Dr. John Mowen, for his guidance throughout his career.

Donald Baack would like to thank his son Daniel for convincing him to make this journey. Eric and Dan made this an extremely enjoyable project. It has turned into a wonderful learning experience and resulted in some great times while completing the manuscript. He would also like to thank his graduate assistant, Matt Carr, and the office staff, including the student workers in his department at Pittsburg State University, for the help they have given. He would also like to acknowledge his other two children, Jessica and David, and his grandchildren, Rile, Danielle, Andy, Emilee, Jason, Tatum, Damon, Joe, and Tommy.

We would like to especially thank our wives, Yen-Wen Kuo, Tara Harris, and Pam Baack, for being patient and understanding during those times when the work seemed monumental. They have been wonderful partners to us over the years.

About the Authors

Daniel W. Baack is an assistant professor of marketing and director of the Integrated Marketing Communications Program at the Daniels College of Business at the University of Denver. Previous positions include Ball State University and Saint Louis University, where Professor Baack received his Ph.D. in international business and marketing.

Professor Baack has published academic research in the *Journal of Advertising, Journal of Advertising Research, Journal of International Management, European Journal of Marketing, Journal of Business Research, International Business Review, Journal of Product and Brand Management, International Journal of Commerce and Management, Journal of Electronic Commerce Research,* and the *International Journal of Emerging Markets*. He serves on the editorial board of the *Journal of Promotion Management*.

Professor Baack is an active member of the Academy of International Business, having attended all but one conference since 2003. When not writing or traveling internationally, Professor Baack stays busy with his Taiwanese wife and their three joint ventures (or children). He also enjoys playing and watching basketball, particularly while in foreign countries.

Eric G. Harris is chair and associate professor in the Department of Management and Marketing at Pittsburg State University. He has also served on the faculty at the University of South Florida. He has B.B.A. and M.B.A. degrees from Pittsburg State University, and a Ph.D. in marketing from Oklahoma State University.

Dr. Harris's academic work has appeared in journals such as *Journal of the Academy of Marketing Science, Journal of Advertising, Journal of Business Research, Psychology & Marketing, Journal of Personal Selling & Sales Management, Journal of Services Marketing, Journal of Business & Psychology, Journal of Consumer Marketing,* and others. He has also contributed to the *Wiley International Encyclopedia of Marketing*. He also serves on the editorial review boards for *Journal of Business Research, Journal of Marketing Theory and Practice, Journal of Services Marketing,* and *Services Marketing Quarterly*, and also serves as a consulting editor for the *Journal of Managerial Issues*.

In addition to *International Marketing*, Dr. Harris has also published *CB "Consumer Behavior" with Cengage Learning* (4LTR Press), which is co-authored with Barry

Babin. He is affiliated with a number of professional associations, including American Marketing Association, The Academy of Marketing Science, Society of Marketing Advances, and Marketing Management Association, and others.

Donald Baack holds the rank of university professor of management at Pittsburg (Kansas) State University. He previously held positions at Southwest Missouri State University, Missouri Southern State College, and Dana College. Baack received his Ph.D. from the University of Nebraska.

Professor Baack is a consulting editor and has published in the *Journal of Managerial Issues*. He has also published in the *Journal of Advertising Research, Journal of Euromarketing, Journal of Nonprofit and Public Sector Marketing, Journal of Customer Service in Marketing, Journal of Professional Services Marketing, Journal of Ministry Marketing and Management, Journal of Business Ethics, Journal of Global Awareness, Human Relations,* and *Journal of Management Inquiry*.

Dr. Baack has authored *International Business* (Glencoe/McGraw-Hill) and *Organizational Behavior* (Dame). He co-authored *Integrated Advertising, Promotion, and Marketing Communications* (Prentice Hall), *Marketing Management* (Sage), and *The Concise Encyclopedia of Advertising* (Haworth) with Kenneth D. Clow. He also has published three popular press books in the area of romance/self-help.

Baack has been active in the Southwest Academy of Management. He was nominated for SWAM's Distinguished Educator award in 2007, 2008, and 2010. He has been recognized as a Distinguished Alumnus at Lincoln (Nebraska) East High School and by Dana College.

PART I
Essentials of International Marketing

1

Introduction to International Marketing

After reading and studying this chapter, you should be able to answer the following questions:

1. What are the meanings of the terms multinational corporation, born-global, home country, and host country?

2. What are the essential ingredients in the marketing mix as they relate to international markets, needs, and wants?

3. How have the drivers of globalization influenced international marketing?

4. How are the factors that create international marketing complexity linked to creating a global mindset for marketing activities?

5. Why are the concepts of sustainability and bottom-of-the-pyramid consumers linked to today's international marketplace?

IN THIS CHAPTER

Facebook.com: Global Marketing Opportunities and Connectivity

VIDEO LINK 1.1:
Facebook's Impact

What online community signs up 700,000 new members each day? The answer—Facebook.com. The Facebook community included 750 million followers by mid-2011.[1] The founder, Mark Zuckerberg, was named *Time* magazine's "Person of the Year" in 2010.

The statistics associated with Facebook take on nearly epic proportions. If Facebook users in January 2011 were members of a country, that nation would have the third highest population in the world, with only China and India ahead. One out of every twelve people on the planet has a Facebook account. And, in the world of Internet hits, one out of every four page views in the United States occurs on the Facebook site. Facebook has caused some dramatic shifts in everyday life, the core of which are new cultural patterns of interpersonal interactions. Marketing professionals have quickly moved into this realm along with the companies they serve.[2]

Many users around the world are familiar with the former Facebook.com opening page. As shown in the photo on page 5, the screen prominently displays the Facebook logo, an important element of its international marketing presence. To maintain interest, the content of the opening photos rotates, giving the website an evolving visual presence. Also, by being user-friendly, the site encourages visitors to try the product. The effective use of the blue, light grey, and white background creates an appealing but simple opening page. The images fit well with the core selling points of the product.

The history of Facebook begins with a nineteen-year-old sophomore attending Harvard University early in the twenty-first century. Zuckerberg built a web service in his dorm to create "an online directory that connects people through social networks at college." In less than a decade, the company grew to the size it now enjoys, dwarfing all other social media, and making Zuckerberg a billionaire many times over along the way. In early 2011, Facebook was valued at nearly $50 billion. As *Time* noted, "We are now running our social lives through a for-profit network."

Numerous domestic and international companies have quickly discovered that a presence on Facebook can be an effective marketing tool. A local restaurant may now invite customers to visit a Facebook page to learn about the menu, and about specials and other marketing offers.

Internationally, marketers know that, while near half of all Americans maintain Facebook accounts, 70% of members are from other countries.[3] The Facebook design team has adapted to differences in these countries. In terms of language, more than seventy translations of the site are now available. Adapting a product to foreign markets constitutes one activity in international marketing. The process requires careful thought and planning.

The opportunities to contact and connect with potential customers in other nations become enormous. At the same time, those with early success in developing popular brand pages represent an eclectic group of companies. In mid-2011, the list of the ten most popular brand pages on Facebook were

1. Coca-Cola,
2. Disney,
3. Starbucks,
4. Oreo,
5. Red Bull,
6. Converse All Star,
7. Converse (brand),
8. Skittles,
9. PlayStation, and
10. iTunes.[4]

Notably missing from the list are companies such as Nike, Sony, Porsche, and other well-established global brands.[5]

The international marketing challenges associated with effectively entering the Facebook domain include both traditional and unique issues. One traditional hurdle in advertising—clutter—remains an obstacle in the new world of social media. Simply getting noticed continues to be difficult. International marketers work to make sure that messages about the company are consistent and reach the appropriate audiences. Social media also present a world in which one dissatisfied customer can quickly contact a worldwide audience. Reacting appropriately to those comments requires a nimble and fast-thinking marketing and public relations effort.

The new world of interactivity means that merely presenting a message to an online target audience may not lead to marketing success. International marketers instead engage in a conversation that is much larger than a dialog. Numerous voices influence perceptions of products, brands, and companies. Fans and friends may be hard to find and harder to keep.

The shifting landscape of international marketing continues to experience the influences of language, culture, political and regulatory systems, economic circumstances, and infrastructure. Facebook is affected by, and affects, many of these features of the international marketplace. Responding to this new global phenomenon constitutes one of the many exciting opportunities future international marketers can explore.

QUESTIONS FOR STUDENTS

1. What websites are Facebook's primary competitors?
2. Do you think Facebook will continue to grow and dominate the world of social media, or will some other format takes its place over time?
3. How would you use Facebook to introduce a brand to a new country?

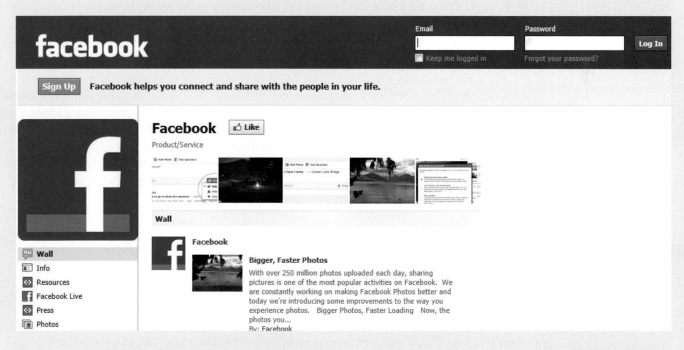

Numerous domestic and international companies have quickly discovered that a presence on Facebook can become an effective marketing tool.

Overview

"The only thing constant in life is change." This roughly translated quote from François de la Rochefoucauld may require an update. More accurately, the only thing constant in life in the twenty-first century is *the increasing rate of change.* The new millennium has witnessed an abundance of dramatic new and newsworthy events. Prior to 2000, no one had used the terms "Facebook" or "Twitter." Technological advances, economic upheaval, political shifts, cultural trends, and a vast variety of smaller innovations have transformed the ways people socialize, work, and shop.

In this turbulent global environment, the field of marketing stands on the cutting edge of the professions required to adapt. Products, methods of production, changes in trade agreements and treaties, financial swings, improvements in methods that can be used to reach customers as well as changes in ways customers shop require the attention of international marketers.

International marketing may be defined as the utilization and adaptation of the best marketing practices for the purposes of conducting commerce in other countries. It includes conducting commerce with customers, clients, partners, society at large, and the *overall global community.*

The first part of this book identifies the basic ideas associated with international marketing. This chapter presents marketing concepts and outlines the plan for the upcoming chapters. Chapter 2 examines economic systems and suggests potential modes of entry into new countries for companies seeking to become involved in international marketing. Chapter 3 studies global trade and integration.

This introductory chapter begins with a review of basic marketing concepts, including the traditional definition of marketing as it relates to the marketing mix. Through a discussion of needs, wants, and demand, the process for creating relationships with consumers can be examined. Next, the grouping of these consumers and the targeting of them with the marketing mix and positioning efforts is described.

With the marketing foundation in mind, the basics of international marketing are introduced. Globalization and greater connectivity are increasing the numbers and types of businesses competing in many countries. The effects of globalization on marketing, specifically in terms of culture, language, politics, law, economics, and infrastructure, are examined. The overall organization of this textbook is provided next. An introduction of the topics of sustainability and bottom-of-the-pyramid marketing within the international context follows, culminating with a discussion of some of the ethical concerns affecting the field.

The Worldwide Marketplace

LEARNING OBJECTIVE #1:

What are the meanings of the terms "multinational corporation," "born-global," "home country," and "host country?"

The majority of consumers purchase a wide variety of items over the course of the week. Some buy coffee or tea to enjoy in the morning. Many people purchase rice and tofu to cook for lunch while others buy fish and chips at small restaurants. People purchase clothes, electronics, insurance policies, and an ever-growing number of items on a regular basis. These products are increasingly sold by companies in other countries. A shirt may have been made in Costa Rica or Vietnam. A pen may have been manufactured in Great Britain, and a purse sewn in China. Globalization has fundamentally changed the ways marketers approach business and how people consume products.

Increasing global competition and opportunities in new countries create complex but exciting choices for marketers. Millions of new consumers can be identified in other countries. Consumers in those countries may be willing to try new products and brands. Companies that effectively market to them may become the global business leaders of the future.

To be successful in the international marketplace, marketers learn about new cultures as they adapt to changes in the environment. Business partners in other countries often speak different languages. Different laws and regulations govern business activities. Consumer wants and reasons for purchasing vary across and even within countries. Marketing in an international context requires comprehension of these and many other forces and factors. This textbook was written to help increase the level of understanding of these marketing and international business elements.

Types of Global Businesses

Many different types of companies are international in scope. The largest are multinational corporations, or MNCs. Multinational corporations conduct business activities in at least one other country that differs from the home country in which the organization is headquartered. Many multinational corporations operate in hundreds of countries. The Coca-Cola Corporation engages in commerce in more than two hundred countries, with different products and brands in many of them.

VIDEO LINK 1.2: Interview with a Global CEO

Multinational corporations can be large in terms of market value, revenues, and numbers of employees. Table 1.1 compares the market value of the top fifteen global multinational corporations to the size of a country's economy, in terms of gross domestic product. The world's largest multinational corporation, Exxon Mobil, has a market value larger than the economy of Pakistan, a nation of approximately 175 million people.

Many international businesses are considerably smaller than the multinational corporations in Table 1.1. These small businesses are often started by entrepreneurs who have experience in international marketing or have worked in multiple countries. These businesses that operate in two or more different countries from inception are **born-global firms**. Often, the founders of these organizations have existing international business relationships or knowledge of international markets that facilitate being international from inception.[6]

Businesses that operate in two or more different countries from inception are born-global firms.

In essence, global business may be as small as a family business selling items in other countries, or as large as the vast expanse of various multinational firms. Many small businesses also partner with multinational corporations to increase international marketing efforts.[7] For each, the **home country** is the nation in which the business is located or the country that houses the company's main headquarters. A **host country** is the nation being targeted for expansion. Nestlé's home country is Switzerland. If the marketing team at Nestlé decides to enter the nation of Belarus by selling its chocolate products, Belarus becomes the host country.

Regardless of the organization's size or its home location, success will be determined, in part, by the effectiveness of the company's marketing operations. Helping students understand and overcome the challenges presented by the dynamic market that currently exists constitutes one of the major objectives of this textbook.

Company Orientation

As companies diversify into a wider numbers of countries, the orientation of the leadership team frequently evolves. What was once a domestic company can take on a new focus and approach to conducting commerce. Four terms used to explain these

COMPANY / COUNTRY	MARKET VALUE OR GROSS DOMESTIC PRODUCT (IN MILLIONS OF U.S. DOLLARS)
Exxon Mobil (United States)	452,505
Pakistan	448,100
PetroChina (China)	423,996
Belgium	381,400
General Electric (United States)	369,569
Sweden	333,200
Gazprom (Russia)	299,764
China Mobile (China)	298,093
Ukraine	294,300
Industrial and Commercial Bank of China (China)	277,235
Norway	276,500
Microsoft (United States)	264,131
Vietnam	258,200
AT&T (United States)	231,168
Royal Dutch Shell (United Kingdom)	220,110
Procter & Gamble (United States)	215,640
Wal-Mart Stores (United States)	210,973
Petrobas (Brazil)	208,390
Berkshire Hathaway (United States)	206,924
Israel	206,900
Nestlé (Switzerland)	197,215
HSBC (United Kingdom)	195,767
Ireland	177,000

Table 1.1: **Largest Multinational Corporations and Equivalent Size Countries**

differences in approach include ethnocentric, polycentric, regiocentric, and geocentric management.[8]

Ethnocentric Companies

When an organization's leaders prefer to use its own employees, both at home and abroad, the company exhibits an ethnocentric leadership style. Management has concluded that nationals from the home country are best able to drive international marketing activities, and a home country orientation becomes the result. The policies and procedures used by the company remain largely unchanged in the host country. The advantages of this type of approach include greater control over the firm and the ability to more quickly transfer core competencies to operations in the host country. The disadvantages may be greater resistance or aversion by employees and consumers from the host country, plus the possibility of expatriate company employees not fully adapting to the host culture.

Polycentric Companies

A polycentric firm employs locals in the host country to conduct operations. The goal is to take advantage of the skills and local knowledge of these individuals to more quickly adapt the company's operations in the host country, shifting the firm's orientation to that host country. Doing so may be less expensive than other approaches to international organization, because fewer expatriate employees will be trained and sent to the host site. The primary drawback occurs when lines of communication and coordination are not carefully constructed and maintained.

Regiocentric Companies

When managers are employed from a variety of countries within a region, such as the Pacific Rim, the company operates in a regiocentric mode, which creates a series of host countries within the region to serve as the primary orientation. The idea will be to transfer some of the knowledge and experience of a region into a specific country. A manager who has successfully worked in a Japanese operation may be able to transfer what she has learned to South Korea or the Philippines. The primary management challenge will be to maintain control over the diversity of employees.

Geocentric Companies

Many global companies seek to find the best employees and systems, regardless of the country in which they are located. Geocentric companies maintain a global orientation without referencing a specific home or host country. Effective geocentric companies adapt to new international circumstances more quickly. The disadvantage may be greater costs associated with more global searches for new employees, plus challenges in the areas of coordination and control.

Implications

Several factors influence the type of orientation exhibited by a company. The firm's age, its number of host countries, the products and services to be marketed, differences and similarities between home and host countries, and management preferences all influence the company's orientation. A firm directed by a CEO who thinks his or her country does things best will most likely remain in an ethnocentric mode. Multinationals are logical candidates for the most geocentric orientation.[9]

The Essence of Marketing

Marketing may be defined as "discovering consumer needs and wants, creating the goods and services that meet those needs, and then pricing, promoting and delivering those goods and services."[10] Using this approach, *consumers and other businesses* are the key targets of the marketing process. Groups of consumers and businesses, or markets, lead companies to produce and merchandise the goods and services they desire.

The American Marketing Association (AMA) notes that marketing activities include a set of institutions, and processes for creating, communicating, delivering, and exchanging offerings that have value for customers, clients, partners, and society at large. This viewpoint expands the overall concept of marketing to include *any* exchange of value. The money that buyers use to make purchases has value, as do the goods and services offered by sellers.

Marketing may be defined as "discovering consumer needs and wants, creating the goods and services products that meet those needs, and then pricing, promoting and delivering those goods and services."

Bosch is a multinational company.

Money represents the most common vehicle used to facilitate a marketing exchange, but it does not need to be present for an exchange to be considered marketing. Individuals trade physical products, such as when an Italian teen swaps an AC Milan team jersey to another for a fashionable jacket made in Germany. Also, two people may barter for services: A man who has difficulty reading and writing could agree to help an acquaintance repaint his living room. In the exchange, the acquaintance helps the illiterate man's child fill out application forms for college. When the two trade these services, a marketing exchange has taken place. In the ideal, an exchange leads to satisfaction for both parties. In this context, the nature of international marketing takes on additional dimensions, including trading goods for services and much more complex trade practices.

THE MARKETING MIX

LEARNING OBJECTIVE #2:

What are the essential ingredients in the marketing mix as they relate to international markets, needs, and wants?

Companies seeking to successfully market items in other countries employ all of the elements of the **marketing mix**, which consists of the major activities used to develop and sell goods and services. The four Ps of the marketing mix are product, price, place (or distribution), and promotion, as shown in Figure 1.1. Effectively combining and managing these four components of marketing means that a company has developed a product consumers desire, the price has been set at a level consumers are willing to pay, the product has been distributed in a way that allows consumers to make the purchase, and the item has been promoted in a manner that makes consumers aware of the product and the value it provides.

Promotion incorporates all of the elements of the *promotional mix*, which consists of all of the activities that transmit messages about a product's value. The promotional mix includes advertising, sales promotion, personal selling, direct marketing, and public relations programs. Trade shows and fairs have become an important part of many international marketing programs.[11] Effective promotional programs are integrated to provide consistent messages to consumers about the nature of the product and the company.

Product	A good or service that satisfies consumer needs by providing value
Price	The value of what is exchanged in return for the product
Place (or distribution)	Movement of the product from the seller to the buyer
Promotion	Communication of product value from the buyer to the seller

Figure 1.1: The Marketing Mix

MARKETS, NEEDS, AND WANTS

A **market** consists of people with wants and needs, money to spend, plus the willingness and ability to spend money on those wants and needs.

Needs are the necessities of life that all humans require for their survival and well-being. Abraham Maslow's hierarchy of needs approach suggests that *physiological* needs include food, clothing, shelter, air, water, and sex for the purposes of procreation (survival of the species). Many products are designed to satisfy these physiological needs. In international settings, especially nations in sub-Saharan Africa, there may be a premium on an item as simple as clean drinking water.

Safety needs are met through products ranging from guns and ammunition to health insurance and life insurance policies. In a nation such as Laos, where the war involving the Hmong insurgency has affected everyday life for the past decade, safety needs become more urgent.

Love and belongingness may not be purchased; however, many products may be designed to assist in meeting these needs, such as flowers and cards for those involved in romances, and taverns, restaurants, or other places for social gatherings with friends. Romantic rituals vary widely by culture, which changes the natures of products that facilitate courtship rituals. Red roses express romantic feelings in the United States and other countries. Red is often the color worn by brides in the East, whereas it is the color of mourning in South Africa.[12]

Self-actualization refers to meeting one's potential and feeling as if one has achieved something valuable by helping others or by performing meaningful work. Finding work that contributes to self-actualization in less- or least-developed countries may be nearly impossible for large segments of the population.

Wants are specific expressions of needs through the desire for specific objects. The need for food, a physiological need, may be expressed by the desire for a plate of lasagna or fresh fruit. Thirsty consumers in the Middle East may desire a carbonated soda to satisfy their thirst need. Depending on the country, Middle Eastern consumers could purchase a variety of local sodas including Mecca, Zam Zam, or Parsi Cola, or a soft drink imported from another nation.

Consumers want many different goods or services; however, not all of these wants can be satisfied. A luxury automobile, for example, may be something that the majority of consumers want. Only a small subset of consumers has the financial ability to satisfy this desire due to the product's high price.

Demand reflects the amounts of a goods or services that consumers will purchase at various price levels. A higher-priced car has a smaller demand because fewer consumers are willing and able to pay what is needed to buy the product.

> Needs are the necessities of life that all humans require for their survival and well-being.

SEGMENTATION, TARGET MARKETS, AND POSITIONING (STP)

Any given product may have several types of customers who might wish to buy it, and they may use the same product in different ways, such as using baking soda for baking or as a tooth cleanser. Consumers may demand or want some products that are their needs, attitudes, and interests is **market segmentation**. Marketers group or segment consumers in ways that allow them to identify specific sets that express or have demand for various products. International marketers also consider differences in nationalities and customs when identifying market segments.[13]

A **target market** consists of a specific, identifiable market segment that a company seeks to reach. The marketing mix can then be used to ensure that consumers within the target market both want the product and are satisfied after purchasing and using it (see Figure 1.2). A company's marketing team might identify ten market segments but choose to only target five of those segments, which is the process of *target marketing*.

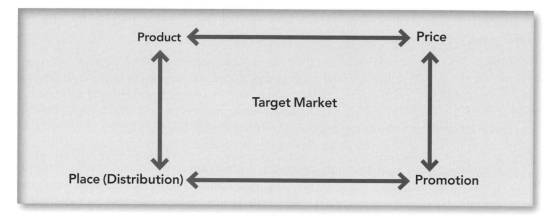

Figure 1.2: The Marketing Mix Applied to Target Markets

> The marketing mix helps establish positioning, which is creating a perception in a consumer's mind about the nature of a company and its products relative to competitors.

The marketing mix helps establish **positioning**, which is creating a perception in a consumer's mind about the nature of a company and its products relative to competitors. Most companies seek to position products as being different from competitors. An emphasis on a unique benefit or component of a product that separates an item from competitors' products results in **differentiation**. Products may be differentiated based on price, innovations, high levels of quality, and many other attributes.

Marketers can control the marketing mix and positioning factors. Other elements in the marketing environment are much less controllable. These external environmental forces are scanned by company leaders seeking to identify the opportunities and threats. These and other forces are considered as part of the segmentation, target market identification, and positioning processes.

Marketing in an International Context

The essence of marketing remains the same, whether in a domestic or international setting. At the same time, entering a new country to sell goods or services requires many adjustments, some of which are relatively minor while others are more dramatic. Employees in a firm preparing to enter foreign markets should first examine the new context to identify the parts of the marketing mix that may require changes along with adjustments to managerial practices, accounting methods, human resource policies, shipping and storage programs, and other activities.

In essence, international marketing involves adapting to meet the needs and wants of consumers in foreign markets. A home country may have a great deal of similarity with the host country in which a target market has been identified. The result would likely be that only small changes or adaptations would be made to the marketing mix. Some marketing writers argue that consumer tastes and preferences are becoming increasingly homogenized as additional products and services are offered globally.[14] In other cases, the host country target market may be markedly different. This would lead to efforts to change aspects of the marketing mix to fit the new environment. Two of the most salient forces that influence the degree of adaptation necessary are

1. the drivers of globalization, and

2. the factors that create international marketing complexity.

These forces combine to create both opportunities and challenges for companies seeking to expand into new countries.

The Drivers of Globalization

Countries around the world are undoubtedly more interconnected now than at any point in history, in spite of terrorism, wars, and conflicts between nations. In the United Kingdom, consumers enjoy computers, games, and toys from South Korea; strawberries from Colombia; flowers from Venezuela; raspberries from Poland; and peas from Kenya.[15] These connections are partly derived from commerce, but are also the result of improved methods of communication, increased travel, and greater ties across borders. The increased interconnectedness of consumers and businesses is **globalization**. Globalization is driven by a variety of forces, including those displayed in Figure 1.3.

LEARNING OBJECTIVE #3:

How have the drivers of globalization influenced international marketing?

Channels of Communication
Lower Transportation Costs
Immigration and Emigration Patterns
Governmental Actions

Figure 1.3: Drivers of Globalization

CHANNELS OF COMMUNICATION

Globalization results from a variety of technological and structural changes. First, technology has fundamentally altered the ways people communicate. The Internet, underwater transcontinental communication cables, and cellular technologies have reduced the costs of communication and created greater access to communication channels, which reduces barriers to communication across borders. Contacts spanning the globe are facilitated by social media outlets such as Facebook. The decreased costs of communication allow employees within a company to interact and work together on projects through technologies such as company intranets and online video conferencing.

Communications between companies and consumers have also been affected. As one example, British consumers calling companies are increasingly talking to customer service representatives in Estonia or Lithuania.[16]

LOWER TRANSPORTATION COSTS

Technology has also decreased the cost of transportation, including the movement of both people and products. Lower costs associated with entering new markets and moving operations to new countries creates new marketing and business opportunities. Shipping costs have been reduced through more effective containerization systems. Containerization is the process of packing goods in such a way that they can fit in a container from the point of manufacture to the point of distribution, with no repacking or complex handling. It is estimated that shipping of a single typical ship-, train-, and truck-interchangeable container from southern China to the western United States costs $2,500. In today's complex global economy, containerization has also become an important part of the production process, supporting global production networks.[17] Reductions in air freight costs have also allowed air transportation to play an increasingly important role in international marketing activities.[18]

Low shipping costs create new marketing and business opportunities.

IMMIGRATION AND EMIGRATION

Globalization has been enhanced by changing patterns of immigration and emigration. Approximately 150 million people lived in countries other than their country of birth at the turn of the millennium. A dramatic increase in movement of people has affected many countries, including Estonians in Finland, Africans in China (including President Obama's half-brother), and Guatemalans in Mexico.[19] This movement increases the ties between countries and widens exposures to different cultures and ideas for many citizens. It also presents marketing opportunities. Someone who has moved into a new country may still desire products from her former home. If a sufficient number of individuals who have left a country share the same want, a company may be able to export that product to their new homes.

GOVERNMENTAL ACTIONS

Governments play an important role in increasing connections between countries. One governmental action has been to reduce barriers to commerce. Lifting barriers was at first designed to stimulate trade. Today, freer movement applies to labor and capital, which has lowered the costs of moving many business processes to low-cost or highly specialized locations.

The increase in the flow of goods, people, and capital has also led, at least to some degree, to economic development in many countries, including China, India, and Brazil. Greater prosperity has paved the way for improvements in education, which in turn strengthens the skills and abilities of laborers in those countries. A cycle of increased connectivity between countries that trade with one another may be the outcome, with the well-being of both enhanced by the trade relationships.

Market liberalization, another form of governmental action, refers to the removal of governmental control over economic activity. Countries that were part of the former Soviet Union, and nations in Eastern Europe, China, and Vietnam, have all experienced some form of market liberalization. Typically, liberalization means the government removes barriers to trade and opens markets to competition. Markets such as China have become primary destinations for foreign investments. China has become a leading global exporter as a result. Map 1.1 presents the exports of countries globally.

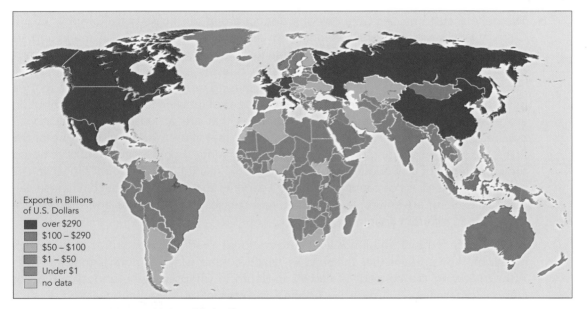

Exports in Billions of U.S. Dollars
- over $290
- $100 – $290
- $50 – $100
- $1 – $50
- Under $1
- no data

Map 1.1: **Exporting Activity Globally**
New major global exporting countries have recently emerged.

Globalization may be viewed as both an opportunity and as a threat. From an international business and marketing perspective, globalization represents a major opportunity. A recent survey of 1,400 CEOs from forty-six countries by Price Waterhouse Cooper revealed that two thirds of respondents thought globalization would have a positive effect on their businesses in the coming years.[20]

The Factors That Create International Marketing Complexity

Marketers face an increasingly complex global context for many business decisions. Complexity may be found in the differences in business environments within each country.

LEARNING OBJECTIVE #4:

How are the factors that create international marketing complexity linked to creating a global mindset for marketing activities?

Each nation has distinct differences, as summarized in Figure 1.4. When conducting international marketing and trade, accounting for these differences and adapting to them represent two of the most important challenges to overcome.

The topics identified in Figure 1.4 are often presented as stand-alone chapters in other international marketing books. In this text, the topics are instead blended in with marketing concepts. The goal is to integrate rather than isolate the concepts, which should help students more clearly understand the links between these external international factors and marketing strategies, tactics, and operational activities.

Culture
Language
Political and legal systems
Economic systems
Infrastructure

Figure 1.4: Factors That Create International Marketing Complexity

CULTURE

The beliefs, customs, and attitudes of a distinct group of people constitute its **culture**. Culture exhibits a powerful influence on all aspects of international marketing. A thorough understanding of and appreciation for culture represents a fundamental aspect of successful international marketing strategy.[21] Tastes and preferences for products, interactions between coworkers, standard purchasing methods, the willingness to try a new product, and comfort levels with different types of retailing and product distribution are examples of differences between countries that are at least partially based on culture. Finding local partners to help navigate these differences should be one of the first steps when expanding operations into a new country. Some researchers have noted the emergence of a "world teen" or "global youth" market, which adopts similar values and tastes regardless of country of birth.[22] Learning about segments such as these can offer an exciting adventure, even as culture increases the difficulties and the costs of marketing in different countries.

Although culture influences all international marketing activities, Figure 1.5 highlights key areas within the field in which culture plays a more significant role. After reviewing the concept of culture in-depth in Chapter 4, the understanding of cultural differences will then be applied to international marketing activities such as market segmentation, or the grouping of consumers into identifiable targets. Culture also strongly influences product positioning efforts, because cultural nuances lead consumers in different countries to view products in unique ways. Often, these culturally based differences lead marketers to change or adapt products to better meet local tastes. Culture plays a substantial role in the promotion of products. In order to be successful, marketing communications such as advertising or social media, sales promotions, and personal selling activities should account for cultural differences.

LANGUAGE

The system used to communicate between peoples, including verbal and nonverbal cues, is a **language**. Consumers may know one or more languages that differ from the one present in the home country for a product. The movement of products across boundaries may require translation and adaptation of advertising, labels on products,

Topic	Found in
Culture In-Depth Review	*Chapter 4*
Segmentation	Chapter 4
Positioning	Chapter 5
Product Management	Chapter 7
Adaptation and Standardization	Chapter 8
Marketing Communications	Chapter 13
Sales Promotion	Chapter 14
Personal Selling	Chapter 15

Figure 1.5: Culture and International Marketing

and basic communication between host and home country marketers. Marketing research programs and other marketing activities often require the assistance of a *cultural assimilator*, a person well versed in the host country's language and culture.

Many classic international blunders have occurred due to language, such as Chevrolet attempting to sell the Nova automobile in Spanish-speaking countries. In Spanish, Nova roughly translates as *"no va"* or "no go." Consequently, the cars did not sell well. Company leaders now recognize the importance of making sure any message will be understood in the way it was intended before sending it out.

Communicating with consumers represents a challenge for marketers in all contexts, especially the marketing activities noted in Figure 1.6. In international settings, language presents a key barrier to success. The topic of language, while included in discussions throughout the book, receives the most in-depth coverage in Chapter 13, the first of three chapters in Part VI on promotion. Language affects marketing communications, personal selling, and sales promotions. Language can become a segmenting tool. Translation will be required when facing language differences, especially when conducting market research.

Topic	Found in
Language In-Depth Review	*Chapter 13*
Segmentation	Chapter 4
Market Research	Chapter 6
Marketing Communications	Chapter 13
Sales Promotion	Chapter 14
Personal Selling	Chapter 15

Figure 1.6: Language and International Marketing

POLITICAL AND LEGAL SYSTEMS

Individual countries use different political and legal traditions. **Political systems** are administered by the people in a government who possess power and maintain the country's power structure. Types of political systems include democracies, authoritarian governments, and anarchies. These governments create laws that regulate commerce and establish trading treaties or arrangements with governments from other countries.

Legal systems constitute the methods for applying and implementing the laws of a country. Legal systems include common law, civil law, and theocratic law, among others. Governmental activities, through both regulations and the actions of governmental officials, constrain what marketers can do within a country's borders. These directives include packaging and labeling requirements, regulation of advertising, and may be as severe as banning certain products.

> Legal systems constitute the methods for applying and implementing the laws of a country.

Political and legal systems influence numerous aspects of international marketing (see Figure 1.7). The concepts are presented separately: political systems are reviewed in Chapter 6 and legal systems in Chapter 8. Political systems are also introduced as part of the process of segmenting or grouping countries, as compared to individuals. Political risk may affect international market research. Both political and legal issues influence the adaptation or changing of products when entering new countries, although legal requirements play a larger role. Political and legal systems regulate international finance and, in turn, affect international marketing activities. Legal systems also influence the information technology capabilities within countries, with many countries restricting, to at least some degree, the flow of information.

Topic	Found in
Political Systems In-depth Review	*Chapter 6*
Legal Systems In-depth Review	*Chapter 8*
Segmentation	Chapter 4
Market Research	Chapter 6
Standardization and Adaptation	Chapter 8
International Finance	Chapter 10

Figure 1.7: Political and Legal Systems and International Marketing

ECONOMIC SYSTEMS

The means by which a country allocates resources, goods, and services to citizens constitute its **economic system**. The types of economic systems present in international commerce include capitalist, communist, and mixed structures.

Each type of economic system will be based, in part, on the role that the government plays in the distribution of resources. Governments are involved in all economic systems. The extent to which a ruling class exerts influence becomes the primary concern in international marketing. In communist systems, the government oversees the means of production and exerts nearly total control over business activities. The interplay between the government and the economic system in communist countries can create additional barriers for companies seeking to enter markets.

In contrast, a capitalist economy invites investment and entrepreneurship. When the system allows for the ownership of private property and protection of intellectual property, market opportunities expand at a faster rate. Marketers consider the economic system of prospective host countries before attempting to enter those markets.

Economic systems affect a variety of international marketing activities (see Figure 1.8). Overall economic systems are presented in Chapter 2 and the chapter then applies economic systems to the process of creating effective mode-of-entry strategies. Segmenting markets is another area where economic systems influence decision-making. Economics also play a key role in the setting of prices and in the overall international finance. Global trade, a key component of international marketing, is also affected by economic systems.

INFRASTRUCTURE

Marketers identify differences in infrastructure in host markets. **Infrastructure** consists of the organizational and physical structures that are essential for societies to operate. Examples of the presence

Highly developed economic systems lead to major urban centers.

or lack of infrastructure include the availability of roads, the degree of Internet access, the percentage of the population owning cell phones, the quality of educational institutions, and the availability of water, electricity, and/or natural gas.

A poor infrastructure can increase production and marketing costs. Roads in India, as one example, are notorious for being underdeveloped and crowded. Infosys Technologies Ltd., a leading Indian technology firm, spent $5 million in 2006 to pay for a fleet of buses, minivans, and taxis to transport its employees in Bangalore. It is estimated that, due to traffic jams, commutes can take as long as four hours per day for employees in that city.[23]

VIDEO LINK 1.3:
Entrepreneurs and Creativity

Topic	Found in
Economics In-depth Review	*Chapter 2*
International Strategy	Chapter 2
Global Trade	Chapter 3
Segmentation	Chapter 4
International Pricing	Chapter 9
International Finance	Chapter 10

Figure 1.8: Economics and International Marketing

A well-established infrastructure presents new marketing opportunities. Most- and more-developed nations grow, in part, by strengthening the infrastructure of the country. Increased investment and greater trade for the nation often result.

Infrastructure influences international marketing in a number of ways. Many times throughout this text, an analysis of infrastructure will be included in the discussion of a marketing activity. Examples of some of these are noted in Figure 1.9. A nation's infrastructure has a dramatic impact on the movement of goods. Consequently, the concept is presented in depth in Chapter 11, the first of the two chapters in Part V, which covers distribution and logistics, or the process by which goods are moved. Infrastructure is also examined in the context of global trade in Chapter 3.

Topic	Found in
Infrastructure In-depth Review	*Chapter 11*
Global Trade	Chapter 3
Distribution and Logistics	Chapter 11
Exporting and Retailing	Chapter 12

Figure 1.9: Infrastructure and International Marketing

IMPLICATIONS

Responding to changes in different countries requires a global mindset. This involves learning about new places, people, and processes, and viewing business activities from a global perspective. Topography represents a key example of an issue that emerges from this broader perspective. Map 1.2 displays key topographic features across the world. Providing the foundation for a global mindset is one intention of this book, while recognizing that maintaining a global mindset should be a continuing process.

Map 1.2: **Global Geography and Topography**
Topographic features can facilitate or hinder relationships between countries.

INTERNATIONAL INCIDENT ///

As part of an international junket, your marketing team stops to visit an important potential new client in Spain. Within a few hours of cordial discussions, the manager of the client company invites you to attend the bullfights the next day as his guest. You have little interest in attending the event and do not like the custom. What should you do? How would you respectfully decline? Or, would you accept and then bow out, claiming illness the next day? Would you consider attending? How would your response change if you were a Hindu from India or Nepal? (Hindus hold all life to be sacred and consider bulls to be religious animals that should never be harmed.)

International Marketing in Daily Life

It may be that most people think of something "glamorous" when the term "marketing" is used. It may feel classy or sexy to consider a marketing program for the newest hand-held mobile technology, a fancy sports car, or designer clothing. At the same time, a case can be made that the majority of marketing opportunities may come from much simpler products and services—those used in everyday life.

One common theme that appears in this textbook is the marketing of products to be used daily or regularly. The approach serves a special purpose: to illustrate how the most commonplace of daily activities can lead to the identification of target markets that companies can reach with products that are adapted to individual cultures and national circumstances. Figure 1.10 lists some of the daily activities described in this textbook. When one of these activities is described, the daily living logo shown below will appear as part of the presentation.

Bathing	Brushing Teeth/Dental Hygiene
Using the Restroom	Wearing Jeans
Sleeping and Beds	Methods of Transportation
Cosmetics	Candy
Dining Habits and Foods	Cooking Methods
Drinks and Milk Consumption	Coping With Headaches
Socialization	Music
Religions	Methods of Payment and Banking

Figure 1.10: Selected Daily Life Activities and Marketing Opportunities Presented in This Textbook

International Marketing in Daily Life

INTERNATIONAL EXAMPLE: MARKETING BATHING PRODUCTS

As an example of the far-reaching impact of globalization on business practices and international marketing, consider this basic human activity: bathing and cleaning. Bathing and cleaning are routine activities worldwide, but the methods and products used vary

Bathing and cleaning are routine activities worldwide.

widely. Among the methods are showers, baths, and washing using only water from a stream or river. Soap products may be solid, liquid, or gels. The same holds true for shampoo. More-specialized items are available to wash a person's face or to clean strong stains, such as oil or grease. Consequently, the simple, common everyday event of washing may present marketing opportunities for numerous companies from a variety of countries, all of them affected by international marketing complexities.

DRIVERS OF GLOBALIZATION: AN ILLUSTRATION

The drivers of globalization and the factors that create international marketing complexity influence the types of products that may be marketed, the places where they are sold, and the methods used to reach customers in order to entice them to buy. Bathing and cleaning products are no exception.

Channels of Communication

The methods consumers use to communicate with companies are changing, as are the methods consumers use to communicate with one another. Methods of cleaning and grooming that are common in one country might be viewed as new and exciting in another.

New channels of communication, such as social networks, allow consumers to gossip about products, form brand communities, and use other methods to describe and discuss products. Customers are able to go online to register thoughts with companies about products. For instance, a customer might inquire about the correct method to use a new soap or cleaning agent for a shower or tub. Website FAQs (frequently asked questions) make it easier to explain product benefits and uses to a wider audience, especially when the website has been translated into more than one language.

Lower Transportation Costs

Reduced shipping costs make it possible for a greater number of companies to enter markets. Unilever sells a large number of personal grooming products around the world. Each can be adapted to the specific needs of a culture, region, or infrastructure. Salespersons from Unilever are now able to travel to remote places seeking out new markets.

Immigration and Emigration Patterns

As a group of people moves from one country to another, the individuals may seek to both maintain their previous cultural norms and adapt to others. For example, a young woman seeking to "fit in" in a Westernized culture may shave her legs for the first time. A young man attempting to adapt might bathe more or less frequently, wash his hair using a different product, and groom himself to become part of the social fabric of a new country.

Governmental Actions

Through liberalization and inner-connectivity, governments may speed up the process of exporting products that are new and innovative. A new soap form, such as a gel that turns into lather, may find a wide marketplace, especially when the container size can be made smaller than a liquid soap. Towelettes that allow for cleaning one's hands without the use of water may reach a wide audience of persons wishing to wash their hands before a meal in arid climates.

FACTORS THAT CREATE INTERNATIONAL MARKETING COMPLEXITY: AN ILLUSTRATION

Even as the drivers of globalization open new markets, the complications remain. Washing and cleaning products require adaptation to meet the needs of consumers in various countries. This includes methods of pricing, promoting, and distributing the products.

Culture

Cultural views of cleanliness vary widely. Strong body odor may be offensive in one nation and acceptable in another. The frequency and duration of cleaning would be affected. Many religions express concepts relating cleanliness to purity. Cleansing and water are used in religious rites, such as baptisms in Christian religions. In India, water holds special meaning to some consumers, especially those from more traditional rural areas. Where water is scarce, baths are infrequent and can be seen as sacred. Many Indians observe a funeral ritual in which the individual's ashes are scattered into the Ganges River. Due to the special nature of water, Indians may find using a hot tub or taking two showers per day to be offensive.[24]

Methods for washing hair and caring for hair are affected by views of aesthetics and beauty as well as practical matters such as hair texture and hair style. In many countries, women do not shave their legs or armpits. The use of deodorants may be widely accepted in one region and not even considered in others.

Language

The term "clean" may have a variety of meanings, depending on the language and culture in which the language is spoken. Language usage would be closely watched as part of any advertising or promotional program for soaps, shampoos, and other items. In a culture with relaxed views toward nudity and sexuality, the image of a bare leg used to promote a bathing product might inspire interest and achieve the desired effect. In a culture with more strict views, such an image would be highly offensive.

Political and Legal Systems

Laws and regulations affect the ingredients that may be included in a product as well as how those ingredients are represented. A dandruff shampoo may be considered medicinal in one country if it contains certain ingredients and might be subject to strict regulation. Packaging and labeling requirements are stringent in some nations and nearly nonexistent in others.

Any cleansing product that injures a customer would be subject to various legal systems. In some countries, a defective or injurious product might result in the execution of the person in the company who was responsible for the problem. Methods of adjudicating lawsuits as well as regulations regarding over compensation for injuries would also vary depending on the government involved.

Economic Systems

In a free enterprise economy, entrepreneurs are encouraged to develop new and better cleaning agents through the market system. This would lead businesses to develop products that not only clean people but also clean the places where people clean. Shower mildew removers may be routinely available in one country but not in another. Glass cleaners and other cleansers may be found where showers with glass doors are available. One innovation driven by economic interests has been liquid soap dispensed from a bottle. Hair care products include shampoo, conditioner, dandruff control, and cleaners that are better suited to hair that has been colored in some way.

Economic systems that are more restrictive may limit the opportunity to develop new products. They may also limit a company's ability to export to that country. A communist or state-driven economy may utilize tariffs and other methods to keep competing companies out.

Infrastructure

Bathing and cleaning are clearly influenced by the availability of water. Where water is scarce, bathing will be less frequent and the emphasis will be on conservation. In some countries, steam showers may be used. Where water is readily available, people may take long, luxurious baths and showers. Water may also be available where electricity or natural gas is not. The result would be cold showers and baths, because the water cannot be heated.

The delivery of products to consumers may be helped or hindered by road and transportation systems. Some countries also have well-developed channels of distribution, including wholesale and retail operations. Others have only scattered and diverse shops and stores.

THE INTERNATIONAL MARKETING CONTEXT

The four drivers of globalization and the five factors that influence international marketing complexity will be featured throughout this textbook. While all of the factors affect every marketing activity, in this textbook these individual concepts are described in greater depth in the sections where they exhibit prominent influence on a specific marketing function.

The Organization of This Book

Figure 1.11 expresses the interactions between the five factors that influence international marketing complexity, with the topics to be described in this textbook. As shown, the marketing mix constitutes the primary set of topics presented, combined with sections about markets and international marketing management. Figure 1.12 lists the topics presented in this textbook. A brief description of each follows.

Figure 1.11: The International Marketing Context

Essentials of International Marketing
Introduction to the Field
Economic Systems and Modes of Entry
Global Trade and Integration
International Markets and Market Research
Markets and Segmentation in an International Context
International Positioning
International Market Research
International Product Marketing
International Product and Brand Marketing
International Product Standardization and Adaptation
International Pricing and Finance
International Pricing
International Finance and Implications for Pricing
International Place or Distribution
International Distribution and Logistics
International Exporting and Retailing
International Promotion and Personal Selling
Globally Integrated Marketing Communications
International Sales Promotions
International Personal Selling

Figure 1.12: Topics Presented in This Textbook

PART I: ESSENTIALS OF INTERNATIONAL MARKETING

This first chapter establishes a foundation for effective international marketing. Marketing is an exchange of value, typically between a buyer and a seller. To provide value, marketers must understand the nature of markets in order to effectively identify the target markets a company intends to reach.

Chapter 2 describes various economic systems. Economic conditions affect the choices of host countries by international marketers. Various modes of entry are explained. Modes of entry constitute the methods marketers use to place products in new host countries.

Chapter 3 investigates the nature of global trade. Various ideas about global trade will be presented. Then, integration, or the agreements between countries to lower limits on the movements of products, capital, and/or labor is described. Free trade has both supporters and critics.

PART II: INTERNATIONAL MARKETS AND MARKET RESEARCH

The second part of this book examines international markets and market research. Chapter 4 describes international target market segmentation and selection. The nature of culture and its effects on segmentation are examined. This includes an analysis of the emergence of ways to identify market segments as a business becomes more globalized. In essence, markets can be segmented at the country level and then at smaller levels, such as by consumer groups and types of businesses.

Chapter 5 continues the presentation of the international segmentation, targeting, and positioning (STP) process by examining methods used to establish positioning. Positioning differentiates products in a consistent fashion across countries. Creating brand equity, the perception that a product is different and better, will be the ultimate goal of positioning. To do so, global products must be positioned to overcome consumer perceptions, including attitudes toward the country of origin of an item, especially when negative attitudes toward specific countries are present.

To provide value to consumers, marketers must first understand what consumers want. International market research, the focus of Chapter 6, is the process marketers use to obtain this information. Market research uses the scientific method and strives for objectivity. Effective market research has a clear problem or objective, balances the costs versus benefits from answering that question, and then develops a research design to collect data. Analysis of these data will provide insights that can begin to solve the initial problem. The data can be from outside sources or can be collected by a market researcher. A great deal of domestic data collection takes place at the micro or individual consumer level. Within an international marketing context, marketers often collect data at the macro or country level. Country-level analysis includes assessing political risk and determining country-level advantages.

PART III: INTERNATIONAL PRODUCT MARKETING

The third part of this text presents product-based issues. Chapter 7 addresses the fundamentals of managing the product component of the marketing mix. The product life cycle is introduced and extended internationally. Product and brand management strategies are reviewed.

Chapter 1: Review and Resources

STRATEGIC IMPLICATIONS //

Top-level managers direct the strategic courses of companies by first employing a SWOT analysis. This analysis involves assessing internal strengths and weaknesses (SW) and opportunities and threats (OT) present in the external environment. Understanding that a company has an advantage based on a superior product and strong brand loyalty represents key company strengths. When that same company lacks the funds to expand further, weakness is present. Predicting changes in economic conditions or shifts in consumer preferences are examples of potential threats or opportunities.

The net result of a SWOT analysis will be the strategic choice of products and services to be offered, because opportunities and threats have been identified, some of which emerge from the analysis of a national or regional culture. Culture presents opportunities in terms of revealing wants and needs held by members of a community. Assuming these individuals have sufficient resources to acquire products that meet these wants and needs, then products can be developed, prices set, delivery systems established, and promotional programs created to reach members in the market.

To complete the strategic design, target markets are chosen with positioning approaches that match the markets. The strategic design outlines the direction the organization will take with regard to both domestic and international markets.

Decisions are made concerning the emphasis on *broad differentiation* of the product as the *low-cost provider* or as the *best-cost provider*. Broad differentiation indicates the product will be presented as being superior as well as different. The low-cost approach features an emphasis on price. A best-cost strategy combines the unique qualities of the product with its price, leading to a focus on the value offered to the customer. After specific target markets are defined, the market niche may also be reached through differentiation, low cost, or best cost. These may be adjusted to fit the requisites of the domestic or international market.

TACTICAL IMPLICATIONS //

Marketing focuses on facilitating exchanges in value by understanding consumer needs and wants, which lead, over time, to relationships with consumers. This process is the same, albeit more complex, for international marketers. International marketing leads to many potential tactical changes. All components of the marketing mix—that is, product, price, place, and promotion—will eventually be adjusted as companies become increasingly international. Advertisement programs will be altered to fit the culture of a host country. Relationships with retail outlets will be formed.

To assist in creating successful tactics, marketers seek to understand how the external environment changes after crossing home country borders. Culture, language, political and legal systems, economic systems, and infrastructure are the primary categories for these changes. By successfully understanding and responding to these differences, marketers can establish connections with consumers.

Changes in tactics should be based on a deep understanding of consumption in each market. Local partners, along with effective marketing research, may help in this regard. Tactics not rooted in an understanding of host country consumers will eventually fail.

Marketers must be willing and able to make rapid modifications to tactics in response to changes in international locales. Predicting responses and risks in host countries is more difficult than in home countries, and it must be assumed that mistakes will be made. By being prepared to respond to these mistakes in tactics, companies will be more successful.

OPERATIONAL IMPLICATIONS //

Day-to-day operations will vary dramatically across markets. In some markets, consumer relationships are built through daily interactions. Methods of payment, body language, bargaining, and other personal contacts affect the conduct of routine business. Over time, these repeated exchanges broker trust and longer-term commitments.

At the operational level, individual advertisements and other promotions will be scrutinized to make sure they fit with the local culture. Shipping methods are studied and adjusted to meet local laws and standards. An overall strategy of broad differentiation results in the local salesperson emphasizing the product's unique features and advantages as part of the sales pitch. The key to effective daily operations will be maintaining consistency with strategic and tactical direction taken by the organization.

TERMS

international marketing	needs	culture
multinational corporations	wants	language
born-global firms	demand	political systems
home country	market segmentation	legal systems
host country	target market	economic system
marketing	positioning	infrastructure
marketing mix	differentiation	sustainability
market	globalization	bottom-of-the-pyramid

REVIEW QUESTIONS

1. Define international marketing and marketing. What is the difference between them?
2. What are the four components of the marketing mix?
3. What components are included in the promotional mix?
4. Define a market and give an example.
5. What is the difference between needs and wants?
6. How do wants lead to demand?
7. What is the market segmentation process?
8. Define target market.
9. What is the relationship between positioning and differentiation?
10. Define globalization and identify the four drivers of this process.
11. What are the five factors that create international marketing complexity?
12. Define culture.
13. Describe how language might influence marketing.
14. Compare and contrast economic systems with political and legal systems.
15. Define infrastructure.
16. Define sustainability.
17. What are the six stages for leveraging sustainability?
18. Define bottom-of-the-pyramid.
19. Define cultural relativism and the justice approach to ethical issues.

DISCUSSION QUESTIONS

1. The marketing mix is manipulated to meet target market needs and wants. How might the following companies use this process to satisfy consumers?
   - Jones Soda
   - Red Bull

- Haeir
- Sony
- Hyundai

2. There are four main drivers of globalization: (1) channels of communication, (2) lower transportation costs, (3) immigration and emigration patterns, and (4) governmental actions. How have these forces influenced your own life? Consider both your social life and your interaction with businesses.

3. Identify, in simple terms, differences in the factors creating international marketing complexity for the following countries. These factors are culture, language, political and legal systems, economic systems, and infrastructure.

- India
- Brazil
- Kenya
- Slovenia
- Mongolia

4. Sustainability is increasingly viewed as a potential driver of firm success. What are the implications of this perspective? Incorporate the framework in Figure 1.7 into your answer.

ANALYTICAL AND INTERNET EXERCISES

1. Visit the following websites. Even though they are in different languages, use the images on the websites to identify the company's target market. Can you also identify the company's position, and how it is differentiated?

   http://news.baidu.com/

   http://www.sony.jp/

   http://www.giant-bicycles.com/zh-TW/

   http://www.mercedes-benz.de/

   http://www.ethiopianairlines.com/en/default.aspx

   http://scf.natura.net/

2. Coca-Cola has an online virtual vendor at www.virtualvender.coca-cola.com/vm/Vending.jsp. Look at the products it sells in at least three countries from each continent. How do these products reflect differences in culture between these countries?

3. Google the terms "sustainability" and "bottom-of-the-pyramid" together. What are the results? What do the results say about how these two concepts interact?

▶ ONLINE VIDEOS

Visit **www.sagepub.com/baack** to view these chapter videos:

Video Link 1.1: Facebook's Impact

Video Link 1.2: Interview with a Global CEO

Video Link 1.3: Entrepreneurs and Creativity

Video Link 1.4: Ethics and Big Business

⊕ STUDENT STUDY SITE

Visit **www.sagepub.com/baack** to access these additional learning tools:

- Web Quizzes
- eFlashcards
- SAGE Journal Articles

- Country Fact Sheets
- Chapter Outlines
- Interactive Maps

CASE 1 ///

Carrefour: Retailing in an International Marketplace

As the second-largest retailer in the world, the French company Carrefour dominates the global retail market. The company's first store opened on June 3, 1957. The name refers to the location of the first store near a crossroads, or a *carrefour* in French. The company expanded at a strong pace within France during the late 1950s and early 1960s. In June 1963, the company revolutionized the retail industry in Europe with the introduction of the hypermarket. A hypermarket combines a grocery store and a department store. As an early pioneer of this retailing model, Carrefour grew rapidly in France, later Europe, and eventually around the globe.

Currently the company faces many international complexities due to culture, language, economic systems, political and legal systems, and infrastructure. To overcome these obstacles, Carrefour leverages local partners when entering new markets. Carrefour was the first Western retailer to enter the Asian market when it began operations in Taiwan in 1989. The company partnered with the local Taiwanese company Uni President Enterprises Corporation. The marketing team focused on learning about the Asian business environment, especially culture, through this relationship. This knowledge led to expansion in six other Asian markets.

The same strategy of seeking local partners was used in other regions. A local partner helped open the first store in Kuwait, and today stores are located in ten Middle Eastern countries. Local partners assist in adjusting to the country's business culture, provide governmental contacts, and smooth the market entry process.

Carrefour recently experienced problems associated with the global recession and increased competition. In 2010, the company sold outlets in Japan to its Japanese partner and closed 21 of 627 stores in Belgium.[31] The experiences of overcoming these difficulties will serve Carrefour well as the company encounters down cycles in the economies of the future.

Retailing behavior may vary greatly depending on the local culture. The willingness to make large or small changes in response to this differences helped Carrefour achieve success. Adapting to cultural differences in consumption in Thailand required the company to move away from hypermarkets. Instead, in 2010 Carrefour introduced a mini-supermarket in Bangkok. These smaller stores still provide ready-to-eat meals, plus groceries, frozen foods, drinks, and household products. The format was created to better meet local Thai needs and leverage the company's strong position in the country.[32]

Carrefour has made changes to account for religious differences. In the Middle East, to generate goodwill and to meet Islamic expectations of corporate giving, the company often donates to local charities. During Ramadan, the company often makes large contributions to the Red Crescent Society. In 2009, in the United Arab Emirates, Carrefour donated food worth AED625,000 (about $170,000) to people in need.[33]

Carrefour deals with many host country languages, which necessitates strong translation skills and sensitivity to local or regional differences in language. At the most basic level, this means successful translation of the company's name, when necessary. In Chinese, while the sounds for the brand

The French company Carrefour is the second-largest retailer in the world.

name remain close to the French pronunciation, the characters used to make up the name Carrefour translate to "Every Happy Family," which reinforces the company's image.[34]

Carrefour operates in countries with vastly different economic systems. Singapore has a more open market economy than Egypt's economy. The company has been active in the relatively strong command economy of China since 1995. In these situations, the marketing program is adjusted to meet governmental restrictions. There may be limitations on the products that can be sold, the price for certain goods may be set by the government, or the company may be required to find a local partner.

Carrefour also faces political and legal difficulties. While the company's home country, France, has a traditional parliamentary democracy, the company operates in countries with less-representative or less-stable systems. Carrefour entered Pakistan in 2009 even though the marketing team faced a situation with high levels of political risk. In other markets, legal actions hinder activities. In the Indonesian market, the firm was found guilty in a recent antitrust case. The company has appealed, but if the appeal is lost, Carrefour will be forced to sell its stake in a local Indonesian retailer.[35]

As a grocery store, Carrefour sources many of its products locally. To overcome difficulties in infrastructure, the marketing and sales departments often couple education with relationship building. In India, relationships with local suppliers of food have been established through camps for Indian farmers. The camps educate farmers on technical farming skills. This creates important bonds with the company, increases the efficiency of Indian farmers, and, most importantly, improves the sources of food.[36]

With the skill to successfully respond to complexity in international markets, Carrefour continues to aggressively pursue opportunities in growth markets. Specifically targeting Brazil, India, and China, the company moved aggressively into these markets. In 2010, Carrefour entered the Indian market using the strategy of leveraging local partners. In this case, the partner was Kishore Biyani of Pantaloon Retail. Local partners may help Carrefour counter moves by the American Wal-Mart and the British Tesco to corner the $390 billion Indian retail market.[37]

Following the same business strategy that fostered success globally, Carrefour's managers hope to continue to be a worldwide leader in retailing. Whether the difficulty faced is cultural, linguistic, economic, political and legal, or infrastructure, the company's acquired abilities suggest a bright future.

1. How is Carrefour's marketing mix kept consistent across markets?

2. What value does Carrefour provide consistently in all of the various countries in which it operates?

3. How do local partners help Carrefour overcome difficulties in new markets? What is the advantage of that approach?

4. Explain the impact of the drivers of globalization described in this chapter with regard to Carrefour.

5. How have the factors that create international marketing complexity both helped and hurt Carrefour? Has the impact been mostly positive or mostly negative?

2

Country Selection and Entry Strategies

After reading and studying this chapter, you should be able to answer the following questions:

1. What two factors drive market economies, and how are these factors different in command economies?

2. How do Rostow's five stages of economic development apply to the concepts of most-, less-, and least-developed economies, emerging markets, newly industrialized countries, and transition economies?

3. What factors help create a national competitive advantage for an economy?

4. How do the five forces that increase competitive rivalries relate to industry-level competitive advantage?

5. How do the various modes of entry balance a company's level of control with its level of risk?

IN THIS CHAPTER ///

Teens and Jeans: Clothing in Transition

Denim continues to be one of the most widely used fabrics in the world. Pants made of denim are sold on most continents. What varies between nations is how the pants are constructed, marketed, and worn. In some countries denim jeans provide protection from the elements as an individual heads off to work in the fields or a factory. At the other extreme, high-end fashion jeans symbolize status, exclusivity, and social connections.

At the nexus of the blue jean industry, teenagers offer a sweeping and diverse target market. In economies where incomes are low and economic development lags behind other nations, teens still want to wear jeans. Years ago, in the former Soviet Union, any individual who could "import" jeans from the Western world had access to a valuable commodity.

Countries experiencing economic development, when combined with certain cultural elements, demonstrate demand for jeans at all price levels. At the high end, Moleton Brazilian style jeans compete with with low-rise and "butt lift" products. An adventuresome tourist might be tempted to try one or more of these local versions. A web surfer could be enticed to buy a pair online. Nearby countries, and possibly more cutting-edge retailers worldwide, may consider importing these sexy, form-fitting products. Other Brazilian citizens with lower incomes will purchase more standard fare. Brazilian and Spanish textile firms have joined together to sell lower-cost Blue Monster jeans targeting this lower-income market.

Russia features a "hip-hop style" retailer, G-Style, that markets jeans to eager teens. Brands include CLH, Akademiks, Live Mechanics, and Apple Bottoms. These products mimic those sold in the West but are offered at more affordable prices.

In developed countries, jean-wearing features even greater social stratification. Designer French jeans such as 2Leep sell for hundreds of *euros*. Trewano Jeans are popular with the young and teens in Germany. Lees and Levis compete for customers with more modest means, as do Old Navy products in the United States.

Beyond economic conditions, jean-wearing faces the same cultural, language, political and legal systems, and infrastructure variations present for other products. Provocative jeans in Brazil may be deemed highly inappropriate in other cultures. Jean brands must adequately translate into other languages to become viable. Jean vendors must adjust to local infrastructure, including delivery of products and the availability of appropriate retail outlets. Size limitations on retailers may limit potential economies of scale, possibly leading to increased prices or smaller profit margins. Levi Strauss jeans often cost more outside of the United States partially due to these space limitations.[1] Governmental regulations and taxes further influence the marketing of local versus international denim products.

The future of jean-wearing on a global basis includes trends that have evolved in some nations but not in others. The Dockers line in the United States, for example, targets older customers who no longer look or feel good in tight-fitting low-rider products. Currently, many social circles seek worn, faded-looking, and even torn jeans. Manufacturers will need to adjust if this trend ends, much as they did when bell bottom pants went out of style. In any case, the world of jeans presents marketing opportunities to local firms as well as to any international company that can catch the wave of a fashion trend.

QUESTIONS FOR STUDENTS

1. How would purchases of jeans be affected by a nation's approach to commerce, such as communism, socialism, or capitalism?

2. How would the marketing of jeans to teens take place in less-developed nations in which people have lower amounts of money but still wish to wear stylish clothes?

3. How should a company export jeans to another country, through local retailers or by using a more elaborate mode of entry?

Jean-wearing faces the same cultural, language, political and legal systems, and infrastructure variations as other international products.

Overview

Marketing across borders involves many different steps. The process begins with the selection of the country to enter. After choosing the country, the next main decision revolves around the specific type of entry mode to employ, along with how the organization's overall structure will be modified to meet the needs of an international expansion.

This chapter opens with a brief presentation of the various types of economic systems present in the global environment. Economic systems are one of the five primary guiding factors used to analyze the context of international marketing (see Figure 2.1). The degrees of economic development and modernization affect the potential to sell within a given nation. Economic systems help identify groups of nations when considering market entry. Various methods of grouping countries based on type and level of economic development are explored.

Marketers consider industry-level factors when selecting countries. Two industry-focused frameworks are of particular importance. The first framework explains how nations create national-level advantages within certain industries. The second framework consists of the forces that increase competitive intensity within one industry.

Following the decision to enter a country, marketers then choose a mode of entry. The various modes of entry and the factors that influence deployment of one approach over the others are explained in this chapter. The dominant theoretical explanations of this strategic international marketing strategic are reviewed. The chapter concludes with an example of mode of entry choice.

LEARNING OBJECTIVE #1:

What two factors drive market economies, and how are these factors different in command economies?

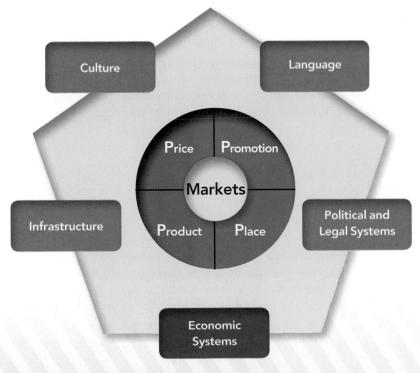

Figure 2.1: The International Marketing Context

VIDEO LINK 2.1:
The Index of
Economic Freedoms

Economic Systems

The economic system present in a country affects the marketing strategies that may be implemented. Economic systems dictate the distribution of resources to members of the society, the ability to accumulate wealth, and levels of purchasing power held by individual consumers. Three basic economic systems are market economies, planned systems, and mixed systems, as shown in Figure 2.2. The terms *capitalism*, *communism*, and *socialism* also apply to these economic systems.

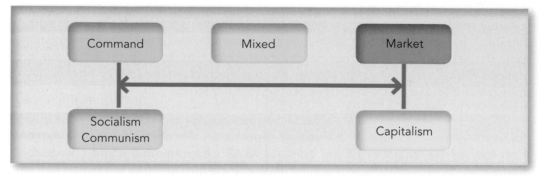

Figure 2.2: Basic Economic Systems

MARKET ECONOMY

An economy in which most economic decisions are made in the marketplace is a **market economy**. The marketplace may be found anywhere money changes hands in a **capitalist economic system**. Purchases are influenced by supply and demand in market economies. *Supply* is the amount of goods and services that producers will provide at various prices. *Demand* is the amount or quantity of goods and services the consumers are willing to buy at various prices. The *market price*, or *equilibrium price*, represents the meeting place between supply and demand. A market economy includes one additional force, profit. Profits take many personal, company, and governmental forms.

> An economy in which most economic decisions are made in the marketplace is a market economy.

Companies earn profits for goods and services when the prices charged create revenues exceed the sum of the costs. The same will be true for individuals or households; profit occurs when income outpaces expenses. Although governments do not make profits, they often encourage businesses to generate them, because company profits are taxed. Governments require tax revenues to pay national expenses. Besides profits, two other forces drive market economies: private property rights and competitive marketplaces.

Private Property Rights

Private property rights allow individuals to buy land, machinery, and other goods. Some of these goods are for personal use, such as houses and furniture, while others can be used to start businesses. A new owner of a restaurant often begins by purchasing or renting a building and the equipment needed to produce and sell the food. An entrepreneur wishing to open a clothing shop will secure a location and then purchase the needed inventory. Property rights are not universal. In China, for example, individuals own the property on the land but only lease the land in various forms of complicated contracts. The leases are for various amounts of time and for specific usages. If the owner of a restaurant in China wants to convert a restaurant into a factory, it may violate the terms of the lease.

Competitive Marketplaces

A free and competitive marketplace means the government does not interfere with prices or sales activities. In any market, some goods cannot be sold without the government becoming involved, such as illegal drugs. Other goods require regulation, including dangerous chemicals. Some countries may set prices for staple items while other countries allow the price to vary. In Venezuela, the prices of bread, milk, and other basic foods are established by the government.[2] In a competitive market economy the government plays a more limited role.

The conservative think tank the Heritage Foundation works with the *Wall Street Journal* to publish a yearly ranking of degree of economic freedom for countries worldwide. Table 2.1 lists the ten most and least economically free countries on this index for 2011.

COMMAND ECONOMY

A central authority makes all key economic decisions in a **command economy**. The government, or a national leader, decides what will be produced, how, and for whom. The two forms of command economies are strong and moderate. Countries with

Ten Most Economically Free Countries, With Overall Score	
Hong Kong	89.7
Singapore	87.2
Australia	82.5
New Zealand	82.3
Switzerland	81.9
Canada	80.8
Ireland	78.7
Denmark	78.6
United States	77.8
Bahrain	77.7
Ten Least Economically Free Countries, With Overall Score	
North Korea	1
Zimbabwe	22.1
Cuba	27.7
Eritrea	36.7
Venezuela	37.6
Myanmar (Burma)	37.8
Libya	38.6
Democratic Republic of Congo	40.7
Iran	42.1

Table 2.1: **Heritage Foundation 2011 Index of Economic Freedom**

Source: Adapted from "2011 Index of Economic Freedom," The Heritage Foundation, Washington, DC, accessed at www.heritage.org/Index/explore.

command economies use socialist economic systems. **Socialism** refers to economic systems where the state owns at least some parts of industry.

In a *strong command economy*, heavy governmental control will be present. Communist states such as Cuba have strong command economies, as do some Latin American and African nations. **Communism** is an extreme form of socialism that bans private ownership of property. Communist states try to reach a goal of full employment, where every citizen who wants a job has one.

Cuba represents one of the last strong command economies in the world. Facing an economic crisis, reforms of the system have been proposed. At present, the majority of the citizens in the country work at state-owned companies. Government officials manage these companies. Governments also regulate land use and permission must be received from officials before idle land can be farmed.[3]

In *moderate command economies* a degree of private enterprise operates. The state owns all of the major resources, which may include mining and ores, other national resources, and some industries such as airlines. Governmental leaders seek the goal of high levels of employment, and often a strong welfare state supports the unemployed.

The distribution of wealth represents one primary difference between a command economy and a marketplace economy. In a market economy, only those who in some way contribute to profits find employment. Often, great poverty and great wealth exist in the same country. In a command economy, differences in wealth may be less dramatic for most of the population, but in many command economies the poor are far poorer than in free market economies.

MIXED ECONOMY

When the marketplace guides part of an economic system, and the government runs the other part, the nation features a **mixed economy**. The government typically oversees defense, education, building and repairing roads, fire protection, and other general services. The marketplace vends other items, including necessities, sundries, and luxuries.

Most countries have mixed economies. One force, the marketplace or the government, tends to be more dominant than the other. In the United States, the marketplace is more dominant than the government. In many European and Latin American countries the government is more dominant. These types of economic systems can be used by the marketing team for an international company to help identify potential customers and to better understand the potential economic regulatory forces the business may encounter.

LEARNING OBJECTIVE #2:

How do Rostow's five stages of economic development apply to the concepts of most-, less-, and least-developed economies, emerging markets, newly industrialized countries, and transition economies?

VIDEO LINK 2.2: The G20 Nations

Economic Development

The degree of economic development present in a region constitutes an important consideration for marketing teams. In the literature associated with evaluation of the economic and social status of a nation, many political and ideological controversies have arisen. At the core, an argument regarding what constitutes "development" and "modernization" continues. These debates are not likely to be resolved by marketers or scholars in the near future. At the same time, it is evident that various nations exhibit differing patterns of work activity, product development and sale, levels of employment, and consumption based on some notion of the "stages" of development or economic activity. These distinctions are often useful in assessing the business potential of a country.

MOST-, LESS-, AND LEAST-DEVELOPED ECONOMIES

The various views of economic development have been summarized by the terms *most-, less-,* and *least-developed*. These categories are used by the United Nations and have replaced the first, second, and third world categorization system that was previously used. Table 2.2 indicates some of the nations that have been identified in each of these categories. Purchases of products and services are affected by the status of each, which in turn affects the ability for international companies to secure new market segments.

The stage of economic development determines the potential to market and sell goods and services in a given region. In a least-developed nation, fewer items may be salable and most would be targeted at basic needs. Greater development affords an increased number of potential products to be sold to an expanding number of

	POPULATION	GDP PER CAPITA (PPP)	NUMBER OF MOBILE PHONES	MOBILE PHONES PER 100 PEOPLE
Most-Developed Countries (Industrialized with high per capita incomes)				
Canada	33,487,000	$38,400	21,455,000	64.1
Germany	82,329,000	$34,200	107,245,000	130.3
United Kingdom	61,113,000	$35,400	75,565,000	123.6
France	64,057,000	$32,800	59,259,000	92.5
Japan	127,078,000	$32,600	110,395,000	86.9
United States	307,212,000	$46,400	270,000,000	87.9
Less-Developed Countries (Industrially developing with some world trade)				
Colombia	43,677,000	$9,200	41,365,000	94.7
Thailand	65,998,000	$8,100	62,000,000	93.9
Chile	16,601,000	$14,700	14,797,000	89.1
China	1,338,612,000	$6,500	634,000,000	47.36
Brazil	198,739,000	$10,200	150,641,000	75.7
India	1,156,897,000	$3,100	545,000,000	47.1
Least-Developed Countries (Industrially underdeveloped, agrarian, subsistence)				
Niger	15,306,000	$2,400	1,677,000	11.0
Chad	10,329,000	$1,500	1,809,000	17.5
Sudan	41,087,000	$2,300	11,186,000	27.2
Myanmar (Burma)	48,137,000	$1,200	375,000	0.78
Cambodia	14,494,000	$1,900	4,237,000	29.2
Haiti	9,035,000	$1,300	3,200,000	35.4

Table 2.2: **Consumption Rates in Most-, Less-, and Least-Developed Countries**

Source: Adapted from the *CIA World Factbook.*

potential customers. A mobile phone "app" that makes it possible to find a restaurant and place a reservation online would be most viable in the most-developed countries, especially Germany and the United Kingdom, which have the greatest number of cell phone owners per capita. In least-developed nations, especially Burma (Myanmar) and Niger, the marketing team would expect few potential consumers for both the app and for restaurants with online booking facilities.

ROSTOW MODERNIZATION MODEL

One view of the manner in which an economy develops and grows was proposed by Walt Whitman Rostow. The model includes five stages, as indicated in Figure 2.3. In the model, a *traditional society* represents the first stage of development. In this type of subsistence economy, farming is the primary occupation and means of production. Limited technology exists, and the capital required to purchase raw materials and create services and industries is not widely available. The term often used to describe this type of society is *underdeveloped*, and citizens have income levels found at the bottom-of-the-pyramid.

Traditional Society
Preconditions for Take-off
Take-off
The Drive to Maturity
The Age of Mass Consumption

Figure 2.3: Rostow Stages of Development

The second stage, *preconditions for take-off*, takes place when the levels of technology within a country begin to emerge. This stage requires the development of a rudimentary transportation system that encourages trade. These two phases signal the earliest signs of a developing economy.

During the third stage, *take-off*, manufacturing industries grow rapidly; airports, roads, and railways are built; and growth expands as investment increases. One of the characteristics of a nation in take-off mode is that a few leading industries can support long-term economic growth. England experienced take-off when the textile industry emerged in the seventeenth century.

In the fourth stage, *the drive to maturity*, growth remains self-sustaining, having spread to all parts of the country, and leads to an increase in the number and types of industries. More sophisticated transportation systems such as modern road systems and airports evolve and manufacturing expands, combined with improved electrical systems and increased access to electricity. This leads to rapid urbanization. Some traditional industries (such as textiles in England) may decline. Mature countries are sometimes called "industrialized."

In the fifth and final stage, *the age of mass consumption*, rapid expansion of tertiary, third-wave support industries occurs alongside a decline in manufacturing. Citizens in these economic systems enjoy abundance, prosperity, and a variety of purchasing choices.[4]

In each stage, the presence and growth of potential target markets changes. Development of an economy typically leads to a wider variety of products and services combined with increasing competition. When a government limits free enterprise, consumers have fewer options, and fewer potential target markets are present.

Social Challenges

Economic development, while beneficial in many ways, may be accompanied by new social challenges. Rising levels of drug abuse, prostitution, and pollution emerge as a greater number of individuals earn more money and have more disposable income. Development may also lead to urban congestion and higher crime rates, making it necessary to add greater police protection.

Social changes result from economic development. Women may marry later, remain employed, and have fewer children. Traditional extended family relationships, particularly between parents and children, are affected. These trends often run counter to traditional social norms.

EMERGING MARKETS

Rapid global economic development has occurred in many countries over the past fifty to sixty years. These nations have passed through most of the Rostow modernization process. As a result, many regions enjoy improved living circumstances for citizens. These nations have emerged as sophisticated markets for foreign businesses. Countries moving through the transformation from developing to developed are termed **emerging markets**. Such economies offer increased access to global goods and services. Mexico, South Africa, and several countries in Asia have been characterized as emerging markets. The term *EMM* (emerging market multinational) is used to describe multinational corporations operating in emerging markets.[5]

> Countries moving through the transformation from developing to developed are termed emerging markets.

A distinct subclass of emerging markets exists: big emerging markets (BEMS). These are countries that have experienced rapid economic development and growth that are also large in terms of population and overall area. The four largest BEMS are known as the BRIC countries: Brazil, Russia, India, and China. Each has become a major economic and political force within its geographic region, due to its relative size. BEMS offer international marketers large markets, lower costs relating to production, and opportunities to learn about rapidly changing marketplaces.[6] Economic developments in these nations improve the economies of neighboring countries that have trade or business ties. The size of each of these markets makes it a more appealing location for foreign investment and market entry. The recent focus on China and India, by both

Newly industrialized countries take advantage of one or more factors of production.

businesses and the popular press, provides an example of the influence of emerging market economies. International marketers carefully research consumers in these nations to assess potential marketing mix strategies.[7]

NEWLY INDUSTRIALIZED COUNTRIES

The two frameworks (most-, less-, and least-developed countries, and the Rostow modernization model) have been criticized for failing to recognize that some nations have experienced rapid economic expansion and industrialization. This means they are neither less nor more developed. Instead, these nations are characterized as being **newly industrialized countries**. Examples include China, Taiwan, South Korea, Hong Kong, Mexico, and Brazil.

Newly industrialized countries are always emerging markets, even though not all emerging markets are necessarily newly industrialized countries. Figure 2.4 indicates some of the characteristics exhibited by newly industrialized countries. The characteristics suggest that governmental forces often dictate the path to development. In contrast, some emerging markets may not exhibit them. Russia offers an example of this type of economy. Russia remains more dependent on commodities, specifically natural gas and oil, than a typical newly industrialized country.[8] National leaders do not focus on exports and have not undertaken many of the legal or economic reform steps that would be found in a newly industrialized country.

Political stability
Strong savings rates
Outward orientation to expand into foreign markets
Advantage in one or more factors of production (land, labor, raw materials, technology)
Presence of growth industries
Emphasis on entrepreneurship
Economic and legal reforms

Figure 2.4: Factors Related to Growth in Newly Industrialized Countries

Most newly industrialized countries have been able to create trade relationships with other nations and to attract foreign investment. Numerous factors contribute to the rapid growth of newly industrialized countries, including those displayed in Figure 2.4.[9] The powerful expansion of trade and increased standard of living present in South Korea, Taiwan, Hong Kong, and Singapore has led to these nations being referred to as the Four Tigers, or the Little Dragons of East Asia.

Newly industrialized countries offer the potential to reach new target markets. Foreign investors and companies build relationships that allow a freer trade environment, which leads to such opportunities.

TRANSITION ECONOMIES

Transition economies occur in what were formally communist countries with centrally planned economies. During the past twenty years, many of these countries, particularly those in Eastern Europe, transitioned from centrally planned communist states to free market economies. In some countries, the conversion was made rapidly and by design. Examples include Poland and Slovenia, which were both were behind the "Iron Curtain." Slovenia was part of Yugoslavia and began the changeover to a separate nation in 1991. Democracy flourished and the country moved rapidly to transition economically. Helped by various factors, including political stability and a geographic location on important trade routes, the country developed rapidly. The first Eastern Europe country to join the European Union, Slovenia was also the first to adopt the *euro*.[10] The changes were accompanied with revisions in political systems. In other countries, such as China, the economic transition has not been coupled with political change and has been more incremental.

Transition economies represent important opportunities for international marketers. Governments in these countries work to improve the standard of living and quality of life for citizens.[11] The countries often exhibit a split in consumption patterns. Younger consumers that grew up in a free market system become more likely to purchase foreign goods. Older consumers, especially those accustomed to a centrally planned economy, remain more resistant to foreign goods and may even call for a return to communism. These individuals often suffer from "transition fatigue."

Corruption commonly constrains transition to a more open market in these economies as national leaders cope with the vestigial remnants of the communist regime. Changing institutions does not necessarily change mindsets. Some governmental leaders worry that a transition that moves too rapidly may lead to democracies without citizens that are ready to participate. Corruption, both at the corporate and consumer levels, then becomes a major obstacle to economic progress. Table 2.3 presents part of the Transparency International survey of corruption in 178 countries. The index ranks countries according to the perception of corruption in the public sector.

Ten Countries With Highest Index Scores	
Denmark	9.3
New Zealand	9.3
Singapore	9.3
Finland	9.2
Sweden	9.2
Canada	8.9
Netherlands	8.8
Australia	8.7
Switzerland	8.7
Norway	8.6
Ten Countries With Lowest Index Scores	
Somalia	1.1
Myanmar (Burma)	1.4
Afghanistan	1.4
Iraq	1.5
Uzbekistan	1.6
Turkmenistan	1.6
Sudan	1.6
Chad	1.7
Burundi	1.8
Equatorial Guinea	1.9

Table 2.3: **Transparency International Corruption Perception Index 2010**

Source: Adapted from "Corruption Perceptions Index 2010 Results," Transparency International, Berlin, accessed at www.transparency.org/policy_research/surveys_indices/cpi/2010/results.

In the case of Poland, where a prototypical transition took place, the nation underwent massive changes in the early 1990s. On January 1, 1990, the Polish government introduced a set of economic reforms that have been called "shock therapy." While the tactics met with criticism, they did lead to a rapid transition for the average Polish citizen. To quote a common and ironic phrase from the country, "The task may be difficult, but the resources are scarce." Although the rapid transition has exacerbated the gap between young and old and rural and urban, it ultimately moved Poland's level of growth to the point that the country now belongs to the European Union.

Transition economies such as Poland's create opportunities for both local and foreign businesses. Management and marketing skills become commodities in themselves, as individuals encountering an entirely new economic system adjust to different circumstances.

Transitions produce opportunities for new companies to fill gaps left over from communist systems. For example, bananas were scarce in Poland before the changeover. The introduction of the fruit to the Polish marketplace led one young boy to ask his father, "What are those yellow sausages?" The first marketer to introduce bananas to the country made a large profit.

A dynamic conversion environment generates entrepreneurship opportunities. In countries including China, Poland, and Slovenia, the activities of entrepreneurs have spurred growth and helped more efficiently allocate resources.[12] Figure 2.5 displays some of the features of transition economies.

Liberalization	Prices set by supply and demand, removal of trade barriers.
Privatization	Previously government-owned industries moved to private ownership.
Legal and Institutional	Legal structures set up to allow for ownership of property.
Reforms	Contracts enforced, and the rule of law allowed.
Budget Reform	Hard budget caps set by governments to help control inflation.

Figure 2.5: Features of Transition Economies

EFFECTS ON INTERNATIONAL MARKETING

The economic system and the level of development present in a country directly affect an international marketing program. As an example, a command economy would not allow the degree of diversity of products that could be targeted at individual groups, as compared to a market economy. When a mixed system exists, the marketing team identifies the products that may be produced in the society and differentiates them from those controlled by the government.

The nature of competition may also be influenced by the economic system. A country producing a single form of a product faces no internal competition. The product will be positioned and sold to target markets in other nations, creating a different type of competition.[13]

INTERNATIONAL INCIDENT ///

An executive from Argentina traveled to Japan to finalize a sale of raw materials. The executive was careful to bow in the appropriate fashion and had memorized a greeting in Japanese. He also had purchased an appropriate gift for the occasion. When negotiations for the final price began, the Argentine executive offered what he felt was an appropriate price. The Japanese management team sat quietly and did not respond. The executive soon began to feel uncomfortable. He offered a lower price just to break the silence. Did he make a good decision, or was he missing something?

The developmental process that countries are undergoing also affects marketing activities. Transition economies do not exhibit the same characteristics as those in newly industrialized countries, which suggests that consumers in these markets will also be different. Transition economy consumers may be uncomfortable with the pricing process or be unaware of basic products and product categories. Higher levels of product and brand awareness are often present in newly industrialized country consumers. At the same time, newly industrialized countries are more likely to have governmental protection of local companies, especially in early stages, which limits the ability of foreign companies to compete.

VIDEO LINK 2.3:
Negotiation

STAGE OF DEVELOPMENT AND BOTTOM-OF-THE-PYRAMID

Low-income, bottom-of-the-pyramid customers are most likely to reside in least-developed economies or in Rostow's traditional societies. When a substantial cluster of low-income individuals is present in a geographic area, it is likely that the infrastructure has not been advanced, that the culture revolves around agrarian life and poverty, that skill sets are low among the majority of citizens, and that the political and legal systems do little to improve living conditions for persons in the area.

In such circumstances, a common item, such as a soft drink, is purchased far less frequently. In Kenya, an average citizen consumes thirty-nine servings of Coca-Cola per year. In the developing country Mexico, the average citizen consumes 665 servings per year. Ned Dewees, a major investor in soft drink common stock shares, concludes that Africa offers an "enormous opportunity" for Coke. As nations begin to evolve in to the take-off stage, consumption rates are expected to rise dramatically.[14]

Many marketers are taking a new look at least-developed, traditional economies. The potential does exist for products that are tailored to consumers in those regions. As an economy moves forward and infrastructure emerges, the opportunities tend to grow and expand impressively.[15]

Global Competition and National Competitive Advantage

International marketers choose which country to enter based in part on the specific features of that country. Beyond the economic development issues above, countries can also be analyzed based on what each does well. Some have built a reputation for technological superiority, such as Japan and Germany,

LEARNING OBJECTIVE #3:

What factors help create a national competitive advantage for an economy?

Demand conditions
Related and supporting industries
Firm strategy, structure, and rivalry
Factor conditions
Government

Figure 2.6: National Competitive Advantage Factors

while others including China and India gain attention based on lower labor costs. Certain industries become the basis of global leadership or **national competitive advantage** for countries.

The theory of national competitive advantage, introduced by Michael Porter, explains the reasons why countries succeed at certain industries and not in others. As displayed in Figure 2.6, Porter's diamond introduces five factors that generate national competitive advantage. The factors move beyond the traditional focus on cost of labor, currency differences, or natural resources and instead concentrate on what leads a country to innovate. The ability to innovate helps establish national competitive advantage. The first four factors drive overall national competitive advantage. The fifth factor, the government, indicates how an administration can leverage and encourage the development of the first four factors.

DEMAND CONDITIONS

Consumers, businesses, and governments demand various goods and services. The unique features of demand in a nation make up that country's demand conditions. By being responsive to domestic consumer needs, nations may be more or less responsive to consumers in other countries, especially when the domestic market is larger or more sophisticated than foreign markets. Consumers who move the global taste in a category or industry help a nation become global leaders in that category.

Consider fashion in France. French consumer tastes in high fashion results in changes in fashion around the globe. Sophisticated consumers force French designers to be cutting edge and provide the nation with an advantage, which has been institutionalized as *haute couture* or "high dressmaking." To qualify for this designation, French law requires each producer to register with the government. Complicated standards must be met to receive this designation.[16]

RELATED AND SUPPORTING INDUSTRIES

Industries need support from various other companies that provide inputs, support production, or facilitate other aspects of the industry. These factors come from related and supporting industries. Nations with this type of support network exhibit one of the conditions required to generate a national competitive advantage in that industry.

Nokia, the world's largest cell phone manufacturer, is based in Finland. Within Finland, Nokia has the support industries needed to be successful, including Codenomicon, which tests the robustness of software; Navicron, a wireless technology company; and Tracker, which provides navigation software.[17] The presence of these other companies provides an advantage to Nokia over competitors, and by extension leads to innovation, which in turn results in a national competitive advantage in cell phone production for Finland.

FIRM STRATEGY, STRUCTURE, AND RIVALRY

Nations also differ in terms of how the government allows companies to be formed, maintained, and structured, including control of domestic and potentially foreign competitors. Firm strategy, structure, and rivalry refer to these features.

National differences exist between the systems in Germany and Italy. In Italy, companies tend to be smaller, family owned, and privately held. German companies, in contrast, often are large and highly structured, and employ managers with technical backgrounds. These differences partially explain the German focus on sophisticated engineering designed to create mass-market products. Italians focus on luxury, high-end products. Multiple companies fall into these designations, leading to intense rivalries between German automakers or between Italian leather companies.[18]

FACTOR CONDITIONS

Factor conditions include components needed for production of goods or services, such as labor and infrastructure. Each industry has specific factors associated with success in that field. Traditionally, these factors were natural endowments that nations possessed without effort. They might be labor or land or various natural resources such as oil or minerals. Increasingly, national competitive advantage grows from resources that have been created. Trained human resources or a strong scientific community are examples of these advantages created resources.

Large labor pools or other natural resources by themselves do not lead to innovation. Japan has been described as "an island nation with no natural resources."[19] The lack of resources led the country's leaders to focus on education and creating the skilled human resources needed to compete globally. Even a country with an ample supply of petroleum needs the technological knowledge necessary to access that resource.

Factor conditions include components needed for production of goods or services, such as labor and infrastructure.

Factor conditions most clearly lead to national competitive advantage when specialization exists. Consider the highly specialized, highly-focused skills needed to succeed in the film industry. The American film industry represents a national competitive advantage for the country, and the various directors, actors, producers, and cinematographers that create these products are arguably the best at the trade globally. As a result, American movies generate money globally. The movie *Avatar* earned more than $2 billion worldwide, including more than $100 million in Germany, the United Kingdom, Russia, France, and China.[20] Films made in India in what is called Bollywood have begun to compete in this marketplace through the introduction of similar technologies and skills, which were best exemplified by the best-selling film *Three Idiots*.

GOVERNMENT

As is the case in a mixed economy, both the government and the free market play a role in creating national competitive advantage. Industry innovation results from competition; however, governmental activities can establish the infrastructure needed to assist in the effort. Governmental support for education, cooperation between related industries, new technologies, emerging industries, and consumer protections all enhance an environment that leads to industrial innovation.

Governments that do not intervene in trade or in competition for resources help expand the foundation for innovation. Laws that limit cooperation between direct industry rivals lead to innovation through competition. In general, policies that increase competition while supporting innovation help create national competitive advantage.

When successful, governmental activities guide a nation with one or more clusters of similar industries that together can generate national competitive advantage. Examples include Silicon Valley software companies and London's financial industry. In new industries, nations may compete to establish the dominant cluster. China's rapid entry into the windmill market positions Beijing as the potential home to the world's leading windmill producers, including Sinovel and Goldwind.[21]

LEARNING OBJECTIVE #4:

How do the five forces that increase competitive rivalries relate to industry-level competitive advantage?

Industry-Level Competitive Advantage

Industries also compete internally. The same theorist who initially described national competitive advantage, Michael Porter, writes about factors associated with industry-level competitive advantage. Five competitive forces influence overall industry competitive intensity (see Figure 2.7). The first four forces work together to increase rivalries among competitors, the last force. Analysis of these forces helps identify the level of competitive intensity in an industry within a country. A country with a highly intense competitive environment may be unattractive for potential entry. The competition lowers potential profit and increases the chance of company failure.

THREAT OF NEW ENTRANTS

The threat of new entrants affects the nature of local, national, and international competition. High profit margins or large potential markets of consumers attract new entrants. The large size of the markets in Big Emerging Markets alone sparks interest and increases the chance of new entrants. For industries in those countries, a larger market size increases the potential for new competitors.

| Threat of new entrants |
| Threat of substitute products |
| Bargaining power of suppliers |
| Bargaining power of consumers |
| Rivalry among competitors |

Figure 2.7: Five Competitive Forces

Barriers to entry can be used by companies to prevent or limit new entrants. In addition, steps that make it difficult to leave an industry or barriers to exit can also limit new entrants. Brand equity, large initial cost requirements, regulations, monopolies over distribution or needed resources, and/or lack of specific, hard-to-learn knowledge can all create barriers to entry.

ZTE is a Chinese telecommunications equipment manufacturer that focused on entering the European market. The company's marketing team recognized that significant barriers limit the ability to be a successful new entrant to the European market. To gain the cultural knowledge needed ZTE found local partners. Some barriers the company encountered were not controllable. European Union officials, in response to pressures from European business competing with ZTE, are considering placing tariffs on some of ZTE's products.[22]

THREAT OF SUBSTITUTE PRODUCTS

The existence of substitute products increases competitive intensity. When consumers can switch from product to product, companies face stronger pressure from competitors to get consumers to make the switch. To respond, marketers may attempt to increase switching costs or seek to retain customers in some other way.

Brand loyalty, product differentiation, and repeat purchase rewards all decrease switching. Increasing brand loyalty, which may be accomplished by exceeding customer expectations and by delivering value, constitutes a key marketing goal in many companies. A hotel in Cameroon that provides Internet access and attentive concierge services, and tailors a customer's stay to his or her personal preferences, exceeds expectations. A restaurant in Spain selling the national dish *paella* might charge a modestly lower price than competitors while offering equal taste and portion size to compete with other restaurants. Both the hotel in Cameroon and the restaurant in Spain discourage competition, especially when no comparable or substitute services (overnight lodging or local cuisine) are available.

Product differentiation occurs when a product achieves the status of being different from the competition. Korean Airlines has made substantial efforts to differentiate the company from other carriers. While travel substitutes exist, none offers the speed and convenience of a trip on the company's jets. An international firm that successfully establishes product differentiation may be able to reduce competition, charge a higher price, and enjoy above-normal profits from its marketing efforts.[23]

Repeat purchases dampen the opportunities to take away market share and to create substitute products. A person accustomed to buying a local flavor of chewing gum will be unlikely to switch to chewing tobacco or some gum from another country.

BARGAINING POWER OF SUPPLIERS

Companies within an industry typically use the same supplier or a small group of suppliers for the resources needed, including labor and raw materials. Suppliers of these resources with strong bargaining power increase the competition within the industry. Bargaining power increases when there is only one or a small number of suppliers. A resource provided by one or a small number of suppliers results in greater power for the producers of that resource. Prices for the resource rise and suppliers, in the worst-case scenario, can refuse to provide the resource.

Marketers may take steps to lower the bargaining power of suppliers. If necessary, companies can buy the supplier or start to supply the resource internally. Companies that find substitutes for the resource or look in other markets, such as in other countries, for potential new suppliers reduce supplier bargaining power.

Wal-Mart, the global chain of retailers, initially signed an exclusive contract with Toronto-based Cott Corporation in 2002 to supply the company with its store brand Sam's soft drinks. Wal-Mart, having more power than the supplier, made the decision to end that exclusive relationship effective January 2012 and pursued an alternate approach in which multiple companies supply soft drinks for the store brand. If the power had rested with Cott Corporation, Wal-Mart would not have been able to make this change.[24]

BARGAINING POWER OF CONSUMERS

Consumers also possess bargaining power. When only a few individuals purchase a product, such as can be the case in business-to-business marketing, those buyers hold more power. As with supplier power, small numbers of consumers increase competition. Industries with high-cost items also face more consumer power because the companies within the industry are dependent on each sale. Price sensitivity increases consumer power due to the increased likelihood of a customer switching to a lower-priced competitor.

Brand loyalty may decrease consumer bargaining power. The same holds true for opening new markets or increasing market share. In general, moving to increase the number of consumers reduces rivalries within an industry. An increase in the numbers of consumers increases the size of the "pie" of revenue that companies compete for. Brand loyalty and growth in market size both shift power from consumers to producer companies.

RIVALRY AMONG COMPETITORS

Together, the four forces above work to increase rivalry among competitors. An industry with high supplier and consumer bargaining power, many substitute products, and a strong threat of new entrants is forced to cope with extreme rivalry among competitors.

An agrarian economy normally features limited travel, primitive technology, and an emphasis on manual labor.

Company-specific factors, outside of the four forces discussed in this section, also increase rivalries among competitors. Widely accessible knowledge and processes result in more rivalry than does specialized, difficult-to-imitate knowledge. Innovation, especially when legally protected, can reduce competition within an industry. The ease of copying the drivers of another company's success provides the impetus to compete.

When every company in an industry competes based on similar, duplicable factors, rivalry becomes more intense. When companies instead compete based on specialized knowledge, rivalry will be reduced. In the pharmaceutical industry in many countries, when a single pharmaceutical company introduces a new medicine, that drug is protected from competition for a set period of time. During that time period, the legal prohibition of copying the drug drastically reduces the level of competition and rivalry. Once the protection is removed, competing pharmaceutical companies are allowed to introduce versions of the medicine, which greatly increases the level of rivalry.

Economic Forces and International Marketing

Economic forces interact with the other primary influences on international marketing, as displayed in Figure 2.1. Culture, language, political and legal systems, and infrastructure combine to determine the overall marketing environment in a country.

Economic forces are strongly linked to *culture*. An agrarian economy normally features limited travel, primitive technology, and an emphasis on manual labor. At the extreme, sons in a patriarchal agrarian society are highly valued for their ability to work, whereas daughters are viewed as an expense. In many areas of China, where government attempts to limit each family to one child, the number of males born far exceeds the number of females. Culture, consumer behavior, and economic development tend to interact with one another. Recent work highlights that the consumer value *materialism* is on the rise in China, in part due to changing economic forces.[25]

Language will also be affected by an economy and by economic development. New terminology associated with technology becomes part of the language. Terms such as "tweet" or "QR code" have been introduced globally in the past few years. In many parts of the world, citizens speak more than one language, which can translate into additional marketing opportunities, but also can increase the threat of entry by outside competitors, because multiple languages facilitate the ease of entry.

Political and legal systems are strongly tied to economic systems through laws that regulate commerce and by granting or withholding private property rights. Governmental activities may also be designed to influence the economic system. Governments can establish protectionist tax codes, seek to keep out international imports, or establish other policies designed to encourage international trade. Some governments go to the extreme of supporting practices such as *dumping*, the deliberate underpricing of goods in order to gain entry into another country. Political and legal systems can speed up or slow down progress to a more sophisticated economic environment, as evidenced by levels of economic change in Poland as compared to China.

Economic growth reflects the addition of more-complex *infrastructure*, including communication systems, roads, and other utilities such as electric power and running water. Infrastructure development plays a prominent role in the Rostow modernization model.

In summary, any marketing team considering entry into a new country should carefully consider its economic environment before taking any additional steps. Many times the economic system in one country will be similar to that of a nearby nation. Countries in the European Union contain such similarities, as do the Four Asian Tigers. The same holds true for the United States and Canada. Comparable economic systems often make entry into a new country easier to accomplish. Whether the system is similar or dissimilar, one of the next projects for marketers will be to select the best mode of entry into that nation.

Sustainability and International Marketing

The continuing focus on sustainability remains likely to continue in international marketing. Consumer demand for green products has grown and marketers realize that serving those needs attracts many consumers. As technologies improve, sustainable business practices lead to lower costs and increased profits.

Several traditional global business giants lead the movement to sustainable business practices. Wal-Mart, a recognized leader in distribution systems, has focused on becoming more sustainable in recent years. In 2010, the company opened a $115 million fresh-food green distribution center in Canada. The advances in the center will save the company approximately $4.8 billion in energy cost by using hydrogen fuel cells for the vehicles in the plant. The plant also features solar, thermal, and wind power. Company plants and stores now feature low-energy or LED lighting, and ammonia can be substituted for Freon in refrigeration systems.[26]

The global economic downturn led to a strong push to buying local, particularly in those countries most strongly affected by the 2008–2009 recession. Motivated by multiple reasons, but particularly by the drive to spend money locally to help maintain local employment, the buy-local movement has reduced the environmental footprints of many businesses. A banana grown in Florida travels a far shorter distance to an American grocer than one grown in Brazil. The reduction in miles results in lower greenhouse gases released into the atmosphere.

Economic development in emerging markets has brought with it large environmental costs. In China, 200 million citizens are projected to move from poverty into the middle class in the coming decade. Significant environmental implications of this growth exist. The building of dams to generate hydroelectric energy to fuel Chinese growth has displaced at least 23 million people and may have caused the Sichuan earthquake that killed 80,000 people in 2008.[27]

Use of virtual water offers a simple example that captures the challenge of sustainability. Production of a product or service requires water. That product or service is then exported. The traded good then represents the transfer of water from one country to another. For example, one ton of beef exported from the United States contains approximately 13,193 metric tons of virtual water.[28] Map 2.1 identifies the net virtual water resulting from trade for countries globally. Map 2.2 displays water consumption footprints, on average, for various countries.

Balancing economic growth with environmental protection may be the largest challenge facing the globe as more countries develop economically. Sustainable business practices, when properly implemented, have the potential to address these concerns. The greatest amount of attention to sustainability is likely to be paid by companies in least-, less-, and most-developed countries.

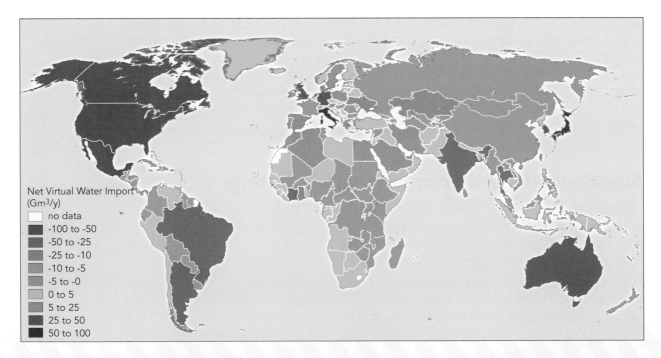

Net Virtual Water Import (Gm^3/y)

- no data
- -100 to -50
- -50 to -25
- -25 to -10
- -10 to -5
- -5 to -0
- 0 to 5
- 5 to 25
- 25 to 50
- 50 to 100

Map 2.1: **Net Virtual Water Globally**
Trade also moves "virtual water," or the water used to produce the good or service being traded.

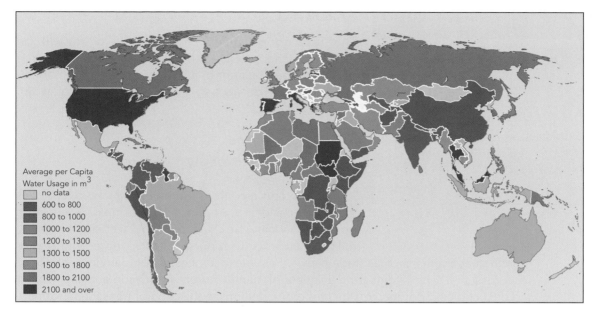

Map 2.2: **Global Water Consumption Footprints**
As countries develop economically, water consumption increases. Sustainability advocates aim to reduce each nation's global water footprint.

INTERNATIONAL INCIDENT //

An international salesperson in Indonesia obtained his college and graduate (MBA) education in the United States, where he acquired a taste for cold American beers. On his first sales trip to Great Britain, where he is seeking to find retail outlets to sell his products, his host offers to buy beers at a famous local pub in Leeds. Thrilled that it appears he is building a cordial relationship with the prospect, the salesperson accepts. The host insists on buying the first round, and glasses of room-temperature ale are served. The Indonesian salesperson had never consumed beer prior to college in the United States. He finds the taste of the beer hard to handle and worries that it might be "spoiled." At the same time, he sees that his host clearly enjoying his glass of ale. The salesperson wonders if he should ask for a cold beer, risking insult to his client. It occurs to him that a cold beer might cost more, or that the pub does not carry any in stock. It might also be possible to use the occasion to reveal a little more about himself and his collegiate background, thereby building the relationship by making light of the situation and even poking a little fun at himself. He also considers simply sipping his ale for a time and seeing if he could adapt to the taste, although it already has upset his stomach a bit. What should the salesperson do?

Modes of Entry

After selecting a country to enter, international marketers then take steps to move the product to that market. Several options exist. The various approaches are called entry modes. Figure 2.8 provides a list. These entry modes have different levels of corporate control, cost, and risk. International marketers balance these concerns and choose the entry mode that best fits the internal environment of the country being entered.

LEARNING OBJECTIVE #5:

How do the various modes of entry balance a company's level of control with its level of risk?

Types of Entry Mode	Concerns
Exporting	Cost
Licensing	Control
Franchising	Risk
Wholly Owned Subsidiary	
Joint Venture	
Strategic Alliance	

Figure 2.8: Types of Entry Mode

EXPORTING

The first option many companies explore will be **exporting** the product, which means the product is shipped in one manner or another into a foreign market. Exporting can be accomplished in a variety of ways, including

- direct sales and
- use of an intermediary.

The rise and growth of the Internet make *direct sales* methods easier to implement. Business-to-business transactions may be facilitated by website contacts, followed by visits from personal sales representatives or meetings at events such as trade shows. In some instances, a company may shop for resources or finished items from a variety of manufacturers worldwide and then select the best choice. Spot markets for crude oil often utilize this type of transaction format.

Individual customers surfing the web are able to locate products that will be directly shipped to any nation with infrastructure that has developed to the point in which routine package delivery takes place. A Swedish tourist who visits Hawai`i and enjoys macadamia nut products there can easily locate ABC Stores or Hilo Hatties, make purchases, and have them delivered by FedEx or some other method to her home.

Numerous *intermediaries* represent products across networks of countries. Agent wholesalers or retailers represent items without taking title to those goods. These types of intermediaries facilitate transactions in business-to-business and consumer markets. An Italian olive oil company can contract with an intermediary to represent the product in any country where olive oil use has begun to rise. A ticket transaction company in Ireland sells tickets to soccer matches to buyers from nearby countries as well as to fans that live farther away.

Merchant intermediaries buy and resell items. Silk cloth woven in Japan may be purchased by wholesalers who vend it to fabric stores and clothing manufacturers in other countries.

VIDEO LINK 2.4:
Market Entry Tips

In these instances, items are exported and sold in other countries without any additional company restructuring or activity. The advantage for exporting lies in its low cost relative to any other form of entry mode. With no large purchases made or long-term obligations to local partners, exporting represents the easiest form of market entry. The concern revolves around lack of control. In some cases, the company literally ships the good and has no further contact with it. No control exists for the retailers that buy and/or sell items. The manufacturer cannot offer input into matters such as product displays or other important elements involved in consumer choice and satisfaction. Without this control, the company risks losing the ability to later enter the market more aggressively.

LICENSING

Instead of entering a country, marketers can chose **licensing**, or a contract that grants a company the legal right to use another company's brand, image, and other marketing components. Many large and successful global brands use licensing to increase revenues. Several professional basketball and soccer teams have licensing agreements that allow other firms to create jerseys, hats, and other items bearing the team's name, logo, and often the name of the star player. In exchange, the teams receive licensing fees.

Fast-food chains can create licensing arrangements to expand internationally.

Popular press books and textbooks are often licensed to other countries. Novels written in Spanish in Paraguay that receive international acclaim will quickly be licensed for translation to other countries. Many textbook providers license books for reprint and sale in other countries, including a translation combined with cultural adaptation. For instance, a photo of a woman dressed in provocative clothing that appears in a Canadian textbook will be removed when the book is sent to a Muslim country such as Saudi Arabia in order to avoid offending students and professors.

Licensing can provide a quick, low-cost method for entering a foreign market. Selling the rights to create a product to a local partner generates revenues for a company. Often the licensee holds additional knowledge about the local market that increases the chance for success. The lack of control constitutes the primary concern with licensing. A local partner, after signing the contract, can detract from the image of the company. Without control over decision-making, the owner of the license has freedom to make what may be poor marketing choices.

FRANCHISING

To increase the level of control over operations in another country, some companies move from exporting or licensing to franchising. **Franchising** involves the contractual agreement to implement a business model. Examples of international franchising include McDonald's restaurants, KFC restaurants, 7-11 convenience stores, Supercuts hair salons, and Jani-King cleaning establishments. While international franchising agreements are common in developed countries, they can also be effective in emerging markets with pent-up demand for high-quality products and services.[29,30]

A contract describes the business model in a franchising relationship. In return for an upfront fee, signees obtain access to the company's colors, images, and products, which offers greater control over the marketing process by the parent company. The risk to the parent company lies in a poor franchisee. The signee to the contract could ignore it or make decisions that hurt the company. The parent company will encounter the costs associated with inspecting and maintaining franchise locations at acceptable levels. Those that do not meet standards are warned, and if the units are not of sufficient quality, the relationship will be terminated. Taking such a step involves adjusting to local legal conditions as they relate to franchise contracts.

JOINT VENTURES

Some companies choose to partner with local businesses when entering a country. When these legal partnerships involve an investment, a division of ownership, and the creation of a new legal entity, the newly created business is **joint venture**. An example is Hindustan-Unilever, a combined India-U.K. company. Joint ventures take many different forms. The categories of joint ventures include (1) majority owned, where the foreign company owns 51% or more of the joint venture; (2) minority owned, where the foreign company owns 49% or less of the joint venture; and (3) 50% / 50%, or an equal split of ownership.

A second form of joint venture involves two companies combining to create and sell a product. It may be a physical good, such as an automobile, or a service. The partnership between Quantas Airlines, which flies to Australia and New Zealand, with American Express has led to the Quantas American Express Classic Card, a joint venture.

Many advantages emerge from joint ventures. Local partners provide access to local connections and understand the local business environment. Sharing of risk lessens potential losses. Costs are lowered. Joint ventures may evolve into stronger relationships, such as strategic partnerships.

Lost or leaked proprietary knowledge represents a key concern with joint ventures because the joint venture partner that now has access to the information and may not keep a patent-protected technology secret. Also, joint venture partners may misappropriate company assets or break the joint venture and then use that knowledge to succeed in separate, independent business ventures. Conflicts between joint ventures partners can also sour the relationship and limit the success of the venture.

STRATEGIC ALLIANCES

Companies may share goals but the leadership team may not want to create a joint venture. In these cases, companies often form strategic alliances. A **strategic alliance** represents a formal agreement between companies to work together to achieve a common goal. Resource sharing, project funding, and knowledge transfer all happen within most strategic alliances. In contrast to joint ventures, a separate legal entity is not created. Instead, an alliance, limited in scope, works toward the overall goal.

Strategic alliances evolve out of other modes of entry. A joint venture arrangement may grow into a more trusting, goal-sharing partnership. Wholly owned subsidiaries, over time, may establish strategic alliances with members of the distribution channel.

Many strategic alliances investigate problems that affect all or most members of an industry. Sharing research on a new technological breakthrough or combining resources to enter a new market are two common goals for strategic alliances.

With less financial commitment than either a wholly owned subsidiary or a joint venture, and with fewer formal legal ties between companies than a joint venture,

> A strategic alliance represents a formal agreement between companies to work together to achieve a common goal.

strategic alliances contain less risk. The entry mode retains less control by the parent company. This increases exposure to a potential partner leaving or stealing technology. The Chinese car company Chery (Qirui) first car, built in the city of Wuhu in 1999, was based on stolen Volkswagen manufacturing blueprints. The company paid a financial settlement to Volkswagen, but the success of the first car allowed Wuhu to grow into one of the largest car manufacturers in East Asia.[31]

WHOLLY OWNED SUBSIDIARY

When a company enters a country by establishing a 100% ownership stake in a business in that country, the company has created a **wholly owned subsidiary**. These units must comply with local regulations, adjust to local cultural standards and mores, operate in the native language, fit with local economic conditions, and be supportable through the local infrastructure. At the same time, the company that establishes the subsidiary can use its own brand, logo, and color scheme, and maintains control over both managerial operations and marketing decisions.

> When a company enters a country by establishing a 100% ownership stake in a business in that country, the company has created a wholly owned subsidiary.

Control represents the primary advantage for the company with a wholly owned subsidiary. The company maintains control of the market entry and does not need to share decision-making or profit with other parties. Although governmental and other external factors influence company success, this success grows from external factors, not from inept partners. The ability to protect proprietary information from potential competitors represents another aspect of control.

The time and money needed to enter another country with a wholly owned subsidiary creates risk. Any failures are absorbed by the company alone. Without a local partner, the entire cost of entry rests on the shoulders of the parent company. Some control may be lost when local expertise is required to help with the transition to the new country. In addition, any learning costs associated with acclimating to the local culture and regulatory environment must be absorbed.

Wholly owned subsidiaries can be divided into either acquisitions or greenfield investments. For *acquisitions*, the company purchases a local business that is then transformed into the subsidiary. In the case of a *greenfield investment*, the company builds the subsidiary from the ground up.

China allows for a unique form of the wholly owned subsidiary—the wholly foreign owned enterprise. Entirely foreign, both in terms of ownership and funding, the subsidiary maintains special economic status within China. These businesses typically manufacture goods solely for export to foreign markets. By giving up access to the Chinese market, less governmental regulation and control applies.

 **International Marketing in Daily Life**

Modes of Entry for Denim Blue Jeans

In the opening vignette to this chapter, denim jeans worn by teenagers were described briefly. As noted, jeans are desired by teens in many parts of the world, regardless of the local stage of economic development. A major Brazilian producer of jeans such as Ellus could consider entry into a new country, such as India, using many of the modes of entry.

Exporting, the low-control, low-cost, and low-risk method, could be accomplished in two ways. The Ellus marketing team could establish a website in India in the Hindi language and sell the items in that manner directly to individual consumers, stressing the sexy fit that has made the brand popular in Brazil. If the company can reach enough consumers through its online activities, this might be an attractive approach.

The company could also contact retail stores in India and offer to sell quantities of jeans shipped in bulk deliveries. Marketers might also identify an intermediary with established relationships with retailers in India to serve as a middleman for the transaction. The risk for the company would be the lack of control. The middleman or the retailer may not promote the product appropriately or may even attempt to reproduce and market a similar design of jean.

Licensing would result in a contract between Ellus and a local company in India. The partner company would manufacture jeans and sell them under the Ellus brand to retailers and/or other intermediaries. Ellus would receive royalty payments for products that were sold. As with exporting, the main concern would be lack of control, especially regarding promotion and potential copying.

Franchising programs might involve selling rights to the Ellus brand by individual jean stores carrying the company name in India. Ellus would ship jeans to the franchise retailers and support those stores with cooperative advertising and other marketing programs. If Ellus already has "Ellus" stores in Brazil, this might offer a viable approach. If not, the effort needed to start franchising might be too large to pursue this option.

A joint venture would involve one of two types of partnerships. First, Ellus could combine with a local jean manufacturer to create a hybrid product to be sold in both India and Brazil. Or second, Ellus could form bonds with a major retail chain in India, such as RPG Retail or Sankalp Retail Value, to sell Ellus jeans, complete with cooperative advertising and other marketing programs.

A strategic alliance might evolve from a joint venture with a retailer. Over time, Ellus and the retailer might come together to form mutual strategic goals, such as selling to bottom-of-the-pyramid consumers or older customers who desired a sexy but less-revealing fit. The focus of the alliance would be on business process innovations, and Ellus would take steps to protect any company-specific knowledge that might be valuable to the partner.

To establish a high-control, high-cost, and high-risk wholly owned Ellus subsidiary, the company would establish a manufacturing system in India. Then, local distribution channels would be developed and Ellus India would retain ties with Ellus Brazil. The advantage would be control; however, the company's executives would need to be sure that a proper level of commitment existed to make such a large, risky investment.

The choice of mode of entry would be influenced by the economic systems in both Brazil and India, and would be influenced by language and cultural differences (and similarities, if any), governmental actions, and the infrastructure of India. Managerial preference by Ellus might also dictate the mode of entry chosen, accounting for risk, cost, and any other relevant factors.

The photo on page 63 provides an example of a website and advertisement for jeans featuring sexual appeal. Notice the use of hearts in red near the words "Hot Sexy Fit.com." In that context, "hot" becomes associated with romance rather than more general sexuality. The opening of a zipper surrounding the words also suggests sexuality without being overt or aggressive. The use of a single model to display various versions of jeans allows the viewer to decide which version might be most complementary to her figure, which is emphasized by the phrase, "Just cuts to compliment your shape." The advertisement also leads to immediate action in two

E-commerce and the Internet may influence entry mode choices.

ways: the first through a website order form and the second by references to four social media websites.

ENTRY MODE FAILURE AND EXIT

Before entering a market, company leaders consider the possibility of potential failure. A plan will be in place regarding market exit pre-entry. The plan includes setting clear, measurable goals regarding entry success with set deadlines for assessing meeting the goals. Failure may not reflect poor planning. Instead, it may result from external, unpredictable forces leading to the entry problems. Regardless, understanding the potential for failure allows firms to assess the amount of acceptable risk or losses, which in turn affects the length of contracts, the pace of the market entry, or the entry mode chosen.

VIDEO LINK 2.5:
Market Entry Failure

When leaving the market, marketers focus on maintaining the relationships built during the time in the country. Contracts should be settled as fairly as possible, for example. Marketers recognize that a company's reputation in one nation may affect the reputation in neighboring countries. Further, the partner in the country being exited might be a potential partner in a separate country, and those individual relationships may be important to future entry success. Finally, it is always possible that the firm will choose to enter the market again at a later date.

Theories of Entry Mode Selection

One widely investigated topic in international marketing research is the factors that influence entry mode selection. Various explanations for this process have been proposed. The three dominant theories are internationalization theory, internalization theory, and eclectic or OLI theory.

INTERNATIONALIZATION THEORY

A core question in international marketing asks why companies expand into foreign markets. Researchers have sought to understand whether a potential explanation exists regarding the steps that are taken, as well as the order in which they are taken.

Internationalization theory represents a theoretical attempt to answer those questions. The theory is strongly associated with the writings of Johanson, Vahlne, Wiedersheim-Paul, and with the Uppsala School, which has led to the internationalization theory also being known as the Uppsala Model. This approach suggests that companies go through four stages during the move to becoming a completely global company: (1) no regular export activities, (2) export via independent representatives, (3) establishment of an overseas sales subsidiary, and (4) foreign production.[32]

The model views global entry as an incremental process. A company's marketers begin by exporting to close, familiar markets. Through these exporting activities, the company leaders gain the knowledge needed to export to other close similar markets. Eventually, sufficient market experience and market knowledge accumulates to increase commitments and resources given to expanding internationally. Over time, the company opens overseas sales subsidiaries and eventually starts producing in foreign markets.[33]

Internalization theory focuses on the reasons company leaders select a specific type of entry mode for a product, such as this combined bathtub and rocking horse.

Psychic distance plays a primary role in country selection under the Uppsala Model. *Psychic distance* refers to the differences between managers from different countries. It includes differences in language, communication styles, legal and political structures, education, and overall cultural values. A focus on cultural value differences—such as the Hofstede values of power distance, individualism/collectivism, uncertainty avoidance, and femininity/masculinity—constitutes cultural distance. While recent academic research has yielded mixed results regarding the specific effects of cultural distance, overall a long managerial tradition of focusing on psychic distance, the differences between managers in different countries when entering new markets, still exists.[34] International marketers who are aware of these differences may be able to reduce communication problems and increase trust, leading to a higher chance of entry success.

INTERNALIZATION THEORY

Internalization theory moves beyond the ordered, staged approach of internationalization theory to focus solely on the reasons a company's leaders select a specific types of entry mode. The underlying assumption is that there are specific advantages to each type of entry mode (exporting, licensing, joint venture, wholly owned subsidiary, etc.) and that these advantages, typically in terms of rent or profit, constitute the reasons a firm's marketing team might choose to export rather than a joint venture or utilize a wholly owned subsidiary instead of licensing a product.

In internalization theory, exporting constitutes a market choice. Supply and demand guide the process, the company exerts little control, and less cost is involved than with other modes of entry. In cases where the market works efficiently, such as in countries where governments are not involved, where there are no unusual risks or uncertainties and; where trusted partners can be found, the market decision represents the best option. In essence, when the company's managers are familiar with the foreign market, there are no extreme external factors limiting the ability to enter that market, and the company's leaders are not concerned that company knowledge will be copied, it will be best to export, because the costs are lower with exporting rather than other modes of entry. Also, in a pure market situation, the risks will be lower. A company can ship the product to the country, make a profit, and keep costs low.

In reality, in most countries governments play a role in trade. Also, in many countries high levels of various types of risk will be present. The situation will be further complicated by the uncertainty in many markets due to cultural differences and the lack of stability. Overall, for many markets, exporting remains excessively risky. In these cases, company marketing managers choose to internalize—hence the name of the theory.

Internalization refers to taking some degree of ownership of the process of entering a country. Typically, doing so involves opening a wholly owned subsidiary or starting a joint venture. Internalization may also be referred to as the hierarchy choice. It represents internalizing the entry into the corporate hierarchy. The costs of this approach can be high, but in many cases those costs are offset by the level of control resulting from ownership. Greater control allows company leaders to better respond to risk and uncertainty. Internalization may also permit the company to exploit market power and protect key assets, especially hard-earned knowledge, from being potentially stolen by competitors.[35]

ECLECTIC OR OLI THEORY

Eclectic or OLI theory was first presented in1976 by Sir Jonathan Dunning at a Nobel Symposium in Stockholm. It seeks to integrate a variety of theoretical explanations of market entry decisions into one integrated model. As with some of the other theories, the eclectic theory assumes that exporting will be the most efficient and preferred form of entry but that inefficiencies or problems in the market mean that in many cases the best decision is another form of entry. These best decisions are based on three factors:

1. Ownership advantages

2. Location advantages

3. Internalization advantages

Ownership advantages can be thought of as the "why" for multinational corporation foreign activities. These advantages represent the reasons marketers spend the time and effort to enter a foreign country. Two types of ownership advantages are present, according to the theory: asset and transaction advantages. *Asset advantages* represent anything the company does well. Asset advantages are in some ways similar to the specific assets discussed in internalization theory. The company can earn money in foreign markets because of its ability to do something that competitors cannot. *Transaction ownership advantages* relate to the ability to capture transactional benefits, such as lower costs, from the common governance of a network of ownership assets. Apple created an innovative product, the iPad, that was difficult for competitors to copy, which became an ownership advantage.

Eclectic theory explains the "where" of entry location advantages. Some markets are more attractive than others and are entered first. Local resources, natural and human; governmental activities; market potential; and lower political risk make some countries more alluring. Many large corporations have begun entering or considering to enter India in the last decade largely because of the 1 billion consumers within the country. This is a location advantage.

The final advantages suggested by the eclectic or OLI theory are internalization advantages. These are the "how" of market entry, and the advantages that come from making the correct entry decision. While exporting is the default option, when companies are considering entering an attractive market (location advantages) and have unique assets that will generate sufficient profit (ownership advantages), the correct selection of entry mode type leads to internalization advantages. To select the right type of entry mode, companies need to balance risk, uncertainty, the ability to exploit economies of scale, and cost.[36]

ANALYSIS

Each of the three theories seeks to explain the factors that might affect a strategic marketing manager's reasoning process when selecting a mode of entry. Internationalization theory logically applies to what might be termed "concentric" expansion, or moving into close, similar markets first, because they will be easier to enter, and then expanding outward to more-difficult, less-similar markets. Internalization theory suggests processes by which managers balance assessments of risk and costs. The process leads managers to select the entry mode that is the most efficient and appropriate. Eclectic theory combines ideas about ownership, location, and internalization that marketers might use to make judgments about which mode of entry would be best for a given company.

Chapter 2: Review and Resources

STRATEGIC IMPLICATIONS //

A commonly used approach to strategic management involves five steps: analysis and diagnosis, strategy generation, strategy evaluation and choice, strategy implementation, and strategic control. The first step, analysis and diagnosis, contains the classic SWOT evaluation, where SW stands for company strengths and weaknesses and OT represents the environmental opportunities and threats.

Assessment of economic conditions takes place as part of the analysis and diagnosis/OT phase. When examining another country's circumstances, the economic system in place may present opportunities or obstacles. Nations engaged in free enterprise and greater degrees of capitalism may offer more open environments for international trade. Communist societies with closed markets are the least inviting. In most cases, mixed economies contain varying degrees of viability. Careful assessment of the economic system in place begins the strategic planning process. Then, evaluation of any national competition advantage informs the marketing team about any impediments that would place the company in a weak competitive position, or identifies the opportunity to enter a market with little resistance.

Considering the modes of entry that could be chosen is part of the second step of the strategic management process, strategy generation. The marketing manager and team evaluates the potential strategic options, such as exporting, licensing, franchising, joint ventures, wholly owned subsidiaries, and strategic alliances across the criteria of cost, risk, and control. Then a strategic method can be chosen.

TACTICAL IMPLICATIONS //

Each economic system requires differing tactics. Free market capitalism will be likely to necessitate advertising and promotions in order to stand out and be noticed in the face of greater competition. Socialist systems often present limits in terms of marketing activities. Tighter controls over matters such as comparative advertising, pricing, and discounting may be present. Communist countries pose the greatest challenges to entry.

Distribution systems vary widely by the level of economic development present in a country. A nation in the most-developed category will feature more-elaborate distribution networks facilitated by more sophisticated transportation and communication systems. Developing and emerging economies will have less-developed systems of distribution, but systems will be under construction over time. A few major industries are present, which may present marketing opportunities in terms of supply materials or supporting companies in those industries in some fashion. In less-developed economies, distribution will be challenging. Consumers at the bottom-of-the-pyramid have less disposable income; however, innovative companies have found ways to reach them with adapted goods and services.

OPERATIONAL IMPLICATIONS //

Economic systems influence the methods used to present products to consumers. The presence or absence of retail chains changes the types of advertising, sales promotions, and pricing systems that will be utilized. In free enterprise systems, selling tactics will vary at the business-to-business and consumer levels due to the presence of competitors.

Pricing and discounting in socialist and communist systems may differ from capitalist economies due to the nature of the competition and of the economic regulatory system. The marketing team studies and adapts to these tactical issues prior to entry into a new market.

Selection of a mode of entry dictates additional operational activities, including the ways in which products are packaged, shipped, and sold. The degree of control present influences how a company moves products from one nation into another.

TERMS

market economy

capitalist economic system

command economy

socialism

communism

mixed economy

emerging markets

newly industrialized countries

transition economies

national competitive advantage

exporting

licensing

franchising

joint venture

strategic alliance

wholly owned subsidiary

REVIEW QUESTIONS

1. Define the terms *market economy, planned economic systems*, and *mixed systems.*

2. Explain the concepts of capitalism, socialism, and communism in terms of market economies, planned economic systems, and mixed systems.

3. Describe the terms *concepts of most-developed, less-developed,* and *least-developed economies.*

4. What are the five stages of the Rostow modernization model?

5. How are emerging markets related to the five stages of the Rostow modernization model?

6. What is a newly industrialized country?

7. Describe a transition economy.

8. Define the concept of national competitive advantage and list the factors that support a nation's competitive advantage.

9. What are the five major competitive forces present at the industry level?

10. Describe exporting, and note which factors make exporting the lowest-cost, lowest-risk, and lowest-level of control international marketing option.

11. How is licensing different from exporting?

12. What are the features of a franchising arrangement?

13. Why does a wholly owned subsidiary feature the highest degree of control coupled with the greatest levels of cost and risk?

14. What two types of joint ventures are possible for international marketing organizations?

15. Describe a strategic alliance.

16. Describe internationalization theory.

17. Describe internalization theory.

18. How does eclectic or OLI theory explain the mode of entry selection processes?

DISCUSSION QUESTIONS

1. Explain how private property rights and marketplace competition are different in market economies and command economies. What might be the difference in these two factors between strong command economies and moderate command economies? Do these economic forms influence the rate of development in less- or least-developed countries? Why or why not?

2. What types of marketing opportunities would be present in BRIC countries that would not be available in least-developed economies? Would the number of bottom-of-the-pyramid consumers in either country influence the ability to move toward becoming most developed? Why or why not? What other factors make it harder or easier for a national economy to grow and expand?

3. Explain how the five main industry level competitive forces would affect marketing programs for the following products:

   - motorbike manufacturers
   - cell phone service providers
   - fast food chain restaurants

   In each instance, how would a nation's economic system impact the five competitive forces?

4. Choose a mode of entry for the following products and defend your choice using one of the three mode-of-entry theories:

- a Mexican salsa product exported to Paraguay
- French automobile batteries exported to Turkey
- Japanese tennis equipment exported to South Korea

ANALYTICAL AND INTERNET EXERCISES

1. As more countries began the process of economic reform and development, analysts struggle to label these new markets in a way as memorable as BRIC or the Four Tigers. The BRIC acronym, which stands for Brazil, Russia, India, China, is now widely accepted. Using the CIA *World Factbook* at cia.gov, create a table comparing these countries in terms of the role of government in the economy, size of economy (in terms of overall GDP and GDP per capita), population, amount of exports, key products exported, and any other variables that may reveal important similarities or differences.[37] Then, based on the numbers, discuss how the countries in BRIC are similar and different. Does one country seem more attractive to international marketers than the other members of the group? Why or why not?

2. Google now offers public data for consumers at www.google.com/publicdata/home.[38] One of the databases provided is called *World Development Indicators,* which was developed by the World Bank. Use the data there to create three graphs that show the developmental process for at least three transition economies. What variables did you choose? Why? For which question did the resulting graphs provide visual evidence?

3. Countries generate national competitive advantages over long periods of time. In many cases, these advantages then become part of the tourist appeals for these countries. For example, the official French tourism website emphasizes French wine (http://us.franceguide.com/). Make a list of five countries and the product(s) that you associate with those countries. Then, using a search engine, find the official tourism promotion website for that country. If you are unable to find the website, select a different country. Does the website promote the national competitive advantage for the countries? How prominently and in what ways?

4. Internationalization theory presents a set, staged model for international expansion. The automobile manufacturer Toyota represents one of the world's largest and most global brands, but the expansion of the company internationally did not begin until the late 1950s. Using the websites below, track the international expansion of each company. Did each company follow the Uppsala School's model?

"History of Toyota," Toyota, Tokyo, Japan (updated 2011), accessed at www.toyota-global.com/company/history_of_toyota/.

"Globalizing and Localizing Manufacturing," Toyota, Tokyo, Japan (updated 2011), accessed at www.toyota-global.com/company/vision_philosophy/globalizing_and_localizing_manufacturing/.

"Role of the Global Production Center (GPC) Fostering Globally Capable Personnel," Toyota, Tokyo, Japan (updated 2011), accessed at www.toyota-global.com/company/vision_philosophy/globalizing_and_localizing_manufacturing/role_of_the_global_production_center.html.

▶ ONLINE VIDEOS

Visit **www.sagepub.com/baack** to view these chapter videos:

Video Link 2.1: The Index of Economic Freedoms
Video Link 2.2: The G20 Nations
Video Link 2.3: Negotiation
Video Link 2.4: Market Entry Tips
Video Link 2.5: Market Entry Failure

🌐 STUDENT STUDY SITE

Visit **www.sagepub.com/baack** to access these additional learning tools:

- Web Quizzes
- eFlashcards
- SAGE Journal Articles
- Country Fact Sheets
- Chapter Outlines
- Interactive Maps

CASE 2 ///

International Marketing in Daily Life

Mobile Communications: Entry Into Africa

Africa represents the fastest growing and most exciting mobile phone market in the international marketplace, with more than 50% growth in market size per year since 2002.[39] More than 28% of African consumers use mobile phones, which represents a larger market than North America.[40] One analyst suggests, "This is a market in the making—as the U.S. was 150 years ago and as China was 20 years ago. If you can get in and if you ride this constantly changing market, there are countless fortunes to be made."[41]

Beyond South Africa and possibly Kenya or Uganda, the rest of the African continent is less- or even least-developed, economically. Several factors account for the rapid growth in generally poor consumers in these countries. The village of Dertu in Kenya is far removed from quality roads and infrastructure. The village does not have effective fixed landlines for telephone service. Instead, the leader of the village, Ibrahim Ali Hassan, describes a mobile phone as his "link with the outside world." When a local farmer was outside of town when his wife went into labor, a mobile phone call rushed him back to take her to the hospital. The baby was healthy and named after the phone company—Celtel. When a young child was bitten by a snake, a cell phone call helped the victim's parents identify the correct antidotes.[42]

Across Africa the same outside access created by mobile phones is possible in isolated communities. Instead of traditional landline phones, consumers have moved directly to mobile communication. Ninety percent of phone subscribers in Africa use mobile phones, often using the more accessible pay-as-you-go models. The pricing system allows consumers more flexibility than a traditional monthly plan. Payments are solely linked to usage rates.[43] Consumers keep multiple SIM memory cards, switching to whichever company provides the best rate for the call being made.[44] Short calls or even

flashing—the act of calling and hanging up after one ring so that the person will not be billed for the call, which also helps keep costs low.[45]

The use of mobile phones differs on the continent from many other parts of the world. For many consumers, mobile technology offers a primary source of information. Cell phones can be used to track the price of crops and to receive reminders to take medicines.[46] They save wasted trips outside of the village.[47] Due to this focus on function, the phones typically strip down many Western phone features and instead only provide the ability to call and send text messages.[48]

Mobile banking also drives increased usage. As traditional banks struggle to penetrate many parts of the continent, mobile banking fills the gap. Vodafone used its m-Pesa (pesa is Swahili for money) mobile banking service to expand into Kenya. In two short years, the product went from introduction to 5 million users.[49] More than 50% of the Kenyan market uses mobile banking for money transfers. While the transactions are small, around 1,500 Kenyan shillings ($20), the lower

Africa offers a potentially rich target market for mobile phone providers.

Country / Countries	Firm	Ownership Structure	Additional Notes
Kenya	Safricom	Private owned	
Mali	Sotelma	State owned	Selling 51% stake
Morocco	Maroc Telecom	Vivdendi subsidiary	
Mozambique	Mcel	State owned	
Mozambique	Vodacom	Subsidiary	
Nigeria	Mtel	State owned	
São Tomé	São Tomé Telecoms	Joint venture	49% state owned 51% Portugal Telecom
Senegal	Sonatel	Joint venture	57% state owned 43% Telecom (France)
Tunisia	Tunisie Télécom	State owned	
Western Africa	Cellcom	Private owned	
Africa	MTN	Private owned	
Africa	Zain	Private owned	

Figure 2.9: Partial List of African Telecommunications Companies[53]

fees than traditional banks have save poor Kenyans an estimated $4 million per week.[50]

In some areas of the continent, mobile minutes have become a substitute for actual money. In Uganda, a villager can transfer money to relatives through the village mobile phone representative. A prepaid card is purchased, which is added to the relative's account, and then, after a fee has been paid, that amount in cash is transferred to the relative.[51]

The African market appears to have given local companies a first-mover advantage. Outside companies entering the highly competitive market have struggled. There are large barriers to entry in terms of cost and governmental approval. Markets tend to be intensely competitive with three, four, five, or even six local providers. The result has been that a large number of the largest companies are local or are from other developing countries.[52]

Various types of ownership structures exist in the African telecommunications industry. Figure 2.9 summarizes some of the important players. Ownership varies from state-owned industries to joint ventures to subsidiaries.

The African cellular phone market's rapid growth exemplifies the potential for all markets, regardless of level of development, to potentially generate profit. Effective international marketers classify markets in an attempt to better understand the market, but not as a method to dismiss markets. The market also provides a clear example of first-mover advantage. Foreign companies find local competitors already in a strong market position. These local competitors use a variety of ownership structures and present a strong challenge to outside competitors.

1. Discuss the difference between the use of cell phones in the African cellular phone market compared with cell phone use in developed-country cellular phone markets.

2. How might the different ownership structures in Africa reflect potential economic systems in the host countries?

3. Would the model for mobile phone expansion apply to other less- or least-developed countries? Why or why not?

4. How do Porter's five factors explain the high level of industry competitive intensity in the African mobile phone market?

5. How might an African government apply Porter's national competitive advantage diamond to further spur cellular phone specialization within a country?

3

Global Trade and Integration

LEARNING OBJECTIVES

After reading and studying this chapter, you should be able to answer the following questions:

1. How does free trade influence the international marketing context?

2. What are the relationships between free trade, integration, and international marketing?

3. What are the major trade agreements around the world?

4. How does protectionism affect free trade?

5. How do laws and ethical concerns affect trade and international marketing globally?

Kikkoman Soy Sauce: A Tradition of Trade

People around the world enjoy soy sauce. The salty condiment plays a role similar to ketchup or salsa and adds flavor to more than just traditional Asian foods. Soy sauce with stir-fried vegetables and rice can be found on dinner tables in many countries.

Soy sauce dates back to *jiang*, a fermented-meat condiment used in the Chinese Zhou dynasty (1122–221 BC). While the condiment traces its roots to China, many of the world's leading soy sauce brands originated in Japan. *Shoyu*, the name for Japanese soy sauce, has been used as a condiment since at least the Muromachi period (1336–1568 AD). *Shoyu* plays a large role in Japanese cooking. To the Japanese, soy sauce contains a fifth taste, called *umami* or "flavor," joining the four traditional tastes of sweet, salty, sour, and bitter.

As Japan developed, the country started exporting *shoyu* in the seventeenth century. Dutch traders shipped barrels from an outpost on an island off the coast of Japan to a Taiwanese trading post in 1647. By 1737, the Dutch East India Company shipped soy sauce to all of Southeast Asia, India, Sri Lanka, the Netherlands, and other parts of Europe. By 1866, the Japanese government charged an export tariff on soy sauce. At least 400,000 barrels were exported a year during the 1860s.[1]

One of the current leading soy sauce producers, Kikkoman Shoyu Co. Ltd., is better known as simply Kikkoman. The company traces its roots to *shoyu* production in Noda, Japan, in the mid-seventeenth century. Noda, located on a large plain, served as the breadbasket for nearby Edo (today's Tokyo). By 1917, the region shipped soy sauce throughout Japan and East Asia. The Kikkoman Shoyu Co. Ltd. emerged from a series of organizations of local *shoyu* producers in 1964 to become the dominant local brand.

The company adopted an aggressive exporting focus following World War II. In 1957, to facilitate exporting to the U.S. market, the company opened a sales base in San Francisco. Expanding rapidly, Kikkoman now produces and exports soy sauce to most of Europe, to China, to North and South America, and to Southeast Asia, creating the leading global soy sauce brand (www.Kikkoman.com).

QUESTIONS FOR STUDENTS

1. What is the role of trade in the spreading popularity of soy sauce?
2. Do the Japanese origins of Kikkoman help or hurt the company's international marketing program?
3. How can a marketing team take advantage of the increasing demand for soy sauce?

Consumers around the world enjoy soy sauce.

Overview

Consumers purchase many products that originate in other countries. The movement of goods across borders ties countries, businesses, and citizens together. The flow of goods increases the diversity of products for people to purchase. Trade creates new competition for local companies. Many governments actively monitor and attempt to influence the exchange of goods.

This chapter focuses on the movement of goods, people, and money, including the two main types of trade. *Exporting* takes place when goods are transferred or shipped to a foreign country. When goods are transferred or enter into a country, **importing** occurs.

The elements associated with free trade are presented first. Next, the process of lowering barriers between countries, or integration, serves as the main focus of the chapter. Legal and political systems affect the distribution of goods, or the place component of the marketing mix (see Figure 3.1).

This chapter continues with a discussion of integration that incorporates broader issues, such as reasons for success of integration activities and the role of the World Trade Organization (WTO). An in-depth review of integrative bodies and trends through the globe follows. Discussion of specific examples highlights the role of integration in influencing marketing activities. Lowering barriers to the movement of goods, people, and money through integration represents a significant change in the international marketing environment.

The concept of protectionism is then introduced with a review of the methods governments use to limit trade. The theoretical advantages and disadvantages from trade are summarized, followed by methods governments use to stimulate trade. The chapter concludes with a review of specific laws and ethical considerations in global trade.

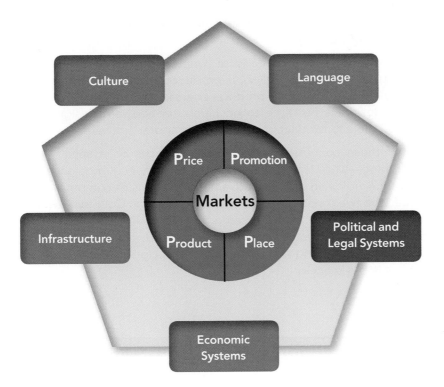

Figure 3.1: The International Marketing Context

Free Trade

LEARNING OBJECTIVE #1:

How does free trade influence the international marketing context?

Goods, money, and people move across the borders of countries. When tourists visit historical sites or other attractions in a country, investors put money into local business ventures, such as gift shops and nearby restaurants. Souvenir t-shirts are shipped from a manufacturer in one country to gift shops in others. This type of fluidity represents a significant component of international marketing activity.

The movement of goods forms the foundation of international marketing activities. **Free trade** occurs when goods travel across boundaries with little governmental interference. The role of free trade stirs debate. Basic questions emerge regarding whether free trade should be encouraged and if it hurts local citizens by leading to the loss of jobs. The essence of the debate focuses on free trade and integration versus protectionism.

Many assert that free trade merits government intervention. Others argue that free trade represents a fundamentally positive force. International trade theory provides the foundation for this discussion, with two theories that serve as guides: absolute advantage theory and comparative advantage theory.

VIDEO LINK 3.1: Principles of Adam Smith

ABSOLUTE ADVANTAGE

One international trade theory is associated with the writings of Adam Smith. **Absolute advantage theory** suggests that a country has an advantage when it can produce more of a good or service than another country using the same amount of resources. The theory draws attention to the advantages countries hold in terms of certain activities.

Country-level absolute advantages lead to trade. For example, Country A has a highly skilled group of twenty computer software designers. These designers work hard, apply their training, and produce high-quality computer software. The twenty designers produce one piece or unit of software. Country A, though, does not possess the ability to produce clothing well. It would take fifty computer software designers to produce one piece of clothing.

Country B has a highly skilled group of twenty clothing designers. The clothing made in this country is the most stylish, is produced more efficiently, and represents the best quality. The 20 designers produce one piece of high-quality clothing. The same group of designers has little to no computer software design skills. It takes seventy-five designers to product one piece of computer software.

For both of these countries, trade allows for focus on a specialty—computer software or clothing—while letting the experts in the other country focus on what they do well. Country A holds an absolute advantage in terms of computer software. The labor input, i.e., the twenty computer software designers in Country A, would produce far more computer software than the same amount of labor input, in this case the twenty clothing designers, would produce in Country B. Therefore, Country A trades computer software for clothing and Country B trades clothing for computer software. Figure 3.2 models this process.

Country A	Country B
Labor Input = 20 software designers	Labor Input = 75 clothing designers
Output = 1 piece of computer software	Output = 1 piece of computer software
Labor Input = 50 software designers	Labor Input = 20 clothing designers
Output = 1 piece of clothing	Output = 1 piece of clothing

Figure 3.2: Absolute Advantage

Trade leads to higher levels of innovation through specialization. Each country focuses on its area of expertise, and more domestic competitors emerge to meet the needs of the global market. All of the countries involved benefit. Eventually, consumers begin to associate the country with a specialty, whether it is Japanese electronics, American movies, or French wine.

COMPARATIVE ADVANTAGE

In the modern international trade environment, many nations trade with less-developed or least-developed countries that do not hold advantages in any type of production. Absolute advantage theory suggests that no trade would occur in these cases. From the example above, if Country A is better than Country C at both software design and clothing production, there would be no mechanism for trade between the two countries. The comparative advantage theory explains how trade might still take place.

The **comparative advantage theory** posits that a country has an ability to produce a good or service at lower levels of opportunity cost than other countries. These opportunity costs are the key component of the theory. A trade-off exists when a

> The comparative advantage theory posits that a country has an ability to produce a good or service at lower levels of opportunity cost than other countries.

country produces two products instead of focusing on just the product that it produces most efficiently. Returning to Country A and Country B, it takes five designers in Country A to produce one piece of computer software, and ten designers to produce one piece of new clothing. The country has sixty designers total. Country B is more efficient than Country A in conducting either activity. It takes thirty designers in Country B to product one piece of computer software and fifteen designers to product one piece of clothing. Although Country A has an absolute advantage in terms of both computer software and clothing design, it would be more efficient to focus solely on computer design, which would be a more efficient use of designers. In terms of total output, as presented in Figure 3.3, two separate conditions emerge. In the first, Country A and Country B do not trade and instead split production duties for the designers evenly.

Country A	Country B
Labor Input = 60 designers	Labor Input = 60 designers
Labor Input Computer = 30 designers	Labor Input Computer = 30 designers
Labor Input Clothing = 30 designers	Labor Input Clothing = 30 designers
Total Output =	Total Output =
3 pieces of clothing, 6 pieces of software	2 pieces of clothing, 1 piece of software

Figure 3.3: Comparative Advantage Production Without Trade

Country A	Country B
Labor Input = 60 designers	Labor Input = 60 designers
Labor Input Computer = 60 designers	Labor Input Clothing= 60 designers
Total Output = 12 pieces of software	Total Output = 4 pieces of clothing

Figure 3.4: Comparative Advantage Production With Trade

In this case, the sixty designers in Country A produce three pieces of clothing (thirty divided by ten) and six pieces of computer software (thirty divided by five). The total output is nine units. In Country B, the same number of designers product two pieces of clothing (thirty divided by fifteen) and one piece of software (thirty divided by thirty), resulting in a total output of three units. How would trade change this process? Figure 3.4 presents that situation.

By focusing on the comparative advantage, Country A does not waste thirty designers producing clothing at a less efficient rate than they would produce computer software. Instead, all sixty designers produce software, resulting in twelve pieces of software (sixty divided by five). The lost efficiency in the case of no trade, as in Figure 3.4, represents the opportunity cost. Country A is better off producing software and then trading some of that software for clothing with Country B. In the case of Country B, the focus on clothing production also increased total output, in this case to four pieces of clothing (sixty divided by fifteen).

Comparative advantage theory presents a strong case for country specialization. The advantages that emerge offer the core benefits from trade. Specializing allows both countries to benefit. Production efficiency increases, consumers in both countries are able to purchase more goods, and, over time, the countries become more skilled at their own specialty.

Governmental Forms

When conducting international trade, marketers consider the types of governments in a specified region or country, including democracies, authoritarian states, or anarchies. A *democracy* vests political power in the citizens of a country, either directly or through elected representatives. Many countries have some form of voting or elections; for a country to be truly democratic, however, those votes or the officials elected through those votes should demonstrate actual political power. Many forms of democracy exist. The United States has a presidential system, whereas much of Western Europe uses a parliamentary system.

Power rests in the hands of a small number of individuals, or even one person in an authoritarian government. These governments include monarchies, dictatorships, and theocracies. A *monarchy*, or a government led by single ruler who inherits the position, is increasingly rare. Many monarchies, such as the one in Great Britain, are constitutional monarchies with a king or queen as a head of state holding only limited political power. Saudi Arabia and Swaziland are examples of absolute monarchies where the hereditary ruler has actual control over the political system.

VIDEO LINK 3.2:
China's Economy ▶

Dictatorships are governments in which the ruling elite or ruling individual holds all the political power. This power results from control of the military, through wealth, or those factors combined with corruption. Examples of dictatorships include those in North Korea, and Cuba. When the ruler or ruling body claims political power due to religious reasons and in many cases is ruled by a religious figure, such as in Iran or the Vatican City, the form of government is called a *theocracy*.

Anarchism occurs when there is an absence of any ruling governmental form. Countries experiencing anarchy may revert to tribalism or warlord rule. Somalia from the early 1990s to the mid-2000s offers an example of anarchy. Businesses are not likely to enter a country moving toward or in a state of anarchy.

When researching potential markets, correctly identifying the situation in the country constitutes one of the primary challenges. Citizens in the People's Republic of China elect 2,987 members to the National People's Congress (NPC), and the NPC votes to elect national figures, including the president. While this may appear to be a functioning democracy, upon closer examination a researcher would discover that 70% of the delegates are members of the Communist Party. Nearly all votes in the NPC are unanimous or nearly unanimous, and delegates from dissenting parties are harassed by the police and often arrested.[2] A quality source for realistic, detailed descriptions of government types is the *CIA World Factbook*.[3] Various government types are presented in Table 3.1.

Governmental forms influence choices made with regard to the allocation of resources. In other words, governmental leaders often dictate whether a country pursues any type of advantage. As an extreme example, the government of North Korea, under dictator Kim Jong-II, concentrates a great deal of national resources on the unreported sale of missiles, narcotics, and counterfeit cigarettes and currency, and other illicit activities, to the detriment of many citizens in terms of their standard of living. Although North Korea may have developed a comparative or absolute advantage, the only beneficiary is the government.[4]

Country	Type of Government
Afghanistan	Islamic Republic
Argentina	Republic
Botswana	Parliamentary Republic
Cuba	Communist State
Kazakhstan	Republic, Authoritarian Presidential Rule
Morocco	Constitutional Monarchy
Qatar	Emirate
Somalia	No permanent national government
United States of America	Constitution-based Federal Republic

Table 3.1: **Countries and Governmental Type**

THE BENEFITS OF FREE TRADE

Using the economic theories of absolute and comparative advantage, many economists have built arguments that conclude free trade offers several benefits. Figure 3.5 presents four of those arguments.

Individual freedom and empowerment often emerge as the primary benefits of free trade. Consumers retain the ability to choose from a range of products from around the world instead of governmental forces leveraging power to reduce choice. Businesses and business owners enjoy a fair, open global market. Government does not constrain business activity, which leads to greater freedom.

Free trade restrains the power of the state and empowers individuals.
Free trade brings people together across distance and cultures, leading to peace.
Free trade makes everyone wealthier.
Free trade encourages basic human rights.

Figure 3.5: Benefits of Free Trade

Trade between countries, at its core, also connects people. A salesperson from Italy interacts with a retailer in Tunisia. An Algerian consumer becomes a fan of a German brand. Small connections such as these multiply around the world, drawing people closer together. Interconnectivity increases cultural knowledge, intertwines countries economically, and reduces conflicts between states. In essence, free trade might increase the chance for peace. Positive economic consequences of international trade for countries combined with pleasant individual-level purchasing activities and experiences may help reduce conflicts between nations.

Free trade may be related to greater wealth, as suggested by the absolute advantage and comparative advantage theories. The ability to specialize, the drive to innovate, and efficiencies due to size will emerge. These factors serve to increase global market wealth. The American automobile industry provides an example. From 1998 to 2005 the number of hours GM spent to produce one car dropped from forty-six to thirty-five hours in response to global competition. The cost of producing the car was lowered and the savings were passed on to American and international consumers. The fastest growth market for GM at the close of the millennium was China, a market opened through a reduction of trade barriers. Foreign companies also shifted production to the United States, employing approximately 335,000 workers in 2007.[5]

An increase in wealth, particularly in a less-developed country, increases freedom for citizens.

The increase in wealth, particularly in less-developed countries, increases freedom for citizens. Wealth often represents power. Given enough wealth, citizens begin to have a voice in politics. If a large enough middle-class with a large enough political sway emerges, the citizens of a country can pressure governments to allow for more political freedoms. The wealth that comes from trade then leads to greater human rights.

GOVERNMENTAL POLICIES SUPPORTING TRADE

Many governments take steps to encourage trade. Trade agreements between countries are the most prevalent form of actions that support trade. Almost all regions of the world have existing trade agreements designed to ease the movement of goods between countries.

> Free trade zones are specially designated areas within a country that have separate laws designed to encourage trade.

Some countries establish free trade zones. **Free trade zones** are specially designated areas within a country that have separate laws that encourage trade. These laws may include a reduction or complete removal of tariffs or fees on goods entering or leaving through the free trade zone. Preferential currency exchange rates, reduction of business start-up fees, and preferential access to distribution channels are additional incentives used in free trade zones. When promoted and developed correctly, free trade zones foster rapid growth. The Ras Al Khaimah Free Trade Zone Authority in Dubai registered 1,740 new companies in 2010.[6] By registering, these companies enjoyed the ability to operate in a free trade zone, seeking business partners for exporting and importing activities.

Many governments establish organizations designed to facilitate trade. These institutions serve an important function globally. The American organization that plays this role is the Export-Import Bank of the United States. The bank, a U.S. governmental entity, provides credit to businesses to assist in financing exporting activities. These exports link to American jobs and help strengthen the U.S. economy. Having helped support more than $400 billion in U.S. exports, with approximately 85% of the businesses involved being small businesses, the Export-Import Bank plays an integral part in promoting global trade.[7]

Integration

Integration allows governments to facilitate trade. **Integration** refers to the process of using agreements between countries to lower limits on the movements of products, capital, and/or labor. Many countries have joined trade agreements. These unions reduce barriers to trade; however, integration refers to more formal, deeper agreements.

LEVELS OF INTEGRATION

Several degrees of the integration or links between countries exist. Figure 3.6 presents various levels.

The first level of integration is a free trade area. **Free trade areas** are created by a group of countries that have entered into an agreement to reduce tariffs, quotas, and other barriers to the movement of goods and services. The North American Free Trade Agreement (NAFTA), consisting of Mexico, Canada, and the United States, established a free trade area.

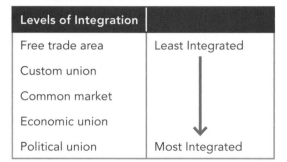

Levels of Integration	
Free trade area	Least Integrated
Custom union	
Common market	
Economic union	
Political union	Most Integrated

Figure 3.6: Levels of Integration

Custom unions produce a more integrated agreement between countries. Members of a custom union agree to remove barriers to the movement of goods and services and consent to a uniform tariff policy toward nonmember countries. MERCOSUR (*Mercado Común del Sur*), or the Southern Cone Common Market, is a customs union with the goal of becoming a common market.

The European Community, within the broader European Union (EU) framework, is a common market. **Common markets** move beyond custom unions by removing barriers to trade within the market, by maintaining a common tariff for nonmembers, and by allowing the free movement of capital and labor within the market. A citizen of France may freely move to Italy to work, without barriers. An investor in Frankfurt, Germany, may move capital from a German bank to a Spanish bank without restrictions.

As countries integrate, the process moves closer and closer to joining as one country, instead of separate countries within a group. The next step is **economic union**. For countries in such a union, economic policy should be harmonized between members, meaning the union attempts to follow the same economic policy. A common currency is also introduced, as is a central bank for the entire union. The EU currently serves as an economic union.

Political union, the complete integration of political and economic policy, represents the final step before the creation of a new country. Presently, no examples of a political union exist, although the European Union has the eventual goal of becoming one.

REASONS FOR INTEGRATION SUCCESS

Many factors influence the success or failure of integrative efforts. Successful past integration builds skills and commitment to the integrative process. Regions including

Geographic proximity creates an advantage for the Singapore–Taiwan relationship.

Western Europe and the Americas trace their integrative traditions to the early 1900s. A cultural disposition toward trade and connections, even in the face of historical conflict, eased those transitions. Post–World War II Western Germany quickly transitioned to participating as a full member in various European integrative activities.

Some countries have experienced historical events and have divergent cultures, which makes increasing ties with neighbors more difficult. Regions such as Asia do not have the same tradition of trade agreements and are less inclined to overlook past conflicts. China and Japan still maintain resentment and conflict over activities, including war crimes, during War World II.[8]

Integration between countries involves the movement of resources across country borders. Often, complementary resources that fill gaps for the countries involved increase the chance of integration success. NAFTA's member countries have some overlap between resources and each country brings unique resources to the group. Mexico features a large population of lower-wage labor; the United States employs innovative technology coupled with a large, rich market of consumers; and Canada has an abundance of natural resources. The synergy reduces conflict between the countries over competition between businesses. Recently, conflicts have arisen in instances in which overlap exists, such as with conflict over Mexican truck drivers driving goods across the border into the United States, taking jobs from American truck drivers.

Physical distance also exhibits an influence. Countries in closer proximity to each other have a natural advantage for trade. Geographic distance increases costs and complicates shipping. Physical distance affects the economic union between Singapore and Taiwan as compared to a union between Singapore and South Africa. The geographic proximity affords an advantage to the Singapore–Taiwan relationship.

INTEGRATION TRENDS

Several trends and global integration processes have recently emerged. The movement in types of products involved represents one of the most significant changes in the past thirty years. Initially, trade deals focused on the movement of manufactured goods. The origins of the European Union revolved around coal and steel. Although manufactured goods still play a large role, as evidenced by the large number of textiles and consumer electronics imported into Western Europe and the United States, increasingly services are traded. Several of the companies involved in the export of services focus on information technology, and many are located in emerging markets. Figure 3.7 lists the top ten information technology service exporters for 2009 in India, the leading country for this process.

In other cases, instead of exporting, businesses offshore manufacturing or business processing. **Offshoring**, which the popular media often incorrectly defines as outsourcing, refers to the movement of a business activity to another country. Offshoring often involves the use of a third party when entering a foreign country. The process is moved "offshore," to another country. Company leaders establish facilities that remain under the overall organizational umbrella. Kikkoman, the Japanese company in the opening vignette, set up sales processes in San Francisco. This is offshoring but in this case the company maintains control. Offshoring is not the same as outsourcing.

Outsourcing refers to relinquishing organizational control of a business process and hiring an external third party to conduct the process. Companies outsource the software development function if a third party, not a group within the company, designs software for the company. This would be considered outsourcing whether the third party resides in the same or in a different country. When the third party resides in a foreign country, the process is called *offshored outsourcing*.

The past twenty years have witnessed an increase in offshoring, particularly business process outsourcing (BPO) activity. BPO activity focuses on business support services. According to the AT Kearney 2011 Global Services Location Index, the top three leading nations for business process outsourcing activity are India, China, and Malaysia. India was the first country to focus on BPO, with activity by GE and Anderson Consulting as early as 1995, and remains an attractive location.[9] Egypt, before the unrest in January and February of 2011, was the fourth most attractive location.[10]

The arguments for and against the outsourcing and offshoring process echo those regarding trade in general. Offshoring results in the loss of jobs in the domestic market, at least in the industry being offshored. The potential economic benefits for both countries result from specialization and better employment opportunities in developing countries.

1. Tata Consultancy Services Ltd.
2. Infosys Technologies Ltd.
3. Wipro Technologies Ltd.
4. HCL Technologies Ltd.
5. Tech Mahindra Ltd.
6. MphasiS Ltd.
7. Patni Computer Systems Ltd.
8. Aricent Technologies Holdings Ltd.
9. CSC India Private Ltd.
10. L&T Infotech

Figure 3.7: Top Ten Indian Information Technology Service Exporters, 2009

Source: Adapted from "Press Release 8/12/2010," NASSCOM, accessed from www.sonata-software. com/export/sites/Sonata/sonata_en/company/ newsroom/inthenews/current/PR_NASSCOM_ FY09-10.pdf.

Bottom-of-the-Pyramid

Integration has important implications for bottom-of-the-pyramid marketing. The reduction of barriers to trade and investment presents an opportunity for companies to target bottom-of-the-pyramid consumers and for those consumers to obtain access to additional goods and services. KFC in Africa targets bottom-of-the-pyramid consumers. Consumers, excited to try American-style chicken, save money to buy a $3 meal of two pieces of chicken and fries.[11] The access to this new product by African consumers resulted from fewer barriers to trade and investment. Increasingly, the draw of these consumers drives business in developing countries to push for integration with less- and in some cases least-developed countries that were not traditionally the focus of trade negotiations.

The World Trade Organization and Integration

The World Trade Organization (WTO) facilitates trade between its 153 member countries. The WTO traces its roots back to the beginning of the United Nations. In 1948, the United Nations Conference on Trade and Employment entered discussions about forming an International Trade Organization (ITO). A compromise structure resulted: the General Agreement on Tariffs and Trade (GATT). For the next forty-seven years, the GATT provided the rules governing trade between signatory countries. The agreement continually evolved. Member countries, including new signatories, met in a series of eight rounds of negotiations (see Figure 3.8). The last of the eight rounds of negotiations, the Uruguay Round, ended in 1994 and created the World Trade Organization. On January 1, 1995, the GATT was replaced by the WTO.

Name	Year	Number of Countries Involved
1. Geneva Round	1947	23
2. Annecy Round	1949	13
3. Torquay Round	1951	38
4. Geneva Round	1956	26
5. Dillon Round	1960–1961	26
6. Kennedy Round	1964–1967	62
7. Tokyo Round	1973–1979	102
8. Uruguay Round	1986–1994	123

Figure 3.8: Negotiation Rounds for the GATT

Source: Adapted from World Trade Organization, accessed from www.wto.org/english/thewto_e/whatis_e/tif_e/fact1_e.htm.

The World Trade Organization primarily focuses on opening member countries to trade. Member countries utilize the WTO as a forum for the negotiation of trade agreements and as the arbitrating party for settling trade disputes. While the WTO is often associated with the removal of trade barriers, the organization supports some trade barriers. The barriers may be established to protect consumers, prevent the spread of disease, to serve as punishment for failing to follow WTO trade rules, or assist developing markets. In cases where barriers exist, the WTO encourages transparency and consistency. Together, these forces increase predictability for outside businesses and investors.

Most-Favored-Nation Status

A fundamental component of World Trade Organization membership is most-favored nation (MFN) status. All member countries with MFN status must be treated equally. The clause is the first article of the original GATT agreement and provides the fundamental benefit from WTO membership. Upon joining the WTO, countries are ensured equal access to all member country markets. Tariffs and other barriers may be in place, but are applied consistently, resulting in a more level playing field. Free trade agreements and special access for developing countries are the exceptions to this rule. The WTO agreement also calls for equal treatment of local and foreign goods.

Tariff Rates

The World Trade Organization helps establish tariff rates. The WTO has not led to, and in some cases does not even call for, the abolition of tariffs. While industrial countries have lowered tariffs rated under both the GATT and the WTO to the point that tariffs on industrial goods have fallen to less than 4%, many tariffs remain in place. In those cases, the WTO focuses on transparency. The WTO asks member states to set ceilings on tariffs for specific goods. As of this writing, 100% of members have upper limits on tariffs of agricultural products.[12]

Dispute Resolution

The World Trade Organization adjudicates trade disputes. It does not have the ability to fine members. The organization can allow the aggrieved party to charge counter tariffs. In 2010, New Zealand won a WTO judgment regarding a ban on exporting apples to Australia. Australian trade officials had claimed that New Zealand apples presented a risk of two diseases, fireblight and European canker, plus potentially the apple-leaf-curling midge, a pest that had not yet appeared in Australian orchards. The WTO ruled that proper packaging of New Zealand apples would remove any risks. The Australian government had two options. It could either remove the ban on New Zealand apples or face retaliatory tariffs by the New Zealand government. As the New Zealand government can decide on which products to place tariffs, politically sensitive products will likely be chosen.[13]

The Future

The World Trade Organization currently has started the Doha Round of member trade negotiations with the goal of further expanding trade liberalization. Negotiations that began in 2001 stalled. As a result, countries are experiencing disagreements regarding agricultural subsidies and intellectual property. The disagreements have become especially prevalent between developed and developing countries. Negotiators hope to conclude the process in 2011.[14]

The WTO serves as a target for protesters and often takes the brunt of complaints regarding trade liberalization or the opening of markets. Protestor concerns echo general arguments for protectionism, including the need to protect jobs, the negative environmental effects from the expansion of international trade, and the weakening of trade union power due to the lack of an effective global labor organization. Some protestors also may hold more extreme views regarding the role of corporations and distant government officials in setting economic policies. In cases where individuals feel as though their voices are not being heard, meetings such as those held by the World Trade Organization permit the powerful to make decisions that hurt the weak.[15]

International Marketing in Daily Life

Beef Exports and Integration

LEARNING
OBJECTIVE #3:

*What are the major
trade agreements
around the world?*

The export of beef provides an example of the complications associated with exporting. Beef is a food staple in many countries. The primary factors that influence the international marketing environment are associated with beef products. Culturally, at one extreme, consumption of beef is part of celebrations and social events. Killing a "fatted calf" as part of a family event is noted in the Bible as part of the Judeo/Christian heritage. At the other extreme, Hindus consider cows to be sacred and would never consume them.

Governmental regulations regarding beef production, exportation, and importation are restrictive in many countries. Care is given to make sure diseases do not pass from one country to another by the movement of live cows or of beef products. The recent mad cow outbreak led to strong restrictions of cattle movements across national boundaries.

Infrastructure dictates the ease with which beef can be moved from one region to another. It may be sold in street markets in one nation and in supercenter grocery stores in others. Beef vendors range from individual farmers and merchants to large beef processing plants.

Language dictates what types of beef are sold. The term "family steak" appears in grocery stores in the United States but not in other countries. Consumption of raw hamburger as *steak tartare* is a popular delicacy in France. Beef Wellington was first cooked in England.

Economic systems lead to situations in which few can afford high-end beef products, such as steak or roast. Even hamburger may not be purchased, or is rarely purchased, by those at the bottom-of-the-pyramid. Economic systems are often supported by products such as beef. Ten percent of U.S. exports are agricultural products. Exporting beef is a growth area for American farmers.[16]

In this section, while examining integration trends across markets, the implications for the exporting of beef will also be considered. Integration, and the theories that support the positive effects from trade, originated in Western Europe. As such, Europe leads the world in terms of overall level of integration. After World War II, the continent followed a continual, gradual path of increased integration. The European Union helped lead this integration.

European Integration

Over the past century, governments have focused on decreasing trade barriers and increasing integration between countries. Although decreasing trade barriers and increasing integration takes place world wide, regional differences exist regarding approaches and degrees of integration. These differences affect how businesses export or choose to enter various markets.

THE EUROPEAN UNION

At the end of World War II, the emerging Cold War between communist Soviet Union and democratic Western Europe raised fears of another continent-wide conflict. To increase economic and political ties, six countries formed the European Coal and Steel Community in 1950. These countries agreed to run all coal and steel industries under common management. With the central role steel and coal production played in creating military *materièl*, the joint management reduced the chance of war between the members.

On March 25, 1957, the members of the European Coal and Steel Community signed the Treaty of Rome establishing the European Economic Community. A common market, the treaty pushed for the removal of barriers to the flow of people, goods, and services between the countries. Figure 3.9 traces the progress over the past fifty years.

The 1960s

In the 1960s, conflict between the West and the Soviet Union increased, and the Berlin Wall that separated West and East Germany was built. In response, the European Economic Community took steps to more rapidly increase ties among members. In 1962, a common agricultural policy was established that set a standard food price and policy across member countries. Six years later, in 1968, the members removed all custom duties or tariffs between each other and set a common tariff for imports

1950	European Coal and Steel Community is founded by Belgium, France, Germany, Italy, Luxembourg, and the Netherlands.
1957	The Treaty of Rome is signed by Belgium, France, Germany, Italy, Luxembourg, and the Netherlands.
1962	A common agricultural policy is introduced.
1968	All custom duties are removed.
1972	Currency exchange rates for member countries are linked.
1973	Denmark, Ireland, and the United Kingdom join the EEC.
1981	Greece joins the EEC.
1982	Spain and Portugal join the EEC.
1986	The Single European Act is passed.
1992	Treaty on European Union is passed.
1993	The European Economic Community is renamed the European Union. The EU agrees on the four freedoms: the free movement of goods, services, people, and capital.
1995	Austria, Finland, and Sweden join the EU.
2002	euro coins and notes begin to circulate.
2004	The Czech Republic, Cyprus, Estonia, Latvia, Lithuania, Hungary, Malta, Poland, Slovenia, and Slovakia join the EU.
	Bulgaria, Romania, and Turkey become candidate countries to join the EU.
	A proposed European Constitution is agreed upon by the heads of government of EU member states, but, over the next few years, fails to be ratified by each member state.
2007	Bulgaria and Romania join the EU.
	Croatia and the Former Yugoslav Republic of Macedonia become candidate countries to join the EU.
	The Treaty of Lisbon is passed.
2010	Iceland becomes a candidate country to join the EU.

Figure 3.9: History of the European Union

from nonmember countries. In effect, the European Economic Community became a customs union.

The 1970s

In the 1970s, major changes within the European Economic Community took place. The currencies of members were linked together in 1972. While each country maintained a separate currency, the fluctuations or movements of value between member currencies were allowed to move only within a set band, which linked currency values.

Three new countries joined in 1973. Around that time, environmental protection laws were introduced. The European Regional Development Fund was created to facilitate development of impoverished areas. The decade ended with the direct election of leaders of the European Economic Community in 1979.

Map 3.1: **European Union Expansion and Current Membership**
The European Union over time has expanded to include the majority of the countries on the continent.

The 1980s

Greece joined the European Economic Community in 1981. Spain and Portugal followed in 1982. To increase the flow of trade, the Single European Act, passed in 1986, started a program to normalize trade regulations across members. The Erasmus Program, which began in 1987, led to funding for students studying in another member country's universities. The decade ended with the Berlin Wall coming down and the beginning of the collapse of the Soviet Union.

The 1990s

As the political landscape of Europe changed, the European Economic Community took steps to expand and to further integrate. The first was the Treaty on European

Union, signed in Maastricht, the Netherlands, in 1992. The treaty set the groundwork for a single currency and increased ties regarding foreign defense policy. It also renamed the European Economic Community the European Union (EU). January 1, 1993, marked six years from the signing of Single European Act. More than two hundred laws had been passed standardizing regulations among members during that time. At that point, the European Union agreed on the four freedoms: the free movement of goods, services, people, and capital.

Austria, Finland, and Sweden joined in 1995, and the Schengen Agreement in the same year allowed for passport-free travel for many EU members. In 1997, the Treaty of Amsterdam was ratified, leading to institutional reforms that further integrated member countries. Also, in that year ten Central and Eastern European countries began the process of joining the union. The original goal of combating the Soviet Union was met. A common currency, the *euro*, was introduced in eleven member countries for financial and commercial transactions in late 1999.

The New Millennium

In 2002, *euro* coins and notes began circulation. The EU moved toward further political union, including sending military units to the former Yugoslavia to assist in peacekeeping. Ten new countries joined and three others became official candidate countries.

The European Constitution in 2004 was designed to reform management of the EU and to create the position of a European foreign minister to speak with one voice for members on foreign affairs. With France and the Netherlands voting against the proposed constitution, the treaty was not unanimously approved. The treaty represented the first major setback toward continual integration. Bulgaria and Romania joined in 2007, with Croatia and the Former Yugoslav Republic of Macedonia becoming candidate countries. With twenty-seven members, the Treaty of Lisbon was ratified in 2007 with the goal of streamlining operations and increasing integration.[17] Figure 3.10 identifies the organization's current members and candidate countries.

ORGANIZATION OF THE EUROPEAN UNION

The European Union constitutes the world's most integrated union of countries. It includes approximately 492 million people and covers a geographic area approximately half the size of the United States. The economy of the EU is the world's largest.[18] Figure 3.11 lists the main institutions and the primary responsibilities of various union institutions.

The European Council serves as the head institution. The European Council has no formal power; however, council leaders normally drive the EU agenda.

The European Council is not the same as the Council of the European Union. The Council of the European Union is the main decision-making body. The Council's ministers represent various activities such as foreign affairs, agriculture, and transportation. The European Council passes legislation jointly, called *co-decisions*, with the European Parliament.[19]

Member Countries	
Austria	Latvia
Belgium	Lithuania
Bulgaria	Luxembourg
Cyprus	Malta
Czech Republic	Netherlands
Denmark	Poland
Estonia	Portugal
Finland	Romania
France	Slovakia
Germany	Slovenia
Greece	Spain
Hungary	Sweden
Ireland	United Kingdom
Italy	
Candidate Countries	
Croatia	Iceland
Macedonia	Turkey

Figure 3.10: European Union Member and Candidate Countries, 2011

The European Parliament consists of 736 democratically elected members. It also has legislative responsibilities, including drafting legislation and, along with the Council, approving the EU budget.[20]

The power to propose legislation rests with the European Commission, the executive body of the European Union. Independent of national governments, the European Commission focuses on serving the best interests of the overall union. The Commission serves for five years before a new one forms. To form a new Commission, the member states propose a Commission president who the European Parliament then approves. The president then appoints members to the Commission who are then also approved by the European Parliament.[21]

The members of the European Union are bound by treaty and agreement to take certain steps. As a result the EU established a court of justice. Focusing on legislation implementation, the court ensures that laws are interpreted and applied consistently. The court has the power to settle dispute between members, and also makes sure countries act as the law requires.[22]

Two additional European Union institutions are present. The first, the Court of Auditors, monitors the use of EU funds. The Court of Auditors has twenty-seven members, one from each member state.[23] The second, the European Central Bank, focuses on monetary policy with the goal of price stability.[24]

European Council	Made up of the heads of state from each member state, it sets the general political direction and priorities of the EU.
Council of the European Union	Made up of the national ministers of member states, the Council of the European Union discusses and, together with the Parliament, adopts EU laws.
European Parliament	Elected every five years, the members of the European Parliament draft legislation.
European Commission	Consists of appointed commissioners and the EU's civil service. The European Commission proposes EU legislation and checks it is properly applied across the EU.
Court of Justice	The Court of Justice applies and interprets EU laws and agreements.
European Court of Auditors	The European Court of Auditors audits the implementation and financing of EU agreements by member states.
European Central Bank	The European Central Bank sets EU monetary policy.

Figure 3.11: Major European Union Institutions

Source: Adapted from EUROPA, "EU Institutions and Other Bodies," accessed at http://europa.eu/institutions/index_en.htm.

BEEF EXPORTS IN THE EUROPEAN UNION

In terms of beef and trade, the high level of economic and political integration in Europe affects marketing activity. Beef and other products only deal with administrative barriers at one point of entry to the European Union. Whether the agricultural product enters through Portugal, Germany, or Greece, access through one country represents access to the entire market.

Labor moves freely within the European Union. A salesperson who legally works in Italy may move to a position in France with limited paperwork. The price of a pound or kilogram of meat stays in the same currency, the *euro*, throughout most of the member countries, which reduces transaction costs and makes trade easier.

Many outside countries have free trade agreements with European Union members. As beef trade moves east, these agreements become increasingly rare. The countries in the Commonwealth of Independent States often maintain larger barriers to trade than do the rest of Europe, which means that Europe represents one of the world's most trade-friendly regions.

Agricultural products, as compared to many other items that are traded, take on special significance. Agricultural subsidies often become the focus of intense discussions during trade negotiations. The inability to compromise around these products has derailed trade agreements that were otherwise supported. In the case of American beef, the European Union takes a strong stand against certain agricultural practices deemed harmful to consumers. Specifically, the EU views the use of certain hormones to promote cattle growth as potentially harmful to humans, and considers one of the hormones typically used in the United States to be a carcinogen.[25] As a result, it is difficult for U.S. producers to export beef to European Union countries. Beef exporting reveals the paradox of the integration of such a large market. While the EU is open to most goods, when the market is closed, outside businesses lose a major exporting opportunity.

The European Union, European Free Trade Association, and the Commonwealth of Independent States are three major trade associations.

OTHER EUROPEAN TRADE ORGANIZATIONS

Other trade organizations are present in Europe. The largest such organization in Western Europe is the European Free Trade Association (EFTA). Iceland, Liechtenstein, Norway, and Switzerland are currently members. If Iceland joins the European Union it will leave the EFTA. The EFTA has limited trade barriers between members and common policies toward nonmembers. These policies include free trade with the members of the European Union.[26]

The other main trade-related organization in Europe is the Commonwealth of Independent States. Its membership includes many Eastern European or Central Asian countries that have not made steps to join the European Union (see Figure 3.12). The stated goals of the Commonwealth are economic integration, including common economic policy and free movement of goods, labor, and capital; however, actual implementation of these practices has been slow.[27]

Azerbaijan	Moldova
Armenia	Russia
Belarus	Tajikistan
Georgia	Turkmenistan
Kazakhstan	Uzbekistan
Kyrgyzstan	Ukraine

Figure 3.12: Members of the Commonwealth of Independent States

In 2009, in an attempt to remove trade barriers, Russia, Belarus, and Kazakhstan formed a customs union. Over time, the countries will put into place a common tariff for nonmembers and remove barriers to trade within the union.[28]

Finally, as part of potential acceptance into the European Union, candidate countries often join the Central European Free Trade Agreement, which was created in 2007. Past members that have then joined the European Union include Bulgaria, the

Czech Republic, Hungary, Poland, Romania, Slovakia, and Slovenia. Currently, Albania, Bosnia and Herzegovina, Croatia, Kosovo, Macedonia, Moldova, Montenegro, and Serbia are seeking membership and actively work to reduce barriers to trade both with each other and with the European Union.[29]

Integration in the Americas

North and South America have major trade organizations. None of the institutions compares to the European Union but they do ease the movement of goods within the Americas. Figure 3.13 lists some of the key trade areas and agreements.

Agreement	Population	Overall GDP
North American Free Trade Association (NAFTA)	456 million	$17.6 trillion
Southern Cone Common Market (MERCOSUR)	142 million	$1.5 trillion
Andean Community	99 million	$869 billion
Dominican Republic–Central America	358 million	$15 trillion
United States Free Trade Agreement Caribbean Community	181,000	$59 billion

Figure 3.13: Key North and South American Trade Areas, 2008

Source: Adapted from Central Intelligence Agency, *The World Factbook*, accessed at CIA.gov World Factbook. https://www.cia.gov/library/publications/the-world-factbook/index.html.

Map 3.2: **North American Free Trade Agreement Members, 2011**
With the three member states of Mexico, Canada, and the United States, the North American Free Trade Agreement is the only trade agreement spanning an entire continent.

NORTH AMERICAN FREE TRADE AGREEMENT

NAFTA is the only agreement spanning an entire continent. The United States, Canada, and Mexico formed NAFTA on January 1, 1994, leading to the world's largest free trade area. As of 2008, it included 456 million people and $17.6 trillion of goods and services. The initial agreement called for the removal of all tariffs and quotas by January 1, 2008. The majority of these goals were met. Increased economic ties between the three countries have been the result, with $1.1 trillion in trade in 2008.[30] NAFTA created an administrative function to oversee implementation, the NAFTA Secretariat, which resolves trade disputes and grievances.[31]

The agreement has not been without controversy. Many claim that the removal of barriers has increased trade and improved standards of living in all three countries. Others believe the treaty has resulted in lost jobs, especially in manufacturing, in the United States. Ongoing disputes regarding Mexican long-haul trucking entering the United States continue as of this writing, with critics citing safety concerns. In response to intense lobbying from American transportation companies and workers, the U.S. government has not allowed Mexican truckers to cross the American border. In response, the Mexican government levied tariffs on American dairy goods entering Mexico.[32] While hope for a resolution exists, it may be difficult to achieve. Map 3.2 displays the current members of NAFTA.

Beef Exporting and NAFTA

Although trucking and milk continue to face barriers, trade in beef has been an important component of NAFTA. Forty percent of America's total value of exported beef went to Mexico and Canada between 2002 and 2005.[33] Even with the ban on U.S. beef for a brief period in 2003 due to concerns about mad cow disease, the reduction of barriers to the movement of beef continued. In the case of Canada, the country initially used two separate tariffs rates—one before and one after a set quota was passed. The quota tariffs were removed as NAFTA was implemented, and eventually all U.S. and Mexican beef was excluded from the quota system in Canada. The United States and Mexico followed suit and also removed tariffs on Canadian beef. This allowed each country to focus on the type of beef it produces best—that is, on its comparative advantage. Mexico does not have the domestic production of large feed grain necessary for grain-fed beef. Instead, the country imports this beef from the United States. Grain-fed beef also is preferred by Canadian consumers, allowing for American beef producers to raise beef prices in that market without losing market share.[34]

Beyond the ability to specialize, the biggest advantage to beef producers in all three countries is with competitors outside NAFTA. These foreign producers of beef face tariffs and quotas, in some cases tariffs as high as 50%, which gives NAFTA members a large cost advantage. Facing high tariffs and a reputation for producing tough meat, Australian beef producers have struggled in the Canadian market.[35]

SOUTHERN CONE COMMON MARKET

The Southern Cone Common Market, or *Mercado Commun del Sur,* was founded in 1991 with the signing of the Treaty of Asunción. MERCOSUR seeks the eventual elimination of barriers to trade, development of joint policies toward nonmembers, and a common currency. Implementation has not met expectations. Members frequently add barriers to trade, and response mechanisms often are ineffective. Some member countries elect to use other organizations to resolve trade disputes instead of using MERCOSUR's administrative function. Map 3.3 identifies the members.

The countries within the trading block also have faced extreme economic and political instability. Argentina's currency crisis and a conflict over a pulp mill on the Paraguay–Uruguay border have caused member states to struggle to maintain commitment to MERCOSUR's principles.[36]

One area of success for MERCOSUR has been in the negotiation of trade agreements.[37] The trading bloc signed a free trade agreement with Israel in 2008 and with Egypt in 2010.[38]

Negotiations are ongoing to create an agreement with Palestine and an ambitious agreement with the European Union.[39] If the EU agreement is approved, it would represent the largest such agreement ever made; however,[40] disagreements over agricultural subsidies must first be overcome.[41]

Beef Exporting and MERCOSUR

Beef also plays a central role in the diet of consumers in MERCOSUR. In 2010, Uruguay passed Argentina as the world's top meat-eating nation, per capita.[42] Beef represents an important component of the economies of Brazil, Argentina, and Uruguay. Beef exports from Uruguay alone were worth $836 million in 2006, with 79% of those exports going to North America. Local competition, especially from Brazilian, Argentinian, and increasingly Uruguayan beef, would make entering the MERCOSUR market difficult. Consumers trust local producers and, with the central role of beef in the economies of these countries, many MERCOSUR countries use high tariffs to protect local producers.[43]

Trade within MERCOSUR faces barriers. Unlike NAFTA or the European Union, beef exports to Argentina or other member states do not automatically gain entry into other member states. Still, with the size of the market large, the role of beef being highly important to consumers, and the economies of many members growing, MERCOSUR has the potential to gain in influence.

ANDEAN COMMUNITY

The Andean Community has deep historical roots of trade integration and cooperation in South America, as reflected in the 1969 Andean Pact. Initially, the Andean Pact focused on protecting local industries from outside competition through high tariffs a practice known as *import substitution.*

Map. 3.3: **South American Free Trade Areas**

In 1989 a shift toward a model of open trade with both member and nonmember states occurred. In 1993, a free trade area was introduced and actions were taken to facilitate trade between members. In 1997, leadership structures were reformed, with a Council of Presidents and of Foreign Ministers being introduced. To reflect these changes, the Andean Pact was renamed the Andean Community.[44] To view the current members of the Andean Community, see Map 3.3.

Although economic volatility has occurred, the Andean Community remains economically strong. In the first half of 2010, trade within the Andean Community increased 36% compared to mid-2009, from $2.6 million to $3.6 million. Trade to nonmember countries also grew by 32% during that period.[45]

The Andean Community and MERCOSUR also both joined, along with Guyana and Suriname, the Union of South American Nations (UNASUR), in 2004. The goals of this pan–South America organization are mainly political, although some discussions of economic integration have taken place.[46] UNASUR shares many goals with the Latin American Integration Association. This organization, whose roots trace back to the Latin American Free Trade Association that emerged in the early 1960s, aims to combine Central and South America into one common market.

Beef Exporting and the Andean Community

Exporting to the Andean Community faces fewer hurdles than exporting to the Southern Cone Common Market. While regulations exist, as do risks, the flow of goods between member states has been greatly streamlined in the past fifteen years. An American beef exporter would face a competitive but relatively open market. The United States exports a large amount of beef products to Colombia and Peru, and these two countries represent a large portion of beef trade to all of South America.[47] With the signing of a bilateral free trade agreement with Peru in 2009, all beef exports to that country became tariff free.[48] Beef plays a central role in the Peruvian diet and beef consumption in that country is high. Important dinners are often marked by the serving of spicy beef dishes, including the local delicacy *anticuchos*, grilled beef hearts.[49]

OTHER TRADE ORGANIZATIONS OR AGREEMENTS

Central American governments have signed several trade agreements. In 2004, the United States signed Dominican Republic–Central America–United States Free Trade Agreement (CAFTA-DR). The agreement slowly entered into force, starting with El Salvador in 2006 and ending with Costa Rica in 2009. Textiles have been an important component of the trade deal, with negotiations focusing on encouraging trade.[50]

The islands in the Caribbean (see Map 3.4) traditionally also focus on removing barriers to trade. In 1965, shortly after many of the islands earned independence, Antigua and Barbuda, Barbados, Guyana, and Trinidad and Tobago formed the Caribbean Free Trade Association (CARIFTA). The initial goals of CARIFTA included economic development and encouragement of trade. In 1973, the group changed the name to the Caribbean Community (CARICOM). In 2001, members signed a revision of the Treaty of Chaguaramas stating a long-term goal of starting a CARICOM Single Market and Economy (CSME). The first step of this process is the CARICOM Single Market, which currently has twelve members.[51] The eight Caribbean countries share a currency, the Eastern Caribbean *dollar*, through the Eastern Caribbean Central Bank (ECCB). These eight countries are Antigua and Barbuda, Dominica, Grenada, St. Kitts and Nevis, St. Lucia, St. Vincent and the Grenadines, Anguilla, and Montserrat.[52]

In the past decade, the United States shifted focus to bilateral or country-to-country trade agreements. Figure 3.14 lists existing bilateral agreements and agreements

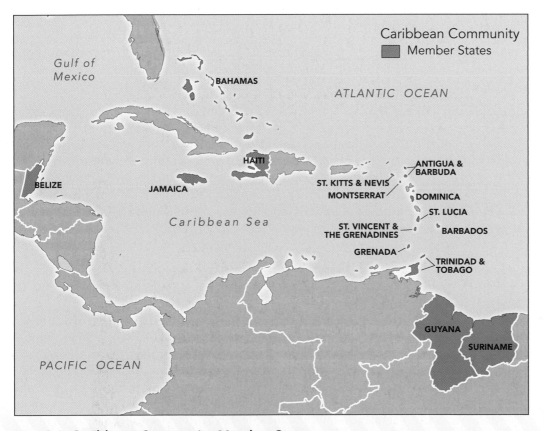

Map 3.4: **Caribbean Community Member States**
The islands in the Caribbean traditionally focus on removing barriers to trade.

Country	Date of Agreement Implementation
Australia	January 1, 2005
Bahrain	January 11, 2006
Chile	January 1, 2004
Colombia	Signed into law October 21, 2011
Israel	September 1, 1985
Jordan	January 1, 2010
Morocco	June 15, 2004
Oman	January 1, 2009
Panama	Signed into law October 21, 2011
Peru	February 1, 2009
Singapore	January 1, 2004
South Korea	Signed into law October 21, 2011

Figure 3.14: Bilateral Free Trade Agreements for the United States

Source: Adapted from "Trans-Pacific Partnership," Office of the United States Trade Representative, accessed at www.ustr.gov/tpp.

that are close to passing. Bilateral agreements involve negotiations between just two countries, making for, in many cases, quicker and easier negotiations.

Integration in Asia, Africa, and the Middle East

Asian, African, and Middle Eastern countries traditionally do not embrace integration to the same degree as European or South and North American countries, but Asia recently has shifted to focusing more on reducing trade barriers. As Figure 3.15 indicates, trading agreements exist, but the degree of integration does not match that present in the European Union or NAFTA countries.

Association of Southeast Asian Nations Free Trade Area
Asia–Pacific Economic Cooperation
Trans-Pacific Strategic Economic Partnership Agreement
South Asian Association for Regional Cooperation

Figure 3.15: Asian Trade-Related Agreements

ASSOCIATION OF SOUTHEAST ASIAN NATIONS FREE TRADE AREA

The oldest trade agreement in Asia, the Association of Southeast Asian Nations (ASEAN), began in 1967. The original member states—Indonesia, Malaysia, Philippines, Singapore, and Thailand—had the goal of banding together to help economic growth and to ensure peace. Over the next thirty-five years, Brunei Darussalam, Vietnam, Laos, Myanmar (Burma), and Cambodia joined. While the ASEAN agreement always focused on increasing economic ties, in 1992, the members officially created a the Association of Southeast Asian Nations Free Trade Area. All members of ASEAN, including those that joined after 1992 (Vietnam, Laos, Myanmar [Burma], and Cambodia), are part of the free trade area.[53] The members of the ASEAN FTA are shown in Map 3.5.

The Association of Southeast Asian Nations focuses on political alliances, defense, culture, and education. Economic integration constitutes one of the group's primary goals. In 2007, an ASEAN economic blueprint called for an eventual ASEAN Economic Community to assist free movement of goods, labor, and capital among ASEAN members and a common trade policy toward nonmembers.[54] Members have taken strong measures to lower tariffs. In Brunei Darussalam, Indonesia, Malaysia, the Philippines, Singapore, and Thailand tariffs have reached some agreement, but the remaining ASEAN countries (Cambodia, Laos, Myanmar [Burma], and Vietnam) lag behind.[55]

The main barrier to further integration for ASEAN lies in the disparate political and economic features of the members. The government of Myanmar, called Burma by the American government for political reasons, suppresses human rights and makes only weak gestures toward moving to a democracy. The other ASEAN member states put pressure on Myanmar for reform, but these political concerns reduce progress on trade issues.[56] National disasters, political unrest, and complicated relationships with other countries, particularly China, have derailed the process in recent years.

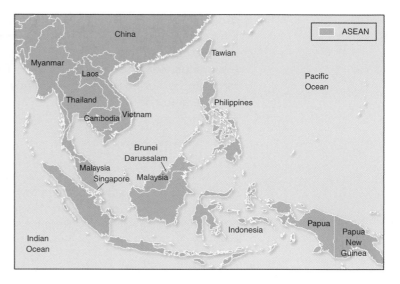

Map 3.5: **The Members of the Association of Southeast Asian Nations Free Trade Area**
The oldest trade agreement in Asia, the ASEAN, began in 1967.

ASIA-PACIFIC ECONOMIC COOPERATION

The Asia-Pacific Economic Cooperation (APEC) group currently has twenty-one members, all of them economies that border the Pacific Ocean. Figure 3.16 lists the members, which account for 40% of the world's population, more than half of the global GDP, and almost 44% of world trade.[57]

APEC, founded in 1990, serves as a connecting group, encouraging dialogue between members. The present members meet annually at the APEC Economic Leaders' Meeting. Discussions focus on the removal of barriers to trade, on opening conversations between business leaders in the member economies, and on an eventual free trade area of the Asia-Pacific region. As of this writing, APEC is focusing on promoting conversations between members. Expansion may follow. A moratorium on new membership expired at the end of 2010 and many new countries may join.[58]

Australia	New Zealand
Brunei Darussalam	Papua New Guinea
Canada	Peru
Chile	The Philippines
China	Russia
Hong Kong	Singapore
Indonesia	Taiwan
Japan	Thailand
Republic of Korea	The United States
Malaysia	Vietnam
Mexico	

Figure 3.16: Members of the Asia-Pacific Economic Cooperation

TRANS-PACIFIC STRATEGIC ECONOMIC PARTNERSHIP AGREEMENT

The United States government increasingly looks to Asia for exports and for growth markets to spur economic development. In 2010, the U.S. government joined the governments of Australia, Brunei Darussalam, Chile, Malaysia, New Zealand, Peru, Singapore, and Vietnam in negotiating a potential Trans-Pacific Strategic Economic Partnership Agreement. A similar agreement already exists for Brunei Darussalam, Chile, New Zealand, and Singapore. The agreement has resulted in the reduction of tariffs and other barriers to trade between those countries. Negotiations for increased membership continue.[59]

SOUTH ASIAN ASSOCIATION FOR REGIONAL COOPERATION

South Asia, as a region, contains few large trade agreements. The largest connecting organization, the South Asian Association for Regional Cooperation (SAARC), has eight member countries: Afghanistan, Bangladesh, Bhutan, India, Maldives, Nepal, Pakistan, and Sri Lanka (see Map 3.6).[60] These countries signed the SAARC Preferential

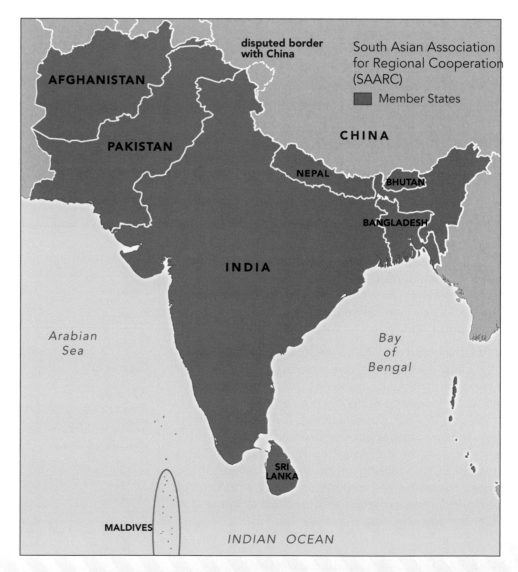

Map 3.6: **Members of the South Asian Association for Regional Cooperation**
The South Asian Association for Regional Cooperation (SAARC) includes eight member countries.

Trading Agreement in 1993 and have discussed a potential SAARC free trade area. Political conflicts between the countries in SAARC, particularly between India and Pakistan, present roadblocks to integration. Consequently, many South Asian countries pursue more easily negotiated bilateral trade agreements. India has signed free trade agreements with Brunei Darussalam, Indonesia, Laos, Malaysia, Myanmar (Burma), Singapore, Thailand, and Vietnam.[61]

BEEF EXPORTS IN ASIA

The exporting of goods to South and East Asia faces many obstacles. A beef exporter to that region would need to deal with tariffs, regulations, and other barriers when attempting to enter many of the markets. Some of the countries have signed individual trade agreements, yet the region does not have a strong, multi-country trading block to facilitate the movement of goods. Until the political and historical reasons for a reluctance to work together are overcome, exporters of beef and other products will find it easier to navigate other markets rather than trying to enter Asia.

Beef has also been the focus of specific protests in various countries in the region. Taiwanese regulators do not allow the growth drug Paylean in imported beef. Recent imports from the United States have included the banned drug, leading to protests and increased screening. The concerns over beef have slowed down talks on a broader trade agreement.[62] Fear of mad cow disease in American beef exports resulted in street protests in South Korea in 2008. The issue remains sensitive, and the 2010 negotiations with South Korea regarding a potential free trade agreement purposely did not include a discussion of removal of barriers to beef trade. The subject is so volatile that it could potentially derail all other negotiations.[63]

INTEGRATION IN THE MIDDLE EAST AND AFRICA

The removal of trade barriers has taken place around the globe. The Middle East and Africa have made progress on integration, although both regions have far to go before trade will flow freely with each region.

Middle East

The Greater Arab Free Trade Area (GFTA), founded in 1997, now encompasses all seventeen members of the Arab League plus Algeria. Figure 3.17 displays the members as well as the members of another key Middle East economic agreement, the Cooperation Council for the Arab States of the Gulf (GCC). The GFTA agreement calls for an eventual uniform tariff between members, sharing of standards, and an aggressive 40% reduction of tariffs. The GFTA operates under the broader Council of Arab Economic Unity.

The Cooperation Council for the Arab States of the Gulf (GCC), founded in 1981, overlaps membership with the GAFTA and CAEU. The council focuses on many issues beyond trade and, to a lesser extent, economic integration. The group put the structure for a customs union in place in 2003. Tariffs were unified at 5% for member nations.[64] Broader goals include eventually having a common market and possibly a common currency.[65]

Cooperation Council for the Arab States of the Gulf
Bahrain, Kuwait, Oman, Qatar, Saudi Arabia, and the United Arab Emirates
Greater Arab Free Trade Area
Bahrain, Egypt, Iraq, Jordan, Kuwait, Lebanon, Libya, Morocco, Oman, Palestine, Qatar, Saudi Arabia, Sudan, Syria, Tunisia, United Arab Emirates, and Yemen

Figure 3.17: Key Middle East Economic Agreements

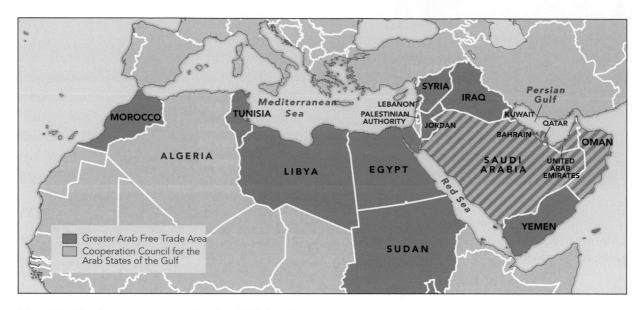

Map 3.7: **Trade Agreements in the Middle East**
Countries in the Middle East have signed various trade agreements.

Africa

Countries on the African continent have traditionally stated lofty integration goals. The oldest customs union in the world, the Southern African Customs Union (SACU), is located on the continent.[66] The vast majority of the countries on the continent are signatories to one or more economic agreements (see Figure 3.18). The Abuja Treaty, signed in 1991, has the goal of establishing the African Economic Community, which includes almost every country on the continent. The Abuja Treaty laid out a series of steps to regional free trade areas leading to a common market and finally to an economic union similar to the EU, complete with a continental currency.

Many regional unions exist throughout Africa. Each of these, as noted in Figure 3.18, exhibits various levels of integration with differing degrees of enforcement mechanisms. The relationships are often superseded by political conflicts and unrest. One success story is the West African Economic and Monetary Union, started in 1994. The International Monetary Fund (IMF) has stated that this customs union is the most integrated of all the various groupings in Africa. The member countries successfully put into place a functioning customs union, including a common external tariffs, and effective administrative oversight.[67]

The East African Community (EAC), which began in 1999 and includes five countries, has also achieved a degree of integration. As is common with many agreements in Africa, the goal of the East African Community is a political federation built on a common market and a common currency among member states. As of 2011, a customs union structure has been developed. Steps are being taken toward a common market among EAC members along with the beginning of discussion of a possible monetary union.[68]

Ties between African countries often trace back to their shared colonial roots. Many countries share a currency that initially served as the regional currency when the states were under the rule of Western powers. The Central and West African *francs* follow this trend. Figure 3.19 lists existing currency unions as well as the proposed West African Monetary Union, which hopes to introduce a common currency, called the eco, in 2015.

Arab Maghreb Union

Algeria, Libya, Mauritania, Morocco, Tunisia

Common Market for Eastern and Southern Africa

Burundi, Comoros, Democratic Republic of the Congo, Djibouti, Egypt, Eritrea, Ethiopia, Kenya, Libya, Madagascar, Malawi, Mauritius, Rwanda, Seychelles, Sudan, Swaziland, Uganda, Zambia, and Zimbabwe

Community of Sahel-Saharan States

Benin, Burkina Faso, Central African Republic, Chad, Comoros, Côte d'Ivoire, Djibouti, Egypt, Eritrea, The Gambia, Ghana, Guinea, Guinea-Bissau, Kenya, Liberia, Libya, Mali, Mauritania, Morocco, Niger, Nigeria, Sao Tome and Principe, Senegal, Sierra Leone, Somalia, Sudan, Togo, and Tunisia.

East African Community—Customs Union

Burundi, Kenya, Rwanda, Tanzania, and Uganda

Economic Community of Central African States

Angola, Burundi, Cameroon, Central African Republic, Chad, Democratic Republic of the Congo, Equatorial Guinea, Gabon, Republic of the Congo, and São Tomé and Príncipe

Economic Community of West African States

Benin, Burkina Faso, Cape Verde, Gambia, Ghana, Guinea, Guinea-Bissau, Liberia, Mali, Niger, Nigeria, Senegal, Sierra Leone, and Togo (Côte d'Ivoire has membership suspended)

Economic Community of the Great Lakes Countries

Burundi, Democratic Republic of the Congo, and Rwanda

Intergovernmental Authority on Development

Djibouti, Eritrea, Ethiopia, Kenya, Somalia, Sudan, and Uganda

Mano River Union

Côte d'Ivoire, Guinea, Liberia, and Sierra Leone

Southern African Customs Union

Botswana, Lesotho, Namibia, South Africa, and Swaziland

Southern African Development Community

Angola, Botswana, Democratic Republic of the Congo, Lesotho, Madagascar, Malawi, Mauritius, Mozambique, Namibia, Seychelles, South Africa, Swaziland, Tanzania, and Zimbabwe.

West African Economic and Monetary Union

Benin, Burkina Faso, Côte d'Ivoire, Guinea-Bissau, Mali, Niger, Senegal, and Togo

Figure 3.18: Economic Ties in Africa

| **Central African** *Franc* |
| Cameroon, Central African Republic, Chad, Republic of the Congo, Equatorial Guinea, and Gabon |
| **West African** *Franc* |
| Benin, Burkina Faso, Côte d'Ivoire, Guinea-Bissau, Mali, Niger, Senegal, and Togo |
| **West African Monetary Union** |
| The Gambia, Ghana, Guinea, Liberia, Nigeria, and Sierra Leone |

Figure 3.19: African Currency Agreements

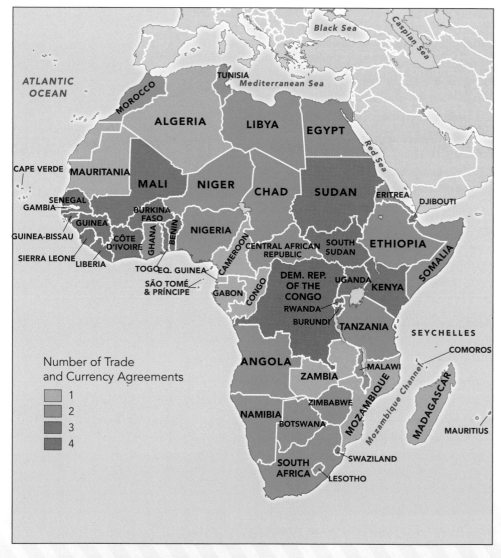

Map 3.8: **African Trade Agreements**
Several African countries have signed trade and currency agreements.

Beef Exports in Africa

Those wishing to export either to Africa or to the Middle East will encounter several obstacles. The limited and inconsistent trade integration in the region does little to alleviate these concerns. An American beef exporter would be hesitant to attempt to enter either market. Beef consumption remains at low levels across the continent. As countries develop, however, the amount of red meat consumed does increase. In Nigeria, 10 million consumers have become middle class in the last decade. These consumers are more likely to purchase meat. As a result, Nigeria has a $9 million market for red meat, the second largest on the continent. Zambeef, a South African beef producer, has moved aggressively into the Nigerian market. With approximately 1 billion people on the continent, further economic development could lead to opportunities for beef exporters globally.[69]

For both regions, the fundamental concern continues to be stability. Political unrest and uncertainty make it difficult to maintain a consistent trade policy. Côte d'Ivoire faced unrest and international pressure over an election that was stolen to allow the president at that time, Laurent Gbagbo, to remain in power.[70] Eventually, Gbagbo was arrested, but only after major disruption. Côte d'Ivoire is a member nation for the Economic Community of West African States and the Mano River Union, and is one of the eight countries that use the West African *franc*. The political and overall instability in Côte d'Ivoire affects the viability of these agreements. The Economic Community of West African States suspended Côte d'Ivoire's membership, and the conflict serves as an example of the political instability undermining increased integration in both Africa and in the Middle East.

Protectionism vs. Free Trade

Protectionism refers to the desire to protect domestic businesses from the exports of foreign firms through governmental policy. Lobbying by the effective domestic companies often creates pressures on governments to respond. In 2010, Brazil announced taxes or tariffs on 102 U.S. products. The tariffs varied in size, with some as high as 100%, and affected around $1 billion per year in trade. The Brazilian government placed tariffs or taxes on these goods in response to what the government saw as unfair tariffs on Brazilian cotton being exported to the U.S. market. The strong American agricultural lobby, especially Southern cotton growers, exerted pressure on the U.S. government to keep the tariffs in place.[71]

LEARNING OBJECTIVE #4:

How does protectionism affect free trade?

GOVERNMENT POLICIES LIMITING TRADE

Governments employ a variety of different tools or devices when trying to reduce imports (see Figure 3.20). Tariffs, essentially a tax on imports, are the most common device. Tariffs can be product or country specific, and are designed to protect local industries. The European Union has targeted tariffs on shoes imported from Vietnam and China to defend the region's footwear industry.[72]

A second governmental tactic is an embargo. Instead of a fee or tax, embargoes either prevent any goods from entering a country or prevent goods from being exported by a country.

Often embargoes are driven by a political conflict, as has been the case with the long-standing embargo on exports to Cuba by U.S. businesses.[73] Embargoes may also be for national security reasons, such as the 2010 Russian embargo on wheat exporting. Facing drought and wildfires, the concern over potential shortages led

> Protectionism refers to the desire to protect domestic businesses from the exports of foreign firms through governmental policy.

| Tariffs |
| Embargoes |
| Quotas |
| Subsidies |
| Import Licenses |
| Other Administrative Barriers |
| Currency Convertibility |

Figure 3.20: Government Policies Limiting Trade

the government to put the embargo in place.[74] Embargoes exist for sensitive technology and materials, including those needed to build nuclear weapons.

In some cases, governments place limits on the amounts of a good that can be either exported or imported. The Chinese government maintains a quota on exports of rare earth elements, including seventeen unique elements used in miniature electronics such as those used in the iPhone. After reaching the quota, no more exports of rare earth elements are allowed during that year.[75]

Instead of limiting the ability of foreign companies to export to a market, some governments attempt to prop up local producers. A subsidy represents the payment of money to domestic businesses. India provides subsidies for food grain–based distilleries.[76] By lowering the operation costs of these businesses, the money or subsidy given to these distilleries creates a competitive advantage over foreign distilleries seeking to export to the Indian market.

Governmental leaders can limit imports by requiring that businesses that wish to import goods purchase an import license. By limiting the number of licenses, the amount of overall imports may be reduced. Indonesia requires import licenses for any business wishing to import clothing, footwear, food and beverages, electronics, and toys.[77]

Other administrative barriers also slow the movement of goods. In Indonesia, the use of import licenses is supplemented by governmental regulations limiting imports to five ports: Belawan in Medan, Tanjung Priok in Jakarta, Tanjung Emas in Semarang, Tanjung Perak in Surabaya, and Soekarno-Hatta in Makassar. At those ports, inspections of the goods delay entry, as does paperwork and other administrative procedures. Between the import license requirements and the administrative barriers, food and beverage imports dropped between 30% to 40% from 2009 to 2010.[78]

The final step a government may take to limit imports revolves around *currency*. Money earned in one country often needs to be exchanged for another currency when it is transferred out of the country. Currency convertibility represents the ability to make currency transfers. Governments may limit the amounts of currency that can be exchanged or even ban the exchange of certain currencies. This action limits the ability of companies that use the banned or limited currency to conduct business in the country.

ARGUMENTS FOR PROTECTIONISM

When other countries employ methods to limit trade, governments often take protectionist steps. Various reasons exist for these actions and some of the reasons overlap. In general, the arguments for protectionism focus on protecting a country's well-being. Figure 3.21 presents a common list of reasons.

The goal of protecting local industries plays a prominent role in many governmental actions. In many countries, defending agriculture spurs protectionism of farm products. Local farmers often represent an iconic component of the country's history. In addition, self-sufficiency for food production may be valued and the agricultural lobby may be strong. Tariffs and other barriers increase the cost of food in Korea and Japan an estimated 1.7 and 1.9 times the global market price.[79]

Infant industries merit protection. Young or new businesses often lack the experience, economies of scale, and overall support to compete with large multinational corporations. Governments may prevent competition from foreign firms until the local infant industry becomes mature enough to compete. Governments in emerging economies often take aggressive steps to protect young, targeted industries. The rationale used is similar to that offered by developed countries in the past. Great Britain used tariffs to protect the infant wool industry in the seventeenth century. In the United States, tariffs were never below 40% for any good from the Civil War to World War I. In the rapid growth of post-war Japan, protectionism was used. One famous example was the unique properties of Japanese snow that led to a ban on foreign ski equipment. Currently countries such as China and India followed a similar path.[80]

Protect local industry, especially infant industry
Respond to local political and popular pressure
Protect national security
Earn revenue
Promote consumer safety
Discourage immoral business practices
Protect the environment with sustainable practices
Protect culture

Figure 3.21: Arguments for Protectionism

Often trade barriers result from local political and popular pressure. Workers who face potential unemployment, business owners with apprehensions about the potential loss of profit or bankruptcy, or local governmental officials who fear the loss of a key local industry may aggressively pressure national governments to put protective barriers in place. Multinational companies often respond by producing the banned or highly taxed good locally. In Nigeria and West Africa in general, the importing of chicken is banned. In response, KFC has contracted with local chicken farms for supplies.[81] The concern for employees potentially losing jobs due to foreign competition also leads local citizens and groups to lobby for protection.[82]

Protectionism may also be justified based on national security concerns. The trade in military goods, or dependency on other nations for resources associated with national defense, represents common justifications for barriers to trade. In 2007, China passed a law requiring all purchases of Chinese companies by foreign businesses to be reviewed for national security implications.[83]

Tariffs, administrative fees, and other trade barriers also earn revenues for governments. In cases of corrupt governments, these fees may go directly into the pockets of governmental officials. This situation creates a powerful incentive for revenue-earning barriers.

Trade barriers may be driven by concerns with consumer safety. Governments often ban or screen products that potentially could harm consumers. The process of product screening adds time and complications to importing, but concerns about consumer protection outweigh these issues. The European Union safety procedure, under the consumer chief, includes a rapid notification system called RAPEX that lessens delays due to safety concerns. The objective is to balance safety concerns with the desire to keep the European Union as open to trade as possible.[84]

Protectionism may be motivated by moral concerns among citizens, particularly the employees, in foreign countries. Severe work conditions, lack of employee rights, and worries about environmental protections represent reasons to limit trade with a country. In many countries, citizens are hesitant to buy products from foreign companies that practice unfair and potentially unethical business practices. Every year at Halloween, U.S. newspapers print articles revealing the use of child labor in West African countries such as Ghana and Côte d'Ivoire to harvest and process cocoa beans, which has led governments to pressure large multinationals to find more ethical sources for cocoa.[85]

Environmental and Sustainability Issues

Increasingly, trade raises sustainability concerns. As sustainability becomes more of a focus for governments, citizens, and many businesses, the differences between

Numerous arguments have been made regarding the need for government steps for or against protectionism.

environmental regulations in various countries draw increasing attention. Environmental regulations may result in an increase in costs, at least short term; companies producing in countries with less-stringent regulations may be able to lower prices for consumers as a result. Environmentally conscious consumers and businesses are sometimes willing to pay the higher prices.

The opening of markets to low-priced products that create pollution has significant environmental implications. In some cases, the companies producing in the foreign markets are domestic companies moving production to avoid environmental regulation. For many countries, the fines for polluting are smaller than the cost of upgrading the production process, reducing any incentive to make a change.[86] The actual transportation of exports also leads to pollution. The estimated amount of sulfur dioxide, the main pollutant linked to acid rain, that is released by global shipping surpasses the amount released by the all of the world's cars, trucks, and buses combined.[87]

Trade potentially affects the cultural identity of countries. The importing of art, entertainment, music, and other similar items from Western countries shifts the culture of a least- or less-developed or a developing country. To protect that local culture and tradition, governments may take protectionist steps.

In Quebec, to protect the local French traditions, strict laws regulate language usage. The Charter of the French Language requires that all business signs include French, and if English is also used, the French component of the sign must predominate.[88] For businesses entering Quebec, these language requirements, and the potential for regulatory activity if the statute is not met, represent increased costs and a barrier to entry.

THE FUTURE

LEARNING OBJECTIVE #5:

How do laws and ethical concerns affect trade and international marketing globally?

Arguments regarding free trade and protectionism are likely to continue. It appears that many national leaders have concluded that regional trade associations are in their country's best national interest, as witnessed by the growth in membership in these organizations. Countries such as North Korea that refrain from joining trade associations tend to join when national leaders or dictators need to do so in order to maintain internal power. Often, the citizens of those countries are at an economic disadvantage as a result.

VIDEO LINK 3.3:
Google

Legal and Ethical Issues

Global trade often places marketers in countries where business practices may involve legally and ethically questionable corruption and bribery. U.S. law outlaws bribery. In 1977, the U.S. Congress passed the Foreign Corrupt Practices Act. It applies to the activities of American business people while abroad. More specifically, it outlaws the payment of bribes to any government official in return for any business preference or favors. In 1998, an amendment to the law increased its coverage to any foreign person or firm that, either directly or through a third party, cause the payment of a bribe in the United States. Any company that lists securities in the United States, such as on the New York Stock Exchange, must abide by the Foreign Corrupt Practices Act. [89]

In 2010, the Securities and Exchange Commission and U.S. Department of Justice together fined companies a total of $1.7 billion for Foreign Corrupt Practices Act violations. More than 90% of the companies fined were non-U.S. firms.[90] One of the more visible of these cases involved Tyson Foods Inc., the world's largest meat protein company. The company's Mexican subsidiary, Tyson de México, bribed two Mexican government veterinarians to certify chicken products for export by hiring their wives. Payments totaled $101,311. Tyson Foods officials not only ignored the payments when first learning of them, but also included the payments as expenses on financial filings. As a result of these actions, Tyson Foods paid a $4 million fine.[91]

The U.S. government prohibits U.S. companies and citizens from participating in any foreign country–sponsored boycott. The regulation is generally referred to as the Anti-Boycott Law. While rooted in concerns regarding potential support of the Arab League boycott of Israel, the law applies to all foreign boycotts. In 2008, the U.K. subsidiary of the Pennsylvanian firm Colorcon was found guilty of supporting the Arab League ban to gain business in Syria.[92]

Governments also commonly regulate businesses to make sure that monopolies do not form. *Antitrust laws* designed to prevent monopolies are common in many countries. In the United States, the primary antitrust laws are the Sherman Act and the Clayton Act. The Federal Trade Commission and the Justice Department enforce the statutes. Similar enforcement structures are common in other countries. In Indonesia, for example, a local company, Temasek Holdings Pte. Ltd., was found to have violated Indonesian anti-monopoly laws through its ownership of stakes in two local cellular companies.[93] In the United States, recent acquisitions by Google have received attention, with concerns that the purchases may lead to monopolistic advantages.[94]

All countries act to prevent the export of technologies related to national security and broader political interests. Whether material associated with nuclear weapons or business innovations, strict control over information transfers exists in all countries. Recently, economic espionage, such as in the case of a U.S. citizen passing on some of Dow Chemical's secret to the Chinese government, has received attention.[95]

The application of laws outside of country borders is called *extraterritoriality*. The passage and application of these laws represents the one final issue with regard to legal restrictions and marketing activity covered in this chapter. Many laws apply to U.S. citizens while acting abroad, such as the Foreign Corrupt Practices Act. Concerns arise when local laws conflict with U.S. laws. International marketers should be aware of the laws they must follow. They should also engage in only the activities with which they feel ethically and morally comfortable.

Chapter 3: Review and Resources

STRATEGIC IMPLICATIONS //

The first step of the strategic management process, analysis and diagnosis, involves assessments of internal company strengths and weaknesses combined with an analysis of opportunities and threats posed in the external environment. The strategic evaluation of global trade provides the backdrop for numerous international marketing activities. Company leaders may examine regions, such as the European Union, MERCOSUR, the Andean Community, or the Pacific Rim, to determine if the region presents a viable area to target with exports. Then specific countries will be studied to see if the local government favors free trade or engages in protectionism. Local laws and customs will be evaluated as part of this analysis. Many times, protections are aimed at specific products or industries, which makes this information valuable to company leaders prior to implementing any strategic exporting decisions.

TACTICAL IMPLICATIONS //

At the tactical level, brand managers, sales managers, promotions managers, and others investigate the best methods to conduct operations in target areas. A financial officer will know that the *euro* is the common currency in the European Union and will incorporate information regarding exchange rates and other financial instruments as part of an exporting program to countries in that region. In a region that does not use a common currency, the financial situation becomes more complex. Preferred modes of shipping vary by region. Laws affecting the movement of goods will be carefully noted as part of the process. Tariffs are to be understood prior to any trade arrangement. Marketing managers at the tactical level take the information gathered for strategic decision-making and adapt it to the area. A brand manager will need to know about any changes in packaging or labeling that will be required. Promotions managers find out which media are most popular with local consumers. Only when tactical operations mesh smoothly with strategic decisions will the exporting process be successful.

OPERATIONAL IMPLICATIONS //

Operationally, companies entering new markets retain employees and other companies to deal with the administrative processes associated with exporting. Individuals may be needed to shepherd shipments across borders. Experience in the paperwork and other processes may speed the border-crossing process. Understanding local regulations, in a broad sense, should be the responsibility of a key individual of a small group in the exporting company. Perishables or other time-sensitive goods will receive special attention. First-line supervisors and entry-level employees carry out the dictates of middle-level marketing managers, including purchasing media time for advertising, working with local shops and stores, and other host-country marketing activities.

TERMS

importing	integration	political union
free trade	free trade area	offshoring
absolute advantage theory	customs union	outsourcing
comparative advantage theory	common market	protectionism
free trade zones	economic union	

REVIEW QUESTIONS

1. Define exporting and importing.
2. What does the absolute advantage theory explain?
3. What does the comparative advantage theory explain?
4. What are the potential benefits of free trade?
5. In global trade, what is meant by the term *integration*?
6. Briefly describe free trade zones, custom unions, common markets, economic unions, and political unions.
7. Briefly describe offshoring and outsourcing.
8. What are the primary activities of the World Trade Organization (WTO)?
9. Outline the primary activities of the European Union (EU).
10. What are the three members of the North American Free Trade Agreement (NAFTA)?
12. On what continent is the Southern Cone Common Market (*Mercado Común del Sur;* MERCOSUR) located?
13. What are the names of the Asian trade-related agreements?
14. What is protectionism?
15. What methods can governments use to limit trade?
16. What arguments are made in favor of protectionism practices?

DISCUSSION QUESTIONS

1. Write an argument for free trade and a counterargument for protectionism. Regardless of your initial perspective on the topic, try equally hard for both arguments. Can you build a legitimate case for both approaches?
2. Trace the history of the European Union, highlighting how each step increased the level of integration. Then consider the organizational structure of the EU. How does the structure reflect the history?
3. Consider the history of integration in the Americas. How do MERCOSUR and the Andean Community compare to NAFTA? How are all three similar and how do all three affect integration in the region?
4. Examine the list of African economic agreements in Figure 3.18. What do you learn from looking at this list? What does the list say about what steps governments need to actually begin to integrate?
5. The Federal Corrupt Practices Act outlaws bribery. Does this law give American businesses an unfair advantage or create a disadvantage when working with foreign governments and businesses?

ANALYTICAL AND INTERNET EXERCISES

1. Some economists look at the role of trade in economic development and conclude that labor standards represent a barrier to economic development. Jeffery Sachs, a famous Harvard economist and a driving force behind the United Nations Millennium Development Goals, was quoted as saying: "My concern is not that there are too many sweatshops but that there are too few."[96] The United Nations also has a standing body focused on labor protection, called the International Labour Organization (ILO). Visit the ILO website or other websites that argue for protectionism (www.ilo.org). Are these arguments convincing? Why or why not?

2. Calculate the comparative advantage each country will get from trade considering the following case:

    Country A
    Labor Input = 15 Workers
    Labor Input Widgets = 10 Workers
    Labor Input Doodads = 5 Workers
    Total Output = 30 Widgets, 10 Doodads

    Country B
    Labor Input = 15 Workers
    Labor Input Widgets = 10 Workers
    Labor Input Doodads = 5 Workers
    Total Output = 10 Widgets, 5 Doodads

    What happens in the case of specialization and trade? Calculate the total output. How can trade then result in a higher amount of each good for each country?

3. The European Union has an animated map of its expansion from 1952 to 2007 at http://europa.eu/abc/history/animated_map/index_en.htm. Visit this map and draw conclusions about the history and the future of the EU based on past trends.

4. Using Google and library resources, research the Free Trade Area of the Americas. What was this agreement? Why did negotiations stall and what does that tell you about potential barriers to further integration globally?

5. Research online a recent antitrust or monopoly case. The case may be in the United States or in another country. How does preventing monopolies potentially help consumers? Is there a counterargument to be made for how a monopoly might help consumers?

 ONLINE VIDEOS

Visit **www.sagepub.com/baack** to view these chapter videos:

Video Link 3.1: Principles of Adam Smith

Video Link 3.2: China's Economy

Video Link 3.3: Google

STUDENT STUDY SITE

Visit **www.sagepub.com/baack** to access these additional learning tools:

- Web Quizzes
- eFlashcards
- SAGE Journal Articles

- Country Fact Sheets
- Chapter Outlines
- Interactive Maps

CASE 3 ///

DHL and Facilitating Small Business Trade

DHL began as a small document currier between the West Coast of the United States and Hawai'i. The company has grown into one of the leading logistics and shipping companies in the world. Named for the three businessmen that founded the company in 1969, Adrian Dalsey, Larry Hillblom, and Robert Lynn, DHL has looked for new opportunities from inception. Recognizing a gap in the market, the company started by shipping papers to and from San Francisco and Honolulu.

The company also focused on international growth. The early 1970s witnessed growth in shipping to the Far East and Pacific Rim, including services in Japan, Hong Kong, Singapore, and Australia. The company expanded into Europe in the 1970s, opening an office in London in 1974 and in Frankfurt in 1977. At the same time, DHL expanded shipping into the Middle East, Latin America, and Africa. In 1983 the company began shipping to and from Eastern Europe. In 1986, DHL became the first express shipping company in China.

The 1990s led to more changes. The German company Deutsche Post became a shareholder in 1998, laying the foundation for eventually becoming the 100% owner in 2002. The company invested aggressively in expansion by opening a $60 million facility in Bahrain in 1993 and by introducing a major information technology center in Kuala Lumpur, Malaysia, in 1998. DHL spent more than $1 billion on a fleet of airplanes for the European and African markets in 1999.

Deutsche Post took over greater operational control in the 2000s and the company focused more on emerging markets. From 2003 to 2008, DHL invested more than $200 million to improve operations in China. In 2004, the company opened an information technology facility in Prague and in the Czech Republic, and also became majority owner of Blue Dart, an Indian express shipping company. By the end of the decade, DHL was conducting business activities in more than 220 countries and territories, with more than 3,000 customers and 300,000 employees, and was generating revenue of more than 46 billion *euros* per year.[97]

A substantial part of DHL's growth resulted from facilitating trade for small- or medium-sized businesses. These organizations often offer products that consumers in other countries would purchase, if the product could successfully reach that market.

DHL offers networking events, website resources, and specialized computer software to support companies that want to trade. A dedicated website (www.DHLsmallbusiness.com) provides additional assistance. The website facilitates the sharing of knowledge between businesses.[98]

One of the key differentiating services is DHL's proprietary software, EasyShip Connect, which was designed for small- and medium-sized businesses. It allows companies to communicate directly with DHL computers to perform a variety of shipping functions, automating the process. The software also fills out American regulatory paperwork required for international shipments of more than $2,500.[99] These services allowed Stretchy Shapes, maker of the recent fad of fun-shaped stretchy bracelets, to use DHL to facilitate international growth. The company estimates that using DHL reduced delivery time by as much as 75%, partially due to faster processing of paperwork.[100]

1. Consider the expansion pattern of DHL. How might this relate to the integration activities discussed in this chapter?

2. Does the reduction of barriers to trade help or hurt DHL's business? Justify your answer.

3. Visit the DHL small business website (www .DHLsmallbusiness.com). What are four activities on the website that facilitate small business trade?

4. Would a supporter of protectionism view DHL's activities as positive or negative? Do you agree with that perspective?

DHL delivery systems assist many small businesses internationally.

PART II
International Markets and Market Research

4 Markets and Segmentation in an International Context

LEARNING OBJECTIVES ///

After reading and studying this chapter, you should be able to answer the following questions:

1. How does a nation's or region's culture, including its origins, characteristics, and values, influence the international marketing context?

2. Why should a marketing team examine cultural imperatives, cultural electives, and cultural exclusives when entering a host country?

3. How does culture affect purchasing behaviors?

4. What are the primary factors used to identify international consumer and business-to-business market segments?

5. How can a marketing team use regional and national segmentation methods to improve a company's global marketing program?

6. What is green marketing, and how is it related to concepts of sustainability?

IN THIS CHAPTER ///

Musical Segmentation

One constant that may be found anywhere on the planet is music. The forms vary, the instruments are similar in some cultures and quite different in others, but songs often feature universal themes and emotions, regardless of where they are sung. International marketers are likely to be involved with music in one way or another as products move across international boundaries.

VIDEO LINK 4.1:
Music and Globalism

Music reflects culture, and culture changes music. The more traditional musical forms have roots that extend far back into history, in no matter which country. In Asia, common traditional instruments include versions of the flute and stringed instruments. The *ruan*, a four-stringed fretted instrument used for opera and other performances, dates back more than 1,600 years in China. The spike fiddle is widespread in the Gobi areas of central Mongolia and among eastern Mongols; the *khuuchir* and the *dorvon chikhtei khuur* are a two- and a four-stringed spike fiddle, respectively.

In Saudi Arabia and other Middle Eastern countries, the flute-like *ney* (or *nay*) accompanies folk songs; the *bandir* (or *bendir*), a type of small drum, keeps rhythm; and the *qanan*, a stringed instrument, enriches the unique sound. African drums create distinctive rhythms that accompany long-standing musical and cultural traditions.

Over time, musical instruments move across national boundaries, as do musical formats. The piano, violin, oboe, harp, trumpet, and numerous other instruments shape classical music sounds across many cultures. Pioneering classical music composers have emerged from a variety of countries, and the music shared between those nations creates cultural contacts and closeness.

Today, forms of folk music and popular culture formats span the globe, moving more quickly due to communication links that make it possible to watch performances as they take place in other nations. Hip-hop artists may be found around the world. Numerous country and western fans reside in Japan. Music connects with language, fashion, cultural change, and other elements of local, regional, national, and international environments.

A variety of international marketing opportunities emerge from music. They include the exporting of musical instruments; the sale of music by Internet, iPod, CD, music video, or on the radio; performances by musical artists touring the globe complete with sponsorships; and the musical backgrounds that accompany advertisements and commercials. Marketing professionals moving into new countries will quickly be exposed to local musical tastes and dislikes.

Musical acts appeal to consumers across the globe. The Dave Matthews Band, as one example, played 1,692 shows globally from 1992 to 2010, selling more than 11 million tickets from 2000 to 2009. The global appeal of the music, and the ability to attract fans in South America, Europe, North America, and elsewhere, allowed the band to gross over $500 million from touring during the 2000s.[1]

To effectively incorporate music into an international marketing program, the marketing team examines the cultural context in which music is performed, including its connections to religious life, festivals, popular culture, and other events. Musical preferences logically link to any number of potential market segments, including distinctions by age, gender, income level, religious affiliation, culture, counterculture, and others. Just as the numbers of songs and musical styles are infinite, the international marketing possibilities created by music are nearly as endless.

QUESTIONS FOR STUDENTS

1. Do you believe music shapes cultural movements, accompanies cultural movements, or merely reflects cultural movements?

2. What types of market segments are associated with various musical forms?

3. What role does music play in international marketing that may be different from marketing in only one country?

Consumers around the world enjoy music.

Overview

Part I of this book was designed to explain the essentials of international marketing. A basic framework was established, economic systems and modes of entry were examined, and the nature of global trade and integration was presented. These factors help form the basis for carrying out all other strategic international marketing functions.

Part II concentrates on international markets. Chapter 4 begins with an analysis of markets and segmentation programs. Chapter 5 analyzes strategic international positioning. Chapter 6 reviews market research, which helps the company's leadership understand the context present in a new target market country. The elements presented in these three chapters combine to assist in an orderly analysis of potential target markets along with the characteristics of persons living in those regions.

A market analysis, the focus of this chapter, begins with answers to basic questions: What do people want? What do people need? Can they afford these items? What influences their cravings and choices? The study of the marketing potential in any country commences with an understanding of the cultural context, the type of economy that exists, and other general circumstances within that nation. These factors make it possible for the marketing team to identify the company's target markets and the characteristics of buyers in those market segments.

The forces that affect market segmentation processes, including a nation's culture, values within the culture, behaviors, and patterns of consumption, are examined first in this chapter. With cultural conditions and other elements of the international marketing context in mind (see Figure 4.1), the methods for identifying target markets or market segments are employed. The intricacies of international market segmentation programs are explored. Finally, the ethical issues that arise in those circumstances are identified.

Figure 4.1: The International Marketing Context

Markets and Segmentation

A **market** consists of people with wants and needs, money to spend, and the willingness to spend money on those wants and needs. International markets vary due to several factors. Marketers consider these factors when developing international segmentation strategies. This chapter focuses on cultural elements associated with markets and segmentation, language, political and legal systems, economic conditions, and infrastructure.

Market segmentation consists of identifying all potential customer groups that are viable for the purposes of marketing products. When identifying market segments, marketers first seek to understand the cultural factors that exist across marketplaces, as well as all of the other forces in the international marketing context.[2]

LEARNING OBJECTIVE #1:

How does a nation's or region's culture, including its origins, characteristics, and values, influence the international marketing context?

Culture

Culture represents the beliefs, customs, and attitudes of a distinct group of people. The term "culture" can be applied to a nation, a region, a city, or a single business. Values, norms, folkways and mores, roles, and behaviors that may be observed through interactions with members of a society express culture (Figure 4.2).

Religion plays an important role in many cultures.

Values	Strongly held concepts that are present in a cultural group
Norms	Social rules that affect behaviors and actions and reflect cultural values
Folkways and Mores	Cultural customs that dictate how people act socially
Roles and Schemas	The enacted "parts" and "scripts" that members of a society play and follow in everyday interactions

Figure 4.2: Elements of Culture

ORIGINS OF CULTURE

Understanding a culture starts with awareness of the factors that created and sustain it. Traditions and customs develop slowly and then become slow to change. Two factors that influence the origins of culture are the history and the geography of a nation or region.

VIDEO LINK 4.2:
Slang

History

Figure 4.3 identifies common characteristics that emerge as a culture develops over time. Language, dialects, and slang have roots that are centuries deep. Each evolves as the context of a nation changes. Consequently, a language such as French now incorporates new technological terminology even as shifts in popular culture influence the nature of slang. These alterations depend, in part, on the nation where the language is spoken. *Francophones*, or French-speaking individuals, may be found in Africa, the Caribbean, and Canada. The dialect and slang vary depending on location. To respond to these differences, Disney introduced a television channel targeted at Francophones in Canada. The programming is in French, and some of the programs spotlight authors from Quebec.[3]

Customs and rituals are closely tied to religions and social institutions and practices. In East Asia, a common custom is to celebrate the new year (which is not on January 1, and instead is based on a lunar calendar) with orange juice for good luck rather than enjoying champagne or other forms of alcohol. Holidays, especially those sanctioned or honored by the government, typically reflect the primary religion of the area. The month-long celebration of Ramadan, in nations where Islam represents the prevalent religion, serves as an example. Social institutions are intertwined with religions and customs. Many schools in Europe include time for prayer, reflecting the official state religions of the countries.

Language, Dialects, Slang
Customs and Rituals
Religions
Social Institutions and Practices
Common Attitudes and Beliefs
Aesthetics (concepts about beauty)
Views Toward Education (for both genders, by wealth, income, or social status)

Figure 4.3: Cultural Characteristics

Not all customs and rituals are religious or were originally religious events. The *La Tomatina* festival in Spain, a massive food fight with tomatoes among members of the local community, began in 1945 with differing origin stories. One group suggests it started as a fracas among friends that included throwing tomatoes and vegetables at their opponents. Others believe that the first tomato-throwing incidents were part of an anti-Franco rally. Eventually, the government sanctioned the event, which takes place in the *Plaza del Pueblo* in the small town of Buñol in eastern Spain. Despite its secular origins, the festival is now considered to have ties to religion as a festival to honor the town's patron saint, San Luis Bertrán, and the Virgin Mary from the Catholic Christian tradition.

Geography

Several factors related to the location and characteristics of a geographic region affect the development of culture. These include topography, population density, climate, and the access to other nations and cultures.

Topography, or the physical surface of a geographic area, influences life styles and the form a culture may take. Mountains and mountain ranges separate people, leading to differences in language, dialect, religious practices, and everyday matters such as finding, growing, and preparing food. The mountainous topography of Switzerland, and the isolation of parts of that country, has led to four official languages within the country over time: French, Italian, German, and Romansch. The unique Romansch language in Switzerland is spoken by less than 1% of the country, and is mainly found in one of the thirteen Swiss cantons, or states.[4]

Deserts and mountainous topographies are often connected to a sparse *population density*. Bodies of water often lead to dense populations of inhabitants near them.

Approximately half of the world's population lives within two hundred kilometers of a body of water, generally oceans, lakes, and rivers.[5] Population density affects patterns of daily interaction and the culture that emerges. High population density creates new target markets for companies, such as restaurants, department stores, big box stores, and specialty shops. Population density often influences fundamental decisions made by individual governments. China's population density has been linked to the government's economic focus on low-cost labor exports.[6]

Climate also has a profound impact on culture. Inhabitants in extremely cold climates such as the First Nations, Inuit, and Metis in Canada lead vastly different lives compared to people in other parts of the world. Hunting and fishing are part of daily life, as is dealing with bitterly cold temperatures. The traditional resident in these regions now has to cope with increased mercury levels in fish, government prohibitions against hunting polar bears, and the introduction of television.[7]

Those near the equator are likely to dress in fewer and skimpier clothes and daily activities are adjusted to cope with intense heat. Smaller differences in climate also create market segments. In countries where sunlight appears only a few hours per day at the height of winter, items such as tanning beds and snow blowers are popular. Countries in warmer climates normally feature a much stronger emphasis on outdoor recreation and may include naps or siestas during the hottest part of the day.

A common beach activity, surfing, was originally part of Polynesian culture and probably originated in either Tahiti or Hawai`i. The climate and geography of the islands—tropical and surrounded by water—facilitated the adoption of the sport.[8] Visitors to Hawai`i began to spread surfing to the continental United States during the 1930s, especially to California. The powerful waves in the Monterey Bay area, especially Santa Cruz, helped spread surfing to the Continental United States.[9]

Access to other nations and cultures affects the culture of a given region. The presence of trade routes creates greater interchanges between collectives of people, and more cross-cultural influences result. Buddhism, the dominant religion in East Asia,

Religious buildings reflect differing cultures.

has its roots in Indian culture. Its founder, Siddhartha Gautama Buddha, was an Indian prince, and the religion spread to East Asia along the ancient Silk Road.[10]

CREATING CULTURAL CONSUMPTION: CARNIVAL

The global celebration of the beginning of the Christian season of Lent, Carnival, represents how history and geography overlap to create culture and consumption. The celebration is Western European in origin and may even predate its Christian roots. The word has two potential origins. It may come from the Spanish words *carne levare* meaning "taking away the flesh," and marks the beginning of the sacrifices during Lent.[11] It may also date to the Greco-Roman festival of Isis, *Carrus Navalis*, which means ship cart or naval car. Early Christians transferred the festival to a celebration of Jesus' mother Mary.[12]

Carnival celebrations are common throughout Europe. The celebration in the Notting Hill area of London is one of the largest in the world. Each country celebrates in unique ways. In Belgium, the celebration dates to at least 1394. Individuals dress up as the Carnival character Gille; the costume includes matching blouses and pants all stuffed with hay, plus masks with glasses and red eyebrow and a mustache. The masked party goers then throw thousands of oranges to the crowd. In Belgium, as in many parts of Western Europe and North America, the celebration is called Mardi Gras, which literally means "fat Tuesday," for the rich, fatty foods usually consumed the day before Lent begins. [13]

Colonization spread the Christian faith and the celebration of Carnival throughout the world. The most famous of these celebrations is probably Carnival in Brazil. The celebrations in that country involve feasts of fatty foods before Lent fasting, parades or *bandas* (troop or group), and dancing. Local culture has influenced the celebration. Samba dancing schools compete as part of the festivities. Samba dances are native to Brazil but have also been influenced by African dancing introduced by slaves that were transported to Brazil. Carnival plays a key role in Brazil's economy, with approximately 70% of all yearly foreign visitors coming for the Mardi Gras celebrations.[14]

Carnival is also observed throughout the rest of Latin America. The capital and largest city in Uruguay, Montevideo, holds a festival for more than a month that involves more than parades: it includes *murga* and *candombe* street performances full of slapstick and sly political commentary.[15]

The Caribbean islands also celebrate Carnival. Trinidad's event rivals Brazil's and includes African culture and calypso and the soca dancing. Venezuela is as close as eight miles to Trinidad, and has been influenced by the Trinidad celebration.[16] The Colombian celebration includes a mix of European, African, and indigenous traditions. The celebration at Barranquilla, Colombia, has been added by the United Nations to its list of ninety activities proclaimed as "Masterpieces of Oral and Intangible Heritage of Humanity."

Colonization eventually spread Carnival to Asia. India, specifically the former Portuguese city of Goa, celebrates every year. The party includes traditional Christian elements but also increasingly reflects India's Hindu roots.[17]

The spread of Carnival and the further adaptation of the celebration to represent local historical components provide a clear example of how culture is formed. The *pastiche* of African slave culture, Western European Christian influences, and local preferences have created unique consumption rituals throughout Latin America. The Mardi Gras celebrations in North America and Europe increasingly represent the blending of Latin American cultures with what started as a Western European ritual.

Culture and Values

A marketing technique or approach that works well in one culture may not work as well in another. Differences in values account for some of this. **Values** are strongly held concepts that are pervasive within a culture. The five main features of values that constitute the common background for social science research about values are (1) concepts or beliefs (2) about desirable end states or behaviors (3) that transcend specific situations, (4) guide the selection or evaluation of persons, behavior, and events, and (5) are ordered by relative importance.[18]

Typical values include freedom, justice, social responsibility, loyalty to family or a spouse, and equality. Various views of the influence of values on those living in a culture and how that influence becomes manifest are available. For years, the most widely cited dimensions of culture were those proposed by Geert Hofstede, as displayed in Figure 4.4. (More detail can be found at www.geert-hofstede.com.)

Power Distance	Distance between leaders and followers; authoritarian versus collaborative relationships
Individualism-Collectivism	Value of personal status versus loyalty to the group Collectivism
Masculinity-Femininity	Male-dominated society versus society with more equal status between genders
Uncertainty Avoidance	Risk-taking versus risk-avoidance societies
Short- or Long-Term Orientation	Emphasis on immediate- versus distant; strategic outcomes

Figure 4.4: Hofstede's Value Dimensions of Culture

Hofstede's dimensions remain widely used in a number of contexts, including international marketing, although criticisms have emerged.[19] Hofstede's data were collected in the late 1960s and, while culture is normally slow to change, the data collected and used as a guide to create the categories predate the introduction of the personal computer, the Internet, the fall of communism, and many other significant global events. A recent approach, Project GLOBE, is an international effort to respond to these criticisms and to identify and measure cultural dimensions. Project GLOBE applies to many areas of marketing strategy, including international marketing issues.[20] Figure 4.5 identifies and defines these dimensions. As shown, elements of the Hofstede analysis continue in the Project GLOBE index.

These dimensions of culture affect everyday lives of citizens. The effects on institutions such as marriage, parenting, education, and governance, as well as daily activities including workplace relationships, are sweeping. For the purposes of international market segmentation, differences in expressions of the values provide a method for grouping consumers in terms of how these values lead to products that will be accepted in a culture and further affect the methods used to identify and reach target markets.

APPLYING CULTURAL VALUES TO MARKETING ACTIVITIES

Research applying the values introduced by Hofstede's work and then further refined by GLOBE research reveals important implications for marketing practice. Marketers

Power Distance	The degree to which members of a collective express comfort with power and differences in status
Uncertainty Avoidance	The extent to which there is an expectation that social norms, rules, and procedures will alleviate future event unpredictability
Humane Orientation	The degree to which individuals are rewarded for being fair, altruistic, generous, caring, and kind to others
Institutional Collectivism	The extent to which institutional practices encourage and reward the collective distribution of resources and collective action
In-Group Collectivism	The extent of pride, loyalty, and in-group cohesiveness individuals have for their organizations and families
Assertiveness	The preference for individual behaviors that are assertive, dominant, and demanding
Gender Egalitarianism	The degree to which a group works to limit gender inequality
Future Orientation	The extent to which future-oriented behaviors such as delaying gratification, planning, and investing in the future are encouraged
Performance Orientation	The degree to which a collective encourages and rewards group members for performance and excellence

Figure 4.5: Culture Constructs Developed in Project GLOBE

can first use cultural dimension scores to provide a broad conceptualization of the cultural values of countries in which a business intends to operate. Figure 4.6 provides examples of high and low scores on Hofstede's typologies. In many cases, countries in a region overlap. Latin American nations, for example, tend to score low on individualism.

Broad implications of these scores may be drawn. Research has linked cultural values to a variety of behaviors. More than six hundred articles have been published regarding Hofstede's values alone, and the findings are diverse. Overall, the research implies that Hofstede's values best predict emotional responses followed by attitudes, perceptions, and behaviors.[21] Evidence suggests that high levels of individualism and uncertainty avoidance lead to slower rates of mobile phone adoption.[22] Cultural values also influence relationships between market channel partners and influence which leadership style to use when managing disagreements.[23]

A large body of research links cultural values to advertising content. Culture influences effectiveness of banner advertising, website design, and television advertising.[24] Differences in perceptions of what is funny in a print advertisement abound.[25] Cultural values also influence the creation of brand meaning and positioning.[26] Cultural values therefore should be considered before beginning any marketing process. Detailed research will reveal how values influence target market responses to marketing activities.

VALUE LEVELS

Additional conceptualizations of values have emerged. The two typologies presented above, Hofstede's and Project GLOBE, concentrate on national-level values. While the

Cultural Dimension	Example Countries With a High Score on the Dimension	Example Countries With a Low Score on the Dimension
Power Distance	Malaysia (104), Guatemala (95)	Austria (11), Israel (13)
	Panama (95), Philippines (94)	Denmark (18), New Zealand (22)
	Mexico (81), Venezuela (81)	Ireland (28), Sweden (31)
Individualism	United States (91), Australia (90)	Guatemala (4), Ecuador (8)
	United Kingdom (89), Netherlands (80)	Panama (11), Venezuela (12)
	New Zealand (79), Italy (76)	Colombia (13), Pakistan (14)
Masculinity	Japan (95), Hungary (88)	Sweden (5), Norway (8)
	Austria (79), Venezuela (73)	Netherlands (14), Denmark (16)
	Italy (70), Switzerland (70)	Costa Rica (21), Finland (26)
Uncertainty Avoidance	Greece (112), Portugal (104)	Singapore (8), Jamaica (13)
	Guatemala (101), Uruguay (100)	Denmark (23), Sweden (29)
	Belgium (94), El Salvador (94)	Hong Kong (29), United Kingdom (35)
Long-Term Orientation	China (118), Hong Kong (96)	Sierra Leone (16), Nigeria (16)
	Taiwan (87), Japan (80)	Ghana (16), Philippines (19)
	South Korea (75), Brazil (65)	Norway (20), Zambia (25)

Figure 4.6: Country Examples of High / Low Scores on Hofstede's Cultural Values

Note: For each of Hofstede's dimensions, a country is given a score. In the table, example countries are listed for each dimension. These examples either score high or low on Hofstede's survey for that dimension.

Source: Adapted from Clearly Cultural, "Geert Hofstede's Cultural Dimensions," updated April 21, 2009, accessed at www.clearlycultural.com/geert-hofstede-cultural-dimensions/.

nation-state arguably represents the most important grouping variable, cultural values have the most impact at the individual level. A micro approach to values can lead to additional insights.

The work by the researcher Shalom Schwartz focusing on the individual level suggests that values may be found in three types of human requirements.[27] First, *biologically-based needs* drive individuals to seek out food, shelter, sex, and other basic survival or well-being requirements. Second, *social interactional requirements* assist in interpersonal coordination and interaction, or, in more common terms, romance, love, friendships, and social relationships in locations such as the workplace or places of worship. Third, *social institutional demands for group welfare and survival* lead individuals to collectively value security, prosperity, and peace. Many times, one value may transcend all three levels. Consequently, basic biological sexual needs are transformed into values related to intimacy and love, and eventually into valuing a peaceful society in which long-term relationships can thrive.

Social motives connect the three levels of values. These motives may be categorized into ten universal and distinctive individual-level values. Figure 4.7 identifies and defines each value.

1. Power	Focusing on attainment of social status, prestige, and dominance over people and resources
2. Achievement	Seeking personal success and proficiency
3. Hedonism	Seeking personal pleasure, particularly physical pleasure
4. Stimulation	Focusing on excitement, adventure, or challenges
5. Self-Direction	Valuing independence in thought and action
6. Universalism	Being concerned with understanding and protecting all people and natural resources
7. Benevolence	Focusing on improving or maintaining the welfare of people, but only those people one is directly in contact with
8. Tradition	Seeking respect and preservation of the core components of one's culture
9. Conformity	Focusing on maintaining order and stable social interactions through observation of social norms
10. Security	Valuing safety, harmony, and stability of society or relationships

Figure 4.7: Individual-Level Values

Source: Adapted from W. Bilsky and S. H. Schwartz, "Values and Personality," in *European Journal of Personality* 8 (1994): 163–181.

The values listed in Figure 4.7 may be categorized as those associated with *individualistic* or *collectivist* interests—that is, with personal versus group well-being. They also may be considered as part of reaching a goal (*instrumental*) or the eventual outcome (*terminal*).[28]

Hofstede's typology and the Project GLOBE cultural factors may be connected to individual level values. Some of the more notable ties are mentioned in Figure 4.8. Relationships between genders are influenced by a culture's masculinity/femininity dimension as well as by values associated with gender equality. Religious teachings as well as the position taken by the government may have influenced these views, reflecting social institutional demands for group welfare and survival. A prolonged war may change values related to gender, when males are away from home and engaged in conflict, because women may find they are asked to work in what had typically been male-dominated occupations. Similar connections between national and individual values can be made for the other items noted in Figure 4.8.

Relationships between genders
Relationships to authority and governance
Importance of the group versus the individual
Levels of equality in the allocation of resources
How aggressively members of a culture approach the environment, including nature
Feelings about fate or destiny

Figure 4.8: Links Between National and Individual Values

Culture and Behaviors

LEARNING OBJECTIVE #2:

Why should a marketing team examine cultural imperatives, cultural electives, and cultural exclusives when entering a host country?

Culture and cultural value affect patterns of daily living and social interactions. These may be observed from matters as simple as greeting friends, strangers, and potential business partners, to far more complex behaviors such as those displayed in family relationships. From a marketing perspective, the most important behaviors are those that affect business relationships. The behaviors can be classified as cultural imperatives, cultural electives, and cultural exclusives.

CULTURAL IMPERATIVES

Cultural imperatives are the business customs and expectations that must be met and conformed to or avoided if international business relationships are to be successful. For example, the significance of establishing friendships in business relationships often becomes a key element in successful international marketing, especially in countries that most strongly emphasize family and group relationships. Building bonds represents a cultural imperative in these countries.

Friendship, human relations, and trust are reflected by language, in the Latin American *compadre*, in China *guanxi*, and in Japan *ningen kankei*. Establishment of these forms of friendship takes place before business negotiations or sales presentations begin. Meetings, entertaining mutual friends, contacts, and spending time visiting develop trust. Friendship motivates local agents to make more sales and helps establish quality relationships with end users.

Also, a person's demeanor can be critical. A cultural imperative in one country may be an imperative to avoid in another. In Japan, making prolonged eye contact is considered offensive. In Arab and Latin American cultures the failure to make strong eye contact may lead to the perception of seeming evasive and untrustworthy. Also, while losing patience and raising one's voice is almost always poor etiquette, in some cultures such an outburst would end a business relationship. Correcting someone in public may have the same results. For instance, in Asian cultures, correcting someone in public causes the person to lose "face," which reflects a sense of personal integrity, an important part of an individual's social identity.

CULTURAL ELECTIVES

Cultural electives relate to areas of behavior or to customs that cultural aliens may wish to, but are not required to, conform to or participate in. The majority of culturally meaningful behaviors fit into this category. Greeting someone with a kiss, eating certain foods, holding hands or touching another person, engaging in gambling activities, and drinking alcoholic beverages are cultural electives that may be graciously declined or avoided.

At the same time, following a given custom might be helpful in building a positive relationship. The symbolic attempt to participate in a custom helps to establish rapport. For example, while a Japanese manager typically does not expect a Westerner to bow or to understand the bowing ritual, the attempt at a symbolic bow indicates interest and goodwill. Greeting an individual in a native language or knowing some small phrases suggests the desire to create a positive tone. In business meetings, Asian businesspeople tend to accept an offered business card with two hands and a slight bow as a sign of respect for the new business connection. The business card is presented with the words facing the person receiving the card, allowing the other person to read it easily during the exchange. Electives such as these can play important roles in international marketing interpersonal relationships.[29]

Culture electives include methods of greeting potential business partners.

CULTURAL EXCLUSIVES

Customs or behavior patterns reserved exclusively for the locals and from which the foreigner is barred are cultural exclusives. Marketers in a foreign country need to know when they are dealing with a cultural exclusive. These often include religious ceremonies in which members of any other religion would not be welcome or when limitations are placed on activities for women. One mosque at the Taj Mahal, the iconic mausoleum in Agra, India, has rules stating that only males are allowed to enter. For visitors to the Parliament building in London, UK citizens may visit year-round while foreign visitors may visit only on Saturdays or during the "summer opening."

Culture and Purchasing Behavior

Cultural influences dictate whether a given region or nation can become a viable target market. Any producer of goods or services first examines culture in order to determine whether those products match the needs and wants of consumers. Culture affects a variety of consumption patterns and purchasing behaviors, including those affected by aesthetics, religious practices, and dietary preferences. The subcultures or countercultures present in a geographic area may also represent an opportunity or an obstacle to expand into the market.

LEARNING OBJECTIVE #3:

How does culture affect purchasing behaviors?

AESTHETICS

Aesthetics, or concepts about what constitutes beauty, affect a vast number of purchases. Items including cosmetics, clothing, and jewelry, spokespersons and models for products, and views of nature are all influenced by cultural views of beauty. In the Caucasus region near Iran, eyebrows that connect across the bridge of the nose are signs of beauty in women. Views of body weight, muscles, and curves vary widely. Colors, fragrances, and art represent cultural preferences. As a result, target markets are selected, in part, based on concepts of beauty. Products, packages, promotions,

Aesthetics vary widely by culture.

websites, and other marketing efforts must also be adapted to fit with a culture.

Differences in aesthetics can lead to marketing opportunities, and these opportunities often center on perceptions of human beauty. Many Japanese consumers believe a thin woman is the physical ideal, which leads to an emphasis on dieting and an attractive market for dieting aids. In 2006, the Japanese dieting scene was buzzing with excitement about the *kanten* plan. *Kanten*, a gelatin made from seaweed, has no calories but does contain fiber, calcium, and iron. The product was promoted as capable of making one feel full, even though no calories were consumed.[30] In other areas of the world, beauty perceptions are quite different. Consumers in many African nations view a heavier person as being more attractive than a slimmer person. Due to the rampant poverty and malnutrition in many African countries, thin people are often viewed as being ill.

Product design can be based on perceptions of aesthetics. Japanese furniture, for example, tends to be relatively austere, with an appreciation for function and straight lines. Tables, chairs, and even beds tend to be short when compared to styles from other countries. In Western cultures, expensive product designs often feature opulence or indulgence.

RELIGION

When a nation or region has one dominant religion, adjusting marketing efforts will be less complicated. The dictates of that religion, including holy days, rituals, foods, gender roles, and other practices, may be examined by a local culturally-sensitive partner or employee to determine if a target market exists, and whether the company's product offerings can be tailored, modified, and positioned to match those markets.

When more than one religion is present, marketing decisions become more complex, especially when ideological differences cause conflicts between the religions. The marketing team decides which religion(s) will become the target market(s) and carefully tries to do so in a way that does not agitate or offend members of other religions.

The fast-food restaurant Chicken Cottage first opened in 1994 in London. The company offers *halal* food, catering to Muslim religious dietary requirements. The company also provides products that appeal to non-Muslim customers. The promotional focus accentuates food quality and innovative offerings. The *halal* component, while in the company logo, is not overly emphasized. This promotional approach allowed the company to grow to 140 restaurants by 2010.[31]

International Marketing in Daily Life

Dietary Preferences

Cultural dictates affect patterns of dining as well as dietary preferences. The primary meal of the day may take place in the mid- to late evening in one culture but at noon in another. Culinary preferences may be quite dramatic, especially in terms of what is deemed a delicacy. In Taiwan, one food, *chòu dòufu* or stinky tofu, has a powerful aroma that many foreigners find difficult to tolerate. Nordic countries serve fish without skinning, deboning, or even removing the eyes. It is not unusual for insects such as chocolate-covered ants to be considered delicacies in various countries. These dietary preferences affect both businesspeople visiting (and eating) in the locales, and businesses that create goods for consumption. In many countries, particularly in Africa, fresh food is preferred to preserved food. There, open-air markets that offer fresh food for sale serve the role that grocery stores play in other regions.

Dietary preferences may also be expressed as part of an individual's religion. McDonald's in India serves neither beef nor pork to meet the dietary restrictions of Hindus and Muslims, two of the dominant religions in the country. Instead, patrons can order a tasty Chicken *Maharaja* Mac.[32]

At the least, the marketing team should make certain that any salesperson or representative visiting another country is aware of dietary differences (see Figure 4.9). These preferences may also influence products to be created and the other elements of the marketing mix that will be used to vend them. Such preferences potentially affect what a salesperson will be served at mealtime when visiting prospective customers.

Kashrut	Jewish dietary law. Kosher foods are "fit" and the law excludes some meats, including pork. Rabbis supervise food production and verify kosher status.
Halal	Muslim law, including dietary restrictions. *Haraam, or* forbidden foods, include pork and alcohol.
Hindu Dietary Law	All Hindus avoid eating beef. Stricter Hindus avoid all meat, and some may avoid dairy products or eggs.
Lacto-ovo Vegetarians	Do not eat meat but do eat dairy foods and eggs. Some Buddhists are lacto-ovo vegetarian on holy days.
Ovo-Vegetarians	Do not eat meat or consume dairy products. Do consume eggs.
Lacto-Vegetarians	Only eat dairy products and vegetables.
Vegans	Do not eat anything derived from animals.

Figure 4.9: Various Dietary Restrictions Globally

SUBCULTURES AND COUNTERCULTURES

Subcultures are groups whose values and related behaviors are distinct and set members off from the general or dominant culture. Each subculture consists of a world within the larger world of the dominant culture, has a distinctive way of looking at life, but remains compatible with the dominant culture. The term *microculture* applies to smaller groups found within an overall subculture or culture.[33]

Ethnic groups often form subcultures featuring their own language, distinctive foods, religious practices, and other customs. Religious subgroups also form subcultures, such as in the differences that exist in the various forms of Judaism. All nations have subcultures, and increasingly these subcultures are found in immigrant groups that may become targets of marketing activities. For example, immigrants from the Ingria region of Estonia constitute a significant subculture in Finland.

Countercultures are groups whose values set their members in opposition to the dominant culture. Countercultures challenge the culture's core values. Some are associated with controversial behaviors or attitudes, such as those present in groups that glorify Satanism or the Nazism. Others simply choose differing lifestyles. Vegans, for example, exhibit dining patterns that most meat-eaters would consider to be benign even though they are part of a counterculture. The Amish avoid advanced technology as an expression of religious values.

> Countercultures are groups whose values set their members in opposition to the dominant culture.

CULTURAL CHANGE

Subcultures and countercultures are associated with the desire for cultural change. Groups that wish to protect animals or the environment, including the People for the Ethical Treatment of Animals (PETA) and Greenpeace, seek to affect laws as well as culture. Other groups may simply push for greater freedom of expression, such as the followers of goth fashion and music in various countries.

There are instances in which subcultures and countercultures represent potential target markets. As part of the assessment of the dominant culture within a geographic area, the marketing team examines the presence of these groups to see if opportunities exist. Companies that successfully market to the dominant culture in one country may be able to effectively market to that same culture as an immigrant subculture in another country. Kingfisher Beer, the largest brewery in India, sells one of every three beers in the country. In the United Kingdom, with its large and growing Indian immigrant population, Kingfisher has become one of the ten fastest-growing beer brands. The company markets the beer to both Indian immigrants and to local consumers.[34]

Two methods may be used by a marketing department to assess and adapt to cultural change. Seeking *cultural congruence*, which means products and marketing approaches are designed to meet the needs of the current culture, constitutes the first approach. Only when change occurs will these factors be adjusted or adapted. The second, and less likely method, involves promoting change within the culture. Such an approach may be viewed as including greater risk and features an increased chance of offending members of a society and the government.

When pizza was introduced in China, it was a food form that had never been seen before. Stories emerged of Chinese consumers attempting to eat the pizza with chopsticks. Realizing that there were gaps between the typical pizza the company served in the United States and the cultural expectations in China, Pizza Hut changed its menus so they were more congruent with the local tastes. This meant adding dishes other than pizza, serving wine at some locations, flavoring dishes with flower petals, using local fish in place of typical Western meats, and offering many other adaptations, including one pizza topped with duck meat.[35]

The Nature of Markets

As noted at the beginning of this chapter, a market consists of people with wants and needs, money to spend, and the willingness to spend money on those wants and needs. Products are typically sold to two major groups: consumers and other businesses. Both groups experience needs for products in the primary areas shown in Figure 4.10.

In addition, both consumers and businesses want or need various services. Services include the items summarized in Figure 4.11.

In any market circumstance, matching wants and needs to specific sets of groups, including consumers and businesses, is one of a company's primary objectives.

THE STP APPROACH

Identifying distinct groups of customers that may be interested in a given product or service remains a key marketing activity, in both domestic and international markets. The company can then create products and brands that provide those customers with a distinct choice in the marketplace. Methods to reach those consumers, based on their unique characteristics, are selected.

Consumer Markets	Business Markets
Convenience	Renewable
Shopping Nondurable Durable	Nonrenewable
Specialty	Finished Goods

Figure 4.10: Consumer and Business Market Needs

Services to Consumers	Services to Businesses
Personal	Legal
Financial	Financial
Sundry and Luxury	Rental Maintenance Specialty

Figure 4.11: Types of Services

One system used to assist in this process is the **STP approach**, or segmentation, targeting, and positioning. *Segmentation* consists of identifying all potential customer groups that are viable for the purposes of marketing products and services. Most companies are not able to create enough products, services, distribution channels, and marketing methods to reach every available market segment. Consequently, the *targeting* component of the STP approach involves selecting the market segments the firm intends to target or reach. *Positioning* is creating perceptions in the minds of consumers about the nature of a company, its brands, and its products and services. Positioning must match the characteristics of the selected target markets.

STP helps the marketing team meet the goal of optimizing sales and profits by reaching the proper audience, both in terms of products served and in the methods used to contact those individuals or companies.[36] This chapter focuses primarily on the strategic international segmentation processes from which a company can select target markets. The next chapter describes international positioning.

The British footwear company Dr. Martens uses the STP approach. The company segments consumers based on footwear needs, targeting those that are attracted to edgy fashion. Footwear positioning emerges from four pillars: creativity, music, fashion, and self-expression.[37]

International Market Segmentation

A company or brand's overall market consists of the cumulative total of all persons and organizations that have a need or want that can be satisfied by the product or service. To more effectively serve the needs of those in the market, various target groups are identified so that the product itself and/or the marketing message can be tailored to each group. A **market segment** is a set of businesses or a group of individual consumers with distinct characteristics.[38] For a market segment to be viable in the eyes of the marketing team, it must pass four tests:

LEARNING OBJECTIVE #4:

What are the primary factors used to identify international consumer and business-to-business market segments?

(1) Those within the segment should be homogenous or have similar characteristics.

(2) The segment must differ from other groups and the population as a whole.

(3) Sufficient demand must be present to make the segment financially feasible.

(4) Methods to reach the market must exist, both in terms of physical delivery of the item and in terms of the marketing messages that would entice customers to make purchases.

International marketers spend a great deal of effort identifying viable market segments.[39] The market segmentation process involves identifying specific groups based on needs, attitudes, and interests. Market segmentation processes apply to consumer groups and to the business-to-business arena, in domestic and international markets.

International Consumer Market Segments

When consumers, or end users, are the primary target market for a firm's offerings, the consumer market segmentation approaches listed in Figure 4.12 are the most common. These groups or categories may be combined in international marketing efforts.

Demographics
Gender
Age
Income
Education
Ethnicity
Psychographics
Geographic Area
Geodemographic Segmentation
Consumer Type
Benefit Segmentation
Usage Segmentation

Figure 4.12: Consumer Market Segments

DEMOGRAPHICS

Demographics are population characteristics. Market segmentation programs often employ demographic variables, especially gender, age, income, education, and ethnicity. International companies can create goods and services to meet the needs of these groups and market to them.

Gender

Previous marketing experience indicates that males and females purchase different products, buy similar products with different features (e.g., hair care items), desire products for dissimilar reasons, and purchase the same products after being influenced by different kinds of appeals through diverse media.

In the international arena, gender takes other dimensions. Males and females play divergent roles, dependent upon a local culture, including which person in the family is the primary shopper. In many cultures, females may play submissive roles within the family structure. These cultural norms, in turn, influence purchasing processes as well as the items sold.

Cultural concepts regarding attractiveness affect the types of products desired in a nation or region. In some cultures, women shave their legs and armpits, while in others they do not. Consequently, target markets for razors and shaving devices vary depending on the dominant culture.

Gender roles within a culture also affect the delivery of services. Purchases of life insurance and other forms of financial protection may vary when cultural norms dictate that all inheritances go to male family members. Child-care services are more widely utilized in cultures where greater numbers of females work outside the home. Personal services, including hair care, beautification, and maid services, will be influenced by the dominant culture of the country or region.

INTERNATIONAL INCIDENT //

As a male company executive traveling to Abu Dhabi, United Arab Emirates, you are interested in exporting a new line of snack foods to various retail stores. While visiting with the CEO of EMKE group, you notice that he stands extremely close to you in face-to-face conversations, to the point where you feel slightly uncomfortable. Then, as you prepare to walk to a restaurant for a light lunch, he takes your hand and walks along the road. How should you interpret his actions? Would your response and reaction be the same if the meeting were taking place in the United States or Mexico?

Age

Many marketing efforts target persons of a certain age, including children, young adults, middle-age adults, and senior citizens. Age is often combined with another demographic, such as gender, to identify market segments. Senior men and women and their younger counterparts purchase different items.

Age may dictate adjustments to marketing efforts in various ways, due to local circumstances. For example, many populations experience much shorter life expectancies, thereby changing the concepts of "old" or "senior citizen." Also, children in affluent, most-developed nations are more likely to have an expanded list of wants and needs as compared to those in less- or least-developed nations.

In many collectivist cultures grandparents play a large role in raising children.

In many collectivist cultures, grandparents play a substantial role in raising children. Consequently, messages targeting parents in one country may be directed at grandparents in others. Also, advanced age may be highly revered in some cultures and perceived as a disadvantage in others. The emphasis on maintaining a youthful appearance will be affected by these circumstances, which in turn affects the products that are sold and the methods used to promote them.

Age affects other purchasing patterns. In some countries younger shoppers are more inclined to purchase products from other nations, whereas older consumers resist foreign products. Younger consumers may be more inclined to spend rather than save earnings, especially in newly industrialized countries and other emerging markets.

Income

Individual or family income is an often-used demographic segmentation variable. Lower-income households primarily purchase necessities, such as food, clothing, and housing needs. In poorer countries, even necessities may be difficult to obtain for some families. As income increases, consumers are able to enjoy some sundry items including vacations, automobiles, more fashionable clothes, and meals at medium-priced or high-end restaurants. In less-developed countries, a trip to a Starbucks coffeehouse can be viewed as a medium-priced, high-status purchase, and Starbucks actively reinforces that image. At the extreme, producers of luxury items such as yachts and private planes target the wealthy.

The distribution of wealth within a nation or region largely dictates the use of income segmentation. In bottom-of-the-pyramid countries, the majority of consumers earn wages so small that even necessities must be adjusted in terms of price and package size. In communist countries large segments of consumers earn nearly equal amounts of money, often with a small wealthy upper class.

Economic conditions affect incomes. Recessions lead to families cutting back on discretionary spending. The marketing team examines economic circumstances prior to launching an effort in a new host country. During the recent economic downturn, research indicates that U.S. companies that increased spending on marketing relative to market size had a 4.3% return on capital whereas those companies that cut marketing spending lost 0.8%. Expenditures on marketing activities that focused on face-to-face contact and relationship building were especially effective.[40]

Education

Income and education are closely related. Educational attainments in populations vary widely. In less-developed countries, a substantial percentage of the population may be illiterate or have completed only the most basic level of education. Consequently, these individuals obtain limited job skills and are likely to receive the lowest wages. As the number of high school and college-educated persons rises, new target markets emerge for a vast variety of products. As a simple example, books may not be widely sought in least-developed economies, whereas popular press books, novels, and printed materials such as special-interest magazines would be desired in emerging economies as well as in most-developed nations.

When advertising returned to Cambodia after decades of war and unrest, outdoor advertising became the primary medium. Local advertisers used images rather than words, or copy, in outdoor promotions. With a high illiteracy rate and low levels of education, the images were more effective than words would have been in promoting various brands.[41]

Ethnicity

Ethnic groups may be present within a given country or nation. These groups often exhibit differing purchasing patterns and product preferences. Ethnicity may be used as a segmentation variable in both domestic and international settings. Products and marketing programs are tailored to individual groups within the area. As has been noted, one method for identifying a market segment would be to seek out a subculture based on ethnicity that is the minority in a country.

Approximately 2.6 million Turkish people lived in Germany as of 2008. With a spending power of €16 billion, this ethnic population has become an attractive target for marketing activity. To reach this group in Germany, some companies advertise in local Turkish-language newspapers and explicitly reference Turkish heritage and culture in promotions.[42]

PSYCHOGRAPHICS

Psychographic profiles emerge from a person's activities, interests, and opinions. Psychographics vary widely by culture because they are influenced by divergent factors such as religious training, customs, language, and even the popularity of local sports.

Psychographics are influenced by cultural differences.[43] They vary with regard to individualism or collectivism, gender equality, humane orientation, and future orientation. Cultures with individualistic tendencies offer opportunities to market personalized products and items that make a person stand out from the crowd. When gender equality is present, fashion and clothing may feature a unisex design. Humane orientation may affect the delivery of products and services that assist people who are disadvantaged and those with disease. Cultures with a short-term orientation may be much less likely to purchase a product featuring long-term usage. Short-term orientation may, in part, reflect life expectancy.

GEOGRAPHIC AREA

Marketing appeals can be made to people in a geographic area or region. Many times differences exist in purchasing patterns in rural versus urban areas, creating unique target markets. Geographic details influence product availability, such as when a region is landlocked.

Germany can be divided into several distinct regions, including Bavaria, the Black Forest, Germany's East, the North and Baltic Sea area, the Rhine Valley, and Ruhrpott. Each exhibits distinct subcultures shaped by cultural factors, economic circumstances, and historical events. The division between citizens of the former East Germany and West Germany continues. Economic circumstances vary, in part due to the levels of affluence attained by those who did not live under the communist regime. The southern and northern regions of Germany are influenced by the presence of a body of water in one but not the other. These differences may dictate the presence of a potential market segment or suggest that one does not exist, even though the regions are part of the same country.

Australia consists of several distinct markets. Wants and needs are different in the Outback area from those in the Highlands regions or the cosmopolitan areas of Sydney or Melbourne. Consumers in the major cities have needs that are similar to the needs of consumers in any major city worldwide. Consumers in the Outback and Highland regions have needs based heavily on climate, topography, and wildlife.

GEODEMOGRAPHIC SEGMENTATION

A hybrid form of geographic segmentation allows companies to enrich geographic approaches to segmentation by adding demographic and psychographic information. Geodemographic segmentation may also be useful when various regions feature differences. In addition to the regional distinctions in Germany, differences exist between Southern and Northern China and between Western and Eastern Europe. Several companies focus specifically on geographic and geodemographic research. ESRI, for example, provides executives with cutting-edge technologies for utilizing data from around the world. Sources such as ESRI help managers to combine geographic and demographic data into useful information for decision-making.[44]

BENEFIT SEGMENTATION

Benefit segmentation focuses on the advantages consumers receive from a product rather than the characteristics of consumers themselves. Demographic and psychographic information can be combined with benefit information to identify segments. A given product may actually feature one benefit in a given country and a separate benefit in another. For example, batteries may offer the benefit of convenience in some settings but generate much greater benefits in regions where power supplies are routinely interrupted. In the Electrolux case at the end of this chapter, various uses and benefits of refrigerators are described. Items are affected by religious and cultural circumstances, economic conditions, and personal income variables.

CONSUMER TYPES

National boundaries have long served as convenient ways to view market segments. More recently, companies increasingly target segments across boundaries. Another method used to identify market segments involves finding concentrations of global, glocal, or local consumers. These individuals have been influenced by cultural circumstances, history, the local political system, and economic conditions.

Global Consumers

Many consumers in different nations earn similar incomes and hold the same social status levels. These individuals often exhibit similar purchasing patterns, suggesting the presence of an international market segment consisting of global consumers. Global consumers typically live in developed countries; however, this segment also includes wealthy consumers in developing and even less-developed countries, especially when those consumers have access to international media and the Internet.

Global consumers are less likely to focus on price and instead buy products that meet global quality standards. They are normally located in urban settings and exhibit high levels of cosmopolitanism. These high-cosmopolitanism consumers view themselves as members of a larger global community rather than as merely maintaining an allegiance to a local culture and community. Global consumers wear similar clothes, use technology in similar ways, and consume similar entertainment. They check the time for the newest American blockbuster movie at the local theater on their iPhones while sipping Cokes and wearing designer jeans.[45]

> High-cosmopolitanism consumers view themselves as members of a larger global community rather than as merely maintaining an allegiance to a local culture and community.

Glocal Consumers

The word "glocal" combines the words "global" and "local." It reflects dual consumption patterns. Glocal consumers buy global products, but the purchase represents a special occasion rather than a typical purchase. They are more likely to purchase products that mimic global products but are priced slightly lower. They may be of a lower socioeconomic status, but their purchasing preferences also reflect strong ties to the local community and local consumption. Glocal consumers might be rural migrants who are relatively new to an urban setting and to the new purchasing opportunities present in that environment.

Glocal consumers are likely to shop at the neighborhood corner market, drink traditional beverages, and enjoy local cultural entertainment. They occasionally go to KFC for a meal or watch an American film. Glocals are more likely to purchase local versions of foreign goods and services, such as staying at a local hotel that mimics a Western chain. International marketers can devise advertisements with glocal themes that appeal to these markets.[46]

Local Consumers

Local consumers rarely consume foreign products. For either economic or taste reasons, these consumers maintain traditional consumption patterns. Many local consumers live in rural settings where they only infrequently have the opportunity to purchase foreign goods. These consumers often exhibit high levels of **ethnocentrism**, or the strongly held belief that one's culture is superior to others. Ethnocentrism is, in many ways, the opposite of cosmopolitanism. Ethnocentric consumers generally exhibit a tendency to avoid purchasing foreign-produced products.[47]

The country of Uganda has one of the highest rates of alcohol consumption in the world. For many locals, the drink of preference is not foreign but local drafts made from some combination of distilled sorghum, millet, maize, sugar, bananas, and pineapples. Even the local word for any sort of alcoholic drink, *waragi*, is a corruption of the colonialist British "war gin" into a more inclusive, Ugandan word. The preference for local spirits then reflects a typical local consumer consumption pattern.[48]

Usage Segmentation

Consumer segmentation can be based on how frequently groups use or purchase the product or service, including the company's best customers, average users, and casual or light users. The objective becomes to provide the highest level of service to the best customers while promoting the company to the other two groups, in the attempt to maximize sales to all groups. In the hospitality industry, hotels in some countries offer frequency programs for vacationers and those who travel more often. For other consumers, taking a trip and staying in a hotel may be a once-in-a-lifetime experience.

Usage segmentation may be found in the hospitality industry.

International Business-to-Business Market Segmentation

The primary goals of business segmentation efforts are to provide better customer service and to group similar organizations into clusters to enhance marketing efforts. Figure 4.13 identifies the various methods used to segment business-to-business markets.

| Industry |
| Size |
| Geographic Location |
| Product Usage |
| Customer Value |

Figure 4.13: Methods of Segmenting Business-to-Business Markets

SEGMENTATION BY INDUSTRY

Many industries extend past national boundaries. Identifying segments by industry, such as health, automotive, financial, or clothing, which represents a common approach to international marketing. Segments can be broken down into smaller subcomponents. An organization selling small appliances such as radios, cell phones, or hair dryers would account for differences in electricity available, such as alternating versus direct current when specifying market segments for items. Major financial and insurance providers, including the Italian provider Generali Group (www.generali.com), offer many financial products and services that vary by industry need.

SEGMENTATION BY SIZE

Market segments can be identified based on the size of a company's sales volume or its number of employees. Large firms with 100,000 employees do not have the same needs as smaller companies with 100 or fewer employees. Typically, selling to a large firm will focus on the company's purchasing department. For smaller firms, the owner or general manager often makes purchase decisions and becomes the target of marketing messages. The marketing team assesses the number of smaller and larger purchasers in a nation or region before developing a program to reach these buyers.

Economic circumstances often dictate the number and types of business organizations of each size (small, medium, large) in a country. Cultural or institutional traditions may exert an influence. Banks in Spain follow a unique organizational structure, called *cajas*, with roots going back to the Middle Ages. Banks are traditionally linked to cities or regions, and some may be controlled by the Catholic Church.[49] Poverty often leads to many small, barely sustainable family businesses. Political-legal conditions favor corporations and multinational firms in countries that lean toward free enterprise, as opposed to communist or state-directed economies.

For years, FedEx did not segment business-to-business customers. In the mid-1990s, realizing that a lack of segmentation was hindering its growth, the company began segmenting based on account size. By 2005, the company had transitioned to one of the most complex segmentation processes in the industry. Mark Colombo, vice president of strategic marketing and corporate strategy, noted, "We look at sizes of segments; opportunities with customers; whether a customer is new; whether we're penetrating, growing, or retaining a relationship; what industry they're in; what distribution model they sell products through; and their geographic locations."[50]

GEOGRAPHIC LOCATION

As with consumer segmentation, identifying business market segments by geographic location can be a successful tactic. This includes larger distinctions such as the Pacific Rim as well as more specific differences, including those countries that use the *euro* as a form of currency as opposed to those that do not. Within a given nation, regional geographic distinctions may also be drawn in order to find target markets, such as the Basque region that spans the border between France and Spain. United States–based global giant General Electric offers numerous business products and services to customers throughout the world and has focused recently on offering infrastructure services to customers in northern and southeastern Asia, segmenting markets based on the needs of these regions.[51]

PRODUCT USAGE

Business markets are segmented based on the manner in which goods and services are used. Some services, including those in the financial and hospitality industries, offer more than one use to customers. In the automobile rental industry, various nations have differing laws regarding the rental process. Cars may be used for business trips, vacations, or entertaining clients. Car fleets are also rented to various organizations. These product usage factors may be used to distinguish various target markets. Thermocouple Instruments, part of the British Rototherm Group, offers a wide selection of business-to-business products pertaining to temperature assemblies, thermostats, and flow instrumentation (www.thermocouple.co.uk). The marketing mix is based on the types of product usage present in various target segments.

CUSTOMER VALUE

Marketers locating business-to-business segments often assign values to customers. Normally, in-depth data about each business customer will be available. A value can be assigned to each individual business through sales records and other sources of data and information, placing them into low-, medium-, and high-value groups.[52] Customer value ratings may also be assigned within or to regions, such as South America or the Eurozone.

The telecommunications industry often uses customer value segmentation, for both consumers and business markets. With the high amount of brand switching (also known as *churn*) to new carriers in the industry, the value segmentation can be linked to the percentage of consumers who are likely to switch as a guide to company marketing activities. For the high-value, high-churn segment, the focus should be on aggressive incentives to retain the business. For high-value, low-churn businesses or the low-value, high-churn business no action is required.[53]

Firms that sell virtually the same goods or services to both consumers and businesses, such as laptop computers, engage in dual channel marketing.

VIDEO LINK 4.3:
Global Currencies

DUAL CHANNEL MARKETING

Firms that sell virtually the same goods or services to both consumers and businesses engage in **dual channel marketing**. The approach fits several situations. One common scenario occurs when a product sold in business markets is then adapted to consumer markets. Products including digital cameras, calculators, computers, fax machines, and cell phones were first sold to businesses and then later to consumers. Also, when individuals who buy a particular brand at work have positive experiences and, as a result, purchase the same brand for personal use, **spin-off sales** occur.

One marketing decision involves how to represent the product in each channel. Similarities between the two markets can be featured unless there are significant differences. When consumers and business buyers value different product attributes or desire different benefits, the marketing team customizes messages for the separate markets. In most cases, business customers and consumers seek the same basic benefits from products.

Dual channel marketing often results from economic development. Emerging economies, newly industrialized countries, and nations with more developed economic systems feature more businesses combined with a larger number of individuals with disposable income. An Italian sales representative who travels throughout the Eurozone may discover she enjoys lodging at the Holiday Inn. When it is time for her family to take a vacation, she might seek out that chain when making travel arrangements. The same scenario will be less likely to take place in least-developed nations. Consequently, the economic status of a country affects potential dual channel markets.

Dual channel marketing can create a major competitive advantage because products are sold in both markets, in terms of both domestic operations and international marketing. Adding customers can lead to economies of scale in production expenses and synergies in messages delivered to consumers and other businesses.[54]

Regional and National Segmentation

LEARNING OBJECTIVE #5:

How can the marketing team use regional and national segmentation methods to improve a company's global marketing program?

Based on the methods for identifying marketing segments that have been selected, international market segmentation programs can be developed. Some are created for large regions, such as the three members of NAFTA or the members of the Eurozone. Others target individual nations and regions within individual countries. In addition, language and regional differences may be used to separate distinct target markets. Further adjustments are made to account for regional differences. An analysis of the definition of the term "market segment" illuminates some of these nuances.

WANTS AND NEEDS

Individual consumers experience wants and needs in vastly different ways depending on specific circumstances. In earthquake-stricken Haiti, wants and needs were reduced to the most basic of human survival issues: water, food, clothing, and shelter. Medical care became nearly a luxury that only a select few could find or afford. Many underdeveloped countries have populations where the vast majority live at this subsistence level. A want in one country may not translate to another. While in many countries, ultrasound meets the desire parents have to know the gender of the baby, this is not always the case. Many health clinics in poorer sections of India refuse to identify the gender of a baby during an ultrasound. The concern is that men may divorce a woman if the child is a girl.[55]

MONEY TO SPEND

Per capita income, or the total income in a country divided by its total population, as displayed in Table 4.1, varies widely by nation. Members of a potential market segment may experience wants and needs in sufficient numbers, yet the ability to pay limits the viability of the market. Per capita income, when combined with the degree of income distribution as dictated by the economic system, dramatically affects the presence or absence of potential target markets. The Gini coefficient index measures income inequality within a country. The higher the Gini coefficient, the higher the income inequality. A coefficient of 1.0 would represent a single individual holding all of the wealth; a 0.0 would represent perfect income equality or distribution.

NATION	PER CAPITA INCOME	LIFE EXPECTANCY FROM BIRTH	GINI COEFFICIENT INDEX
Brazil	$7,350	73	56.7
Denmark	$59,130	78	29.0
Greece	$28,750	80	33.0
Haiti	$660	61	59.2
Libya	$11,590	74	36.0
Russian Federation	$9,620	68	42.3
Thailand	$2,840	69	43.0
United States	$47,580	78	45.0
Zimbabwe	$362	45	50.1

Table 4.1: **Selected Per Capita Incomes in Various Countries**

Source: "Key Development Data and Statistics," The World Bank, accessed at www.worldbank.org.

VIDEO LINK 4.4:
Poverty and Inequality

WILLINGNESS TO SPEND

The figures in Table 4.1 indicate a wide disparity among select nations which in turn affects wants and needs, money to spend, and the willingness to spend money. Consumers in Denmark and the United States are more likely to desire many more items beyond necessities. Sundries and luxuries may be made available to a number of patrons. In Greece and similar nations with less-dramatic differences in wealth, sundries would be desired by many, with a limited number wishing to obtain luxuries. Haiti and Zimbabwe exhibit a far different type of economy, one in which the vast majority of citizens generate incomes at the bottom-of-the-pyramid.

LANGUAGE

Citizens in many parts of the world speak a relatively common language, such as Spanish. The individuals and countries may constitute a large market segment. In other circumstances, an individual country may feature numerous languages. Switzerland lists four official languages: German, French, Italian, and Romansch. India recognizes one official language, Hindi, but the number of other languages spoken across the nation may number in the low thousands. The continent of Africa has complex overlaps between languages and countries. Many of the world's complicated languages are found there, including Xhosa, the "click" language of the San, or "bushmen," of the Kalahari Desert.[56] The country of South Africa alone has eleven official languages: IsiZulu, IsiXhosa, Afrikaans, Sepedi, English, Setswana, Sesotho, Xitsonga, isiNdebele, Tshivenda, and siSwati.[57]

Successful marketing to African consumers requires navigating these complicated languages. The goal of the segmentation analysis would be to make sure that the products and messages match with a viable group of people speaking a common language.

GLOBE Societal Clusters	Ronen and Shenkar Clusters
Nordic Europe (three countries)	Near Eastern
Eastern Europe (eight countries)	Nordic
Sub-Saharan Africa (five countries)	Germanic
Southern Asia (six countries)	Anglo
Latin Europe (six countries)	Latin European
Germanic Europe (six countries)	Latin American
Latin America (ten countries)	Far Eastern
Middle East (five countries)	Arab
Confucian Asia (six countries)	Independent

Figure 4.14: Cultural Clusters

REGIONALLY BASED MARKET SEGMENTS

The segmentation variables discussed above can be used to group countries into regions. Countries in several regions of the world have similar cultures, consumption patterns, and languages, which leads to regional groupings. Often these groupings are based on culture. Two versions of the clusters that have been suggested as groupings are displayed in Figure 4.14.[58]

These groupings allow for regional segmentation based on similarities across markets. Companies can introduce products across the regions, knowing that consumption patterns and business processes will be fairly consistent within the region. Success in one country within the region will lead to skills that will transfer well within that cluster. Expanding within the cluster will typically be less costly than expanding to countries in another cluster.

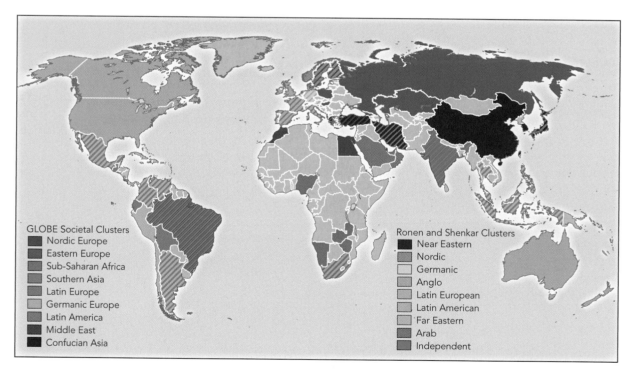

Map 4.1: **Cultural Clusters**
The GLOBE academic study and the research by Ronen and Shenkar (1985) revealed the following cultural clusters.

Segmentation and the Bottom-of-the-Pyramid

The final global segment consists of the 4 billion people worldwide that live on $2 per day or less, the bottom-of-the-pyramid consumers (see Figure 4.15).[59] These individuals experience wants and needs but have only limited money to spend. Still, opportunities

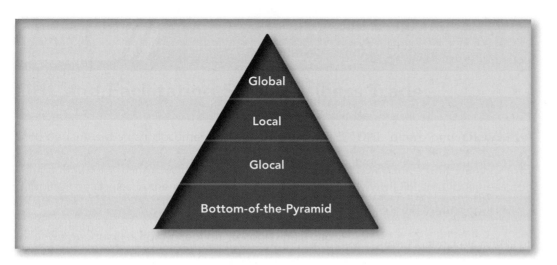

Figure 4.15: International Income Segments

are present. Even with a small profit margin, the large size and equivalent large potential volume makes this segment increasingly attractive. Even a $0.01 margin can result in millions of dollars in profit. To segment this group effectively, the marketing mix must be adjusted, including changes in products, prices, and delivery systems, and, in some cases, brands. The goal of these changes is to create the capacity to consume by lowering the barriers to purchase.

PRODUCTS

One approach to marketing to those at the bottom-of-the-pyramid involves changing the product, either in terms of the design of the item to meet a slightly different need or by simply lowering the quantity offered per purchase. In India, for example, local companies have produced more eco-friendly, single-usage packages or sachets of laundry detergents; foreign multinational corporations now also produce these items.[60] This packaging lowers the price, allowing consumers with limited incomes to purchase the product.

PRICING

Pricing may also be adjusted to match the market segment. While it is important to lower the price to allow for expression of demand, there is evidence that persons at the bottom-of-the-pyramid are also brand conscious. Therefore, pricing based on price-quality relationships remains viable.

Exchange systems, or the methods of facilitating payment, may vary within the economies of bottom-of-the-pyramid countries. For example, more extensive use of *barter* may be present, whereby an individual trades one good or service for another. Use of money *or* currency will take place by customers who are able to accumulate sufficient amounts to make payments. Also, debit cards rather than actual currency are the norm in many countries. The use of credit may be more dependent on individual relationships than on any company offering such a service (credit cards) to facilitate purchases. Providing credit for purchases that seem relatively small, the equivalent of $10 to $15, can help create the capacity to consume.

Companies targeting the bottom-of-the-pyramid market often focus on cutting costs to create price reductions. Cost cutting can be the result of changes in product

> Exchange systems, or the methods of facilitating payment, may vary within the economies of bottom-of-the-pyramid countries.

design. Hindustan Unilever Ltd.'s marketing team set the goal of cutting the price of ice cream in India in order to reach low-income consumers. Realizing that refrigeration constitutes 40% of the cost, the company introduced a salt-based heat shield that was less expensive to produce, provided more insulation, and contained fewer pollutants, which reduced costs and the price.[61]

DELIVERY

Reaching target markets involves finding delivery systems that match a local region. This includes identifying traffic systems, the presence of electricity on a routine basis, and even more basic elements such as running water. Product modifications match delivery systems when effectively reaching target markets of low-income members of a country. Bottom-of-the-pyramid segments often face problems with electricity access, which necessitates innovations in refrigeration, batteries, and more-efficient energy consumption.

PROMOTION

Promoting products to market segments at the bottom-of-the-pyramid creates distinct challenges. These consumers are less likely to be exposed to mass media and may not be reachable in most ways. Literacy and overall levels of education may be limiting factors. Word-of-mouth endorsements and other less-traditional promotional tactics become valuable tools to contact and persuade these customers to make purchases. At the same time, for many brands, bottom-of-the-pyramid consumers already exhibit

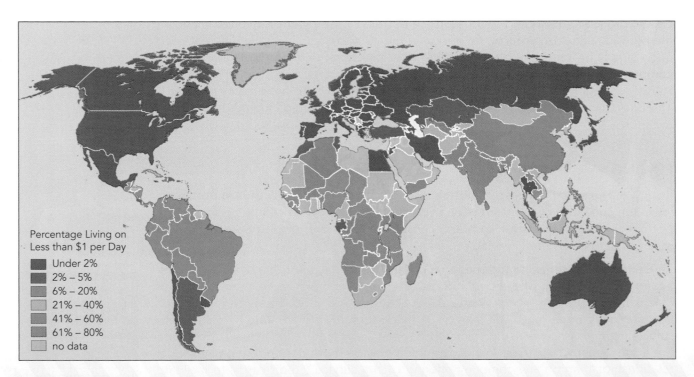

Map 4.2: **The Percentage of Country Population Living on Less than $1 per Day**
Even with a small profit margin, the large size and equivalent large potential volume of consumers making less than $1 per day makes the bottom-of-the-pyramid segment increasingly attractive.

brand awareness and demand for the product, making promotion more focused on messages that remind or inform potential customers about a new, lower price.

Green Marketing and Sustainability-Oriented Segments

In the past two decades, an increasing number of more environmentally friendly products have been developed in the international arena. When conducting a market segmentation program for these items, the distinction may be drawn between consumer preferences for green products when as a matter of choice versus when it becomes a matter of necessity.

LEARNING OBJECTIVE #6:

What is green marketing, and how is it related to concepts of sustainability?

CONSUMER PREFERENCES

One of the primary challenges facing green marketers has been the inability to entice consumers to spend more for environmentally safe products. In essence, the majority of customers only purchase green products when the item maintains the same level of price, quality, convenience, and performance.[62]

GREEN BY NECESSITY

In many bottom-of-the-pyramid nations, sustainability has become a driving force in purchases. Any item that saves or reuses water, runs on solar power or renewable batteries, or helps in some other way to preserve natural resources has a better chance to be accepted and purchased. Part of the reason for this advantage is that such products also save the consumer money. A growing amount of evidence suggests that sustainable products create one of the largest marketing opportunities in nations where the majority of citizens live below the poverty line.

SC Johnson has focused on developing sustainable agricultural processes for the production of a key ingredient, pyrethrum, to the company's botanical pesticides. The company sources much of this ingredient, which is made from chrysanthemums, from East Africa. Working with farmers in the region, the company established sustainable practices that are ensuring its own profit and long-term viability of the crop for East African farmers.[63]

In sum, numerous forces influence segmentation processes by affecting what consumers want or need, how much money they have to spend, and subsequently the willingness to spend that money. These factors can be used to develop regional and national segmentation strategies.

A Market Segment Analysis

Three terms may be used to help understand the potential of a target market. *Market potential* represents the total number of individuals or businesses that could purchase a product in a given area. *Market demand* consists of the total sales of all brands sold in an area or within a product industry. *Company or brand demand* is the estimated demand for a company's brand. Company demand may also be called *estimated market share*.

The following statistics would emerge from an analysis of the potential sales of solar-powered personal computers in South Africa:

> *Market potential* = 27 million households that might purchase solar personal computers
>
> *Market demand* = 3 million households that have purchased solar personal computers
>
> Sales of Sony solar computers = 750,000 units
>
> $$Company\ demand = \frac{Sales\ of\ Sony\ computers}{Market\ demand}$$
>
> $$= \frac{750\ thousand}{3\ million}$$
>
> $$= 25\%$$

These calculations indicate that Sony's market share, or its company or brand demand, is one fourth of all computers sold in South Africa. One additional factor may be of interest: the product's *penetration rate.*

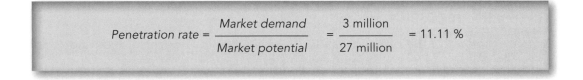

$$Penetration\ rate = \frac{Market\ demand}{Market\ potential} = \frac{3\ million}{27\ million} = 11.11\ \%$$

Calculating these statistics may assist the marketing team in making decisions about entering nearby nations or expanding operations within South Africa.

ASSESSING MARKET POTENTIAL

When examining the potential of a region for expansion, five market potential factors should be assessed:

1. Availability of financial resources
2. Availability of potential substitutes
3. Ability to offer attractive benefits
4. Current product availability
5. Consumer awareness of the product

When the marketing team examines the market penetration of South Africa, the firm would either expect to provide the necessary financial resources or would believe access exists to obtain those resources in nearby nations. Based on the Sony market share within South Africa, the company's leaders would assess whether a 25% share would be sufficient to expand into a new country, or if too many potential substitutes are available. Then, Sony's marketers, working with production and other parts of the company, would seek to understand whether Sony's products could be differentiated in some way to offer attractive benefits. The competition would be assessed to identify all competitors that could affect current product availability. Finally, consumer awareness in the nation would be examined to determine whether those in the nation are *aware* of the value of a solar-powered personal computer, which would continue to work during power outages and in remote regions where electricity is not available.

The target market or market segment for a solar-powered personal computer would be assessed, notably by examining age, income, and educational level of potential consumers, and possibly by examining geographic factors. If the marketing team determines that sufficient potential exists, then expansion may be justified.

ASSESSMENT CRITERIA

A second method that may be used to study the potential benefits of entering a new market is to examine the segment across four criteria, as follows:

Measurability: Can the segment be quantified and identified?

Accessibility: Can the segment be reached?

Profitability: Is the segment large enough to generate profits?

Actionability: Can a marketing program be designed to stimulate interest and behavioral responses (purchases)?

No matter which method is used to evaluate the potential of a new market segment, the marketing team should consider the context. It may be that, in the short term, a market may not seem viable. The strategic question to be posed in those circumstances is whether entering might elicit benefits in the long range. For example, entering the market may preempt the competition from doing so, thereby gaining a first-mover advantage in a growing or emerging economy. In essence, the final decision to enter a new target market combines an understanding of current circumstances with other judgments.

When an international company is able to capitalize on these opportunities and match them with innovative products, international marketing success often results. Montreal's *L'Oréal* preempted international competitors by introducing the world's first two-step hair coloring product, *L'Oréal Paris' Couleur Experte*, by becoming the lead innovator and first-mover in the industry. The development of the patent for the product, along with superb international marketing, led to quick consumer acceptance and marketplace success.[64]

Ethical Issues in International Segmentation

Many of the ethical issues associated with domestic markets also appear in discussions of international segmentation. For example, one common complaint is that any segmentation program featuring demographics creates the potential to reinforce stereotypes. This tendency might emerge when ethnicity becomes the basis for a market segment, especially when marketing messages play to stereotypical images, both in the dominant culture and in any subculture or counterculture.

A closely related issue occurs in the area of gender discrimination. Females are confined to submissive and subservient roles in many cultures. When a company from a different country, one with opposing views, markets to women, the question arises as to which cultural customs should be observed. For instance, packages and labels for feminine hygiene products may be strongly regulated based on cultural norms; a company may at the same time wish to be able to portray the benefits of the products, however, especially when those benefits include health advantages. The package might also assist less-educated women in identifying exactly what they are buying through the use of a drawing or photo, but the problem remains that any such figure or image might be culturally objectionable to some.

Targeting lower-income segments may be viewed by some critics as being the process of creating overconsumption by people who least can afford to do so. This includes encouraging purchases of less-healthy food products such as fast food, clothes designed to create status rather than to offer functionality, and modes of transportation that are less practical but at the same time are associated with a higher social standing.

Conversely, market segmentation programs may limit access to certain goods or services, especially when the process takes places at the nation level. When only the rich are entitled to educational services or access to free Internet service, there may be ethical problems associated with a form of discrimination based solely on income or entitlement.

Chapter 4: Review and Resources

STRATEGIC IMPLICATIONS //

An international marketing program includes all of the elements of a domestic program. Marketing professionals identify target groups that match with tactics to reach the most viable audiences for products and services. Doing so requires an investigation of the regional or national context, in terms of culture, economic conditions, and local customer characteristics and preferences. Completing these processes allows for a program targeted at those who are most likely to welcome a new product or service to a given area.

Effective market segmentation programs, whether domestic, international, or both, require an alignment of all of the elements of the marketing mix. Products, prices, distribution systems, and promotional efforts are matched with target markets and are positioned accordingly. At the global level, distinct strategic decisions are made with regard to either a standardization or adaptation approach. Ford features an international global brand, and Proctor & Gamble adapts products to individual nations and cultures.

The strategic direction of the company dictates either a differentiation or a low-cost approach to product development, pricing, and promotional programs. Companies may seek to serve a more general population through differentiation, presenting items as being different and better than competitor products. Others may choose to compete based on low cost to serve the needs of consumers that are price conscious and those that are constrained by their incomes. The local culture has a strong impact on this choice. Where consumers are most resistant to international companies, a differentiation approach may be less viable.

TACTICAL IMPLICATIONS //

Numerous tactical efforts are undertaken to support the strategic position dictated by strategies. For example, the product's packaging and label will be altered to fit the legal and cultural dictates of a nation and a given target market. Legal requirements vary as to any promise of a product benefit as well as labeling of content. Promotional programs would be adjusted as well. This may lead to segmentation approaches based on usage or benefits.

Cultural preferences influence other tactical choices. Beyond the actual products, pricing methods and discounting programs may vary substantially. Some cultures take a dim view of the use of coupons. What may be considered a "sale" price might be determined by local laws and customs. Many cultures inject bargaining into purchase processes. The marketing team accounts for these nuances as well as exchange and payment systems. Further, some cultures and nations strongly discourage comparative advertising. Distribution systems are adjusted to local conditions and the infrastructure present in international markets. Many countries do not have big box super stores. Local small companies dominate instead, which affects order sizes and methods of transportation to be used.

Additional tactics include the selection of sales methods. This would include attending trade shows. When presenting a product to a potential new target market, company employees should first understand that in some international trade shows that executives attend, sales are made on the spot. In others, only information will be collected by lower-level operatives.

In situations where the target market consists of members at the bottom-of-the-pyramid, tactics with regard to packaging may lead to a smaller size and a lower price. As has been noted, many consumers in this market do respond to strong brands, which may at the strategic level indicate that a price-quality relationship focus is viable. The tactics that might succeed would potentially include pricing discounts or offers.

OPERATIONAL IMPLICATIONS //

Day-to-day operations will be influenced by cultural imperatives, electives, and exclusives. Sales force activities, including calling on prospective clients, will be influenced by the dictates of the culture that is present. This includes greeting prospective clients, engaging in social activities, making the actual sales presentation, dining, and even exchanging business cards. Careful preparation should be made before making contact with potential buyers in a new target market. This includes awareness of differences in language and slang.

Other operational activities associated with target markets include promotions. Consequently, any advertisement, coupon, website posting, sponsorship, public relations event, or alternative marketing tactic such as product placement in a television program or movie should be carefully inspected by a cultural assimilator to make certain the promotion meets the standards of the local culture.

Company activities are also adjusted to meet the norms of a local culture, including understanding of when to close for holidays and adapting to religious preferences and cultural nuances such as whether and when to make eye contact, and the physical distance to maintain between a buyer and seller during the purchasing process.

In summary, market segmentation and target market selection activities in international settings may be viewed as being "distinctively similar" to those in domestic markets. The processes used to identify target markets will be largely the same; differences emerge when segments are assessed to understand how to adapt the marketing mix to meet the needs and wants of a group with money to spend and the willingness to spend that money on a product being sent to a new country or region.

TERMS

market	subcultures	ethnocentrism
market segmentation	countercultures	dual channel marketing
culture	STP approach	spin-off sales
values	market segment	exchange systems
aesthetics	cosmopolitanism	

REVIEW QUESTIONS

1. Define the term *culture*.
2. What two factors often affect the origins and development of culture in a given area?
3. Define the term *values*.
4. How are Geert Hofstede's value dimensions of culture different from the culture constructs identified by Project GLOBE?
5. What three levels of values exist in a society?
6. Define the terms *cultural imperative, cultural elective,* and *cultural exclusive.*
7. In what ways does culture affect purchasing behavior?
8. Describe subcultures and countercultures.
9. Define markets.
10. Define market segment and market segmentation.
11. What factors are used to identify consumer market segments?
12. What methods are used to segment business-to-business markets?
13. What do the terms *dual channel marketing* and *spin-off sales* mean?
14. Define the global consumers, local consumers, and glocal consumer concepts.

15. How is cosmopolitanism related to ethnocentrism?

16. How can the marketing mix be adjusted to meet the needs of those at the bottom-of-the-pyramid?

17. What types of consumers are most likely to buy green or sustainable products in industrialized countries?

18. What ethical issues are present in market segmentation programs?

DISCUSSION QUESTIONS

1. Which element of culture do you believe has the greatest impact on shopping habits? Which has the greatest impact on the production of products, including selecting a brand name for the product? Which has the greatest impact on advertising and promotional programs? Do your answers vary based on the country involved? Explain your answer.

2. Three methods can be used to select employees to sell products or manage marketing operations in foreign markets. *Expatriates* are persons employed by the exporting company who are asked to move or travel to foreign lands. *Locals* are individuals from the target country. *Third-party nationals* are persons who live in neither the home country nor the target country. Which do you think would be best suited to use in an international marketing program focusing on developing new target markets? Why?

3. How would cultural imperatives, electives, and exclusives affect the development of new target markets? How would they affect personal selling? How would they influence advertising programs?

4. Your company provides gift baskets that are given by hosts and visitors in various business relationships. Describe how your product must be modified based on cultural circumstances in the following countries:

   - Taiwan
   - Iran
   - India
   - Honduras

   Then, describe the form of business-to-business segmentation you believe would work best in each of those countries.

5. Think of circumstances (industries or products) that serve as examples of when to use the following types of business segmentation:

   - Industry
   - Size
   - Geographic location
   - Product usage
   - Customer value

ANALYTICAL AND INTERNET EXERCISES

1. Visit the Project GLOBE website (www.globe.gov). Write a report about how you believe information from the project can be used to identify market segments, based on the information about market segmentation in this chapter.

2. Choose a country from three of the regions presented in Figure 4.14. Using the Internet, collect as much information as you believe is needed to identify the potential for market segments based on age, income, and product usage for the following products:
   - bottled water
   - iPod or similar device
   - frozen pizza to be baked at home
   - life insurance

3. Calculate company demand and the penetration rate using the following statistics:

   Market potential = 130 million

   Market demand = 41 million

   Company sales = 17 million

   Explain what the numbers mean and why they are important.

4. Using the Internet, identify consumer market segments in India for two types of music:
   - traditional Indian folk songs
   - music from other countries, including classical, rock, hip-hop, and country and Western

   Then, match each of these forms of music using the various forms of consumer market segmentation presented in this chapter.

 ONLINE VIDEOS

Visit **www.sagepub.com/baack** to view these chapter videos:

Video Link 4.1: Music and Globalism

Video Link 4.2: Slang

Video Link 4.3: Global Currencies

Video Link 4.4: Poverty and Inequality

STUDENT STUDY SITE

Visit **www.sagepub.com/baack** to access these additional learning tools:

- Web Quizzes
- eFlashcards
- SAGE Journal Articles

- Country Fact Sheets
- Chapter Outlines
- Interactive Maps

CASE 4 ///

Electrolux: Refrigeration and Segmentation

The Elektrolux company began operations with the introduction of a new type of vacuum cleaner. It started when founder Axel Wenner-Gren came across an unwieldy Santo vacuum cleaner in Vienna. He went to work for the company that produced the item. Later, Wenner-Gren returned to his home in Stockholm to begin work on what became Lux 1, the world's first household vacuum cleaner, introduced in 1912.

Later, the invention of the absorption refrigerator led to the firm's growth and expansion. Swedish engineering students, Baltzar von Platen and Carl Munters, from the Royal Institute of Technology in Stockholm, presented an invention, a machine that produced cold through heat, using a new application of the absorption process. The machine could be driven by electricity, gas, or kerosene. In 1925, the first Elektrolux absorption refrigerator was launched and Elektrolux started in its quest to be the largest household appliance producer in the world, directed by the marketing genius of Axel Wenner-Gren.

After changing the name from Elektrolux to Electrolux in 1957, the firm became a global leader in household appliances and appliances for professional use. The company now sells more than 40 million products to customers in more than 150 markets each year. The management team focuses on innovations that are thoughtfully designed, based on extensive consumer insight, to meet the real needs of consumers and professionals.

Electrolux products include refrigerators, dishwashers, washing machines, vacuum cleaners, and cookers or stoves sold under esteemed brands such as Electrolux, AEG-Electrolux, Eureka, and Frigidaire. In 2009, Electrolux had sales of SEK 109 billion in Swedish kroner, or about $16 billion in U.S. currency, and 51,000 employees.

The global marketplace for refrigerators is diverse and complex. Many factors influence the types of refrigerators consumers are willing to purchase. The products must be adapted to the type of electricity present in a country (alternating versus direct current) and to many other factors. These include dining habits, shopping habits, and matters as simple as the size of living quarters.

The first consideration, dining habits, refers to what people eat and how they wish to enjoy the item. A beverage as simple as beer may be sold to customers who prefer it to be served warm or others who want it ice cold. The same holds true for a variety of foods. Preferences regarding what is fresh, what is cooked, and how leftovers are stored vary widely.

Shopping habits are tied to both dining habits and to the size of living quarters. In Europe, it is not unusual for a family to purchase only one or two days' worth of dining supplies at any given time, shopping daily at a local market. Needs for a refrigerator are relatively small, and the unit purchased reflects this daily cultural event, in which socialization becomes a large part of the shopping event. Americans, in contrast, often shop at large retailers and need a larger space for a refrigerator that can store larger, less-frequent purchases. Further, many cultures feature patterns in which women are the primary, if not only, household shoppers for food. In cities, living spaces are often quite small. A refrigerator must be adapted to fit in a tiny space. The company has also introduced a refrigerator that keeps ice frozen for up to six hours during a blackout for regions that have electricity infrastructure problems.

Refrigerator sizes vary by country and region.

Many religions dictate that individuals fast at certain times or certain days. The fast may last from dawn until dusk, or take place during a religious holiday or festival. Storing food for times when the person is allowed to eat becomes a consideration in selecting a refrigerator.

Electrolux offers a variety of refrigerators to meet the needs of various markets and customers. The company's ongoing success may be determined, in part, by the influence of new, emerging markets, changes in technology related to sustainability, and other unforeseen forces.[65]

1. Discuss how issues of culture, language, and slang would affect marketing programs for Electrolux refrigerators in international markets.

2. How might religious differences influence the type of refrigerator to be sold as well as its size in international markets?

3. How would topography influence the production and sale of refrigerators by Electrolux?

4. What potential market segments can you identify from the information provided in this case?

5. Would there be a refrigerator market for bottom-of-the-pyramid customers? Why or why not?

5 International Positioning

LEARNING OBJECTIVES ///

After reading and studying this chapter, you should be able to answer the following questions:

I. What two primary elements shape a product's positioning in the global marketplace?

2. What are the main approaches to international product positioning?

3. How can a product's position become an asset in an international marketing effort?

4. What additional challenges affect international product positioning programs?

5. What steps and tactics are used to establish positioning, evaluate positioning, and conduct repositioning in international markets?

IN THIS CHAPTER ///

The Wide World of Tea

What does the word "tea" mean to you? For most citizens of the United States, the answer would likely be along the lines of a "refreshing summertime drink." Companies including Lipton and Nestea sell a relatively limited line of teas made either to be brewed from bags or to be prepared from a powdered, instant form with variations such as caffeine free and lemon and raspberry flavors. Even so, tea consumption varies domestically. Iced tea remains popular in some areas, hot tea in others. Also, someone from New Jersey or another northern state visiting Georgia might be surprised to discover that iced tea is typically presweetened with sugar in the Deep South.

In the global marketplace, tea has more uses and meanings. In Asia, specific gestures and methods are used in the brewing, serving, and selling of tea in restaurants and other locations. The tapping of a cupped hand, fingers down, signifies a thank you for being served more tea without a word being spoken. Tea may be served during courtship rituals and as part of engagement and marriage ceremonies. Drinking tea with family and friends remains a longstanding form of socialization.

Teas are brewed for medicinal purposes throughout the world. Green tea and oolong tea have been suggested to help numerous health concerns. Both contain antioxidants. Green tea's antioxidants, catechins, scavenge for the free radicals known to damage DNA and contribute to cancer, blood clots, and atherosclerosis. Green tea features minimal processing; its leaves are withered and steamed and not fermented (as oolong teas is), which makes green tea's catechins, especially epigallocatechin-3-gallate (EGCG), more concentrated.[1] Some dieticians suggest green tea can also help with weight loss.

Tata Tea is made by a company in India that suggests its products can help lower rates of heart disease and strokes and may lower the risk of oral, pancreatic, and prostate cancer. Another common form of tea includes ginseng, which is believed to boost health by helping with digestion.

While many associate tea with Asian countries, others may remember Earl Grey tea, which is named after British diplomat Earl Charles Grey, as the favorite brew of Captain Jean-Luc Picard from the star ship *Enterprise* (*Star Trek*). Earl Grey is a form of black tea combined with ingredients from Vietnam and China. The tradition of afternoon tea is common in England and throughout former British colonies. In Europe, tea may be served plain, with sugar, or with milk or cream.

Tea consumption is also common in the Middle East and Africa. Together, those two regions consumed 13.8% of all tea worldwide in 2009.[2] In North Africa, particularly Morocco, heavily sugared green tea with mint leaves is popular. Ingrained in the culture, the male head of the household typically serves the tea to welcome guests.[3]

Tea is made from actual tea leaves and from other plants. "Tea snobs" will argue that brews made from flowers and other plants, such as chamomile (a flowering plant from the daisy family) and lavender tea (made from the lavender plant), are not the real thing. Proponents of both teas say that the health properties are similar to those of regular teas.

Tea has also become part of the culture of social responsibility. The Honest Tea Company delivers a variety of tea products while seeking to support local farmers and business people (www.honesttea.com). The company's statement of corporate social responsibility states, "Honest Tea seeks to create honest relationships with our employees, suppliers, customers and with the communities in which we do business." The company actively participates in a "Fair Trade" program with its suppliers. Honest Tea also promotes lower sugar content in its products and the corresponding health benefits as part of its marketing efforts.

Tea movement reflects the degree of development of infrastructure. Many early tea routes by sea helped establish trading relationships among countries. As cultures continue to intermingle, a potential outcome may be an increasing variety of teas in various countries, even those in which the drink has been less popular. Any company's marketing team that seeks to sell tea in other countries will start by carefully considering the positioning strategy to take. The product's characteristics will be compared to local and global competitors. The product must be differentiated in ways that drive consumers to purchase it, in order to get them to change their brewing and tasting habits.

QUESTIONS FOR STUDENTS

1. How would the time of day influence the consumption of tea?
2. Should a company selling tea emphasize price, taste, or some other feature when establishing international product positioning?
3. Which countries would have a natural advantage or disadvantage when selling tea to consumers in other nations?

Tea is consumed daily worldwide.

Overview

The company name "Toyota" may be related to several different perceptions. Some consumers might think of the company and brand as being a high-quality option in the automobile market, backed by a strong warranty program. Others may express fears based on safety problems and recalls of the automobiles in the United States. Others still have not formed much of an opinion. Product positioning, the focus of this chapter, summarizes these attitudes and beliefs. A product's, company's, or brand's position consists of the general perceptions the public has about it relative to the competition.

If marketing is rooted in satisfying consumer needs with goods or services, positioning is how the marketing team instills the assumption in consumers that they will indeed be satisfied. Perceptions form the foundation of positioning. Through the marketing mix and strategic decision-making, marketers work to create a consistent brand position in the minds of consumers.

This chapter begins with a discussion of the basic approaches to positioning in the international marketplace and some of the considerations involved in the process. International positioning, including consumer feelings and activities about global businesses plus the influence of the country of origin, which are components of this procedure, are described next. Culture, language, economic systems, political and legal systems, and infrastructure (see Figure 5.1) all affect approaches to reaching international markets through various positioning efforts. These external global issues are applied throughout the discussion of international positioning.

After laying this foundation, the actual process of positioning will be examined. This includes examples of domestic and international positioning maps, along with the incorporation of global competitors. The chapter concludes with a discussion of the ethical issues surrounding international positioning.

LEARNING OBJECTIVE #1:

What two primary elements shape a product's positioning in the global marketplace?

Figure 5.1: The International Marketing Context

LEARNING
OBJECTIVE #2:

*What are the main
approaches to
international product
positioning?*

The Nature of International Product Positioning

Chapter 4 introduced the STP (segmentation, targeting, and positioning) process. Market segmentation includes identifying distinct consumer groups. Targeting is selecting the groups with which the company intends to engage. Positioning represents the final part of the program. Product positioning involves creating a perception in the consumer's mind regarding the nature of a company and its products relative to competitors. Positioning plays a vital role in international marketing by helping a brand stand out among domestic and international competitors.[4]

The positioning process creates a unique place for the product in comparison to competitors. **Product position** summarizes consumer opinions regarding the specific features of the product. Product position represents what currently exists. **Product positioning** states the goal that marketers have in mind. Marketing activities can be designed to shape a product's position over time. The airline Virgin Blue in Australia was perceived by consumers as focused on meeting the needs of leisure fliers, which constituted the brand's position. Virgin Blue's marketers used the product positioning process to include meeting the needs of business travelers. To create this position, the company introduced a new business cabin class, and increased its flights on key routes for business travelers. The marketing goal was to shift the company's position through positioning activities.[5]

Numerous variables influence positioning, including the features of the product, the price, methods of distribution, packaging, the support services provided, and interactions with members of the company. Two key elements of product position are the way customers view the product and the product's standing relative to competitors.

Positioning Statements and Approaches

A one- or two-sentence summary of a company's positioning strategy is its **positioning statement**, which serves as the basis of the positioning process. The positioning statement focuses on the key benefits the product provides to consumers. "Nike will provide authentic, innovative products that improve athletic performance" serves as an example.

Effective positioning can be achieved in at least seven ways (see Figure 5.2). In international marketing, emphasizing one of these approaches consistently across markets whenever possible remains the most advisable approach. This allows for reduction in production and marketing costs, reduced consumer confusion when visiting other markets, and can lead to increased marketing expertise in building the product's position.

Product Attribute
Competitors
Use or Application
Price-Quality Relationship
Product User
Product Class
Cultural Symbol

Figure 5.2: Product Positioning Approaches

PRODUCT ATTRIBUTES

A trait or characteristic that distinguishes one product from others is a product attribute. It can be used to position a product, such as a "reduced fat" food item or a "no ironing needed" feature for a piece of clothing. Marketing efforts emphasize the attribute as the key selling point.

Japan's Sony Corporation was able to expand into foreign markets by creating a series of quality product attributes. The company has consistently focused on picture quality as the key product attribute driving successful international positioning. In 1968, Sony introduced the Trinitron. The television used what was, for that time, revolutionary "color aperture grille cathode ray rubes" that led to a clearer picture than other technologies. Following this international positioning based on the attribute of picture quality, Sony offered the Bravia flat screen television in 2005, again positioning the product as the television with the best picture. In this case, the sets had "color like no other."[6]

COMPETITORS

Competitors can be used to establish position by contrasting the company's product against others. Legal and/or cultural pressures may limit direct comparisons with a competitor, such as through comparison advertising; however, competitor positioning may still be emphasized in other ways.

Companies in multiple countries often face a complex and differing combination of competitors in each market. Competition arises from other international brands or locally produced brands. The country in which the product was manufactured may also enter into consumer evaluations. When products ranging from drywall to children's toys made in China reached U.S. markets with major defects, many Chinese brands suffered in various global markets, and some were sued by injured consumers.[7]

The soda market in Turkey provides an example of how local competitors can affect positioning. The local soda, Cola Turka, has used the American actor Chevy Chase to position the product as strongly "Turkish." In one spot, Chevy Chase sips the soda and then starts to sing a local song in Turkish. The commercial ends with the actor growing a bushy mustache.[8]

USE OR APPLICATION

Use or application positioning involves creating a memorable set of uses for a product. Bleach may be used as a cleaning product for clothes in one country, as a "germ-killer" in another, and as a way to extend the life of cut flowers in yet another. Use or application positioning requires the identification of the target markets that purchase the product and then notes how those products are used in other countries.

PRICE-QUALITY RELATIONSHIP

A price-quality relationship approach may be used for positioning purposes when businesses offer products at the extremes of the price range. At the high end, the emphasis becomes quality. In the low range, price will be emphasized. Price-quality perceptions may also be affected by the nation in which an item is produced. Many technological innovations that are exported from Japan enjoy favorable views about quality due to the country of origin. German-made automobiles often possess the same price-quality status.

New Year celebrations throughout the world often include the consumption of champagne. Many consumers only purchase a bottle once each year. For this product, the price-quality relationship may drive purchase due to the signal of quality. In 2010, a food critic survey of champagne in Birmingham, a city in England, revealed that the price of champagne at local groceries ranged from £14.99 to £27.99 a bottle. Even though the critic argued that the most expensive champagne did not merit such a high price,

Scooters may be marketed with product user segmentation strategy.

consumers shopping for the beverage would assume that the high price positioned the most expensive champagne as high quality.[9]

PRODUCT USER

The product user positioning method distinguishes a brand or product by clearly specifying who might use it. In transition economies, companies that differentiate by targeting younger consumers as part of a "global" market segment may position products as being more universal or worldly. Services such as hotels, credit cards, and airline travel can be positioned as favoring business travelers or vacationers. Whereas some product users may drink tea for its potential health benefits, more infrequent users may only consume tea for ceremonial reasons.

In the past, marketers of the automobile brand Buick discovered that the cars were typically sold to U.S. consumers who averaged sixty years of age; however, the same brand, when sold to buyers outside the United States, reached a market with an average age of thirty-seven. Consequently, the company started an aggressive promotional campaign targeting younger, Generation X consumers in the United States. The goal was to shift to a newer, younger product user profile.[10]

PRODUCT CLASS

Product class indicates a general category of items within which the good fits. For example, "undergarments for men" include t-shirts and underwear. Other product class groups include "soft drinks" and "energy drinks." Perceptions of product class vary by the culture and the economic circumstances of a country or region. Silk pajamas are targeted to a different set consumers than those made of cotton.

Tofu offers an example of product class differences. In many parts of East Asia, tofu is a staple food, similar to bread or milk in Western countries. Millions consume it on a daily or weekly basis. In Western countries, tofu does not hold the same status. Instead, it is perceived by many as a foreign product to be only occasionally consumed. Hodo, a Californian company with Asian roots, attempted to move the product class position of tofu to that of a luxury good. The company produces high-end, organic tofu that looks far different from "the white lump" that most see in grocery stores.[11]

CULTURAL SYMBOL

Cultural symbol positioning involves an item or brand achieving unique status within a culture or region. Cultural symbols reflect a characteristic of a nation or region and may evolve from popular culture, religion, or other factors that make an area distinct. Any product endorsed by the sports stars Yao Ming in China or Pelé in Brazil would have the potential to be positioned as a cultural symbol.

Consumers often buy a product when it is viewed as a cultural symbol. The spice curry is a cultural symbol to many consumers in India, even though the history of the spice involves several countries. Curry is a combination of spices, usually including turmeric, coriander, and cumin, among others; it was at least partially created by the British. Consumers around the world purchase curry when the goal is to cook "Indian-flavored" dishes.[12]

International Positioning Objectives

International positioning, at its core, involves changing or creating attitudes. Establishing differentiation constitutes one goal of positioning. **Differentiation** results from emphasizing a unique benefit or component of a product that separates it from competitors. Differentiation can be associated with the actual product, or it may be part of an organization's image. Differentiation may develop from perceptions of the product or in terms of support services. Marketers for Casas Bahia, a retailer in Brazil, differentiated the company from competitors by being the first to allow consumers to purchase products on credit.[13]

Differentiation is not the same as the STP process. Segmenting, targeting, and positioning programs seek to identify target market segments containing a homogenous group of members. Each segment is unique and unlike other segments. The product will be positioned within that target market in terms of various benefits or attributes. In some cases, competitors may share some of these benefits or attributes, such as sugar-free or diet soda.

In contrast, differentiation notes the *specific* benefit or attribute that makes the product unique when compared to competitors. This differentiation typically applies *across* various target markets. When performed correctly, marketers establish a point of difference and value proposition that applies to all markets segments, including global target markets.

The search engine Google has achieved differentiation across global markets, even as Bing, Baidu, and other competitors seek to create forms to set themselves apart. Google focuses on the company's position as the top search engine globally. The company's reputation for providing fast searches, for maintaining the innovative edge, and for having vast resources at its disposal creates differentiation. Many market leaders become synonymous with a product category. Google has achieved this status in online searches: the brand name has become a verb, as in, "I Googled it."

LEARNING OBJECTIVE #3:

How can a product's position become an asset in an international marketing effort?

The Hershey's Kiss is used to represent the brand.

BRAND EQUITY

A second goal of positioning programs is to engender **brand equity**, or the unique benefits that a product enjoys due solely to its brand name. Consistent positioning leads to global brand equity. The benefits of brand equity include the ability to charge a higher price and the presence of increased consumer loyalty; in addition, the company's stock price often will be higher than brands without similar levels of equity. These positive outcomes result from the ways consumers view the brand, seeing it as providing a unique benefit. The sources of differentiation or *points of difference* are the strong, favorable, and unique associations consumers have with the brand.

Figure 5.3 highlights some of the strongest global brands. Each has achieved a level of differentiation based on a point of difference. The iconic Marlboro Man represents a cultural symbol that created a unique position for the company, especially with male smokers. The image was initially used to position Marlboro's new filtered cigarettes as being masculine. The popularity of the image was used to expand globally, because the Marlboro Man also emphasized the American origins of the cigarette.[14]

Mercedes Benz holds a strong position and brand due to perceptions of superior engineering, safety, and customer satisfaction. This point of difference has been established around the world. A recent survey revealed it to be Germany's strongest automotive brand. Sony's position begins with perceptions that the company produces superior products across a series of items due to Japan's perceived technological expertise.[15]

BRAND PARITY

Brands without points of difference or unique benefits are inclined to experience perceptions of brand parity. **Brand parity** exists when brands within one product

> A second goal of positioning programs is to engender brand equity, or the unique benefits that a product enjoys due solely to its brand name.

category are viewed as similar or undifferentiated. When all products are deemed to be basically the same, companies are forced to compete with price or other marketing enticements that reduce revenues per sale, such as coupons, premiums, contests, or bonus packs.

Consider the differences between consumer perceptions of airline travel and of automobile brands. Most airlines suffer from brand parity, because most consumers believe there is little to no difference between companies. The brands are not differentiated, which means other marketing approaches will be needed. Airlines often compete based on price. In contrast, some automobile brands are the strongest in the world because they are highly differentiated. Consumer perceptions of differences in the brands Ferrari, Ford, Bentley, and Hyundai are relatively easy to identify.

International Product Positioning Challenges

Attempting to undertake product positioning has one thing in common with many other international marketing efforts: the process is largely the same as in domestic markets. Additional differences arise in response to other factors. The influence of changes in technology, country-of-origin issues, regulations, plus packaging and labeling complications all affect international product positioning programs. These elements reflect the cultural, language, political and regulatory, economic, and infrastructure influences in the international marketing environment that were displayed in Figure 5.1.

CHANGES IN TECHNOLOGY

International positioning has been strongly influenced by the development of new technologies, some of which improve a nation's infrastructure. One of the primary changes has been that marketing messages transmitted in one country will be seen in others. Television and radio signals in Italy are likely to reach Switzerland, Austria, and France. Consequently, *consistency* has become a key element in successful international product and brand positioning. Positioning statements help maintain consistency.

Conflicting positioning approaches in various countries would likely damage the brand of any company seeking to make in-roads into these markets, which may lead to making changes to brand names in order to become consistent across markets. The Twix bar is one of the leading candy bars made by Mars. Until the early 1990s, the bar was named Raider in Germany, France, and other parts of Western Europe. Due to increased media bleed across borders and to support more-consistent positioning, Mars changed the brand name to Twix in its European markets.[16]

Brand	Country of Origin
1. Coca-Cola	United States
2. IBM	United States
3. Microsoft	United States
4. General Electric	United States
5. Nokia	Finland
6. McDonald's	United States
7. Google	United States
8. Toyota	Japan
9. Intel	United States
10. Disney	United States
11. Hewlett-Packard	United States
12. Mercedes Benz	Germany
13. Gillette	United States
14. Cisco	United States
15. BMW	Germany
16. Louis Vuitton	France
17. Marlboro	United States
18. Honda	Japan
19. Samsung	South Korea
20. Apple	United States
21. H&M	Sweden
22. American Express	United States
23. Pepsi	United States
24. Oracle	United States
25. Nescafé	Switzerland
26. Nike	United States
27. SAP	Germany
28. Ikea	Sweden
29. Sony	Japan
30. Budweiser	United States

Figure 5.3: Leading Global Brands in 2009

Source: Adapted from "Interbrand Ranking of the Best Global Brands of 2009," *Business Week.*

LEARNING OBJECTIVE #4:

What additional challenges affect international product positioning programs?

VIDEO LINK 5.1:
Global Markets

The Digital Divide

Technological differences and comfort levels with new technologies can also influence the manner in which a product is positioned in global markets. Less-developed economies suffer from the digital divide, or the gap in technology that limits the ability of countries and regions to develop.

One example comes from personal computer usage. It is estimated that in three fourths of low-income countries, there are fewer than fifteen personal computers per one thousand people. In poverty-stricken and remote areas, other issues arise. Cases have been reported in which ants have eaten through hard drives. Oftentimes earthquakes disrupt Internet service for entire regions.[17] Positioning personal computers with these limiting factors changes the methods a marketing team might use.

Consumer Reluctance

Consumers may also be reluctant to try new product and technologies. Whether it is a mobile phone, a soda, or a solar panel array, many of the billions of consumers in emerging or least-developed markets view these products as innovations. Somewhere a consumer is picking up a digital camera for the first time. For marketers, this means that these products are automatically viewed as foreign, innovative, and new. For established companies, these perceptions may be contrary to some well-established points of difference and might lead the company to reposition the product.

In contrast, consumers in more-developed countries take various products for granted, such as mobile phones, Internet access, and computers, and these products play significant economic and social roles in the country. Entering these markets probably means targeting a more sophisticated set of consumers with higher incomes and educational attainments, and positioning the product accordingly.

In India, the potential market for dental care is large and penetration rates are low. The marketing objective may be to convince reluctant consumers to pay more for value-added product attributes such as gels or teeth whitening. For poorer, bottom-of-the-pyramid consumers, the challenge will be getting consumers to switch to using toothpaste itself instead of the more commonplace toothpowders.[18]

COUNTRY-OF-ORIGIN EFFECTS

As companies attempt to establish positioning globally, one common concern will be the product's country of origin. The **country-of-origin effect** summarizes the response a consumer has to a product due to the country that is the source, in the consumer's mind, of the product. Depending on the home country and the country being entered, the country-of-origin effect can drastically alter the position of the product in the minds of consumers. Country-of-origin effects originate in four different areas, which are displayed in Figure 5.4.[19] Together, these factors work to create the sources of country-of-origin positioning effects.

Home country: The influence of a consumer's home country on his or her beliefs
Origin country: The country that the consumer generally associates with a certain product
Made-in country: The country listed on the "made in" label of the product
Designed-in country: The country in which the product was designed

Figure 5.4: Sources of Country-of-Origin Positioning Effects

Country-of-origin effects can be positive or negative. Many multinational corporations, such as Coca-Cola, Levi Strauss, and Sony, leverage positive country-of-origin effects to help differentiate products. Some evidence suggests that the country-of-origin can be more important than brand name to consumers. One set of consumers may be willing to pay a price premium for goods when they have positive attitudes toward the country-of-origin.[20] Country-of-origin also affects perceptions of quality, which can be used to reduce feelings of purchase risk, and also to increase the likelihood to buy.[21] Country-of-origin effects are part of the cultural context of international marketing.

Country Image

Country-of-origin effects are often based on stereotyped conceptions consumers have about countries, or the country image. **Country image** consists of the attitudes and knowledge consumers have about a country. Some countries have positive and consistent images globally, including Switzerland's reputation for quality engineering or France's reputation for style. Most-developed countries generally have more positive country images. Less- and least-developed countries often struggle with poor country images. As a result, country-of-origin may limit the ability to market products in more-developed countries.

Negative country-of-origin attitudes can be changed over time, as was the case of the South Korean automaker Hyundai. When Hyundai models first entered the American market in 1986, the marketing team faced negative country image problems. Jay Leno joked that filling up a Hyundai with gas doubled its value.[22] The automaker realized consumers were reluctant to buy a car that was "Made in Korea," and was perceived similarly to the Yugo, which was manufactured in the former Yugoslavia. To counter this perception, Hyundai introduced a 100,000 mile, ten-year warranty, the most comprehensive in the industry, in 1998. Finbarr O'Neill, Hyundai Motor's America president and CEO, stated in 2000, "We have to make it OK to drive a Hyundai into the driveway without being apologetic to your neighbors."[23] The warranty, coupled with an increase in quality and an aggressive advertising campaign designed to position the company's cars as being highly reliable, led to a remarkable turnaround. While other automobile companies were losing market share at the end of the decade, Hyundai increased sales and gained market share. The Genesis model was voted 2009 "North American Car of the Year" at the 2009 Detroit Auto Show, suggesting that the negative effects of country image had been largely eliminated.[24]

Country image problems can emerge in several ways. Figure 5.5 lists some of the more common problems. Each can influence a company's ability to effectively position its products. Country-of-origin attitudes are shaped, in part, by cultural differences, language differences, and political or ideological divergence. Each of these four differences is part of the international marketing context.

VIDEO LINK 5.2: Language

| Ethnocentrism |
| Animosity |
| Nationalism |
| Religiosity |

Figure 5.5: Attitudinal Factors Influencing Country Image

Ethnocentrism

Cultural values influence international positioning. Country image varies among consumers within a country. While there are general trends, marketers also need to know the specific attitudes of consumers in the target market. Consumers exhibiting high levels of ethnocentrism or the attitude that their country is better than others pay more attention to country-of-origin labels and are more likely to buy products produced in their home countries.[25]

Animosity

Relationships between countries can confound positioning efforts. Tensions between or within nations arise in many parts of the world, including those between Greece and

Turkey, Pakistan and India, and Israel and the Palestinians living in the West Bank and the Gaza Strip. These conflicts undoubtedly influence consumer attitudes and behaviors.

When the United States invaded Iraq in 2002, various countries throughout the world, especially in Western Europe, expressed disapproval. A survey completed in 2004 revealed that nearly 20% of consumers abroad said they would avoid U.S. companies and products such as McDonald's, Starbucks, American Airlines, and Barbie dolls (Mattel's) because of the war. At that time, the more American a product was perceived to be, the more resistance it encountered.[26]

Any **animosity** or anger toward a country can be worsened by political, economic, or military conflicts between countries. A considerable amount of evidence suggests that animosity toward a country strongly influences consumers.[27] In the United States, animosity with regard to objections to the Iraq war reached a level in which Congress circulated a resolution to change the name of the French fries in the congressional cafeteria to "Freedom fries," because France had expressed strong opposition to the war at the beginning of the conflict.

Nationalism

At times, animosity toward another country may be coupled with nationalism. **Nationalism** refers to the strong pride and devotion citizens have in a country or nation. Nationalism can be the internal response to activities that can also lead to animosity as consumers examine products from other countries. Nationalism should not be considered as a purely negative or positive attitude. It may be associated with heroic sacrifice, loyalty, and group cohesiveness. From a marketing perspective, it can also lead to a preference for purchasing local goods and services. Conversely, nationalism can lead to boycotts, protests, and even acts of violence toward another country or a company conducting business in a foreign land. Nationalistic consumers often perceive that buying imported goods is wrong because it negatively impacts the domestic economy.[28]

In May of 2010, millions of Indonesian farmers threatened to boycott Nestlé products. Angry at a move by Nestlé to stop buying crude palm oil from Indonesian farms, an action that would potentially severely hurt the Indonesian economy, the farmers expressed national pride and attempted to protect their community.[29]

Religiosity

International Marketing in Daily Life

Religions

Attitudes toward countries can also be influenced by religion and religious similarities between countries. Increasingly, **religiosity**, or the degree to which consumers within a country or region are religious, has become a factor some marketers consider when positioning products. Religiosity affects shopping behaviors, attitudes toward advertising, purchase information-search processes, and product preferences.[30] A list of the major religions and the percentage of the population that follows each in select countries is presented in Table 5.1.

Each of these religions practices differing dietary programs, holds religious ceremonies in differing ways, exhibits varying viewpoints regarding the status of

COUNTRY	RELIGIONS
Afghanistan	Sunni Muslim 80%, Shia Muslim 19%, other 1%
Argentina	Roman Catholic 92%, Protestant 2%, Jewish 2%, other 4%
Botswana	Christian 71.6%, Badimo 6%, other 1.4%, none 20.6%
Cuba	85% Roman Catholic prior to communist takeover
France	Roman Catholic 83%-88%, Protestant 2%, Jewish 1%, Muslim 5%–10%, unaffiliated 4%
India	Hindu 80.5%, Muslim 13.4%, Christian 2.3%, Sikh 1.9%, other 1.8%
Kazakhstan	Muslim 47%, Russian Orthodox 44%, Protestant 2%, other 7%
Morocco	Muslim 98.7%, Christian 1.1%, Jewish 0.2%
Qatar	Muslim 77.5%, Christian 8.5%, other 14%
Somalia	Sunni Muslim near 100%
Taiwan	Buddhist / Taoist 93%, Christian 4.5%, other 2.5%
United States	Protestant 51.3%, Roman Catholic 23.9%, Mormon 1.7%, other Christian 1.6%, Jewish 1.7%, Buddhist 0.7%, Muslim 0.6%, other or unspecified 2.5%, unaffiliated 12.1%, none 4%

Table 5.1: **Religions in Select Countries**

VIDEO LINK 5.3:
Economies in Transition

women and children, and has unique holy days. Product positioning efforts account for these cultural, language, and daily life variances.

By measuring ethnocentrism, nationalism, animosity, and religiosity, marketers have a better understanding of the potential effects of country image and country-of-origin image. This increases the potential to successfully position products that are ready to export to other countries.

Consumption of simple products, such as drinks, may reflect religious beliefs. American politics, particularly in the Middle East, have led come consumers to want an alternative to Coca-Cola sodas. Mecca Cola, which is sold in parts of Europe and the Arab world, positions itself in terms of religion. The brand name, Mecca, and the cola's slogan "Don't drink stupid. Drink committed," both reflect targeting of Muslim consumers.[31]

Mecca Cola, which is sold in parts of Europe and the Arab world, positions itself in terms of religion.

REGULATIONS

Regulatory environments present one of the more important differences between nations as marketers respond to the international context. Each country's government has sovereignty over business activities within national boundaries. **Sovereignty** means that the government has authority or control within its state. Foreign businesses must respect this sovereignty and follow the regulations and rules within the country.

Regulations may keep a company from positioning a product in terms of a new benefit or attribute, or in some cases, from entering a market at all. In Canada, Tropicana orange juice with added calcium is not classified as a food but instead as a drug. Each container is required to have a drug identification number on the label.[32] The regulation limits the potential position of this product in the mind of consumers as simply a tasty or healthy beverage. It might be difficult to market the drug "orange juice with calcium," complete with a drug number, to consumers.

PACKAGING AND LABELS

Product of
Made in
Designed in
Packaged in
Assembled in
Certified made in

Figure 5.6: Country-of-Origin Label Wordings in the United States

Another difficulty associated with international marketing may be found in packaging and especially labeling regulations that are part of the political or regulatory international marketing context. A salmon caught by a fisherman in the United States that is shipped to Thailand for skinning and deboning and ends up on a grocery store shelf in Brazil has three potential points of origin. The question arises as to which country of origin should be printed on the label. A Braun shaver sold in Wal-Mart is made with parts from Germany, Ireland, and Hungary, and was probably assembled in China.

In the United States, differing country-of-origin labels are allowed (see Figure 5.6). The labels may reflect where the product was produced or where the product was assembled. As is the case in many countries, a product can be labeled "certified made in the U.S.A." even when at least part of the product was manufactured in other countries. The key is that virtually all parts and processing are of U.S. origin. The "assembled in" label can be used if the last substantial transformation happened in that country. In general, what this means is that many product packages, even ones with "made in the U.S.A." on the label, were probably partially produced or assembled elsewhere.[33]

International Positioning Methods

LEARNING OBJECTIVE #5:

What steps and tactics are used to establish positioning, evaluate positioning, and conduct repositioning in international markets?

The positioning process, whether international or domestic, includes a series of steps, as is summarized by Figure 5.7. First, the company's marketing team identifies target markets. These targets identify the group of consumers whose perceptions form the basis for the company or the product's position. Members of various target markets may have different perceptions of the company. A company may be well positioned in one target market but not in another. Next, competitors are identified. Finally, the marketing team conducts an analysis of target market characteristics to identify points of difference. Techniques such as positioning maps are used to further clarify the position a product or brand holds in the marketplace. Depending on the results of the analysis, efforts to enhance or to reposition the brand may be undertaken.

IDENTIFY TARGET MARKETS

The second element of the segmentation, targeting, and positioning (STP) approach is target marketing. After a group of market segments has been identified, the marketing team chooses which market segments to pursue. Market segments may have been established based on demographics, psychographic similarities, geographic area, geodemographics, consumer type, product benefits, or product uses. A set of these segments, typically with a common element, constitutes the target markets that best fit with the company's marketing program.

A key concern marketers have about any target market is when consumers in the group will be willing to spend their money on the product. Positioning, especially in terms of unique product benefits, often signals a certain price point. In Japan, Tod's, the Italian leather goods house, is positioned as a high-quality, high-price product.[34] Members of Tod's target market are affluent, aspiring, global consumers, whether in Japan, the United States, or China. These individuals are willing to spend money on quality products.

A company such as Toyota, with a larger, more-price-sensitive target market, becomes more concerned with the price signal that is sent. The price should not signal a level of quality that is higher than members of the target market believe they can afford. This issue becomes particularly important when the marketing team targets local and bottom-of-the-pyramid consumers.

1. Identify target markets.
2. Analyze competition within the target market.
3. Identify points of difference.
4. Enhance or reposition, if necessary.

Figure 5.7: The Steps of Product Positioning

ANALYZE COMPETITION WITHIN THE TARGET MARKET

One key concern for a company's marketing team involves identifying all potential competitors. Nearly every product or service sold encounters several levels of competition internationally, including product versus product, product line versus product line, brand versus brand, company versus company, and industry versus industry. These perceptions in turn affect positioning efforts.

Product vs. Product

At the most basic level, a product first competes with similar products. In the United Kingdom, a variety of home cooking, fast-food, and upscale restaurants offer fish and chips, a standard British fare. There are now around 8,500 fish and chip shops across the United Kingdom; which is eight for every one McDonald's outlet, making British fish and chips the nation's favorite take-out food.[35] Automobile companies first compete at the product versus product level, as a buyer considers a Nissan Altima, Toyota Camry, or Hyundai Sonata. When positioning products globally to compete with other products, careful attention should be paid to issues of quality, product differences, and price at the product level.

Product Line vs. Product Line

A product line consists of similar products within a particular category. Canned fruits may be sold by a company offering a product line that includes mixed fruit, pineapples, peaches, grapes, mandarin oranges, pears, and apples. Typically, a house mark brand represents all of the products in a line. In the United States, Dole's line of canned fruit competes against Del Monte and others. In Thailand, another of Dole's competitors is Bangkok Companies and its subsidiary Thai Fruit Company.

Product lines compete with depth and breadth, both of which affect positioning. The *depth* of a product line is the total number of products in that line. If Thai Fruit Company offers ten varieties of canned fruit, ten becomes the depth of the line. *Breadth* refers to the number of lines offered by the company. The Thai Fruit Company also offers fruit drinks; Dole benefits from a strong association with fresh fruits, especially pineapples from Hawai`i. Dole also offers canned vegetables and packaged salads, creating greater breadth.

Depth and breadth can create a stronger brand image, as the increased number of product offerings leads to the company becoming known to a wider variety of

Fruits and fruit products can be offered using product line target market positioning.

customers. Depth and breadth also contribute to positioning at the product line versus product line level of competition. As depth and breadth expand, customers enjoy more choices and can rely on a brand when shopping, reducing purchase time, and quickly eliminating other purchase alternatives. By offering quality salads, Dole increased the odds that those who purchase the salads will also buy its fresh fruit, canned vegetables, or any new product the company introduces.

Brand vs. Brand

Well-known companies with powerful brand names enjoy key advantages in positioning efforts. This may be due, in part, to consumer considerations as one company is compared to another. Brand equity contributes to positioning and becomes a major asset in brand versus brand competition. A strong brand makes product diversification processes more manageable. When Sony introduces a new electronic device, consumers are likely to transfer the trust they have in the brand to the new product.

A brand name with negative connotations may experience some difficulties. The Exxon-Mobile Corporation has been vilified by various critics since the 1989 oil spill disaster in Alaska. BP, the British Petroleum brand responsible for the largest oil spill in world history (2010), undoubtedly will share the same fate in the coming years.

Global brands compete against each other across markets. The toothpaste brands Crest, which is owned by Proctor & Gamble, and Colgate, which is owned by Colgate-Palmolive, battle for the same consumers globally. China represents the largest toothpaste market by volume, and toothpaste marketing activities in the country are particularly aggressive. Consumer reluctance to brush daily continues, and only 20% of bottom-of-the-pyramid rural Chinese consumers do so. Many Chinese view toothbrushing as providing cosmetic rather than health benefits. In response, both toothpaste brands try to establish position in terms of health benefits. Crest had plans to make a television advertisement where half of a white egg is brushed with Crest toothpaste. The egg is then lowered into an acid bath for an hour. After the hour, the side of the egg coated with toothpaste is strong while the other side is brittle and breaks. Colgate's marketing team discovered the potential ad and preempted Crest by making a similar commercial using a seashell instead of an egg.[36]

Company vs. Company

When engaging in positioning activities, a foreign company may face an advantage, disadvantage, or relatively neutral outcome when competing with local firms. In some instances, where consumers are more cosmopolitan, a foreign entity may be more readily accepted; in areas where ethnocentrism prevails, a foreign competitor begins with a strategic disadvantage.

Although marketing teams in multinational corporations from developed economies may believe that at all they need do is enter an emerging market to enjoy success, the

INTERNATIONAL INCIDENT ///

An employee of the 7-11 Convenience Stores company, you travel to Mexico looking for new potential franchisee partners. A meeting is held with a local businessman to gauge his interest. The opportunity seems to be attractive to him, but one concern is raised. A certain amount of animosity exists toward the United States in parts of Mexico. He is nervous that this partnering will hurt the company's position in the country. This places you in a potentially awkward position. Your company, 7-11, is actually a Japanese company. How do you respond to this issue? Should you correct him? Does the high power distance culture, in which status differences have significant meaning, in Mexico affect how you should respond? More broadly, animosity toward 7-11, even if it is based on a false perception, might constrain moving into the Mexican market. How would you address this problem?

opposite may be true. Outside companies often encounter difficulties when entering emerging markets and struggle to compete with local competitors in those countries.

Multinational firms face institutional voids in emerging markets. In other words, these organizations do not have the structures or support needed to enter an emerging market and the country cannot meet those needs with local resources. The emerging market country may lack the data or delivery services required to meet the needs of the market. A lack of access to local capital or human resources might create another challenge. Local firms can often access the same developed country markets for capital or talent. Managers of these companies can talk to angel investors in California or list the company on the New York Stock Exchange.

Local firms, by definition, already meet the needs of local markets. In contrast, multinationals encounter additional costs, in terms of both time and money, to adapt activities in order to meet the same local needs. The costs and risks associated with entering these markets rise as a result, and may impede attempts at positioning.[37]

A multinational firm hiring local talent in India might experience an institutional void. With the boom in services, talented workers are becoming increasingly rare. With little knowledge of local institutions, and no valid ranking systems available, the company faces the institutional void problem.[38]

Industry vs. Industry

In any economy, an individual, family, or business has a finite number of dollars to spend. Choices are made on a daily basis. The decision to purchase an expensive cup of coffee in the morning may lead the consumer to skip lunch or to buy only a bag of potato chips at noon.

Understanding the product's industry as well as other industries that may take customers away will be part of the position process. Recreational activities compete internally (watching a professional soccer match versus going to the movies), and with other businesses where consumers spend money on sundries. During economic slumps, a family may forgo traveling on vacation and instead purchase a new smoker or barbeque grill.

Careful positioning means accounting for all levels of competition. The most powerful influence will be similar products; however, brand names and other factors can change a company's approach. Comparisons with similar brands and products from other industries will include pricing considerations.

IDENTIFY POINTS OF DIFFERENCE

After identifying target markets, evaluating competitors, and reviewing other influences, the marketing team analyzes the company or product's current position. Market research will be conducted, normally beginning with consumer surveys regarding attitudes about a product. Attitudes are assessed across a variety of features and benefits, both tangible and intangible.

Tangible product benefits are the value drawn from the physical components of the product. The popular Brazilian soda ingredient Guarana accounts for more than one third of Brazilian carbonated drink sales. The bubble-gum-tasting fruit ingredient has high caffeine content and is also rumored to create romantic benefits. The product provides many tangible benefits including taste and energy.

Intangible product benefits are the value drawn from the social, emotional, and nonphysical aspects of consumption. Within the Brazilian market, there are also important intangible benefits to purchasing Guarana, including prestige, patriotic pride, and connections to local communities.

> Intangible product benefits are the value drawn from the social, emotional, and nonphysical aspects of consumption.

Most products offer tangible and intangible benefits to consumers. An analysis of the benefits can become complicated as a result. To organize the process, marketers often employ positioning maps. **Positioning maps** are tools used to map the company and its competitors in terms of consumer attitudes or perceptions. Typically the marketing team examines factors that drive purchases and influence purchasing decisions. Positioning maps can be important tools for international marketers, helping them understand how a company's products and brands are perceived by consumers in other countries.[39]

Figure 5.8 displays a traditional positioning map featuring price and quality perceptions within the automobile industry. The map indicates that perceptions of quality increase as the price of the product rises. The positioning map also suggests that quality signals price. Most maps that utilize price and quality as the main factors look basically the same across product categories. In the map as shown, Toyota, which had experienced problems with safety (that have been since resolved), may have seemed overpriced at that time, due to quality perceptions. This positioning map is not based on data. It was created by the authors as a sample for illustrative purposes.

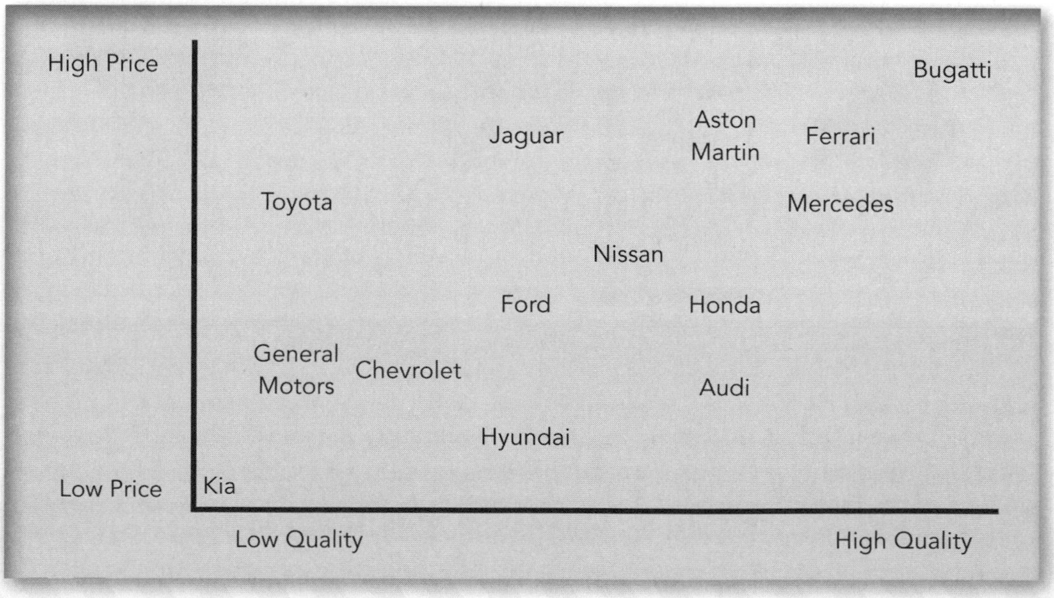

Figure 5.8: A Price-Quality Positioning Map

Positioning maps should be designed to identify attitudes related to a company's source of differentiation. Instead of using price, actual product attributes can be examined. The positioning map featured in Figure 5.9 includes the same automobile brands that appear in Figure 5.8, but instead this second map uses consumer impressions of speed and safety as its basis. The map does not display the same relationships as the price-quality map but rather the map suggests clusters of brands. The luxury sports cars cluster together on the high-speed feature but, as a result, engender lower perceptions of safety.

The family car brands such as Ford and Nissan cluster in the middle of the map. These brands are all perceived as being relatively safe but also relatively slow. The brands that do not cluster are differentiated in terms of speed or safety. Audi has the reputation as a safe car, which is how it differentiates from competitors. This position is reflected on the map. When Toyota experienced problems with accelerator pedals (that have now been fixed), consumers may have viewed the product more negatively, as shown in this example. This positioning map (Figure 5.9) is not based on data. It was created by the authors as a sample for illustrative purposes.

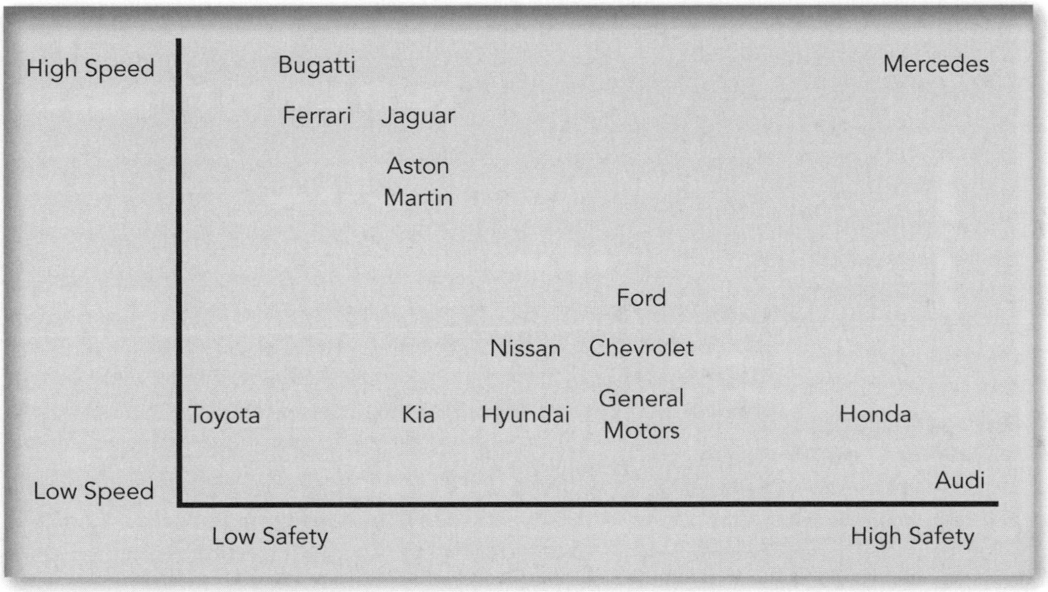

Figure 5.9: A Speed-Safety Positioning Map

Share of Mind and Share of Heart

Two additional variables may be used to examine the position of a product or brand: share of mind and share of heart. *Share of mind* refers to the product's position in terms of brand awareness. A product with low share of mind is not readily recalled when a consumer considers brands in a product category. A brand with high share of mind will immediately emerge when a consumer thinks about the same category. When consumers are asked to name the top athletic shoe companies, typical responses are likely to include Nike, Reebok, Adidas, and perhaps one or two more brands. These brands feature a strong share of mind, which may be based on the tangible attributes of the shoes.

Share of heart focuses more on the emotional components of the consumer attitudes. These include the ways consumers experience the product and its social context. Share of heart suggests that relationships, emotions, and experiences are part of a product's position. When a basketball player continues to wear Air Jordan basketball shoes because he had worn them in high school, the shoes have achieved share of heart.

A product exhibiting high share of mind combined with high share of heart holds a strong marketing advantage. Vegemite, a yeast extract spread, is sold in Australia. Leftover brewer's yeast extract, a by-product of beer manufacture, is combined with various vegetable and spice additives. Vegemite appears dark reddish-brown, almost black, and provides a rich source of Vitamin B. It is thick, similar to peanut butter, very salty, and has achieved nearly cultural icon status. Numerous sources note that Vegemite is to Australian children what peanut butter is to kids in other countries. Vegemite clearly has strong share of mind and share of heart in that market. If a pocket of Australian immigrants were to emigrate, they would undoubtedly constitute a target market for Vegemite based on this strong position.[40] Figure 5.10 displays a share of mind/share of heart example for Vegemite, Sanitarium Peanut Butter, Kraft Jelly, and Philadelphia Cream Cheese in Australia.

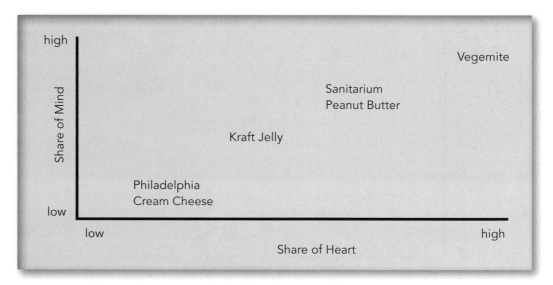

Figure 5.10: Share of Mind and Share of Heart

As shown, Vegemite enjoys both high share of mind and high share of heart. Positioning efforts would be dedicated to maintaining that standing. Sanitarium Peanut Butter holds nearly as much share of mind, but has less share of heart, because it does not possess cultural icon status. The company holds a strong position and would likely seek to enhance one or more of the features, perhaps by emphasizing price-quality relationships, product user status, such as children versus adults, or some other positioning approach. Kraft Jelly has a diminished place in terms of both share of mind and share of heart. Should the marketing team discover that share of heart is lower due to perceptions that it is an "American" product with no particular appeal to Australian customers, marketing efforts can be made to improve share of heart and create greater loyalty to the brand by linking the brand to Australia. The marketing team with the biggest challenge would be the one selling Philadelphia Cream Cheese. A logical approach would be to begin with improvements to share of mind, thereby increasing consumer awareness of the product and its many uses. Share of heart and brand loyalty might then grow over time.

The same share of mind and share of heart map, if produced for the United States, would reveal dramatically different results. Most American consumers only know about Vegemite sandwiches due to a line from a Men at Work song from the 1980s ("He just smiled and gave me a *Vegemite* sandwich"). In the United States, Kraft's peanut butter and jelly products would occupy the position held by Vegemite. Consequently, each company's marketing team can use the map to understand a product's position in other countries. Philadelphia Cream Cheese's advertising company recently undertook a massive marketing effort to reinforce the concept that the product could be used in a variety of ways beyond being a spread for crackers, because the marketing team believed the company held strong share of heart status. The results were a change in share of mind, based on new uses for the product, and increased sales.

ENHANCING POSITION OR REPOSITIONING

Following the analysis of a company or product's current position, the decision will be made regarding enhancing a current position or seeking to reposition the brand. Most of the time, a position that has been previously established will be reinforced or enhanced. Repositioning normally will be undertaken only when circumstances indicate that a more radical approach is in order.

Tata Motors is an Indian automobile manufacturer. A few years ago, Tata Motors began the process of introducing the Nano in the United Kingdom. In India, the Nano is an austere and simple $2,500 car targeting relatively impoverished consumers. To be successful in the British market, the marketing team understood that the car would require some adjustments. First, it would have to meet more stringent safety standards. In response, the company added extra foam and structures behind parts of the car, reinforced sections of the body, and installed air bags. After passing safety tests, upgrades to the Nano's engine and brakes were considered. The modifications would be designed to achieve a new position, one in which the same brand name is attached to a radically different and more expensive car. Company leaders believed the car, as adapted, would attract British customers.[41]

Enhancing Position

Enhancing position involves all standard and nontraditional marketing approaches. A brand featuring a *unique product attribute* will be marketed with a strong emphasis on the feature. When targeting a new market in another country, the marketing team ascertains whether the feature or attribute is known and valued by those in the market. Over time, a description of or reminder of the attribute may appear in point-of-purchase displays; it might be described on any social networking forum that becomes available; advertising could be used to highlight the feature; and customer loyalty programs may be designed to encourage repeat purchases. Attempts will be made to build on the unique benefit, especially if a celebrity or well-known company purchases and endorses the item in the target market country.

Positioning based on *competitors*, as part of an international program, likely will concentrate on local competitors first. The product will be differentiated in some way, typically avoiding denigrating the competition so as not to offend locals. An established product that has achieved a niche may continue to compete by fending off any new entries into the marketplace while seeking to enhance the status of the product relative to competitors.

Enhancing *use or application* positioning constitutes a relatively straightforward process. It can be accomplished through the training of salespeople to emphasize various product uses. Advertising can demonstrate those uses. When additional uses for the same product have been identified, the number of potential customers expands. Arm & Hammer baking soda has been successfully marketed in the United States for many years. Growth in sales resulted, in part, from advertising campaigns that touted its many uses. It can be used for cooking, for deodorizing refrigerators, and as a household cleaning agent. Baking soda is viewed differently worldwide. It is not commonly used for baking purposes in France. Rather, *bicarbonate de soude* and the more common *la levure chimique* are used. Promoting alternative uses may be a creative way for the product to gain sales in countries such as France.

Price-quality relationship positioning may be emphasized through various tactics aimed at the position chosen. When a product carries a high price and implies high quality, premium programs allow the marketing team to offer a sales enticement without reducing the price. At the extreme, it may be possible to develop social networks of fans of high-priced items. Conversely, at the low-price extreme, a continuing emphasis on price remains the primary marketing tactic. For those products of medium price and quality, the approach features value as the primary selling point. These methods are highly similar in both domestic and international markets.

Product user positioning in international marketing may center on psychological, sociological, or spiritual values held by potential consumers. Psychological values may include feelings of cosmopolitanism, positive attitudes toward the country-of-origin, or pleasant feelings associated with the actual use of the product. Products that are considered to be "everyday" in one country can be perceived quite differently in others. American jean marketers, such as Levi-Strauss, realize that their products are quite fashionable in many European countries. Wearing Levi jeans makes a statement about the consumer in these countries. Sociological distinctions include the emphasis on feelings of belonging, social status based on use of the product, or connections to family, such as by purchasing insurance to protect them. Heineken, from Holland, is marketed as a premium product in the United States and is positioned to appeal to the upscale consumer. Religious values are also sometimes expressed in the use of some products, such as unleavened bread and kosher meats.

Product class international positioning may rely on a universal endorsement, such as ISO (International Organization for Standardization) 9000 or 14000 standards. These notify buyers that an item is of sufficient quality to be considered as competitive with other products in the same class. Retaining ISO distinction maintains a product's position. ISO standards apply to both products and services. Hospitals may seek ISO certification to become known for delivering the highest quality in health care to patients.

Cultural symbol positioning can be an effective international marketing strategy.

Cultural symbol positioning may be based on a local icon, such as Yannick Noah. Noah was a professional tennis player and is now a singing sensation in his native France. Cultural symbol positioning may rely on association with a specific national feature, such as the spectacular sunsets on the Greek Isles of Mykonos. As long as the celebrity maintains that status or a national feature remains popular, associating a product with the symbol may enhance the status of the product.

Consistency remains the key to enhancing product positioning using any of these methods. Strong brands stand on continual emphasis of the same features. A product's position remains stable unless unforeseen events, competitor actions, or other external forces change it.

Often enhancing a product position involves overlapping concerns. Phillips has been successful in the Malaysian kitchen appliance market with three separate brands: Comfort, Cucina, and Essence. Essence is Phillips' premium brand. Though both Comfort and Cucina are affordable and positioned as top performers at a reasonable price, Cucina is positioned as the higher-quality, higher-priced brand. Products carrying the brand are high end, with sophisticated technology. For all three brands, Phillips balances the price-quality position while emphasizing unique product attributes and use positioning.[42]

Bottom-of-the-Pyramid Positioning

Positioning within the bottom-of-the-pyramid markets can be complicated. Consumers typically already have awareness of the product and the benefits it provides. The challenge is not differentiation, at least no more so than in any other international market segment. The concern become shifting the company's focus. For many strongly positioned, premium global brands, the process of creating those brands leads to a high-quality position. The natural concern will be that within the bottom-of-the-pyramid market the position also signals a high price. Such a perception may lessen consumer interest because they will believe that they cannot afford the product.

Positioning in the bottom-of-the-pyramid involves educating consumers about the steps the company has taken to adapt to the consumer's level of income. Doing so requires repositioning the product or brand as being attainable in terms of price without losing the differentiation in terms of quality or product features. It may entail the introduction of a new brand that then can be positioned in the minds of consumers.

Ginger Hotels in India are part of the large Indian conglomerate, the Tata Group. Before introducing Ginger Hotels, the company's marketers mainly focused on the

INTERNATIONAL INCIDENT //

You are visiting Russia as part of an executive exchange program. Upon arrival, you witness two Russian executives engaging in a hug as they greet one another. Assuming this is proper protocol, you hug the two executives and receive a chilly response. Soon after, you offer an apology, explaining that you thought it was the cultural norm to hug as a greeting. The executives laugh and explain that they are old friends. In business settings, a firm handshake is in order. Later, during the meeting, one of the two executives laughs during a light moment and touches you on the arm. What should you conclude?

luxurious Taj Hotel brand. Ginger Hotels, in contrast, are positioned as "smart basic" hotels that are highly functional but with no frills. The target is bottom-of-the-pyramid consumers.[43]

Every positioning activity will be pursued while looking for the most low-cost approach. Unlike more-developed countries or regions that have more expensive labor, companies seeking to serve the bottom-of-the-pyramid often use local salespeople or contacts in order to minimize selling costs. Beyond the social employment benefits, these individuals can turn into strong advocates for the product or company.

Repositioning

> Repositioning is the process of changing consumer perceptions of a brand relative to competitors.

When a product or brand's position creates an unfavorable circumstance, the company's marketing team may seek to reposition it. **Repositioning** is the process of changing consumer perceptions of a brand relative to competitors. It involves a sweeping process that must be implemented at the strategic level, thereby affecting every part of the company. It cannot simply be a marketing ploy, which might arouse the suspicions of consumers.

In the positioning map shown in Figure 5.9, Nissan did not have an advantage with regard to either safety or speed. The marketing department, after seeing the results, might try to reposition Nissan on the variable of safety. Repositioning would involve improvements in the safety features of the automobile (in the design and manufacturing departments), a promotional campaign to inform consumers of these changes (marketing), public relations releases announcing the results of new safety tests when they favor the company, and an overall company focus on safety. Such a strategy includes informing all employees about the new approach and rewarding those who suggest innovations and improvements related to safety of the automobiles. If successful, a future positioning map would show Nissan moving up on perceptions of safety.

The Hyundai example from earlier in this chapter serves as an example of effective repositioning. The company moved from perceptions of being cheap and low quality to a new position based on improved consumer perceptions of quality.

Repositioning cannot be viewed as a quick and easy fix. It takes time to change public views of a company, especially when the organization has experienced brand damage in some way, when consumer preferences have changed, or when international events, such as a war or an economic shift, have taken place. Some evidence suggests that it can take up to six years for consumer perceptions of quality to shift.[44]

In 2004, Findomestic, an Italian bank, began to reposition the service as one that stressed responsibility. Support was provided to consumers that wanted guidance on how to use credit more responsibly. A code of ethics was established for the company and a guide was provided to consumers about financial responsibility. Even with these steps, the company's leaders were disappointed in the results and so, to better communicate with consumers, in 2010 the first television campaign in the history of the company was rolled out. Time will tell if the repositioning effort will be successful.[45]

Sustainability and International Positioning

Sustainable business practices can be a method to differentiate a business from its competitors. Positioning a company, business practice, and product as being more environmentally conscious allows the organization to occupy a unique space in the minds of consumers. Sustainable business practices have become popular around the world.

The potential benefits created by a sustainable position have led to growing concerns about greenwashing tactics. **Greenwashing** is the practice where company leaders exaggerate or even fabricate the degree of the sustainable or green activities taking place in the organization. Treating sustainability as a fad, instead of a core value of the company, can lead to greenwashing. Figure 5.11 below provides examples of greenwashing "sins."[46]

> Greenwashing is the practice where company leaders exaggerate or even fabricate the degree of the sustainable or green activities taking place in the organization.

Greenwashing Sin	Explanation
Hidden Trade-Off	Emphasizing one environmental issue at the expense of another
No Proof	Using assertions not backed by evidence or certification
Vagueness	Using a phrase such as "All Natural" that has no meaning
Worshipping False Labels	Using images that look green but have no meaning
Irrelevance	Emphasizing a green activity unrelated to the product or not allowed by law
Lesser of Two Evils	Being green with a product that by nature is not green (e.g., organic cigarettes)
Fibbing	Making outright false statements or claims

Figure 5.11: Seven Deadly Greenwashing Sins

Many activities can help a marketing department respond to concerns about greenwashing and effectively position brands as being genuinely sustainable. When a company appears to be sincere and authentic, and to communicate sustainable practices, consumers are more inclined to believe the message. Doing so may involve a complete reinvention of the brand.

For many years, General Electric held the reputation of being a polluter and an aggressive corporate citizen. The view was partially due to management's refusal to clean up the Hudson River that the company helped to pollute. In 2005, General Electric's management team began the attempt to reposition the company as being sustainable and green. First, the company launched the Ecomagination initiative program, which included a variety of product innovations. The research and development department invented a solar-powered water purification unit that is now being used in Haiti to help supply water to that country following the 2010 earthquake. Next, the company renovated its headquarters in Vancouver to be more sustainable by adding a system to catch rain, a wastewater-treatment system, and a rooftop garden.[47] These activities build trust with consumers; company actions have repositioned General Electric as sustainable and socially responsible.

Truly green programs are accepted and acclaimed in many international settings. In future years, going green may become less of a positioning advantage if most companies follow the trend.

Ethical Issues in International Positioning

In the area of positioning, two ethical concerns have arisen. The first is the role that positioning can play in encouraging consumption. This may drive consumers to purchase things they do not need or to envy those who can afford the product. In essence, positioning may be viewed as leading to envy and greed.

Second, positioning often seems to make the promise that the consumer will become younger, prettier, or more popular. The ethical issue is in regard to body image and self-image when products are marketed in terms of intangible benefits that are based on social standing. Positioning based on social status has been criticized as unethical and a driver of low self-esteem. Instead, critics argue, products should be differentiated in terms of benefits present in the product or its use that are not based on social status or unrealistic hopes for improved personal appearance. The issue becomes magnified when consumers in less- or least-developed countries are the target market.

Chapter 5: Review and Resources

STRATEGIC IMPLICATIONS //

As has been described earlier, three basic strategic approaches to the overall direction of a company include cost leadership, differentiation, and focus. These strategies represent the broadest, most strategic perspective on positioning. A business that emphasizes differentiation will use the approach to position all of its products, even when the point of difference changes from product to product. In the international marketplace, effective generic strategy positioning will be a key element in the success of an operation.

When entering a new market, a key element will be establishing an effective position. The specific positioning present in one country may not be ideal in others. Many fast-food restaurants cannot be positioned as low-cost leaders in emerging markets because the cost of a meal represents a sundry purchase to many consumers. Instead, in many countries McDonalds has repositioned itself as a high service, "American" place to eat.[48]

Strategic positioning focuses on the benefits or value that a product or company provides to customers. The most ideal circumstance occurs when this benefit transfers across national boundaries. An important consideration is the role of country-of-origin effects as companies enter new countries. The country image for the company or the brand may hinder the company's ability to position itself in the same way as it does in a domestic market.

Most of the time, a local company will already occupy the position sought by the competitor entering the market. To respond, the marketing team might undertake repositioning based on some other attribute, or the company could aggressively compete with the local competitor. Repositioning may injure the company's image, especially when marketing messages are viewed in other markets. Aggressively competing with local competitors risks alienating the exact customers a company intends to pursue.

TACTICAL IMPLICATIONS //

Tactical efforts are undertaken to support the position a company's marketers wish to reach. The product's package and label will be altered to fit the legal and cultural dictates of a nation and a given target market. Legal requirements vary as to any promise of a product benefit as well as labeling of content, including statements about country of origin. Promotional programs would be adjusted as well. Cultural differences often dictate more careful wording of advertisements when seeking to position, reposition, or enhance the position of a product.

The French culture is quite open about sexuality, but the French do not view sex as something that should be presented in a humorous fashion. Any product or service that has an element of sexuality would be positioned without the use of funny ads in order to be successful in that market.

Other promotional tactics can help create and maintain positioning. A promotion such as a contest may be construed as essentially "gambling" in a given culture, which would in turn affect the brand's image and position. Promotions represent an opportunity to communicate to consumers about the attributes and benefits of the product.

The core of product positioning at both the strategic and tactical levels rests with the product itself. Effective positioning should be based on what the product itself does well in comparison to competitor products. This lowers barriers to consumer acceptance of promotional activity, and grounds consumer attitudes in product features. Benefits may be intangible or tangible, but attempts to position products in ways incompatible with the actual features of the product will eventually fail.

OPERATIONAL IMPLICATIONS //

Successful positioning is best supported at the operational level through communication and consistency. Individuals working with the company should be aware of the position of the brand. Position should be reflected in all operational activities, including distribution, sales, promotion, and all other components of the marketing mix. The focus on positioning ensures a consistent message at all contact points.

Positioning processes become more complicated in international settings. A company should, whenever possible, present consistent positioning in all markets. With travel and relatively global communications, consumers will eventually be exposed to messages from different countries or regions. These communications should support the overall positioning of the firm.

In summary, international positioning processes should be consistent with those used in domestic markets. The underlying characteristics of the product plus the expertise of the company should drive this consistency. Emphasizing a product attribute in one product and a different attribute in another, or trying to leverage one company skill in one market and a different skill in another, becomes costly and problematic. Efficiencies can be gained from consistency and focus; the position that emerges for the company and brand helps lead to long-term success.

TERMS

product position	country-of-origin effect	tangible product benefits
product positioning	country image	intangible product benefits
positioning statement	animosity	positioning maps
differentiation	nationalism	repositioning
brand equity	religiosity	greenwashing
brand parity	sovereignty	

REVIEW QUESTIONS

1. Define product positioning.
2. What are the two key elements of product positioning?
3. Define differentiation. What are some examples?
4. How does differentiation help create brand equity?
5. Define brand parity and give an example.
6. In what ways does technology influence global positioning?
7. Define the country-of-origin effect.
8. What do the terms *animosity* and *ethnocentrism* mean?
9. Define nationalism. How is it different from animosity?
10. Define sovereignty.
11. What are the different country-of-origin label options?
12. What are the complicating factors for identifying country of origin?
13. What is product versus product positioning?
14. Define product line.
15. What is product line versus product line positioning?
16. What is the difference between brand versus brand positioning, and company versus company positioning?
17. How does positioning relate to price?
18. Describe tangible product benefits and intangible product benefits concepts.

19. How do positioning maps show differentiation?

20. What is the difference between share of mind and share of heart?

21. What are the different ways to enhance a product's position?

22. Define repositioning.

23. Define greenwashing and name the seven deadly sins of greenwashing.

24. What is the change in focus some companies need to make when positioning at the bottom-of-the-pyramid?

25. What ethical concerns does positioning present?

DISCUSSION QUESTIONS

1. There are at least six effective methods for positioning products: (1) competitors, (2) use or application, (3) price-quality relationship, (4) product user, (5) product class, and (6) cultural symbol. Identify two brands associated with the following countries:

   - United States
   - Mexico
   - United Kingdom
   - Japan
   - Netherlands

   Identify the positioning strategy each uses, then suggest an alternative strategy.

2. Choose a product category and make a list of five brands, three of which are not made in the United States. Identify two attributes that are common across these five brands. Using the perspective of a college student (meaning you are part of the target market), create a positioning map for these brands and then interpret the map.

3. Identify two products that compete at each of the following levels, in at least two countries besides the United States. Explain how the competition might influence positioning strategies.

   - Product versus product
   - Product line versus product line
   - Brand versus brand
   - Company versus company
   - Industry versus industry

4. Ethnocentrism, animosity, nationalism, and religiosity all influence consumer perceptions of products. Consider how these factors influence positioning for the following brands when entering France, Thailand, and Saudi Arabia:

   - Royal Dutch Shell
   - Starbucks
   - Haier
   - Carrefour

5. Visit a local retailer and find five products with country-of-origin labels. What countries are they from? How does country of origin relate to product attributes or sophistication? How does it influence the position for the product?

ANALYTICAL AND INTERNET EXERCISES

1. Many companies do not emphasize home country status. As a result, many consumers are unaware of the country or origin for many brands. Research online the home countries for the following companies or brands:

   - Firestone
   - 7-11 Convenience Stores
   - Ben & Jerry's Ice Cream
   - Samsung
   - The Wall Street Journal
   - Smith and Wesson

- Rolls Royce
- Adidas
- Lego
- Burger King
- Huffy Bicycles
- Nokia
- Red Bull
- Volvo

2. Differentiation can be created and/or reinforced by promotional activities. Visit the websites of the following companies and use the home pages to identify how they are differentiated.

- Sony (sony.com)
- The Tata Group (tata.com)
- Hyundia (hyundia.com)
- Starbucks (starbucks.com)
- Mango (mango.com)
- The Mandarin Oriental Hotel Bangkok (mandarinoriental.com/Bangkok)

3. Food is subject to a particularly high level of regulation. Examine the Food and Drug Administration food labeling requirements website (www.fda.gov/Food/GuidanceComplianceRegulatoryInformation/GuidanceDocuments/FoodLabelingNutrition/FoodLabelingGuide/default.htm). What is the benefit of the labeling process? What is the cost? How might it influence international positioning?

4. One product that has enjoyed international success is Turkish Delight candy. Many companies, including Nestlé, produce versions of the product. In Turkey, firms such as Tatlisumak and Pinar Kuruyemis produce and sell the delicacy both domestically and in other countries. Most Turkish citizens are proud of their local culture and products. Construct individual maps exhibiting share of mind and share of heart for Nestlé, Tatlisumak, Pinar Kuruyemis, a British confectioner that produces "lumps of delight" for Turkey, Great Britain, and Mexico. Explain how differences in status in these countries would affect positioning or the product as well as other international marketing programs for them.

▶ ONLINE VIDEOS

Visit **www.sagepub.com/baack** to view these chapter videos:

Video Link 5.1: Global Markets

Video Link 5.2: Language

Video Link 5.3: Economies in Transition

🌐 STUDENT STUDY SITE

Visit **www.sagepub.com/baack** to access these additional learning tools:

- Web Quizzes
- eFlashcards
- SAGE Journal Articles
- Country Fact Sheets
- Chapter Outlines
- Interactive Maps

CASE 5 ///

TOTO: Positioning Plumbing Products Globally

TOTO is the world's largest manufacturer of toilets, producing more than 7 million units each year. The Japanese company was founded in 1917, with "TOTO" being an abbreviation of the two Japanese words forming its full name: Toyo Toki. Although the company manufactures a complete line of plumbing supplies, the company is best known for its high-end, innovative toilets.[49]

TOTO enjoys a consistent position across markets, and differentiates from competitors by being the leader in innovation. With 5% of revenues going to research and development (R&D) and an army of 1,500 engineers, the company remains at the cutting-edge of toilet technology. The company's Washlet Zoe was listed in the Guinness Book of Records as the world's most sophisticated toilet in 2005.[50]

TOTO holds its position based on beliefs about company innovations combined with an emphasis on sustainability. The company began designing water-conserving toilets before many governments began to focus on this improvement. The Aquia introduced in 2005 has a 1.6-gallon flush for bulk waste and a 0.9 gallon flush for light or liquid waste. The Aquia saves an estimated 20% more water than an ultra-low flow toilet.[51] TOTO also invented and introduced the tankless toilet, which leads to less material waste in manufacturing and a more efficient flush.

TOTO's success has been largely based on its patented invention of the Washlet, an automated, remote-controlled cleaning nozzle. A consumer pushes a button and a nozzle extends to warm-water rinse and then warm-air dry. The nozzle moves back-and-forth resulting in a clean so thorough that the company claims that no toilet paper is needed. This makes the nozzle not only innovative but also green—it eliminates paper waste. The nozzle then retracts and self-cleans before the next usage. The products were first introduced in 1980 and have sold 18 million units worldwide. Washlets are highly popular in Japan and hold 60% of the market share for toilets.[52]

The Washlet is one of many company innovations the company has made. TOTO also features "smart toilets" that offer various luxury features such as a heated-seat, hands-free automatic flushing, tank-less toilets, built-in air-purifying systems, remote control adjustable heated seat temperatures, an energy-saver timer that turns off the toilet during low usage time periods, and even medical sensors to measure blood sugar, pulse, and blood pressure. In Japan, a popular feature in women's restrooms are small speakers that play music to mask any sounds made while the consumer uses the toilet.[53] Two other recent innovations are the automatic closing and opening lid, which the company markets as a "marriage saver," and a rimless design for the bowl, which keeps the bowl cleaner longer.[54]

As TOTO has become increasingly dominant in the Japanese market, with over 70% of households using the company's products, global expansion has become necessary to continue growth.[55] The company currently operates in the following countries:

- China
- Taiwan
- Thailand
- United States
- Indonesia
- Vietnam
- India

TOTO enjoys a consistent position across markets, and differentiates from competitors by being the leader in innovation.

TOTO has maintained a consistent position as it has moved into the new markets. Targeting the high-end, "global" market segment, the company emphasizes innovation and sustainability consistently in all of these markets. The newest toilet added to its product line, the Neorest, can cost up to $5,900 in the United States and has been called the world's most expensive toilet.[56]

In the United States, the company has taken specific steps to project an innovative, green position. To maintain this green reputation, TOTO continues to sell green products and actively participates in the United States Green Build Council. The company has built ties with local communities in Atlanta, where TOTO USA is headquartered, and in the company's manufacturing plant in Morrow, Georgia. The plant has many innovative sustainable components. The water used at the plant is cleaned before being returned to the county.

TOTO has also attempted to remove American consumer resistance to its innovations, especially the Washlet. In 2007, the company started a promotional campaign to encourage Washlet usage. The company used a comparison to dirty dishes at the core of the campaign. It asked the question "Would you use toilet paper to clean dishes?" The company placed a billboard in Times Square in New York with six naked buttocks and the phrase "Clean is happy. No ifs, ands, or . . . " blocking the more potentially scandalous part of the image.

The company's marketing team realizes that one promotional campaign will not be enough to remove the taboo surrounding its products and use of the Washlet. Instead, a long-term view has been taken.

The Washlet faced the same resistance in Japan when TOTO first introduced the product in the early 1980s. TOTO used a similar promotional message "Oshiri datte arattehoshii" (Even buttocks want to be cleaned) to promote the product when it was introduced in Japan. Critics respond that the concern is not the taboo, it is the time involved. Americans are not as technology oriented as the Japanese and focus more on convenience. The Washlet may seem interesting, but consumers in the United States may settle for the convenience and speed of toilet paper.[57]

Regardless of initial success or struggles in the American market, TOTO continues to be positioned as the global leader in toilet technology. This positioning, across all markets, differentiates the company globally, and provides the foundation for future success.

1. Discuss the challenges TOTO might encounter when seeking to maintain a consistent position globally.

2. How might regulatory activities affect TOTO as it enters markets?

3. Create a positioning map for the TOTO using the attributes green and price.

4. TOTO targets high-end consumers in their markets. What are some other potential segmenting factors for the company's target market?

5. It is possible that competitors may follow TOTO's lead by focusing on innovation and green products. What will need to happen before TOTO should consider repositioning? What is a potential attribute that the company could emphasize if repositioning? Would share of mind and share of heart become part of this analysis in some way? Why or why not?

Market Research in the International Environment

LEARNING OBJECTIVES

After reading and studying this chapter, you should be able to answer the following questions:

1. How can market researchers effectively employ the scientific method to improve the quality of a marketing program?

2. What are the steps of the marketing research process?

3. What roles do primary data, secondary data, validity, and reliability play in the process of designing an international marketing research program?

4. What techniques can be used when developing samples and collecting data for international marketing research?

5. What factors complicate the analysis and interpretation of data in international marketing research?

IN THIS CHAPTER

Focus on Cosmetics

Notions of "beauty" carry a wide variety of concepts, interpretations, contrasts, and cultural idiosyncrasies. Differing opinions regarding what is "beautiful" vary by individual taste, family collectives, regions, and nations, whether the topic is art, music, geographic landscape, or human attractiveness. The vast divergence in views of beauty creates numerous marketing opportunities.

Cosmetics and make-up products are sold worldwide. Evidence of make-up and cosmetics are found in ancient Egypt, when women changed their hair color with henna and drew kohl around their eyes. Members of society in Rome and Greece also used various forms of make-up.

In some countries, wearing cosmetics is considered to be culturally unacceptable, except under highly restricted circumstances. Still, some women seek to adorn themselves. Iran recently banned women from wearing make-up while on television, because according to national leaders, doing so violated the Sharia, or Islamic law.[1] In nations with less strict interpretations of Muslim law, women are allowed to wear make-up only in the presence of their husbands or with other women, but not in public. Even then, moderation is the guideline.

At the opposite extreme, high fashion often includes the outlandish use of eyeliner, lipstick, rouge, or other colors and enhancers, foundation and make-up. Highly visible fashion shows include displays of the latest cutting-edge cosmetics. Often these trends move into the entertainment industry, high society, and eventually into other public segments.

Factors such as skin color influence make-up choices. African women may prefer golden natural make-up combined with long false eyelashes.[2] The traditional Japanese form of make-up includes a white powdery foam coupled with bright lipstick.

Currently, many new forces shape or have an impact on what women seek to wear. The Internet and social media make it possible to see how others dress up around the world. Fashion trends that begin in Great Britain may soon find their ways into department stores and cosmetics counters in a variety of countries.

To take advantage of the many opportunities presented by the cosmetics industry, careful market research will be in order. The marketing team examines what women in any given target market seek to wear based on local tradition and culture, religious and governmental regulations, emerging trends, concepts of beauty, and other factors, such as levels of disposable income.

The marketing team will seek to understand the context under which wearing make-up is acceptable. This includes noting the standard age at which young women begin using cosmetics. Special ceremonies, such as weddings, may merit more elaborate make-up; everyday life often requires little, if any.

Marketing cosmetics also deserves careful scrutiny. It may not be advisable, for example, to sell cosmetics in public places in some countries. Males may or may not be welcome salespersons. Selling methods might include a full-fledged makeover in one country but not even touching the customer in another. Advertising programs should be modified to meet local cultural constraints, as will packages and labels for cosmetic products.

In more-developed countries, make-up and cosmetics industries have started ethics debates. Some companies have been criticized for using animals to research allergic reactions to cosmetics products, creating a backlash from groups such as PETA (People for the Ethical Treatment of Animals). Others have faced reproach for *age compression marketing*, whereby younger and younger girls are encouraged to dress like adults, including the elaborate use of cosmetic products. The argument is to "let girls be girls," without all of the social pressure associated with meeting adult glamour standards at a young age.

To discover these and other cultural features, both quantitative and qualitative research will be needed. Focus groups can help a company's marketing team understand the meaning and significance of make-up in a given culture. Then, projections regarding potential sales may be made.

As is the case with other products, effective marketing of cosmetics will not occur unless company leaders understand the cultural context and other key elements of local conditions. Then, products can be designed, imported, and marketed to meet the ongoing demand many women express by purchasing the things that help them feel beautiful.

QUESTIONS FOR STUDENTS

1. How does the concept of beauty apply to cosmetics in physical, emotional, and social terms?
2. What types of market research would be best for studying cosmetics in a new country?
3. Do concepts of beauty apply to males and, if so, what type of international marketing opportunities would become available to cosmetics companies?

The use of make-up varies by country and culture.

Overview

Market research plays a vital role in connecting businesses with customers. The adage "knowledge is power" only holds true when valid information can be attained. Decisions to engage in any international marketing activity are more likely to succeed when they are based on valid and reliable market research information. Obtaining such information can be challenging. In the international context, differences in language, culture, economic systems, political and regulatory systems, technological development, and marketing infrastructures make data collection more complex (Figure 6.1). What works well in one country might not work at all in another.

International marketing researchers face an additional obstacle: the rapid pace of change occurring worldwide. Many global events quickly alter the business landscape. These developments change the types of information to be gathered as well as the methods used to collect, analyze, and store the data.

In this chapter, the scientific method and the basic international market research process are discussed first, along with differences between primary and secondary data, micro- and macro-level analysis, and qualitative and quantitative research. Next, the goals of validity and reliability in international research are described. Finally, various types of research are assessed, including all of the elements of a marketing program. Product, pricing, promotion, and distribution research are important ingredients in successful global marketing.

LEARNING OBJECTIVE #1:

How can market researchers effectively employ the scientific method to improve the quality of a marketing program?

Figure 6.1: The International Marketing Context

Market Research

Market research is the systematic gathering, storing, and analyzing of marketplace information for use in strategic decision-making.[3] The market research process links the organization with various constituent groups. Companies seeking to satisfy the wants and needs of customer groups must first understand them, which requires quality marketing information. Completing the task begins with understanding what research methods will and will not work in a targeted country, culture, or specific market. Use of the scientific method assists in collecting quality international marketing data.

The Scientific Method

> Market research techniques are based on the scientific method, a term that describes how researchers use observations, empirical evidence, and knowledge to objectively study various phenomena.

Market research techniques are based on the **scientific method**, a term that describes how researchers use observations, empirical evidence, and knowledge to objectively study various phenomena. Conducting quality research in domestic and international markets requires objectivity. It also accounts for the rapid rate of change in the global environment.

OBJECTIVITY

Objectivity plays a key role in the scientific method. Researchers try to remain objective when developing research designs and questions when collecting data, and when arriving at conclusions based on the outcomes. An objective approach requires an impersonal viewpoint of a project and the ability to avoid letting personal feelings or emotions interfere with the work.

Remaining impersonal and objective can be difficult when performing international market research. One factor that affects objectivity, the **self-reference criterion**, occurs when someone applies his or her own cultural values and background to the assessment of the behaviors of others.[4] Self-reference can lead to stereotyping members of other cultures or to unfounded beliefs about them, such as when someone believes all persons from Latin America are hot-tempered and highly romantic. The researcher seeks to set aside such stereotypes and unfounded beliefs about consumers in other cultures. This includes working to make certain language in questionnaires and other research methods is not biased and does not inflame or artificially influence the subjects in a study.

Failure to recognize the existence of these stereotypes can doom marketing efforts. In the United States, some women have a sense of obligation to achieve a degree of career success before starting a family. In contrast, many women in Spain feel less pressure to start a career and are more comfortable when making the decision to not work outside the home. These differences affect the images of women advertisers might use. A woman balancing work and children would be better received by American women than by Spanish women, for example.[5]

> One factor that affects objectivity, the self-reference criterion, occurs when someone applies his or her own cultural values and background to the assessment of the behaviors of others.

THE PACE OF CHANGE

The pace of global change should also be taken into account when conducting international research. Cultures, and cultural influences, evolve over time. What was true about a particular culture in the last decade, or even the last year, may not be true today.[6] As an example, the use of social media such as Facebook has dramatically influenced a variety of cultures through connections between persons from other cultures and countries. The effects of music, world views, and other aspects of daily life should not be underestimated. Effective market research can help ensure that the marketing strategies are based on facts and not on opinions or stereotypes.

Types of International Market Research

International marketing research is used in managerial decision-making across the entire marketing program. In this way, product, pricing, promotion, and distribution decisions are all influenced by international marketing research. Each type of research discussed below is presented in Figure 6.2.

VIDEO LINK 6.1:
Facebook

PRODUCT RESEARCH

Companies that develop products or make alterations to existing product offers often utilize product research programs. Cultural differences also affect this type of

Type	Sample Issue Addressed
Product	What product design would be most appropriate?
Pricing	How sensitive are consumers to the price?
Promotion	How do consumers react to advertising campaigns?
Distribution	What is the best method for distributing the product?

Figure 6.2: Types of International Marketing Research

international market research. Consumer responses to various products change over time. For example, the American staple, the hamburger, was once frowned upon in France. Now, however, the burger has become much more acceptable in the French culture, offering new market opportunities for American fast-food franchises.[7] Product research helps marketers stay current on changing international tastes and trends.

Taste preferences should also be considered. Coca-Cola introduced a line of drinks in China that included traditional Chinese herbal ingredients.[8] Being a truly global brand, Coca-Cola took advantage of its international market research program by adapting to the differences in taste revealed by the findings.

International product research focuses not only on consumer needs but on legal requirements and restrictions as well. Toyota adapted the engine size of its luxury brand, Lexus, in China by producing a smaller version with a sub-three-liter engine. The decision was based largely on the Chinese government's decision to raise sales taxes on vehicles with engines larger than three liters.[9] In this instance, the international legal environment changed and research helped to address the problem that was created.

PRICING RESEARCH

When the effects of pricing decisions, including the impact on consumer demand, are examined, pricing research will be used. The price of a product often represents a statement of value or worth, and signals the quality of the item being sold. The meaning of "price" varies across cultures. Cultural influences should therefore be carefully considered and researched before international pricing policies are set.

Researchers have discovered that consumers in Poland generally view price as a positive signal of quality. Consumers are less likely to connect a product's price with quality in the United States. This finding would suggest that marketers in the United States commonly use pricing as a method to entice quick sales. In Poland, price changes, especially discounts, may be used less often.[10]

PROMOTION RESEARCH

When researchers study the effectiveness of promotional messages, the method is called promotion research. In international marketing research, cultural differences dictate that researchers should take careful steps to make sure the message in an advertisement is the message that the company intended to deliver. The marketing team at Pizza Hut realized that changes needed to be made in the way the brand was promoted in Hong Kong. Consumers sought not only good food but also more involvement in the process of how the food was delivered. After the advertising messages were adjusted to this cultural nuance, sales for the chain began to take off.[11]

One particularly relevant area in promotion research is cultural sensitivity to what advertising messages are considered to be either acceptable or unacceptable in foreign cultures. Given that many advertising campaigns are now implemented on a global scale, market researchers assess how consumers in other countries react to advertising campaigns. The use of overtly sexual imagery in television commercials, for example, is generally viewed as being offensive in some East Asian cultures.[12] Consumers in collectivist cultures such as China react differently to advertisements than would consumers in more individualistic cultures, including Germany. One recent study addressed this issue and revealed that, in general, Chinese consumers more often rated offensive advertisements as uncomfortable, disgusting, and impolite than did their German counterparts.[13]

A nation's topography affects international marketing research programs.

DISTRIBUTION RESEARCH

Distribution research examines the most effective methods for distributing products to consumers on an international scale. Distribution research takes on special importance because infrastructure development varies greatly around the world. As a result, gaining a better understanding of the physical distribution methods available in a targeted country constitutes an important task for the market researcher.

Many countries worldwide suffer from poor transportation capabilities, often due to economic deprivation or topography. Nepal, for example, is largely a mountainous country. The mountains and rugged hills make public transportation difficult. Roads are generally concentrated in the eastern and central regions of the country. Although air and rail transportation are available, difficulties exist in the physical distribution of goods and services in Nepal and similar countries.

Distribution research can also be used to gain a better understanding of the efficiencies of existing distribution systems. One recent study revealed a significant level of cost inefficiency in the retail grocery distribution system in Spain.[14] Consequently, distribution strategies aimed at improving efficiency would greatly benefit marketing programs in Spain. Consumer behavior, as it relates to distribution management, should also be considered. In China, many grocery shoppers arrive at supermarkets on foot, thereby limiting the amount of goods they can carry home.[15] Shopping is different there than in many regions of Europe and much of North America.

The International Market Research Process

Although market research projects can vary based on a situation, the market research process normally follows a well-established set of steps, which are highlighted in Figure 6.3. The process can take a good deal of time. International marketing decisions require

LEARNING OBJECTIVE #2:

What are the steps of the marketing research process?

Step 1	Define the problem or situation.
Step 2	Complete a cost/benefit analysis.
Step 3	Develop a research design.
Step 4	Develop a sample.
Step 5	Collect data.
Step 6	Analyze and interpret data.
Step 7	Formulate conclusions and write a report.

Figure 6.3: The Market Research Process

careful deliberation. Samsung Electronics, for example, began market research in India a full year before attempting to enter the marketplace.[16] In international marketing terms, a single year can be considered to be a relatively short time frame. To ensure that marketing managers capture the best information possible when considering international marketing strategies and tactics, ample time should be allowed.

Define the Problem or Situation

Defining the problem or situation that an organization faces constitutes the first step in the market research process. Correctly defining the company's market research issue will be critical to the success of any market research project. An inadequately or hastily defined problem or situation can lead to flawed data and conclusions.

Researchers take cultural differences into account early in the process. A problem in one culture may simply not exist in another. For example, the marketing team may decide that a sales promotion did not succeed in a domestic market due to declining sales levels across the product category. This may be a non-issue in other countries, however, because sales promotions have never been used as extensively in those countries. The sales promotion problem does not exist in the foreign market, but other marketing issues may be present. Consequently, it may be difficult for managers to communicate the problem effectively across varied markets and stakeholders. Correctly identifying the problem represents a continuing concern for market researchers, made worse by language, behavioral, and cultural differences in an international context.

Another roadblock to precisely identifying a problem emerges from the ways products are evaluated. Consumers in Portugal may report they are satisfied with a brand of toothpaste whereas consumers in Canada report they are not. Portuguese consumers may base their answers on satisfaction on good breath, whereas Canadians base their responses on perceptions of healthy teeth. In other words, differing criteria regarding the same product have been used during the evaluation. As a result, a research team from Portugal might not understand why the product struggles in Canada.

Marketers can define and assess a problem by asking if the problem as stated represents the actual issue or merely a symptom of the problem. Declining sales may be the symptom of a larger problem such as negative publicity, a design defect in the product, or an innovation by a competitor. American Apparel, the trendy, edgy clothing company, faced declining sales in 2010. The marketing team tried to discover whether the apparel was no longer popular or if lower sales resulted from the recent recession. At the time, the company had aggressively expanded, which might also have been the cause of the problem. The marketing team used discounts and sales promotions to clear out inventory at about the same time, which possibly influenced consumer perceptions of the company. To try to understand what actually transpired, marketing research should be conducted.[17]

Complete a Cost/Benefit Analysis

In most business decisions, the costs and benefits of engaging in an activity are assessed early in the process. The same holds true for international market research. In general, international decisions require a degree of research. Some research projects may be performed at a relatively low cost. Other international research techniques involve significant monetary investments.

Making the decision to proceed with research requires the marketing team to compare the importance of obtaining the required information and the time frame within which the information will be collected against the value of the benefits of acquiring the information and the overall difficulty in obtaining the data.[18] The availability and type of data needed to address the problem can drive up costs. The overall research budget influences these decisions. Whenever possible, sufficient resources should be made available to conduct quality research.

Develop a Research Design

Several issues emerge when developing the design of the research, in both domestic and international markets. Decisions revolve around the use of secondary or primary data, reliability and validity, micro- or macrolevel analysis, and quantitative or qualitative research.

SECONDARY DATA

In many cases, data can be gathered from various external research sources. **Secondary data** are collected by an outside agency and are made available free of charge or for a fee. The information can be relatively inexpensive to obtain and many sources of secondary data are available.

One powerful source of secondary data comes from the U.S. Department of Commerce website (www.stat-usa.gov). Other important sources include the Department of Commerce International Trade Association (www.trade.gov) and Euromonitor (www.euromonitor.com). Several secondary sources of international market research information are listed in Figure 6.4. Information may be obtained from many of these sites free of charge.

Although secondary data sources offer convenience, this type of data often presents problems when used to make many marketing decisions. While all of the sites listed in Figure 6.4 are reputable, secondary information should always be scrutinized carefully. Marketers may struggle to find details regarding the collection of data for government statistics. For instance, the Chinese National Bureau of Statistics keeps many of its data collection methods secret. In response, private research agencies often calculate separate measures of key country-level statistics. In 2011, this private research revealed that property prices more than doubled from 2004 to 2010, but the National Bureau of Statistics generated results suggesting only a 50% increase.[19] Outside marketers would want to study both sources of data and consider whether either source would be motivated to skew the figures.

When examining international markets, it can be difficult to compare data and information from one country to another. Consider the problem of accessing market viability. Researchers can easily obtain secondary data about imports and exports in a market. Simply knowing the level of imports and exports in one country versus another provides limited information regarding the market attractiveness of either country. Imports may be low in a particular country, but the demand for a specific product may be high. Consequently, the researcher will try to obtain additional information to be able to draw informed conclusions about the market's viability.

LEARNING OBJECTIVE #3:

What roles do primary data, secondary data, validity, and reliability play in the process of designing an international marketing research program?

U.S. Department of Commerce, www.commerce.gov/
U.S. Department of Commerce International Trade Association, www.trade.gov
Euromonitor, www.euromonitor.com
Organisation of Economic Co-operation and Development, www.oecd.org
International Monetary Fund, www.imf.org
CIA-The World Factbook, https://www.cia.gov/library/publications/the-world-factbook/index.html
World Information, Ltd., www.worldinformation.com
The World Bank, www.worldbank.org
United Nations International Trade Statistics Yearbook, http://unstats.un.org/unsd/trade/default.htm
Europa, www.europa.eu
World Economic Forum, www.weforum.org/en/index.htm
GlobalEdge, http://globaledge.msu.edu/
Economist Country Briefings, www.economist.com/topics (search for specific countries within the topics)
The World Bank "Doing Business," http://doingbusiness.org/
Transparency International, http://transparency.org/
Internet World Stats, http://internetworldstats.com

Figure 6.4: Secondary Sources for International Market Research

Many secondary resource services are available in the United States. Although secondary sources may be offered in other developed nations, far fewer sources will be available in less-developed countries. Some of the data may not be available for specific regions of a country. Even when they are, these data may not be offered a form that will be useful to the research team. This makes data collection from only secondary sources more challenging.

PRIMARY DATA

Primary data are gathered by the researcher or research team. They are collected in the form chosen by the researcher and can be gathered in practically any region of the world. Primary data can take many forms, as displayed in Figure 6.5.

A questionnaire can be given to members of a potential target market. The items should be carefully translated to the language of the target market to make certain no confusion emerges. Telephone and Internet surveys serve the same purpose. The data gathered will only be as effective as the skill levels of those conducting the interviews. Primary data can be drawn from interviews of customers in a store after they have purchased an item (the mall intercept method) or by questioning members in a focus group. Cultural norms should be carefully followed. For instance, in some nations

Questionnaires
Telephone and Internet Surveys
Interviews of Customers
Ethnographic Studies
Observational Studies

Figure 6.5: Primary Sources for International Market Research

interrupting someone after the individual purchases an item may be perceived as an aggressive invasion of privacy.

Other forms of primary data collection are ethnographic studies and observational studies. An ethnographic study takes place when a researcher studies respondents in their native environment by living with them. Observational studies focus on observing consumers as they shop, as they interact in the marketplace, or as they use products in the home. Researchers can also quietly observe in-store signage and displays, pricing methods, tactics used by members of the sales force, and methods of payment. By performing a store visit, the researcher can also make a purchase to observe sales experience in person.

Primary data can be difficult to collect in certain regions, and can also be costly. Effective primary data collection requires a staff of trained and experienced researchers. When the company budgets adequate resources, primary data may prove to be more valuable than data available from secondary sources. The value of primary data is that they are collected in exactly the form as desired by the researcher. Primary data may be especially valuable in international marketing because secondary sources vary dramatically by country and by region.

RELIABILITY AND VALIDITY

In any research design, reliability and validity constitute important standards. Without these two factors, research results become far less useful. Marketing professionals endeavor to make sure both criteria can be met when developing a research project.

Reliability

In survey research, **reliability** refers to the degree to which the items used to measure a concept are internally consistent with each other and the extent to which the findings are repeatable over time. Measures are considered to be internally consistent when they appear to measure the same concept.

> In survey research, reliability refers to the degree to which the items used to measure a concept are internally consistent with each other and the extent to which the findings are repeatable over time.

To demonstrate reliability, a researcher will use more than one measure when assessing marketing concepts. In a situation in which a researcher seeks to measure a consumer's perception of "media accuracy" in her home country, the decision could be to ask the respondent to agree or disagree with research statements, such as

- In general, the media in my country are credible.
- I feel a good deal of confidence in the news I read daily.
- The newscasters in my country do not attempt to lead their viewers astray.

These items appear to be consistent with one another. A scale demonstrates reliability when results are similar across times. In other words, if the survey were given again, answers from the original persons who took the survey should be consistent with persons taking it for the first time.

Validity

In survey research, **validity** refers to the extent to which responses to a measure reflect the actual differences in the concept found across respondents, or the overall level of accuracy of the measure itself. A measure can be internally consistent, or repeatable, but not valid. A scale in a bathroom, for example, could consistently reveal someone's weight to be 210 pounds. If so, it could be said that the scale is reliable. If, however, the person's true weight is 190 pounds, the scale did not indicate a valid finding.

Reliability and validity constitute important concepts for marketing experiments as well. Two types of validity influence the outcomes of experiments. **Internal validity** results when *cause-and-effect* relationships have been correctly identified by the research. A study that accurately predicts that lowering prices by 10% will increase the likelihood a customer in South Korea will immediately buy a new cell phone by 25% is internally valid.

External validity means that the statement of cause and effect would apply to other situations or settings. In other words, if a 10% price reduction would also increase the likelihood of a customer purchase by 25% in Paraguay, the study would exhibit external validity. The most powerful external validity emerges if the research indicates that a 10% price reduction of *any item* would result in the same level of change in buyer behavior, regardless of the country involved. The reliability of an experiment is assessed by the degree to which the findings are replicated using subjects drawn from the same population.

> Internal validity results when cause-and-effect relationships have been correctly identified by the research.

Validity and reliability are more difficult to assess when using secondary data because the researcher does not control the method used to collect the data. Primary data allow the researcher to assess reliability and validity using various statistical techniques.

MICRO-LEVEL ANALYSIS

A micro-level analysis seeks to understand the attitudes, preferences, motivations, lifestyles, and intentions of individual consumers. Many companies perform this type of analysis for international market research projects. Primary data fit with the micro level of analysis. Micro-level analyses account for language, culture, and other factors that affect or influence individual consumers.

MACRO-LEVEL ANALYSIS

A macro-level analysis often occurs at the country level. The selection of a country to enter requires research devoted to political and legal risk, which, in turn, affect the selection of target markets in various countries. Secondary data can often be used to research macro-level factors, including governmental forms and entry risk.

Political Risk

VIDEO LINK 6.2:
Unions and
Collective Bargaining

Governmental stability and governmental interactions with businesses are topics of concern for international marketers. When entering a market, **political risk**, or the potential for political forces and governmental activities to hamper and harm business activities within a country, should be considered. Political risk reflects the stability of the country being analyzed. Assessing this type of risk involves answering important questions, as displayed in Figure 6.6.

A complete on-the-ground research effort would be the best method to answer these questions; however, it may be expensive and time-consuming. For preliminary market screening, a variety of sovereign credit rating services are available. Moody's and Standard & Poor's provides information that focuses on currency stability, which can be used as a proxy measure of overall country risk.

When assessing political risk, the marketing team considers how the product relates to the government in question. Alcohol, for example, remains a politically sensitive product and is outlawed in many Islamic countries. Other products are allowed but are likely to be highly regulated. These include children's toys, pharmaceuticals, and birth control products.

- What is the chance of a governmental collapse?
- What is the potential for a different government to take power through democratic or other means?
- What effects would a change in government have on business activities?
- What is the role of labor unions in the country?
- What are the limits on corporate political activity?
- Is the country's currency stable?

Figure 6.6: Assessing Political Risk

Terrorism, or the use of violence and the threat of violence as a means to gain political advantage, runs rampant in several countries. Business leaders consider the potential for a terrorist attack as part of the study of a country. The Pakistani government estimated an economic loss in the billions from 2004 to 2010 due to terrorism. From July of 2009 to April to 2010 the country experienced a 45% drop in foreign direct investment largely due to security concerns.[20] Many companies avoid countries with elevated levels of terrorist activity.

Legal Risk

Legal risks are those associated with the laws present in a country, and the enforcement of those laws. Legal systems vary dramatically across the globe. Not all countries have well-defined laws and marketers cannot assume that legal infractions will always be pursued by authorities.

In the area of legal risk, the extent to which patents, copyrights, and intellectual property rights are protected in various countries remains an important issue for international marketers. Many countries do not offer these protections. Others have such laws but fail to enforce them.

Glodok, a section of Central Jakarta in Indonesia, was the target of high-visibility intellectual property raids in 2010. These raids were touted by the government as signs of enforcement, but many viewed them as only cosmetic. Experts estimate more than 550 million counterfeit CDs and DVDs were sold in 2008. The sales result in 1.4 trillion *rupiah* ($154 million) in lost revenues. The raiding of a small number of vendors selling pirated goods does little to stop the problem, and the legal risk remains for foreign companies entering the country.[21]

 **International Marketing in Daily Life**

Methods of Transportation

Traveling continues to be a basic human need. Modes of transportation vary widely. In many parts of the world, a motorbike represents the most practical and economical choice, which creates a large target market for many companies. The recent Honda Diamond Blue motorbike introduced in Vietnam in September of 2010 is an almost perfect replica of the Vespa LX, which is manufactured in Vietnam by the Italian company Piaggio. Some critics might argue that Honda was infringing on Piaggio's intellectual property. In fact, Honda had nothing to do with the Honda Diamond Blue. Instead, the motorbike is manufactured by Vietnam Shipbuilding Industry and Motorbike Corporation (Vinashin Motor) who copied Vespa's design and used Honda's brand name. Vietnam is signatory to international intellectual property treaties with Italy and Japan governments in both countries are considering taking legal action. The odds of success in legal actions are low, because Vinashin Motor is a subsidiary of a state-owned company and the Vietnamese government has already signaled that it will support the company's actions.[22]

In summary, numerous factors should be considered when making decisions about marketing in other countries. Most research projects that assess other countries require both micro- and macro-level data collection. Macro-level information can often be gathered from secondary sources whereas micro-level information may need primary data collection.

QUALITATIVE AND QUANTITATIVE RESEARCH

Numerous research designs are available to international marketing researchers to collect micro-level information. Researchers begin by choosing to use qualitative research, quantitative research, or a combination of both. The major types of qualitative and quantitative research methods are presented in Figure 6.7.

Qualitative Methods
Ethnographic Research Design
Observation
Focus Groups
Personal Interviews
Delphi Technique
Quantitative Methods
Survey
Experiments
Test Markets

Figure 6.7: Qualitative and Quantitative Research Methods

QUALITATIVE METHODS

The focus will be on obtaining information without relying on numerical expressions or measurements when **qualitative research designs** are employed. These research methods center on understanding the meanings of consumer responses to the researcher's questions. The information gained can prove to be valuable in an international context. Qualitative research designs are particularly useful when seeking to understand a given culture.[23]

Deriving meanings from consumer responses requires the researcher to interpret data from various groups of people. Qualitative methods are *researcher dependent*, which means that the researcher subjectively analyzes the information that has been collected. The use of a qualitative research design typically limits the number of respondents or research subjects included in a sample. The sample size or response rate needed has a strong impact on the decision to use qualitative research designs.

Cultural norms can preclude the use of many qualitative research designs. In some cultures, consumers are hesitant to express their opinions in front of others, due to factors that might not be considered by the researcher. In China, workers with young children may receive higher salaries than those without. Some workers may lie about having children, which in turn may make them reluctant to reveal the truth when talking to a researcher.[24]

Ethnographic Research Design

In some circumstances, only certain types of qualitative research designs are useful. As discussed previously, an ethnographic research design is one in which the researcher studies respondents in their native environment by living or interacting with them. This provides a viable option in certain situations. What emerges are "thick descriptions" of

Cultural limitations can preclude the use of many qualitative research designs, such as journals.

cultural patterns, shopping habits, and other features of the area. Marketing managers at Unilever's Indian subsidiary, Hindustan Lever, are required to spend two months living in rural villages after being hired. Doing so allows them to see how consumers interact with the company's products.[25]

Observational Studies

Observational studies involve a researcher watching consumers as they shop and make purchases. This approach may prove to be fruitful for some international studies. One difficulty can be that in some cultures staring at another person is considered to be rude and consumers might be uncomfortable when they discover that they are being observed. As with other international decisions, researchers carefully consider the customs of consumers in the targeted countries before proceeding. While there may be difficulties for an obvious foreigner to surreptitiously observe others, observational data can be an effective method to garner rich, in-depth data, which may be especially helpful when attempting to overcome the self-reference criterion problem.

Focus Groups

Focus groups are semi-structured or unstructured group discussions that generally take place in groups of eight to twelve. A focus group *moderator* facilitates the discussion and does his or her best to ensure that each member of the focus group has an opportunity to contribute and give opinions. Focus groups are used extensively in market research, in both domestic and international marketing research contexts. Researchers are advised to consider the specific issues and challenges that emerge when conducting focus groups.

Focus group moderators in international settings consider language differences across cultures, nonverbal cues, and cultural customs.[26] A focus group held in China should include a number of younger consumers mixed in with older consumers in order to minimize peer pressure to yield to older consumers' opinions as a sign of respect.[27]

Eye contact, touching other persons, and posture may all affect a focus group. Staring someone in the eyes may be viewed as aggressive in one culture but essential in another. Raising one's voice may be expected in an African or Latin American focus group but considered rude and boorish in Asia.

Focus groups can offer an effective method of obtaining information directly from consumers. When conducting focus groups in other countries, the marketing team includes native speakers to help analyze what has been said in order to ensure the correct meanings are extracted from the focus group data.[28] Although the use of these groups in international research presents some challenges, the benefits of this approach often outweigh the costs. As with other qualitative techniques, additional research approaches are generally needed to supplement the information obtained from focus groups.

Personal Interviews

One-on-one discussions between a researcher and a respondent represent the personal interview method. Cultural nuances may affect the interviews. Consumers in the United States are generally quite open to expressing their honest opinions; subjects in other countries might not be as open with their feelings. Gender roles are an additional factor, and the gender of the actual interviewer should be taken into account. Women in many cultures are hesitant to answer interview questions and may not respond when a male is present. In some countries, women are not allowed to speak with a personal interviewer. A male interviewer may be viewed as intimidating to a female respondent. A female interviewer may be treated harshly by a male respondent in a more misogynistic culture.

Delphi Technique

Experts often provide a unique and valuable perspective on a topic. The Delphi technique method taps expert opinions. The technique involves a market researcher who assembles a panel or group of experts on the topic of interest. The experts then answer a series of questions regarding that topic. Typically, these questions forecast or predict future behavior. As with any group, disagreements occur. Using the Delphi technique, the researcher then asks the experts to respond and come to a consensus. The final report presents convergence regarding the underlying agreed-upon answer and strongest prediction. The Delphi technique might be used to help forecast external market concerns such as growth rates in specific markets, potential for economic unrest, or political election outcomes.

QUANTITATIVE METHODS

Numerical measurements and analyses are used in **quantitative research design** formats. These methods, including surveys, experiments, and test markets, require skill in designing questions for research subjects and in using statistical techniques to analyze the answers.

Surveys

Sets of questions are asked in various settings in surveys, which are widely used market research tools. Survey instruments can usually be given to large numbers of consumers with relative ease. Administering surveys can be more challenging in international settings. Approximately 760 million people worldwide are illiterate, and two thirds of those are women.[29] Also, some consumers are difficult to reach in more remote locations. Others are reluctant to record their true opinions or feelings on a survey instrument. These consumers may provide responses biased by cultural norms, which complicates the survey process.

There also may be issues regarding interpretation of figures. Arabs write and read graphics from right to left. A graphic that displays the stages of a process that reads from left to right might cause Arabic survey participants to think the end of the process is the beginning and the beginning is the end.

Conceptual equivalence problems create additional difficulties. These occur when a concept in one country has a different meaning in another. The word "household," for example, has different meanings in various countries. A household may be interpreted as consisting of a father, mother, and children in one country, but may include grandparents, aunts, uncles, and cousins in another.

Careful translation of survey questions constitutes a key ingredient in international survey research. Questions that are misunderstood or deemed offensive in some way may hurt the ability to obtain quality information. To make sure questions are correctly stated, two types of translation techniques are available.

Back translation is a process in which a survey is translated from an original language into a targeted language—for example, from Italian to Portuguese—and then back into the original language by a different translator. The second translated document is then compared to the original version in order to check for accuracy and meaning. Back translation is widely used when developing international market surveys.

Parallel translation is a process in which two or more translators are used for each step of the back translation process. If different translations result, the research team discusses the results and selects one final translation. Parallel translation helps to account for the subtle nuances present in each language.[30]

> Parallel translation is a process in which two or more translators are used for each step of the back translation process.

Experiments

Experimentation offers another viable quantitative market research option. Experiments are research techniques that allow researchers to discover cause-and-effect relationships by manipulating certain variables and controlling others. When utilizing experimentation techniques, researchers seek to identify the effect of one or two independent variables on a dependent variable.

One experimental technique often used by marketers is the *purchase simulation* method. A room is given the appearance of a retail store. Then, the research team can test variables such as color, methods of displaying merchandise, and selling techniques for effectiveness. Researchers can also explore how different price levels (an independent variable) affect consumer intentions to buy (the dependent variable).

VIDEO LINK 6.3:
Color and Marketing

Advertisements and marketing materials are tested using *portfolio* techniques. Researchers may show consumers a series of commercials dispersed throughout a television program, then test attitudes and recall to see if the ad achieved its desired effect. The same basic methodology can be used with arrays of newspaper or magazine advertisements. Portfolio experiments assist the marketing team in understanding if an advertisement that is effective in one country will be equally as successful in another.

Experimentation can be utilized in international market research, although they are generally difficult to administer and control. One criticism of experiments is that they are too artificial when conducted in a laboratory setting.

Test Markets

One special type of experiment that can address the problems associated with an artificial environment is a **test market**, a type of experiment that is constructed within realistic marketplace conditions. In essence, results from an experiment in a small area, such as a small township in South Africa, are used to predict what would happen in a larger area, including all small townships or the entire country.

Companies use test markets in order to better understand cause-and-effect relationships in a marketplace. A company may sell a product at one price in a test market and a higher price in a second market to discover the level of price elasticity that is present. Another marketing team might assess the impact of a coupon program in one area compared to a bonus pack program in another. A third firm can test the effectiveness of an advertising program in a region. In each instance the cause or independent variables (price, promotions, or advertising) are linked to effects or dependent variables (sales figures).

Quantitative research designs are generally considered to be more objective than qualitative research designs. The numbers speak for themselves. Quantitative research designs tend to work well when the intent is to reach large sample sizes. Surveys can be distributed to large numbers of consumers if the infrastructure of the country allows for such distribution. It is generally more difficult to reach a large number of consumers through focus groups or personal interviews.

Many international marketers combine qualitative and quantitative methods to obtain richer answers to difficult marketing questions. Recently, the British music magazine and website NME (www.NME.com) hired a new editor that wanted to make many changes. Before moving forward, the head of marketing, Tom Pearson, used both a series of focus groups and a survey of customers to gauge the potential effectiveness of those changes.[31]

Approximately 1.7 billion consumers have Internet access worldwide.

ONLINE RESEARCH: A HYBRID APPROACH

Online research offers exciting new opportunities for international researchers. Approximately 1.7 billion consumers have Internet access worldwide as of 2010.[32] Asian countries make up the highest number of Internet users, followed by European countries, and then the Americas. Internet data collection can work well in these regions.

Developed regions tend to experience high levels of Internet usage. Other regions do not have the same adoption rates, especially in less- or least-developed countries. The latest estimates reveal that fewer than 1% of consumers in the African countries of Liberia, Malawi, Ethiopia, Burundi, or Niger currently have Internet access.[33]

Several problems have been associated with Internet market research programs. These include the lack of Internet capabilities and high illiteracy rates in some countries. Also, any Internet survey must be constructed to meet the cultural norms of the target audience. Careful translation and examination of the visual parts of the website will be necessary. The Internet offers several online sources of secondary data. The information can be combined with primary online research to gain a better understanding of a target market.

Develop a Sample

Sampling is a process wherein members of a population are selected for inclusion in a research study because they will be representative of the larger group. Sampling techniques can be used to survey a small subgroup rather than the entire population, but at the same time draw inferences about the entire population based on the results. Several well-established sampling techniques make it possible to have confidence in findings generated by samples.

LEARNING OBJECTIVE #4:

What techniques can be used when developing samples and collecting data for international marketing research?

Researchers generally choose between probability and nonprobability sampling methods. A **probability sample** is one in which each element in the population has a known, nonzero probability of being selected for a study. A *random sample* is a type of probability sample in which each element has an equal chance of being selected for study; it involves setting up a process or procedure ensuring that each person in the population has an equal probability of being chosen for the sample.

Random samples are particularly effective when the researcher seeks to make statistical inferences. *Statistical inference* means that the research results obtained from a sample apply to the larger population, a common objective in international marketing research projects.

Simple examples of random selection include picking a name out of a hat or choosing the short straw. Researchers can use computer programs to generate random numbers as the basis for random selection.[34] A stratified sample process divides the population into different categories and subsamples for further analysis. Using this technique, a researcher would categorize the residents of Great Britain into Labour Party, Conservative Party, or Liberal Democrat Party, then would take a subsample of respondents from within each category. The research team could even specify the percentage of final respondents that they prefer in the final sample. For instance, the research team could target a final sample of 40% Labour, 40% Conservative, and 20% Liberal Democrat.

A **nonprobability sample** is one in which the probability of an element of the population being included in a sample is unknown, which means a random sample cannot be used. The goal remains to make the sample as representative of the larger population as possible. Various tactics may be used. *Snowball techniques* are nonprobability techniques in which one respondent refers the researcher to the next respondent, and so on. Generating a *convenience sample* is a nonprobability technique in which researchers sample the respondents that are the easiest to reach without regard for how people are selected.

Obtaining a true probability or random sample in most international settings will be difficult, because methods used to reach people create biases. Some citizens do not own telephones, others do not have access to the Internet, and others still are illiterate and cannot read mail. Dispersed populations make selecting a random sample even more problematic.[35]

Some results are biased because researchers only reached the most readily available consumers. These individuals may not be representative of the true population being investigated. With international research, two key areas relate to age and education. Young, college-aged consumers in the Middle East may not have the same attitudes as their elders. Older, conservative consumers in Russia may not share similar opinions with younger consumers. Researchers using nonprobability samples should carefully consider these issues.

SAMPLING ISSUES IN INTERNATIONAL RESEARCH

International sampling introduces several difficulties for the international market researcher. One issue pertains to the lack of availability of accurate demographic information. For many countries, such lists, or sample frames, are not available. Less-developed countries often do not keep valid demographic information. Collection methods can be severely limited or deliberately altered by the ruling government.

Deriving the correct type of sample based on the information needed remains a key part of international marketing research. The overall aim of the research project dictates the type of sampling procedure to be used. In general, four types of research considerations should be addressed: descriptive research, comparative research, contextual research, and theoretical research.[36]

The *descriptive research* method allows the researcher to examine attitudes and behaviors that are relevant to one specific country. Descriptive research applies when, for example, a marketing team seeks to understand the attitudes of consumers in South Korea toward automobile makes and models. Researchers focus on describing the attitudes and actions of consumers in that country.

Comparative research takes place when the researchers examine *differences between* cultures or countries. Comparative research would be used when marketers compare attitudes of consumers in South Korea with attitudes of consumers in India. Efforts are focused on ensuring that the results reveal valid differences in attitudes between these two countries.

Contextual research may be performed when the research team attempts to study cross-national groups and how consumers behave in a selected context. The focus with contextual research is not necessarily on uncovering differences in consumers across different countries: instead, researchers concentrate on how consumers think or act within a specific context, such as within a certain political system.

Theoretical research examines the extent to which a theory garners support across cultures and national boundaries. The type of research chosen will be based on a specific academic research question. Academic institutions normally perform theoretical research, but the results may be applied to business settings. An international researcher might want to study how various satisfaction theories apply in certain countries or cultures, and the information could ultimately help solve marketing problems.

CALCULATING THE SAMPLE SIZE

A review of the statistical theory behind sampling is beyond the scope of this text. It is clear, however, that international issues influence both desired sample sizes and the confidence intervals associated with research findings. To illustrate, consider the formula for determining a required sample size for a mean (or average) score given a particular level of confidence and acceptable error. This formula is

$$n = (ZS/E)^2,$$

where

n = required sample size,

Z = standardized value based on confidence level (1.96 for a 95% level of confidence),

S = standard deviation of a population of interest, and

E = acceptable error.

Assume that a researcher wants to survey consumer satisfaction with a particular brand in a specific culture such as satisfaction with computer brands in Malaysia. A question on a survey might be, "Please indicate your level of satisfaction with Brand X on the following scale." The scale endpoints are 1 = very dissatisfied and 10 = very satisfied. The researcher desires an error term of no more than 0.25 points and a level of confidence of 95% (corresponding to a z-score of 1.96). The researcher will make some assumptions about the standard deviation of the population on the statistic. One rule of thumb is that a standard deviation for a population can be assumed to be approximately one-sixth of the range of responses.[37] If the researcher assumes a standard deviation of 1.5, and the researcher assumes that the phrase "Please indicate your level of satisfaction" conveys the appropriate meaning in the focal culture, the required sample size would be $[1.96(1.5)/.25]^2 \approx 137$.

Notice that the sample size actually obtained in the research project also influences the confidence level of the statistic that is obtained. For example, consider the confidence interval formula for a given mean. The formula is

$$\mu = \text{average} \pm Z\,[S/\sqrt{n}\,],$$

where

μ = true, unknown, average score for an entire population,

average = average score obtained from a sample,

Z = standardized value based on confidence level,

S = standard deviation of sample, and

n = actual sample size obtained.

From this example, assuming that 137 consumers responded to the survey with an average satisfaction score of 6.0 and that the standard deviation of the sample actually equaled 1.5, the 95% confidence interval for average satisfaction of this population would then equal

$$\mu = \text{average} \pm Z\,[S/\sqrt{n}\,],$$

$$\mu = 6.0 \pm 1.96\,[1.5/11.7],$$

$$= 6.0 \pm 1.96\,[.13] = 6.0 \pm .25 \approx (5.75 \longleftrightarrow 6.25).$$

In this example, the researcher would be 95% confident that the true population average for satisfaction would be between 5.75 and 6.25.

The entire population of a country or region can generally never be reached with a certain research question. Consequently, international market researchers rely heavily on sampling methods and statistical theory. If a research team could contact *every* consumer that they actually wanted to learn about, there would be no need for the types of statistics described in this section. They would simply know exactly what they want to know about the consumers. If the team was only able to survey 137 randomly selected consumers in Malaysia, then the marketing team would need to understand how to use these techniques. If the results obtained came from a study of these consumers, the researcher would have an estimate of consumer satisfaction along with a level of confidence with which to gauge the findings.

Collect Data

Data collection will be the next step of the international marketing research process. The ability to collect data depends on local customs and technological infrastructure. The proliferation of telephone and Internet communications has changed the landscape of data collection in many countries, but usage rates still vary widely around the world. In Latin American and Caribbean nations, estimates suggest that fewer than 50% of consumers have fixed-line telecommunication access.[38] In other parts of the world, telephone proliferation is even lower. Kenya has about 665,000 fixed-line telephones in the country with a population of over 40 million.[39]

The recent growth of mobile phone usage in some countries may lead to new marketing research opportunities. In the past decade, 30 million consumers in Nigeria have purchased cell phones. On the African continent, more than 280.7 million subscribers, or about 30.4% of the overall African market, had signed up for service by 2007.[40]

Internet access also varies worldwide. In Latin American countries, only 30% of consumers have access.[41] This estimate is relatively high when compared to African countries, where only 7% of residents enjoy Internet access.[42]

International market research may be further complicated by language and cultural barriers. Estimates reveal that only 29% of consumers in Niger are literate, 39% in Senegal, and 52% in Liberia.[43] These rates are substantially lower than in industrialized countries. Companies often also may have to hide foreign origins. In Iraq, polling companies may need to hide the fact that Americans have employed them to complete the surveys.

Another difficulty occurs when attempting to use maps to find addresses. Some Western cities, such as London, are famous for being difficult to navigate, even with a map. In less-developed countries, the maps themselves are often outdated and incorrect. Addresses can create additional complications. A region may not use addresses, per se, and other parts of the world may have strikingly different addressing traditions. In East Asia, addresses normally start with the zip code, followed by county or metro area, followed by the city, then the ward or town, then the district, then the block, then the building number, ending with the apartment number if necessary. The order is exactly opposite of that found in most Western countries.[44]

In summary, limitations of technology and consumer literacy mean that international market researchers should be careful to ensure that data collection methods are appropriate for the country, culture, or market under consideration.

Analyze and Interpret Data

The next phase of international market research involves analyzing and interpreting the data that have been collected. Ensuring that data are actually comparable continues to be an important issue when examining findings across countries and cultures. Two common problems at this point are linguistic difficulties and metric equivalence issues.[45]

LEARNING OBJECTIVE #5:

What factors complicate the analysis and interpretation of data in international marketing research?

LINGUISTIC PROBLEMS

Linguistic problems, or those associated with different meanings for terms, often complicate international market research. Frequently used concepts such as "satisfaction" and "feelings" should be carefully examined to understand how these terms might differ across cultures. The concept of "late" has a variety of meanings, influenced by both language and culture. In French, *en retard* translates as "not on time." The concepts of later and latest roughly translate as "more not on time." Arriving thirty minutes late in Brazil would not be considered rude but rather something approaching normal. Any research questions related to time and punctuality in other countries require careful consideration by the marketing team.

METRIC EQUIVALENCE ISSUES

Metric equivalence issues arise when respondents from different countries systematically score interview or survey questions differently.[46] Cultural differences in response styles can greatly affect research results.[47] In a culture with strong tendencies toward humane orientation, respondents may be much more likely to offer favorable answers to questions, always granting the benefit of the doubt. Countries low on the same cultural characteristics may have respondents who are harsher in their evaluations of items such as product quality, brand loyalty, or other attitudes, feelings, and emotions.

Cultural differences in response styles can greatly affect research results.

American consumers are willing to express extreme positions on measurement scales, which may not be the case for consumers in other cultures. In collectivist societies, consumers are less willing to express extreme attitudes in either face-to-face or survey research, which affects research results in places such as China, Vietnam, Korea, or Taiwan. One study revealed, for example, that Korean consumers prefer to respond to survey items at the midpoint of a scale.[48] Some evidence suggests that cultural patterns, such as individualism or uncertainty avoidance, are related to consumers from various countries being more likely to respond at the extreme end of survey scales.[49] Problems such as these can restrict or alter the range of responses from one culture as compared to those in another culture. Restriction of range of responses can lead to problems with several statistical procedures and affect the required sample size.

The sample size formula shown earlier in this chapter reveals the problem. From the previous example in which the researcher was assumed to be studying the level of consumer satisfaction with computer brands in Malaysia, a smaller sample size was needed when the standard deviation of responses was assumed to be small.

For example, if the researcher assumes a standard deviation of 1.2 rather than 1.5, the desired sample size for the same level of confidence (95%) and precision (0.25) will be dramatically reduced to approximately 88 ($n=[1.96(1.2)/.25])^2$, rather than 137 consumers. When the standard deviation of responses is reduced (as would be the case when most consumers respond near the midpoint of a scale), the required sample size decreases. Larger sample sizes would be required for a sample performed in cultures where consumers are more willing to express extreme positions (assuming a given level of precision).

Notice what this change in the standard deviation of responses would do to the confidence interval that is obtained. In this case, the confidence interval would be narrowed as shown in the following equation: (again assuming an average score of 6.0 on a 10-point scale):

$$\mu = \text{average} \pm Z\,[S/\sqrt{n}\,]$$

$$\mu = 6.0 \pm 1.96\,[1.20/11.7]$$

$$= 6.0 \pm 1.96\,[.10] = 6.0 \pm.20 \approx (5.80 \leftrightarrow 6.20).$$

SOCIALLY DESIRABLE RESPONSES

A related complication with analyzing data from international markets is the problem of socially desirable responses, which occurs when respondents bias their opinions by what they believe are the most culturally acceptable ways in which to respond to a question. As noted, consumers in collectivist cultures tend to be reluctant to express their true feelings in survey research. If they simply respond near the midpoint of a scale, it becomes problematic for the researcher to ascertain whether these responses indicate their true feelings, or if they are responding in the ways they feel they should.

One problem for data analysis, then, is that even when the researcher selects the proper sample size for a proposed standard deviation level in the population, the true score on the statistic may still deviate from the actual opinions of the respondents, which, in turn, would affect any analysis of the data. In that instance, problems would exist with the validity of the findings even though the researcher believes she has secured the desired degree of error and sample size. Consequently, the use of multiple methods, including both qualitative and quantitative techniques,

INTERNATIONAL INCIDENT ///

You are performing a market research project in a collectivist culture, Korea. Product sales in the region have been slipping and your supervisor has given you the task of identifying the reasons behind the lagging sales. The research team has decided that a consumer survey is the best method for collecting data from consumers. The team ultimately finds that the majority of the responses on the survey question are quite favorable regarding the satisfaction consumers express toward the company's product. When presenting the results to the supervisor, what would you tell him? What would you suggest?

becomes critical when performing international market research. Monitoring cultural differences to the various research approaches generates results of a better quality.

Formulating Conclusions and Writing Reports

The final step in the international market research process is formulating conclusions and writing the research report. Decision-makers reach conclusions regarding whether the firm should expand marketing efforts internationally. If so, they can then choose the best method to enter a country. The research report should be written in a direct and informative way that assists the international marketing in making decisions. In general, the conclusions presented in international market research reports should be both complete and concise.[50]

In an international context, this step poses the same communication issues that have been part of the entire process. Often, one of the difficulties is in re-creating an environment that many of the readers of the report will never have visited. Consequently, those readers may be initially reluctant to accept the findings.

VIDEO LINK 6.4:
The Rise of China

In a recent marketing research project report, the team noted that bottom-of-the-pyramid consumers in China used clothes washing machines to clean vegetables. A Western executive might be hesitant to believe this finding. It would be the responsibility of the marketing researcher to present this information in a manner that earns the executive's confidence. When this finding was reported to the Chinese company Haeier, instead of being skeptical, the executives responded by introducing a machine specially designed for cleaning vegetables. The company later introduced a machine that assists in making cheese from goat's milk.[51] These products were introduced because the marketing team believed research findings and used them to guide strategic decisions.

Ethics and International Market Research

International market researchers have an obligation to ensure that their activities are ethical. Ethical responsibilities go beyond simply being objective when performing research. Researchers who are ethical protect the rights and privacy of research participants. They also work to keep confidential information from being leaked to outside parties.

Researchers who engage in experimentation focus on protecting the safety and well-being of research subjects and ensure that no one is harmed in any way by the research project. While most market research projects are relatively harmless, it would be harmful to manipulate consumers while engaging in a research project. Ethical researchers also make certain that research activities are not misrepresented in any harmful way. One unethical tactic is to engage in "sugging." Sugging is selling under the guise of research. A researcher that suggs begins asking a respondent questions and then attempt to sell the person a product. Practices such as sugging are frowned upon in international market research.

Bottom-of-the-Pyramid and International Market Research

International market researchers seek to gather the opinions of bottom-of-the-pyramid consumers so that the findings can be incorporated in various marketing efforts. Many of these consumers may be unable to respond to surveys or Internet research programs, because they do not have access to computers, and many more may be illiterate. Data collection techniques may be adapted, relying more on qualitative methods such as personal interviews or ethnographic methods in order to tap the attitudes and behaviors of this segment.

Pricing research takes on a new meaning when researching bottom-of-the-pyramid consumers. Rather than studying the effect of a pricing change on purchasing behaviors, researchers should instead seek to identify what price consumers are actually able to pay for a particular product or service.

Product research may focus on finding gauging consumer responses to cost-saving changes to product design, and may explore differences in purchasing frequency. Smaller quantities per purchase may result in more frequent purchasing of the item. Instead of buying a six-month supply of soap, market research may find that bottom-of-the-pyramid consumers prefer buying single-use sachets as needed.

Distribution and promotion research also varies in context for bottom-of-the-pyramid consumers. Many bottom-of-the-pyramid consumers are rural; research should highlight how the consumers access the product. Promotion research in these countries should examine the effectiveness of word-of-mouth efforts rather than advertising, mass media, or Internet marketing campaign approaches.

Control of the International Market Research Process

Another concern in international market research is how to structure the research task from an organizational standpoint. Should an organization conduct all international research activities from a centralized location, or should the efforts be decentralized? A *centralized* structure brings the management of these tasks "in house" to a corporate headquarters location. A *decentralized* structure allows research tasks to be managed in offices in, or near, the foreign region under investigation. Although there are valid arguments for each type of structure, the main advantage of the decentralized method is that the researcher will be closer to the subjects being studied and may be more sensitive to market-specific issues. An argument can be made for maintaining research expertise in both the home and foreign country so that research results from each country may be more appropriately compared.[52]

Another alternative for the international market researcher is to hire an external research firm to conduct research. This option presents a method of combining secondary and primary data. By employing an external research firm, management can draw from the significant expertise of successful market research companies. Two benefits of hiring an external firm are convenience and expertise.

Hiring an external research firm can be costly. As such, the decision-maker should decide whether the benefit of convenience and expertise is worth the cost of the project. The website www.greenbook.org provides a directory of potential international marketing research firms. Table 6.1 presents a list of major global market research firms.

A. C. Nielsen	United States
Arbitron, Inc.	United States
GfK AG	Germany
IBOPE	Brazil
IMS Health	United States
Information Resources Incorporated	United States
INTAGE Inc.	Japan
Ipsos Group	France
J. D. Power and Associates	United States
The Kantar Group	United Kingdom
Synovate	United Kingdom
Video Research	Japan

Table 6.1: **Major Market Research Firms (listed alphabetically)**

Chapter 6: Review and Resources

STRATEGIC IMPLICATIONS //

Given the importance of international marketing research, decision-makers should ensure that the overall international marketing program is guided by solid data and information. International market research should be recognized as an essential component of the overall organizational strategy. In order to identify potential targets for international expansion, as well as viable market segments for products internationally, solid research is needed.

To collect quality information for the purposes of international marketing, macro- and micro-level studies are necessary. Undertaking these forms of research requires the commitment of top management. Company executives should allocate the necessary resources to ensure that adequate support is given to international market research. A systematic process of collecting both secondary and primary data should draw support from upper-level managers, who guide the strategic direction of the firm.

TACTICAL IMPLICATIONS ///

Each of the four types of international market research described in this chapter regarding products, pricing, distribution, and promotion helps the firm to achieve its overall international marketing strategy. Tactical decisions for international market research are based on the overall corporate strategy. Following either a differentiation or low-cost provider strategy, for example, requires the collection of both pricing and product research in the target country or region. When differentiation is the goal, qualitative methods help researchers understand whether local citizens perceive the differences. The overall international strategy of the firm will likely fail in the absence of valid and reliable international research aimed at the various parts of the marketing mix. International market research tactics play a vital role in ensuring that the overall international marketing strategy is successful.

OPERATIONAL IMPLICATIONS ///

Day-to-day international market research operations are guided by both strategic and tactical decisions. Ongoing research activities are necessary to address cultural differences, regional preferences, and consumer attitudes toward a company's products. Researchers can spend a great deal of time each day analyzing international survey or focus group data, as well as drawing conclusions and writing research reports. Researchers also should daily analyze macro-level events that occur in targeted countries or regions.

The pace of global change has increased. Daily events can drastically alter the marketing environment in any given country. This leads researchers to monitor world events on a daily basis.

In summary, international market research plays a vital role in international marketing. The demand for valid and reliable market research information is greater than ever, and international business decisions require that this information be gathered in the most effective and efficient method available. Cultural differences should always be taken into account when attempting to perform any international market research project. The control of this process is an important issue as well, with many firms opting for a combination of both in-house and field arrangements.

TERMS

market research	secondary data	validity
scientific method	primary data	internal validity
self-reference criterion	reliability	external validity

political risk	back translation	probability sample
qualitative research designs	parallel translation	nonprobability sample
focus groups	test market	
quantitative research designs	sampling	

REVIEW QUESTIONS

1. Define market research.

2. Explain the scientific method.

3. What factors would lead a researcher to be biased when performing international research?

4. How does the self-reference criterion relate to international market research?

5. What are the steps in the market research process?

6. What types of information are included in secondary data and primary data?

7. Define both validity and reliability and explain how the terms apply to surveys and experiments.

8. What are some of the most commonly used sources of secondary data for international market research?

9. What is the difference between a macro-level and a micro-level analysis?

10. What is the difference between qualitative and quantitative international market research?

11. What are some of the popular qualitative research designs commonly used in international market research?

12. Describe a focus group along with the challenges that come with performing focus groups on an international scale.

13. What are some of the popular quantitative research designs commonly used in the international market research?

14. What are the major advantages and disadvantages of quantitative research design?

15. What are the main differences between back translation and parallel translation?

16. What is the difference between a probability sample and a nonprobability sample?

17. What is the difference between descriptive research and comparative research?

18. What is the difference between contextual research and theoretical research?

19. Describe the four main types of international market research discussed in this chapter.

20. What are some of the factors to consider when addressing the control of the international market research process?

21. What are the major legal restraints on performing international market research?

DISCUSSION QUESTIONS

1. Discuss the advantages and disadvantages of secondary and primary research. Which type of research is probably best for micro-level analysis? For a macro-level analysis?

2. Discuss the various types of quantitative research designs. What types of research would be appropriate in developed countries? In lesser-developed countries?

3. Describe the basic market research process. What types of issues should a researcher consider during each phase with regard to international market research? Which phase is most important?

4. How is a desired sample size affected by response characteristics of a particular population? Are confidence intervals affected by these issues? If so, how are they affected?

5. If you had to select between experiments, surveys, personal interviews, or Internet research, which type(s) would be best for research performed in lesser-developed countries?

ANALYTICAL AND INTERNET EXERCISES

1. Determine the appropriate sample size for a research project that is focused on finding the average purchase intentions of consumers for a particular brand that is measured on a 10-point scale ranging from 1 = *Definitely will not buy* to 10 = *Definitely will buy*. The researcher wants to be 95% confident and allow an error of not more than 0.15 points.

2. Assume that the researcher in Exercise 1 achieved a sample of size 150. The standard deviation for purchase intentions was 1.25, and the average was 5.0. Find a 95% confidence interval for these results.

3. Visit a number of the Internet resources that present secondary data for international market researchers, including U.S. Department of Commerce (www.stat-usa.gov), U.S. Department of Commerce International Trade Association (www.trade.gov), Euromonitor (www.euromonitor.com), Organization of Economic Cooperation and Development (www.oecd.org), and the International Monetary Fund (www.imf.org). What type(s) of information do you find? How do you think these sources could be used for international market research?

4. Visit the websites of several market research firms that specialize in international market research such as A. C. Nielsen; Arbitron, Inc.; GfK AG, IBOPE, and INTAGE Inc. Compare the type(s) of research that these firms perform. What are the advantages to using these specialized firms?

5. Enticing consumers to spend more for environmentally friendly products remains one of the primary challenges facing green marketers. International market research can play a key role in identifying potential consumers and market segments for green marketing strategies. Survey techniques can be used to identify segments such as the "true-blue greens," "greenback greens," and "sprouts" that have been identified in most-developed nations. Experiments and test markets can be devised that gauge the effectiveness of offering green products in these cultures. Determining consumer openness to green marketing and sustainability initiatives will be a crucial part of international marketing research for environmentally sensitive companies. Describe the research methods you would use to conduct sustainability research in the following countries:

   - Canada
   - South Africa
   - Morocco
   - South Korea

▶ **ONLINE VIDEOS**

Visit **www.sagepub.com/baack** to view these chapter videos:

Video Link 6.1: Facebook

Video Link 6.2: Unions and Collective Bargaining

Video Link 6.3: Color and Marketing

Video Link 6.4: The Rise of China

🌐 **STUDENT STUDY SITE**

Visit **www.sagepub.com/baack** to access these additional learning tools:

- Web Quizzes
- eFlashcards
- SAGE Journal Articles

- Country Fact Sheets
- Chapter Outlines
- Interactive Maps

CASE 6 ///

The "Mobile You" Breathalyzer

The X275 Mobile You Breathalyzer is a portable, handheld breathalyzer device made by Youtoi Industries of Japan.[53] The product is marketed directly to consumers who are concerned about drinking and driving. Whereas some breathalyzers can be attached directly to automobiles of consumers who have had prior drunk-driving convictions, the Mobile You offers an inexpensive alternative for consumers who simply choose to be safe drivers. The product has been marketed successfully in Japan and in several other countries. The Youtoi company has recently decided to try to enter the European marketplace. In particular, the company's marketing team has chosen to focus on Germany.

Germany is well known for its beer and beer-friendly environment. Public drinking is more acceptable in Germany than in many other countries. The legal drinking age in Germany is sixteen, but children as young as fourteen may drink alcohol if they are accompanied by their parents. Alcopops, or alcohol mixed with soda pop, have become increasingly popular.[54] The acceptance of the alcopop, which is also marketed in other areas of the world, reflects the casual attitude that prevails in the German market regarding youth consumption of alcohol.

Although alcohol is more widely accepted in Germany than in other countries, several problems are associated with its consumption. Some argue that the general lenient societal attitude toward drinking has created troubles, and especially with regard to young adults. Approximately 25% of male mortality in the fifteen to twenty-nine age group is related to alcohol consumption.[55] Drunk driving continues to be a serious problem. The legal limit in Germany is 0.05 blood alcohol content; penalties can be assessed for blood alcohol content as low as 0.03, however, if there are signs of driving impairment.[56]

Due to problems associated with drinking and driving among young adults, the German government has recently moved to adopt a zero-tolerance policy regarding young drivers. Under this initiative, young drivers that have had a license less than two years face a fine of up to 125 *euros* (about $170) and license probation extension of four years. The goal is to motivate young drivers to monitor themselves closely to stay out of legal trouble. The makers of the Mobile You believe that this represents a genuine opportunity to market the voluntary breathalyzer to this target market.

Japan has also strengthened its drunk-driving laws. Japan's Amended Traffic Law went into effect on September 1, 2007.[57] The law is strict. It doubles fines and increases jail time for drivers who are guilty of driving under the influence (blood alcohol content 0.05). In addition, the law increases both jail time and the financial penalty for driving while impaired (blood alcohol content 0.03). The law also states that individuals can be prosecuted for failing to prevent someone from driving under the influence or for providing a vehicle to a drunk driver.

Marketing a voluntary breathalyzer to young consumers will be challenging. Marketing the product across cultures adds additional challenges to the venture. The first issue is to simply convince consumers that the product is worth the price. Cultural differences cause difficulties in this process. Legal issues can also complicate the issue because

Patterns of alcohol consumption vary by country and culture.

laws differ across national boundaries. Overall, the issue becomes clear: Can a Japanese company successfully market this product in a German market?

1. How would the self-reference criterion apply to this case?

2. What type(s) of research would need to be performed in order for Youtoi to have the best chance of successfully marketing the Mobile You breathalyzer in Germany?

3. Describe the research design process as it pertains to marketing the breathalyzer in Germany.

4. What kinds of macrolevel factors should be obtained before introducing the product in Germany?

5. How could a sample of consumers be selected for this study? What type(s) of sample should be obtained?

6. What would the appropriate role of qualitative data be in this case?

7. To what extent should formalized research be attempted in the case? Should it be attempted at all? Why or why not?

8. To what extent should product, pricing, promotion, and distribution research be utilized in this case?

PART III
International Product Marketing

7

International Product and Brand Marketing

After reading and studying this chapter, you should be able to answer the following questions:

1. What basic product categories and product dimensions are available in domestic and international markets?

2. What types of decisions must be made with regard to a company's international product mix?

3. What types of international business products and services are available?

4. What types of patterns exist as new products move from introduction to eventual decline?

5. What role does brand development and management play in international marketing?

IN THIS CHAPTER ///

A Good Night's Sleep

For the 7 billion people currently living, some common denominators exist. As a simple example, nearly everyone sleeps. Most sleep at night, but the number of variations in resting patterns might seem surprising. The differences also create international marketing possibilities.

Sleeping patterns offer cultural contrasts. Bed times vary widely, often within the same region. A farmer most likely will turn in fairly early and rise possibly before dawn. City dwellers stay up later to enjoy nightlife. In hotter regions, taking a siesta or nap in the afternoon is more common. In many cultures, especially those in East Asia, children are likely to sleep in the same beds as their parents. Not surprisingly, then, African Americans and Hispanics are ten times more likely than East Asians to have sex before falling asleep. African Americans are the most inclined to pray prior to turning out the lights. Caucasians are most likely to allow pets in the bedroom.

Other patterns vary by individuals. Some read at night. Others watch television. Some take sleep-inducing medications, and others exercise or meditate. Sleeping disorders range from falling asleep unexpectedly (narcolepsy), to snoring (sometimes a symptom of sleep apnea), to sleepwalking (somnambulism).

Sleeping patterns change as people age. Children require the greatest amount. Seniors require the least. A growing percentage of married couples in the United States now spend the night in separate beds.

A number of studies have been conducted regarding sleep deprivation and its relationship to anger, depression, and other outcomes. Researchers have examined those who work at night and try to sleep by day. The effects of exposure to light on sleep have also been studied.

Numerous marketing opportunities emerge from sleep and rest. Items such as pajamas and nightgowns, night-lights, sheets, pillows, comforters, soothing agents, medications, and more can be sold to those hoping to rest comfortably. Most notably, beds represent a marketplace consisting of billions of people. Beds come in a variety of shapes and sizes. Mattresses are made from many ingredients, including air, water, foam, wool, bamboo, and straw.

The Japanese market a unique form of bed that combines a series of elements. The *shiki* futon is the essential component of the Japanese bed, because it critically influences the overall comfort level of the Japanese sleeping system. A *shiki* futon will be quite different from a Western-style futon filled with foam and wool. The *shiki* futon consists of 100% organic cotton and varies in thickness from two to four inches. In the United States, a *shiki* futon can be expensive. The manufacturing process is meticulous and the materials must be top quality for the futon to hold its shape and firmness.

On top of the *shiki* futon will be a *kakebuton*, which is similar to a comforter. A Japanese *kakebuton* typically will be filled with hand-pulled silk, which makes it extremely lightweight while efficiently retaining body heat throughout the night. It provides a pleasant sleeping experience because it exerts little pressure on the body.

No Japanese sleeping system would be complete without a *soba gara makura*, which is a buckwheat hull pillow. The pillow helps provide a comfortable night's sleep by perfectly adjusting to the contour of a person's head and neck. *Soba gara makura* materials were used in the original Tempur-Pedic mattresses.

Although not required, many people, especially Westerners, prefer to sleep with a tri-fold mattress underneath the *shiki* futon. The thick foam mattress pad provides a perfect solution for adding an extra layer of comfort to the Japanese sleeping system.

Finally, many people use a *tatami* (straw mat) or a platform bed to support the entire Japanese bed. The choice between these two elements can either make a portable and foldable sleeping system that can be stored in the closet, or create a stunning structure in the bedroom radiating with authentic Japanese imagery.

The Japanese bed is but one example of how an everyday experience, sleeping, also presents a major marketing opportunity. With increasing interactions between cultures, the international marketing potential for sleeping products continues to grow.[1]

QUESTIONS FOR STUDENTS

1. Which product feature should companies that make beds emphasize the most—price, comfort, health, or a good night's sleep?

2. How would culture influence the sales of bed in international markets?

3. What is the most effective way to build brand loyalty for products, such as beds, that are purchased infrequently?

Beds and sleeping habits create new international marketing opportunities.

Overview

Part I of this textbook provided a backdrop for the field of international marketing. Culture, language, infrastructure, economic systems, and political and legal systems influence any domestic or global marketing operation. In Part II the central core of Figure 7.1 was examined: the market. Concepts of target market segmentation and product positioning were explained, along with international market research methods to emphasize the starting point for any marketing program: identifying consumer wants and needs.

The third part of international marketing, as shown in Figure 7.1, is the development of the physical goods and intangible services that meet the needs of those in the target market. Products are designed and sold within the context of the cultural, linguistic, economic, political, legal, and economic constraints imposed by any country in which a global marketing firm intends to operate.

In this chapter, product and brand management activities are detailed. Chapter 8 expands the discussion by incorporating the concepts of product and service adaptation. Making certain a product fits with a specific country and its culture helps the product compete in the international marketplace.

International product marketing involves first understanding the types of products that companies sell and the main dimensions of those products from the viewpoint of the consumer. Next, product mix decisions regarding the number of products in a line (depth) and the number of product lines (width or breadth) are made. Product packaging and labeling concepts are integrated into all product decisions, as are choices with regard to the number and types of business-to-business products to be offered. In addition, marketers carefully evaluate product support services to ensure consumers and business customers receive quality attention during and after the purchasing process.

International services constitute a growing segment of international marketing efforts. Companies providing financial, insurance, transportation, health-care, personal,

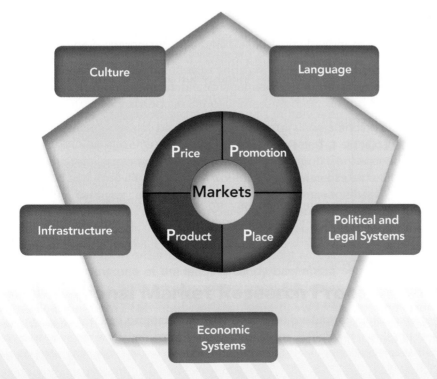

Figure 7.1: The International Marketing Context

and tourism services engage in the same marketing activities as those that manufacture and sell physical goods.

LEARNING
OBJECTIVE #1:

What basic product categories and product dimensions are available in domestic and international markets?

Strategic brand management begins with choice of a brand name, assigning names to individual products and product lines, and with decisions regarding how to brand new products. Building powerful global brands involves moving consumers from brand awareness to perceptions of brand equity and feelings of brand loyalty. Brand valuations assist the marketing team in understanding how well a brand is received in the marketplace.

Finally, international marketing managers can make strategic, tactical, and operational decisions. Product and brand management efforts will be a major determinant of a company's eventual success or failure.

Types of Products

A **product** consists of a bundle of attributes that provide value for exchange partners. Products offer value in many ways. International marketers conceptualize value in terms of tangible, intangible, and symbolic elements. A product as simple as a screwdriver allows consumers to solve a tangible, basic problem (assembling a bicycle) while potentially delivering both intangible benefits (a feeling of safety) and symbolic benefits (the feelings associated with owning a nice set of tools).

A product can be either a good or a service. A **good** is a physical product sold to and used by an individual, household, or business. Distinctions can be drawn between durable and nondurable goods, as well as between consumer and business products. *Durable goods* are items that are consumed over time. Televisions and household appliances are durable goods. *Nondurable goods* are consumed more quickly. Toothpaste and food items are nondurable goods. Many nondurable goods are consumed in daily life.

Businesses sell *consumer products* to consumers either directly or through a market channel that employs intermediaries. The buyers, or end-users, are individual persons or families. *Business products* are marketed to the other businesses, which are the end-users.

A **service** is an intangible product that generally centers on an act or performance that delivers value to individuals, households, and businesses. Services play a major role in the global economy. Consequently, understanding the roles tangible goods and intangible services play in international marketing helps a company operate more effectively in the global economy.

Classifications of Products

Products can be categorized as convenience, shopping, and specialty items. The essential elements used to create these categories are how consumers behave regarding products, including purchase frequency, along with the degree of effort consumers are willing to expend to make purchases.

CONVENIENCE PRODUCTS

Convenience products are inexpensive and frequently purchased. Consumers do not spend much time or effort when shopping for them. Marketers normally make the items widely available, using an intensive distribution strategy, because a consumer generally will not go out of her way to buy them.

Impulse products and staples are special types of convenience products. Many convenience products are *impulse products*, or items purchased spontaneously with no preplanning for the enjoyment that the purchase provides. This contrasts with *unplanned purchases*, which are also not planned but provide no pleasure. Buying toilet paper when a promotional display reminds a consumer about a low household supply is an unplanned purchase; buying ice cream when a promotional display reminds a consumer how much pleasure one receives from eating ice cream is an impulse purchase. *Staples* are goods that are used regularly and tend to be replenished often, such as sugar, flour, rice, millet, salt, and soap. These products are often widely distributed as well. Staple products differ in countries. Chickpeas are a staple part of the diet in India, sorghum and yam are staple foods in parts of Africa, and sweet potatoes and cassavas are staple foods in parts of South America.[2]

 **International Marketing in Daily Life**

Candy

A popular convenience product in many countries, candy, presents a contrast in the nature of convenience goods. What consumers consider to be "candy" varies from country to country. In the United States, most candy contains heavy sugar content, which is not the case in other nations. In many regions, candy can be spicy or sour. A popular treat in Indonesia, for example, *Ting Ting Jahe*, is a spicy candy made from ginger and potato starch. The Violet Crumble, a chocolate bar, is popular in Australia. Regional differences such as these should be taken into account when marketing convenience products internationally.

Convenience products are often sold in convenience stores, which have grown in popularity worldwide. East Asian markets have demonstrated a great deal of promise for the convenience store industry. China, in particular, has witnessed relatively rapid growth in this sector. Popular convenience stores in China include 7-11, Kedi, and FamilyMart, which is one of the largest convenience store chains in all of Asia. In Japan, *combinis* (the Japanese word for convenience store) are everywhere, offering convenience products to a large population. Other areas of growth include India, Turkey, Vietnam, and Russia, which presents marketers with the opportunity to take advantage of an increasing demand for convenience products worldwide.

SHOPPING PRODUCTS

Consumers expend more effort when searching for and purchasing shopping products. Shopping products are more expensive than convenience products and are purchased less frequently. Consumers compare several brands and more carefully consider prices. Marketers typically employ selective distribution strategies for shopping products, which means retail outlets are chosen for each geographic region.

International marketers pay close attention to cultural differences and how they affect consumers as they relate to shopping goods. Successful marketers often offer features and specifications that match distinct countries or regions for shopping goods such as appliances. For instance, washing machines in many European countries typically use only cold water. Market research plays an important role in discovering that type of difference.

Candy is a convenience good.

Department stores and shopping malls often carry shopping products. Stockmann, the largest department store in Nordic countries, has become a well-known source for shopping products in Finland. Other large destinations include MetroCentre, the largest shopping center in the United Kingdom, and the world's largest mall, the New South China Mall in Dongguan, China. The mall includes more than 7 million square feet of retail space. The Mall of America near Minneapolis, Minnesota, attracts over 40 million visitors per year, making it a more popular destination than the Disney theme parks in the United States.

Shopping products include services. Hair care, spa treatments, insurance policies, and numerous other services tend to invite comparisons between providers. Tour guides for various popular locations, such as the Colosseum in Rome, compete with one another for consumer patronage.

SPECIALTY PRODUCTS

Specialty products are items consumers spend a great deal of time searching for, and generally they will not accept substitutes. These products tend to be expensive and are marketed with a significant degree of exclusivity. Only a select few retailers offer them in any one country or region, which increases perceptions of exclusivity. Consumers generally do not consider competing brands, as they usually have chosen one particular alternative and expend effort to purchase the preferred brand.

Fender Musical Instruments Corporation, a major musical instrument marketer located in the United States, is the world's leading guitar manufacturer (www.fender.com). The company sells its instruments worldwide. Consumers are usually willing to spend much effort, time, and energy in shopping for Fender guitars, although a guitarist may compare prices at various retailers before purchasing a Fender Stratocaster.

Luxuries represent a subcategory of specialty products that are marketed with high prices and a high degree of exclusivity. Hermès scarves and handbags from France are well-known specialty products worldwide. For those consumers in this target market segment, price deserves little consideration. Some Hermès scarves retail for several hundred dollars, and Hermès handbags sell for several thousand dollars.

Product quality becomes the primary marketing issue for luxuries and specialty products. Consumers are willing to pay extra for the quality associated with the goods. Patek Philippe SA, a watch marketer located in Plan-les-Ouates, Switzerland, offers world-class timepieces of uncompromised quality. The company's customers willingly pay higher prices for the world-class craftsmanship.

The term "specialty product" also applies to services. Lloyds of London provides insurance policies for high-end buyers with specific needs, such as when a soccer player has his legs insured in case of injury. Lloyds of London insures higher-risk items in more than two hundred countries with its 360 Risk Insight program.

Product Dimensions

Products often display three key dimensions: the core product, packaging, and auxiliary dimensions (see Figure 7.2). The *core product* satisfies or remedies a basic need. A screwdriver is a core product, as are candy bars and lawn mowers.

Packaging includes the elements of the product that are used to communicate the brand name, logo, and trademark, as well as to protect the core product. Marketers adapt packaging and labels in response to differences in legal systems, local traditions, and cultures.

The *auxiliary dimensions* include warranties, instructions, company contact information, as well as the image of the particular brand. Shopping products sometimes are differentiated based on auxiliary dimensions. An inexpensive automobile may deliver the same basic benefit as a more expensive model, thereby offering the same core product but unique auxiliary dimensions. Marketers normally devote a substantial amount of attention to auxiliary dimensions as they present shopping products to potential customers. All dimensions of the product offering deliver benefits to the consumer, or end-user.

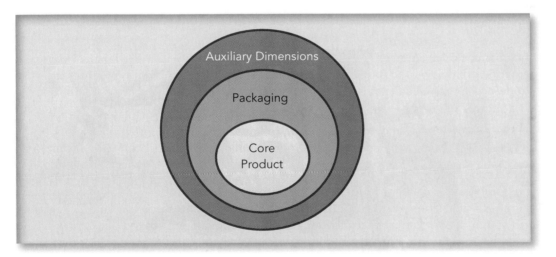

Figure 7.2: Product Dimensions

International marketers often consider the *total value concept*, or the complete set of values from products that customers receive.[3] An example of the total value concept can be found with Europa Park in Germany. Guests at the popular German amusement park enjoy rides and entertainment. At the same time, they experience family fun and create life-long memories. The park is conveniently located and is easy to find. The park provides instructions for bicyclists who want to visit. Value comes from the many roller-coasters and thrill rides, but also from family bonding and togetherness. Recognizing that different market segments perceive value differently, the park offers special activities targeting seniors, children, families, and teenagers.[4]

International Product Mix Management

International marketers face numerous decisions pertaining to brand and product management. Many global companies develop individual products and product lines. Effectively managing portfolios of these products and brands constitutes a key strategic international marketing activity.

PRODUCT LINES AND MIX

Product lines are groups of similar products within a particular category, such as the Maddog line of surfboards manufactured in Australia. The **product mix** refers to the total number of products that a firm carries. Maddog also offers an apparel line and scuba accessories. The *depth* of a product line refers to the total number of products in that line. If Maddog sells four types of surfboards, the depth of the surfboard line is four products. The *width* (sometimes called the breadth) of the product mix refers to the total number of product lines that the company offers. If Maddog sells surfboards, surfing apparel, and scuba equipment, the width would be three lines.

Bosch International, a leading global supplier of technology and services with headquarters in Germany, sells products and services to the automotive and industrial technology and to consumers. The company also offers products for various building technology industries. The combination of these products across all segments constitute Bosch's product mix.

PACKAGING

Packaging decisions represent a key aspect of international product marketing. When exporting or shipping goods, the product's package serves to protect the item until it arrives safely. Packaging facilitates the movement of products through the distribution channel—from the factory to the consumer. Packaging can become an aspect of a brand's identity, thereby affecting the relationship between the customer and the brand.[5]

Packaging should be adapted to individual markets based on consumer tastes, preferences, and culture. Matching the package to the market can become the deciding factor in a product's success, because consumers actually make many purchase decisions at the point of purchase. A recent study of Thai consumers indicated that packaging technology, such as the convenience of the package, was the most important determinant affecting the intention to buy a product. Other package determinants include packaging shape, product information, color and graphics, and layout of product information.[6]

Many marketers view packaging as a place for innovation. In the case of wine, protective elements are important, because the product will spoil and turn into vinegar if exposed to air, heat, and light. In the past, wine was packaged in large, air-proof casks. It was then served from the cask or put into glass bottles to transport home for consumption. The younger the wine, the fresher and more preferred. The invention of cork closures allows consumers to store wine at home and has led to a preference for older, matured wines. The introduction of a screw top reduced the risk of cork contamination, while the use of bags-in-a-box allows European consumers to keep open wine fresh for weeks. The South African packaging company Mondi recently introduced wine bottle made from PET plastic. While the bottles look like glass, the lighter plastic lowers the shipping costs and the carbon footprint associated with shipping. Making plastic requires less energy than glass production. Leveraging the green components of the packaging, the Backsberg winery introduced the Tread Lightly label using the PET plastic bottles.[7] Other examples of innovative packing include fridge packs for sodas, liquid soap with a pump, and Apple's innovative iPad2 smart cover.

Packages contain at least four elements, including visual elements, informational elements, protective elements, and symbolic elements.

Visual Elements

Elements such as shape, color, font usage, and pictorials help to communicate brand meaning to customers and differentiate the product from the competition. Much of the sensory experience of consumers comes from the visual elements, which plays an important role in package design. Today's technology permits marketers to incorporate eye-catching colors and shapes that can increase purchase likelihood.

Informational Elements

The package transmits vital and legal information regarding the contents of the package and the product. Marketers should ensure that the language used on the package will be suitable for the selected target market. Some countries have adopted language labeling laws. Canada requires the use of both French and English on packaging. Products marketed in the European Union must be packaged with metric measurements. Information included on packaging can also build valuable brand associations.[8]

Protective Elements

Protective elements, such as plastic, must be carefully considered by international marketers due to regional restrictions and sustainability issues. As an example, restrictions in the European Union help reduce unnecessary and hazardous waste, restrict package size, and encourage reusable materials in packages.[9] The restrictions are a part of the Packaging and Packaging Waste Directive of the EU.

Seafood presents special considerations for packaging and protection. Producers often distribute seafood over thousands of miles, and product protection is at a premium. The successful international seafood marketer Royal Greenland A/S understands the importance of delivering high-quality seafood from the farthest reaches of the Earth's oceans to consumers worldwide. The company, headquartered in Nuuk, Greenland, offers high-quality seafood for international delivery while maintaining strict packaging guidelines for sustainability (www.royalgreenland.com).

Symbolic Elements

Package shapes and features help the consumer recognize the brand. The symbolic nature of packaging not only appeals to a consumer's inner needs but also helps to convey desired images to others. Perfume and scent manufacturers, such as Dubai's Al Arabiya Al Swissriya (Arabian–Swiss) fragrance company, spend considerable time and energy

Packages and labels influence purchase decisions.

creating the proper bottle for the product and for the box that holds the bottle. The company matches symbolic elements with local culture and customs.

LABELING

Labeling serves several communication purposes. Consumers cannot judge the attributes of many products until after the purchase. Labeling helps potential customers learn about various aspects of the product prior to buying it. Consequently, designing a label is an important marketing process that becomes magnified when the product ships to another country.

Cultural factors also affect designs of labels, including the use of art, various colors, images, and wording. Marketers respond to these variations in taste by changing labels. In the United States, a picture or drawing of a squirrel may be used as part of a logo or display with the intent of leading the consumer to believe she is being prudent or thrifty. In other countries, however, squirrels are considered to be rodents similar to rats. Placing the picture of one on a label would not conjure the desired image.

Aesthetics

Aesthetics are concepts of beauty. Countries and groups within countries have diverse views of beauty. What is considered beautiful in one country may be considered garish or unattractive in another country. Colors are important aesthetic ingredients in packaging and labeling decisions. Marketers pay close attention to the meaning of color in different cultures. Red, for example, symbolizes happiness and good luck in China, whereas it symbolizes caution in the United States and Canada. The color green has special meaning for Muslims.[10] Several Islamic countries use green as a national color because it has a strong association with the Muslim faith. Using green as part of a label should be carefully considered. Marketers should make sure the label does not offend religious sensitivities, which could lead to lost customers.

Legal Requirements

A label provides information about a product's country-of-origin, which often plays an important role in international product success. A recent study of Greek wine consumers revealed that information linking a product with a specific place will be one of the top pieces of information that wine consumers seek on a product label.[11] The same holds true for region of origin: French wines labels often carry the name of the province or region in which the grapes were grown to assist wine connoisseurs.

One essential part of labeling in the European Union, the "CE Mark" (a French acronym for *Conformité Européenne*), signifies that a product has met EU health, environmental, and safety requirements.[12] The mark allows the product to flow freely throughout the European Union. In the United States, companies must adhere to the Fair Packaging and Labeling Act, which sets mandatory requirements for labeling and encourages voluntary labeling and packaging standards.

Labeling standards vary significantly by product type. In many Muslim countries, feminine products cannot display pictures of the item. Other products require express and complete ingredient descriptions, plus any warnings and/or warranties. Cigarette manufacturers in the United States must place the surgeon general's warning on each pack; in late 2010, the Federal Drug Administration proposed that cigarette manufacturers begin putting graphic images associated with the health effects of smoking. These included images of a corpse, diseased lungs, and children suffering from second-hand smoke. In some countries, the warnings are even more explicit or dire; in others, either no policy exists or the policy in place is not enforced.[13]

Sustainability and International Product Marketing

VIDEO LINK 7.1: Sustainable Communities

The two major areas of sustainable product management are product design and packaging. Product design can become more sustainable by using recycled or recyclable materials, identifying areas where fewer materials can be utilized, and ensuring that production techniques are as efficient as possible.

Several countries and organizations have taken steps to address sustainability issues related to packaging. In 2010, the Consumer Goods Forum released the report "A Global Language for Packaging and Sustainability" that describes how packaging can be designed holistically with the product to optimize overall environmental performance.[14] Focusing on sustainable packaging not only helps the environment but also can improve consumer perceptions and lead to increased sales. Country-specific guidelines are available. The Packaging Council of Australia developed a comprehensive program of actions to implement a Towards Sustainable Packaging program in 2007. The program seeks to reduce the harmful effects of packaging products nationwide.[15] In the United States, organizations such as the Sustainable Packaging Coalition work to encourage environmentally friendly packaging.[16] The ISO 14000 guidelines address various elements of environmental management and provide a general framework for product management as it pertains to sustainability.

Ecology Coatings of the United States provides environmentally friendly standards for coatings and other materials for business buyers.[17] Coatings and resins are particularly important in package design and production. Companies that reduce excessive packaging materials, increase use of biodegradable materials, and incorporate packaging materials that have been produced from energy-efficient operations and production techniques are building a solid foundation for future operations.

Many consumers prefer green packaging. Some larger businesses have made changes to meet this demand. In Australia, KFC has started to serve food in compostable bags. After six months in a landfill, the bags will have completely converted to carbon dioxide and water.[18] In the United Kingdom, retailers are considering using a milk container made almost completely from recycled and recyclable paper. This new packaging would greatly cut the amount of plastic in U.K. landfills.[19]

Consumer demand for environmentally friendly products remained strong even during the recent turbulent economy. One study reported that 44% of consumers stated that their green buying habits did not change despite difficult economic times.[20] This unwavering commitment from consumers highlights the importance of sustainable product designs.

LEARNING OBJECTIVE #3:

What types of international business products and services are available?

International Business Products

Consumer products tend to garner more attention in popular press books and magazines; the business-to-business sector plays an equally important role in international marketing. Business products consist of items in the categories presented in Figure 7.3.

Raw Materials
Maintenance, Repair, and Operating Supplies
Component Parts
Accessory Equipment
Business Services
Process Materials
Installations

Figure 7.3: Categories of International Business Products

RAW MATERIALS

Materials used in the manufacture of end products and including natural resources (minerals, ore, chemicals, and fuel) and farm products (beef, cotton, poultry, milk, and soy beans) are all raw materials. Mercatto Group of Brazil supplies leather goods from the vast resources of southern Brazil to companies throughout the world.[21] Leather is used in numerous products globally and remains an important raw material in international trade.

MAINTENANCE, REPAIR, AND OPERATING SUPPLIES

Maintenance, repair, and operating supplies are marketed to businesses for use in production and other operations. Examples of maintenance, repair, and operating supplies would include cleaning products and standard repair tools. H. E. Williams, Inc. of the United States is a major supplier of innovative lighting solutions for businesses (www.hew.com). Lighting equipment facilitates the production of nearly all factory-produced items.

COMPONENT PARTS

Finished products that eventually become parts of other products are component parts. These products are common, for example, in the automotive industry, and include radios, tires, and other essential parts of the vehicle. Comstar in India supplies component parts for several automotive companies including Ford, Mazda, and Volvo.[22] Many consumers are familiar with the brand names of MP3 players and GPS systems that are added to new cars, such Garmin or iPod.

International business products include component parts, accessory equipment, and process materials.

ACCESSORY EQUIPMENT

Products that help facilitate the production of other products but that do not become a part of the products themselves are forms of accessory equipment. Examples include office equipment such as computers and fax machines that help the manufacturer conduct daily operations. The Taiwanese company Anoma Corporation is a worldwide leading manufacturer and supplier of custom power supplies for clients throughout the world such as Siemens (Germany), Samsung (Korea), Philips (Netherlands), and Sony (Japan).

BUSINESS SERVICES

Business services assist companies in normal business operations, either with the production or maintenance of goods, or with general business operations such as delivery services, telecommunication service, or logistical services. MTU Aero Engines of Germany has become a worldwide leader in commercial aero engine maintenance services (www.mtu.de/en/index.html). Business services are a crucial part of the international service sector.

PROCESS MATERIALS

Materials that become a part of other products in an unidentifiable way are process materials, such as food additives and resins. Industrial Resins Sdn Bhd of Malaysia supplies industrial resin products worldwide.[23] Other companies focus on providing coatings and other materials for the manufacture of products. Nearly every manufactured product has some type of coating, creating a large international marketing opportunity.

INSTALLATIONS

Major capital equipment products used directly in the manufacturer of other products are installations. Heavy machinery and assembly line equipment are examples. Advanced Machining & Automation, Inc. of the United States designs and manufacturers automated equipment for industrial customers.[24] Heavy machinery and other capital installations continue to be mainstays of industrial marketing.

DISTINCTIONS BETWEEN BUSINESS AND CONSUMER PRODUCTS

Although distinctions have been made between business and consumer products, many international marketers offer the same product to both businesses and consumers. The Canadian company Agrium, Inc. markets agricultural products and services through both retail and wholesale channels. The agricultural products help growers worldwide to increase crop yields. The same product can be used as a component process material that is sold to other businesses. The company sells urea, which provides nutrients for plants and can also be used as a resign by lumber companies or to assist in the recycling of aluminum.[25]

Many products are both business products and consumer products. The categorization depends on the use of the product by the customer. A stapler is a good example. It may be used at home or in an office. Marketers of products such as this often use multiple distribution channels even though there are no differences in the product itself.

Bottom-of-the-Pyramid International Product Marketing

Several opportunities exist regarding the management of products and brands as they pertain to bottom-of-the-pyramid consumers. A central issue will be the price-quality relationship. Traditional market logic assumes that consumers are willing, sometimes more than willing, to pay premium prices for high-quality products. Some consumers will go out of their way to buy specialty and luxury items.

An alternative approach is to rethink the price-quality relationship and design products that offer basic essentials at minimal prices. To do so requires that the company carefully consider its obligation to both shareholders and the world community. One concern will be that by offering stripped-down product versions, the company's image will suffer.[26] Marketers weigh slim profits in the short run against the long-term goodwill that may come with serving bottom-of-the-pyramid markets.[27]

Manufacturers should consider product costs carefully, as transaction costs and logistical costs can be higher in less-developed regions.[28] Marketing remanufactured products presents one opportunity to reach these regions. *Remanufactured products*, used products that have been refurbished through manufacturing processes in order to be restored to acceptable functioning, often fit with the needs of bottom-of-the-pyramid consumers. Used products about to be discarded are part of this category. The millions of computers, televisions, and cell phones that would have otherwise been thrown away in developed countries each year represent a realistic opportunity for marketing to bottom-of-the-pyramid consumers.

Another opportunity may be found in offering smaller package sizes and quantities.[29] This strategy can be successful for international marketers. Marketers in rural areas of India have found success by following such strategies.[30] One recent study indicated that easy-to-carry packages that are also easy to understand are critical for influencing the buying behaviors of bottom-of-the-pyramid consumers.[31]

International Product Support Services

One additional element of product marketing attracts the attention of the marketing team: product support services accompany a vast number of consumer and business purchases. Support services include installation, maintenance, servicing and repair, providing credit, answering questions by telephone or over the Internet, assisting businesses with inventory management, and more general activities such as providing market information.

The phrase "service after the sale" often appears in advertisements for shopping goods including automobiles and appliances. High-quality product support generates goodwill for a variety of domestic and international companies: the experience of dining at a restaurant can be made more pleasant by an attentive server or ruined when a patron's credit card is wrongly rejected by the restaurant's cashier system. Currently, the German company SMA sells some of the more reliable inverters that are needed to turn direct current from solar panels into alternating current (www.sma.de/en). Providing effective servicing of the inverters in other countries is an important part of SMA's international marketing success.

Many companies selling copiers and other image-reproduction equipment also offer maintenance and service agreements. The key product support services help build longer-term relationships with customers, making the sale of the next product easier.

INTERNATIONAL INCIDENT //

In Taiwan, purchases, especially large ones, are rewarded with thank-you gifts. These gifts are branded to serve a promotional benefit. A gasoline purchase may be rewarded with a gift of a box of tissues. Someone who makes a large purchase at a retailer takes the receipt to a special prize section in the store, often near the exit, and gets to choose from a variety of prizes. The rewards are small and simple, such as an alarm clock, house decoration, or a low-cost children's toy. The retail environment in an emerging market often features a high level of personal service, in part due to low labor costs. Stores have elevator attendants and a large sales force. A shopper may receive assistance from two or three sales people at one time. What would happen if you took a Taiwanese immigrant or a travelling businessperson to visit an upscale U.S. retailer? The visitor would expect great service and might receive little or no attention from the salesperson in some stores. The shopper would also expect a gift or prize for making a purchase and would not receive one. How would you explain this to your shopping companion?

The term "service" can create confusion. In this context, product support services are not directly sold to customers. Instead they provide added dimensions to the sale of a physical good or intangible service. In the next section, services that are sold to customers and businesses are described.

International Services

The global economy has largely shifted toward a services base.[32] Services are intangible products that are based around some act or performance that delivers value. Effectively marketing them in new countries presents many challenges. Services include those displayed in Figure 7.4.

A growing interest in the international marketing of services has emerged. Table 7.1 presents data for the worldwide export value of merchandise and commercial services trade. Although exports of merchandise still dominate world

Type of Service	Example
Transportation	taxi, air travel, bus, rickshaw, boat
Financial Services	credit/lending, credit/debit card, investment, checking account, savings account
Telecommunication	landline, cell/mobile phone, Internet connectivity
Insurance	policies for health, life, property, business, shipping
Health Care	hospital, family doctor, walk-in clinic, eye care
Personal Services	hair care, spa, massage, concierge
Recreation/Cultural	museums, art districts, theater, opera
Business Services	accounting, consulting
Tourism	theme parks, tourist attractions, beach, tour guides, destination gambling

Figure 7.4: Types of Services

VIDEO LINK 7.2:
Offshoring

	VALUE ($ BILLION)		% CHANGE		
	2009	2005–2009	2007	2008	2009
Merchandise	12,147	4	16	15	–23
Commercial Services	3,312	7	20	12	–13

Table 7.1: **Exports of Merchandise and Commercial Services**

Source: World Trade Organization (July 27, 2010), accessed at www.wto.org/english/news_e/pres10_e/pr598_e.htm.

France	77.6%
United States	76.9%
Belgium	76.1%
United Kingdom	75.6%
Portugal	73.7%
Denmark	72.6%
Italy	71.0%
Japan	69.3%
Germany	69.0%
Spain	68.3%
Brazil	65.3%
Mexico	59.1%
El Salvador	58.4%
Honduras	55.4%
Norway	52.6%
Chile	52.3%
Ethiopia	42.4%
China	40.1%
Bhutan	35.2%
Angola	25.7%
Azerbaijan	23.8%
Liberia	21.9%

Table 7.2: **Services as Percentage of GDP**

Source: "Services, etc., Value Added (% of GDP)," The World Bank (2011), accessed at http://data.worldbank.org/indicator/NV.SRV.TETC.ZS; data presented from 2008 indicators.

trade, the marketing of services has risen, even as both merchandise and commercial services trade has been severely influenced by the recent global recession. Many multinational corporations also outsource various services to companies offshore in other nations that have an expertise in that service.[33]

Economies generally progress from agrarian to manufacturing to services over time. Worldwide, services account for an average of approximately 70% of GDP.[34] Services, as a percentage of GDP, tend to dominate the economies of developed countries. Services often play a smaller role in lesser-developed countries.[35] Table 7.2 presents data for services as expressed as percentage of GDP for several countries.

Tourism often plays an important part of international marketing; it exhibits a major influence on the gross domestic product (GDP) of many countries. The impact of tourism can readily be observed in developed countries. Canada (8.9% of GDP), France (9.7%), Germany (7.5%), Greece (15.5%), Italy (9.3%), Japan (9.1%), Spain (15.3%), the United Kingdom (9.7%), and the United States (9.1%) all have major tourism industries.[36]

Many governmental leaders recognize the potential importance of tourism to local economies. Copenhagen, the capital of Denmark, has recently refocused efforts to increase tourism to its locales through the Wonderful Copenhagen campaign, an attempt to increase the number of tourists to 1 million per year by 2014.[37] Table 7.3 presents the top tourism economies worldwide.

International Product Quality Standards

Offering high-quality products, both physical goods and intangible services, should be a key goal for international marketers. As competition intensifies in many industries, the only sure method of achieving marketing success involves paying close attention to product quality. The term "product quality" can refer to many different aspects of a product. Figure 7.5 on page 244 presents the various dimensions of product quality.

The value of each of these dimensions varies by product, country, culture, and individual consumer. To some, durability may be the primary factor influencing a purchase decision, because the product represents a major purchase, and consumers may have limited funds. For others, aesthetics could be the key decision variable, especially for items that become part of a household's decor. At the least, the marketing team should attempt to identify the most salient features of product quality in the culture of a new country.

QUALITY STANDARDS

Many consumers look for methods to ensure that products sold across national boundaries are of comparable quality. As a result, demonstrating that a product meets a quality standard can become a key ingredient in international marketing success. Individual companies, countries, and regions seek to meet or exceed quality standards when marketing internationally. The *International Organization for Standardization (ISO)* provides standards that guide management practice as it relates to quality management and assurance (www.iso.org). The ISO organization includes more than 160 member nations. ISO standards are widely used in the European Union.

The *American Society for Quality (ASQ)*, a global community of experts in quality management, is also the sole administrator of the Malcolm Baldrige National Award (www.asq.org). The annual award is presented in manufacturing, services, small business, education, health care, and nonprofit sectors. Figure 7.6 lists the winners for 2010. The award pertains to product quality and other areas of management including leadership, strategic planning, customer focus, knowledge management, human resource focus, process management, and business performance.

In the automotive industry, the J. D. Power & Associates Initial Quality Study continues to be considered by many to be the industry benchmark for annual new car quality ratings (www.jdpower.com). Consumers are asked to rate their automobiles on both mechanical and design quality. The results are highly valued in the industry. Automobile companies operating internationally pay close attention to J. D. Power ratings.

COUNTRY	$ BILLIONS
United States	1,344.35
Japan	473.74
China	445.47
France	265.77
Germany	259.71
Spain	229.76
United Kingdom	220.48
Italy	204.86
Canada	120.96
Mexico	114.81

Table 7.3: **Top Tourism Economies, 2009**

Source: "Economic Data Search Tool," World Travel & Tourism Council (2010), accessed at www.wttc.org/eng/Tourism_Research/Economic_Data_Search_Tool/.

Many governmental leaders recognize the potential importance of tourism to local economies.

The Product Life Cycle

The product life cycle can be used to represent the "life" of a product as it progresses through four stages: introduction, growth, maturity, and decline (see Figure 7.7). The life cycle concept applies to physical goods and intangible services, to entire product categories such as mobile phones, and to specific brands of products (for example, Toshiba). The assumption that every product has a "life" may not be the case. Some products used in daily living do not appear to ever reach a point of decline or death, including coffee, tea, sugar, and salt; although the companies selling these items may follow the cycle.

LEARNING OBJECTIVE #4:

What types of patterns exist as new products move from introduction to eventual decline?

Dimension	Description
Performance	degree to which the product performs its key functions
Features	auxiliary dimensions beyond the core product
Conformity	extent to which the product is produced according to specifications
Reliability	consistency of product performance over time
Durability	overall product usefulness over its life
Aesthetics	appearance and design of high-quality product
Serviceability	convenience and ease of service of the product

Figure 7.5: Product Quality Dimensions

Source: Adapted from David A. Aaker, *Managing Brand Equity* (New York: Macmillan, 1991); also David Garvin, "Competing on the Eight Dimensions of Quality," *Harvard Business Review* (1987, Nov.–Dec.), 101–108; Kevin L. Keller, *Strategic Brand Management* (Upper Saddle River, NJ: Prentice-Hall, 1998).

Company	Category
MEDRAD	Manufacturing
Nestlé Purina PetCare Co.	Manufacturing
Freese and Nichols Inc.	Small Business
K&N Management	Small Business
Studer Group	Small Business
Montgomery County (Maryland) Public Schools	Education
Advocate Good Samaritan Hospital	Health Care

Figure 7.6: 2010 Malcolm Baldrige National Award Winners

Source: "Baldridge Performance Excellence Program," National Institute of Standards and Technology (2011, July 19), accessed at www.baldrige.nist.gov/Contacts_Profiles.htm.

Various products may be at different points in the life cycle across different countries and cultures. Televisions may be in the maturity phase the United States but in the growth stage in developing countries. Each of the lifecycle stages presents opportunities and challenges.

DEVELOPMENT

Development takes place before the product life cycle actually begins. Prior to a product's introduction, the development process involves creating and testing a product concept. In most cases, a well-thought-out and executed developmental program is needed to successfully bring a product to market. Development requires companies to commit significant resources in terms of human capital, financial investment, and market research. Profits are nonexistent at this point, because the product has not been sold to consumers. Only the expenses necessary for successful development are present.

A small percentage of products introduced each year continue to be marketed five years later. Most products do not last in the marketplace, and some fail very quickly.

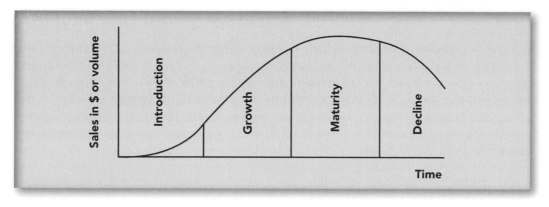

Figure 7.7: Product Life Cycle

In the vast majority of cases, the product's failure results from insufficient or poorly executed market research. Consequently, careful attention should be given during development.

Some firms attempt to become the pioneers of new innovations. The **pioneering advantage** refers to all of the benefits that result from being the first mover in a market. Haier, a major Chinese manufacturer and worldwide leader in household appliances, achieved a great deal of success by developing processes that enable the firm to respond to market demands quickly and efficiently.[38] Responding quickly to market demands is an important part of capturing the pioneering advantage. To be a pioneer also means that the company carefully monitors its investments in research and development. Innovative companies spend a great deal of resources on new product introductions. South Korean giant Samsung pays close attention to its allocation of resources across its new product innovations as well as to its new product success ratio.[39]

> The pioneering advantage refers to all of the benefits that result from being the first mover in a market.

INTRODUCTION

When the product has been initially released to the targeted market segment, the introduction stage commences. Educating the target segment about the new product will be one key activity. The focus turns to establishing *primary demand*, or demand for the generic product itself rather than necessarily the specific brand being introduced. To move consumers to that point, marketers explain the benefits of the new product. Marketing costs tend to be high during the introduction stage due to the expenses associated with promoting the product, acquiring adequate distribution channels, and recouping production and research and development costs. Profits are normally not realized during this stage.

International marketers may attempt to introduce products at different periods in different countries and/or regions, thereby staggering demand for the product. The strategy is popular for products forecasted to have huge global demand. As an example, Apple's iPad was first released in the United States. The product was introduced to the United Kingdom, Canada, Germany, France, Switzerland, Italy, Spain, Japan, and Australia approximately one month after the U.S. release. Other markets were targeted months later.

GROWTH

When sales begin to grow more rapidly and profits are realized, the product has entered the growth stage. Competition begins to enter the market during this stage. Competing firms, or followers, enter the industry after pioneering firms have developed and introduced a product.

Firms that introduced the product are forced to develop defensive strategies that concentrate on retaining current customers. For pioneering companies, retaining current customers will be more efficient than obtaining new ones. The iPad drew considerable international competition from Sony (Japan), Samsung (South Korea), and Motorola (United States), pushing the tablet market quickly through the growth phase of the product life cycle. During the growth stage, primary demand ceases to be the focus and market differentiation becomes the key. Competitors in the tablet market quickly developed points of differentiation, including unique operating systems and features.

MATURITY

When sales begin to increase at a decreasing rate and market saturation begins, the product has reached the maturity stage. Due to saturation and intense competition, the only way marketers can obtain new customers will be by taking them from competitors. Prices generally begin to drop during this phase due to the intense competition and resulting increased marketing efforts aimed at customer retention. Laptop computers quickly moved from the growth phase of the life cycle to maturity, even as some consumers moved on to tablet models and smartphones.[40] Laptop sales, however, were healthy and they eventually exceeded desktop sales internationally.[41]

During the maturity stage, marketers attempt to hold the company's current market share or entice customers away from competitors. The goal becomes to maintain a company's share in a growing market, thereby increasing sales, or to capture share in a stagnant market in order to increase sales.

Many consumer durables, such as appliances, have reached the maturity phase in developed countries. Appliances including washing machines, clothes dryers, microwave ovens, and televisions are commonly found in most households in these nations. Households in lesser-developed nations, especially where bottom-of-the-pyramid consumers are concentrated, do not experience the same level of consumption of durables.

Market saturation in one country leads many international marketers to consider introducing a product in other countries. The cell or mobile phone provider industry quickly reached the maturity phase. Statistics indicate there are now more than 5 billion mobile phone connections worldwide, with the penetration rate exceeding 100% in some countries. In other words, there is more than one connection for each person in some countries.[42] Opportunities to market cell phones and provider services are present in developing and bottom-of-the-pyramid regions. Price and technological infrastructure development issues are the most significant obstacles to expansion into these regions.

Firms may attempt to extend the maturity phase in a number of different ways, including increasing the number of users by expanding the overall market, finding new uses for the product, or attempting to increase the frequency of product usage. These strategies fall under the general category of market penetration. Firms may also introduce quality improvements, feature improvements, or style improvements in order to prolong this stage.[43]

DECLINE

The decline stage occurs when a gradual or rapid drop in sales takes place. As consumer tastes change and new innovations are introduced, product sales fall. During this stage, the company's marketing team begins to decide how long to stay in the market. Sometimes, a company will completely discontinue a product, as was the case with film-based cameras. The Eastman Kodak company stopped selling most film cameras in Canada, Europe, and the United States.[44] Kodachrome film, a well-known product from Kodak, was also discontinued in Europe and North America in 2010, and the final processing facility in the United States closed in that year. Desktop computers, long thought to represent a growth industry, have begun to show declines in sales worldwide as laptops, tablets, and smartphones earned quick consumer acceptance. Although once thought to be inconceivable, it is possible that the desktop computer will become a thing of the past.

Product Cycle Theory

Raymond Vernon first introduced product cycle theory in the field of international economics in 1960. The theory explains how products and production move from developed countries to lesser-developed countries.[45] It separates regions into lead innovation nations, developed nations, and developing nations.

According to the theory, a new product is first developed, produced, and consumed in a *lead innovation nation*, such as Japan. Over time, as the product becomes widely accepted, the manufacturer realizes production efficiencies as foreign demand for the product emerges. The manufacturer then exports the product to other *developed nations* or regions that exhibit sufficient demand, such as the European Union. Production gradually shifts to these overseas markets, and eventually the manufacturer exports the product from these markets to both the original market and to lesser-developed countries. Finally, production again shifts, this time to lesser-developed or *developing nations*. Then companies from the original, developed countries devote capabilities to new innovations.

Product cycle theory has been criticized for relying on studies of the United States as the lead innovative nation. The research appears to neglect the current trend in which many products are launched simultaneously around the world. Companies that are international in scope from their inception are born-global firms. Product cycle theory does not appear to fit products introduced by these firms. In addition, companies often target emerging wealthy customer segments in developing markets early in the product cycle. Later, the company may begin to target other market segments, as predicted by the theory. Even with these criticisms, product cycle theory does explain some patterns of international trade over time.[46]

Market/Product Matrix

An important part of international product and brand management will be strategically matching the product portfolio to the various markets that a firm serves. A useful tool for conceptualizing the various strategies is the market/product matrix, as presented in Figure 7.8. Each of these strategies fits with a unique set of circumstances.

Products		Markets	
		Existing	New
	Existing	Market Penetration	Market Development
	New	Product Development	Diversification

Figure 7.8: The Market/Product Matrix

MARKET PENETRATION

A firm uses a market penetration strategy when it attempts to increase sales of existing products in existing markets. One market penetration tactic is developing and promoting new uses for existing products. Baking soda may be used in cooking, to deodorize a refrigerator or freezer, or in toothpaste.

An alternative strategy for successful market penetration, *repositioning*, is the process of changing perceptions of the product in the minds of consumers. Philips, the Dutch multinational electronics marketer, recently repositioned its products under the theme of "health and well-being" from an earlier "sense and simplicity" theme that was developed for its electronics lines. The idea was to reposition the company away from television and electronics into products that improve everyday living through innovation. Repositioning a company and its product offerings can help the firm to better connect with its customers and may lead to higher levels of market penetration.

PRODUCT DEVELOPMENT

Product development strategies take place when the marketing team attempts to introduce new products to existing markets or to enhance existing products with new features or options. Product development strategies are highly popular in international marketing. Many firms actively engage in product development. Japan's Sony Corporation develops several new products each year for existing markets. Ford Motor Company developed the Kuga SUV specifically for European markets as part of a product development strategy. Optimal Energy of South Africa has plans to market the Joule electric car, the first vehicle to be developed and manufactured by a South African company, with export plans to the United Kingdom and Commonwealth countries by 2013.[47]

DIVERSIFICATION

Firms employ a diversification strategy by marketing new products in new markets. Company leaders often choose this strategy as a response to perceived opportunities or as a way to defend against increased competition in existing markets and product lines. The Vortex Engineering company in India developed a new form of ATM specifically for rural markets. The machines simplified the process of obtaining cash by including fingerprint-reading technologies.[48] To date, the venture has been successful.

The Taiwanese corporation Wistron announced in 2010 that it was diversifying from its notebook computer business into handheld devices, flat-panel televisions, and three-dimensional televisions. A move such as this would allow the company to expand into new products and markets as a response to intense competition in the company's main business.[49]

MARKET DEVELOPMENT

A market development strategy occurs when a firm attempts to market existing products in new markets. This international marketing strategy allows a company to minimize problems with local or domestic market saturation by expanding into new countries or regions.

TeaGschwender, a German specialty tea company, grew its business from an original location in Trier, Germany, to more than 130 shops in seven countries.[50] The strategy has proven to be successful in making the company a leader in specialty teas.

Starbucks has also become well known for its aggressive market development strategy. The company operates thousands of outlets worldwide, with several hundred in Japan and China. The coffee giant currently maintains approximately 5,500 stores outside the United States.[51] Harley Davidson, the American motorcycle icon, currently earns more than one third of its retail sales outside the United States.[52]

IMPLICATIONS

International product development and management presents an ongoing set of opportunities and obstacles. The marketing team continually evaluates individual products and product lines, the product mix, packages, labels, and the stage in the life cycle for each product in domestic and international markets. Marketing efforts are then adjusted to economic circumstances, cultural trends, political shifts, and technological innovations within industries and various countries. One tool that can become a major asset in the process of managing products is effective management of a company's name and brands.

International Brand Management

The name, sign, symbol, and/or design that identifies the products of a firm and distinguishes it from competition is the company's **brand**. A *brand name* is the verbal part of a brand that can be spoken (the name Nike), and a *brandmark* is comprised of the nonverbal elements that signify the brand (the name Nike combined with the Nike swoosh). A *trademark* is a legally protected brand name and a *servicemark* is a legally protected service name. A global brand is a brand that is common across countries and is recognizable worldwide. Coca-Cola, Sony, and Mercedes-Benz are well-known global brands.

LEARNING OBJECTIVE #5:

What role does brand development and management play in international marketing?

Brand-building is a key element of international beverage marketing efforts.

FAMILY AND INDIVIDUAL BRANDING

International marketers can choose between family branding and individual branding. **Family branding** means a number of products in a line or mix share the same brand name worldwide. LG, the South Korean electronics giant, uses the family branding approach. The LG name appears on televisions, home theater products, washing machines, clothes dryers, and cell phones. The family brand approach capitalizes on the company's reputation and its trusted, established name. Japan's Toshiba, Inc., uses a family branding strategy for lines of televisions, digital video recorders, laptops, and electronic accessories. Marketers should ensure that the brand name fits the basic product concept to avoid consumer confusion. Family branding holds the advantage of transferring trust in a brand to new products. When Black & Decker offers a new power tool, people who have used other products recognize the name and are more willing to try the new product.

An **individual branding** strategy involves creating distinct brand names for the individual products created by a company. The international giant Proctor & Gamble utilizes an individual branding strategy for most of the company's products. In its household care line, the company offers brands such as Bounce, Bounty, Charmin, Cheer, Dawn, and Downy. Each product has a unique brand name. An individual branding strategy works when the brands do not share common features or uses. In international marketing, distinctive brands are developed for individual countries. Proctor & Gamble sells many laundry detergents with familiar names; until recently, however, the Ariel brand was only sold in certain markets. Individual branding allows for more-specific targeting of a name that matches a specific geographic region or culture.

> An individual branding strategy involves creating distinct brand names for the individual products created by a company.

BRAND AND PRODUCT LINE EXTENSIONS

Marketers frequently face the decision of when and how to extend brands and product lines. Two distinct methods may be used. A **brand extension** strategy takes the brand name and adds it to a new product. Britain's Virgin Group Limited has successfully extended the well-respected Virgin brand name across numerous product categories and industries, including airlines, entertainment, and mobile media (www.virgin.com). The company has recently moved into space travel, representing an extension of the travel options already associated with the brand.

A **product line extension** strategy means products are introduced that are in a related product category and that respond to specific opportunities in the marketplace. Germany's Adidas Corporation recently announced that it would extend its outdoor product line into high-end mountaineering jackets as it strives to be a leading brand for performance sports gear. The movement into the jacket product line allows the company to claim that Adidas products increase performance for all types of active endeavors.[53] Other examples of product line extensions include PepsiMax, Coke Zero, Dannon fat-free yogurts, Yoplait Go-Gurt, and Honey Nut Cheerios.

COBRANDING

The practice of placing two or more brand names on the same product, or **cobranding**, has become a popular international marketing strategy. The Wendy's/Arby's group recently announced plans to form an agreement with Al Jammaz Group, a Saudi Arabian franchisee, to open 135 cobranded Wendy's/Arby's restaurants in nine countries in the Middle East and North Africa.[54] The two companies merged in

2008; the cobranding agreement presents an opportunity for synergies between the established names. Cobranding strategies can follow ingredient, cooperative, or complementary approaches.

Ingredient Cobranding

Ingredient cobranding occurs when one brand becomes a "part" of another brand's final product. The Intel processor receives special mention for all the computers that contain it. NutraSweet is another ingredient brand. In some cases, an ingredient brand may be used in a wide range of usage conditions. Kevlar, the synthetic fiber developed by DuPont, is used in armor for soldiers, in musical instruments, in brakes, and as an especially durable type of rope.[55]

Cooperative Cobranding

Cooperative cobranding agreements are reached when two brands receive equal attention and promotion. Team names for professional basketball in Europe are often cobrands, such as Armani Jeans Milano.

Complementary Branding

Brands that enter into complementary cobranding agreements are promoted to suggest they use both brands. Bulgari beauty products are included at Ritz Carlton hotels as part of a cooperative marketing agreement, under the Luxury Division of Marriott International. If one British company sells fish to grocers and another sells chips, it would make sense for the two firms to engage in complementary branding.

Building Powerful International Brands

Developing and maintaining strong brands offers benefits in both domestic and international markets. Marketers recognize that it is much less costly to retain customers than it is to attract new ones, and that a strong brand can be the key to customer loyalty.[56] The bottom line is that strong brands contribute to higher sales and profits. Powerful international brands extend these benefits to other countries. Building them takes time and careful planning.

BRAND AWARENESS

A series of steps help lead consumers to favor a brand. First, **brand awareness** results from marketing efforts that place the brand in a consumer's mind. Instilling brand awareness begins with creating simple recognition. Brand recognition in global markets helps create marketing success. Germany's automobile manufacturer, Audi, recently worked with its advertising agency to increase brand recognition in the U. S. auto market.[57] Although the company had been selling its cars in the United States for years, the marketing team determined that it needed to increase brand recognition with American consumers. Consumers must be aware of the brand before sales will increase.

> Brand awareness results from marketing efforts that place the brand in a consumer's mind.

Over time, the brand may be recalled with some help, or aided recall. Brand associations assist in building recall. The associations include all of the attributes, images, and symbols that a consumer mentally attaches to a brand. Eventually the brand will be remembered without assistance, or through unaided recall.

BRAND MEANING

Next, the marketing team attempts to create the perception that the company's brand represents a product that is different from and better than what the competition offers. The unique benefits a product gains solely due its brand name create *brand equity* for the company. Much of brand equity results from **brand image**, or the perceptions consumers have of the brand.[58] Brand image includes perceptions of brand quality. Brand quality refers to both the degree to which a product is free from defects and the characteristics of the product that bear on its ability to satisfy targeted needs.[59]

One threat to brand equity, *brand parity*, exists when consumers believe all products in a category are essentially the same, regardless of brand. Brand parity often leads to competition solely based on prices, discounts, and other consumer promotions.

Brand equity takes time to build. It only results from paying consistent attention to product quality, offering excellent customer service, and exceeding the expectations of consumers. Advertising and promotional efforts can then be used to support the message by providing compelling evidence and testimony that a brand is indeed different and better than the others.

BRAND LOYALTY

When a company's product enjoys the benefits associated with brand equity, it becomes easier to move consumers to a third stage: **brand loyalty**. Brand loyal customers seek out a specific name and often are willing to pay a higher price for the product than what the competition charges. Brand-loyal customers are less likely to switch brands or be enticed to try other brands due to marketing tactics such as coupons, discounts, bonus packs, and other methods. Two elements associated with brand loyalty include brand preference and brand insistence.

McDonald's enjoys brand loyalty in many international markets.

Brand Preference

Brand preference has become an important concept in international marketing as global competition intensifies. Brand preference goes beyond simple liking to a mental ranking in which the brand's attractiveness becomes foremost in the consumer's mind. Marketing managers assess brand preference from the target market's perspective. One study revealed that Swedish consumers indicated no difference in liking or preference for domestic brands over international brands.[60]

Brand Insistence

In order to maintain brand loyalty, international marketers seek to instill brand insistence in customers. As the term implies, brand insistence occurs when the customer accepts no substitutes for the preferred brand. Bucchelli is one of the largest U.S. importers of high-quality hair-cutting shears that imports products from Japan, Germany, and Asia. The company encourages its customers to "Insist on the best!" when purchasing hair-cutting products (www.bucchellishears.com).

DOUBLE JEOPARDY

Double jeopardy can emerge as a problem smaller firms experience regarding brand loyalty. Double jeopardy, as it pertains to product management, occurs when small market-share firms encounter low levels of customer loyalty. A recent study in the United Kingdom sportswear market confirmed this effect there: smaller brands experienced lower loyalty than larger brands.[61] Double jeopardy exists because small firms need to build brand loyalty to grow larger, but the very fact of being small makes such growth difficult, if not impossible, to achieve.

BRAND VALUATION

Brand equity and brand loyalty become part of **brand valuation**, which is the process of estimating the financial value of a brand.[62] While brand valuation has been a controversial issue worldwide for years, the ISO (International Standards Organization) produced ISO Standard 10668 in 2010 as an effort to reach agreement on how brand valuation should be reached. According to the ISO approach, three types of analysis are required for brand valuation: *legal analysis*, including assessments of the legal protections of the brand; *behavioral analysis*, including the contribution of the brand to purchase decisions as well as the attitudes of all stakeholder groups; and *financial analysis*, including market values, cost, and income figures.[63] Table 7.4 presents the brand rankings of the top twenty global brands from a financial perspective.

> Brand equity and brand loyalty become part of brand valuation, which is the process of estimating the financial value of a brand.

IMPLICATIONS FOR MANAGERS

Brand management involves a consistent effort by the marketing team working in conjunction with manufacturing, sales, support services, public relations, and other departments to create a consistent, inviting image of the company. A brand that has moved from awareness, to brand meaning, to brand loyalty enjoys a variety of advantages related to sales and profits. As a cautionary note, although it can take years to build and maintain a strong brand, that brand can quickly be damaged or destroyed. BP has undoubtedly suffered a great deal of brand damage due to the 2010 oil spill. Toyota may have suffered as well when questions about the safety of the company's automobiles emerged in the same year. The management and marketing

VIDEO LINK 7.3: McDonalds' International Strategy

VIDEO LINK 7.4:
World's Most
Valuable Brands

COMPANY	OWNERSHIP	BRAND VALUE ($ MILLIONS)
1. Coca-Cola	United States	$71.9
2. IBM	United States	$69.9
3. Microsoft	United States	$59.1
4. Google	United States	$55.3
5. General Electric	United States	$42.8
6. McDonald's	United States	$35.6
7. Intel	United States	$35.2
8. Apple	United States	$33.5
9. Disney	United States	$29.0
10. Hewlett Packard	United States	$28.5
11. Toyota	Japan	$27.8
12. Mercedes-Benz	Germany	$27.5
13. Cisco	United States	$25.3
14. Nokia	Finland	$25.1
15. BMW	Germany	$24.6
16. Gillette	United States	$24.0
17. Samsung	South Korea	$23.4
18. Louis Vuitton	France	$23.1
19. Honda	Japan	$19.4
20. Oracle	United States	$17.3

Table 7.4: **Brand Rankings, 2011**

Source: Adapted from "Best Global Brands 2011," Interbrand, accessed at www.interbrand.com/best_global_brands.aspx?year=2009&type=desc&col=6&langid=1000.

teams of both organizations, and others that have endured the same type of damage, have been put into a position that will take concerted effort and careful marketing activities to restore the brand in the minds of consumers.

Ethical Issues in International Product Marketing

As with other areas in international marketing, ethical issues arise in international product management. Companies are sometimes criticized for knowingly selling unsafe or even recalled products in other countries in order to increase international sales or to offset sagging domestic sales. Toys, electrical appliances, motor vehicles, and clothing are major categories of products that are often found to be deliberately dumped in foreign markets. International marketers should go beyond international rules and regulations to ensure that dumping of unsafe products does not occur.

The unsafe products may not be perceived as unsafe in the market where sold. Problems with tobacco usage by children, even those as young as two years old, have brought international attention to Indonesia.[64] Two of the top tobacco companies in the market are Philip Morris International and British American Tobacco.[65] Most agree that it is unethical for the companies to make profits from selling cigarettes to children in any country.

Packaging itself can be an ethical concern. If wasteful or if used to mask the contents, packaging can come under attack. The use of air to make packages seem fuller and the waste associated with plastic bottles of water are two recent examples of ethical concerns about packaging. Using imagery on the package that targets children when the product may not be appropriate for that age group can be another packaging issue.

Treatment of animals in product testing garners much attention. Organizations such as People for the Ethical Treatment of Animals (PETA) often protest the use of animals to test make-up or other beauty products. Animal suffering seems like an unfair price to pay when balanced against the personal benefit of looking more attractive.

The product line itself may be an ethical issue. Companies may choose not to sell the full product line in certain markets, denying those consumers access to the benefits from some products. If medicines, healthier foods, or similar products are involved, it may appear that companies are wrongly selecting which consumers will have better health or other positive outcomes. When less-developed countries or certain races do not have access to such life-giving or life-enhancing products, the company's motivation may come into question.

Chapter 7: Review and Resources

STRATEGIC IMPLICATIONS //

International product and service decisions require strategic direction. The biggest strategic decisions revolve around the market/product matrix, the product life cycle, and decisions to market to bottom-of-the-pyramid consumers.

Many marketers pursue the market development strategy by offering existing products in new and foreign marketplaces. The strategy can be effective particularly in the maturity phase of the product life cycle, because it presents growth opportunities for otherwise stale product sales.

Diversification strategies present viable options for many firms. As noted, the strategy was employed by Vortex Engineering when company leaders decided to produce ATMs for consumers in rural India. Strategy makers also consider the relative advantages of being a market pioneer or follower brand. A pioneering advantage often awaits the market pioneer.

Brand strategies begin with the decision to carry one house mark on all products or instead to feature different names on each product offered. Then, brand strategies are matched with product line strategies. When a product line is extended, a matching brand approach will be needed. When expanding product line breadth or width, a similar branding decision will be in order. Decisions to cobrand are also strategic choices, especially those that involve creating relationships with other companies. International cobranding represents the new horizon. Companies with strong global brands enjoy many advantages in the worldwide marketplace.

TACTICAL IMPLICATIONS //

Tactical decisions pertaining to international product marketing must follow the overall strategies set by policy makers. At this level, managers consider how best to carry out market development, diversification, penetration, and product development strategies. The strategies are supported by tactical techniques, including promoting new uses for products or finding new markets to enter. Tactical decisions also focus on the core benefits and auxiliary dimensions that products will offer.

Packaging and labeling choices are often tactical decisions. After a product has been developed, marketing leaders carefully consider package design and labeling choices. The decision to create a new package or label constitutes a change in tactics designed to support a modification in strategic direction. A service company that develops a new logo and company mission statement will also modify letterhead, billing statements, and other components of the company's operations.

OPERATIONAL IMPLICATIONS //

Much of the work at the operational level focuses on tracking consumer perceptions of quality. These daily activities are important for international product and service marketing. These efforts include market research activities.

Operational decisions work to ensure that the implementation of product plans made at the strategic and operational levels are carried out effectively and efficiently. Consumer reactions to branding strategies also receive consideration. Entry level employees should pay attention to consumer reactions to the firm's brands. First-line supervisors carry the responsibility of making sure the company's brands are presented in a positive light. Managers that train new employees make sure the company's product lines are well understood, so that the ideal item is presented to a business or retail consumer.

TERMS

product	brand	brand awareness
good	family branding	brand image
service	individual branding	brand loyalty
product line	brand extension	brand valuation
product mix	product line extension	
pioneering advantage	cobranding	

REVIEW QUESTIONS

1. Define the term *product* and name the three elements that are part of a product.
2. What are the three categories of products?
3. What are the three key dimensions of a product?
4. What is meant by the total value concept?
5. What is the difference between a product line and a product mix?
6. How do the main elements of packages affect international marketing programs?
7. What are the main categories of international business products?
8. How can remanufactured products become part of an international marketing program aimed at the bottom-of-the-pyramid?
9. What roles do international product supports play in reaching target markets?
10. What is the role of the service sector in international marketing?
11. Describe the product life theory and explain how the concept applies to international marketing.
12. How are the strategies that make up the market/product matrix used in international marketing?
13. Describe brands, brand names, brand marks, and service marks.
14. Describe the concepts of family branding and individual branding in relation to international brand management.
15. What three forms of cobranding can be used in domestic and international marketing?
16. Describe brand equity and brand parity.
17. Define brand loyalty and name the factors that influence it.
18. How does the concept of brand valuation relate to international marketing?
19. What ethical issues are present in international product marketing?

DISCUSSION QUESTIONS

1. Explain how international marketers can utilize the total value concept in marketing the following products:
   - A theme park in Brazil
   - A rock concert in Ireland
   - An online newspaper in the United Arab Emirates
   - A bicycle in Japan

2. Discuss how international companies can use market penetration and market development strategies for the following products in developing countries:

   - Hand soap
   - Paper towels
   - Shampoo
   - Glass cleaners
   - Toothpaste

3. How could the product life cycle be extended internationally for the following products?

   - Cassette recorders
   - Coffee percolators
   - 35-millimeter cameras
   - Typewriters
   - Videocassette recorders

4. Would you use family branding or individual branding for each of the following product categories? Defend your answer.

   - Canned foods
   - Insurance products
   - Mobile phones
   - High-end wedding gowns

ANALYTICAL AND INTERNET EXERCISES

1. Visit the websites of several popular shopping malls worldwide. Some examples are below. What differences do you notice in shopping malls across various cultures? What similarities do you see? How do they compare to the malls in your home country?

   - South China Mall (China), www.southchinamall.com.cn/english/index1.jsp
   - West Edmonton Mall (Canada), www.wem.ca/#
   - The Dubai Mal (Dubai), www.thedubaimall.com/en
   - SM Megamall (Philippines), www.sm-megamall.com/megamall/index.php?p=1262
   - Berjaya Times Square (Malaysia), www.timessquarekl.com/
   - Mall of America (United States), http://mallofamerica.com

2. Search tourism websites for various countries or regions. Some examples are below. What are the main selling points for tourism in these countries?

   - United Kingdom, www.visitbritain.com/
   - France, www.franceguide.com/
   - Australia, www.australia.com
   - Japan, www.jnto.go.jp/
   - India, www.tourismofindia.com/
   - Spain, www.spain.info

3. Search the website of major international marketers and find information about the products they offer in various countries. Discuss how each company's product lines vary by country or region for the following:

   - Coca-Cola, www.cocacola.com
   - Proctor & Gamble, www.pg.com
   - Honda, www.honda.com
   - LG, www.lg.com
   - Samsung, www.samsung.com

4. Visit the J.D. Power & Associates "Initial Quality Study" website (www.jdpower.com/Autos/ratings/Quality-Ratings-by-Brand). Discuss the various aspects of quality that led to the ratings for several of the brands. Are you surprised by the findings? Why or why not?

ONLINE VIDEOS

Visit **www.sagepub.com/baack** to view these chapter videos:

Video Link 7.1: Sustainable Communities

Video Link 7.2: Offshoring

Video Link 7.3: McDonalds' International Strategy

Video Link 7.4: The World's Most Valuable Brands

STUDENT STUDY SITE

Visit **www.sagepub.com/baack** to access these additional learning tools:

- Web Quizzes
- eFlashcards
- SAGE Journal Articles

- Country Fact Sheets
- Chapter Outlines
- Interactive Maps

CASE 7 ///

Interface: Prize-Winning, Sustainable Modular Flooring

When the inaugural Sustainability Survey was released by Globescan and SustainAbility in 2009, one relatively unknown corporation made the very top of the list. Ahead of corporate giants such as General Electric, Toyota, and Wal-Mart was Interface, Inc., a global corporation that markets modular carpet under the FLOR brand. The corporation's website states that the company is "the worldwide leader in design, production and sales of environmentally responsible modular carpet for the commercial, institutional, and residential markets, and a leading designer and manufacturer of commercial broadloom."[66]

Interface conducts operations in numerous countries, including InterfaceFLOR in Europe, InterfaceFLOR in Asia-Pacific, and InterfaceFLOR in the Americas, based in Atlanta, Georgia.

In Europe, InterfaceFLOR has manufacturing facilities in Craigavon, Northern Ireland; Halifax, West Yorkshire; and Scherpenzeel, the Netherlands. In addition, it has sales offices in most major European cities. InterfaceFLOR Asia operates in China, Hong Kong, Japan, Malaysia, and Singapore.

To be placed at the top of this list of sustainability-focused companies is no easy feat. The survey, which was distributed to a panel of sustainability experts throughout industry, government, and nongovernmental agencies, centers heavily on a credible commitment to sustainability grounded in the mission of the company.[67] Interface clearly meets these requirements.

Whereas the overall idea seems straightforward—innovation through sustainability—the implementation of the strategy can be difficult. What is essential to the success of such a strategy is the overall connection of the company with its mission and its products. Product development must be monitored very closely to ensure that the sustainability goals are met. For modular carpet products to remain competitive, the flooring must meet durability standards, must have stain resistance levels present in competitor products, and also must be attractive and marketable to consumers and businesses.

Production processes are keys as well. Company leaders examine the entire marketing channel from suppliers of raw materials to the final installation of the product. Methods of delivery of carpet, installation protocols, and inventory control become part of the program. The supply chain will also be monitored, along with the ultimate disposal of the company's core products. Used flooring and carpet to be discarded should be made to be recyclable or at least not damaging to the overall environment.

Further, the process itself must be continuous. With sustainability, a company cannot simply rest on its laurels. Rather, an ongoing commitment is required. Interface understands and continues to implement this concept.

The commitment dates back many years. Founder and chair Ray Anderson devoted Interface to an effort entitled Mission Zero, which was essentially a mission to only take from the Earth what could be replenished by the Earth. The pledge was powerful, essentially promising that the company would be the first name in industrial ecology worldwide. The results of the effort have been outstanding: the company has decreased greenhouse emissions by

Interface is a major manufacturer of a sustainable product: flooring.

more than 80% and lowered the use of fossil fuels by 60%. The Mission Zero initiative carries a promise that the company will eliminate any negative impact it has on the environment by the year 2020.[68] These efforts naturally garnered considerable praise by many. *Fortune* magazine recently listed the company as one of the most admired in America.

While many business thinkers assume that the sustainability initiatives ultimately raise overall costs, Interface reports that such may not be the case. As Ray Anderson explains, the choice between "economy" and "environmental" constitutes really nothing more than a myth, as the company has realized decreased costs and increased synergies from the common purpose found in Mission Zero.[69] Interface's sustainability program resulted in dramatic sales increases followed by a major growth in profits.[70] To realize these results also requires an authentic focus on innovation, as the entire business model must be reexamined from top to bottom.

Maintaining a leadership position in sustainability continues to present an ongoing challenge to the company. With strong leadership and a well-accepted mission statement, Interface appears poised to maintain its position for many years to come. As consumers worldwide continue to demand green products and sustainability-focused business models, the future appears bright for other sustainability leaders as well.

1. What product category best matches carpeting, convenience good, shopping product, or specialty product? Does the company's sustainability program influence your answer? If so, how? If not, why not?

2. Explain how the core product, the packaging, and the auxiliary dimensions of carpeting produced in a sustainable fashion might create a marketing advantage for Interface.

3. Where is carpeting in the product life cycle? Using product cycle theory, where would sustainable modular carpet products fit? (You may visit www.interfaceglobal.com to help prepare an answer.)

4. What product support services would be crucial for Interface?

5. Should the marketing team at Interface seek to build and enhance brand awareness? If so, how? If not, why not?

6. How could Interface's sustainability program generate brand loyalty or brand equity, especially when the brand is less-well-known than other carpet manufacturers?

8 International Product Standardization and Adaptation

After reading and studying this chapter, you should be able to answer the following questions:

1. How do legal systems influence international marketing programs, including standardization and adaptation strategies?

2. How are international marketing disputes resolved within various legal systems?

3. When is standardization the most viable international marketing strategy?

4. How can adaptation help a marketing team succeed in reaching target markets in a host country?

5. How can standardization and adaptation programs combine to achieve greater international marketing effectiveness?

6. How can global innovation and patterns of diffusion assist the marketing team in reaching target markets, including those consisting of bottom-of-the-pyramid customers?

IN THIS CHAPTER ///

McDonald's Global Expansion: Adaptation and Differences in Taste

VIDEO LINK 8.1:
The Fast Food Market

McDonald's restaurants have been part of the American culture since the first store opened in 1940. By 1949, carhops replaced drive-in service and the world first tasted the iconic McDonald's French fries. In the 1950s, the company pioneered the franchising process and rapid expansion began. Global expansion was not far off. After becoming the leading restaurant in the United States, McDonald's opened restaurants in Puerto Rico and Canada in 1968. The company's rapid globalization continued in the 1970s and 1980s, with entries into Japan, Spain, Denmark, and the Philippines. By 2010, the company was conducting operations in 118 countries.

McDonald's global success offers an example of effective marketing. While the company retains the core elements of its operations, each country requires changes in response to local tastes and conditions. McDonald's has managed to balance the need to maintain a core identity with making changes to fit local markets (www.mcdonalds .com).

McDonald's brand strategy remains consistent in all 118 countries. An identical logo appears in each country, the arches are part of the store facades, and tasty French fries are sold in every location. Consumers can purchase Happy Meals to mollify the kids in the familiar red and yellow containers. Even though the language is different, consumers recognize the iconic McDonald's packaging. The Ronald McDonald brand character has been a global figure. Local actors have portrayed the brightly colored clown as a universal component of McDonald's operations.

Providing high-quality service permeates McDonald's global efforts. The prices of food items may shift the company's position to a more premium product in emerging markets, but all of the company's restaurants focus on friendly, fast service. Being greeted with a smile from an employee continues to be part of the McDonald's experience worldwide. The company also emphasizes cleanliness, particularly of restrooms, as a unique selling point.

Even as McDonald's overall brand strategy remains consistent across markets, the company adapts the menu to local circumstances. The Big Mac is not sold in India; McDonald's restaurants do not offer any beef or pork products, in response to Hindu and Muslim dietary restrictions in India. Instead, consumers can buy food that contains chicken, lamb, or *paneer*, a type of cheese unique to India. In Taiwan, consumers can buy a hamburger with a bun made from rice instead of bread. The Chicken McDo with spaghetti is popular in the Philippines. The McPalta (or "McAvocado" in Chilean Spanish) chicken sandwich sold in Chile features *palta* (avocado) sauce.[1]

In all of these settings, McDonald's marketing leadership recognizes that food preferences are culturally unique. To be profitable in a foreign country, McDonald's adapts the menu. By selling beer in Europe and soy sauce in East Asia, meeting local tastes has led to success in international markets. McDonald's relies on detailed consumer research to identify local tastes, and then creates menu items to satisfy them.

Global expansion is one key to McDonald's continuing profitability. According to Jim Skinner, McDonald's chief executive officer, the company's "performance demonstrates the popular appeal of McDonald's relevant menu choices. We're delivering great tasting food to our 60 million customers around the world every day with the outstanding value and unmatched convenience they expect from McDonald's."[2]

QUESTIONS FOR STUDENTS

1. What parts of McDonald's operations are the same across markets, and what parts are changed to meet local tastes?

2. Do you think McDonald's should adapt marketing messages such as commercials and contests to other countries?

3. Should McDonald's executives worry that adapting too many things will dilute the McDonald's global brand?

McDonald's combines aspects of standardization and adaption to succeed globally.

Overview

Differences between markets occur across and within countries. Consumer needs vary, competitors introduce new products, and governmental regulations regarding marketing activities evolve over time. Marketers entering new countries as well as those conducting continuing operations in other countries adjust to these conditions. The forces that shape the international marketing context play a major role in shaping strategic decisions about product standardization and adaptation (see Figure 8.1).

This chapter begins with a brief review of legal systems, an important cause of change in other markets. Legal systems affect patents, copyrights, and other intellectual property protections. Disputes over these and other matters often arise in other countries. Methods to resolve these disputes are presented. Next, an examination of how to balance the goal of being responsive to local needs by changing goods, services, and brand positions against cost savings derived from a standardized approach is provided.

A country's legal system often creates the necessity of adapting a marketing program. Changes in the product potentially lead to changes in the communications used to promote that product. These decisions are interrelated. The product and communication model of adaptation can help resolve these issues.

Product changes often result from innovations, and the process of new product development is the final topic of the chapter. Differences in consumer acceptance of a new product are examined and related to diffusion of innovations. Finally, strategic, tactical, and operational implications for marketers are reviewed.

Figure 8.1: The International Marketing Context

Legal Systems

LEARNING OBJECTIVE #1:

How do legal systems influence international marketing programs, including standardization and adaptation strategies?

Legal systems dictate the methods used when applying and implementing the laws of a country. The systems are rooted in the history of the country and in developing countries are often based on colonial ties. Legal considerations influence a number of international marketing activities, including the decision to enter a country.

A **common law** system relies on legal precedents and usage traditions to form the basis of law. It can be found in the United Kingdom and in former British colonies. The written law applies to disputes and other issues; however, the interpretation by the judicial system coupled with the implementation of the law gives the written law meaning.

The most prevalent legal system, **civil law**, utilizes statutes based on written words or a legal code. It can be traced back to its introduction by Justinian, the Byzantine emperor, in Justinian's Code. Laws are written to be comprehensive with clear instructions for how to handle exceptions. Precedent or usage plays no role.

Legal systems based on religious writings practice **theocratic law**. Islamic law provides an example. Written Islamic law is *Sharia* law. The interpretation of the law or Islamic jurisprudence is called *fiqh*. Theocratic law is the least common legal system worldwide.

Figure 8.2 provides examples of countries following various legal systems. The systems can be roughly categorized into the three categories, although many countries practice a combination of the systems. Nigeria has a tradition of common law but also uses some components of Islamic law, especially in the north part of the country. In the United States, common law remains the dominant form, but the state of Louisiana follows a form of civil law.

Legal System	Example Countries
Common Law	United States of America, The United Kingdom, India, Australia, Belize, and Malaysia
Civil Law	France, Bolivia, Brazil, Russia, China, Angola, and Chad
Theocratic Law	Iran, Saudi Arabia, The Holy See (Vatican), and Libya

Figure 8.2: Country Examples of Legal Systems

Legal systems affect marketing activities. Consider the case of property ownership. Depending on the country, ownership can be based on either *prior usage* of the property or official *registration* with legal authorities of the property ownership. In a prior usage context, which is more typically found in common law countries, a person who has used a property is more likely to succeed in an ownership claim over someone who has registered the property. In a registration context, registration becomes more important than usage. To be safe, a company should always register ownership of all property regardless of the legal context in which it operates.

International Intellectual Property Protection

Protecting intellectual property continues to be a primary challenge to marketers when operating in other countries.[3] **Intellectual property** consists of creations of the mind or the intangible property that results from thought. Examples include a song by a popular singer, a new type of electrical plug outlet, or a more efficient process for protecting an individual's identity.

Various tactics are employed to protect intellectual property in international markets. In general, the main methods include copyrights, trademarks, and patents. These three are all protected under the Agreement on Trade-Related Aspects of Intellectual Property Rights (TRIPS), which is a covenant that all members of the World Trade Organization sign. The governments of all of the world's major economies are signatories. While some complaints regarding enforcement continue, especially in some emerging markets, the extension of the TRIPS protections into a greater number of countries reflects the growing focus on intellectual property protection globally.

Copyrights are granted to authors of creative works, such as songs and novels. When a copyright expires, the work enters the public domain. Until then, the work can only be used for profit with the author's or authors' permission. *Trademarks* apply to the symbols, words, phrases, and logos that are attached to brands. These brand marks identify products to consumers and can only be used by the companies that own them. *Patents* apply to inventions, which range from business processes to physical products, or to unique improvements in either one.

One critical form of international protection, the Madrid Protocol, is an international treaty that allows a company or trademark owner to seek registration and protection in a number of countries by filing a single application. The International Bureau of the World Intellectual Property Organization administers the system. Currently forty-eight countries participate in the agreement.[4]

Intellectual property protection will be a priority for international marketers. Many companies possess unique assets, such as inimitable technologies or brand equity that requires protection from outsiders. The potential to lose those assets may dissuade a company's executives from entering a market, especially in countries that exhibit poor intellectual property protections.

INTELLECTUAL PROPERTY PIRACY

The unauthorized use or reproduction of intellectual property that has been legally protected is **intellectual property piracy**. Oftentimes piracy takes the form of a close replication of existing products, or *counterfeiting*. A wide range of products are pirated or counterfeited worldwide. Attempts to stop the activity depend largely on the country involved. Many Western nations work vigorously to prevent counterfeiting, whereas China and some other Asian nations do not.

CORPORATE SPYING

While global travelers may be familiar with seeing knock-off or counterfeit goods in other countries, intellectual

Products such as the iPad and the iPod have been counterfeited in some countries.

property piracy also refers to more serious acts of corporate spying. Corporate spying or espionage involves a company intentionally stealing the designs or business processes of a competitor. Estimates indicate that corporate spying costs the thousand largest global companies more than $45 billion each year.[5] The corporate espionage phenomenon has led to more FBI investigations of cases, mainly corporate, than were made during World War II.

In response to corporate spying concerns, the U.S. Congress passed the U.S. Economic Espionage Act of 1996. The law makes the theft or misappropriation of a trade secret a federal crime. Penalties include a maximum of fifteen years in prison and/or a fine of $500,000. One of the earliest uses of the law involved prosecuting executives at Four Pillars, a leading Taiwanese adhesive company, for paying an employee at Avery Denison $160,000 to steal $60 million worth of trade secrets. The executives were fined $5 million and ordered to return the materials.[6]

REVERSE-ENGINEERING

In some cases, technical experts reverse-engineer a product or create a replica by breaking down the original and deducing how to manufacturer it. Reverse-engineering has become highly prevalent worldwide. It has reached a point at which reverse-engineering of computer software, such NextEngine's 3-D program, is possible.[7] Reverse-engineering may be found in the entertainment gaming industry, with copies of Xbox 360s and PlayStation 2s prevalent in Latin America.[8] Currently, a growing consulting industry that concentrates on preventing reverse-engineering has emerged.[9]

COUNTRY DEVELOPMENT

A complicated relationship exists between intellectual property protection and a country's development. Many of the world's emerging markets are known for lax intellectual property protections. Piracy has allowed some nations access to unique assets and has driven innovation within them. On the other hand, a potential link exists between strong intellectual property protection and innovation-driven development. As Table 8.1 indicates, many countries that rank high on industrial technology industry competitiveness have strong intellectual property protections. In contrast, many of the lowest-ranking countries have problems with computer software being stolen.

As countries shift to a more innovation-focused economy, greater intellectual property protection may aid in the process. Some evidence suggests that increased intellectual property protection attracts higher levels of investment from foreign companies and leads to a greater transfer of knowledge between countries.[10] China's current intellectual property protection, which is weaker in practice than its laws would suggest, echoes Japan's intellectual property protections in the 1950s and 1960s. Some expect China to follow the Japanese path and to more strictly enforce intellectual property laws as the country becomes more economically developed.[11]

A contrary opinion regarding intellectual property development has emerged. The *free culture movement*, most strongly associated with Harvard professor Lawrence Lessig, argues that intellectual property protection constrains creativity and limits freedoms. The continual extension of the expiration of copyright, the extension of copyright protection to Internet communication, and the limitations on the ability to copy protected works are all points of contention for the free culture movement.[12]

COUNTRY	INFORMATION TECHNOLOGY COMPETITIVENESS RANKING	PERCENTAGE OF SOFTWARE PIRATED
United States	1	20%
Japan	2	23%
South Korea	3	43%
United Kingdom	4	26%
Australia	5	28%
Switzerland	10	25%
Ireland	15	34%
Israel	20	32%
Poland	30	57%
Romania	40	68%
Sri Lanka	50	90%
Pakistan	60	84%
Vietnam	61	85%
Azerbaijan	62	92%
Nigeria	63	82%

Table 8.1: **The Relationship Between Intellectual Property Protection and Technology Success**

Source: Adapted from "The Fifth Annual BSA and IDC Global Software Piracy Study, 2007," accessed at www.nationmaster.com/graph/cri_sof_pir_rat-crime-software-piracy-rate#source; and "The Means to Compete: Benchmarking IT Industry Competitiveness 2007 Report," the Economist Intelligence Unit, accessed at www.bsa.org/country/Research%20and%20Statistics/~/media/12EB624EB30C486FBEA0A4B653D D5E89.ashx.

For large multinational companies, piracy can lead to *brand dilution*. When consumers purchase a counterfeit of poor quality, their negative attitudes toward the knock-off may affect perceptions of the original brand. Over time, this problem can weaken the company's brand equity and dilute the company's brand image.

International Dispute Resolution

Legal actions, including those designed to protect a company's intellectual property, are part of doing business. Within one country, disputes can be handled through the local legal system or through professional dispute resolution organizations. As greater numbers of companies enter new countries, the process of dispute resolution becomes more complicated. The process begins with deciding which country's courts should be involved and how court decisions will be enforced. The possible parties involved are citizens, companies, and governments. The interactions between the three entities complicate any dispute resolution process. Issues include those displayed in Figure 8.3.

LEARNING OBJECTIVE #2:

How are international marketing disputes resolved within various legal systems?

| Protection of Intellectual Property |
| Contract Terms/Interpretations |
| Payment Disputes |
| Responsibility for Products Damaged in Shipping |
| Responsibility for Product Liability |
| Mergers/Acquisitions |
| Control of a Company |

Figure 8.3: Types of Disputes in International Marketing

VIDEO LINK 8.3:
Economic Espionage ▶

JURISDICTION

The first step to dispute resolution, the establishment of **jurisdiction**, defines the power to apply the law or local statutes. In the case of a legal dispute, the laws of the country in which the incident took place hold jurisdiction. Jurisdiction questions can also apply at the state, province, country, or city levels. Some detective television shows touch on the concept of jurisdiction when the lead actor tells the pushy FBI agent, "This happened in New York City. I have jurisdiction here."

Establishment of jurisdiction for legal disagreements can be included in contracts. The setting or location of the jurisdiction may become a point of contention during negotiations. Each company wants to establish jurisdiction in the legal system that gives it the greatest advantage. Typically, it will be in the company's home country, where its legal team has the most experience and comfort, but it can also be in a third country.

Laws can also attempt to establish jurisdiction. The U.S. Economic Espionage Act of 1996 provided extraterritorial jurisdiction for cases when the offender or the victim is a U.S. citizen. This means that the U.S. legal system would have jurisdiction when a United States citizen is involved. The concern, in both the case of this law and in all cases of jurisdiction, is that when the other party ignores the jurisdiction provisions the only recourse will be legal action in the other party's legal system. In many cases, doing so creates a disadvantage for the party seeking recourse in the foreign system.

METHODS OF DISPUTE RESOLUTION

Companies may use three different methods to resolve disputes: conciliation, arbitration, or litigation. It is not unusual to begin with one process and move to another. In all three cases, the marketing team seeks to balance risk and cost against achievement of the most positive outcome.

Conciliation

Many companies prefer conciliation as the first step in resolving a dispute. **Conciliation** applies to the various forms of mediation or conflict resolution that companies can pursue before resorting to a more formal arbitration process. A third party typically mediates between the two companies involved in the dispute. Contracts may include specific wording about how the conciliation process will work. The third party collects information, meets with the two parties involved in the dispute, and presents a possible solution. If the two parties agree, the conflict is resolved and business resumes.

Conciliation offers important advantages over other approaches. The proceedings are confidential, which protects intellectual property and the privacy of the parties involved. Instead of conflicts being played out in the business press, the media pays little to no attention. Conciliation can be an effective approach in emerging markets where relationships are paramount and where loss of public face can be a major concern.

Recently, textile companies in South Africa faced strikes from the 55,000 members of the Southern African Clothing & Textile Workers Union. The strikes shut down production, and smaller businesses in South Africa began to close due to the lack of revenue. The employers and the union used conciliation, specifically the Commission for Conciliation, Mediation & Arbitration, to negotiate the dispute and reach an agreement.[13] The approach shortened the time period for the strike and kept the negotiations private.

Arbitration

When conciliation does not succeed, the parties typically move to arbitration. The **arbitration** method is a formal conflict resolution process in which both parties agree to abide by the decision of a third-party arbitrator. The process differs from conciliation in that, instead of making a suggestion, the arbitrator declares a binding decision. Both parties sign a statement, often as part of a contract, that agrees to use arbitration before any conflict emerges. The process has recently received attention from the press due to its use by professional athletes to adjudicate contract disagreements with team owners.

> The arbitration method is formal conflict resolution process in which both parties agree to abide by the decision of a third-party arbitrator.

Arbitration's popularity has increased. Numerous arbitration providers are available (see Figure 8.4). Providers are located throughout the world and, as with jurisdiction, company leaders typically prefer to arbitrate in their home countries or in countries where they have much experience. Arbitration clauses in contracts can be highly detailed, including the arbitration provider to be used, the number of arbitrators involved, and the place hearings will be held.

Arbitration offers many advantages. The proceedings are confidential, protecting industry secrets and keeping the conflict private. The process itself presents both parties with the opportunity to make a case to an impartial third party, much like a legal proceeding, but without the costs associated with going to court. The arbitrator's binding decision will normally be followed by both companies. The one difficulty with arbitration can be that, at its core, the arrangement remains a contractual relationship. When one of the parties disagrees with the arbitrator's finding, the contract can be broken. At that point the only recourse will be litigation.

Reliance Industries, one the largest conglomerates in India, was founded by Dhirubhai Ambani in 1966. When Ambani died in 2002, his two sons began battling for control of the company. The company was split into Reliance Communications and

International Court of Arbitration Dispute Resolution Services www.iccwbo.org/court/arbitration
European Court of Arbitration http://cour-europe-arbitrage.org/content.php?lang=en&delegation=1&id=1
The Inter-American Commercial Arbitration Commission (IACAC) www.sice.oas.org/dispute/comarb/iacac/iacac2e.asp
The Commercial Arbitration and Mediation Center for the Americas (CAMCA) www.adr.org
World Intellectual Property Organization Arbitration and Mediation Center http://arbiter.wipo.int/center
Association of International Arbitration www.arbitration-adr.org/news/
Hong Kong International Arbitration Centre www.hkiac.org/

Figure 8.4: Arbitration Providers

Reliance Industries, with each brother controlling one part. The dispute over how to structure two entities escalated to the point where one of them refused to participate in conciliation, and it became unclear as to whether arbitration would be effective. Both brothers attacked the arbitration process as well.[14] Eventually, the brothers' mother became involved and the dispute was resolved.[15]

Litigation

A legal proceeding through a judicial system, **litigation**, normally will be the course of last resort for companies. Higher risks and costs are associated with litigation. Legal proceedings can last for years and legal fees can be millions of dollars. Often what becomes even more important than the costs is that the litigation becomes public. Company secrets and "dirty laundry" may be publicly aired, which can hurt a company's image and brand.

> A legal proceeding through a judicial system, litigation, normally will be the course of last resort for companies.

Jurisdiction creates a major concern during litigation. Foreign courts follow different norms, which may be confusing to an outsider, giving an advantage to one of the parties. In some cases, the courts themselves may not be fair or unbiased. Even in cases where the findings of litigation are positive, collection of a judgment may not occur. The company can protect itself through bankruptcy by hiding assets in another country, or by leaving the country entirely, thereby removing the jurisdiction needed for collection.

MARKETING IMPLICATIONS

A key decision to be made when entering a foreign market will be whether to offer a product in its current form or to adapt that product to a nation's unique circumstances. Legal systems contribute a major unique circumstance. As a simple example, beautification products encounter various legal circumstances in nations practicing or being influenced by Islamic law. Turkey's population is mostly Muslim. Still, cosmetics and other beauty products are widely available in Turkey even though strict religious practice lead some citizens to reject using such items. Turkey's legal system is not theocratic. In strongly theocratic nations, legal restrictions prohibit or limit the use of many cosmetics and beauty products.

The marketing and management teams examine the prevailing legal system, including methods of intellectual property protection and conflict resolution, prior to taking any other action with regard to offering standardized or adapted products. Where little protection from counterfeiting exists, careful consideration will be given as to whether a strategic investment in a new country would be worthwhile. Company leaders concerned about conflict resolution give careful thought to any country in which the company might operate at a disadvantage. In essence, standardization and adaptation processes are similar for the product itself as well as for the legal system under which the product will be sold.

LEARNING OBJECTIVE #3:

When is standardization the most viable international marketing strategy?

Standardization

One common approach used in international marketing, **standardization**, is the process of applying the same marketing mix to all markets.[16] A single production process, brand, and appeal are used. While this may seem less responsive to consumer needs in a given country, it decreases costs and increases efficiency. With standardization, the company can focus on perfecting a single approach. The benefits of this method have been discussed by international marketing writers for many years.[17] Theodore Levitt argued that the success for companies comes from "concentrating on what everyone wants rather than worrying about the details of what everyone thinks they might like."[18]

The cost savings from standardization result from economies of scale and scope. **Economies of scale** refer to a reduction in the cost per unit as the total volume produced increases. A range of efficiencies emerge as a company produces more of a single product. The efficiencies result from increased purchasing power, spreading of fixed costs across a larger volume of units, the potential for managers to be more efficient as they specialize, and the company's ability to use the same promotional materials for a larger market. For companies that standardize, economies of scale reduce costs, which often leads to greater profits (see Figure 8.5).

> Economies of scale refer to a reduction in the cost per unit as the total volume produced increases.

Jones Soda	Coca-Cola
Produces 100,000 bottles of soda	Produces 1,000,000 bottles of soda
Cost per soda = $0.50	Cost per soda = $0.25
Price per soda = $1.00	Price per soda = $1.00
Profit for one soda = $0.50	Profit for one soda = $0.75

Figure 8.5: Example of Economies of Scale

In contrast to economies of scale, **economies of scope** emerge from producing a variety of similar products, which allows for at least parts of the production process and management activities to apply across the product line. For example, the consumer packaged goods company Unilever has a large, sophisticated brand management group. These marketing professionals work on many different Unilever brands at once, creating efficiencies due to economies of scope.

Increased standardization may be the result of **cultural convergence**, or the growing similarities between global consumers. Debates occur with regard to the actual degree of convergence present worldwide. Some agreement exists that consumers are becoming more alike in terms of consumption behaviors. Movies, soft drinks, fast-food restaurants, and other products have experienced growing global markets. As potential markets increase in size, the incentive to take advantage of savings that standardization of products offers becomes amplified.

In the case of renewable energy, sustainable sources of energy are sought by countries and companies around the world. Convergence in demand for these resources has risen. The state-owned energy company in Indonesia, PLN, builds solar- and hydro-powered sources of energy. Recently, the country's legislature announced plans to spend $84 million on 250 solar power plants.[19] The convergence in demand for solar energy has led to a larger market and greater savings due to economies of scale.

Cultural convergence may lead to increasing sales of soft drinks.

SERVICE STANDARDIZATION

Many services are offered in standardized form. Airline travel serves as an example. Many international carriers operate under a single brand on a worldwide basis. Other services, such as insurance, financial services, credit and debit cards, and banking often cross national boundaries without major changes. The same holds true for parcel delivery services such as UPS and FedEx.

Standardization, and the efficiencies associated with it, can be a powerful marketing force. Citibank standardizes many components of its credit card business across markets. As a result, the company has become a leading global financial institution. UAE-Citibank, a subsidiary, has the largest number of credit cards in use in the United Arab Emirates.[20]

Adaptation

LEARNING OBJECTIVE #4:

How can adaptation help a marketing team succeed in reaching target markets in a host country?

When entering new markets, success often hinges on how much goods and services change in response to the differences in those markets. Changing of any component of the marketing mix to better meet the needs of a local market is **adaptation**.[21] Changes or adaptations can be as minor as adjusting the information about the product to meet local labeling requirements, or as significant as adding new ingredients or creating unique new brand names.

Responding to local needs as closely as possible constitutes the primary goal of adaptation. Many benefits may emerge as a result. Adaptation can lead to more satisfied consumers, build brand image, and increase sales. Adaptation also incurs costs. Changing the marketing mix may require designing an entirely new advertising campaign or developing an expensive new ingredient. These costs may be higher than the potential return.

 International Marketing in Daily Life

Food Products

Many food products require adaptation. Everyone needs to eat, which makes food a basic necessity. Few things play as large a role in daily life, and few product categories are as difficult to sell in a different country or even a different region. In marketing, taboo or forbidden foods are key concerns. The prohibitions on pork for Muslim and Jewish consumers are well known, as is the Hindu prohibition on eating beef. Less-well-known are Jainist requirements. Jainism is practiced by 4 million people, mainly in India. The religion is strictly vegetarian; in addition, followers typically do not eat tubers or other vegetables that are killed as part of the harvesting process. Some Taoists follow a similar ban on vegetables in the alliaceous family, such as garlic and onion.

Individuals in Western countries also avoid taboo foods. Americans do not eat horsemeat, even though it is common in parts of Europe. Most people in Western cultures do not eat insects or grubs, but the practice is common in Southeast Asia and in the jungles of Latin America. Dogs and cats are pets in part of the world and dinner in others.[22]

The examples of taboos show the breadth of differences in food consumption globally. One group's "nasty" food is another's favorite chocolate-covered snack, such as Japanese chocolate-covered grasshoppers and ants. Beyond excluded foods, large differences are present in the role food plays in daily life. Some countries start the day with a large breakfast. Others prefer a light breakfast and a large lunch, followed by a nap. Visitors to Brazil often comment on the country's tradition of eating dinner late in the evening, leading most restaurants to not even open until around 8:00 p.m.

Methods of serving food change from country to country. Traditional Chinese meals are served on a large rotating "Lazy Susan," and each person takes turn serving himself or herself. Ethiopian cuisine is also often shared in a communal manner. The dishes are usually served on top of *injera*, a spongy flat bread. Dining involves using the fingers, not utensils. In cases of friendship, individuals may feed someone a bite to indicate closeness. The use of fingers instead of utensils is common throughout Africa, the Middle East, and South Asia. Some believe that the oils from fingers add extra flavor to food.

LAWS AND ADAPTATION

Laws often govern marketing activities. Marketing communications, product attributes, green marketing, organizational forms, and interactions between businesses and packaging are all affected by laws. The legal system of a country in which the company operates applies to marketing activities as do the laws of the country in which the company is headquartered. For instance, U.S. companies must follow both American laws that apply to businesses abroad and the laws of any host country. Problems arise when American laws conflict with the laws of the host country.

Marketing Communications

Marketing communications present a common legal concern for marketers. Many countries enforce legal restrictions on advertising to children or on advertising potentially unhealthy or addictive substances. False advertising and medicines are also often regulated or prohibited. The 2010 World Cup football tournament in South Africa drew attention to the country's advertising regulations. The country has strict laws, especially regarding health claims. Advertisements are not allowed to claim that a product will help a person slim down or any similar claim.[23]

Product Attributes

Product attributes are also influenced by laws. These laws frequently focus on safety; children again are a primary group to be protected. In some cases, product attributes are allowed but claims about those attributes may be limited. In other cases, products that are accepted in one country are forbidden in others. In strict Islamic countries, this includes a prohibition on alcohol. Brazil has taken an aggressive approach to tobacco regulation. The country has limited the tar, nicotine, and carbon monoxide levels allowed in cigarettes, added a more severe warning on packages, and became the first country in the world to outlaw the use of "descriptors that may induce complacency in consumers regarding the consumption of tobacco products." Descriptors include the words "light," "ultra light," and "mild."[24]

Organizational Structure

Laws also apply to organizational structures. Governments often have concerns regarding the degree of influence multinational corporations can exert. In these cases, multinational corporations may be required to have local partners, or limits on ownership for foreign companies may be in place. The requirements often target specific industries, especially those deemed important and in need of protection. India's government deems telecommunications to be such an industry. Foreign ownership of any telecommunications company is limited to 74%. When the U.S. company Qualcomm entered India, a joint venture called Long-Term Evolution was created with two local Indian companies, each of which owned 13% of the new venture.

The other main effect on organizational structure from governmental activity is antitrust regulation. *Antitrust laws* prevent companies from becoming monopolies. Most countries limit the size of a business to restrain monopolies and preserve competition. The threshold for governmental actions will be different in each region and can even change from case to case. The European Union's approach to antitrust law is often more stringent than that of the United States. Recent actions by the EU included fining Intel $1.44 billion for attempting to drive AMD, Intel's main rival, out of the market.[25] In addition, an investigation aimed at Apple sought evidence that the company violated antitrust laws by not allowing Flash to be used in any of its products.[26]

Adapting Packages and Labels

A product rarely enters a new, foreign market without changes being made to packaging. Many of these alterations are in response to the legal requirements present in a country. Legal requirements regarding product size, materials used, and other components are common. Products are consumed differently in other cultures, necessitating changes to the packaging. Various shapes or materials may be typical in different countries. Glass bottles are more common for soft drinks in some countries. Tall skinny bottles may be associated with energy drinks in one culture and used for different types of drinks in another. Juices may only be sold in glass containers in one country and in aluminum cans in others. Preliminary market research can identify these kinds of cultural nuances and can lead to appropriate adaptation (see Figure 8.6).

Legal stipulations affect product labels. Each country enacts its own labeling requirements. Often these can be complicated and require significant adaptation. Recently, the government of South Africa passed a consumer protection law. One provision required retailers to inform consumers of the risk from potentially hazardous products, particularly from those risks that consumers could not "reasonably be expected to be aware of." These risks must be on the labels for the products, and the labels must use "plain and simple language." In response to the law, retailers began updating labels on products, often with guidance from a lawyer.[27]

| Legal Requirements |
| Warranties |
| Cultural and Aesthetic Factors |

Figure 8.6: Packaging and Labeling Adaptation Factors

Warranties are an additional component of product labeling that differs substantially from one country to another. Warranties are not common in many less-developed or developing countries. In developed countries, especially for high involvement purchases and expensive products, the quality and type of warranty can be a key part of the customer's purchase decision-making process. Regulations regarding warranties are common. In the European Union, consumer protection laws require a two-year warranty for thousands of products. Each must carry understandable instructions.[28]

Cultural and aesthetic factors will be adapted as packages and labels are developed for individual countries. Colors, shapes, and sizes are designed to fit local circumstances. They should also mesh with the brand and product name.

Green Marketing and Labels

As consumers increasingly buy products based on environmental or green claims, the need for consumer protection has grown. Greenwashing, or fake green claims, essentially defrauds customers. In response, regulations have been introduced to control this type of labeling. Green marketing regulations are constantly changing as governments struggle to keep up with a rapidly growing industry.[29]

Adaptation of Services

It might be easy to think of services as being nondurable products, but that may not be the case. Several services are durable. Insurance services are consumed year-round, even though premiums and claims are generally paid infrequently. Similarly, business accounting services are usually "consumed" year-round.

Intangibility is not the only product feature that makes services unique. As a general statement, services differ from tangible goods due to intangibility, heterogeneity, simultaneous production and consumption, and perishability elements, as described in Figure 8.7.

Characteristic	Description	Example
Intangibility	Services cannot be touched or easily displayed.	Manulife Indonesia is a major financial service provider offering intangible services in Indonesia.
Heterogeneity	Delivery of service is not standardized and is dependent on social interaction.	Bright Ideas Event Coordinators Ltd. is a leading event planning company in Vancouver (Canada) that produces unique corporate and special events.
Simultaneous Production and Consumption	Customers co-create services along with the provider.	AnticaPesa is a top restaurant in Rome, Italy, whose atmosphere is co-created by both staff and guests.
Perishability	Services cannot be stored, and they depend heavily on supply and demand.	Hemavan is a favorite ski resort in Sweden, where demand is dependent on the geographic surroundings.

Figure 8.7: Characteristics of Services

Service firms utilize several approaches to deal with the unique aspects of service offerings. Malayan Banking Berhad (Maybank) is the largest banking group in Malaysia. The company won 2009 Promotion Marketing Award of Asia for the development of its Maybank Treats Fair, an event that centered on a four-day shopping extravaganza in a carnival-like setting.[30] By bringing consumers together in a physical location, the company was able to make tangible the intangible.

Ocean Park, a popular tourist water park in Hong Kong, recently revamped its website by relying largely on interactive technologies to allow the consumer to become more engaged with the company, which allowed customers to co-create the experience with the provider.[31] International airlines often focus on ensuring on-time arrivals of

Services such as banking may require international adaptation.

flights to make a brand stand out. Japan Airlines won three On-Time Performance Service Awards in 2010 for delivering a high percentage of on-time flights, adding to the prestige of the brand.[32]

Services are adapted to meet legal and cultural constraints.[33] For example, in places where theocratic law prevails, charging interest is prohibited, which affects banking and credit card services. Other banking regulations influence how loans may be granted, the definition of usury, and collateral requirements. Further, laws regulating accounting practices vary, causing the need for adaptation of the service.

Strict terrorism laws in Israel substantially affect the nature of air travel into and out of the country. Personal services including grooming are affected by cultural considerations. In some countries, women and men do not visit the same salon for hair care. Tourism services also adjust to local conditions. At the extreme, women cannot own property in some countries, thereby affecting all of the services associated with ownership.

In many instances the service itself will be adapted, as will the messages used to market those services. The portrayal of women affects numerous advertisements and marketing for services worldwide. Marketers consider both the product and its communications prior to beginning service provider operations in various countries.

SERVICE QUALITY

Service quality consists of the outcome of an evaluative process in which a consumer compares the service she expected to receive with her perception of the service as provided.[34] A popular approach to measuring service quality is the SERVQUAL method, which measures the concept across various dimensions.[35] The dimensions can be conceptualized using the "RATER" acronym, which stands for reliability, assurance, tangibles, empathy, and responsiveness, as described in Figure 8.8.

Dimension	Description
Reliability	Provider provides service dependably and accurately.
Assurance	Provider conveys feelings of trust and knowledge.
Tangibles	Provider has appealing facilities, equipment, and personnel.
Empathy	Provider conveys a feeling of caring and individual attention.
Responsiveness	Provider is willing and able to provide prompt service.

Figure 8.8: Dimensions of Service Quality

Source: Adapted from A. Parasuraman, V. Zeithaml, and L. Berry, "A Conceptual Model of Service Quality and Its Implications for Future Research," *Journal of Marketing* 49 no. 4 (1985): 41–50.

ADAPTATION AND SERVICE QUALITY

Service quality perceptions are influenced to a significant degree by cultural differences, as are perceptions of the relationship between service provider and customer.[36] In general, reliability constitutes a key element of service quality in the United States, but not necessarily in other cultures.[37]

One recent research effort examined the extent to which each of Hofstede's cultural dimensions relates to the service quality dimensions in various cultures.[38] Using this method, the data suggest that cultural profiles with large power distance and high collectivism rated the assurance dimension as the most important feature of service, whereas cultures exhibiting smaller power distance and high collectivism gave equal importance to each dimension. Also, cultures with smaller power distance and high individualism rated reliability and responsiveness as most important. Cultures with large power distance and medium individualism viewed tangibles as most important. Small power distance and medium individualism cultures preferred reliability and responsiveness and view empathy as moderately important.

In another study, the research revealed that in cultures where openness and frankness are widely accepted, such as in Germany and the United States, consumers feel more comfortable expressing their emotions and openly stating how they feel. In contrast, in cultures where maintaining group harmony is expected, including Japan, the same behaviors were frowned upon.[39]

A study of Taiwanese consumers revealed that sincerity, generosity, and courtesy underscored perceptions of service relationships. These consumers were particularly focused on *chin-chieh*, a Mandarin Chinese concept that broadly translates into "warm politeness." These studies indicate that the interpersonal element of service relationships differs across cultures.[40]

In summary, the quality of a company's products and services often determines its future success. Quality represents the starting point. From there, other elements, such as advertising, promotion, and other marketing activities, help sell the product and build relationships with customers over time.

Some musical forms of musical presentation require international adaptation, as may have been the case for Fergie and the Black Eyed Peas during their concert at Morumbi Stadium in Sao Paulo, Brazil.

Music: Legal Systems, Standardization, and Adaptation

Some form of music can be found in nearly every culture. As methods of communication have become more immediate and sophisticated, musical products have begun to regularly move across national borders. Consequently, legal systems, standardization, and adaptation come into play.

When a music company or performer seeks to sell works in other countries, the actual product itself will first be considered. Sheet music may require translation of the words on the page. Recorded music can be offered in a series of formats, including vinyl albums, cassette, compact disc (CD), or as downloadable music for electronic players such as an iPod. The music can be left in its standardized original language or adapted and recorded to match the language of the host country. Musical performances will be subject to the availability of concert venues, logistical issues, and other local circumstances.

Where cultures are relatively similar, standardization may be possible. A Canadian musician seeking to break into the British or U.S. market would be able to sing in English, and the format, package, and label could remain the same, assuming French is not the artist's primary language. A Mexican songster might consider rerecording a tune into English in order to reach a wider audience.

Culture also affects the degree to which musical content will be accepted in a country. What may be suitable to people in one region might be offensive to citizens in another. Cultural considerations should be taken into account prior to exporting music in any format.

In addition, the role of radio might influence the music company and the artist. In a country where stations are state owned, it might be difficult to achieve airtime. In more capitalist countries, access to radio airplay will likely be easier to achieve.

VIDEO LINK 8.4:
Video-On-Demand Services

LEGAL ADAPTATION

Following the development of the music format, an additional concern when entering a new country will be the legal system in the host country. Legal nuances affect the degree to which a product or service can be standardized, or whether it must be adapted. When music moves from one country to another in various formats, the overall legal system influences the process. Common law, civil law, and theocratic law treat music in different ways, considering

- content of the music,
- restrictions on live performances,
- packaging and labeling requirements, and
- intellectual property protection.

Musical Content

The degree to which freedom of expression exists largely depends on two factors: local cultural norms and the legal system. Censorship in some form appears in nearly all legal systems, most notably in the regulation of obscenity. In Europe, music videos can include nudity and other more graphic images. In the United States, obscene words may be heard on a recorded version of a song but will be removed if the song is played on the radio or on television. At the extreme, theocratic law would limit the type of language to be used as well as references to women and religious values.

Restrictions on Live Performances

In 2011, China announced a ban on Western music. Handel's Messiah and other religious songs were not allowed at the country's International Music Festival. In response, the Sinfonica Orchestra di Roma dropped plans to play Mozart's Requiem in the Sichuan earthquake zone in honor of the dead and to raise money for survivors of the 2008 earthquake.[41]

National governments also limit dissent produced in the form of music. Music has a long and storied history of presenting lyrical protests. Oppressive governments work to prevent some music from being performed. In Iran, musical promoter Yaghub Mehrnahad was executed for his role in protest concerts.[42]

Performances are also scrutinized by governments. Highly sexualized musical show performances are popular in Brazil and banned in Libya. A touring band should carefully adapt any musical show to meet governmental restrictions.

Packaging and Labeling Requirements

As is the case with any exported item, local restrictions exist for packages and labels. Portrayals of women and other culturally sensitive figures should be carefully considered. Album covers or CD labels often must be changed to fit local circumstances.

Intellectual Property Protection

Copying music without paying for it has been a problem in the music industry for many years. Tape recorder technology made it possible to copy songs from the radio or from an album onto a reel-to-reel recorder many years ago. More recently, Internet downloading capabilities have made musical piracy even easier. In Canada, a major court ruled that P2P (peer-to-peer) file sharing was legal, although uploading files for larger distribution was not.[43] In the United States, the file-sharing website Napster faced major governmental intervention. The rationale for limiting file sharing is that the intellectual property of the musician and the music company that recorded the song has been taken without compensation.

Today consumers globally are increasingly pirating entertainment goods such as music. In India, the illegal downloading of music to mobile phone chips has become a growing problem. One estimate suggests that the music industry lost *Rs 300 crore* in 2009 due to mobile chip piracy (300 million *rupees*, or approximately $6.4 million).[44] Table 8.2 identifies piracy rates in selected countries.

Music piracy can severely injure a local music industry, which in turn can drastically impact the export of music. France and Spain have been hit hard by music piracy. Local artists from these countries have a difficult time producing new music due to a culture of tolerance toward music piracy. The lack of local music affects international trade in the industry.[45] In many countries, file-sharing technologies threaten the existence of music production companies.

At the same time, various countries allow for legal downloading of music, including Argentina, Australia, Chile, and Hong Kong. With Internet access, it is possible for most people around the world to gain access to music files. Thus, even though legal protection among many countries exists in the form of the Agreement on Trade-Related Aspects of Property Rights (TRIPS), the practicality is that file sharing cannot be stopped on an international basis. No real recourse to collect lost royalties is in place.

Individual countries, however, can still take actions for downloading within their borders. Many countries have taken legal steps to reduce music piracy. One relatively new method, the "graduated-response" approach, has been used in South Korea, England, and France. One or two warnings are given before criminal charges are brought against consumers infringing on intellectual property rights. The laws include pressure on Internet service providers to record information about

COUNTRY	PERCENTAGE OF SOFTWARE PIRATED
United States	20%
Germany	27%
Singapore	37%
Italy	49%
Croatia	54%
Mexico	61%
India	69%
Albania	78%
China	82%
Pakistan	84%
Iraq	85%
Sri Lanka	90%
Armenia	93%

Table 8.2: **Piracy Rates**

Source: Adapted from "The Fifth Annual BSA and IDC Global Software Piracy Study 2007," accessed at www.nationmaster.com/graph/cri_sof_pir_rat-crime-software-piracy-rate#source.

the individuals or businesses that are using Internet connections inappropriately. These individuals or the businesses themselves face fines or other consequences.[46]

As indicated, music in all its forms requires decisions regarding standardization and adaptation, both in regard to the actual product as well as to the legal system that governs the marketing of that product in an individual country. Marketing professionals work to make sure any good or service fits with the constraints of the local host nation.

Combining Standardization and Adaptation

While the standardization versus adaptation debate may be presented as an either/or situation, in practice marketers often combine the two approaches. The **contingency approach** suggests that marketers should do what is appropriate for each market, which typically leads to a combination of both standardized and adapted components.[47] By taking this approach, companies are able to effectively meet the needs of local consumers while still offering some degree of global standardization. Marketers then attend to the factors of the marketing mix that should be adapted or standardized. The default will be standardization because it offers cost savings, although some degree of adaptation often becomes necessary to generate product demand. The conflicting objectives of saving costs versus creating product acceptance are balanced, and the most effective marketing mix will be deployed.

Domino's Pizza utilized a product extension-communication adaptation approach.

THE PRODUCT AND COMMUNICATION ADAPTATION MODEL

When expanding into new markets, adaptation decisions can be broken down into two separate but related components. First, the same product can be extended into the market—that is, a standardized product may be offered to the new market. Second, communication and promotional materials can be extended into the market. The other options are to adapt the product, communications, or both. These two decisions are coupled and represent four strategic approaches (see Figure 8.9).

Product/Communication	Extension	Adaptation
Extension	Dual Extension	Product Adaptation-Communication Extension
Adaptation	Product Extension-Communication Adaptation	Dual Adaptation

Figure 8.9: Product and Communication Extension or Adaptation Model

Product and Communication Extension

Product and communication extension, or a dual extension, is the strategy in which the same product and communications are extended into the new market. Standardization of everything possible becomes the marketing goal. By using the same product and communications, often not even changing the language, marketing messages focus on the product's attributes. Another by-product of this strategy will be an increased consumer interest in a product's country of origin. The dual extension strategy may be found in exporting, which is the process of shipping goods to foreign markets. Exporting companies, especially those beginning the process of entering markets, use a dual extension strategy to lower the costs and risks associated with that market entry.

Clinique and Bacardi are companies that employ product and communication extension strategies.[48] In some cases, products can meet a global need or be used without change across borders. The Chinese computer power manufacturer Huntkey introduced a universal power strip in March of 2010 with a unique plug design that allows it to work in more than 240 different countries.[49] The global appeal of the product allows the company to feature the product and communication extension method.

Product Extension-Communication Adaptation

When marketers keep the same product but make changes to the communication, a product extension-communication adaptation approach has been utilized. Coca-Cola and Pepsi Cola typically apply this strategy. The product remains the same, other than possibly using locally sourced ingredients, but the communication changes. A visit to Coca-Cola's various country-targeting websites reveals how the company adapts communication but keeps the product standardized. The same iconic bottle appears, the color of red is the primary color in most of the websites, and the product is positioned as "happy" and "refreshing" across the majority of markets.

Product Adaptation-Communication Extension

Product adaptation-communication extension involves adapting the product but retaining the same communications program. This often includes keeping the same basic theme for the advertising, such as testimonials or humor, but changing the product's brand name or adding an additional attribute to the product. It is a common strategy for large consumer goods companies. Not long ago, Unilever in Japan introduced a new brand of Lipton tea. The company adapted the traditional product by adding the amino acid theanine to the tea. The company's communications claim was that the additive allows the consumer both to relax and to focus. The new tea has been branded Lipton *Hirameki*, which means "I've got an idea" in Japanese.[50]

INTERNATIONAL INCIDENT ///

You have a longtime business contact in an emerging market who is always excited about the latest technical device. The problem is that he typically does not know how to really use the gadget. You recently traveled to meet with him and found him proudly displaying his new Blackberry Torch 9800. You are frustrated that he appeared to have purchased it for reasons of conspicuous consumption and not utility. The phone has 3G, built-in GPS mapping, powerful web-searching tools, and a multi-touch screen. Your contact mainly sees it as a shiny phone. Over the course of the day, there are a variety of times when the phone's abilities would have been helpful. You could have used the GPS when lost and the web function to get extra information before a sales meeting. At the very least you just wanted to be able to send an email to your contact. You are sensitive to insulting your contact, but it is reaching the point of real frustration. Do you say anything? Why or why not? If you decide to bring it up, how do you broach the topic?

Product-Communication Adaptation

The final approach involves adapting the product and communications, the product-communication adaptation, or the dual adaptation strategy. Large demand and large target markets often are best served by adapting products specifically to individual markets. Cosmetics can be adapted to respond to demand for unique attributes in new markets. In East Asia, white skin is seen as the beauty ideal. Many cosmetics companies have adapted products to include a whitening version. The market leader is the American brand Oil of Olay, which offers the Olay White Radiance product. The traditional face cream with a whitening additive effectively reaches the target market. Communication for the product can be adapted to use local models, language, and appeals.[51]

In extreme cases, to be successful in a new market companies invent a new product to meet the needs of new consumers. This can be thought of as an extreme version of dual adaptation. While creating an entirely new product may be difficult, it might be necessary when the firm faces a vastly different but large or strategically important market.

VIDEO LINK 8.5:
Recycling ▶

Sustainability and Adaptation

Two approaches to sustainability are practiced as part of adaptation. The first, adaptation of the product, includes all of the methods used to design and market items that can be reused or recycled. Electronics, appliances, automobiles, and other durable goods are logical candidates for recycling efforts. Component parts, including ink jets for copiers and printers, can also be manufactured to be reused. Disposable batteries may be replaced with rechargeable forms, and power sources for other products can be adapted to include wind, solar, or other renewable forms of energy.

In many instances, the packaging can also be adapted into a more sustainable form. Chinese companies that were engaged in recycling cardboard products noticed significant declines in orders during the most recent recession. The trend will likely reverse as economic conditions improve.

The second approach to sustainability involves changing the production process. Many firms have designed manufacturing plants and office buildings to save energy through the use of solar panels, new types of roofing, and other innovative energy-savers. Further, by placing plant locations strategically and seeking more-efficient forms of transportation, shipping costs can be greatly reduced.

In the future, the movement toward sustainable products and production methods is expected to expand. Companies on the forefront of the trend may realize substantial marketing advantages by becoming the first mover or innovator in sustainability.

銀獎

Trash pack for outdoors

戶外用三角垃圾包 用途：垃圾桶

三角包裝誕生自瑞典，日本
國內多年來常見於機關學校
供餐時的牛奶容器，早已廣
為人們所熟悉。運用其三角
造型特色，兼具安定及隱蔽
性，能輕鬆立穩且袋內垃圾
不容易被看見，可當作露營
及野餐的戶外最佳幫手。

Elements of adaptation affect sustainability efforts.

Global Innovation

Many companies increasingly emphasize innovation as a source of advantage over competitors. The position of innovation manager has been added to many organizations as part of an in-depth innovation strategy. A key component of innovation and marketing, new product development, is the process of creating a new product. New product development helps renew a company and assists the marketing team in effectively responding to changes in customer tastes. With estimates as high as nine out of ten new products failing, new product development can be costly and entail a great deal of risk, but creating new products may be a necessary strategy for long-term firm success.

The Brazilian Zeebo gaming console product is about the size of a paperback book. It plays online games. The console has been positioned as a gaming console for emerging markets, as a less expensive product when compared to consoles made by Microsoft, Nintendo, and Sony. Fierce competition exists and the risk for failure is high, a typical scenario for new product introductions.[52]

Several types of "new" products can be introduced. *New-to-the-world products* are the inventions or discoveries most strongly associated with new product development. The fluorescent light bulb, the personal computer, and the digital music player are all types of new-to-the-world products.

A company may also create a product for an existing product category. These are *new category products*. Microsoft's introduction of the Xbox 360 was a new category product for the company and counts as an example of this kind of new product development.

Another form of extension is an *addition to the product line*. Additions are made to protect a lead brand in the product category from competitors or to fill a gap in the product line. Product lines frequently differ from country to country; an addition to a product line in one country may be an existing product in other. When Samsung introduced two top-of-the-line "beyond smart mobile phones" capable of running thousands of different applications, these were additions to the product line.[53]

In many cases, especially when entering new markets, a producer makes small changes to an existing product. *Product improvements* may be considered a type of new product development. In China, Sprite sells a ginger-flavored product named Sprite on Fire, in reference to the burning sensation from the ginger in the soda.

The final type of new product development, *repositioning*, refers to finding a new use or application for an existing product. This increasingly occurs as companies that sell existing products to bottom-of-the-pyramid consumers offer the items in developed countries. Nestlé repositioned its Maggi brand of dried noodles, which was

LEARNING OBJECTIVE #6:

How can global innovation and patterns of diffusion assist the marketing team in reaching target markets, including those consisting of bottom-of-the-pyramid customers?

a top seller in rural India and Pakistan, as an inexpensive but healthy food in Australia and New Zealand.[54]

In some cases, an established product in the home market will be viewed as a new product in the country being entered. For established businesses, this means viewing what may be a traditional, old product as something new and innovative. Resistance to the new, especially the foreign, often accompanies the introduction of these products in new markets. The problem will be more likely to occur in certain market segments, such as rural consumers in emerging markets, or older consumers in transition economies. Increasingly, new products become popular in developing countries and are then introduced into developed countries. Fanta, the second-best selling soda in Africa, is a Coca-Cola brand that has not become popular in the United States. The company rolled out an aggressive marketing campaign around a product launch in 2001, but the brand is still only the eighth-best-selling soda in the American market.[55]

TYPES OF ADOPTERS

When entering a market, an effective tool for marketers comes from targeting the different categories of adopters (see Figure 8.10). Marketers can segment consumers based on speed of new product adoption. *Innovators*, the group of consumers who start using new products first, represent approximately 2.5% of any market. The next group to try something new, *early adopters*, make up about 13.5% of the market. Marketers often combine efforts aimed at early adopters and innovators when introducing a new product. These two groups represent around 16% of the overall market. Success with these groups often serves as a signal of sales in the overall market.

Early adopters and innovators can be targeted using promotions designed to ensure adoption. Postpurchase surveys are used to gauge satisfaction with the new product, and, if needed, changes will be made before targeting the overall market. The largest two segments of adopters are the *early majority* and the *late majority*, each consisting of about 34% of the market. Penetration into these markets signals successful product introduction and the movement toward a mature product. The final segment, *laggards*, represents 16% of the market. Laggards may never start using the product. In many cases it is more cost effective to not target this segment and instead to focus on successful introduction of a different new product. This begins the cycle of adoption all over again.

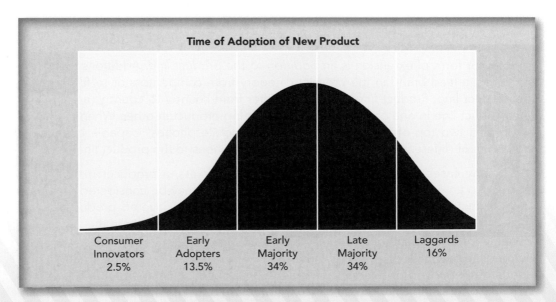

Figure 8.10: Types of Adopters in New Product Diffusion

GLOBAL PRODUCT DIFFUSION

The process by which an innovation slowly spreads through a culture or group is **diffusion**. It is comparable to the spreading of a blot of ink that is dropped on a sheet of paper. The ink slowly diffuses into the paper. The same process applies to new products and new uses for existing products. The knowledge reaches a few individuals—the innovators and early adopters—and then diffuses, sometimes slowly or sometimes quickly, to the early majority followed by the late majority, ending with laggards.

Four factors should be considered with regard to diffusion. First is the innovation itself. The marketing team identifies how similar the innovation is to existing products or processes. The larger the disconnect with existing consumer behaviors, the slower the rate of diffusion.

The second factor will be the effectiveness of communications about the innovation. The best mousetrap ever invented cannot sell without effective promotion. Consumers should be exposed to communications designed to encourage trial purchases, and they must understand the message.

Time represents the third key component of diffusion. All innovations take time to spread within a culture. Appropriate marketing mix activities can speed up this process. Poor marketing activity leads to slower diffusion.

The final factor emerges from the members of the society within which the product is introduced. Effectively marketing to them will be particularly challenging in foreign markets. A lack of deep understanding of consumers and how the product might be used hinders efforts to introduce a new product.

Acceptance of hybrid electric vehicles has gone through the diffusion process. The technology for hybrids can be traced back to the turn of the twentieth century when electric, hybrid, and gasoline cars all fought for acceptance. The second car built by Dr. Ferdinand Porsche, the founder of Porsche Vehicles, was an electric-gas hybrid. The modern history of the hybrid begins with the introduction of the Audi Duo III hybrid in 1998. The car was priced out of the mass market and was not a success, but it marked the rebirth of the hybrid category.

At about the same time, Toyota began to mass-produce the Prius, but at that point it was only sold in the Japanese market. The first global mass market hybrid was the Honda Insight, which hit the market in 1999. The car, a three-door hatchback, was a limited success. Consumer innovators and early adopters with a passion for

The Toyota Prius has successfully penetrated markets and gained acceptance by consumers.

environmental issues purchased the car, and the hybrid innovation began to diffuse throughout society.

In 2000, Toyota released the Prius four-door sedan hybrid in its major global markets. The introduction was successful and the model was declared the 2004 Car of the Year by *Motor Trend* magazine. At that point, the early majority had started purchasing the car. By 2009, hybrid technology had diffused across much of society. Ford, Honda, Toyota, Mazda, Nissan, General Motors, BMW, Hyundai, and Mercedes-Benz all manufactured some form of hybrid vehicle.[56] Coming full circle, Porsche announced on January 28, 2010, that it would be manufacturing the Porsche 918 Spider, a plug-in hybrid.[57]

New Product Development and the Bottom-of-the-Pyramid

New product development is an important part of effective marketing to bottom-of-the-pyramid consumers. Often, creating the capacity to consume necessitates marketers designing a new, less expensive version of an existing product. In many cases the product can then be reintroduced back in developed markets as a less-expensive, downscaled version of the original product. This approach reverses the traditional model of new product development. The product is introduced to the masses in the less-developed world and then moves into more economically advanced countries.

GE is the world's leading manufacturer of electro-encephalograph (EEG) machines, with 34% of the global market. The company introduced the MAC 800, a low-cost, stripped-down version of the typical EEG machine used in developed countries. The MAC 800 was developed for emerging markets. To fit the needs of developed country health professionals, a few features were added, such as Ethernet, USB, and telephone ports, but introducing the updated machine was an estimated $1.8 million less expensive than developing a new machine.[58]

Ethical Issues in Standardization and Adaptation

Adaptation of products can lead to ethical concerns. A major concern may be found at the intersection of religion and ethics. Religion can be one of the primary sources of ethical values in any culture; as companies go abroad, however, religious values in the host country often conflict with those values in the home country. The question remains as to which values the company should follow. The issue becomes whether marketers should be expected to adapt to controversial or potentially unethical practices. For example, managers of satellite campuses for Western Universities in the Middle East wonder if they should require women to wear head coverings and traditional Muslim dress, regardless of their religions. Food providers might examine social norms against eating certain animals or insects before making the decision whether to offer certain products.

ETHICS AND LAWS

Ethics may differ from laws. Some laws (or the lack of a laws) conflict with ethical values. When a company operates in many dissimilar legal environments, conflicts can arise between the company's values and the laws of the country in which the company is doing business. For example, child labor takes place in many countries. Ethically, a company's management team may feel the need to enforce stricter guidelines than the legal limits in the country. The same may apply to minimum wages, worker safety, and the role of women in the workplace.

Chapter 8: Review and Resources

STRATEGIC IMPLICATIONS //

When entering a new country, the marketing team's first step will be to determine the unique legal requirements of that locale. After studying the legal environment, voluntary adaptation choices can be made. Then, the main strategic question for global marketers will be how much to change. Marketing leaders decide on the degree of adaptation necessary to achieve the desired level of local responsiveness, which will be balanced with the efficiency gains from standardization. Regulations and the adaptation necessitated by them are not optional. If the requirements are too stringent, the best strategic choice may be to not enter the country.

International marketers should foster a clear conceptualization of each brand's global position. Questions will be asked regarding what needs to be constant across borders and what should be changed. The marketing team identifies what the brand means and how well that meaning transfers to another culture. Branding decisions are coupled with the communication strategy. One of the product/communication strategies will then be chosen.

TACTICAL IMPLICATIONS //

Adaptation and standardization decisions are based on deep understanding of consumers in each market. Market research and local partners, often tied together, help marketers understand local consumer tastes. With this knowledge, product adaptation becomes more likely to succeed. Keeping the global brand goals in mind, products are changed and new products are introduced. Packaging is updated and labels are changed. Warranties may or may not be added.

Market research will be used to identify early adopters and innovators. These consumers can be targeted for the introduction of adapted products, new-to-the-country products, and new-to-the-world products. Understanding these consumers will speed the diffusion of innovative products throughout the country.

OPERATIONAL IMPLICATIONS //

Communication of brand meaning to all employees globally is crucial. Consistent positioning can only be achieved through effective communication. The communication should be two-way. Decisions will be transmitted to employees, bearing in mind that individual workers may discover valuable potential adaptations that can only be seen by individuals with on-the-ground experience.

Local workers should be carefully trained with regard to local laws and statutes. Host country employees can assist in training expatriates. The training should extend beyond legal requirements to include cultural and ethical differences.

Standardized products are often best served by individual training of first-line supervisors and employees, especially those not familiar with an exported product. The benefits of any item that has been adapted to fit the needs of the local community should be carefully explained by those who design advertisements and other communications, as well as the sales force and others making contacts with customers.

TERMS

common law	conciliation	cultural convergence
civil law	arbitration	adaptation
theocratic law	litigation	contingency approach
intellectual property	standardization	diffusion
intellectual property piracy	economies of scale	
jurisdiction	economies of scope	

REVIEW QUESTIONS

1. Describe the three main legal systems: common law, civil law, and theocratic law.
2. Define intellectual property and name the treaty that seeks to protect intellectual property.
3. Describe copyrights, trademarks, and patents.
4. What is counterfeiting?
5. Describe corporate spying and reverse-engineering.
6. What is the relationship between intellectual property protection and economic development?
7. Define jurisdiction and explain how it applies to legal actions.
8. Describe conciliation and arbitration.
9. What are the advantages and disadvantages of arbitration?
10. What are the disadvantages of litigation?
11. Define standardization and name the primary reasons for its use.
12. Describe economies of scale and economies of scope.
13. Define cultural convergence.
14. Define adaptation.
15. Explain how laws affect adaptation and the product areas affected by regulations.
16. How is packaging adapted?
17. How are labels adapted?
18. Describe the contingency approach with regard to standardization and adaptation.
19. What are the four different approaches to the product and communication adaptation or extension model?
20. Define new product development and name the different types.
21. How can adopters of new products be categorized?
22. Define diffusion and explain the factors influence the speed of diffusion.

DISCUSSION QUESTIONS

1. Explain the advantages and disadvantages of the three primary legal systems—common law, civil law, and theocratic law. Is one of these systems more conducive to marketing activity than another? Explain your answer.
2. Many individuals in both developed and developing countries have violated intellectual property protections. Choose a side and make a case for why violating intellectual property is either wrong or right.
3. Litigation is often the least attractive of the conflict resolution choices. Create a table listing the advantages and disadvantages of conciliation, arbitration, and litigation, then pick the best possible resolution option for a business seeking to protect a patent. Defend your choice.

4. Whether to standardize or adapt a product will be one of the central decisions an international marketer makes. Consider a global product that you recently purchased. What was standardized or adapted? Why did the marketing team make these choices? What was legally required?

5. New products fail at an increasingly high rate. How can the graph of new product adaptation be applied to ensure higher acceptance of a new product?

6. Think of a new product you recently purchased. What factors influenced your decision to purchase the product? Does the product seem to be one that diffuses quickly or slowly across a target market?

ANALYTICAL AND INTERNET EXERCISES

1. Search the Internet for "Coca-Cola virtual vendor." Using this online tool, list at least ten of Coca-Cola's global versus national brands. Why were these choices made? Do you agree or disagree with Coca-Cola's overall brand strategy? Justify your answer.

2. The concept of aesthetics is not easy to explain. Using Google or another online search engine, search for various examples of art and architecture from at least one country from each continent (excluding Antarctica). What does the search reveal about differences in aesthetics?

3. Find a recent example of a case of conciliation or arbitration. Why would the companies involved have preferred this conflict resolution method to litigation? Now find a recent litigation example. What did the companies risk from litigating the dispute?

4. Using the Internet, track the rate of diffusion internationally for the following products:

- cell phones
- laptop computers
- professional basketball
- credit and debit cards

▶ ONLINE VIDEOS

Visit **www.sagepub.com/baack** to view these chapter videos:

Video Link 8.1: The Fast Food Market

Video Link 8.2: Brands and Globalization

Video Link 8.3: Economic Espionage

Video Link 8.4: Video-On-Demand Services

Video Link 8.5: Recycling

🌐 STUDENT STUDY SITE

Visit **www.sagepub.com/baack** to access these additional learning tools:

- Web Quizzes
- eFlashcards
- SAGE Journal Articles

- Country Fact Sheets
- Chapter Outlines
- Interactive Maps

CASE 8 ///

AB InBev: Adapting Beer Products in Global Markets

Budweiser, the world's best-selling beer brand, proudly promotes its American heritage. To American consumers, Bud and Bud Light are iconic national brands. In July 2008, the $52 billion purchase of Anheuser Busch cast the company's brand into question. The purchaser, InBev, is a multinational corporation with roots in both Brazil and Belgium. The company is now headquartered in Leuven, Belgium, and the Anheuser-Busch brand has been added to the company name.

The history of InBev explains part of the frustration with the acquisition. The beginnings of the corporation can be traced to three Brazilian investors who purchased a local brewer, Brahma, in 1989. The investors increased the efficiency of the brewer and aggressively expanded in Brazil, including merging with another large Brazilian brewer. The next step was a merger with Interbrew in 2004, a Belgium brewer with roots in that country going back to the year 1366. InBev purchased Anheuser-Busch in 2008 and became AB-InBev, the largest brewer in the world. It has the highest or second-highest market share in twenty-five of the world's top thirty-one beer markets.[59] After refinancing the debt from the decade of mergers and acquisitions, the company is poised for rapid global growth. The planned growth involves adaptation and standardization decisions.

The first decision for AB InBev was how to manage the complex global brand portfolio. As shown in Table 8.3, many different brands are sold in various markets. Overall, the company owns more than two hundred brands, including global best sellers: the best-selling American beer (Budweiser), the best-selling Canadian beer (Labatt's), the best-selling German beer (Beck's), and the company's initial flagship brand, the best-selling Belgium beer (Stella Artois). A variety of Latin American beers, including the Brazilian leaders Skol and Brahma, and the leading beer in Argentina, Quilmes, are also company products. In addition, recent legal activity may give the company majority ownership of Grupo Modelo, owner of the world's leading Mexican beer Corona.[60] This does not include the numerous local brands the company also owns.

To structure the brand portfolio, the company picked three global brands to focus on as "jewels": Budweiser, Beck's, and Stella Artois. These three brands will be standardized globally and are the focus of much of the marketing activity for the company. In addition to the global brands, AB InBev will sell multi-country or regional brands. Leffe Hoegaarden will continue to focus on the European market, where it is already strong, and Brahma and Pilsen will focus on the Latin American market. For the remaining one hundred plus brands, which AB InBev calls "local champions," some will be divested and others will become key brands within only those markets.

Innovation will be an important part of the global strategy. Various new products are in development. The company introduced Stella Artois Black in Belgium and now exports it to other major markets. The golden lager products represent continued commitment to innovating around the Stella Artois brand.[61] Zenda, a new beer, was launched simultaneously in Ecuador and Peru in 2008. The company also leveraged the positive perception of Belgian brewers and pub life by opening more than fifty Belgian beer cafés throughout Europe, and in Australia and New Zealand.[62] Some brands have been divested. Bass, once the best selling beer in Britain, is for sale, as might be the Boddingtons and Flowers brands.[63] AB InBev is also selling Croatian operations and rebranding operations in Romania.[64]

InBev's original brands included Brahma and Antarctica Sub Zero.

COUNTRY	VOLUME (MILLIONS OF HECTOLITERS)	MARKET SHARE	NUMBER OF EMPLOYEES	LOCAL CHAMPIONS SOLD SOLELY IN THAT MARKET
Argentina	12.9	74.4%	4,700	Quilmes, Andes, Norte, Patagonia
Belgium	5.6	58.6%	2,700	Belle-Vue, Jupiler, Vieux Temps
Bolivia	4.1	98.1%	890	Huari & Ducal, Paceña, Taquiña
Brazil	76.2	68.7%	23,000	Antarctica, Bohemia, Skol
Canada	11.2	42.4%	3,000	Labatt Blue, Kokanee, Alexander Keith's, Lakeport
Chile	36.6	N/A	380	Baltica, Becker, Malta del Sur
China	48	11.1%	40,000	Harbin, Sedrin, Jinling, Tangshan, KK, Double Beeer, Jin Long Quan
Cuba	1.1	46.6%	550	Bucanero, Cristal, Mayabe
Dominican Republic	1.5	13.6%	1,600	No local brands, instead importing the regional brands Brahma Light and Brahma Ice brands
Ecuador	192.7	8.7%	250	Zenda
France	1.8	10.0%	250	Boomerang, Loburg, la Becasse
Germany	9.2	9.4%	2,900	Löwenbräu, Diebels, Haake-Beck, Hasseroder, Gilde, Spaten
Italy	1.3	8.0%	130	No local brands, instead importing regional German brands
Luxemburg	0.2	49.3%	100	Diekirch, Mousel, Belle-Vue
Netherlands	2.2	15.8%	550	Dommelsch, Hertog Jan
Paraguay	2.3	98.5%	500	Baviera, Ouro Fino
Peru	0.96	8.14%	1,200	No local brands, instead importing regional brand Brahma
Russia	16.5	15.8%	8,800	Klinskoye, Sibirskaya Korona, Bagbier, T Tolstiak
Ukraine	10.4	39.8%	3,000	Chernigivske, Rogan, Yantar
United Kingdom	12.6	21.8%	1,400	Boddingtons, Whitbread, Mackeson
United States	122.3	48.9%	18,000	Michelob, Busch, Natural Light, Shock Top, Landshark Lager
Uruguay	0.9	N/A (#1)	500	Pilsen, Patricia, Noteña, Zillertal
Venezuela	0.8	4.1%	700	Zulia

Table 8.3: **AB InBev's Global Business**

Source: Adapted from the country fact sheets at ab-inbev.com.

Turning around the slumping global Budweiser brand will be the next step. The company previously had success reviving the Stella Artois brand, and the marketing team expresses confidence about success with the iconic American beer. The revival will include standardizing much of the brand in all markets. This includes its red color, the beechwood aging process, and its association with Clydesdale horses.[65] Brazil is being considered as a target market for the growth of the brand.[66]

Overall, Brazil and other emerging markets will be the main sources of growth for AB InBev moving forward. In 2010, although overall sales were down 6.8% for the company, volume rose by 5.1% in China; profits and more than half of all revenues came from emerging economies.[67] In emerging markets, the company has a consistent approach of using local partners to learn how to adapt to local tastes.

In China, entry started through a technology transfer agreement with Zhujian Brewery in Guangzhou. Additional partnerships with other leading brewers allowed the company to continue to expand while learning more about the Chinese beer market. In May 2006, the company became more aggressive through its acquisition of Fujian Sedrin Brewery, which doubled AB InBev's sales in the country. The company now has set its sights on the Indian market, and again is using a joint venture approach. In May 2007, it started a joint venture with RKJ, an Indian brewer. To build a market for its global brands, the company contracted with Dasappa in southern India to produce Beck's and Tennets for the Indian market.

AB InBev faces various legal regimes and issues in all of its markets. Alcohol is a highly regulated product, and these regulations can vary greatly from market to market. Each country within the European Union, for example, has different regulations for alcohol.[68] Beyond alcohol regulations, the company faces regulation of its corporate structure in each market. In fact, as of April 2010 there were still legal suits filed by individuals fighting over whether the company can buy Anheuser Busch in the United States.[69]

Another legal activity is prohibition of alcohol, which is common in many Muslim countries, but can also be found in other markets. The United States has its own history of prohibition. A legacy of the activity of organized crime during prohibition is the unique three-tiered system in the U.S. market. The system means that producers are allowed to sell only to wholesalers, wholesalers are allowed to sell only to retailers, and only retailers are allowed to sell to consumers. This structure leads to more efficient collection of taxes, among other benefits. It has come under recent scrutiny because it also limits a brewer's ability to sell alcohol online.[70] Other countries also use prohibition as a political tool. Indian politicians, for example, sometimes campaign on prohibiting alcohol and have succeeded in having it banned in the state of Gujarat.[71] Hugo Chávez, president of Venezuela, generated a great deal of press recently when he banned sales of alcohol after 5:00 p.m. for ten days during Easter week, and all day on Holy Thursday, Good Friday, and Easter Sunday.[72]

Taxation constitutes another major issue. A traditional form of revenue in many countries, taxation reduces demand and can influence revenue. In 2009, Russian alcohol taxes increased up to three times the initial rate, depending on type of alcohol. This resulted in a drop in profit and revenue in the Russian market.[73]

The success or failure of the recent creation of the mega AB InBev brewer will depend on effective brand adaptation and standardization globally. The company, which describes itself as "an international company with Belgian roots that go back to 1366," hopes to build on almost 650 years of success to become the brewer of both the best global and the best local brands in each market.[74]

1. Is the decision to focus on Budweiser, Stella Artois, and Beck's the correct one? Were any of the brands incorrectly chosen? Why or why not?

2. What country is AB InBev's home country? Is it possible that the company has no country of origin? Justify your answer with details from the case.

3. Consider Table 8.3. Using Google or another search engine, research five of the brands on the table. Is AB InBev still selling the brand? What is the brand's current status?

4. What steps can AB InBev take to mitigate legal risk? How should the company react to steps to prohibit alcohol in markets?

5. The United Kingdom has recently considered more-aggressive alcohol regulation. What steps should the company take in response to this activity? Should AB InBev react at all?

6. AB InBev is in the major emerging markets. What country should be the company's next target for expansion? Justify your answer.

PART IV
International Pricing and Finance

9 International Pricing

After reading and studying this chapter, you should be able to answer the following questions:

1. What forms of pricing exist, and how do perceptions influence views of prices?

2. What are the most common strategic objectives associated with prices, and what methods may be used to achieve those objectives?

3. What types of pricing discounts are available to international marketers?

4. What factors influence decisions about price changes in international markets?

5. What ethical concerns are associated with international pricing programs?

IN THIS CHAPTER

Wind Turbines in Finland:
Pricing Sustainability and Economic Incentives

The Scandinavian nation of Finland was once a province and then a grand duchy under Sweden from the twelfth to the nineteenth centuries, and an autonomous grand duchy of Russia after 1809. It won its complete independence in 1917. The nation had to defend its freedom and resist invasions by the Soviet Union during World War II and lost territory during that war. The country shares a major boundary with Russia.

During the second half of the twentieth century, Finland transformed from a farm and forest economy to a diversified modern industrial economy. The country's per capita income ranks as one of the highest in Western Europe. Finland became a member of the European Union in 1995 and was the only Nordic state to join the *euro* system at the time.

Currently, the key features of Finland's economy include a high standard of education, equality promotion, and a national social security system. Its challenges include an aging population and the fluctuations of an export-driven economy. The nation, which is approximately the size of Montana, has an extensive shoreline with a cold climate featuring long days of sunlight in the summer and long, dark nights in the winter. In 2010, the estimated population of the country was more than 5 million citizens, with more than two thirds of the population living in urban areas. Persons living in Finland can expect to reach the age of eighty. Nearly the entire population is literate.

Finland is home to Tuulivoimala Finland LTD, one of several major corporations devoted to sustainable energy. These efforts address the threats of air pollution, acid rain, and water pollution from power plants and agricultural waste. The company also reaches a lucrative market consisting of neighborhoods wishing to base electric systems on methods other than the national power grid.

A group of Finnish scholars recently made presentations to several regional universities in the United States. The educators described the advantages and challenges associated with setting up neighborhood associations owning their own wind turbines. The advantages included improved property values, because any buyer would know he or she would not have an electric bill to pay each month along with feelings of satisfaction knowing one's home was more environmentally friendly.

One of the primary challenges was pricing. Each turbine costs in excess of $1 million and would serve approximately fifty homes. While a household would not have to pay an electric bill, it would be required to pay for the system itself, normally financed with a thirty-year bond, plus its share of maintenance and operational costs. Each household would take about twenty years in terms of savings on electric bills to recover the purchase price of the system. Then, however, the household would only pay maintenance costs with all other electricity being free, and at times would receive a stream of revenue from excess electricity sold back to the nation's power grid.

An additional pricing challenge came from negotiating with the government. On the one hand, Finland's government benefits from reduced pollution and not being forced to create additional power supplies for the population and local industries. On the other, revenues from the electricity being sold and taxes on that electricity would be reduced. The question arose as to whether the government of Finland should help subsidize purchases of the wind turbines with tax incentives, since doing so was, at least in some ways, in the nation's interests.

The final complication arose from making price decisions for homes that were already built versus new construction. How much should the neighborhood association charge existing homes, which required some adaptation to become part of the self-contained grid, as compared to those built with the features included?

The visiting scholars concluded by saying that, whereas pricing issues in these circumstances are complex and require careful calculations incorporating the life the wind turbine and the houses, they were well worth the effort, for both home buyers and the larger country.[1]

QUESTIONS FOR STUDENTS

1. What should the government of Finland do—provide tax incentives for energy reduction or leave the system as it is?

2. How do energy savings increase the sale price of a house?

3. Is energy a fixed cost or a variable cost in a household's budget?

Wind turbines owned by individual citizens create unique pricing challenges.

Overview

Part IV of this textbook considers pricing and financial issues in international marketing. At first it might not seem that pricing should be a complicated process. One simply needs to know how much it costs to produce an item, identify the desired amount of profit, and affix a price tag. Such an approach ignores a number of factors. Even in domestic-only markets, other influences, including supply and demand, the distribution of wealth, economic conditions, political shifts, and taxation policies all affect pricing programs. Figure 9.1 indicates the background for pricing and its connections to the other aspects of international marketing.

Figure 9.1: The International Marketing Context

Culture affects methods of setting prices, methods of bargaining, and perceptions regarding what price indicates (quality, exclusivity). Pricing language, especially with regard to what constitutes an "established" price or a "discount," varies. Governments regulate prices for domestic and international products. Supply and demand are economic forces that shape prices in many nations. A country's infrastructure influences product costs, delivery charges, and therefore subsequent prices.

Financial considerations are identified in Chapter 10. Financing plays a sweeping role in strategic international marketing decision. Financing affects decisions to enter countries and the costs of doing business. Financial markets affect profits and subsequent deliberations about whether to expand operations or leave a market.

In this chapter, strategic pricing issues are considered. The essentials of pricing and international pricing are described first, then methods of discounting and changing prices are explored. Pricing of both new and ongoing products will be examined.

The complications that arise when pricing in the international marketplace also are explained. International business-to-business pricing programs also receive attention. Finally, quantitative methods for studying pricing as well as the unique aspects of pricing to consumers at the bottom-of-the-pyramid are presented.

The Nature of Price

Why is the price of milk different in the countries shown in Table 9.1? As shown, a great deal of variation exists. Discovering the reasons for the differences constitutes one of the goals of this chapter, along with explaining how and why prices change.

A **price** is the amount a person, company, or government charges for a good or service. Prices may be established for a single item (a canola), a set of items (a six-pack of Thums Up soda), a combination of products (a six-course meal), a single service (a haircut), a combination of services (air fare and hotel in a one-price package), an event (a performance of Chinese opera), a season or time period (soccer/football tickets for the entire year), and other less common possibilities.

COUNTRY	PRICE
Brazil	$0.71[a]
Jamaica	$0.57[b]
Japan	$2.48[c]
South Africa	$1.24[d]
United States	$1.01[e]

(All prices have been converted to U.S. dollars.)

Table 9.1: **Price for One Liter of Milk in Various Countries in 2010**

Source: a.CLAL, "Brazil: Farm-Gate Milk Prices," accessed at www.clal.it/en/index.php?section=latte_brasile.

b. Mark Titus, "Farmers, Milk Processors Bicker Over Price," *The Gleaner* (Jamaica, WI), August 10, 2010, accessed at www.jamaica-gleaner.com/gleaner/20100813/business/business4.html.

c. "Tokyo Travel Guide," About.com, accessed at http://gojapan.about.com/od/dailylifeinjapan/a/costlivingtokyo.htm.

d. "Cape Town Cost of Living," accessed at www.expatcapetown.com/cape-town-cost-of-living.html.

e. Christopher Leonard, "Global Milk Glut Squeezes Dairy Farmers, Consumers," *The Missourian* (Columbia, MO), May 25, 2009, accessed at www.columbiamissourian.com/stories/2009/05/25/global-milk-glut-squeezes-dairy-farmers-consumers/.

For products moving through the market channel, the first price will be the one offered by a manufacturer to middlemen, typically wholesalers and distributors. These organizations then resell the item to retailers at the *wholesale price*. Retailers mark up the item, and the final price becomes the *retail price*. Brazilian retailers are allowed to mark up the cost of essential medicines by as much as 30% over the wholesale price to create the retail price.[2]

Service prices are charged to other businesses, to the government, and to retail customers. Another business may purchase a health insurance program and offer it to employees. The government buys services from vendors for a variety of situations, including clean-up after a major storm, independent snow plowing operations, and others. Retail customers are charged retail service prices for a wide variety of products, from insurance, to personal care, to entertainment.

Another variation on pricing that can be especially well received in some markets is *leasing*. A product, typically a big-ticket item, may be leased for a specified number of years, usually five, with accompanying servicing, spare part, and repair agreements. Leasing opens markets for manufacturers and provides foreign companies with the opportunity to use equipment while making level monthly or annual payments. As has been noted, in China property is not owned: instead, it is leased for a certain amount of time, often seventy years in the city or thirty years in rural areas.[3] In all cases of leasing, by establishing a finite time period, purchase risk becomes lower for the company leasing the equipment. Manufacturers may seek out leases to defend against fluctuations in currencies or political risks.

INTERNATIONAL PRICES

Each of the forms of pricing may be adapted to international operations. When prices are set in other countries the complications of payment systems, discounting programs, types of currencies and currency value fluctuations, methods of payment, and other differences such as negotiation and bartering occur. In essence, marketers spend a great deal of time and energy establishing prices for products sent to other nations.

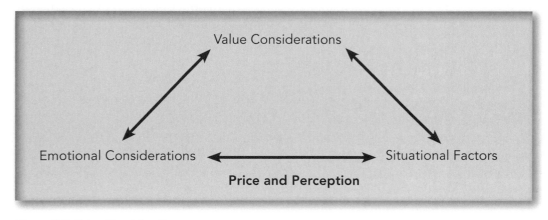

Figure 9.2: Price Considerations

Price and Perception

Prices represent a combination of circumstances and perceptions. As depicted in Figure 9.2, three items influence perceptions of price. A consumer may go through complicated interactions between these variables as she considers a price in terms of fairness or as an incentive to make the purchase. The deliberations can be altered at any time, based on changes in the buyer's level of income, mood, or even the time of day. International marketers seek to find an attractive price at the right time for the largest number of consumers.

VALUE CONSIDERATIONS

Among the first thoughts a buyer may have about the price of a product or service is whether the amount charged represents a reasonable portrayal of the item's value. Perceptions of value are most dramatically influenced by comparisons of the item's price to its quality. A hotel room with a scenic view of the Dardanelles in Canakkale, Turkey, charges a substantially higher price than a comparable room that offers no view, even when the hotels are on the same street. A serving of fish sold in a high-end restaurant in Tokyo carries a higher price, because customers believe it will be prepared by the finest chef cooking with the best ingredients.

Price can convey either that a product is "cheap" or that it is a worthy bargain due to the lower amount being asked. A London tavern selling the exact same ale at a lower price than all competitors expects to make up some of the difference by selling more glasses. Other low-priced items may be viewed as simply trinkets or junk.

Many purchases result from a consumer's conclusion that the relationship between an item's price and its level of quality are in synch. In many cases, rational reasoning leads to the decision. There will also be comparisons with competitors' prices, past purchases, and other experiences. One productthat has become increasingly popular is the Icelandic-style, *skyr* strained yogurt. The Siggi brand's rapid growth in the United States has not been hindered by its relatively high price—$2.68 for a six-ounce cup at Whole Foods Markets. Many consumers conclude that the unique taste of Siggi *skyr* makes it worth the price.

VIDEO LINK 9.1:
Cars and Competition ▶

A Price Perceptual Map

One of the tools international marketers use to examine a brand's image and market position relative to the competition is a **price perceptual map.** The map depicts various companies or products along two dimensions, typically price and quality. Figure 9.3 provides an example of a price perceptual map for hotels in the city of Buenos Aires, Argentina.

As shown, three well-known multinational chains offer hotels in the city. These units tend to charge the highest prices per stay. In this city the Hilton does not have the biggest advantage, however, because consumers perceive Caesar Park as being of higher quality and a lower price. A risk exists for Hilton that frequent travelers and locals might conclude Caesar Park offers a better price-quality relationship as experience is gained with the local hotel. Hilton's marketing team might seek to

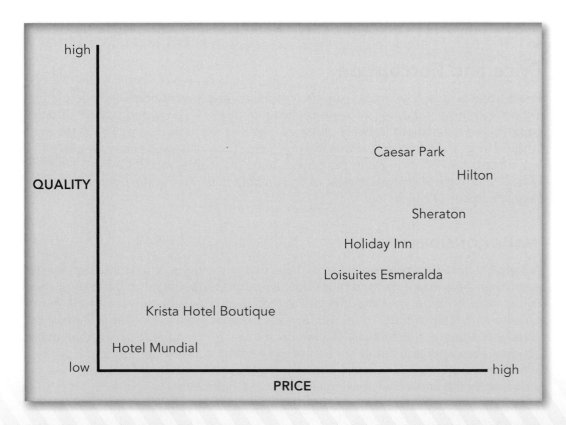

Figure 9.3: Price Considerations

respond to this perception by highlighting or enhancing the quality of the hotel or by targeting groups that are brand loyal and therefore be less inclined to stay at Caesar Park. A loyalty program would assist Hilton in this effort.

The marketing team at the Holiday Inn might discover that perceptions of its quality over Loi Suites Esmeralda are primarily the result of a more well-known brand name. This might lead to similar attempts at improving quality in some way or through other means to strengthen loyalty to Holiday Inn. Loi Suites' marketers would be able to promote the concept that travelers are receiving the same quality at a lower price.

Creating a pricing perceptual map allows the marketing group to provide a visual portrayal of the relationships between price, quality, image, or other variables. Then, pricing and other strategic marketing decisions on what they have observed. Focus groups and other forms of market research assist in developing pricing perceptual maps. The groups will consist of travelers to Buenos Aires from other countries, locals, or both.

EMOTIONAL FACTORS

At times reasoning and rational thought do not drive purchase decisions. Many goods and services contain emotional components that affect value judgments and influence purchase decisions. After the British Petroleum (BP) oil spill in the Gulf of Mexico, some angry consumers boycotted the company; 500,000 Facebook users "liked" the Boycott BP page, even though many industry experts pointed out the boycott would hurt local gas station owners, not the large multinational.[4] It would not be surprising to discover that some consumers decided to change their gasoline purchasing habits.

Emotional components exist in services, such as hair care, personal finance, and insurance. Hair care may be associated with beauty and sensuality, personal finance with individual success, and insurance purchases with feelings that one has "protected" his or her family.

The same holds true for physical products. Clothes sold in a high-fashion district, such as the *huitième arrondissement* (eighth municipal district) in Paris, likely hold the emotional value related to feelings of being *chic*. An automobile purchase often reflects both rational and emotional instincts.

The market leader in Russia, the Lada brand of automobiles (Vladimir Putin drives one), has a cult following in the United Kingdom even though the brand has not been available in that market since 1997. The brand was infamous for being Spartan and inexpensive; some models were incapable of breaking the speed limit on highways. Even with all of the jokes about the car, including the classic "What do you call a Lada at the top of a hill? A miracle!" the low price for the car meant it was often the first car someone in the United Kingdom purchased. Those emotional ties remain strong for some in the United Kingdom and may allow for successful reintroduction of the brand.[5]

SITUATIONAL FACTORS

Price also reflects an individual's immediate circumstances. A tourist lost in the streets of Budapest, Hungary, might be willing to spend a large amount of money for a taxi to take him back to his hotel. *Impulse buys* are those made on the spot. A unique-looking drink that is red in color being sold in a small establishment on the streets of Sitges, Spain, might cause a thirsty and adventuresome tourist to make a purchase without

VIDEO LINK 9.2:
Oil Spills

having any idea about its taste. Common wisdom suggests that money has a different value and is spent differently when a person is on vacation.[6] Other situational factors include the consumer's physical situation, the social setting, the time of day, and the consumer's mood.

International Pricing Methods

LEARNING OBJECTIVE #2:

What are the most common strategic objectives associated with prices, and what methods may be used to achieve those objectives?

Pricing decisions will typically be made following consultations and discussions with several individuals and company departments. Members of the marketing and management teams choose the method to be used in setting the price and eventually determine the price itself. One of the first activities will be to establish strategic pricing goals. Figure 9.4 lists common pricing objectives.[7]

Objective	Measures
Profitability	Total Dollar Profit
	Return on Investment
	Percentage Increase From Previous Year
	Contribution to Overhead
Market Share	Product Market Share
	Product Line or Brand Share
	Company Market Share
Enticing New Customers	Number of New Customers
	Percentage of Total Company Customers
Retaining Current Customers	Repurchase Rates
Counter Competitive Actions	Market Share Statistics During a Specific Campaign
	Number of New Competitors Entering the Market
Attract Competitor's Customers	Purchases by New Customers

Figure 9.4: Pricing Objectives

Each of these goals can be modified to fit international operations. Companies also set different goals in various markets. Unilever may seek differing goals in diverse markets. The goal of a company in Cambodia might be to gain market share quickly, because the company just began selling products there. To help meet this objective, products may be sold at lower prices and in smaller packages.[8] In the European market, where the company is more established, profitability may be the goal. In response to recent increases in production costs, the company might raise prices to maintain profits levels, even if market share goes down slightly.[9]

Following the establishment of pricing objectives, various methods are available for establishing a product's base price. Several pricing methods may be used to help a firm to reach its pricing goals. They include

- cost-based pricing
- demand-/supply-based pricing

- competition-based pricing
- profit-based pricing

Each serves the purpose of identifying the most viable price.

COST-BASED PRICING

Cost-based pricing begins with a careful assessment of all costs associated with producing and selling an item. *Fixed costs* remain constant regardless of volume sold. Rent payments, installment payments on machinery purchases, interest on debt, and licensing fees remain the same regardless of the level of production. In addition to total fixed costs, an estimate can be made of the number of units the company seeks to produce and sell. Fixed costs can then be allocated to each unit, as fixed costs per unit.

Variable costs are those associated with the production and sale of each item. Raw materials, labor costs, storage, shipping costs, and commissions all vary with the number of units produced and sold. *Total costs* constitute the total dollar amount assigned to a product, and are calculated by adding total fixed costs to the sum of all variable costs. Marketers may then use various methods to establish a price based on those costs, including break-even analysis, cost-plus pricing, and markup pricing.

Break-Even Analysis

A common method employed to discover the relationships between costs and price is a **break-even analysis**. The calculations apply equally well to international expansions and other situations. Ray-Ban markets a luxury brand of sunglasses. If upper-middle class customers in Kenya appear to be a viable market segment, the company's marketing might consider manufacturing and selling sunglasses within the country. To determine how many pairs of glasses would need to be sold to cover the cost of expansion, the company could conduct a break-even analysis, as shown in Figure 9.5.

> A common method employed to discover the relationships between costs and price is a break-even analysis.

Ray-Ban's marketing team would then assess the size of the market segment. If they conclude that 20,000 or more pairs of glasses can be sold in Kenya, the company would break even. Each pair of sunglasses sold after that number would result in additional revenue that contributes to profit.

Cost-Plus Pricing

Cost-plus pricing involves setting the product's price based on fixed costs, variable costs, plus the desired profit margin for each item. Cost-plus pricing can be employed in cases where costs are unknown or hard to predict, and when company leaders want to ensure a certain level of profit regardless of the costs incurred. Contractors, lawyers, and business consultants often use this method.

Cost-plus may be used when pricing chili peppers in Sulawesi, one of the main islands in Indonesia. Much of the island's population is Manadonese who are said to "breathe fire" because 90% of local dishes contain chili as a spice.[10] While demand is high, the cost of producing chili peppers can be highly variable because it is influenced by Indonesia's weather. In response to this variability, producers could sign a contract with Starbucks, who uses the peppers for sachets of chili sauce, which prices the peppers at a 15% profit margin. Regardless of the end costs, the producer would be assured a 15% profit. Figure 9.6 provides an example of a cost-plus calculation of price.

$$\text{Break-Even Point (units)} = \frac{\text{Fixed Costs (total dollars)}}{\text{Price per unit} - \text{Variable Costs per unit}}$$

$$= \frac{60,000,000 \text{ KES}}{8,000 - 5,000}$$

$$= 20,000 \text{ units}$$

Where: Fixed Costs   = plant rent
                        cost of machinery
                        interest on debt

        Variable Costs = plastic and ingredients to make glasses
                        shipping cost per unit
                        packaging cost per unit
                        increased advertising costs per unit
                            (ads in Kenya)

Figure 9.5: A Break-Even Analysis

Note: The Kenyan *shilling* (*KES*) is the Kenyan currency.

Total Fixed Costs   = 45,000,000 Rp^{a}

Fixed cost per unit @ 5,000 units (1 kg^{b} of chili)
            = 45,000,000 Rp -:- 5,000 Rp
            = 9,000 Rp

Variable cost per unit for 5,000 kg of chili   = 5,000 Rp
Total Variable Costs   = 25,000,000 Rp
Total Costs   = 70,000,000 Rp

Desired Profit Margin   = Total Costs * Percentage Profit Margin
            = 70,000,000 * 0.15
            = 10,500,000 Rp

Profit per Unit   = Total Profit -:- Units Produced (5,000 kg of chili)
            = 10,500,000 Rp -:- 5,000
            = 2,100 Rp

Unit Price = Fixed cost per unit + Variable cost per unit + Desired profit per unit
            = 9,000 Rp + 5,000 Rp + 2,100 Rp
            = 16,100 Rp

Figure 9.6: Cost-Plus Pricing

Note: a. *Rp* stands for rupiah, the currency of Indonesia. b. kilogram.

Markup Pricing

In cases where costs are known, markup pricing can be used. **Markup pricing** offers a straightforward pricing method that adds a standard markup to the costs assigned to a product. The approach may be best suited to retailers stocking large numbers of products and manufacturers that produce large quantities of goods. In those cases, tracking demand per item will be difficult and setting a price for each item would be cumbersome and time consuming. Markup pricing is a simple, quick method to price many goods. The markup approach typically features a percentage as the margin of profit per good. Note that the percentage profit is taken from the costs and not from the final price, a common error. Figure 9.7 presents an example.[11]

Total Cost per Unit	R$2.00[a]		
15% Markup	R$0.30	Final Price	R$2.30
20% Markup	R$0.40	Final Price	R$2.40
25% Markup	R$0.50	Final Price	R$2.50

Figure 9.7: Markup pricing for a 2.5-liter bottle of Guaraná Antarctica soda in Brazil (R# =)

Note: a. R$ stands for Brazilian *reals*.

The markup pricing approach may be most useful when the company's marketing team has determined that consumers are not strongly affected by price. Cost-plus pricing also has value when the company leaders seek to recover start-up or expansion costs first.

Some marketers criticize the cost-based pricing methods, break-even, cost-plus, and markup for focusing on costs rather than demand. While demand may be hard to predict, demand-based priced pricing can be more precise and allows for more efficient price setting. Cost-based methods may over- or under-price a product relative to demand, which results in decreased market share when an item is overpriced or lost profits when it is underpriced.

DEMAND-/SUPPLY-BASED PRICING

The second pricing approach takes advantage of calculations normally associated with economics. The method requires an estimation of *demand*, or the amount of items that will be purchased at various price levels, and *supply*, or the amount producers of items are willing to provide or sell at various prices. The *equilibrium point* reflects the intersection of the demand and supply curve, as displayed in Figure 9.8.

Calculating supply and demand can be difficult. Typically, a research format such as a test market will be used to determine demand. By pricing an item at various levels in differing markets, it might be possible to at least estimate corresponding levels of demand. Thus, in the Asia-Pacific market the average price for beer is approximately $2.20 per liter, whereas in Western Europe it is $4.90 and in the United States it is $3.70. Price differences can be partially linked to the lower demand for beer in Asian countries. The average consumption in China, as one example, is thirty liters per capita per year compared with eighty liters in the United States and Western Europe.[12]

Price elasticity of demand measures the impact of price differences on sales and demand. When *inelastic demand* exists, consumers are not strongly affected by price. They make purchases within a price range in which smaller price differences do not affect the willingness to buy. These goods are often staple items. Wheat, for example, is a staple item in the United Kingdom used to produce many types of food. In August of 2010 the price of wheat went up 40%, leading to consumer calls for governmental action, because no substitutes were available, keeping the demand inelastic even at the higher price.[13]

> Price elasticity of demand measures the impact of price differences on sales and demand.

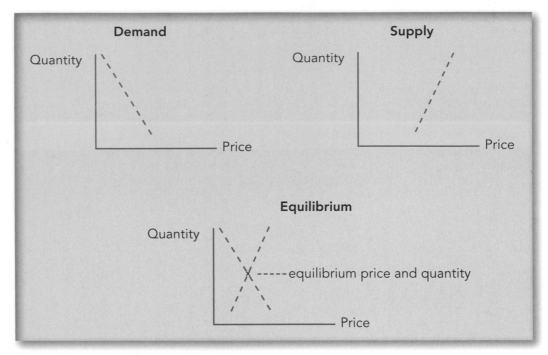

Figure 9.8: Demand, Supply, and Equilibrium

Supply and demand equilibrium explains the price of milk in various countries.

Highly elastic demand occurs when consumers are extremely price sensitive. A small price increase drives consumers away, and a small price decrease attracts them. In 2009, Kirin, the Japanese brewer, introduced the zero-alcohol beer Kirin Zero in the Japanese market. Non- or low-alcohol beers have traditionally struggled in the Japanese market, but the brand has become surprisingly popular. Price created part of the appeal. At around 148 *yen* (about $1.90), a bottle of Kirin Zero is cheaper than regular beer.[14] Due to the elasticity of demand for a product such as beer that has many substitutes, the low price resulted in increased demand for the new product.

In international markets, demand, supply, and elasticity will all be affected by local conditions. Fashionable items experience a different demand curve due to emotional features such as price and status. Demand may be lower because fewer individuals can afford the item, such as an automobile in a less-developed economy, yet the price may be higher, because only the affluent can afford to purchase a car. When coupled with a lower supply and the costs associated with shipping a vehicle to another country, the price changes.

Local customs and traditions often affect elasticity. When a family requires a specific item to perform a religious ceremony, such as a specific type of incense for a Buddhist ritual, that family may be willing to pay a great deal for the product because no substitute exists and the item carries a high emotional value.

International Marketing in Daily Life

Calculating Supply and Demand Equilibrium

Discovering the exact impact of various prices on supply and demand is often not possible. The marketing team instead attempts to develop estimates of the relationships. The chapter began with a chart of different prices for milk in various countries (Table 9.1). These differences in price are at least partially due to differences in demand and supply. Table 9.2 portrays supply and demand in Brazil, which has a low, inelastic price for milk.

PRICE ($)	DEMAND (LITERS PER WEEK)	TOTAL REVENUE ($)
$0.60	1,000,000	$600,000
$0.65	975,000	$617,500
$0.70	800,000	$560,000
$0.75	500,000	$375,000
$0.80	350,000	$280,000

Table 9.2: **Demand, Price, and Total Revenue for a Liter of Milk in Brasília, Brazil**

In this instance, the optimal price would be $0.65 per liter of milk, because it yields the highest total revenue.

A second calculation reveals price elasticity. The equation for price elasticity of demand is

$$\text{Price elasticity of demand} = \frac{\text{percentage change in quantity demanded}}{\text{percentage change in price}}.$$

Table 9.3 was developed for milk in Japan, where dairy milk consumption is not as common as it is in Brazil. Milk substitutes are available, including a traditional preference for soy milk. The market difference leads to differences in price elasticity. As shown, a price of $1.90 per liter results in projected sales (demand) of 1,100,000 liters annually. If the price rises to $2.00, the percentage increase is 5.27% ({$2.00—$1.90} / $1.90). Elasticity in that instance is calculated by examining the decline in sales, from 1,100,000 to 1,000,000, as ({1,000,000—1,100,000} / 1,100,000), which equals –9.09 %. When the percent change in demand (–9.09%) is divided by the percentage change in price (5.27%), the elasticity value becomes –1.72. The absolute value of this number, 1.72, is the elasticity of demand.

An elasticity value of 1.0 represents the point of *unitary* elasticity of demand, because the change in demand is equal to the change in price. Any value below 1.0 represents *inelastic* demand, because the change in demand is lower than the change in price. Any value over 1.0 means *elastic* demand is present, because the change in demand is greater than the change in price.

Most items have an elastic demand to some degree. Consumers at some point become unwilling to purchase the product and look for an alternative. In Table 9.3, when the price is set above $2.00, customers become less willing to pay for the product and look elsewhere.

PRICE ($)	DEMAND	PERCENT CHANGE		
		PRICE (%)	DEMAND (%)	ELASTICITY (%)
$1.90	1,100,000			
$2.00	1,000,000	5.27	−9.09	1.72
$2.10	900,000	5.00	−10.00	2.00
$2.20	800,000	4.76	−11.11	2.33
$2.30	700,000	4.37	−12.50	2.86
$2.40	600,000	4.17	−14.29	3.43
$2.50	500,000	4.00	−16.67	4.17
$2.60	400,000	3.85	−20.00	5.19
$2.70	300,000	3.70	−25.00	6.76

Table 9.3: **Price Elasticity of Demand for Milk in Nagoya, Japan**

Marketers are likely to discover that elasticity varies by country or by regions within a country. In the case of the Brazilian market, demand for milk will be more inelastic because drinking milk is more culturally the norm and fewer similar substitutes exist than in the Japanese market. For the initial price increase from $0.60 to $0.65, the elasticity was 0.60 (–5.0% drop in demand / 8.3% increase in price), which reflects inelastic demand. Brazilian consumers are less sensitive to changes in the price of milk than are Japanese consumers.

Other factors can also influence elasticity. Per capita income and income distribution dramatically affect the willingness and ability of consumers to pay within various price ranges. In Paraguay, hair care will be more commonplace in urban areas and elasticity may be lower. In rural areas, hair care prices may be highly elastic and prices will be set at a lower range, due to reduced incomes. When the price rises beyond a certain point, the consumer will be inclined to have a family member cut his hair rather than paying for it.

International Diversity of Demand

International marketers know that demand curves will be different in various countries. Factors such as trade barriers, governmental activities and differences between those activities across markets, and the costs associated with shipping and/or moving into a new market influence the nature of demand. Also, variances in consumer tastes and preferences between markets due to cultural and environmental influences mean that demand curves do not transfer well across international boundaries. The demand for a product in one country may be totally different from the demand for that product in another. As a result, the strong potential exists that each country will exhibit a different equilibrium point between supply and demand and a different level of elasticity.

In some cases, governments may take actions that increase or decrease demand or elasticity. Th!nk City, an electric vehicle that was designed in Norway, is manufactured in Elkhart, Indiana. The U.S. price for the vehicle, approximately $38,000, is essentially equivalent to the automobile's price in other markets. The U.S. government, seeking to promote cars that do not run on gasoline and, at the same time, create manufacturing jobs, offers incentives that reduce the price to about $30,000. The price drops to $25,000 in California, where the state government offers additional incentives.[15] These governmental rebates have increased demand.

Global Marginal Analysis

To apply demand differences to a marginal analysis, remember that the demand curve predicts the response to a drop in price. If the curves change from market to market, the marketing team will need to estimate a different curve and conduct a separate marginal analysis for each market. International markets also typically incur different costs, especially if adaptation is needed, if there are tariffs that must be paid, or if there are any other potential increased costs. These factors will also change a marginal analysis of supply, demand, and elasticity across various prices.[16]

COMPETITION-BASED PRICING

In domestic settings, competition-based pricing remains relatively simple. The marketing team chooses from one of three options:

- below the industry average,
- at the industry average, or
- above the industry average.

Pricing below the industry average indicates that price will be the primary marketing tactic. Big box retail giants, including Vishal Mega Mart in India, Carrefour, and Wal-Mart, employ this method.

Pricing at the industry average occurs in oligopolistic situations or when brand parity exists. Producers attempt to make price a less-relevant variable in the purchasing situation and turn the focus to other features, such as convenience or other differentiating product attributes.

Pricing above the industry average usually seeks to convey the message of exclusivity and high quality. Luxury hotels worldwide feature this approach. Other services may be marketed in the same way, as will high-end dining.

In new markets, new layers should be considered when pricing based on competition. The new calculations include

- pricing versus domestic competitors,
- pricing versus foreign competitors, and
- pricing versus domestic and foreign competitors combined.

In these circumstances, the marketing team will be charged with understanding the types of customers involved. If the majority of customers only purchase domestic products in the product category, then foreign competitors are largely ignored. When Nabisco began exporting Oreo cookies to the United Kingdom to compete with British biscuits (cookies), most locals exhibited low levels of interest in the new items.[17] As a result, local bakeries could afford to largely ignore the competition.

Pricing against foreign competitors may occur in circumstances where international bids are being made for a contract. The marketing team will try to identify any incentives given by the government to assist a company in winning the bid. For example, many companies in numerous countries offer water purification products. Should the government of Ghana seek bids for a system, several companies might enter the competition. If a company in Russia receives governmental support to respond to the request for a bid, the company may be able to offer a lower price for a comparable water purification system. At the same time, if relations between Ghana and Russia are strained for some reason, then price will not be the only issue involved.

Pricing versus foreign and domestic competitors combined takes place in many markets. Shoe giants Nike and Reebok face both local and foreign competition when trying to place athletic shoes in local stores and when trying to sell the shoes to high school, college, and professional sports teams. In these instances, factors beyond price arise. When some shoes are produced in less-developed nations in factories where workers receive low wages, tariffs may be imposed, trade disputes can arise, and other emotional forces may become involved.

COMPETITION-BASED PRICE SETTING FOR NEW PRODUCTS

Any time a new product launches, the key pricing decisions involve how to position the product using price, how to capture market share, and how to recover start-up costs. The same methods apply to entering a new country with ongoing products. The two extreme positions are known as skimming, or skim-the-cream, and penetration pricing.

Skimming

At one end of the new-product-price continuum, **skimming** represents the attempt to recapture start-up costs as quickly as possible. Setting the price as high as the market will bear allows the manufacturer or exporter to generate the most revenue possible in a short period of time. Skimming works for unique products that cannot easily be duplicated. Competitors are discouraged by various barriers to entry, including government regulations, patent protections, and, in the case of international marketing, access to channels of distribution.

Skimming prices tend to invite competition; Other companies see the high price and higher mark-up, and some eventually find their way into the marketplace, which drives the price down. Companies may take preemptive action and lower the initial price in staggered steps to maintain market dominance. Sony used a skimming approach to pricing the various PlayStation consoles with the goal of earning a higher profit on brand-loyal, hardcore video game players before dropping the price to attract more-casual users.[18]

Penetration Pricing

> Penetration pricing occurs when the entrant charges the lowest price it can afford.

The other extreme new-product-price approach, **penetration pricing**, occurs when the entrant charges the lowest price it can afford. The method discourages entry by competition, because larger margins do not appear possible. Also, penetration pricing helps a company quickly build sales figures and establish a larger market share, and provides time for consumers to develop brand, product, and company loyalty. The company then can allow the price to drift up, especially if price elasticity remains low.

Penetration pricing makes it more difficult to recover start-up costs. It will take more time due to the smaller margin per product sale. The creators of Zeebo, the low-cost, emerging-market gaming device, selected a price of $240 for introduction in the Brazilian market. With competitors typically priced up to $1,000, partially due

Penetration pricing may be used to quickly capture market share for beauty products.

to tariffs, the low price should allow the company to gain as much market share as possible as quickly as possible. The company will experience a loss for the first few years, but the marketing team believes the risk is worth the potential long-term market position.[19] Figure 9.9 presents the ways prices tend to move using both skimming and penetration pricing approaches.

PROFIT-BASED PRICING

Profit-based pricing examines pricing from the perspective of what consumers are willing to pay rather than the cost of the item. Three situations fit with profit-oriented pricing. The first occurs when an organization operates in a monopolistic competition environment. The second involves pricing to quickly recover start-up costs. The third exists in markets in which prices are set to achieve a balance between demand and supply while generating optimal profits.

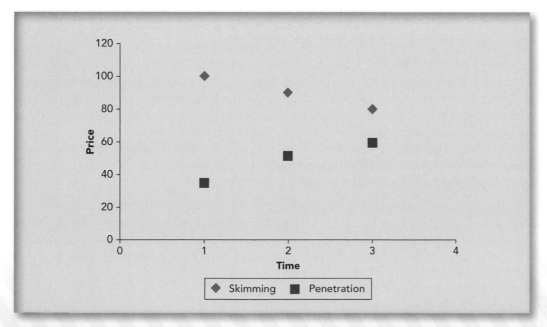

Figure 9.9: Skimming vs. Penetration Price

In monopolistic competition situations, a form of break-even analysis may be used. Instead of break-even occurring at the point where fixed and variable costs have been covered, profits are added to the formula, as displayed in Figure 9.10.

Premier League Soccer / Football Tickets to One Match

Fixed Costs   = £30,000,000[a]

Desired Profit   = £3,000,000

Variable Costs   = £50.00 per unit

Desired tickets sold = 60,000

$$\text{Break-even point for 60,000 tickets} = \frac{\text{Fixed Costs} + \text{Desired Profit}}{\text{Price} - \text{Variable Costs}}$$

$$60,000 = \frac{£30,000,000 + £3,000,000}{\text{Price} - £50.00}$$

$$\text{Price} = £600 \text{ per ticket}$$

Figure 9.10: Profit-Based Pricing Break-Even Analysis

Note: a. £ stands for the pound sterling, the currency in the United Kingdom.

This formula would only apply to circumstances in which the team marketers were certain 60,000 tickets could be sold at the desired price of £600 each.

In the second circumstance, a company may have incurred high start-up costs and might want to recover those costs quickly. This might happen when managers believe competitors will quickly enter the marketplace or when the start-up costs have pushed the company to the brink of financial problems. Oftentimes, the start-up costs associated with moving into a new country are high. Beyond the development of a physical location such as plant and equipment, various fees and taxes may be present. Costs associated with relocating employees or hiring local workers are also involved. Profit-based pricing becomes viable when demand remains sufficiently inelastic for the company to recover costs by charging a higher price.

Using prices to achieve a balance between demand, supply, and profit becomes an option when demand is elastic. A musical group that plans a concert tour in Europe will first examine the venues for the concerts. When an arena can hold 30,000 patrons, the price can be set high enough to encourage that many purchases. When the price is set too low, many fans wishing to buy tickets are turned away, causing frustration and possibly attempts at gate crashing or scalping. If promoters raise the price, some consumers will decide the event is too costly. Optimal profits are achieved because supply and demand match at the higher price.

When singer Barbra Streisand announced her European tour, demand was high and prices for tickets were as high as $1,200. This price was appropriate for the level of demand in the United Kingdom, and that show sold well. For the Rome concert, the price did not fit demand. Consumer groups protested, sales were slow, and the concert was cancelled.[20]

Target ROI Pricing

Another popular method of profit-oriented pricing, **target return on investment (ROI) pricing**, resembles markup pricing because it uses unit costs as a basis for determining the final price. The difference is found in the markup portion of the formula. With target ROI pricing, information will be required regarding the capital investments associated with production of the product. The goal is to set the price at the proper level to achieve a predetermined ROI. For example, consider the following information from a Swiss manufacturer of designer alarm clocks:

Investment   = $500,000

Expected sales = 50,000

Unit cost   = $15.00

Targeted ROI   = 20%

Target ROI price = Unit Cost + [(Target ROI Percentage * Investment) / Expected Sales]

Target ROI price = $15 + [(.20 * $500,000) / 50,000]

$\qquad\qquad\quad$ = $17.00 per clock

With sales of 50,000 units, total revenue would equal ($17 * 50,000) = $850,000 and costs would be $750,000. Profit would be $850,000—$750,000 = $100,000, which is a realized return of 20% (0.20 * $500,000 = $100,000). Again, these calculations depend heavily on accurate market research information.

INTERNATIONAL CONSIDERATION IN PRICING GOALS

As has been noted, pricing becomes more complicated when products are sold across international boundaries. Variable costs rise due to additional shipping, more expensive sales calls, tariffs and taxes, and other items. From a marketing perspective, two concepts deserve consideration as part of international pricing processes. The first requires balancing of short- and long-term goals. The second, which closely connects, is consideration of emotional and situational factors. The same product will be priced differently in each market as was shown in the price comparisons for milk in various countries in Table 9.3.

Short-Term vs. Long-Term Goals

Each of the international marketing goals presented earlier in Figure 9.4 receives consideration when making pricing decisions. Profitability concerns will naturally emerge. For products that have been sold over a period of time, additional market share objectives may be pursued. Prices may be designed to attract new customers in some circumstances and retain customers in others. Prices may be set to counter competitive actions or to attract the competition's customers.

One primary concern will be to balance short-term goals versus longer-term strategic objectives. When entering a new country, profit objectives may be stated as limiting projected losses until the product or company becomes established. Other objectives, such as brand awareness, rise to the forefront. Once an item receives attention, price can become the final element in the decision whether to try the entrant product. Sampling, coupons, and other enticements can be tied to prices to encourage trial. The longer-term strategic objective will be to establish a presence in the new country and to build on that presence over time, with the assumption that profits will eventually accrue due to the establishment of a strong market presence.

VIDEO LINK 9.3:
Food and Culture

Building Relationships vs. Profits

The emotional and situational elements of pricing apply to relationships as well. The Gulf of Mexico area experienced the devastating impact on the BP oil spill in 2010 and the spill affected prices for seafood. In that situation, some international suppliers experienced the opportunity to build relationships with restaurants and grocery chains by keeping prices as low as possible. While forgoing some short-term windfall profits, seafood providers could establish relationships and develop bonds that will last for years. In many countries, relationships are more important than profits. Business partners will pay a higher price or take a loss during periods of stress in return for future business contacts or a reciprocal drop in price when the business environment stabilizes.[21]

In summary, the four methods used to set prices, based on costs, supply and demand, competition, or profits, apply equally well to domestic and international pricing activities. Each takes place in the context of variables beyond just the amount charged for the item.

The idiosyncrasies of a country or region, combined with the desired objectives displayed in Figure 9.4, affect price-setting in each situation or market. For example, if *profitability* represents the primary strategic objective, then the marketing team is likely to set prices using costs or profit-based methods. For new products, the marketing team would be inclined to price to near the ceiling by using skimming methods. Enhancing *market share* suggests that pricing will probably be related to or based on competition in some way. Pricing to *retain current customers* may be competition-based or designed to find the supply/demand equilibrium for the volume a company intends to deliver. Should the goal be to *entice new customers* with a new product, then a penetration pricing approach would apply. Competition-based pricing or supply and demand approaches would apply to ongoing products and markets. When *countering competitive actions* is the goal, penetration pricing matches new products and competition-based pricing would be the best method for continuing products. To attract competitor customers, pricing would utilize a competition-based method.

In each of these instances, marketers should remember that price represents more than depictions of quality or standing relative to the competition. Prices also contain emotional and situational components. Economic conditions change situations. When recessions occur, substitute products become more viable as those challenged by lower incomes look for bargains and other ways of cutting personal expenditures. Governmental regulations may further complicate pricing decisions for both new and ongoing products. This means that pricing will be an ongoing operation for the marketers and managers in other departments.

Individual airlines may use different methods to set prices.

International Marketing in Daily Life

Pricing Air Travel

In most of the world, airline travel is available to domestic and international travelers. Any competitor in this industry would be subject to the various objectives and pricing methods. Each airline's marketing team chooses from the more common pricing goals, including earning profits, improving market share, retaining current customers, enticing new customers, or countering competitive actions. The choices will be based, in part, on the airline's financial status, country of origin, age, reputation or image, level of governmental protection and investment, and relevant degree of competition.

The pricing methods, based on costs, supply and demand, competition, or profitability, all fit with pricing for airlines. The complicating factors are that prices, especially fuel prices, can change quickly and dramatically. Supply and demand will be influenced by shifts in economic conditions. Competitors and competitive actions vary widely, as carriers enter and leave the marketplace, while some merge in various types of alliances. Profit targets become difficult to establish in such volatile markets.

PRICING TO BOTTOM-OF-THE-PYRAMID CONSUMERS

When pricing to those with the lowest incomes, new variables become prominent. Beyond the price and quality associated with an item, the unit size and payment method constitute important considerations. Effective international marketing to these groups results from a clear understanding of how individuals make purchase decisions.

Capacity to Consume

Capacity to consume refers to the power to use goods and services in the satisfaction of human wants. It consists of wants, goods and services available, time and energy, and purchasing power.[22] In the past, the method used to create the capacity to consume among the poor has been to provide the product or service free of charge. Some argue the approach has the feel of philanthropy. While charity may feel good, it may not be the best marketing tactic. Instead, when marketing to consumers with meager incomes, C.K. Prahalah suggests that increasing the capacity to consume will be the best approach.

> Capacity to consume refers to the power to use goods and services in the satisfaction of human wants. It consists of wants, goods and services available, time and energy, and purchasing power.

Consumption and choice at the bottom-of-the-pyramid can be encouraged by making unit packages that are small with affordable prices, because these consumers typically experience unpredictable income streams. Many subsist on daily wages and use cash cautiously.

Single-serve packages match the needs of this population. Consequently, single-serve packages are much more prevalent in less-developed economies. In India, where large pockets of low-income consumers live, single-serve sachets have become the norm for a wide variety of products, including shampoo, salt, biscuits (cookies), coffee, tea, ketchup, fruit drink concentrate, mouthwash, skin cream, and even bread.[23]

Marketing with smaller units carrying a lower price represents a strategic attempt to reach a large group of consumers. While the approach may appear to contain elements of altruism, the goal truly is to expand a company's customer base through effective packaging and pricing. The three key elements required by this method are affordability, access (reaching people in their standard shopping places), and availability, or having the product on hand when the individual has cash and is ready to buy. Pepsi has started to develop anti-anemia health drinks targeting bottom-of-the-pyramid consumers in India. To remove price-related barriers, the company plans to charge between Rs1 and Rs2 (1 to 2 *rupees*, or $0.02 to $0.04) per serving.[24]

Pricing meals by time of day allows customers to pay lower prices.

Credit

A second pricing pillar needed to build sales with bottom-of-the-pyramid consumers, providing credit, may appear to be counterintuitive. It may not seem logical to give credit to persons with uneven and unpredictable income streams; default rates among the poor, however, are lower than they are among their more wealthy counterparts. In Mumbai, some lenders charge 600% to 1,000% interest on loans to customers with low levels of income. A bank charging 25% interest can attract these consumers as customers and cover the costs of potential defaults at the same time. Providing access to credit supports pricing decisions and allows bottom-of-the-pyramid customers to upgrade their living conditions. Many use such credit to improve home lives by financing items such as televisions and mobile phones. Some rent these products to others to help make the payments.

Several companies employ creative tactics. In India, small grocers were not able to afford the $440 price for generators as a back-up source of power during outages. Unable to get loans, the shopkeepers had few options. A Honda Motor Co. distributor in the state of Uttar Pradesh came up with a unique solution. Twenty shopkeepers formed a group and each of them paid the distributor $22 per month. Every month, enough money was collected to buy one generator, which was awarded to one of the retailers through a lottery. After twenty months, every participant owned a generator.[25]

Marketing to bottom-of-the-pyramid customers can engender strong feelings of brand loyalty, especially when the company exhibits trust and dignity, and combines those values with appropriate product sizes, features, and prices.

International Pricing Discounts

Price discounting begins at the same place as setting prices in the first place: stating the desired objective. Discounts are not given randomly or without careful consideration. The amount and type of discount provided will be determined by the reason for the discount. When the primary rationale is to defend against the actions of a competitor, price reductions are made with the competitor in mind. When prices are discounted to build or reward customer loyalty and frequent purchases, other discounts become more effective. The French retailer Carrefour allocated 600 million *euros* to discount prices in France in 2009. The objective was clear: with sales having dropped in France by 3.4% in the third quarter of that year, the marketing team designed the discounts to increase demand and traffic in the stores.[26] Pricing discounts may be adapted to suit the needs of international marketing. The main types of pricing discounts are identified in Figure 9.11.

LEARNING OBJECTIVE #3:

What types of pricing discounts are available to international marketers?

LOSS LEADER

In retail stores, pricing certain items at or below cost in order to build store traffic remains a common marketing tactic. **Loss leader** pricing relies on regular prices for other items in the store in order to generate profits. The loss-leader system also creates sales for other businesses. To attract an order from a wholesaler or retailer, a manufacturer can offer one loss leader designed to encourage a series of purchases of additional products at the regular price.

Loss Leaders
Seasonal Discounts
Quantity Discounts
Early-Payment Discounts
Other Channel Discounts

Figure 9.11: Types of Pricing Discounts

At times, loss leaders are tied with other pricing programs. A *promotional price* takes the form of a price reduction associated with a promotion, such as a pre-Christmas sale. An *introductory price* features a discount for trying something new. A restaurant offering a new menu item may at first sell the product at a discount to lure patrons to try the newfood product.

Loss leaders offer the advantage of generating interest. They also move consumers to action by traveling to the store, often to the back of the store, in order to take advantage of the low-price items. Typically other purchases follow. Loss leaders help fend off competitive attacks by appealing to store customers to remain loyal, even as other offers are made. In Canada, a typical approach used by car dealers is to sell subcompact cars at a loss to attract new customers and to maintain the loyalty of repeat purchasers.[27]

The use of loss leaders applies equally well to international marketing. Companies seeking to enter or build share in another country can provide loss leader offers to accompany a catalog or list of products. Ryanair, the low-cost Irish airline, has announced plans for flights from United Kingdom to the United States priced at £ 10 in the near future. These loss leader flights are offered in the attempt to gain a foothold in the British market.[28]

Loss leader pricing is often used in retailing.

SEASONAL DISCOUNTS

Seasonal discounts are often associated with tourism and the hospitality industries. Vacation resorts, dining establishments, fishing and boat rental services, and entertainment venues including theme parks and music shows often experience peak sales and attendance during warmer months. To entice patrons at other times, companies such as these can offer off-season discounts. An international marketing firm might be able to balance seasonal fluctuations by conducting operations in several parts of the world. The summer season in Australia and Brazil takes place during the winter months in North America and Europe, and vice versa.

Seasonal discounts apply to physical products as well. Lawn care and gardening items sell well in warm seasons. Discount offers can discourage regular customers from shopping around during peak seasons. When cool weather appears, off-season discounts entice customers to stockpile or purchase items such as a new shovel or hoe for future use.

Sports and entertainment have well-defined seasons. Basketball is played at certain times of the year. Theater productions often shut down during part of the year. Of course, these seasons will vary country by country. Advance ticket purchases at a discounted price generate cash flow during off seasons.

QUANTITY DISCOUNTS

Quantity discount offers apply to retail purchases and sales by manufacturers and other suppliers to various channel members. The simplest form of quantity discount, a buy-one-get-one-free offer, encourages retail customers to stockpile items and/or use them more frequently.

Manufacturers offer quantity discounts to wholesalers and retailers. The price per unit declines as the volume of purchases rise. Volume discounts are particularly helpful to some international marketing programs. Rather than a series of sales calls followed by a series of shipments, producers can bundle purchases into larger amounts and offer the savings to the wholesaler or retailer.

Quantity discounts also appear in advertising programs. Most media companies reduce the price per advertisement as the volume of ads rises. Newspapers allow advertisers to accumulate column inches over time, with the price per inch lowered at various levels of volume. A company ordering one hundred column inches pays $5 per inch, whereas an advertiser buying one thousand column inches during the course of the year may only pay $2 per inch. Television sells sets of commercial packages that reduce the price per spot with increased volume. The same discounting method applies to magazines, billboards, and other venues.

International marketers use quantity discounts to build relationships. By granting discounts based on volume over time, the buyer is encouraged to make repeat purchases. Lines of communication remain open and the sales team may be able to reduce visits to the company, because there is no need to begin a totally new sales approach each time.

EARLY-PAYMENT DISCOUNTS

Another form of discounting, based on early payment, can be offered on an invoice. The term "2/10 net 30" reflects a 2% discount when an invoice is paid in ten days or less. The balance becomes due in thirty days. Early-payment discounts provide buyers with the opportunity to "earn" a lower price through prompt payment. When one firm offers more generous terms (3/20 instead of 2/10) the discount might be the deciding factor in a purchase. Early-payment discounts are more difficult to offer when international shipments are made, due to time differences and more lengthy delivery schedules. Electronic payment systems have reduced some of these complications. A 2005 survey revealed that a fourth of all U.S. companies offer early-payment discounts, with small businesses being more likely to do so.[29]

CHANNEL DISCOUNTS

Manufacturers offer additional enticements designed to generate sales to middlemen and retailers, known as *trade promotions*. These programs include trade allowances and trade incentives. One form of trade allowance is an off-invoice allowance, or a per case rebate paid to retailers for an order. Manufacturers also vend bonus packs with additional merchandise per pack to obtain and retain customers. These approaches reduce the wholesale price per item.

Channel discount offers sometimes include promotions such as free shipping and handling. The total price charged becomes lower. Free shipping discounts are popular in international marketing, where shipping costs are often high.

International marketers also take advantage of zone or region channel discounts. A price discount provided to all countries in the Pacific Rim will be attractive when shipping costs are reduced by combining orders on the same mode of transportation. Also, when several countries have similar channels of distribution, such as the Japanese *sogo shosha* (general) trading companies, it becomes possible to send larger orders to a single company or inter-firm risk-sharing organization for further distribution within the country.

LEARNING OBJECTIVE #4:

What factors influence decisions about price changes in international markets?

Price Changes in International Markets

Certain circumstances require companies to change prices permanently rather than temporarily through discounts or surcharges. Prices may be raised or lowered due to

Actions or Reactions of Competitors
– domestic
– foreign
Company Status as Industry Leader or Industry Follower
– domestic
– foreign
Impact on the Brand's Image
Impact on Revenues and Gross Margin
Reactions of Customers
– domestic
– foreign

Figure 9.12: Factors to Consider When Changing Prices

a variety of circumstances, including increased costs of raw materials, increased shipping costs, economic changes, and changes in currency exchange rates. Note that prices may at times move lower and at times may rise. Figure 9.12 identifies the factors marketers consider when making permanent changes to prices of existing products.

PRICE REDUCTIONS

A price may be permanently reduced in one or more of three situations. The first occurs when production costs decrease, which results from economies of scale as the firm expands the scope of its operations. It may also take place when start-up costs have been recovered or when the price of a raw material or component part declines.

Increased competition can trigger a permanent price reduction. Typically the response takes place when a company begins to lose market share to competitors. Lowering prices as a reaction to competition should not proceed without careful thought. A marketing team may be able to identify ways to maintain share without lowering prices and losing profits.

Telstra, the largest Australian telecommunications company, sells the majority of landlines in the country. Recently, the company faced severe competition from mobile and Internet phone competitors. In response, Telstra's marketing team focused on improved customer service and on negotiating higher fees with the government.[30] These steps were taken before the company considered lowering prices.

When product demand declines, prices sometimes fall. The primary concern will be whether the demand declined due to the entry of a new competitor or the development of a substitute product. Declining demand results in lower revenues. When a product reaches the later stages of its life cycle, the marketing team might look for foreign markets that are not in the same stage as a way to maintain sales rather than lowering price as the only response.

When the Volkswagen Beetle lost popularity in Western markets, the company shifted focus to Latin America, especially Brazil and Mexico. The iconic automobile became popular in those markets, easing the process of removal from other markets. By the time production stopped in Mexico in July of 2003 the automobile was the best-selling automobile in the history of the world.[31]

PRICE INCREASES

Price increases most often result from increases in production costs, including prices of raw materials, labor, and energy. When increasing prices, the company's marketing managers first review the company's pricing objectives and make note of international considerations such as the short- and long-term consequences in foreign markets. Adobe, the software company, charges more in European markets than it does in the United States or in Mexico—as much as 170% higher—due to the cost of maintaining local offices in those countries.[32] The price differential in this case is due to labor cost differences.

Price increases are made incrementally over time or as a single increase. Incremental changes may not be announced to customers in the hope they will not notice or

When the Volkswagen Beetle lost popularity in Western markets, the company shifted focus to Latin America, especially Brazil and Mexico.

become upset due to the gradual nature of the increase. Attention is paid to the response of competitors that may or may not follow suit. Should they not, the company may reconsider the price increase.

When a price is raised in a single action, customers, especially business-to-business clients, should be notified. Effective explanations should be provided to lessen the impact of the price increase. Contacting business customers in international markets about price increases indicates the company's intentions to be above-board in those relationships, where trust is at a premium. When trust is violated, business can be lost.

Mittal Steel, a company in India, is the largest producer of steel in the world. Recently, the company raised the price of steel sold to the government of India government three times without an explanation. In response, the Indian government threatened to bring in competitors to bid for the governmental purchases.[33]

WEBER'S LAW

German physiologist Ernst Heinrich Weber studied the link between a physical stimulus and a desired response. Weber's Law has been transferred to pricing. It suggests that for a price change (a stimulus) to be noticed and to elicit a response, it must be greater than 10%. For those who believe such a relationship is true, the implication would be to try to hold price increases to less than 10% and to make price decreases larger than 10%. The latter often will have a negative impact on the bottom line.

In international marketing, the question arises as to whether Weber's Law applies equally well to every culture. Given that economic systems vary widely, as do personal financial circumstances in a population, the 10% figure may seem arbitrary. At the same time, the general principle, that a threshold exists at which prices go noticed or unnoticed, may be valid.[34]

INTERNATIONAL INCIDENT ///

You are traveling in Mexico with a very good friend who lives in Japan. Your friend finds a sombrero he likes very much. He asks the vendor the price. The salesperson suggests a number that you know is ridiculous, expecting to bargain down to the amount he actually wishes to receive. You also know that your friend's culture is highly deferent and nonconfrontational. How can you suggest to your friend that he needs to look the salesperson right in the eye and demand a lower price? Or, should you tell the vendor that your friend is uncomfortable with bargaining? Or, should you simply do the bargaining yourself on behalf of your friend?

Ethical Issues in International Pricing

LEARNING OBJECTIVE #5:

What ethical concerns are associated with international pricing programs?

Many of the pricing practices that raise ethical concerns in domestic markets apply to international markets. Among the more common are collusion, predatory pricing, and deceptive pricing. These practices could be legal in some countries yet still violate ethical standards within a company or in the mind of the marketing practitioner.

COLLUSION

In oligopolistic markets, a set of major competitors experiences the temptation to set prices at uniform levels either overtly or covertly, through **collusion**. While collusion may be allowed or even expected in countries, the net result can be that prices do not reflect costs or other considerations, yet consumers have no recourse or alternatives. Price collusion continues unless or until new competitors reach the market, which may be difficult due to powerful barriers to entry. Mongolian flour manufacturing companies were accused by governmental regulators in the country of colluding to raise the price of flour in the country and were fined 250,000 tugrik (approximately $190).[35]

PREDATORY PRICING

Predatory pricing involves the direct attempt by a major competitor to drive other companies out of business by setting prices unrealistically low. When smaller competitors cannot withstand the loss in sales, the firms eventually become at risk and eventually go out of business. Predatory pricing practices are especially harmful when foreign companies are competing against domestic firms with fewer resources, especially in less- or least-developed nations.

DECEPTIVE PRICING

Another ethically questionable practice, **deceptive pricing**, takes place when the marketer promotes one price, yet due to hidden charges, add-ons, or higher prices for products with more than the bare minimum of features, the actual price is much higher. Automobile manufacturers have often used the phrase "starting at" to set prices for models with little or no common accessories, such as a radio or an automatic transmission. Service providers, especially credit card companies, have become notorious for add-on charges and late fees, raising interest rates without notification, ATM usage fees, and other attempts to increase revenues in secretive ways. A common practice among airlines is to label airline fees, which count as revenue for the company, as "taxes." A lawsuit filed against British Airways accuses that airline of the practice and states that the pricing is deceptive.[36]

Each of these issues is present in domestic and international markets. Company standards and individual moral judgments apply to the use or misuse of pricing practices.

DUMPING

One more purely international ethical pricing issue involves **dumping**, or the practice of selling goods below costs in another country or pricing a product in one country lower than the price of the product in another country. The goal in both cases is to capture the market in the country with the low price. The company may experience a loss on the sales; the goal, however, is to eliminate competitors through the low price. The net result of removing customers will be to be able to eventually charge higher prices and generate higher profit margins.

Many governments and the World Trade Organization have outlawed dumping, yet it continues to exist. Ethical firms refrain from such practices and should notify the WTO or the local government when they take place. [37] Dumping accusations are often brought by governments in response to actions of foreign businesses within their borders. Recently, Chinese Ministry of Commerce found what it believed was evidence of dumping by South Korean and Thai producers of terephthalic acid, a chemical used in clothing and plastic manufacturing.[38]

Chapter 9: Review and Resources

STRATEGIC IMPLICATIONS ///

Pricing decisions are, at the core, strategic decisions. Three primary competitive forces are price, quality, and the price-quality relationships. These three forces dictate the strategic direction of the organization. Price conveys meaning. It becomes part of a corporation's image and a brand's position. Strategic managers identify relationships between cost and price. A small restaurant owner chooses ingredients that create the best quality for the price she wishes to charge. A microchip manufacturer in Japan is likely to insist on the highest-quality materials in order to create the most durable and efficient product, at which point company leaders would feel comfortable charging a higher price for that item.

At the other extreme, lower costs and prices are vital to success in the discount retail business. An industry giant such as Wal-Mart attained its status by delivering "everyday low prices." Marketing to consumers at the bottom-of-the-pyramid requires pricing strategies that fit the needs of those with the most modest incomes.

TACTICAL IMPLICATIONS ///

International pricing tactics take place in three major areas: setting prices, discounting prices, and changing prices. Each is based on the company's primary pricing objectives and strategic position. Pricing based on costs reflects a different tactical approach from one based on demand/supply, competition, or profit motives.

The same holds true for discounting. The marketing team considers not only the objectives for discounts but also the legal and cultural implications in each country. A marketer knows that Islamic countries frown on charging interest, which leads to the use of other charges or fees as part of the price. Many governments regulate what can be termed a "sale" or "discount" as it relates to the "regular" price.

Price changes also begin with a review of pricing objectives. Methods for raising and lowering prices reflect the company's desire to achieve short- and long-term goals as well as to build relationships with other businesses and individual consumers over time.

OPERATIONAL IMPLICATIONS ///

Individual storeowners need to understand local customs with regard to pricing items. Should the price be displayed, or only conveyed verbally? Are prices fixed, or is bargaining expected? Methods of advertising discounts and price changes should be studied. A company's image and reputation can be quickly damaged when local norms are ignored.

Sales representatives making presentations to other businesses should be equally aware of pricing protocols. Methods for presenting prices, discounting prices, agreeing to price, rejecting a price offer, and finalizing the deal should be well understood before the sales call ever begins. Salespeople that are trained to know and convey the company's strategic and tactical intentions will make sales calls that are more effective. They will know when price will be the primary force in the sale, or represent only one smaller element in building markets and creating long-term relationships with businesses in other countries.

TERMS

price	price elasticity of demand	loss leader
price perceptual map	skimming	collusion
cost-based pricing	penetration pricing	predatory pricing
break-even analysis	profit-based pricing	deceptive pricing
cost-plus pricing	target ROI pricing	dumping
markup pricing	capacity to consume	

REVIEW QUESTIONS

1. Define price and name the various types of prices described in this chapter.
2. What three main considerations influence perceptions of prices?
3. What are the typical objectives associated with pricing programs?
4. What four factors can become the basis for a pricing program?
5. How can a break-even analysis assist in developing an international pricing program?
6. Define price elasticity of demand, elastic demand, and inelastic demand.
7. When pricing based on the competition, what three approaches are available?
8. Describe skimming and penetration pricing in international marketing and explain how penetration pricing is different from dumping.
9. What three circumstances match with profit-based pricing?
10. Describe the international considerations in pricing programs noted in this chapter.
11. Define the term *capacity to consume* and explain how it is part of marketing to the bottom-of-the-pyramid.
12. Identify the main types of pricing discounts offered to consumers and businesses.
13. How is a loss leader different from dumping?
14. When making price changes, what factors should the marketing team consider?
15. How does Weber's Law apply to price changes?
16. How do negotiation systems and countertrade arrangement affect business-to-business pricing programs?
17. What four main ethical issues affect international pricing programs?

DISCUSSION QUESTIONS

1. Discuss the value considerations, emotional considerations, and situational factors associated with prices for the following items, specifically as they would relate to international marketing:
   - accidental death insurance policy
   - suntan lotion at the beach priced far higher than in local retail stores
   - tickets to a rock concert featuring a popular band
   - designer undergarments
2. A pricing perceptual map typically depicts products based on relationship involving price and quality. Describe quality for the following items:
   - one-night stay in a hotel in Uruguay
   - fishing tour guide in Cambodia

- fish and chips for a British citizen visiting Slovenia
- candy for a child in Sudan

3. From the list of pricing objectives stated in Figure 9.4, which would be most important for an exporting company in the following situations? Defend your choices.

- just entering the market with an unknown brand
- just entering the market with a well-known brand
- established company facing new domestic competitors
- established company facing new international competitors
- product in the take-off stage of the product life cycle in a foreign market
- product in the maturity stage of the product life cycle in a foreign market
- product in the decline state of the product life cycle in a foreign market

4. Which pricing method (cost, demand/supply, competition, profit-based) would you recommend for the following items to be sold in other countries? Defend your reasoning.

- tennis balls by a manufacturer in the Philippines
- retail store to open with 20,000 sku (stock-keeping units) in Luxembourg
- cell-phone services in Chile
- solar panels in Canada

5. Which types of discounts should be given by each of the following companies? Explain your answers.

- Hilton International Hotels
- AFLAC in Japan
- Perrier bottled water sold in South Africa
- Bulldozers sold by Caterpillar

6. Describe the differences and similarities between dumping, penetration pricing, and predatory pricing. How might Weber's Law be relevant to this discussion?

ANALYTICAL AND INTERNET EXERCISES

1. Draw a pricing perceptual map for these products in international markets, naming the major competitors and placing them on the map. Use the Internet to identify the major competitors, if necessary.

- automobiles
- athletic shoes
- cell-phone service
- farm tractors

2. Calculate the break-even point in units for the following product:

Price per unit = $10.00

Variable cost per unit = $2.75

Fixed costs = $15,000

3. Using markup pricing, calculate the price for cell phones to be sold in Argentina:

Total fixed cost = $400,000

Units to be sold =   50,000

Variable cost per unit = $50.00

Markup on price = 20%

4. A company sells packaged cookies in Hungary. The price is €2.50 per package. The company's marketing team believes that in Romania, price elasticity of demand would be €1.67. In contrast, price elasticity of demand in Ukraine would be €0.88. Which country offers the most lucrative market, especially in terms of recapturing start-up costs? Which pricing strategy would be viable in Romania: skimming or penetration pricing? Which would work best in Ukraine?

5. Prepare a report on the advisability of using quantity discounts and early-payment discounts businesses in the following countries, based on cultural norms and governmental regulations:
   - Mexico
   - Niger
   - Saudi Arabia
   - Italy

6. Using the Internet, investigate sales methods, including negotiation tactics and practices and countertrade arrangements for the following countries:
   - South Korea
   - Australia
   - Iran
   - Brazil

▶ ONLINE VIDEOS

Visit **www.sagepub.com/baack** to view these chapter videos:

Video Link 9.1: Cars and Competition

Video Link 9.2: Oil Spills

Video Link 9.3: Food and Culture

STUDENT STUDY SITE

Visit **www.sagepub.com/baack** to access these additional learning tools:

- Web Quizzes
- eFlashcards
- SAGE Journal Articles

- Country Fact Sheets
- Chapter Outlines
- Interactive Maps

CASE 9 ///

La Poste: Pricing Banking Services

La Poste began as the government-owned postal service provider to citizens of France. It has become one of the top three logistics, corporate services, and financial providers in Europe, behind Germany's Deutsche Post and ahead of the United Kingdom's Concordia. The company, which is now independently operated, holds the number three position for electronic mail services in Europe, the number three spot in the European parcels and logistics sector, and one of the top positions in the French financial services market. These activities combined to produce more than €17 billion in 2001. Among the company's assets is its network of more than 17,000 post offices, which provide mail services, financial services, and Internet access and email services throughout France.

The company offers all major banking services, including checking and savings accounts, debit cards, credit cards, online banking, automatic transfers and savings programs, sales and purchases of common stock in France and other countries, domestic and international money orders, and international banking services, including currency exchanges.

The strength of *La Poste* has been its operations in Europe, most notably France, Germany, and the United Kingdom. In France, patrons enjoy the convenience of taking care of post office needs and banking activities in the same location. Recently, however, company leaders have discussed the possibility of expansion into other French-speaking nations.

Two possibilities emerge. First, *La Poste* could seek to enter Canada or other developed countries in which both English and French are spoken. Citizens and potential patrons would be more affluent and would be familiar with the large range of banking services normally offered by financial institutions. The primary impediment would be competition. Consumers would have no vested interest in trusting their money to a foreign bank. Consequently, price would become an important consideration. To encourage customers to open accounts, La Poste would expect to offer discounts on some services combined with any potential advantages the bank could offer.

The second type of expansion includes less-developed Francophone countries such as Haiti, Cameroon, and the Democratic Republic of Congo. These nations experience high levels of poverty and unemployment. Investments may be considered more risky.

Additional opportunities also exist, most notably in the area of microfinancing, in which a small investment is provided to a local entrepreneur starting a small-scale business, such as making soap to sell in the local marketplace. Among the advantages of microfinancing are high levels of repayment at profitable rates plus considerable favorable publicity both in the nation involved and in the home country of France.

La Poste's marketing team notes that the company would not enjoy the advantage of providing mail service combined with banking in either type of location. Canada has a well-developed postal

La Poste combines banking with financial services.

system. While less- or least-developed nations have poorer systems, the government would undoubtedly be protective of these interests. The potential would exist to provide Internet access and email stations for patrons in those situations.

It might also be possible to establish package-delivery programs in both circumstances, as long as these did not conflict with governmental interests and protections. Canada would pose stronger competitive threats, whereas Haiti and Cameroon would have less-developed roads and mapping systems and so other companies would pose less of a threat.

The final alternative available to *La Poste* would be to seek further expansion in European countries. About 21% of the population of Switzerland speaks French, for example. Other elements of culture may be similar to what is present in France. Clearly the marketing and management teams had a great deal to consider as the company formerly known as *Société Générale* (the General Society) moves forward into a new era.

1. If the company begins operations in Canada, which type of pricing system would be most viable: that based on cost, supply/demand, competition, or profit?

2. In Canada, would any type of discounting program work? If so, which methods?

3. In Canada, would loss leader tactics be advisable? How would they be delivered?

4. If the company commences operations in Haiti or Cameroon, which type of pricing system would be best, based on cost, supply/demand, competition, or profit?

5. In the Democratic Republic of Congo, would any type of discounting program work? If so, which one?

6. Which situation should the marketing and management teams from *La Poste* choose? Why?

10 International Finance and Pricing Implications

LEARNING OBJECTIVES

After reading and studying this chapter, you should be able to answer the following questions:

1. How do currencies and currency exchanges affect international business and international marketing programs?

2. What factors affect currency movements in the international marketplace?

3. How do the law of one price and purchasing power parity affect international marketing activities?

4. How do governmental activities influence international finance?

5. What are the relationships between international finance and the elements of the marketing mix?

IN THIS CHAPTER

Pricing ArcelorMitall Steel Globally: The Effects of Currency Changes

Who claims the title of the richest person in the world? Although Bill Gates and Warren Buffet are still near the top of the list, recently a new name, Lakshmi Niwas Mitall, owner of ArcelorMittal, has emerged. He founded his company in 1989 in India, and, in just a little more than twenty years, it has grown into the largest steel manufacturer in the world. With operations in all of the major steel markets plus ever expanding mining activities globally, more than sixty countries, the firm faces challenging international marketing issues due to international finance complexities.

ArcelorMittal conducts business using a variety of currencies (see Figure 10.1). Changes in the value of any of these currencies can affect ArcelorMittal's marketing activities and profitability. The company's leadership attempts to cope with fluctuations in currency exchange rates, but the price of steel and other goods moves up or down as currency values change. Shifts in exchange rates affect product positioning, demand, and other strategic international marketing factors. As variable and fixed costs increase or decrease, profit margins may rise or fall. The company may be paying steel workers in Argentina while selling a large supply of steel in China. If the Argentinean *peso* suddenly changes to be worth far more than the Chinese *yuan*, the costs of production increase and the value of the company's revenue decreases. In sum, currency affects the company's entire marketing strategy.

In response to changes in currency values, the company's financial team hedges or attempts to lessen currency risk. Purchasing various financial instruments makes it possible to offset some of the risk of currency movement. Mitall views the expense of these instruments as necessary to provide currency stability. Without hedging activities, the company's marketing goals would be more difficult to achieve.

Argentina: Argentine *Peso*	Morocco: *Moroccan Dirham*
Australia: Australian *Dollar*	Oman: *Omani Rial*
Bahrain: Bahraini *Dinar*	Poland: *Polish Zloty*
Canada: Canadian *Dollar*	Qatar: *Qatari Riyal*
China: *Yuan*	Russia: *Russian Ruble*
Czech Republic: *Czech Crowns*	South Africa: *South African Rand*
European Union: *euros*	Thailand: *Thai Baht*
Hong Kong: *Hong Kong Dollar*	Trinidad and Tobago: *Trinidad and Tobago Dollar*
India: *Indian Rupee*	Ukraine: *Ukrainian Hryvnia*
Israel: *Israeli New Sheqel*	United Arab Emirates: *UAE Dirham*
Kazakhstan: *Kazakhstani Tenge*	United States: *U.S. Dollar*
Kuwait: *Kuwaiti Dinar*	Venezuela: *Strong Bolivar*
Mexico: *Mexican Peso*	

Figure 10.1: Examples of Countries and Currencies in Which ArcelorMittal Operates

Note: For details on the Strong Bolivar, see www.economist.com/node/15287355.

Governmental regulations also play an important role in limiting or controlling currency movement. ArcelorMittal encounters various currency regulations. The company's international marketing strategy accounts for and responds to these regulations. The South African Reserve Bank has strict rules regarding the South African *rand*. The Bank must approve a variety of business activities involving the *rand* while it also monitors payments for trade. The National Bank of Kazakhstan maintains even stricter regulations. To change the local currency, the *tenge*, into a foreign currency, the company must obtain approval for each transaction on a case-by-case basis. The Central Bank of Algeria does not allow cash surpluses to be invested outside of the country. Brazilian law allows currency exchange through only one exchange, and only with a license by the Brazilian bank. Argentina does not permit the country's *pesos* to be converted into any different currency. In some instances domestic companies must even transfer profits from goods shipped from the country back into the *peso* within 360 days.[1]

At the same time, based on Mr. Mittal's financial standing, it seems clear his company has effectively responded to the complex marketing and business challenges associated with currency.

QUESTIONS FOR STUDENTS

1. How are the concepts of risk and currency values related?
2. Why would governmental leaders become involved in managing currency exchange rates?
3. How would international financial decisions affect the operation of ArcelorMittal?

ArcelorMittal conducts business using a variety of currencies.

Overview

Many aspects of pricing programs influence international marketing decisions. The previous chapter examined international pricing from the perspectives of setting prices, discounting, and changing prices. International marketers recognize that those three activities are often dramatically affected by outside forces. One primary influence comes from financial considerations in the home and host countries.

Financial conditions affect all international marketing activities. From currency issues to access to capital, understanding international finance helps increase marketing effectiveness. This chapter reviews methods for responding to international finance issues within the context of international marketing. Effective responses assist international companies in building effective marketing programs.

The chapter begins with an overview of money and types of currencies. Next, international finance is described in terms of the basics of capital markets and the financing of transactions. The nature of currency exchange and exchange rates are then reviewed, as are the factors that affect currency movement. The factors include individual and business transactions, trade and investment activities, trade deficits or surpluses, inflation, and interest rates.

The role of government in attempting to control the value of a country's currency is then described. Currency regimes, including floating and fixed exchange rates, constitute one of the primary tools governments can use to manage currencies. A brief history of currency control as it relates to the gold standard and other methods of currency pegging will then be presented.

Currency risk and movement often lead to international marketing problems. Methods for predicting currency fluctuations are examined, including hedging and futures contracts. The basics of international finance funding, including acquiring capital, financing ongoing trade operations, methods of countertrade, internal pricing, and shadow pricing, are described.

The conclusion of this chapter relates international finance to international marketing, as is highlighted in Figure 10.2. Financial effects on markets, product, prices, distribution systems (place), and promotional programs are analyzed. The strategic, tactical, and operational implications of the interactions between marketing and finance are noted.

Figure 10.2: The International Marketing Context

Money and Currency

LEARNING OBJECTIVE #1:

How do currencies and currency exchanges affect international business and international marketing programs?

The basis of international finance and its relationship to international marketing begins with money. *Money* is the unit of value people accept as a form of payment. The exchange of value is at the core of international marketing. Money has taken many forms, including salt, stones, seashells, and beads. For something to be considered as money, it should have five characteristics, as displayed in Figure 10.3. Money serves many purposes, including being used as a measure of value, as a medium of exchange, and as a savings mechanism.

CURRENCY

Currency represents the form of money used by a specific country or region. Currencies change and evolve over time. When East and West Germany reunited in 1990, the *deutsche* mark was used instead of the former East German currency, the East German

Acceptability	It is accepted as payment by a group of people.
Scarcity	When a product is scarce, it becomes more valuable and it takes more money to purchase the product, as only a limited supply of money is available.
Durability	It will not spoil or become damaged.
Divisibility	It can be divided into smaller units.
Portability	It is small enough that people can easily carry it around.

Figure 10.3: Properties of Money.

mark. Now, however, German's currency is the *euro*. Various symbols signify a currency. The $ sign represents the U.S. dollar and the Mexican *peso* due to a common origin with the symbol for the Spanish *peso*. In fact, some claim that Mexico used the symbol before the United States.[2]

The use of money represents a constant part of life for most of the world.

International Marketing in Daily Life

Methods of Payment and Banking

Various currencies circulate globally. The use of money represents a constant part of life for most of the people in the world. In most countries, money contains both bills and coins. The green bills used in America are plain compared with the colorful pink, blue, and purple notes used in other countries. Coins often can be made from multiple alloys and have striated edges. The penny, nickel, dime, and quarter may be replaced by one penny, two *pence*, five *pence*, ten *pence*, twenty *pence*, and fifty *pence* coins in the United Kingdom. The dollar coin may be reserved for vending and parking machines in the United States, but the use of such coins is more common in other countries. The one-, two-, and five-*pound* coins in the United Kingdom or the one-, two-, and five-*rupee* coins in India are both examples. The currency names and symbols for the world's ten largest economies can be found in Table 10.1

In the modern economy, consumers use physical currency less and less frequently. Between computer and mobile devices, many purchases are made electronically. This also holds true for businesses. The spending of millions of dollars involves the clicking of buttons, not the physical movement of briefcases of money.

COUNTRY	CURRENCY NAME	CURRENCY SYMBOL
United States	Dollar	$
China	*Renminbi*	¥
Japan	*Yen*	¥
India	*Rupee*	*Rp*
Germany	*euro*	€
United Kingdom	*Pound*	£
Russia	*Ruble*	руб
France	*euro*	€
Brazil	*Real*	R$
Italy	*euro*	€

Table 10.1: **Currency Name and Currency Symbol for the Top Ten Largest World Economies**

Currency is at the core of marketing. Business activities involve the use of local currency in terms of incoming revenues (sales to consumers), salaries paid to employees, and payments of company expenses. The currency earned through marketing often will be converted or exchanged for a different currency. This may be to bring profits back to the home country, transfer funds to a third country to pay for expansion, or move the money to yet another country to deposit in a bank. Figure 10.4 summarizes the ways that business uses currency.

Before entering a new country, the marketing team considers the nature of the currency in the target nation. Decisions regarding methods of payment and forms of investment are made based on the presence of either a hard currency or a soft currency.

| Bank Deposits and Withdrawals |
| Conversion to Move Across Borders |
| Employee Salaries |
| Expenses |
| Sales |
| Taxes and Fees |

Figure 10.4: Currency and Business Activity

Hard Currency

A **hard currency** can be exchanged for other currencies worldwide. *euros, riyals, yen,* dollars, and other foreign hard currencies are traded for each other at set rates in financial centers such as Paris, London, and Tokyo. Hard currencies are also known as *convertible currencies.* Hard currencies stabilize marketing operations because the partners in a trading or sales relationship can rely on relatively manageable currency risk. Hard currencies allow confidence in the prices and costs of various marketing programs, including the value of a coupon or discount, the amount that will be charged for advertising time, and the cost of distributing products through a network of intermediaries.

Soft Currency

A **soft currency** is unstable and will not be traded at major financial centers. A soft currency can be exchanged or used for purchases within a country, but has limited or no use in other countries. Soft currencies are more commonplace in less- or least-developed nations. Soft currency values fluctuate more and create uncertainty in a marketing program. In order to adapt to a soft currency, the finance department will undertake additional efforts to find methods for managing currency.

After discovering the form of currency that will be used in a foreign operation, international marketers consider other international finance factors. Among them, exchange rates for money, exchange regimes, and global currency institutions are considered. The topics form the basis of international finance.

International Finance

International finance involves the study of currency exchange, investments, and how these processes influence business activities. Actors in global international finance include governments, international organizations, commercials banks, central or government banks, large and small corporations, and individuals. Managing the exchange of currency and gaining access to funds are necessary for all international businesses. This includes access to capital to conduct operations as well as the financing of transactions.

CAPITAL MARKETS

Any location, online or physical, where businesses or individuals can raise funds becomes a **capital market**. The funds pay for entry into foreign markets, trade with foreign partners, research and development, a physical presence such as an office building or manufacturing plant, and a long list of other domestic and foreign expenses.

Companies raise two types of funds in global or local capital markets: debt and equity. *Debt* refers to funds that may be paid back or that are owed. Debt takes the form of loans, and structured loans by governments or companies are called *bonds*. Typically debt includes the money borrowed plus some interest or fees. The use of fees is common in Muslim countries, where religious law forbids charging interest. Granting a degree of ownership, typically in the form of stock, in return for an investment of money, results in *equity*. Important international differences exist regarding usage of capital markets. American firms tend to raise funds more through equity markets than they do through loans and debt. European firms have a stronger tendency to raise funds through debt rather than equity.

Companies gain advantage through access to international capital markets. By being able to access multiple markets, firms can access the most efficient and lowest-priced sources of debt and equity. When funding cannot be found in a company home capital market, the firm's leaders may look in other countries.

Company finance officers work to attain the best balance of debt and equity, considering local taxes, regulations, and other variables. When a company balances debt, which carries greater risk, with equity, which has a higher cost, across international capital markets, the finance department is seeking to diversify the degree of risk a company assumes. Reducing risk applies to lenders, investors, and companies. As more and more international companies enter global capital markets, greater choice allows for less risk. In addition, by being in multiple countries, companies suffer less vulnerability to country-specific economic problems, such as a recession.

THE FINANCING OF TRANSACTIONS

When customers make purchases, currency exchanges facilitate the transactions. The use of money within a nation's boundaries normally means a company will take a common currency as payment, and the trade is relatively simple. Most foreign travelers quickly adjust to prices, currency values, and other issues such as making correct change when purchasing goods.

Complications emerge when transactions take place across national boundaries. Purchases will be affected by the values of the currencies involved. International transactions are affected by currency values, changing currency values, and other factors. Transactions between businesses, with governments, and with individual consumers are all influenced by the value a currency holds in relation to currencies in other countries.

The Nature of Currency Exchange

A currency's **exchange rate** is the rate at which one country's currency can be traded for another country's currency. Consider a German marketer wanting to purchase advertising time in the British television market. The price of a thirty-second commercial on the BBC network will be stated or denominated in British pounds. To purchase the time, the marketer will pay in pounds. It is likely that much of a German firm's cash will be held in *euros*; however, BBC may not accept *euros* as a means of payment. Instead, the German marketer exchanges *euros* for British pounds to complete the transaction. A certain number of pounds will be equal in value to a certain number of *euros*. In September of 2010, 1 *euro* was worth around 85 *pence* (100 *pence* equals 1 *pound* much as 100 cents equals 1 dollar).

A currency's exchange rate is the rate at which one country's currency can be traded for another country's currency.

Marketers can use a variety of sources to identify the value of an exchange. Typically, the bank or a similar institution that completes the currency exchange will provide the rate. Exchange rates can also be found in a newspaper or online. The rates in these examples are called spot rates. *Spot rates* are a set rate of exchange for a delivery of currency within two days of the agreement to exchange currencies. Many of these exchanges are immediate, but for large purchases, businesses may need the extra two days to complete the transaction. The exchange rates that tourists use are often the spot rates plus a premium to allow for a small profit.

Currency conversion exchange rates take the form of direct and indirect quotes. *Direct quotes* calculate the home currency price per unit against that of the foreign currency. Using this method, the example above would be 1 *pound* = 1.17 *euro*. *Indirect quotes* are calculated using the value of the foreign currency. Direct quotes are the more commonly used, but indirect quotes are used by the Euro zone, Australia, and New Zealand.[3]

A potentially complicating calculation occurs when the currencies involved vary widely in terms of value, because the exchange rate can be confusing. Consider the Japanese *yen*. A kilogram of rice in the country may cost around 225 *yen*.[4] This does not mean that rice is expensive. It just means that the value of a single *yen* is lower than the value of a single U.S. dollar or a single *euro*.

The value of the Japanese *yen* is less than 1 *euro* penny.

In Japan, the direct quote for the *euro* would be 111.98 *Yen* = 1 *euro*. This means it requires approximately 112 *yen* to purchase 1 *euro*, and that one kilo of rice costs around 2 *euros*. In Japan the indirect quote would be 1 *yen* = 0.0089 *euro*. This means that 1 *yen* is not worth even 1 *euro* "penny."

COMPUTING EXCHANGE RATES

A key variable that marketers consider is the percentage change in a currency's value over a period of time. Continuing with the previous example, a marketer may want to know how much the value of the *euro* relative to *yen* has changed over the past month. In other words, a *euro* may be able purchase more or less *yen*, depending on market movements.

Different formulas must be used to calculate percentage change in the currency depending on whether a direct or indirect quote is used. Figure 10.5 presents the formula for both calculations. Regardless of formula, the same percentage change should result.

Regardless of the method used, the same outcome has occurred: the *euro* lost 13% of its value relative to the *pound*. To rephrase, the *pound* is now worth 13% more in *euros* than it was at the beginning rate.

In international marketing, exchange rates affect prices of goods, values set for promotional items such as coupons and discounts, the use of credit including terms of repayment, and more general issues. A product's positioning often reflects a price/quality relationship. When a currency increases in value due to a shift in the exchange rate, a product may suddenly become more of a bargain or less attractive, not because the product has changed, but because the relationship between the price and the product's quality has been affected.

Beginning Rate: 1 pound = 1.17 *euro*
Ending Rate: 1 pound = 1.02 *euro*

$$\text{Direct Quote} = \frac{\text{ending rate} - \text{beginning rate}}{\text{beginning rate}}$$

$$\frac{1.02 - 1.17}{1.17}$$

$$= \frac{-0.15}{1.17}$$

$$= -13\%$$

$$\text{Indirect quote} = \frac{\text{beginning rate} - \text{ending rate}}{\text{ending rate}}$$

Beginning Rate: 1 *euro* = 85 pence
Ending Rate: 1 *euro* = 98 pence

$$\frac{85 - 98}{98}$$

$$= \frac{-13}{98}$$

$$= -13\%$$

Figure 10.5: Direct Quote and Indirect Quote Percentage Change Formulas

Factors That Affect Currency Movement

LEARNING OBJECTIVE #2:

What factors affect currency movements in the international marketplace?

Currency values move. The exchange rate between two currencies changes over time. The underlying reason for this is supply and demand for money. Figure 10.6 provides a list of currency movement drivers or factors, excluding the governmental activities that will be discussed later in this chapter.

In the transaction described earlier in this chapter, a Germany company's *euros* were exchanged *euros* for pounds to facilitate the purchase of BBC advertising time. Currency movements might have an impact on the transaction. An increase in the demand for the *pound* will change its value, just as increased demand for a product might cause the product's price to rise. Should the value of the *pound* relative to the *euro* rise, the cost of purchasing advertising time will be affected.

The typical small daily individual transactions that increase demand for a currency will not move its value; approximately $3.2 billion worth of currency are bought and sold each day.[5] Consequently, the value of a single currency can change greatly depending on these transactions. Several factors affect currency value. Various forces cause some currencies to be purchased and others to be sold.

The currency exchange process can be viewed as being a tug-of-war, albeit a highly complicated one. On one side are those buying a currency. When one side wishes to make purchases of a currency, the demand for that currency will rise. In essence, that team pulls the rope in the direction of a more expensive or valuable exchange rate. On the other side are those wishing to sell the same currency, or those who are pulling the rope in the opposite direction. These forces lead to a lower price or a weakening of the currency.

The various actors pulling on the rope, including individuals, companies, and governments, can switch sides if needed or if a potential benefit arises, which further complicates the process. Someone or some group might switch when they believe money can be made by speculating on a weaker currency. Governments may intervene due to the possible political implications of a change in a currency's value. A follow-the-leader mentality can emerge in which everyone switches to one side when it becomes apparent that it is going to "win." Other external factors also influence the game. Inflation, interest rates, and trade activities all affect the process of currency valuation and currency exchange.

| Individual and Business Transactions |
| Inflation |
| Interest Rates |
| Trade and Investment Activity |

Figure 10.6: Nongovernmental Factors That Affect Currency Movement

Taken as a whole, this tug-of-war will be a great deal more complicated and the winner will be much more difficult to predict than when a game is played by children in a backyard. Some argue that the outcome is impossible to predict. This means that although it is possible to examine the factors that influence currency values and currency exchanges, there are no rigid rules. Prediction is possible; however, certainty about the accuracy of that prediction is not.

Even with those difficulties, understanding currency movements represents a fundamental element of international marketing. A South Korea automaker may be exporting to South Africa. Due to the strength of the South African *rand* compared to the South Korean currency, the *won*, the Korean company's exports become priced too high for the South African market. The company's chief financial officer might predict that the *rand* is going to devalue relative to the *won*, which would lower the price of the automobiles. Based on this prediction, the company will continue to export to the market and wait for the currency to devalue. If the company predicts that the *rand* will continue to stay strong, the company may decide to start manufacturing within the country. By manufacturing within the nation's boundaries, the company's costs would be in *rands*, which might make it possible to lower the price of the cars in the market.

INDIVIDUAL AND BUSINESS TRANSACTIONS

General economic health can lead to more pulling on the "supply" or the "demand" side of the currency tug-of-war. When economies are doing well, consumers spend more, companies are more likely to make foreign investments, and greater transaction demand for currency occurs. *Transaction demand* refers to demand for the currency needed to conduct business activities, such as importing goods or investing in a country's stock market. The opposite is also true. When economies are weak, lower demand for the currency will be present. There will be lower consumer and business spending, fewer imports, and investors will view domestic companies as less appealing.

While much of the demand for currency results from individual and business transactions, speculators make some currency purchases with the goal of profiting from the transaction itself. Basically, they hope to purchase the currency at a low price and to sell it later at a high price. The attempt to make money in the currency market is called *currency speculation*. These investments are made based on predictions of future changes in the currency's value. After the recent financial crisis in 2008,

The currency exchange process can be viewed as being a tug-of-war, albeit a highly complicated one.

speculation has come under criticism for not providing any value and for leading to currency movement based purely on profit for speculators. Others argue that speculators play an important role in balancing out both sides in the tug-of-war.

TRADE AND INVESTMENT ACTIVITY

Business transactions take the form of trade and investment activities. Countries track these activities using a balance of payments statement. The statement catalogues all of the currency-related activity within a country. It allows international marketers to obtain a broad overview of the trade activity within a country and the country's economic ties with the globe. Central to international marketing, trade consists of the exchange of goods and services across borders.

Trade plays a central role in a country's overall economic position globally. Some countries, such as China or Germany, have a tendency to save, to keep large reserves or savings of currency, and to export. Others, such as the United Kingdom, import many goods and have high consumer spending rates. A look at the balance of payments statement would reveal this. Figure 10.7 provides an example.

Countries buy and sell goods and services as well as financial assets. A balance of payments statement tracks these activities. The balance of payments statement contains five components: current account, capital account, financial account, net errors and omissions, and reserves and related items.

The current account catalogues trade in merchandise, services, income, and current transfers. Current transfers refer to any transfers of currency that are not capital-related such as gifts and grants. The 400 million Saudi *riyals* (*SR* 400 million) given by Saudi

U.S. International Transactions 2009 (in millions of dollars)	
Current Account	
Exports of goods and services and income receipts	2,159,000
Imports of goods and services and income payments	–2,412,000
Unilateral current transfers	–124,943
Capital Account	
Capital account transactions, net	–140
Financial Account	
U.S.-owned assets abroad, excluding financial derivatives	–140,465
Foreign-owned assets in the United States, excluding financial derivatives	305,736
Financial derivatives, net	50,804
Net errors and omissions	162,008

Figure 10.7: Abbreviated Balance of Payments Statement for the United States

Source: Adapted from Bureau of Economic Analysis, "U.S. International Transactions Accounts Data" (September 15, 2011), accessed at www.bea.gov/international/bp_web/simple.cfm?anon=71& table_id=1&area_id=3.

Arabia to Pakistan during the 2010 floods would belong under the current account or as a current transfer.[6] Trade balance statements refer to the current account. A surplus or deficit means a trade surplus or deficit. Map 10.1 displays the current account balances of various countries.

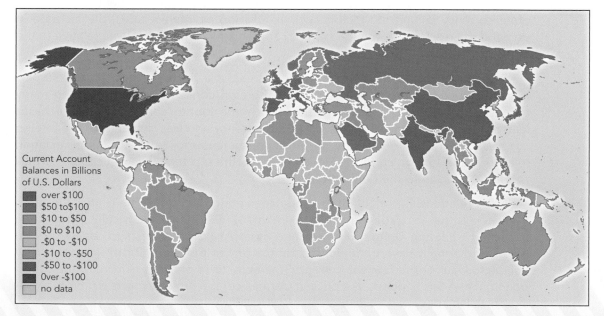

Current Account Balances in Billions of U.S. Dollars
- over $100
- $50 to$100
- $10 to $50
- $0 to $10
- -$0 to -$10
- -$10 to -$50
- -$50 to -$100
- Over -$100
- no data

Map 10.1: **Current Account Balances Globally**
The current account catalogues trade in merchandise, services, income, and current transfers.

In contrast, the capital account contains capital transfers, nonproduced assets, and nonfinancial assets. Typically, not much activity takes place in the capital account.

More activity can be found in the financial account. The account tracks direct investments, portfolio investments, and other financial assets. This includes buying bonds or stocks, and foreign direct investment such as buying a factory or an existing company.

Ideally, the balance of payments would balance the activity in the current account with activity in the capital and financial account. Compilers of the balance of payment statement typically cannot acquire all of the information needed to finalize the statement. The incomplete information may be due to unreported activity, timing problems, or simple mistakes in filling out forms. To make sure the statement balances, net errors and omissions are added.

The final item on the balance of statements is reserves and related items, or the represents reserves held by official governmental authorities. The reserve currency refers to the currency most commonly held in reserve accounts. Most commonly, countries hold the U.S. dollar in reserve.

TRADE DEFICITS

Trade consists of exports and imports. *Exports* are goods or services that are shipped from a home country and sold in a foreign market. Goods or services shipped from a foreign country into the home market are *imports*.

> A trade deficit exists when a country imports more than it exports.

Depending on the relationship of exports to imports, a country experiences a trade surplus or a deficit. A country can have a trade surplus or deficit overall, or the trade relationship between a pair of two countries can lead to a deficit or surplus between just those two actors. A **trade deficit** exists when a country imports more than it exports. In that case, local consumers are spending the local currency on imported goods. These goods all have to be initially purchased in the currency of the country of origin, which leads to increased demand for the foreign currency rather than the domestic currency. Barring activity by one or both of the governments, or possibly other currency influencing factors such as inflation or interest rates, the increase in demand will result in the foreign currency appreciating or rising in value relative to the domestic currency.

A country with more exports than imports enjoys a **trade surplus**. A trade surplus has the opposite effect of a trade deficit. Foreign consumers are purchasing many domestically produced goods using the local, home country currency. Local purchases lead to increased demand for the domestic currency and less demand for the foreign currency. The resulting pressure on the domestic currency leads to an appreciation relative to the foreign currency. Figure 10.8 lists the top ten trade deficit and surplus nations in relation to the United States.

Trade relationships affect international marketing decisions. The United Kingdom traditionally has a trade deficit with Germany. Germany historically focuses on exporting while the United Kingdom and other Anglo countries such as the United States traditionally have trade deficits.[7] In the United Kingdom, British exporters may decide to wait for the German currency (the *euro*) to appreciate relative to the British *pound*. When this happens, the price in Germany of the British exports will drop, which in turn will increase export levels.

Trade Surplus (U.S. dollars)	Trade Deficit (U.S. dollars)
1. Hong Kong (17.6 billion)	1. China (29.5 billion)
2. Netherlands (16.2 billion)	2. Mexico (5.3 billion)
3. Australia (11.6 billion)	3. Japan (4.9 billion)
4. United Arab Emirates (10.6 billion)	4. Germany (3.6 billion)
5. Belgium (7.8 billion)	5. Nigeria (2.4 billion)
6. Singapore (6.6 billion)	6. Ireland (2.4 billion)
7. Brazil (6.1 billion)	7. Russia (2.2 billion)
8. Panama (4.1 billion)	8. Venezuela (1.8 billion)
9. Turkey (3.43 billion)	9. Saudi Arabia (1.6 billion)
10. Chile (3.41 billion)	10. Italy (1.5 billion)

Figure 10.8: Top Ten Trade Deficit and Surplus Nations With the United States

Source: Adapted from Daniel Workman, "Top 10 Export Trade Surpluses by Country 2009" (April 16, 2010), accessed at www.suite101.com/content/top-10-us-export-trade-surpluses-by-country-2009-a226355; and from "Top Ten Countries With Which the U.S. Has a Trade Deficit: For the Month of July 2011," Foreign Trade, U.S. Census Bureau, accessed at www.census.gov/foreign-trade/top/dst/current/deficit.html.

INFLATION

Inflation occurs when the price of goods and services increase. Inflation affects whether a currency will strengthen or weaken. Rates of inflation vary by country and are partly a result of supply and demand for a currency. Price increases within a country are not always accompanied by salary increases in that same country. For consumers, this means that goods and services become more expensive as inflation rises. As a result, governments often take steps to control inflation by manipulating the currency supply in a country. Governmental spending and taxes influence currency supply and demand indirectly. Officials can take steps using these tools when needed.

> Inflation occurs when the price of goods and services increase.

In other cases, governmental leaders conclude they can help an economy by increasing the supply of money. In these cases, a federal reserve or a national bank will introduce more money in the system to increase supply for the domestic currency. Currency values move in response to inflation, both current and predicted. Inflation that is expected in the future weakens the purchasing power of a currency, and the exchange rate will reflect that weakness. In India, year-to-year inflation was 10.5% in June 2010, which meant that, on average, the price of all goods rose 10.5% as compared to the previous year. The price of milk went up approximately 1.8 *rupees* to 29.4 *rupees* per container.[8] The price increase has the most profound effect on bottom-of-the-pyramid consumers. The result was that inflation increased pressure on the *rupee*, which led to concerns about currency weakness.

Inflation concerns international marketers because it influences price. A company in a country such as the United States with a low inflation rate may encounter difficulties when payments are delayed from a firm in a nation with a higher inflation rate. In essence, the U.S. company will be paid with a "cheaper" currency. The R2C

Corporation, makers of the popular Thomas the Train Engine toys, experienced lower profits in 2010 due to currency inflation in key markets.[9]

INTEREST RATES

Interest rates are defined as the percentage rate charged or paid for the use of money. The amount of interest charged by lenders relates to currency demand. Rising or lower interest rates influence the tug-of-war between the weakening and strengthening of a currency's value. Many consumers have an interest rate attached to a savings or checking account. Governmental debt or bonds also earn interest, and typically the governmental interest rate determines the interest rates offered by other lenders within the country. Countries with high interest rates, all else being equal, will experience a higher rate of foreign investment in bonds and other instruments linked to this interest rate. The result can be an increased demand for the currency.[10]

Inflation also affects interest rates. The *Fisher effect* states that the nominal or stated interest rate of a country is equal to the actual interest rate plus the rate of inflation. As inflation reduces the value of a currency, interest rates need to reflect both elements. The formula for the Fisher effect can be found in Figure 10.9.

Nominal rate = real rate + inflation
Nominal interest rate in Mexico = 5%
Inflation rate in Mexico = 2%
5 = x + 2
3 = x
Real interest rate in Mexico = 3%

Figure 10.9: Fisher Effect Formula

Overall, interest rates serve an important role in international marketing. When borrowing internationally, interest rates set both the cost of much debt and the return on savings. By influencing currency demand, the difference in interest rates between countries will typically be offset by the differences in exchange rates.

INTERNATIONAL INCIDENT ///

Your company has started to actively conduct business in Venezuela. The country, while an attractive market in many ways, maintains strict limits on currency conversions. In practical terms, you are unable to transfer your earnings from Venezuelan *strong bolivars* into the *euros* needed to repatriate the money to your Belgian headquarters. Your local partner does not support the Venezuelan government and tells you about a currency black market where you can exchange the money. While the black market operator charges a higher rate to cover the increased risk, it would give you the opportunity to move the revenue out of the country. Do you politely thank your friend for the advice but turn down the offer? Do you consider the offer? The Venezuelan government has begun taking over foreign companies with little to no compensation. Does that affect your decision?

LEARNING OBJECTIVE #3:

How do the law of one price and purchasing power parity affect international marketing activities?

The Law of One Price and Purchasing Power Parity

Anyone traveling to a foreign country realizes that exchange rates do not always link to what can be purchased with a country's currency. Textiles may be relatively less expensive, while electronic goods may be relatively more expensive. These differences are contrary to the law of one price. The law of one price states that identical products should be priced identically in different markets, once the price is converted to the same currency in each market. Consider a staple product such as bread. The price for bread in Poland may be 1.5 *zloty*. In Belarus, the same loaf of bread may cost 1,500 Belarus *rubles*. If the exchange rate is 1 *zloty* equals 1,000 *rubles*, then the products actually have the same price. The apparent difference is due to currency differences. Figure 10.10 provides details.

| Price of Bread Poland = 1.5 *zloty* |
| Price of Bread Belarus = 1,500 *rubles* |
| Exchange rate: 1 zloty = 1,000 *rubles* |
| Price of bread in Poland converted to Belarus *rubles* |
| 1.5 * 1000 = 1500 *rubles* |

Figure 10.10: Example of Law of One Price

Now consider if the price of the bread was 1,500 *rubles* in Belarus and 2 *zloty* in Poland. Using the same exchange rate, the price of bread in Poland can be converted to Belarus *rubles*, as shown in Figure 10.11. The resulting price is 3,000 *rubles*. This means that the price of bread, once currency differences are accounted for, is higher in Poland than it is in Belarus. In other words, the *zloty* does not go as far in Poland as the *ruble* does in Belarus, at least for a loaf of bread.

| Price of Bread Poland = 2 *zloty* |
| Price of Bread Belarus = 1,500 *rubles* |
| Exchange rate: 1 zloty = 1,500 *rubles* |
| Price of bread in Poland converted to Belarus *rubles* |
| 2 * 1,500 = 3,000 *rubles* |

Figure 10.11: Example of Law of One Price Not Applying

PURCHASING POWER

The law of one price often does not apply. A soda or a candy bar or bus rides all frequently are more or less expensive in other countries due to purchasing power differences. Purchasing power refers to the amount of goods a unit of currency can purchase. If hypothetically 1 *euro* could be exchanged for 1 Japanese *yen*, this would not mean that the currencies would purchase the same amount of a good, a bowl of rice, for example, in the respective home markets. Purchasing power reflects the strengths of different currencies in terms of their abilities to purchase goods. Marketers are concerned with purchasing power because these differences influence costs and prices across markets. The Big Mac Index is released periodically by *The Economist* magazine. The index compares the price of the Big Mac (or a comparable sandwich) in all of McDonald's markets. The price of the burger should be relatively the same, but the Big Mac Index indicates otherwise. Price differences may be due to different costs for the various components of the burger, unequal labor costs, increased or decreased demand for the sandwich, cost of transportation of goods, consumer psychology within a country, or governmental activities, particularly taxes on imports.

PURCHASING POWER PARITY

Purchasing power measures using a single item or product can be flawed. Specific product features or issues surrounding that product might explain the unique high or low relative cost. Instead, the price for a basket of goods can be used to identify differences in purchasing power. This approach is referred to as purchasing power parity.

The Organization for Economic Co-operation and Development (OECD) creates more exhaustive measure of purchasing power using the prices for a basket of more than one thousand goods and services. Figure 10.12 displays the similarities and differences in the ranking for the OECD and Big Mac indices.

Purchasing power can drastically influence costs and revenues. Understanding purchasing power can lead to more effective methods for comparing costs, prices,

The OECD and the Big Mac Index		
	OECD PPP[a]	Big Mac Index
Top Five	Japan (1)	Norway (1)
	Switzerland (2)	Switzerland (2)
	France (3)	Brazil (3)
	The Netherlands (4)	Euro Area (4)
	Sweden (5)	Canada (5)
Bottom Five	South Africa (36)	Philippines (21)
	India (37)	Malaysia (22)
	Turkey (38)	Thailand (23)
	Iceland (39)	China (24)
	Russia (40)	Hong Kong (25)

Figure 10.12: A Comparison of the Weakest and Strongest Currencies

Source: Adapted from "Consumer Prices (MEI)," OECD (October 6, 2011), accessed at http://stats.oecd.org/Index.aspx?querytype=view&queryname=221; and "When the Chips Are Down," The Economist (July 22, 2010), accessed at www.economist.com/node/16646178?story_id=16646178.

Note: a. PPP stands for purchasing power parity.

and sales across countries. The process at least partially removes the role of currency exchange from the comparison. During the Mexican currency crisis of 1994, the amount of Mexican *pesos* that could be bought by 1 U.S. dollar dropped 37% from December 20, 1994, to January 5, 1995. The drop in currency value affected consumption, but it did not decline by 37%. By considering the actual purchasing power of the currency instead of its value relative to the U.S. dollar, companies were able to maintain a more realistic perspective on the market.

Purchasing power parity scores can be used as another way to calculate price. Instead of focusing on established currency exchange rates, marketers can instead use purchasing power parity to convert to an appropriate price for the new market. Purchasing power parity scores can be treated as a form of currency conversion.

Price of Bread Poland = 2 *zloty*
Price of Bread Belarus = 1,500 *rubles*
Purchasing Power Difference: 3 *zloty* = 3,000 *rubles*
1 *zloty* = 1,000 *rubles*
Price of bread in Poland converted to Belarus *rubles* using purchasing power conversion
2 * 1,000 = 2,000 *rubles*

Figure 10.13: Purchasing Price Parity Example

Consider the example of the price of bread in Poland and Belarus. If 3 *zloty* purchase the same basket of goods in Poland as 3,000 *rubles* do in Belarus, the ratio of 3 *zloty* to 3000 *rubles* can be used to establish an exchange rate. If bread costs 1,500 *rubles* in Belarus and 2 *zloty* in Poland, the difference in terms of purchasing power parity is 500 *rubles*. Using the exchange rate, as in Figure 10.13, the difference is 1,500 *rubles*. A company considering selling bread in Belarus would be well served to consider the purchasing power parity price of bread when entering the market. Setting the price only based on exchange rates might price the bread out of the market.

Governmental Activity and International Finance

Currency and currency exchange are part of the foundation of an economy. Consequently, governments often play active roles in currency management. Governments can be viewed as referees or even the commissioner of the tug-of-war contest over currency values. Almost all global currencies are created and backed by the government in which they are used. This allows governments to play the most central role in the control of currency value. Through central banks or federal reserves, governments have an almost limitless supply of money. When a government needs more currency, more can be created, which increases the supply of the money and can lead to inflation. Governments can also purchase large amounts of foreign monies or domestic currencies. These purchasing actions increase demand for the currency.

Consider a situation in which the European Central Bank believes that the *euro* is too strong relative to the *pound*. This may limit investments in Germany and other European countries from the United Kingdom because the weak *pound* increases costs for members of the European Union. In an attempt to move the currency value, the European Central Bank increases the number or supply of *euros*. A higher supply of any good, even currency, should lead to a decrease in price. Basically, governments often attempt to influence the tug-of-war and the overall value of currencies.

Governments take steps to influence the value of a domestic currency; however, non-currency-related motives often drive these actions. Governments often increase the supply of money within a country to help spur economic growth. The increased supply of domestic money can weaken the currency on the global market. During the Irish economic downturn of 2009, the Irish government accused the United Kingdom of expanding the money supply in an effort to devalue the *pound*. The devaluation caused economic problems in the Irish Republic.[11] Marketers in both countries that followed the currency activity were better able to predict the resulting economic issues, which might lessen the effects of the governmental action taken by the U.K.

CURRENCY REGIMES

Governments also actively set up controlling structures or regimes around domestic currencies. Officials decide which regime to use and then employ governmental instruments to maintain the regime. The type of regime influences the manner in which the currency exchange rate moves and the activities that governments take to maintain that regime. This movement and these actions in turn affect marketing activities. Broadly, the structures can be classified into two different methods for establishing and monitoring the domestic currency's exchange rate: floating exchange rate and fixed exchange rate regimes.

Floating Exchange Rates

The first type of exchange rate regime, a **flexible** or **floating exchange rate**, occurs in circumstances in which the value of the currency is allowed to respond freely to market forces. Forces of supply and demand apply. Governments may act to influence the tug-of-war and may even have stated goals regarding currency value, but governments do not set hard limits regarding how far the rope can be pulled in one direction or the other.

The float allows the currency to move in value. When there is increased purchasing of a currency by another currency, such as more *euros* being bought by pounds, the

LEARNING OBJECTIVE #4:

How do governmental activities influence international finance?

VIDEO LINK 10.1:
Banks and Debt

Floating exchange rate occurs in circumstances in which the value of the currency is allowed to respond freely to market forces.

exchange rate changes and the value of the currency being purchased will increase. The rise in the value of one currency relative to another is *appreciation*. In contrast, if the number of purchases of one currency by another decrease, representing a drop in demand, the value of the currency being purchased goes down. The decrease in the value of one currency relative to another is *depreciation*.

Beyond demand, supply also affects the tug-of-war or currency value in a flexible exchange regime. If the central bank or a similar governmental institution increases the supply of a currency in the world market, the increased supply should result in currency depreciation across the board. If the government instead takes steps to purchase its own currency to remove it from the currency market, supply decreases and the currency appreciates. In September 2010, Japan increased the supply of *yen* in order to depreciate the currency. The value of the *yen* decreased by 3.1% against the dollar and 3.4% against the *euro*.[12]

Fixed Exchange Rates

> The other method governments can use to control the tug-of-war is called a fixed or pegged regime.

The other method governments can use to control the tug-of-war is called a **fixed** or **pegged regime**. Under this regime, a predetermined band or par value establishes the value of a currency. The government sets limits as to how far the rope can move in either direction during the tug-of-war. These limits can be thought of as lines in the sand. As long as the movement is between the lines, the government does not act. If it appears that the rope is going to move too far in either direction, the government takes aggressive steps to ensure that the currency does not move outside the designated range.

Supply and demand still apply to currencies that are pegged, but the governments act more aggressively in response to potential movements in value. The movements may occur in the black markets that typically spring up for controlled currencies due to the appeal of uncontrolled movements. Central banks intervene in the currency market through purchasing of currency or creation of more currency in response to the potential for the currency to no longer maintain par value.

Revaluation and Devaluation

In some cases, the government cannot prevent the rope from moving past the line in the sand. Think of the government as one person all alone on one side of the rope while everyone else gangs up and pulls on the other end. Even the largest of governments typically cannot keep the rope from moving past the band. In these cases, the central bank will set a new par value or line in the sand. *Revaluation* refers to a government increase in the par value of a currency under a fixed-rate regime. *Devaluation* refers to a government decrease in the par value. In late 2010, the Vietnam currency, the *dong*, faced aggressive activity in the black market for the currency. In response, the Vietnamese central government devalued the *dong* by 2% against the U.S. dollar setting the new exchange rate at 18,932 dong for 1 U.S. dollar.[13]

Analysis

Advantages and disadvantages exist for both exchange regimes. For a fixed exchange regime, marketers can be mostly sure of short-term stability. The value of the currency should stay within the prescribed band. The risk with a fixed exchange regime lies in the underlying supply and demand features of currency. If the par value becomes too disconnected from the demand or the supply for the currency, the peg can be "broken." This occurs when the central bank for a government can no longer maintain a peg. Think of it as the government falling down while pulling on the rope. The currency can wildly change in value, leading to drastic losses in value in some case, which can cause significant economic problems.

Possibly the most famous example of a peg being broken happened on Black Wednesday, September 16, 1992, to the prestigious British *pound sterling*. The United Kingdom had entered into the European exchange rate mechanism, which pegged the sterling to various other European currencies that also were part of the agreement. Being unable to maintain the peg, the government left the exchange rate mechanism on this date.[14] The rumor at the time was that George Soros, the famous currency speculator, was responsible for breaking the *pound sterling*. Not only did he potentially break the peg, but also he possibly made $1 billion for his efforts.[15]

For a flexible exchange regime, the opposite concerns exist. The float tends to be protected from extreme fluctuations in value. Instead, daily market forces tend to move the currency up or down. Short-term risks are relatively high, but over the long term the currency should remain relatively stable. Flexible exchange regimes cannot be broken, but tend to be far more difficult to predict in the short term. For example, while the overall trend for the Canadian dollar has been appreciating versus the dollar, with the value of the currency rising by 50% from 2002 to 2008, on any day the value of the Canadian dollar may drop.[16] Predicting the long-term trend is easier than predicting day-to-day changes. Figure 10.14 provides some names of fixed and flexible regime countries.

Fixed Regimes	Flexible Regimes
Belize	Algeria
Bolivia	Brazil
Brunei	Egypt
China	*euro* Zone
Ecuador	India
Hong Kong	Japan
Iran	Kenya
Lebanon	Mexico
Lesotho	Nigeria
Malawi	Philippines
Panama	Sudan
Rwanda	Switzerland
Syria	Thailand
Turkmenistan	United Kingdom
Uzbekistan	United States

Figure 10.14: Sample of Countries With Fixed and Flexible Regimes

Source: Adapted from "Annual Report on Exchange Arrangements and Exchange Restrictions 2008," International Monetary Fund.

Global Currency Institutions

Due to the importance that governments place on currency and currency values, throughout history governments have banded together to stabilize currency values. The history of currency controls and regimes continues to be a key area where politics affects marketing activities. Within the United States, some citizens and politicians have recently made calls to return the country to the gold standard, the historical system for valuing money.[17] A brief review of the recent history of currency provides the background needed to understand why the current system exists. By better understanding the history of the system, marketers can better predict potential future changes and comprehend the historical roots of governmental actions. Figure 10.15 lists key points in the history of currency exchange.

Pre-1914	Gold standard pegged to the British sterling.
1914 to 1944	Unstable period with most currencies floating.
1944 to 1971	Gold standard pegged to the U.S. dollar.
1971 to Present	Major world currencies float with some emerging markets pegged.

Figure 10.15: Highlights of Currency Exchange Control

Before 1914, gold was typically the underlying medium of exchange between countries. Most countries pegged their currencies to a certain weight of gold or to the British sterling, the dominant global currency. The sterling was convertible to gold at the Bank of England, and many other countries held sterling for that reason. By the time World War I started, it was clear that the Bank of England did not actually own enough gold to cover the obligations on all of the sterling in circulation, and countries stopped using the gold standard based on the British sterling.

The period from World War I to the end of World War II was marked by currency instability. The majority of currencies floated, and the global depression of the 1930s made the return to the gold standard not feasible. Many European countries then used currency manipulation to spur economic growth during the 1930s and to attack their enemies during World War II.

After World War II, the Allies agreed that steps should be taken to ensure currency stability during the postwar period. The various governments met in Breton Woods, New Hampshire, in 1944 to deal with these issues. The meeting created the International Monetary Fund and the International Bank for Reconstruction and Development, which is also known as the World Bank. These institutions established separate but related missions.

The primary responsibility of the International Monetary Fund is currency stability. The organization provides short-term loans in response to currency crises and works diligently to monitor currency activities. Loans from the International Monetary Fund may be denominated in *special drawing rights*, the value of which reflects a basket of the member country currencies. The World Bank concentrates on long-term development. Initially, the Bank gave loans and grants to European countries to fund reconstruction. More recently, the Bank's focus has shifted to less- and least-developed countries.

The United States does not rely on the gold standard for currency valuation.

The Bretton Woods agreement also established a global currency system. The signatories agreed to fix the value of their currency in terms of either the U.S. dollar or a certain weight of gold. In turn, the U.S. dollar was always convertible to $35 per one ounce of gold (the "gold standard" that politicians refer to). This American gold standard stayed in place until the early 1970s, when forces put pressure on the peg. The American government had to pay out gold and other reserves to protect the peg but eventually was unable to continue this activity broadly because of an insufficient amount of gold being held in U.S. reserves. The system collapsed and the U.S. dollar and many other countries moved to a flexible exchange regime.

The International Monetary Fund continues to actively monitor currency activities. In 2010, Greece faced country-level economic concerns. The currency for Greece is the *euro*. A disconnect ensued between the unique economic events within Greece and the value of the *euro*. The resulting stress on the *euro* threatened the viability of the currency and led many to suggest that Greece should leave the Euro zone.

In response, the International Monetary Fund took steps to stabilize both the Greek economy and the value of the *euro*. A loan of €110 billion ($143 billion) plus strong recommendations for governmental actions together helped to stabilize the situation.[18] Tourism makes up almost one fifth of the Greek economy.[19] Marketers in this industry would obviously be concerned with currency and overall financial stability in the country. In this case, marketers would carefully watch International Monetary Fund actions before determining whether to leave the country or to hope to ride out the instability and maintain a position in the market.

Managing Currency Risk

Effective strategic international marketing management leads to revenues and in most cases profits. Currency fluctuations can wipe out those profits. Costs can increase within the country, or if the costs of manufacturing the good are in a separate currency, costs can go up while the value of the currency goes down. As a company's activity in a country increases, the exposure to currency risk increases. A 10% drop in the value of a currency causes problems when a company has revenues of $200,000 in the country. A 10% drop in the value of a currency is a catastrophe when revenues are $20 million (a $20,000 loss versus a $2 million loss). Successful international marketers take steps to limit monetary risks.

PREDICTING CURRENCY RISK

The best international marketing strategies can fail due to uncontrollable currency changes. Successful prediction of currency risk in itself can increase firm profits. One common way to predict currency risk involves consideration of how the currency market perceives different currencies. *The Wall Street Journal* and *The Financial Times* typically list two different exchange rates. The first rate listed is the spot rate, or the exchange rate with a guarantee of two-day delivery. The second rate or set of rates are forward rates. **Forward rates** are the exchange rates for the delivery of the currency at a specific time in the future, which is typically 30, 90, and 180 days using what are called *forward contracts*.

Usually differences exist between the spot and the forward rates. The differences result from market predictions of future currency movement. A forward rate lower than the spot rate indicates the presence of a *discount*. A forward rate that is larger than the spot rate is called a *premium*. The efficient market theory posits that in cases of complete openness and knowledge, exchange rates would reflect this knowledge, market predictions would be accurate, and speculation would not lead to profit. A thirty-day forward contract, according to this theory, would perfectly predict the actual exchange rate in thirty days. Research on the topic fails to find evidence of this effect.[20] Instead, speculators attempt to make money in exchange markets by taking advantage of a misalignment between the spot rate and the forward rate.

Debt ratings offer a second country-specific predictor of currency risk. **Sovereignty debt ratings** assign a score that represents the chance that a country will default on governmental debt. The ratings assess the overall fiscal stability of a country, which directly ties into currency stability. Moody's and Standard & Poor's provide two of the most commonly used sovereignty ratings. Much like ratings for corporate debt, a country with a AAA sovereignty rating has less risk than a country with a lower rating

Country	Rating
Argentina	B–
Belgium	AA+
Canada	AAA
Colombia	BBB
Fiji	A
Honduras	B
Malaysia	A+
Pakistan	B–
Qatar	AA
Spain	AA
Uganda	B+
United Kingdom	AAA
United States	AA+
Venezuala	BB–
Vietnam	BB+

Figure 10.16: Examples of Standard & Poor's Sovereignty Ratings

Source: Adapted from "Sovereigns Ratings List," Standard & Poor's, accessed at www.standardand poors.com/ratings/sovereigns/ratings-list/en/us? sectorName=null&subSectorCode=39.

VIDEO LINK 10.2:
Global Markets and Sovereign Debt

such as AA or BBB. A drop in rating can change the behavior of the global currency market and lead to more selling of the country's currency on the global market. Figure 10.16 provides the sovereignty ratings for select countries.

For international marketers, the importance of sovereignty ratings includes guiding decisions whether to enter new markets. The lower the probability that a currency will devalue, the lower the risk of conducting business in that country. Currency values affect sales prices, valuations assigned to inventories, the costs of marketing activities such as advertising and promotions, and eventual bottom-line profits.

HEDGING CURRENCY RISK

Currency risk can be lessened through various hedging techniques. **Hedging** refers to any financial process that lessens financial risk. In the context of currency risk, hedging involves purchasing various financial instruments. Forward contracts can be used to lock in an exchange rate for thirty, sixty, or ninety days. If a company has a set amount of profit it wishes to convert within a set period, a forward contract for that amount can be purchased guaranteeing the exchange rate.

Companies may also purchase currency futures contracts. **Futures contracts** allow the company to sell or buy a certain amount of a foreign currency at a set exchange rate on a specific date. Futures and forward contracts are similar but differ in two important ways. Forward contracts are for specific transactions, so they are customized to specific amounts. Futures contracts are for standardized amounts. Forward contracts, while listed for thirty-, sixty-, and ninety-day contracts, can be purchased for a set date. Futures contracts have a small number of maturation dates, four typically, in a given year. The advantage of futures contracts is that only a percentage of the contract needs to be presented to purchase it. This allows the money that would be needed to purchase a forward contract to be used for other business needs.

International marketers use hedging and futures contracts to ensure the success of a marketing effort. Should a Thai company ship one thousand units of a product to Saudi Arabia to be sold at a value of 40 Thai *baht* per unit, these contracts help guarantee that payment in the Saudi Arabian *riyal* will equal those 40 *baht*.

The Basics of International Finance Funding

When entering new markets, companies require capital. Capital will be required to set up office space, establish distribution channels, purchase warehouse inventory, and fund any other long-term purchases designed to support activities in a new country. Often that capital comes from internal sources of funds. When the new business is structured as a subsidiary, the funding comes from the parent company in the form of loans or transfers of funds.

Several additional sources of financing may be used. When the source of expansion capital will be equity, companies can seek investors at the three dominant exchanges in London, Tokyo, and New York. Frankfurt and Hong Kong are also hubs for financial activity. In each of these centers, shares of stock are sold to raise capital for the venture.

When the company wishes to use debt to expand operations, bonds may be sold in a variety of markets. Two types of international bonds can be issued. Bonds issued outside of a country but are denominated in a currency different from the country of purchase are called *Eurobonds*. A bond for a company or country that is sold outside the home country and that is denominated in the currency of the country of issue is a *foreign bond*.

| U.S. Agency for International Development |
| Asian Development Bank |
| African Development Bank |
| European Bank of Reconstruction and Development |
| European Investment Bank |
| Inter-American Development Bank |
| Overseas Private Investment Corporations |
| U.S. Export-Import Bank |

Figure 10.17: Partial List of Regional Developmental and National Banks

Source: Adapted from Suk H. Kim and H. Kim Seung, *Global Corporate Finance*, 6th ed. (London: Blackwell Publishing, 2006).

When internal funding through internal company loans or sales of common stock is not sufficient for the expansion, external sources of funds may be sought. Debt may be borrowed locally. If necessary, the parent company can provide a guarantee in order to achieve approval for the loan. When local or international banks are not sufficient, developmental banks may also be a source of funding. The World Bank is one place to obtain funding. Regional and national developmental banks such as the Inter-American Development Bank, the African Development Bank, or the U.S. Export-Import Bank can also provide funding. Figure 10.17 lists some regional and national developmental banks.

FINANCING ONGOING TRADE OPERATIONS

The transfer of either goods or currency is at the core of foreign trading. **Terms of payment** refers to the agreed-upon payment in return for the goods or services. While currency is the dominant payment form, other methods can also be used. In the case of cash terms of payment, the cash can be COD (cash on delivery of the goods) or it can be CBD (cash before delivery of the goods). In many cases, the seller provides credit to facilitate transactions.[21] Negotiating credit terms is an important part of international pricing.

A unique aspect of international pricing occurs when two companies and countries engage in **countertrade**, where goods are traded or exchanged without the use of hard currency. The four forms of countertrade include

- barter,
- buy-back,
- compensation deals, and
- counter-purchases.

Barter involves the direct exchange of goods between two companies involved in a transaction. If Honest Tea were to trade finished tea products made in the United States for raw ingredients from an African nation without cash changing hands, a barter arrangement has been reached.

Buy-back countertrades are agreements to sell one set of goods and services used in the production of products for another set of goods and services. A price for each will first be negotiated. The seller agrees to buy some of the goods and services being produced as part of the payment system. Should a South Korean DVD manufacturer sell production equipment to Thailand and agree to buy finished DVD systems from the company in Thailand as part of the payment price, a buy-back agreement exists.

Compensation deals include both cash payments and exchanges of materials. A Chinese company requires lithium cobalt oxide to manufacture lithium batteries. The company could purchase the ingredient from a supplier and make payment in the form of finished batteries and cash.

Counter-purchases require two contracts. The first specifies the selling price for the item. The second spells out a period during which the buyer is able to resell the item in combination with other goods and then repay the original seller with the proceeds. Counter-purchases are also called offset trades and are often made with firms in less- or least-developed nations.

Countertrade benefits various countries by allowing countries with lower levels of foreign exchange to attain improved technologies. When Russia trades oil for automobiles, the Russian economy benefits from the technologies in the vehicles that are being exchanged for an abundant resource.[22]

The challenges of pricing in countertrade arrangements include finding common ground on the prices of the items to be exchanged, the exchange rate or monetary value assigned to the goods, and the volume of goods sent to each party. Individual company leaders, such as the automobile manufacturers selling to Russia, may feel constrained by the terms of the countertrade.

The Russian economy could benefit from the technologies in the automobiles that are exchanged for an abundant resource, oil.

INTERNAL PRICING

Due to the wide variety of companies engaged in partnerships, joint ventures, integrated distribution systems, licensure arrangements, and other intra- or intercompany connections, managers in these organizations seek to reduce costs and lower the impact of governmental restrictions. *Transfer prices* help achieve these goals. In intracompany pricing, a commodity sold by one subsidiary of a company to another section in a second country features a set price that bypasses taxes and tariffs by simply shifting funds internally. Many governments have become aware of these programs and have introduced methods to collect taxes by claiming unreported profits.

Sustainability advocates increasingly push for shadow pricing for internal financing. *Shadow pricing* means that the opportunity and environmental costs are included in prices, such as water or air pollution. Developing country officials might complain that the environmental costs, especially in terms of carbon output, of foreign manufacturing should be included in assessing price.

Companies also may move money to certain countries that have low to no tax. Called *tax havens*, increased international attention focuses on stopping corporations from avoiding taxes.

International Finance and International Marketing

As the world of commerce becomes increasingly based on global interactions, the role finance plays in international marketing has grown in importance. Any company seeking to sell goods in other countries will be faced with finding ways to integrate a financial system with the marketing program. Failure to do so may lead to the frustration of finding customers, contacting them, successfully generating sales, but then not making profits due to financial problems rather than problems with the marketing program.

To fully develop an international marketing program that accounts for financial concerns involves adjustments to all parts of the marketing mix. Financial issues affect markets, products, prices, places (distribution systems), and promotions. This section provides a review of some of the major concerns.

LEARNING OBJECTIVE #5:

What are the relationships between international finance and the elements of the marketing mix?

MARKETS

Target markets in other countries may be skewed due to currency changes. Weaker purchasing power may shift the price-value relationship and might result in a need to target a different segment. For example, inflation in a country can limit the ability of consumers to purchase houses. Suppliers of building materials would be noticeably affected by increasing costs and prices. Inflation in Brazil during the 1990s was severe. Those seeking to build homes would purchase materials as soon as they could afford them, because waiting would result in a higher price for each item. The net result was sets of neighborhoods with partially built houses.

Currency values influence the selection of market segments to target in foreign markets. Rapid changes in currency values often lead to reconsideration of market segmentation. Marketers of necessities are more likely to adjust package sizes in response to fluctuating currencies. Companies offering sundries tend to shift sales to more stable currency markets or use other means to ensure profits.

Price sensitivity defines bottom-of-the-pyramid consumers, which makes this segment particularly vulnerable to currency fluctuations. Marketers are hesitant to increase prices, because the capacity to consume largely drives demand for bottom-of-the-pyramid consumers. With small margins, currency changes may lead marketers to stop targeting the bottom-of-the-pyramid segments.

International financial issues also influence access to debt and capital markets. In many cases, limits are placed on the amount of foreign currency that can be exchanged in a country. In those cases, local sources of financing become necessary. The lack of sophistication in local financial markets and the inability of foreign companies to access those markets may reduce the feasibility of entering a market or cause struggles after entering.

PRODUCTS

Price and quality drive perceptions of products. Positioning relative to competitors depends on effective management of these perceptions. Purchasing power differences can make positioning difficult to manage when entering a market. To maintain a sufficient level of profit, company leaders may need to raise prices. The new price leads to repositioning, which must be reflected in the rest of the marketing mix, including promotional activities.

Access to financing constrains the ability of marketers to research new products within a country. New product development can be expensive and often requires an injection of capital. In essence, it may not be possible to develop and sell some products in foreign markets due to financial constraints. An investigation of financial circumstances should precede any decision to enter a new market.

PRICES

Financial conditions strongly affect international pricing programs. Currency exchange and credit influence the prices of products and of the resources needed to produce and distribute those products. The marketing team works in concert with financial experts to make sure prices can be set to achieve company goals.

Fluctuations in currency create one marketing challenge. Currencies may change in value unpredictably and quickly. Argentina recently experienced a major currency crisis. On January 7, 2002, the government devalued the country's currency, the Argentine *peso*, by 29%.[23] The *peso* continued to devalue in world markets for the rest of the year. Any company conducting business in Argentina needed to make adjustments to try to maintain profits. Firms that positioned products based on price were strongly affected.

| Exchange Rate Fluctuations |
| Price Escalations |
| Administered Prices |

Figure 10.18: International Finance Factors That Affect Pricing

Inflation constitutes another of the major threats to international pricing programs, especially when the currency for the exporter's country has a manageable rate of inflation but the host country's rate is high. When this situation occurs, a product may be sold at a price that does reflect the item's true value. In addition, the basic components of international finance and the effects of these factors on international pricing, as displayed in Figure 10.18, deserve additional consideration.

Exchange Rate Fluctuations

In the early part of the 2000s, the value of the dollar against the *euro* made purchases in *euro* zone countries more expensive. When the trade rate was at nearly $1.30 for 1 *euro*, dollar buying power was substantially reduced. American tourists traveling to popular destinations noticed their dollars would not buy as much. For some, this led to travel to other places. Others purchased fewer items while visiting places such as Spain, France, or Italy.

By the end of the decade, economic circumstances in Europe resulted in an exchange rate of less than $1.00 for 1 *euro*, thereby increasing dollar buying power in *euro* zone countries. American travelers were enticed by marketing campaigns noting that going to Europe could be visited at "bargain" prices. When pricing items, exchange rates affect what people buy and the methods marketers use to reach them.

Price Escalations

As a product moves from one country to another, the costs of transportation, middlemen charges and markups, tariffs, and other expenses cause the price of the item to rise (Figure 10.19). A bottle of Spanish wine may sell in Madrid for the equivalent of $5, yet sell for $10 or more in other countries due to these uncontrollable factors. Price escalations make competing in foreign markets more difficult for many exporters. Many countries seeking to support more open trade will establish foreign trade zones or fee ports in which various tariffs and taxes are not charged, which helps control price escalation in those zones. When a market is large enough to justify the risk and expense, companies may begin manufacturing within the country to avoid some of these costs. Price escalation may be particularly problematic when targeting bottom-of-the-pyramid consumers. Increased costs often put marketers in a position where either the profit margin must be greatly reduced or the product price becomes too high for consumers to afford.

Transportation Costs	Cost of Transporting to the Market
Tariffs	Governmental Fees
Importer Margins	Profit to Cover Process of Importing
Wholesaler Margins	Cost Associated With Inventory Management and Distribution
Retailer Margins	Mark-Up in the Retail Store
Taxes	Value-Added or Other Government Taxes

Figure 10.19: Causes of Price Escalations

Administered Prices

Administered prices are set by individual governments, often in an attempt to weaken foreign competitors by setting prices for an entire market. Critics argue administered prices are simply a form of price fixing, with governmental approval. Some international agreements allow for administered prices, which tends to stabilize trade relationships between countries, even though the lowest prices may not be offered to consumers in any of the nations involved.

Administered prices may also be used for sensitive, high-demand, or essential products. Governments can set the price for rents in densely populated areas or for staple foods such as milk or rice to ensure appropriate access. In some cases, governments do not set the prices. Instead, when a government is the largest purchaser of the item, it can influence the product's price. By being a large purchaser, the government can negotiate a lower price. For instance, the Russian government recently asked for a 15% reduction in HIV drug prices from the pharmaceutical company GlaxoSmithKline.[24]

PLACE (DISTRIBUTION)

Differences in purchasing power lead to different distribution costs. One type of transportation may be more expensive than another in a foreign market. Packaging may also cost more in one market than another.

The ability to distribute or move currency in and out of a country may also be different in various markets. The ability to change the local currency for a foreign currency is called *currency convertibility*. As noted in the opening ArcelorMitall vignettes, many governments limit currency convertibility and some completely forbid it.

PROMOTION

Consumer promotions depend on stable costs and prices. The success of coupons and other similar discounts results from the perception of increased value due to decreased price. Currency fluctuations during a consumer promotion can alter this relationship and decrease the effectiveness of the promotion.

The same applies to trade promotions. Trade promotions aimed at distributors typically consist of discounts. With larger purchases being made, trade promotions may be even more vulnerable to shifts in value due to shifts in exchange rates.

In sum, international finance directly relates to the marketing process. It influences the entire marketing mix and affects the firm's bottom line. Profit, a core component of business activity, can be drastically impacted by international finance issues, especially currency movements. Careful planning and coordination between the marketing team and those in finance are required in order to manage these issues.

Chapter 10: Review and Resources

STRATEGIC IMPLICATIONS //

International marketers face international finance concerns when entering or maintaining a presence in a market. The stability of the local currency will influence the initial decision to enter the market. Unstable currencies may defer entry to a later date. Once in the market, currency control measures will be an important strategic consideration for company leaders. These hedges have costs. The marketing and finance teams must decide whether the currency risk is extreme enough to warrant hedging, or if the company's exposure is large enough to justify the additional costs.

Effectively finding sources of financing as well as balancing debt and equity remainas key strategic issues for international marketers. Equity gained by selling shares of stock relinquishes ownership and some degree of control. Debt has a specific cost. While activity in global markets provides for access to more sources of capital, it does not remove the need to select the best combination of financial instruments.

TACTICAL IMPLICATIONS ///

Hedging currency risk can be complicated. The tactical choices include the types of contracts to buy, the size of the contracts, and timing the maturity of the contracts with the need for the currency. These short-term transactions can become a juggling act. International marketers work with the finance department to ensure effective timing of the flow of money to support marketing transactions.

When the financial instruments are in place, marketing activities can be undertaken. Establishing distribution systems, creating supportive programs such as coupons or premiums, and preparing advertising campaigns will proceed with greater confidence. Understanding when monetary transactions will take place helps the marketing manager understand when the company can expect to receive revenues and when it will render payments to suppliers and others in the target market country.

Product positioning efforts are affected by international finance. The price/quality relationship can be altered by inflation, devaluations of currency, and other shifts in monetary markets. Consequently, the marketing team should remain in constant contact with the finance team in order to be able to adjust to monetary differences and maintain the desired position in the marketplace.

OPERATIONAL IMPLICATIONS ///

Individual employees deal with currency issues on practically a daily basis. International marketers responsible for a specific country or region will normally know the approximate exchange rate without needing to look it up. The exchange rate is used to calculate sales, costs, and profit.

Individual salespeople should be trained in the basics of international finance. Potential customers in other countries are likely to ask about methods of payment and how each side will be protected from currency risk. In essence, these financial concerns represent part of the price to a foreign buyer.

Expatriate employees will require training in the areas of exchange rates and currency fluctuations. These employees will need to adjust to the monetary system in the country to which they are sent. They will be affected by other issues such as the currency in which they receive their salaries and expense reimbursements, and will also be influenced by transaction fees charged to move money back to their home countries.

In essence, every person, from the CEO to the first line person serving in a foreign country, will be better served by having a working understanding of how international finance affects them and their company.

TERMS

currency	trade surplus	sovereignty debt ratings
hard currency	inflation	hedging
soft currency	interest rates	futures contracts
international finance	flexible or floating exchange rate	terms of payment
capital market	pegged or fixed regime	countertrade
exchange rate	forward rates	
trade deficit		

REVIEW QUESTIONS

1. What are the five properties of money?
2. What is the relationship between money and currency?
3. Define hard currency and soft currency and note how the two types of currency are dissimilar.
4. Define capital market, and explain the roles debt and equity play in capital markets.
5. Define direct currency exchange rate quotes and indirect currency exchange rate quotes.
6. What are the four factors that affect currency movement?
7. How do transaction demand and currency speculation affect currency values?
8. What are the five components of the balance of payments statement?
9. Define inflation and explain how it affects currency values.
10. How does the government influence currency value?
11. Describe a fixed or pegged currency exchange and contrast it with a flexible or floating regime.
12. What were the outcomes from the Bretton Woods agreement?
13. What does a low or high sovereign debt rating mean?
14. Define futures contracts and forward contracts.
15. Define hedging and note how it is used in international marketing.
16. Where can companies find capital?
17. What are common forms for the capital?
18. Define terms of payment and list examples.
19. Name the types of countertrade.
20. Define internal pricing, shadow pricing, and explain how they are different from one another.
21. How does international financing affect markets?
22. How does international financing affect products, prices, distribution systems, and promotional programs?

DISCUSSION QUESTIONS

1. Brainstorm and list all of the various ways that businesses use currencies. Is there any part of international marketing that is not affected by currency?
2. The Indonesian *rupiah* has recently weakened. Explain how each of the following is related to the weakening in value: (1) individual and business transactions, (2) inflation, (3) interest rates, and (4) trade and investment activity.

3. Examine the U.S. balance of payments statement in Figure 10.8. Using the numbers there, calculate the American trade deficit. How does this trade deficit then influence the value of the U.S. dollar? If other forces do not prevent this change, what should the long-term value of the trade deficit be?

4. What are the advantages and disadvantages of a fixed or flexible currency exchange regime? How can international marketers use the type of exchange regime to predict potential currency movements?

5. Trace the history of the global currency exchange controls from 1900 to the present. The movement in general has been from fixed systems to flexible systems. Study Figure 10.11. The majority of countries that are classified as "developed" have what kind of exchange regime? Why might that be?

6. As the brand manager for a large Brazilian company, you are concerned about exposure to currency fluctuations hurting your profit in Mexico. What steps could you take to hedge this risk?

7. There are three international finance factors that affect pricing (see Figure 10.17). Discuss them and steps international marketers can take to limit these effects.

ANALYTICAL AND INTERNET EXERCISES

1. You are an Australian marketer whose company is entering the Indian market. One Australian dollar is worth 43.34 Indian *rupees*. Is this an indirect or direct quote? Calculate whichever quote it is not. When the company first entered the Indian market, the exchange rate was 1 Australian dollar = 44.56 Indian *rupees*. Calculate the percentage change in the rate.

2. One of the most significant currency events of the past twenty years was the Asian currency crisis of 1997. Complete online research regarding the crisis. Were fixed or flexible regimes involved? What was the role of the International Monetary Fund in responding to the crisis?

3. The CIA World Factbook (https://www.cia.gov/library/publications/the-world-factbook/index.html) includes current account balances for countries. It also lists top exporting and importing trading partners. Look up a country of your choosing. Find out whether it has a trade deficit or trade surplus, then find the country's top trading partners. Finally, look up exchange rates for the country of interest, and its trading partners. How well does the exchange rate reflect the trading relationships between the countries?

4. Using Google, find a currency that has weakened or strengthened relative to the *euro* in the past year. How would this change in value effect international marketers interested in doing business in the European Union? How would it affect the marketing mix, particularly price?

5. Currency values can become political issues. The value of the Chinese *yuan* or *renminbi* is historically a source of conflict between the country and its trading partners. Research the conflict and provide an update on recent steps regarding the value of the Chinese currency.

▶ **ONLINE VIDEOS**

Visit **www.sagepub.com/baack** to view these chapter videos:

Video Link 10.1: Banks and Debt

Video Link 10.2: Global Markets and Sovereign Debt

Video Link 10.3: Microcredit

Video Link 10.4: Fighting Global Poverty

🌐 **STUDENT STUDY SITE**

Visit **www.sagepub.com/baack** to access these additional learning tools:

- Web Quizzes
- eFlashcards
- SAGE Journal Articles
- Country Fact Sheets
- Chapter Outlines
- Interactive Maps

CASE 10 ///

Microfinance and Bottom-of-the-Pyramid Consumers

For most consumers in developing countries, credit is an afterthought, an easily accessible component of making a purchase. Certainly credit scores are tracked and access to credit can be limited for individuals with a bankruptcy or foreclosure. Still, for the majority of consumers, the next loan is the swipe of a credit card away.

Obtaining credit is difficult for bottom-of-the-pyramid consumers in developing markets. It is estimated that two thirds of the world's population cannot obtain access to credit from banks. Instead, credit, if available at all, can only be accessed through loan sharks and other forms of organized crime.[25] This debt comes with a hefty cost. Interest rates can be extremely high.[26]

The lack of reasonably priced credit has implications for international marketers. It keeps many consumer stuck in poverty. It limits purchasing power, constrains development, and is a key component of bottom-of-the-pyramid markets.

For years, individuals and groups have looked for ways to respond to the global credit access problem. In 1976, Nobel Prize winner Muhammad Yunus came up with a solution—microfinance. On a trip to his home country, Bangladesh, Professor Yunus conducted an informal survey of the loan shark loans to local villagers. The total amount of the average loan was a small $27. The pain associated with this debt in terms of the amount of interest charged was unequal to the value. The banks in the country would not lend to the villagers because they were not "credit worthy." They had no collateral and low earnings. The profit on a $27 loan also seemed too small for them.[27]

Stepping into the void in the market, Professor Yunus loaned the $27 himself. From there microfinance was born. The concept of microfinance is simple. By fixing the institutional gap, credit can be made available to impoverished individuals. This provides them the funding needed to start businesses and earn their way out of poverty. Women are more likely to repay loans, which makes them the target market for the majority of microfinance loans.

Mallamma was a forty-two-year-old entrepreneur in Hyderabad, India. She used a microfinance loan of 10,000 *rupees* to start a fish business. In one year she grew the business to the point that she is seeking a second loan of Rs 50,000 to hire an employee and continue expanding. In Hyderabad, another borrower, Geetawati, used an Rs 10,000 loan to buy a sewing machine after her husband passed away. In one year, she grew the business to the point that she earns Rs 100 per day and has an employee. Both women repaid their initial loans.[28]

Professor Yurus founded the Grameen Bank, which now lends more than $1 billion each year. Ninety-seven percent of their borrowers are women, and all of the loans are self-financed, making the bank highly stable. The company also keeps costs very low. Advertising or other promotions are not used. The simple product coupled with the social goal of helping the disadvantaged allows them to be highly efficient.[29] This efficiency has allowed the Grameen Bank to start loaning to poor consumers in developed countries, including the United States.[30]

> **VIDEO LINK 10.3:** Microcredit

Microfinance has boomed in the past decade. In India alone, the sector grew at a 50% to 70% annual rate from 2006 to 2009. More than eight hundred microfinance institutions now operate in

Obtaining credit is difficult for bottom-of-the-pyramid consumers in developing markets.

NAME	COUNTRY
ASA	Bangladesh
Bandhan (Society and NBFC)	India
Banco do Nordeste	Brazil
Fundación Mundial de la Mujer Bucaramanga	Colombia
FONDEP Micro-Crédit	Morocco
Amhara Credit and Savings Institution	Ethiopia
Banco Compartamos, S.A., Institución de Banca Múltiple	Mexico
Association Al Amana for the Promotion of Micro-Enterprises Morocco	Morocco
Fundación Mundo Mujer Popayán	Colombia
Fundación WWB Colombia—Cali	Colombia
Consumer Credit Union "Economic Partnership"	Russia
Fondation Banque Populaire pour le Micro-Credit	Morocco
Microcredit Foundation of India	India
EKI	Bosnia and Herzegovina
Saadhana Microfin Society	India

Table 10.2: Top Fifteen Microfinance Institutions

Source: Adapted from Matthew Swibel, "The 50 Top Microfinance Institutions" (December 20, 2007), accessed at www.forbes.com/2007/12/20/microfinance-philanthropy-credit-biz-cz_ms_1220 microfinance_table.html.

the country.[31] There are 183 members of Sa-Dhan, a network of microfinance lenders, and for this group the amount of loans grew from *Rs 3,456 crore* to *Rs 11,734 crore*.[32] Microfinance has become a key component of the Indian economy. It has led to some migration from cities to rural areas to take advantage of the jobs created by microfinance.[33]

Professor Yunus started a global movement. More than 150 million bottom-of-the-pyramid consumers have borrowed money from a microfinance institution.[34] The average microfinance loan is $1,026

and only 3.1% of loans default. The default rate is better than that for many banks lending to developed market consumers. The amount of finance tripled between 2004 and 2006 to $4 billion globally. The majority of lending goes to women and 85% of lending is conducted in Asia where the movement originated. Growth is fast in other regions, especially Latin America. Even with this growth, it is estimated that 95% of the potential market for microfinance has borrowed money. In markets where microfinance has deep roots, such as Bangladesh, 60% to 75% of the market borrows, which suggests that there is great potential for growth.[35] Table 10.2 lists the top fifteen microfinance institutions globally.

Microfinance has been criticized. As global banks move into the market, many worry that the social roots of the process will be lost. For example, CompartamosBanco, a Mexican microfinance focused bank, was criticized for using an initial public offering to raise $1 billion in credit. Professor Yunus started microfinance by doing the opposite of what banks do. CompartamosBanco instead acts more like a bank, including charging high interest rates of up to 80% a year.[36] Other critics point out that many microfinance borrowers may have been successful without the loan. The loan is not the root of their success. Instead, their success resulted from successful business and marketing strategies coupled with a great deal of hard work.[37]

Even accounting for the criticisms and changing nature of microfinance, Professor Yunus started a significant social and financial movement. Providing access to credit has the potential to help pull least-developed countries out of poverty and increase purchasing power for billions of consumers. The vast implications for international businesses and marketers continue.

1. Is the goal of microfinance profit or a social benefit? Can it be both?

2. Consider how you use credit on a daily basis. How would your life be different without this credit?

3. Conduct an online search of the world's poorest countries. Do you think microfinance will be effective in these markets?

4. What business benefits are there from increased wealth in least-developed countries?

VIDEO LINK 10.4: Fighting Global Poverty

5. Do you agree with the criticisms regarding banks moving into the microfinance market? Why or why not?

PART V
International Place or Distribution

II International Marketing Channel Management

LEARNING OBJECTIVES ///

After reading and studying this chapter, you should be able to answer the following questions:

1. What are the essential elements of an international marketing channel?

2. What key marketing channel decisions must be made in order to efficiently and effectively reach customers in other countries?

3. How can the marketing team successfully manage international channels of distribution?

4. What international marketing channel functions do various intermediaries perform?

5. What are the 5 Cs of selecting channel members?

IN THIS CHAPTER

Fruit Around the World

One common product consumers around the world enjoy is fruit. Bananas, oranges, apples, grapefruit, and other popular fruits are a food staple people have consumed for thousands of years. Today, the production of fruit remains a multibillion dollar industry annually, making it an inviting opportunity for international trade.

For many consumers, eating fruit continues to a matter of necessity, tradition, or culture. For others, a healthy lifestyle includes fruit consumption, as many varieties deliver unquestioned health benefits. Fruit consumption has been shown to lower the risk of heart disease and cancer and can be an important part of a weight management program.

The cultural significance of fruit can be found in the roles it plays in various religions. Buddhists in Myanmar (Burma) use green bananas as a part of a religious offering. In Hindu nations, coconuts symbolize God's fruit, and some offer them as a prayer offering. In Christianity, some believe the pomegranate represents resurrection and eternal life.

Fruit consumption depends upon product availability and therefore on infrastructure. Most fruits are grown in only a few, select regions of the world but are consumed worldwide. Many products that are marketed internationally can be manufactured in any number of countries worldwide, which is not the case for fruit. Automobiles are built in many countries including Japan, South Korea, Germany, Brazil, the United States, and Italy; however, coconuts grow only in climates that offer present abundant sunlight and rainfall including countries such as the Philippines, Indonesia, and India. Grapes thrive in the wine-producing areas of Europe, including France, Italy, and Australia, but do not grow well in dry climates.

Distributing fruit within one nation can be difficult. U.S. farmers grow oranges primarily in Florida, grapefruit in Texas, and grapes in California. These products are in demand across the country, and are delivered by truck, railroad, and, in some cases, barges. While managing the distribution of these fruits can be complicated, the challenge pales in comparison to distribution in international markets.

Fruit reaches the far corners of the world in various ways. Grocery stores in Montreal sell bananas. Oranges make their way to Finland. Coconuts are delivered to Ireland. Consumers in China use oranges to symbolize good fortune while celebrating the New Year. All of these outcomes result from well-managed international marketing channels.

Bananas, which are grown primarily in tropical regions and countries such as Brazil, Costa Rica, Ecuador, and the Philippines, are consumed in many developing regions, but they also have a high demand in countries such as the United States, England, and throughout the European Union. Managing the production, distribution, and marketing of the fruit is not easy. Producers harvest bananas before they become ripe and carefully store them in climate-controlled warehouses or distribution centers before loading them onto trucks or ocean-going vessels. Delivering the product before it spoils or becomes overly ripe is the goal. The ability to ensure wide distribution of fresh products in international markets contributes to the success of the Chiquita company.[1]

Producers, transportation agencies, distributors, and retailers all play important roles in the international distribution of fruit. For most consumers worldwide, growing a favorite fruit is usually not an option. For this reason, consumers rely on all of these marketing channel members to meet their needs. International marketing channels, including those utilized for the worldwide distribution of fruit, are the focus of the current chapter.

QUESTIONS FOR STUDENTS

1. What is the role of distribution in the consumption of fruit?
2. Historically, how has the potential scarcity of fruit contributed to the development of various cultures?
3. Examine the fruit in your house, apartment, or dorm room. Where did it come from?

Fruit consumption depends upon product availability and therefore infrastructure.

Overview

Strategic international marketing channel management plays a critical role in global marketing success. International marketing strategies succeed when effective and efficient international marketing channels are established and managed. International marketing channel decisions revolve around the consumer's or end user's needs.

Part V of this textbook examines the place or distribution aspect of strategic international marketing (see Figure 11.1). This chapter considers international marketing channel management. Chapter 12 concentrates on exporting, physical distribution, and retailing. As is the case with every element of the international marketing mix, marketing channel decisions are influenced by culture, language, political and legal systems, and economic conditions; the most profound influence on distribution, however, is the *infrastructure* present in a target country or market. These ingredients are considered when international marketing strategies are designed and implemented.

The extent to which company products will be distributed worldwide constitutes one of the first decisions that international marketers make as part of international marketing channel management. Methods include intensive, selective, and exclusive distribution systems. Next, the marketing team identifies international marketing channel partners. Power issues with the partners are identified and negotiation processes are prepared. This chapter concludes with a review of the functions performed by intermediaries and a review of the 5 Cs used when selecting channel members.

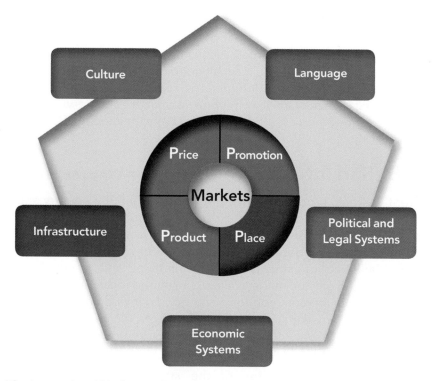

Figure 11.1: The International Marketing Context

International Marketing Channels

The distribution of products to other nations helps spur the global economy. Products require methods to reach international customers. An **international marketing channel** consists of the marketing system that promotes the physical flow and ownership of products and services from producer to consumer.

LEARNING OBJECTIVE #1:

What are the essential elements of an international marketing channel?

Marketing channel management integrate two key areas in marketing strategy: distribution and logistics. **International distribution** is the process by which products and services flow between producers, companies that act as intermediaries, and consumers, and includes the transfer of ownership. **International logistics** refers to the strategic management of the flow of products and services among marketing channel members, including both upstream and downstream activities. *Upstream activities* focus on bringing a product or supplies into a company, while *downstream* activities concentrate on sending a product or supplies to another channel member, usually for resale. The tendency may be to devote the greatest amount of thought to downstream efforts of a marketing channel; however, upstream activities such as ordering raw materials and inbound delivery contribute equally to strategic international marketing channel management.

Distribution systems revolve around the marketing channel's structure combined with logistical decisions. Marketing channel structure and logistics present a variety of challenges to international marketers. Channel decisions affect, and are affected by, other marketing decisions. When a company's marketing team concludes that the company can distribute a product worldwide, decisions regarding the rest of the marketing mix will follow. Promotional efforts may utilize a standardized message in all markets or adapted to strategy to each particular market. Price increases may be required in order to cover distribution costs.

LEARNING OBJECTIVE #2:

What key marketing channel decisions must be made in order to efficiently and effectively reach customers in other countries?

International Marketing Channel Decisions

A variety of factors in the international marketing environment influence the development of distribution channels. Nearly every country has an existing distribution model, or structure, in place for almost all goods and services. Japan is well known for its complex distribution system. International marketers seeking to conduct business in Japan will first become familiar with the system in that country. Figure 11.2 displays the decisions made when establishing international marketing channels.

Distribution Intensity

The extent to which products are distributed throughout a country and the number of intermediaries utilized to carry a good constitutes the product's **distribution intensity**. Strategic decisions pertaining to level of distribution intensity are made on a country-by-country basis, because demand for products can vary greatly across countries. Marketing infrastructures differ greatly as well. In developing countries, some products can only be made available in limited locations. Open-street markets are common for many goods, including grocery items. In open markets, consumers come to a place, often in the middle of a town, to buy necessities. Oftentimes consumers haggle over prices with the vendors.

Regardless of the stage of development, international marketers consider the overall demand for company products. Consumer demand greatly influences the overall distribution strategy that a firm employs. In general, the three distribution strategies that a firm can utilize are highlighted in Figure 11.3.

Distribution Intensity
Selection of Distribution Channels
Managing Distribution Channels
Physical Distribution

Figure 11.2: International Marketing Channel Decisions

Intensive distribution is an international marketing strategy in which products are distributed through as many wholesalers and retailers as possible in a particular market. Marketers prefer this approach when the company offers items that appeal to a mass market of consumers. Soft drink manufacturers such as Coca-Cola or Pepsi Cola use intensive distribution on a worldwide basis. Marketing efforts focus on making the product widely available. Usually, the items are low-price products that retailers sell with relatively high volume. Convenience products, such as candy, soft drinks, cigarettes, chips, aspirins, cough drops, and packaged doughnuts or pastries are often intensively distributed in global markets.

Intensive Distribution
Selective Distribution
Exclusive Distribution

Figure 11.3: International Marketing Distribution Strategies

A strategy of using only a limited number of channel intermediaries in the international marketing program is a **selective distribution** system. Producers normally exert fairly strong control over channels that utilize selective distribution because close relationships develop among channel members. Shopping products are usually marketed worldwide using selective distribution methods. Marketers who focus on selling products such as appliances worldwide often choose this approach. When the international cosmetic dentistry company REMI entered Saudi Arabia, the company partnered with a local health-care company, Thimar Al Jarzirah, to access the selective distribution networks necessary to successfully enter the market.[2]

> A strategy of using only a limited number of channel intermediaries in the international marketing program is a selective distribution system.

Exclusive distribution is an international marketing strategy that focuses on offering products through only one wholesaler or retailer in a particular market area. Prestigious products are often offered through an exclusive distribution strategy. French luxury-goods manufacturer LVMH markets several prestige products worldwide utilizing exclusive distribution networks. The French firms Louis Vuitton, Céline, and Guerlain market clothing and accessory products at exclusive upscale retail establishments worldwide (www.lvmh.com).

Strategic distribution intensity choices rely primarily on the factors of price, quality, and competition. Marketers match these factors with exclusive, selective, or intensive options. In international markets, the same basic approaches are viable, depending on the infrastructure of the host country and any mitigating factors, such as legal restrictions on imports.

Selection of Distribution Channels

Distribution channels dictate the flow of products from the manufacturer or producer to the final end user. Often, the end user will be a retail customer who purchases the product for personal consumption or use. Other end users include businesses and governmental entities. Company leaders choose channels of distribution based on several factors, including business precedent, local conditions, the availability of intermediaries, and managerial preference. Figure 11.4 depicts some of the most standard types of direct and indirect distribution.

DIRECT MARKETING

A primary option for many international marketers, especially those just entering a new host country, is to engage in direct marketing. A *direct marketing channel* relies on direct selling of a product or service to consumers or end users without the use

Ferrari is distributed exclusively.

Consumer Channels

Direct Channel   Producer ⟶ Consumer

Indirect Channel   Producer ⟶ Retailer ⟶ Consumer

                                  Producer ⟶ Wholesaler ⟶ Retailer ⟶ Consumer

Business-to-Business Channels

Direct Channel   Producer ⟶ End user

Indirect Channel   Producer ⟶ Industrial agent ⟶ End user

                                  Producer ⟶ Industrial merchant ⟶ End user

Figure 11.4: Direct and Indirect International Channels of Distribution

of wholesalers, retailers, industrial agents, or industrial merchants. In many domestic markets, direct channels utilize mail systems and catalogs as the primary promotional element. Telemarketing also qualifies as a direct marketing tactic. In international operations, the Internet has allowed marketers to directly reach consumers, especially through email and by social media. Consumer use of the Internet depends heavily on the availability of Internet technologies in a given country.

Consumers around the world are familiar with direct marketing. In Germany, more than 80% of companies provide some form of direct marketing.[3] Telemarketing, email, and direct marketing programs are common in Brazil. Business-to-business goods are also often distributed through direct marketing channels. China's Agri-Business, Inc. focused on direct sales channels in an effort to strengthen relationships with farmers and to increase market share of the company's organic agricultural application products in China. The effort reportedly amounted to 84% of the company's sales during the first six months of 2010.[4]

Direct marketing channels also grant the firm greater control of the image of a brand. An example is wine marketing. Wineries can control brand identification through direct marketing efforts.[5] A recent study of French wineries revealed that, particularly for small producers, direct marketing enabled firms to control both costs and quality while nurturing mutually beneficial relationships with individual customers.[6]

INDIRECT CHANNELS

When indirect channels are used, the goods and services move through one or more intermediaries. **Intermediaries** are organizations that move products for producers to consumers and end users, as shown in Figure 11.4.

> **VIDEO LINK 11.1:** China's Currency

In general, two types of intermediaries may be employed: agent middlemen and merchant middlemen. **Agent middlemen** do not take title or ownership of the products. Agents, or brokers, bring buyers and sellers together in a particular country. These channel members generally work on a commission basis and facilitate international sales. Agent wholesalers may or may not take physical possession of the products that they market. Agent retailers also represent services, such as insurance policies, travel tickets (airlines, cruises), and tickets to entertainment events. These retailers do not have ownership of the services to be rendered. In the airline industry, electronic middlemen such as Orbitz or Expedia typically earn a $3 commission per flight leg sold online.[7]

Merchant middlemen assume title and ownership of the products being marketed. These organizations generally take possession of the products. Merchant wholesalers take title and possession of products, which makes their activities more difficult for producers to influence or control. One type of merchant wholesaler, an *import jobber*, purchases products from producers in one country and sells them to established distribution system members in another country. Merchant retailers purchase goods for resale and then market those products to consumers. Merchant middlemen play a large role in the diamond industry. The luxury diamond company Tiffany & Co. purchases about 50% of the diamonds sold in Tiffany's retail outlets from merchant middlemen.[8]

> Merchant middlemen assume title and ownership of the products being marketed.

Consumer Channels

Many larger international companies, when the option is available, will ship products directly to retail outlets, bypassing any local wholesale operations. The reasons for this option include cost and control. Wholesalers charge markup prices to retailers, which raises the final price to consumers. Eliminating the wholesaler allows the manufacturer or producer to charge less. Conversely, shipping to a wide array of retail outlets will likely increase transportation costs, because items are not sent in bulk to a single wholesaler location. A manufacturer that negotiates directly with retail outlets retains greater control over company products marketed in host country stores. Wholesalers often market goods from more than one manufacturer, which further lessens the degree of control one producer can exhibit.

Trading companies are common in the Pacific Rim. These organizations provide intermediary activities that include marketing services, financial assistance, and information flow. The Japanese *keiretsus* trading companies act as a family of firms with close relationships and, often, shared ownership. The *keiretsus* constitute an important part of the Japanese business culture. Four of the largest in Japan are ITOCHU, Maruberi, Mittsui, and Mitsubishi. The companies also act as intermediaries for Japan's exports and have expanded operations to include operations in the areas of mining, oil and gas exploration, and information technology.[9] The *chaebols* of South Korea are similar in many ways and play an important part in South Korean politics and business culture. International marketers targeting these countries carefully consider these organizations when making mode of entry and other strategic marketing decisions.

Other marketing teams may select the *traditional international marketing channel*, which consists of producers, wholesalers, and retailers. In developed countries, distribution systems tend to be more institutionalized and focus on the traditional roles of producer, wholesaler, and retailer. Prices are generally set by the marketing channel members and little price negotiation occurs. Use of international and domestic channels may begin to decline, especially in most-developed nations, as Internet companies emerge around the globe.

Business-to-Business Channels

Many countries house large industrial agent and merchant companies. The manufacturer's marketing team selects those that reach the company's target market most effectively. Local conditions and considerations, including legal restrictions, the availability of delivery systems, and the potential to create quality partnerships, affect these decisions.

International marketing channels may include a series of different wholesalers and retailers. Also, several types of firms assist in the physical flow of products through the channel. These firms, known as facilitating agencies, assist in various aspects of negotiation, financing, documentation, physical distribution, and warehousing of products internationally. Figure 11.5 displays examples.

Freight forwarders	provide shipping, documentation, customs clearance and brokerage, consolidation, storage, and insurance.
Transportation companies	specialize in moving products through various modes of transportation.
Customs brokers	represent importers/exporters in dealings with customs, including obtaining and submitting all documents for clearing merchandise through customs, arranging inland transport, and paying all charges related to these functions.

Figure 11.5: Types of Facilitating Agencies

Marketers examine the various options when making distribution channel decisions. A balance between what has traditionally been the marketing channel in a given country with new possibilities created by improved infrastructure and emerging technologies will be needed. Then, products are directed to consumers and business-to-business end users using the best available format.

CHANNEL LENGTH

Marketing channel length refers to the number of intermediaries that a product goes through before reaching the consumer. In the traditional channel, two intermediaries are utilized: the wholesaler and the retailer. Direct marketing represents the shortest channel length, as the product moves directly from the manufacturer to the retail customer.

International marketing channels differ significantly in both length and complexity. The intricate Japanese distribution system utilizes a number of wholesalers. Also, Japanese consumers tend to make many trips to retailers, and as a result, numerous small retailer stores can be found throughout the country. In lesser-developed countries it may not be practical for consumers to make several trips to a retailer. In these areas, consumers either produce necessities themselves, or stock up on goods when they have the chance to visit a store. Consumers in the very poorest regions of the world often either go without, or produce their own items. Bottom-of-the-pyramid consumers in struggling countries such as Niger, Bangladesh, and Ethiopia are examples.

Products that are intensively distributed tend to have longer international marketing channels. When a company distributes a product in many different outlets, longer channels can be more effective than shorter channels. In situations such as these, it may take several marketing channel members to ensure that a product will be made available at many distinct retail outlets. Exclusively distributed products often have shorter channels as retailers often order directly from producers. The exclusive nature of these channels allows such dealings to occur. When supermodel Gisele Bündchen introduced her own cosmetics brand, Sejaa, in Brazil, the Droga Raia chain of drugstores and the Internet retailer Sacks were its exclusive distributors.[10]

SELECTION FACTORS

Figure 11.6 lists some of the primary factors that affect distribution channel choices. The type of product and its price affects the choice of an intensive, exclusive, or selective distribution strategy. For selective and exclusive products, competitors and brand image become more important variables. These all influence and are influenced by the desired product position and target market. The relationship between price and quality will be one of the primary considerations when making the distribution channel choice.

Type of Product
Price
Competition
Brand Image
Desired Product Position
Target Market
International Considerations
     Available Intermediaries
     Image of Distributors
     Domestic vs. Foreign Issue
     Legal Restrictions
     Taxes on Transportation and Delivery

Figure 11.6: International Distribution System Selection Factors

In international markets, additional variables arise. Most important will be to understand whether intermediaries are available. Retailers hold lesser and greater levels of prestige and consumer confidence, depending on the host country. The same holds true for wholesale companies. Legal restrictions influence the ability to market products in various countries, including any quotas or embargoes that exist. Taxes on transportation and delivery systems affect costs and prices to be charged. Marketing professionals consider local circumstances and the effects on distribution before going forward with other activities, such as establishing channels of distribution. Agricultural goods sold in the United Kingdom must deal with the strong negotiating power of the four major supermarkets that dominate the market: Tesco, Asda, Sainsbury's, and Morrisons. These companies sold 75% of the £ 120 billion worth of groceries purchased in 2008.[11]

VIDEO LINK 11.3:
Distribution Channels ▶

STANDARDIZATION OF CHANNEL STRUCTURE

As the global economy becomes increasingly integrated, distribution channels in each country are likely to become increasingly similar. Not all distribution channels will become standardized. Differences will remain across distribution channel types. Nevertheless, as multinational companies continue to expand worldwide, distribution channels will also likely evolve.

ENVIRONMENTAL FACTORS AND INTERNATIONAL MARKETING CHANNEL DECISIONS

Political, geographical, economic, and cultural differences influence international distribution decisions. Governmental instability represents a major environmental factor in many countries. State-owned distribution networks are common in many countries. These variables affect marketing channel decisions. The privatization of the distribution network in Russia after the fall of the former Soviet Union led to major changes in the system, with many firms now involved with international marketing channels in the region (www.lvmh.com).

China presents an example of the ways geography can affect international marketing channels and distribution. Mainland China's mountainous regions create difficulties for physical distribution. India faces a similar situation. Motor carrier and railroad transportation systems do not reach many citizens. Also, air transportation is limited in many countries, leaving international marketers with fewer distribution alternatives. Costs and the availability of functioning channels influence the distribution system.

In some countries, geographic hurdles such as mountains are removed or, in the case of Switzerland, tunneled through. To ease the transportation of goods through the country, which sees much trade between southern and northern Europe pass through its boundaries, Switzerland has begun an aggressive tunnel-building project through the Alps. When finished in 2017, more than three hundred trains daily will travel through the tunnels, including the 35.4 mile Gotthard Base Tunnel, which will be the longest in the world when completed.[12]

EXISTING CHANNELS

Managing international distribution networks means that companies utilize unique distribution structures in each country. A channel structure may work well in one country but not in another. Understanding the distribution systems present in target countries constitutes a crucial element in developing a successful international distribution system.[13] In some situations, the company will establish an entirely new distribution system. The Swiss pharmaceutical company Novartis developed a cherry-flavored malaria drug called Coartem Dispersible for children in developing countries. The company faced challenges in distributing the drug. Many children in rural areas are not part of the network of national medical facilities that the company traditionally uses when introducing a new medicine. Consequently, the marketing team worked directly with local sellers in rural areas, establishing relationships and using subsidies to encourage drug distribution.[14]

International marketing professionals work to ensure that the international distribution channel meets the needs of all parties involved. The system should effectively serve producers, wholesalers, retailers, and consumers. Analyzing the distribution channel from the perspective of the various constituent groups will be the first step. Channel members often use market research to more clearly understand distribution patterns in target markets.

FUTURE CHANNELS

Discussions about infrastructure in international marketing often concentrate on the availability of road, rail, and air transport systems; water, electricity, and natural gas; and other physical features. Deliveries of products and even the availability of those products are often influenced by the presence or absence of highways and railroad cars along with other modes of transportation. Map 11.1 presents the major roadways linking countries across the Western Hemisphere. As these types of infrastructure increase in number and quality, trade between countries becomes easier.

The future of physical delivery systems contains promise and problems. In terms of promise, high-speed rail systems, more-elaborate ground transportation companies, GPS tracking devices, and other innovations have made it possible to distribute a greater number of products to a larger number of customers in a wider variety of countries. When accompanied by better refrigeration systems and greater access to electricity and other sources of power, the potential to find new markets and develop products that fit those markets continues to grow, especially, as has been noted, in areas of the world inhabited by bottom-of-the-pyramid customers.

The problems associated with physical infrastructure are connected to political and legal systems as well as economic downturns. Even as better methods of delivery continue to evolve, many governments limit access to some citizens, and economic recessions reduce the ability to take advantage of technological improvements. International marketers will continue to assess conditions in various target host countries, seeking opportunities associated with more sophisticated infrastructure systems while also finding ways to overcome obstacles to the movement of goods.

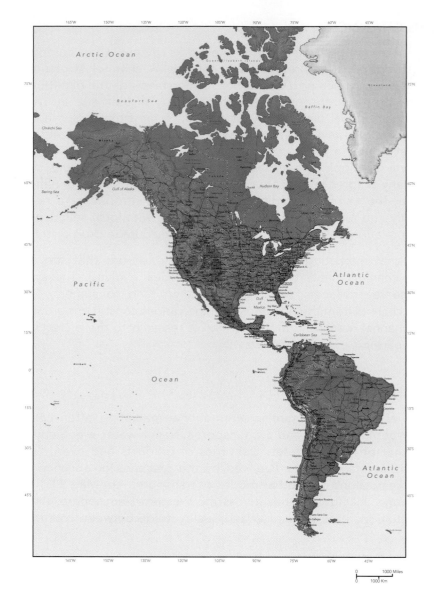

Map 11.1: Major Roadways in the Western Hemisphere
The increasing number of roadways linking countries together eases trade between countries in the Western Hemisphere.

LEARNING
OBJECTIVE #3:

*How can the marketing
team successfully
manage international
channels of distribution?*

Managing International Distribution Channels

Managing the supply channel involves a series of strategic decisions and activities. Each should concentrate on the ultimate goal, which is reaching the target market effectively and efficiently. The key elements involved are

- establishing international channel strategies,
- selecting intermediary arrangements,
- making channel arrangements and choosing channel partners, and
- managing channel power.

VIDEO LINK 11.4:
Physical Delivery
Systems

The future of physical delivery systems contains promise and problems.

ESTABLISHING INTERNATIONAL CHANNEL STRATEGIES

A manufacturer or producer of a service faces a series of issues when marketing an existing product in an existing area, vending a new product in an existing marketing, or when entering a new country or market. Employing a pull or push strategy constitutes the primary choice involved.

A *pull strategy* means that the producer concentrates on stimulating consumer demand through extensive advertising and consumer promotions. The goal, building demand, leads others in the marketing channel to carry additional stock, because customers are asking for the product. When this occurs, the product has been pulled through the channel by the end users.

A *push strategy* focuses on providing intermediaries with incentives that will lead them to cooperate in marketing the product. Discounts, sales contests, training programs, and other methods entice the wholesaler or retailer to order in greater quantities, thereby pushing the product through the channel to the consumer. When customers find the product in the store and the salesperson is enthusiastic about the item, chances of generating greater sales improve.

In international markets, both push and pull strategies may be used. Push strategies can assist in overcoming intermediary resistance to foreign products. Pull strategies increase consumer demand by making an item seem desirable, easy to use, exotic, or in limited supply. Television advertising remains a popular method for stimulating consumer demand. Television advertising laws vary widely throughout the world, and international marketers work to ensure that the laws are followed. In 2010, Taiwan moved to become the first country in the world to ban junk food advertisements during children's television programming. The move was motivated by the desire to combat consumer obesity.[15]

SELECTING INTERMEDIARY ARRANGEMENTS

The second strategic choice is whether to use traditional intermediaries or to create an in-house distribution channel. Several possible intermediary arrangements exist. Three of the most common are

- vertical integration,
- horizontal integration, and
- vertical marketing systems or international strategic alliances.

Vertical Integration

> **Vertical integration means that one member of the market channel merges with or acquires another intermediary.**

Vertical integration means that one member of the market channel merges with or acquires another intermediary. Backward vertical integration occurs when a retail chain develops or acquires its own wholesale distribution system. Forward vertical integration strategies involve manufacturers establishing wholesale distribution systems or company-owned retail outlets. The U.S. coffee giant, Starbucks, recently won a court case in which the company was allowed to bring the distribution of its products in house. Such an effort can lead to higher overall profits for the channel leader.[16]

The Spanish clothing retail chain Zara produces more than half of its clothing products in house, a backward integration strategy. Zara clothes are created in a manufacturing center and then completed by seamstresses from four hundred local cooperatives. A constant flow of information between the cooperatives and the marketing team ensures the most desired fashions reach the stores.[17]

Backward vertical integration occurs when a retail chain develops or acquires its own wholesale distribution system.

Horizontal Integration

When a company acquires or merges with another company at the same level of the distribution channel, the strategy is **horizontal integration**. These efforts include manufacturers joining with other manufacturers, wholesalers acquiring other wholesalers, or retailers merging with or acquiring other retailers. In 2006, the retail chain Best Buy acquired Chinese giant Five Star. The first decision was whether to retain the two brand names and operate independently or to merge the brands. The Best Buy brand was unknown in China and Five Star was well known. Strategic choices such as these accompany horizontal integration efforts.[18]

Vertical Marketing Systems and International Strategic Alliances

A **vertical marketing system** distribution arrangement involves the producer, wholesaler, and retailer performing marketing activities as a unified system. These systems are planned to the extent to which functions are integrated throughout the system. Often vertical marketing systems include partial ownership between the cooperating companies.

> A vertical marketing system distribution arrangement involves the producer, wholesaler, and retailer performing marketing activities as a unified system.

Some marketers have opted for what are known as *international strategic alliances* that, like vertical marketing systems, create enduring cooperative arrangements between firms that utilize resources from distinct firms that are headquartered in two or more countries.[19] By utilizing international strategic alliances in a distribution channel, firms establish a more effective means of ultimate product delivery.[20] As firms continue to search for long-term relationships with international channel members, international strategic alliances continue to grow in usage.[21] Siemens Worldwide, located in Germany, partnered with China's Huawei to form an alliance aimed at competing in China's 3G mobile technology market. Alliances such as these can be effective when a company enters a foreign marketplace.

GRAY MARKETS

A **gray market** is the practice of distributing products through distribution channels that were not authorized by the marketer of the product.[22] In international marketing, the process is often referred to as *parallel importing*, or the use of gray market tactics across international borders.[23]

With parallel importing, international distributors begin to sell a product in either unauthorized countries or through unauthorized retailers. Wholesalers buy a product in one country at a low price and resell it in other markets, or to unauthorized retailers, for profit. A gray market creates a problem when a producer markets products in a home country and in foreign countries. The producer ends up competing domestically against its own brands that were imported into the country by overseas distributors.

In general, gray marketing is legal. It does, however, violate almost all marketing channel agreements. Marketers also lose control over key parts of products, such as a manufacturer's warranty, when gray markets are present. While consumers and retailers selling gray market goods may get lower prices and access to goods, the manufacturer and the retailer with exclusive rights both suffer from gray markets. Sony Corporation of Japan filed and won a lawsuit in 2005 claiming that Nuplayer of United Kingdom was utilizing parallel exporting tactics with its distribution of the game consoles. Nuplayer was ordered by the High Court of Justice in London to discontinue selling the consoles.[24] Control over international distribution continues to be an important strategic issue.

INTERNATIONAL INCIDENT //

While working for an international company that conducts business in Ethiopia, you discover that a major wholesaler is selling your products to retailers that your company does not authorize. Also, the prices are lower than those charged to the authorized retailers. The wholesaler plays a major role in distributing your products in the region and is one of your biggest channel members worldwide. A small authorized retailer hears about the practice and has threatened to stop carrying your product until the problem is resolved. Your company has experienced problems with the wholesaler in the past, but you badly need its business due to its size and expertise in the region. You must balance the needs of the small, authorized retailer with the unauthorized actions of the wholesaler. What do you do? How do you address the power imbalance between the two intermediaries? What types of power do you think your firm can exert? Would it be wise to do so?

MAKING CHANNEL ARRANGEMENTS AND CHOOSING CHANNEL PARTNERS

A *channel arrangement* guides the administration of the marketing functions that will be performed in the distribution system. *Channel partners* are organizations with relationships that help move products from producers to consumers. Three forms of channel partner systems are contractual, administered, and partnership. Each results in unique relationships between organizations in a channel arrangement.

A *contractual channel arrangement* consists of a binding contract that identifies all of the tasks to be performed by each channel member with regard to production, delivery, sorting, pricing, and promotional support. International contractual arrangements also specify legal elements of the relationship, including the country with jurisdiction over disputes. These types of contracts tend to include well-defined details with little room for interpretation. The agreements assist companies of all sizes with international marketing campaigns and are particularly useful for smaller companies attempting to expand internationally. Phoenix Footwear Group (U.S.) entered into a contractual channel agreement with the Canada Shoe Corporation for an exclusive footwear distribution arrangement for the Canadian marketplace.[25]

An *administered channel arrangement* includes one dominant member in the distribution channel. *Channel captains* coordinate the marketing tasks provided by the channel members. Powerful manufacturer brands often become channel captains. Many vertical marketing systems feature channel captain arrangements. South Korea's Samsung is a channel captain for international marketing channels.

A *partnership channel arrangement* allows members of the channel to work cooperatively for the benefit of all firms involved. Sharing of information will be one key element of an effective partnership channel arrangements. Developing these arrangements in international markets can be difficult due to the complications of the global environment, including differences in technology and infrastructure, legal restrictions, and cultural nuances.

MANAGING CHANNEL POWER

Two major types of channel conflict occur in international distribution channels, horizontal conflict and vertical conflict. **Horizontal channel conflict** emerges when conflict occurs between members of a marketing channel at the same level, for example, between retailers carrying the same product. One retailer may be upset about unfair pricing between the outlets. **Vertical channel conflict** occurs when there are disputes between channel members at different levels in the system, such as between a wholesaler and a producer, or between a producer and a retailer.

One way in which control can be maintained by channel members involves using various power bases. **Marketing channel power** is the ability of one channel member to control the marketing decisions of another channel member.[26] Five sources of marketing channel power are displayed in Figure 11.7.

Legitimate

Legitimate power exists most frequently in the form of contracts and formal agreements between marketing channel members. Legitimate power results from contractual channel arrangements. Channel members agree to certain conditions of distribution and yield to the legitimate power of other channel partners. M4 Science Corporation of the United States recently signed an international distribution agreement with Fukuda Corporation of Japan to establish distribution channels in the Japanese market.[27] Legitimate channel power for M4 Science results from the specifics of the distribution contract.

| Legitimate |
| Referent |
| Expert |
| Reward |
| Coercive |

Figure 11.7: Power Bases in International Marketing Channels

Referent

Referent power may be found when channel members desire to be associated or identified with a particular producer or product. Marketers of prestigious products hold referent power. This form of power emerges from the likelihood that several potential channel members will be interested in carrying and promoting the product. Any retailer wishing to carry Sony products might defer to the referent power held by the Sony Corporation.

Expert

Channel leaders are able to exert expert influence when channel members perceive the leader to be an expert in the marketing of the product or service. Expert power can also reside with other marketing channel members. In international settings, expertise results from having the best understanding of local conditions. Local intermediaries in host countries often enjoy power based on expertise. The successful children's apparel chain Mamas & Papas of the United Kingdom entered into a franchising deal with Al Tayer Group of the United Arab Emirates.[28] The expert knowledge that the Al Tayer Group has in the Middle East region represents a valuable asset in the relationship.

Reward

One straightforward type of power in the international marketing channel is reward power. Producers can reward international marketing channel members by offering better profit margins, providing product incentives, and assigning exclusive channel member agreements with members. Rewards in the marketing channel are often based on the principle of equity, which suggests rewards in the marketing system in the form of some type of compensation should be based on a channel member's contribution to overall channel success.[29] Celplas Industries Nigeria Limited, a leading household products company in Lagos, recently rewarded its distributors in the country for exceptional performance by giving items including automobiles, motorcycles, appliances, and televisions to them. Rewards including these can help to foster improved relations throughout the marketing channel.[30]

Coercive

Coercive power will be present when a channel member can sanction other channel members for failure to perform various marketing duties. Quite commonly, reductions in discounts, allowances, or profit margins may be instituted by channel leaders as forms of coercion in the marketing channel. The retailer Wal-Mart plays a large role in the Mexican economy and business environment. The company sells almost 30% of all supermarket food in Mexico, and overall sales make up 2% of the Mexican gross domestic product. As such, the company leverages its size and importance to coerce other channel members to give the company favorable terms.[31] The disadvantage of using coercion comes from the potential for a decline in trust, which would be particularly damaging for a company trying to establish a positive relationship in a host country.

TRUST AND COMMITMENT IN INTERNATIONAL MARKETING CHANNELS

Power struggles and imbalance may lead to instability in the marketing channel.[32] Effective marketing channels are based on mutual trust and commitment rather than on the display of any type of channel power. *Marketing channel trust* refers to the willingness to rely on other marketing channel members, and *marketing channel commitment* reflects the desire of channel members to continue channel relationships.[33] Both trust and commitment lead to improved cooperation and coordination of marketing channel activities.

Cross-Cultural Negotiation and International Marketing Channels

International marketing involves negotiation, which means the successful management of international marketing channels requires close attention to negotiation. International marketing cannot take place without at least two parties negotiating, each from a different country.[34] Cultural differences greatly impact the negotiation process. International marketers work to control or at least limit the potentially negative effects of these differences.

In Japan, South Korea, and Mexico, the buyer is king. In negotiations, the cultural expectation will be that the buyer will get a more beneficial deal solely because that individual is making the purchase. Negotiation simulations across countries suggest the presence of this bargaining advantage.[35]

STAGES IN THE NEGOTIATION PROCESS

Negotiations typically follow the process displayed in Figure 11.8. While stages in the process can be longer or shorter or can have varying importance depending on the countries or marketers involved, in general the same stages apply to any negotiation.[36]

Negotiations commence far before the involved parties meet. The preparation stage marks the beginning of negotiations. In this first stage, marketers prepare for the negotiation task and devise plans for successful negotiating. This may involve role playing or practicing the negotiation, collecting information regarding the company and country involved in the negotiation, or setting written guidelines regarding the outcome of the negotiation. Many successful negotiations result from detailed, thoughtful preparation.

After marketers complete preparations, relationships can be built with the other party. Cultural variables strongly influence the tactics used in relationship building. Collectivist countries focus on relationship building prior to any discussion of bargaining issues. Conversations may take place about families, countries, or key contacts within either company that both negotiators know. In many countries, the relationship building stage of the negotiation process can last a long time and over multiple meetings. Negotiations should typically be between members of a company with the same level of status, particularly for high-power distance countries, in which status differences are regarded as important factors in a meeting. If the other partner is sending the chief marketing officer to make the deal, the counterpart should also hold the rank of chief marketing officer or a similar title.

Preparation
Relationship Building
Information Gathering
Information Using
Bidding
Closing the Deal
Implementing the Agreement

Figure 11.8: Stages of Negotiation

As relationships form, marketers attempt to gain as much information as possible about the other party through continual research or discussions with the negotiation partner through information gathering. One goal of this process is to gather information regarding the agreement the other party seeks.

The information gathered can be used by the negotiator in the information-using stage. Arriving at a successful negotiation outcome results from leveraging the preparation, the relationship built, and information gathered.

When a deal is closed, the parties formalize an agreement in a culturally recognized or legal fashion.

To reach that final agreement, the negotiation involves bidding. In this stage, the negotiating parties make gradual steps from their most preferred positions or desired outcomes to an actual, or final, agreed-upon outcome.

If the bidding stage ends successfully, the negotiators then close the deal. Here, the parties formalize an agreement in a culturally recognized or legal fashion. For some cultures, a handshake represents a finalized deal. In others, the deal is not complete until contracts are signed. Negotiations often plan for a BATNA or best alternative to a negotiated agreement. BATNA represents an option that can be used if the optimal agreement cannot be reached. As such, it becomes a source of power for a negotiating party. Negotiating parties have a great deal to gain by understanding each other's BATNA position.[37]

The final step of the negotiation involves actual implementation of the agreement. As with other aspects of international marketing, the implementation of agreements for international marketing channels or other marketing components require that actions be undertaken in accordance with the overall agreement. Both parties in the negotiation ensure that they perform the agreed-upon actions. In some cases, the negotiated terms will not be successfully implemented. In those cases, both sides should try to break the agreement as graciously as is possible. For cultures that focus on relationships, maintaining that relationship when implementation fails may lead to more beneficial terms in later negotiations.

CULTURAL INFLUENCES ON NEGOTIATIONS

Cultural variables influence international negotiations in many ways. Key areas of concern include interests, behaviors, and desired outcomes; relationships, communication, and perceptions; negotiation context; Hofstede's dimensions; thought processes; and the overall negotiation culture.

Interests, Behaviors, and Desired Outcomes

Culture affects negotiations in many ways, including the interests and priorities of the negotiating parties, the strategic behaviors of the parties, and the patterns of interactions between the parties.[38] All individuals have interests and priorities, as will the organizations involved in the negotiation process. Specific behaviors and patterns of interaction, such as choice of direct/confrontational or indirect/cooperative interactions follow. The negotiating parties choose tactics based on the cultural context. As an example, collectivist and high-context cultures lead to interaction processes that differ from individualist and/or low-context cultures.

Relationships, Communication, and Perceptions

Four key areas receive attention when dealing with cross-cultural interactions.[39] These areas can dramatically influence the negotiation process:

- relationships
- communication
- time perceptions
- space perceptions

In the area of relationships, negotiators need to know whether long-term connections are desirable in the other culture. They should understand whether communication will take the form of a cultural high-context or low-context. Time perceptions, the third area, include whether the culture is polychromic or monochromic. Space perceptions involve the role of personal space in interpersonal interactions and negotiations.

Negotiation Context

The overall negotiation context or climate affects each of the four key areas. Researchers have suggested that both the environmental context and the immediate context significantly influence the negotiation process.[40] The environmental context includes variables that cannot be easily controlled by the parties. These include issues such as legal and political developments, international economics, ideological differences, and culture. Factors in the immediate context include those things that are easier to control, such as the bargaining power of the participants, relationships, and the processes by which potential conflicts are resolved.

Hofstede's Dimensions

Cross-cultural negotiation research provides some guidelines that can be used for successful international negotiations. Hofstede's cultural dimensions prove useful for the international negotiator.[41] Regarding power distance, negotiators should carefully consider the social class of their potential customers and show proper respect when it is expected. Negotiators should work to convince partners that a person of equal status attends the bargaining sessions. Some cultures, such as those found in China and Japan, are high in uncertainty avoidance, and as a result, buyers or channel partners from these cultures will likely demand rules and procedures for dealing with uncertain events if they should arise.

Buyers or partners in collectivist cultures, such as those found in China or Japan, value negotiating teams over one-on-one negotiations. The inclusion of a marketing team, rather than a reliance on individual salespeople, can help to form solid business relationships. Finally, gender roles should be considered. Although the role of women in business is evolving and many women have assumed roles of great power, some cultures still prefer to conduct business primarily with men.

Thought Processes

People from various cultures perceive the world and think in different ways.[42] Thought processes are shaped heavily by culture, tradition, and the educational system in play in the specific country, and are critical to negotiations. Western cultures tend to rely more heavily on logic when arriving at conclusions than do Eastern cultures. Eastern cultures tend to view negotiations holistically, whereas Westerners tend to focus on specific parts of a problem or negotiation issue.

Significant time, resources, and attention will be given to the entire international negotiation process. Negotiating teams are carefully selected and given appropriate training. The negotiation process should be monitored very carefully to ensure that agreements that are reached are beneficial for all parties involved.

Overall Negotiation Culture

Two different approaches to culture exist. Information-oriented cultures view the negotiation process as rooted in information sharing. Marketers from relationship-oriented cultures perceive negotiations as an opportunity to build relationships.[43] Figure 11.9 identifies features common to these two types of cultures.

The two approaches lead to different behaviors during negotiation. Israeli and United Kingdom negotiators are more likely to promise something during negotiations, while Brazilian and Korean negotiators are less likely to do so. French and Taiwanese negotiators, on the other hand, are more likely to reveal personal details about themselves. Japanese negotiators tend to reveal little personal information. German negotiators typically give commands during negotiations. Brazilians are likely to use the word "no" while the Japanese and Chinese almost never use the word during a negotiation. American negotiators also avoid using the word no, and are likely to refer to the opposing negotiator as "you," whereas negotiators in other countries will not. [44]

Information Oriented	Relationship Oriented
Focus on Competition	Focus on Increasing Trust
Low Context	High Context
Less Respect for Authority	Authority and Position Play Key Roles
Individualism	Collectivism
Impatient	Less Focused on Time

Figure 11.9: Information-Oriented and Relationship-Oriented Negotiation Cultures

Source: Adapted from Hernandex William Requejo and John L. Graham, *Global Negotiation: The New Rules* (New York: Palgrave Macmillan, 2008).

As this summary of negotiation suggests, effective bargaining in an international context requires attention to detail. Negotiators should be chosen based on personality characteristics that indicate they enjoy working with people who are different from themselves, and that they are intrigued by cultural differences. Ethnocentrism likely will stall nearly any bargaining session.

International Marketing Channel Functions

LEARNING OBJECTIVE #4:

What international marketing channel functions do various intermediaries perform?

International marketing channel members perform many value-added activities. Overall, marketing channel members bring efficiency and a level of continuity to what would otherwise be a chaotic process of delivering goods from producers to consumers. The various functions of international marketing channel members are presented in Figure 11.10.

Research market needs	determine buyer needs and ability to purchase
Promote products to end users and channel members	use financial and marketing incentives to increase purchases
Fulfill order-taking duties	includes order entry, order fulfillment, and order delivery
Communicate with other channel members	share information about customer buying patterns and preferences along with local market research information
Warehousing, inventory control, and materials handling	store products until they are sold, keep track of items, move products within both the manufacturing and the warehousing systems
Address discrepancies of assortment	manage demand for a wide array of products by consumers with producers' desire to manufacture a limited array
Secure payment and extend credit	provide reassurance that payment will be made, and follow through with actual payment
Transport products to channel members and end users	select method of transportation

Figure 11.10: Functions of International Marketing Channel Members

 **International Marketing in Daily Life**

International Example: Marketing Electric Toothbrushes

As an example of how the members of an international marketing channel provide the various functions that would facilitate the entry or sale of a product to foreign consumers, consider electric toothbrush products. Many dentists agree that the use of an electric toothbrush would advance oral hygiene significantly. Patients would suffer lower levels of gum disease and removing plaque is easier with an electric toothbrush. In addition, increasing evidence suggests that quality dental care is strongly related to overall health.

All of the factors that influence international marketing would become relevant. The importance of dental hygiene and care could be influenced by cultural trends, particularly with reference to the importance of having bright shiny teeth and a white smile. Language barriers might come into play in explaining what exactly an "electric" toothbrush is. Political and legal forces would define whether the product would be considered a medicinal item, thereby making it subject to local medical laws and statutes. The economic status of a target nation would be a factor in terms of the number of citizens that could afford such a purchase. Infrastructure affects the sale and delivery of items, in terms getting the actual product into the hands of consumers, the type of electric currency delivered to homes, as well as its availability on a daily basis. Battery technology is often placed into electric toothbrushes so they may be charged and used when needed. The marketing channel would help to overcome these challenges.

The Proctor & Gamble toothbrush brand, Oral-B, is a worldwide leader in electric toothbrush technology. The brand has successfully penetrated markets globally, including Central and South America, Europe, and the Asia Pacific region. The company is currently making in-roads in the Middle East by overcoming the various cultural, technological, promotional, and distribution challenges.[45]

RESEARCH MARKET NEEDS

Intermediaries would be able to help Proctor & Gamble as they seek to export the Oral-B by providing information about the degree of dental care in a region and the availability of retail outlets willing to place the product prominently before potential consumers. Intermediaries can also identify the number and type of individuals that might be convinced to try this new form of dental care. Where economies are less developed, questions pertaining to infrastructure would be addressed as part of this analysis.

PROMOTE PRODUCTS

When promoting the product to other channel members, at the retail level, and to end users, intermediaries can offer a great deal of assistance. Proctor & Gamble could promote products to both wholesalers and retailers. Assistance to intermediaries might take the form of volume purchase incentives, cooperative advertising, and any other method that would convince them to carry the product. In some countries, wholesalers might help promote the toothbrushes to retailers. Retailers would then promote

P & G's Oral-B electric toothbrush is making in-roads in the Middle East by overcoming the various cultural, technological, promotional, and distribution challenges.

products to the ultimate consumer by use of discounts, coupons, premiums (free item given with the purchase of a toothbrush), contests (best smile), sweepstakes (drawings for free products), bonus packs (toothbrushes in combination with toothpaste), and perhaps even free samples, such as in-store demonstrations of using the product. These types of promotional activities are a large part of marketing channel responsibilities.

ORDER PROCESSING

Order processing consists of all the activities associated with fulfilling a customer's order, including order entry, order fulfillment, and order delivery. Technological developments, including Internet and mobile technologies, have greatly influenced this area of distribution. In many contexts, order processing technologies have significantly influenced order-time-to-delivery cycles. This may be particularly relevant if small initial purchases are made by intermediaries, to be followed up with larger orders should the toothbrush achieve market penetration.

The group of people involved with order processing, termed the *operational network*, also plays a vital role in order fulfillment.[46] While technology rapidly changes the international marketing landscape, people continue to play a vital role in international marketing success.

COMMUNICATE WITH CHANNEL MEMBERS

Channel members communicate frequently with other members of the international marketing channel. Sharing information about customer buying patterns and preferences would be one key part of marketing electric toothbrush products. Some consumers may indicate that a great deal of purchase risk would be associated with buying an item that totally changes their dental care and morning or evening grooming routines. Local market research information would also be helpful. Should the number of local dentists be limited, it might be helpful for Proctor & Gamble's marketing team to find additional ways to transmit information to local customers about the health benefits of the products, possibly through physicians or small medical clinics. Information on local markets becomes a crucial part of revising current marketing strategies.

INTERNATIONAL INCIDENT //

As a student in college, you took four years of Spanish and believed you were fluent in the language. You travel to Brazil on a business junket. Upon arrival, you notice that most of the Brazilians are speaking Portuguese, a language that is similar enough to Spanish that you can follow much of the conversation. In an attempt to break the ice, you offer a phrase in Spanish meant to compliment them. Instead, they seem miffed. What did you do that was culturally inappropriate?

WAREHOUSING, INVENTORY CONTROL, AND MATERIALS HANDLING

Warehousing is the process of storing products until they are sold. Electric toothbrushes would not require a great deal of storage space, which would mean a warehouse may not be needed. Marketing channel members also focus on inventory control. Maintaining an optimal inventory of products that will meet consumer demand without burdening the system with excessive stock constitutes a challenge for logistics managers. In the case of electric toothbrushes, identifying the amount needed in order to always have products in stock without an excess would be the key. Materials handling includes all activities associated with moving products within the manufacturing and warehousing systems.

ADDRESS DISCREPANCIES OF ASSORTMENT

One fundamental concern in all domestic and international marketing channels is the discrepancy of assortment problem. The problem results from the simple idea that producers generally desire to produce a large number of a limited variety of products, while consumers usually desire limited quantitiesof a wide variety of products.[47] To remedy this discrepancy, channel members engage in what is known as the *sorting function*. The sorting function includes sorting out, accumulating, allocating, and assorting, as described in Figure 11.11.

By performing these functions, channel members are able to ensure that the needs of all parties, including producers, wholesalers, and retailers, are met by the channel structure. Intermediaries may sort electric toothbrushes in combination with other small electronic consumer products, such as electric razors and hair-cutting devices. They may also sort them to be combined with other dental products, including pre-rinse, mouthwash, toothpaste, and dental floss. Wholesalers would divide larger inventories of electric toothbrushes into smaller units to be purchased within the local retail distribution system, such as drug stores, department stores, and possibly grocery stores or other outlets.Retailers would then be able to accumulate these personal care items to provide an assortment of products to consumers.

Sorting Out: Channel members break heterogeneous deliveries into relatively homogeneous stocks of products.
Accumulating: Channel members accumulate products for retailers and retailers accumulate products for consumers.
Allocating: Channel members break down large inventories into smaller units that are demanded by downstream members.
Assorting: Channel members build assortments of various goods for distribution throughout the marketing channel.

Figure 11.11: Revolving Discrepancies of Assortment

SECURE PAYMENT AND EXTEND CREDIT

Documentation plays an important role in order processing. In particular, a **bill of exchange** can be used to facilitate order processing and payments. A bill of exchange represents an agreement between parties in which one party, a *drawer*, directs a second party, a *drawee*, to issue a payment to yet another party, a *payee*. A bill of exchange creates a secure transaction for both parties.

Another instrument that facilitates order fulfillment and payment, a **letter of credit**, is a document issued by a bank to signal the creditworthiness of a buyer to a seller. The letter of credit ensures the seller of the buyer's creditworthiness by stating that the bank backs the buyer's credit. These agreements would be made between the electric toothbrush manufacturer and any intermediary (wholesalers and retailers) that would purchase and resell the product.

TRANSPORTATION

The global transportation of products will be an important part of international marketing channels. Products must be delivered reliably and effectively. Deliveries are reliable when they are on time. Deliveries are effective when the shipments arrive with good quality, undamaged by the mode of transportation. Several transportation modes are available for the international marketer. The Oral-B toothbrush might be delivered in larger quantities using delivery trucks or possibly even the mail system in smaller packages.

International Marketing Channel Structure

LEARNING OBJECTIVE #5:

What are the 5 Cs of selecting channel members?

International marketers consider a number of factors when selecting and motivating channel members and managing the overall distribution network. Issues pertaining to the financial *costs* of the system, the *coordination* of marketing efforts, distribution *coverage*, channel member *cooperation*, and channel control are all important. These components are known as the 5 Cs of selecting channel members, as displayed in Figure 11.12.

COST

Two types of costs are relevant when determining international marketing channel structure. First, some costs are incurred when establishing the channel and choosing members. Second, there are costs associated with maintaining the system, which typically center on encouraging channel members to remain members of the system.

International distribution expenses consist of more than just costs associated with moving products from country to country. The costs associated with storing, packing, preparing, and documenting product sales are also included in distribution costing.

The task of transporting goods between countries presents additional difficulties. International distribution systems are often more expensive than those found in purely domestic settings due to the costly nature of moving products between countries or continents. It has been estimated that as much as 30% of the price of a product can be directly attributed to distribution costs for products shipped between continents.[48] Distributing products in geographically-dispersed countries such as Nepal add to the overall cost of products. Marketing infrastructure will have a major impact on international marketing channel success.

Cost
Coordination
Coverage
Cooperation
Control

Figure 11.12: Issues Pertaining to Marketing Channel Structure

COORDINATION

Coordinating the marketing efforts that must take place at each level of the system constitutes an important part of managing the international marketing. Here, decisions are made as to what promotional and logistical activities each member will perform. Marketing channel coordination requires an efficient international distribution process.

COVERAGE

Marketers examine questions pertaining to the extent to which channel members cover certain territories. Channel member roles differ according to the country being served, and as a result, distribution strategies will likely vary from country to country. When addressing coverage, international marketers consider intensive, selective, and exclusive distribution strategies. When intensive distribution is selected, channel members will be expected to cover a wider and more intense territory than would be the case for an exclusive distribution strategy.

COOPERATION

Although it is difficult to assess, channel leaders attempt to assess the cooperation of potential channel members prior to the formation of a formalized marketing channel. The reputation of potential members, along with evidence of previous marketing success in targeted regions or countries, becomes critical. The extent to which marketing channel members simply trust one another becomes the primary determinant of cooperation between parties in a marketing channel.[49]

CONTROL

The extent to which channel members exert marketing channel control represents another issue in international distribution. International marketers lose some control over the physical movement of goods when goods are shipped domestically. Monitoring the movement of goods and ensuring their safe delivery brings about extra expenses.

All members should work together to create an efficient distribution system. Unfortunately, marketing channel members are often apt to protect their own interests rather than the well-being of the overall marketing channel. *Opportunism* reflects the tendency for channel members to pursue self-interests rather than those of other members of the marketing channel. Consequently, producers monitor the activities of channel members. Monitoring and controlling the activities of channel members allows the producer to ensure that marketing activities are carried out as planned. A producer can exert some control over an international marketing channel by exerting forms of channel power when conflict occurs in the system.

Channel leaders can also consolidate international distribution systems in order to maintain better control and cooperation among channel members. Sony recently consolidated its distribution efforts in the UK market by selecting two specific distributors, Imago and Midwich, with the goal of improving customer service while increasing channel efficiency.[50]

Chapter 11: Review and Resources

STRATEGIC IMPLICATIONS //

Choosing and managing channels of distribution and retail outlet formats are strategic decisions. The marketing team matches products, prices, and other variables with target markets in other countries. International market research information becomes especially important in this effort. Then, decisions are made regarding how the international marketing channel will be integrated into the company's existing channel structure. The first key decision for policy makers pertains to the appropriate level of distribution intensity in each country. The match between the firm's existing channel structures and the structures required in the targeted country is also considered. Company leaders make decisions regarding the methods to be used in managing distribution channels, including push and pull strategies, and channel arrangements, such as vertical integration, horizontal integration, or a vertical marketing system, in advance of entering a new host country. They also examine issues related to physical distribution to make sure customers can be efficiently and effectively reached.

TACTICAL IMPLICATIONS //

Marketing managers are designated to make arrangements with international marketing channel members. The issues present in the 5 Cs are considered—cost, coordination, coverage, cooperation, and control. Managers may work with existing channel members, if possible, or attempt to find new members to handle the international operation. Managers also consider the appropriate match of international retailers to the international strategy set forth during the formation of the overall marketing strategy. Many varieties of international retailers operate in various countries and the choice of retailer is important. Managers at the tactical level are also instrumental in assessing channel member performance and, when necessary, discontinuing channel relationships and contracts.

OPERATIONAL IMPLICATIONS //

Entry-level employees and first-line supervisors work constantly to ensure that the product flows efficiently through the marketing channel. Managers monitor the daily operations of the system, with a particular focus on maintaining positive relationships with international wholesalers and retailers. Managers also inform those at higher ranks about issues pertaining to maintaining control of the channel, performing channel leader duties, dealing with channel conflict, and exerting channel power when necessary. First-line supervisors work to ensure that valid information is shared among channel members, with special attention paid to local market conditions.

TERMS

international marketing channel	exclusive distribution	gray market
international distribution	intermediaries	horizontal channel conflict
international logistics	agent middlemen	vertical channel conflict
distribution intensity	merchant middlemen	marketing channel power
intensive distribution	vertical integration	BATNA
selective distribution	horizontal integration	bill of exchange
	vertical marketing system	letter of credit

REVIEW QUESTIONS

1. Define the term *international marketing channel*.
2. Describe international distribution and international logistics.
3. What three distribution intensity strategies can marketers employ?
4. Describe the direct and indirect international channels of distribution.
5. How is an agent middleman different from a merchant middleman?
6. What factors influence the choice of international distribution systems?
7. Describe a push strategy and a pull strategy.
8. What three types of channel arrangements can marketers use?
9. What power bases are found in international marketing channels?
10. What is a gray market?
11. What marketing channel functions are necessary in global marketing?
12. What are the 5 Cs of marketing channel structure?

DISCUSSION QUESTIONS

1. What type of distribution tactic, intensive, selective, or exclusive, do you think should be used for the following products?
   - milk in the United Kingdom
   - luxury jewelry in France
   - high-end automobiles in Germany
   - cigarettes in Mexico

2. Describe how channel leaders can exert each of the power bases, legitimate, referent, expert, reward, and coercive, on marketing channel members who market televisions in selected retail outlets in Europe.

3. Figure 11.8 provides a list of the functions of international marketing channel members. Apply the list to the following companies, industries, or situations.
   - automobile manufacturers
   - disposable pens and cigarette lighters
   - exclusively distributed goods
   - selectively distributed goods

4. The 5 Cs of channel member selection represent key components in the strategic distribution process. Apply the 5 Cs to the following products.
   - school supplies
   - sports equipment
   - fast food
   - perfume

ANALYTICAL AND INTERNET EXERCISES

1. Search the Internet for website of major international marketers, such as Carrefour from France. What can you learn about the international marketing channels for these companies and countries? Suggested websites include
   - Carrefour, www.carrefour.com/
   - General Electric, www.ge.com
   - Samsung, www.samsung.com
   - Hyundai, www.hyundai.com/kr

2. Find a product that is intensively distributed in a country of your choice. Look for this information on the Internet. What can you say about its distribution channels in that country?

3. Using the Internet, go to a search engine and find three international marketing channel logistics providers. Examine the websites and note the services these companies offer.

4. Using websites such as www.cia.gov and other resources that explain cultural components, examine the following countries. Explain how the 5 Cs of channel selection would be affected by what you find.
   - Pakistan
   - Sweden
   - Japan
   - South Africa

▶ **ONLINE VIDEOS**

Visit **www.sagepub.com/baack** to view these chapter videos:

Video Link 11.1: China's Currency

Video Link 11.2: Shipping

Video Link 11.3: Distribution Channels

Video Link 11.4: Physical Delivery Systems

🌐 **STUDENT STUDY SITE**

Visit **www.sagepub.com/baack** to access these additional learning tools:

- Web Quizzes
- eFlashcards
- SAGE Journal Articles

- Country Fact Sheets
- Chapter Outlines
- Interactive Maps

CASE 11 ///

JDA Software Services

In 1978, James D. Anderson founded JDA Software Services in Canada. The initial goal of the company was to provide software solutions for the retailing industry, but the company rapidly expanded into a full-service, global supply chain management company. By 2010, the company had transformed the distribution processes of more than six thousand companies in industries including manufacturing, wholesale distribution, third-party logistics, retail, passenger travel, and cargo and freight. Global in scope, the company maintains offices throughout North America, Latin America, Asia, Australia, and Europe, including locations in Brazil, Mexico, Chile, Singapore, Taiwan, India, China, and the Philippines.[51]

One of the main factors leading to the company's success has been an aggressive acquisition strategy. The company has acquired many of the leading brands in the logistics field including i2 Technologies, Manugistics, E3, Intactix, and Arthur. With these services, the company can assist clients in almost all distribution-related problems.

The company also focuses on providing services to mid-sized companies. Often these companies face costs or infrastructure barriers to adopted complicated logistics-related software. To remove these barriers, JDA offers its branded Supply Chain Now solution. The software, hosted via the JDA Private Cloud, leverages cloud computing to avoid the costs and time consumed by onsite technology set-up.[52]

The company recently won a 2010 Green Supply Chain Award from the magazine *Supply & Demand Chain Executive*. The award was based on the company's supply chain strategist solution. The process optimizes a company logistics while accounting for carbon emissions, carbon taxes, cap and trade structures, and other sustainability-related components of the process. Compared to competing tools, the JDA approach allows companies to actively monitor these various issues to find the best possible solution.[53]

The use of this software then gives JDA clients a competitive advantage. More channel captains, such as Wal-Mart, require suppliers plus the companies supplying those companies to meet a sustainability code of conduct. Without meeting these guidelines, Wal-Mart will stop ordering. The overall industry trend is the same. One estimate claims that 6% of leading companies deselected suppliers failing to account for carbon in 2010, while more than 50% of companies are committed to do so in the future.[54]

Photo 11.7 displays the opening web page for JDA. The use of a blue background provides a sense of calm and order in what is a turbulent environment. The web page notes a tie-in with OfficeMax, which creates credibility through the name recognition attached to the company. The credibility angle is further reinforced through the reference to JDA granting an award to OfficeMax, which places JDA in a position of authority. Among the many services offered in the banner, "thought management" jumps out and invites viewer inquiry. Notice that a language option is available for international customers.

Facing a rapidly changing environment, JDA Software has made aggressive moves in terms of both acquisitions and sustainability leadership. Together these efforts led to first quarter 2011 revenues of $163.6 million, a 24% increase from the previous year, and to the company generating approximately $260 million in cash to fund future actions.[55] With more than six thousand current customers, the company has a global customer satisfaction rating of 95%, and has become a global leader in channel management technology.[56]

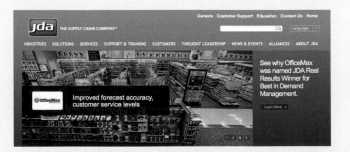

JDA Software Services is a full-service, global supply chain management company.

1. Sustainable distribution practices, particularly the management of carbon emissions, have become increasingly important. What role have channel captains such as Wal-Mart played in this process?

2. JDA Software provides services to a broad range of industries. Why do the company's services apply to such a large range of companies?

3. JDA operates on nearly every continent, and in many different countries within those regions. How might a global reach give the company an advantage over competitors?

12

International Distribution: Exporting and Retailing

LEARNING OBJECTIVES ///

After reading and studying this chapter, you should be able to answer the following questions:

1. Why do companies export?

2. What methods of entry into foreign markets can companies use?

3. What are the documents needed for exporting?

4. How can the marketing team effectively operate the five tasks associated with the physical distribution of goods?

5. What factors influence the choice of retail outlets in host countries?

IN THIS CHAPTER

Exporting and the Business-to-Business Market: Alibaba.com

> ▶ **VIDEO LINK 12.1:**
> Alibaba and Online Selling

Yahoo.com once represented the online giant everyone wanted to copy. Now, up to three fourths of the company's value comes from an investment made in the online Chinese trading website Alibaba.com. The site earned *renminbi* 5.55 billion ($856.7 million) in 2010, and *China Economic Review* named it as the top company in China.[1]

The company's roots are in Hangzhou, southwest of Shanghai. It was founded by Jeffrey Ma in 1999, a former schoolteacher. Ma came-up with the idea for the business-to-business website while searching for "Chinese beer" on a U.S. search engine. Recognizing a gap in the marketplace, Jeffrey started an online platform to connect U.S. importers with Chinese suppliers. Over the next decade, the company grew to employ eight thousand people. In 2007, Alibaba.com was listed on the Hong Kong Stock Exchange for $1.7 billion, the largest initial public offering since Google.com.

Alibaba.com achieved success by targeting small- to medium-sized Chinese businesses that need assistance in exporting to the larger global market. Instead of focusing on advertising revenues, the company charges a membership fee and a fee for value-added services.[2] With approximately 61 million registered users in more than 240 countries and regions, Alibaba.com has become the leading online export company.[3]

Distribution plays a key role in the company's success. Alibaba.com headquarters include its famous monitoring room. In the room, maps and moving charts track, in real time, transactions, with larger orders making a larger "ripple."[4] The company also has its own logistics and shipping service called Fulfillment. Multiple orders are combined into one international shipment, and buyers can track the orders. The savings to small- and medium-businesses are as high as 30%.[5]

With a 69% market share in the Chinese business-to-business e-commerce market, Alibaba.com's focus has shifted to expanding into new businesses. The company offers China's largest online shopping website (Taobao.com) and its own online version of Paypal.com (Alipay.com), and hosts classified ads (Koubei.com). Jeffrey Ma jokes that the company wants to be Google, eBay, Amazon, and Craigslist all at the same time.[6]

QUESTIONS FOR STUDENTS

1. How has Alibaba.com leveraged innovations from other companies?

2. Why would Alibaba.com invest in software to assist with the distribution of products for suppliers?

3. Alibaba.com focuses on small- and medium-sized businesses. Why would this be a particularly effective strategy in emerging markets?

The online Chinese trading website Alibaba.com provides exporting assistance to small and medium size Chinese businesses.

Overview

Many products purchased by consumers enter the country through exporting processes. Exporting involves the shipment of the finished product from a foreign country to the country of final purchase. This chapter begins with a review of the exporting process (Figure 12.1). The reasons for exporting are reviewed, as is the process of selecting markets to enter. The type of export system used, including direct or indirect, and the different types of intermediaries involved are discussed next. Once in the market, setting of export price takes place. This chapter continues by comparing how an export price relates to the domestic price. A review of the documentation needed to export follows.

The chapter then moves to discuss the process by which products and supplies are shipped to foreign buyers. The five tasks of physical distribution are reviewed. The final home for the exported good is often a retail store where the consumer finds the product to be purchased. A review of international retailing concludes the chapter.

Figure 12.1: The International Marketing Context

Exporting Choices

Marketers can use various approaches when a company enters a foreign market. To limit risk and cost, in many cases company leaders select *exporting* or shipping a product to a foreign market, regardless of the method of delivery. In 2010, global exporting totaled $14.95 trillion in value.[7] Bringing a foreign product into a market is *importing*.

Relationships between exporting and importing can be complicated. Many of the items shipped across boundaries are the parts or resources businesses need to produce

LEARNING OBJECTIVE #1:

Why do companies export?

products. The completed products may then be exported. Winget Limited (Seddon Group, U.K.) is a major international supplier and exporter of the heavy equipment and mixing products used in the production of other products. The company offers products that can be used in the manufacture of artificial and architectural stone products.[8]

Whether internal, business-to-business, business-to-consumer, or the growing consumer-to-consumer market, exports result from demand in a foreign market. In some cases, the desire for the product is latent or is the type of demand in which consumers have a need for an item but are unaware that the product exists.

INTERNAL REASONS FOR EXPORTING

One of the first questions to consider is why companies export. At the most general level managers decide to export when they believe a company's products can meet a consumer demand while making a profit. Within that general rationale, several more specific explanations for beginning to export exist. Internal reasons often drive a company to export, including those provided in Figure 12.2.

Managerial Urge
Unique Product Characteristics
Economies of Scale
Extension of Sales
Lower Risk
Overcapacity

Figure 12.2: Internal Firm Reasons for Exporting

Managerial Urge

The first rationale for exporting, managerial urge, suggests that a managerial champion begins an exporting effort. Often a single person makes the decision to export. The individual may have experience in the foreign market being targeted or may have had experience exporting with a separate business. It can be that the person simply has a strong motive to enter foreign markets with the product. Red Bull creator Dietrich Mateschitz, from Austria, expressed the drive to enter the European and U.S. markets with his high-energy drink. In just a few years sales to exceeded $140 million annually in the United States, and the company held a 70% share of the market for similar energy drinks by 2001.[9]

Unique Product Characteristics

At times the product itself leads to exporting. The possession of a unique asset that consumers want to purchase increases the potential to make a profit by exporting a product. When competitors are unable to copy the product easily or consumers have low levels of brand awareness that can be increased, the potential to earn profits rises. Other business skills, such as a talented sales force or a leading distribution approach, add further protection from competition and may spur exporting. In the film industry, 3-D movie players are starting to become available. These players possess unique features that would be hard to copy, thereby providing an exporting advantage to companies that manufacture them.

Economies of Scale

Exporting to foreign markets increases the size and scope of the business. Due to economies of scale—the decrease in per unit cost resulting from an increased number of products manufactured—company profits often by exporting to foreign markets. Using as much of a standardized marketing mix as possible best leverages advantages based on economies of scale. An international confectionary company producing chocolate, such as the Swiss company Chocoladefabriken Lindt & Sprüngli AG, can increase profits by spreading the fixed costs of making high-quality candy by selling goods around the world. The company leverages the reputation of Swiss chocolates to reach a wider, global audience.

Extension of Sales

Seasonal sales often present business cycle pressures for companies. Many products face this hurdle including textiles, sports equipment, and tourism. Exporting to a foreign market can help smooth out the spikes in demand. Ski equipment can be sold in North America during fall and winter and then exported to markets in South America during the North American off season. Wide and Tall Plastic Company, from Hong Kong, exports snow rings, snow ski equipment and tools, and inflatable sports equipment to countries around the world, relying on its website and placement on the Alibaba.com search engine to locate individual customers and distributors in various countries. The organization also serves a trading company in the Asian region.

Lower Risk

With economic downturns, government unrest, and various other external risks in both the domestic and foreign markets, exporting of products to multiple countries lowers risk for the firm. Instead of over-dependency on one market, exporting dilutes risk by operating in several markets. Diamond traders found India to be an attractive market, even though demand for diamonds in other countries, such as the United States and the United Kingdom, exhibited only a modest recovery from the 2008 economic downturn. Analysts forecast that the demand for diamonds in India will continue.[10]

Numerous internal and external advantages lead companies to export.

Overcapacity

In some cases, a steep drop in domestic demand can lead to overcapacity or market saturation in one country that makes exporting to other countries more attractive. Domestic demand may drop due to recessions, changing consumer tastes, or changes in governmental policies that affect a product, such as when the United States moved to high definition rather than analog television signals. Instead of taking a loss, firms with warehouses full of products often turn to exporting to sell excess inventory.

EXTERNAL REASONS FOR EXPORTING

While internal reasons may drive firms to export, factors external to the firm can influence the decision to do so. The global business environment and other forces influence the choice to export. Figure 12.3 lists the four main external factors.

Change Agents

Change Agents
Foreign Market Features
Domestic Market Features
Unsolicited Orders

Figure 12.3: External to the Firm Reasons for Exporting

Outside change agents often have the goal of increasing exports. Trade associations, governmental agencies, port authorities, and many others may contact a business with the goal of inducing a business to export. Often these organizations play key roles by providing the information the firm needs to consider entering a market. In the case of visiting trade delegations, key business decision-makers meet with governmental representatives from the foreign market. A face-to-face meeting can be a particularly effective way to bridge differences and establish the relationships needed to feel comfortable about exporting to a market. One such delegation from Bangladesh visited the Philippines as an attempt to increase trade between the countries, particularly in certain industries. Some of the main industries targeted included plastics, garments, chemical products, and seafood.[11]

Foreign Market Features

The features of potential foreign markets also drive exporting. In some cases, the foreign country contains a large group of consumers clamoring for the product. In other instances, foreign market similarities with the domestic market increase company confidence regarding the potential to succeed in the market. In still other circumstances, features of the country lead to a desire to export. The country may have a large population, may be wealthy, or may just be the "in" country to export to.

The Saudi Arabian market serves as an example. Wealthy oil merchants in that nation crave many of the luxuries found in the rest of the world. Consequently, producers from a variety of countries export expensive automobiles to Saudi Arabia. More recently, horse racing has grown dramatically in popularity. The Equestrian Club Riyadh lists races, horses, trainers, jockeys, and other information for enthusiasts around the world on its Facebook page. Tourists now travel to the country to enjoy the sport in the luxurious racing venues in major cities.

Domestic Market Features

Features of the domestic market may also lead to exporting. A small or limited means of exporting may present the only viable expansion opportunity. The domestic market may also be stagnant, saturated, or experience declining demand. Facing difficult domestic conditions or limited opportunities for growth, ambitious companies often look to exporting to increase sales and to present new challenges. The National

Basketball Association in the United States has a history of targeting China due to its immense population, the popularity of the sport, and market saturation in the domestic market.

Unsolicited Orders

With the increased availability of communication across national boundaries, many marketers receive unsolicited orders for products. These orders commonly start with the company's website or through promotional activities that reach foreign markets. Overall, unsolicited orders are the most common reasons for firms to begin exporting. Having received the request for the product, concerns regarding demand and risk lessen, and business leaders can be more confident of success in the to-be-entered market.

Market Selection

Once a company commits to exporting, the market to be entered will be selected. Often, the process of committing to exporting itself dictates the countries chosen to be entered, such as in the cases of unsolicited orders or change agents or managerial connections to the market. In situations where a marketing team seeks to enter multiple countries, the options will require screening. Countries can be categorized using the various segmentation processes discussed in Chapter 4. Market research can be used to examine the size of the potential market and demand for the product. Such information often results in more effective market screening. Exporting to countries that are close, both culturally and geographically, helps reduce risk and lowers shipping costs. Consequently, many companies start by first exporting to neighboring countries.

A choice also exists between market concentration and market spreading. **Market concentration** occurs when a company exports to a small number of markets or one key market and then slowly expands into additional countries. **Market spreading** involves growing exports in many different markets simultaneously and rapid expansion to new markets.

Market concentration and spreading represent two extreme approaches. Most companies use a method that is somewhere in between. One key consideration is the amount of first-mover advantage that is present. When barriers can be created to keep competitors from exporting to the market, market spreading may be the best approach. In contrast, if many competitors already exist, market concentration will lead to higher market share, which will then give the company a stronger competitive position.

> **Market concentration occurs when a company exports to a small number of markets or one key market and then slowly expands into additional countries.**

Export Entry Modes

In general terms, two modes of exporting, direct and indirect, are possible. **Direct exporting,** or *export marketing*, involves the producer or supplier being in charge of marketing to foreign buyers. **Indirect exporting**, or *export selling*, means the manufacturer sells the product to intermediaries that then handle the foreign selling of the product. The choice will be based on specific company features, the characteristics of the target market country, and the quality of potential intermediaries in that market. Marketers compare the costs associated with direct exporting against the loss of control with indirect exporting.

LEARNING OBJECTIVE #2:

What methods of entry into foreign markets can companies use?

HOME-BASED DIRECT EXPORTING

Figure 12.4 lists various methods for direct exporting. Each will be discussed individually, but marketers often combine different methods. Many companies establish a home country–based department that will be responsible for the exporting program. These are built-in departments, the simplest of structures. The department contains salespeople responsible for selling the product to buyers in the foreign market, often retailers, but many of the other marketing functions are handled by preexisting, domestic-focused departments. A built-in department approach works well for small firms, firms new to exporting, firms with low exporting volume, or firms with a low commitment to exporting.

The second home country–based option involves using a separate export department. These departments carry out all of the marketing functions needed to successfully export to the foreign country, including promotional activities, pricing, distribution, and the ability to adapt the product. For complex firms exporting to a large number of markets, many of which are different from the domestic market, this approach may be best.

Export sales subsidiaries may be established when a firm has a strong export focus with a large amount of export business. The subsidiary operates independently from the parent company, almost as a separate firm. The subsidiary also has complete control over profit and costs, which in some cases can be more efficient.

> Home Country–Based Activities
>   Built-In Department
>   Separate Export Department
>   Export Sales Subsidiary
>
> Foreign Country–Based Activity
>   Foreign Sales Branch
>   Foreign Sales Subsidiary
>   Foreign-Based Distributors and
>   Agents/Representatives

Figure 12.4: Methods for Direct Exporting

FOREIGN-BASED DIRECT EXPORTING

Companies may also choose to use the foreign country–based direct exporting structures shown in Figure 12.4. The most common of these is direct exporting using a foreign sales branch. These branches typically cover a set area with responsibility for the marketing mix within that area. Having a branch in the region facilitates buyer visits, builds stronger relationships, and in some cases may circumvent government regulations on foreign company activities.

In cases of a large amount of exporting business, company leaders may make the decision to change the foreign sales branch into a foreign sales subsidiary. This approach grants more authority and independence to the foreign exporting activities.

The final foreign-based direct exporting method is using foreign-based distributors and agents/representatives. The distinction between distributors and agents revolves around possession of the title or ownership. Distributors take ownership or represent customers for the exporter while agents do not take ownership and instead work to connect the exporter to buyers. In both cases, the foreign location of the distributors or agents means that using these intermediaries counts as direct exporting. The use of domestic-based intermediaries, on the other hand, is classified as indirect exporting.

International Marketing in Daily Life

VIDEO LINK 12.2:
Exporting Chopsticks

Exporting Chopsticks

Chopsticks are used as utensils worldwide. Companies that manufacture them invest in forests and other wooded areas. Wood or bamboo is cut and honed into the final product. In Indonesia, the PT Multisentral Gemilang company produces square-head chopsticks. Should the company decide to export on a wider basis to restaurants and other customers, the home country–based approaches would be available. Company executives could authorize some members of the sales department to seek out Asian restaurants in other countries. Multisentral could also create a separate export department for that purpose. The company would employ export sales subsidiaries until it establishes a stronghold in a region, such as Europe.

Larger-scale operations selling chopsticks might include the use of a foreign sales branch, possibly located in a major metropolitan area, such as New York or Quebec. It is unlikely that Multisentral would expand beyond such an approach to a foreign sales subsidiary or use sales agents or merchants, unless the company also expanded the scope of products offered.

INDIRECT EXPORTING

When exporting indirectly, marketers choose between either merchants or agents. Merchants take ownership or title to the product while agents do not. Figure 12.5 lists the common types of merchants and agents.

Merchants

The marketing team may select from between two main types of merchants. The first, export merchants, buy from multiple companies, often in many different countries. While called "export" merchants, these merchants typically both import and export products. With operations in many countries, these merchants often have relationships globally and choose from multiple companies when buying. Focused on easily sold products, export merchants often buy commodities or products where the brand plays a limited role.

Merchants
    Export Merchant
    Trading Company

Agents
    Export Commission House
    Resident Buyer
    Broker

Figure 12.5: Methods for Indirect Exporting

As noted in Chapter 11, trading companies can be found in many different countries, particularly in emerging markets and in Japan and Korea. The key concern for exporters will be making sure that trading companies do not hold a monopoly on exporting to a country. When such a situation exists, the exporting company will need to work to establish a relationship with individuals at the trading company.

Agents

The three main types of agents are listed in Figure 12.5. The first, export commission houses, represent foreign buyers in the domestic market. Contracted by foreign companies, export commission houses act as purchasing agents. Using these houses represents a simple and often efficient method of exporting products to foreign markets.

An exporter may also choose to use resident buyers, which are similar to export commission houses except they are permanent employees of the buyers, instead of the temporary, purchase-oriented export commission employees. This creates the opportunity to build relationships between the manufacturer and the resident buyer, which increases the potential for repeat business and the reduction of any cultural differences that might create difficulties.

Brokers play a different indirect exporting role. These agents work to bring a buyer and seller together. Brokers focus on introductions and facilitation of contractual arrangements rather than on handling the product. Typically, brokers are paid a commission on each sale they facilitate. Export Trade Brokers (United States) helps clients to identify foreign buyers for products and services while establishing overseas contacts that bring buyers and sellers together.[12] Services such as these are valuable for international marketers.

INTERNATIONAL INCIDENT ///

A Danish construction engineer took on a major building project in India. He hired three local engineers to assist in the development and oversight of the endeavor. After a few weeks, the Dane, thinking he was building rapport with the engineers, used some mild profanity while talking with them. His idea was to help them relax while working. Later in the same week, he was trying to attract the attention of one of the engineers on site. He snapped his fingers to signal the person and then beckoned him with a curled forefinger. The engineer stormed over, and said, "I am tired of being treated like a dog. I quit." How could a cultural assimilator have prevented this unfortunate event from taking place?

Pricing Exports

When entering a foreign market, pricing the product presents unique challenges. Companies may choose to use export prices that are lower than domestic prices, higher than domestic prices, or on par with domestic prices. Each of these approaches presents advantages and disadvantages to the company. Consequently, a company may use different pricing approaches in various markets.

Lower prices than domestic may be needed in cases of low consumer awareness of the brand or product category. A lower price encourages product trials and helps gain initial market share. Lower prices may also be necessary when local competitors leverage local, low-cost resources to offer a less expensive version of the product being exported. Entering a market with low prices is similar to penetration pricing for new products.

Charging higher prices than domestic companies often results from the costs associated with exporting. Governmental duties, transportation expenses, market research in the foreign country, and various other expenses all lead to higher exporting costs. The higher price helps to cover the expenses. A higher price also may lessen the additional risk from exporting to new markets. Charging higher prices when entering a new market is similar to skimming pricing for new products.

Keeping the prices the same in the domestic and foreign market represents the easiest pricing choice. When companies initially enter markets, using a par price often allows for the use of the same overall positioning and marketing approach. Matching competitor prices can be especially helpful if the company does not have the ability or time to learn about the market before entering, such as in the case of unsolicited orders.

LEARNING OBJECTIVE #3:

What are the documents needed for exporting?

Exporting Documentation

Various types of paperwork must be completed as part of the exporting process. Some of these result from government regulations. Others help finalize the actual business transaction. Effective international marketing programs include careful attention to making sure shipments are not held up due to poorly filled-out or missing documents.

REGULATIONS AND DOCUMENTATION

Governments require documentation before goods can enter a country. Ports-of-entry customs officials expect proper documentation and often may selectively search some of the containers entering a country. One advantage of using indirect exporting is that the intermediary assumes the responsibility and has the expertise needed to manage customs entry requirements.

Governments have the power to limit imports and exports. Such restrictions may be for national security reasons, economic concerns, or to protect political constituencies. Maintaining strict restrictions on the import of drugs across national boundaries is a major international concern. As an example, the importation of prescription drugs into the United States from unapproved foreign sources is generally against the law. Recently drug purchases from Canada gained public attention because many Canadian drugs are less expensive than the same drugs in the United States. Companies also may face paying custom duties or taxes on the product before being allowed to bring it into the country.

EXPORT AND IMPORT LICENSES

One of the primary documents required for exporting from a country is an export license. For many countries, such as the United States, these may be general or validated licenses. The differences between the two licenses are driven by the type of product, the final destination for the product, and the use or user. General licenses apply to products that are not highly regulated. The licenses typically declare the product, its value, and final destination. Validated licenses are more complicated and contain far more information pertaining to the various regulations that apply to the product being exported. Most countries also require import licenses, which also vary in type and regulation.

Understanding that companies seeking to export often feel overwhelmed by the various licensing requirements, various electronic services may be used to help deal with the process. Systems include the Electronic Request for Item Classification (ERIC), System for Tracking Export License Applications (STELA), the Export License Application and Information Network (ELAIN), and the Simplified Network Application Process (SNAP).

FINANCING

The other documentary concern for exporters is financing. In some cases, exporters receive payment through an open account. Basically, open accounts operate in a manner that is similar to an exchange in the domestic market. The exporter trusts the creditworthiness of the buyer and ships the goods without worrying about receiving payment. The exporter may also ship the products on consignment, which involves simply sending a demand for payment, basically an invoice, with the expectation of payment.

Many transportation companies assist in the financing of exporting by using cash on delivery or COD. For this process, the buyer pays for the goods when the carrier delivers them. The carrier has systems to accept the payment and transfer it to the manufacturer. No official title of ownership or bill of lading is part of this process. Similar to COD, a cash with order system involves the official documentation of ownership transfer. The buyer makes a payment, sometimes a partial payment, before the order ships. Often the payment covers the cost of transporting the product both to and from the buyer, should it be returned for some reason.

In all of the examples above, the manufacturer assumes all of the payment risk. In other cases, the exporter does not have enough information to be confident about the creditworthiness of the buyer. The concern exporters have is that the buyer may not pay for the shipment, may not be willing to take ownership if the goods are damaged in transit, or may not be willing to take responsibility for other increases in costs, such as currency movement or increased custom duties. At this point, a third party, typically a bank, becomes involved to ensure payment. The various documents and processes that may be used are the following:

- Drafts
  - Documents Against Acceptance
  - Documents Against Payment
- Letter of Credit / Documentary Credit

The core document for many exporters is a draft for payment. Often, this documentation is sent to both the buyer's bank and to the buyer. Drafts can vary based on the unique needs of the buying situation. In general, drafts serve as documentation of the order being placed. Having a draft does not represent the guarantee of payment by the bank, but it does provide proof of an agreement if a dispute occurs.

Drafts can be of a type called documents against acceptance. These refer to drafts in which the buyer agrees to pay the exporter by a certain time; the agreement must be signed before the buyer receives title to the goods. Drafts may also be documents against payment, where the buyer must pay for the goods before receiving title. For many countries, customs officials will not release goods to the buyer without a signed draft. The buyer can refuse to sign the draft, which results in the exporter having to pay to ship the goods back.

The most secure option for exporters is a letter of credit. For this documentation, the bank receives payment in return for providing credit guaranteeing the purchase. The buyer applies for the credit by providing specifics regarding how the payment will be made to the exporter. The exporter bank reviews the agreement and then, if no problems exist, extends payment to the exporter. The advantage of letters of credit lies in the agreement between the two banks. Both institutions are backing the payment. Figure 12.6 presents some of the unique features of letters of credit.

Revocable vs. Irrevocable	Refers to whether the importer bank can cancel or change the terms of the agreement without getting approval from all parties
Confirmed vs. Unconfirmed	Refers to whether the bank explicitly confirms the credit in writing on the letter of credit
Transferrable vs. Nontransferable	Refers to whether the letter of credit may be transferred to another party
Revolving	Refers to a letter of credit that applies to regular, ongoing shipments
Deferred Payment	Refers to a letter of credit where payment to the exporter is paid at a specified date or dates after the shipment is received

Figure 12.6: Features of Letters of Credit

Physical Distribution

The term **logistics** applies to all of the activities in the physical movement and storage of goods from the producer to the consumer. The ultimate objective of a logistics program will be to meet the needs of customers in a convenient and timely fashion at the lowest possible cost. Five tasks (see Figure 12.7) are associated with logistics and the physical distribution of products.

MATERIALS HANDLING

Part of physical distribution involves handling the in-flow of raw materials. Company leaders balance the costs of holding raw materials against the problems associated with running out. In global markets, materials handling becomes a major part of the decision to use a mode of entry that involves manufacturing items in different countries, such as franchising, wholly owned subsidiaries, and joint ventures. A nation's infrastructure will be the primary factor in this analysis. As is the case with other aspects of physical distribution, materials handling has largely been automated in many industries, although human factors still play key roles in materials-handling activities.[13]

The manager of a company's receiving department will be responsible for raw material orders, counting them and preparing them for use. A *bill of lading* specifies the exact amount of raw materials that are in a shipment. The exporter must take care of bills of lading prepared in different languages.

INVENTORY LOCATION

The production team identifies the most efficient and effective methods for storing finished goods before shipping to other businesses and customers. A *warehouse* facility stores products before they are placed into the distribution channel. Three alternatives are available: a private warehouse, a public warehouse, and a third-party warehouse.

Private warehouses are owned or leased and operated by firms storing products. In some countries, where real estate prices remain low, a private warehouse represents a cost-effective method of storing inventory.

Public warehouses are independent facilities that provide storage rental and related services for companies. When these are available in a host country, the costs tend to remain low. Also, when a company runs with lower levels of inventory, storage space may be rented only when needed.

Third-party warehouses involve a firm outsourcing the warehousing function. A company that specializes in inventory and warehousing can provide the service, thereby relieving the manufacturer of the task. This option matches with a variety of exporting operations. Van Bon Cold Stores Beneden-Leeuwen BV of the Netherlands offers customers a number of warehousing and logistical services for customers shipping products to Europe.[14]

Distribution Centers

Distribution centers are not warehouses, because they are not designed to store products. Instead, a flow of goods moves through the system. Delivery costs from distribution centers usually comprise a large portion of overall distribution costs. The physical location of a distribution center will be important. Most are located

LEARNING OBJECTIVE #4:

How can the marketing team effectively operate the five tasks associated with the physical distribution of goods?

| Materials Handling |
| Inventory Location |
| Inventory Control |
| Order Processing |
| Methods of Transportation |

Figure 12.7: Five Tasks of Physical Distribution

Warehouses take several forms and are utilized based on company needs.

near major transportation routes, ports, or terminals. Many international marketers maintain distribution centers worldwide. Some of these centers are wholly owned by the producing firm, while others are public warehouses. Small-sized products are often sent through distribution centers.

In general, distribution center activities are focused on receiving products, storing them, preparing them for delivery, and shipping. One growing trend is the use of *3PL* (*Third Party Logistics*) for inclusion in warehousing activities. 3PL firms provide warehousing and other logistics activities for firms without taking ownership of the products.

Warehousing and inventory control activities have been significantly impacted by improved technologies. New technologies such as automated warehousing systems have drastically changed these activities. Automated warehousing systems vary greatly, but often expedite the loading process of products from storage locations to delivery docks. In this way, automated warehousing systems also assist in the materials handling function of physical distribution. Polish footwear marketer New Gate Group (NG2) recently built one of the largest automated warehousing facilities in Eastern Europe. The mammoth facility allows for distribution efficiency for Poland's leading footwear company.

INVENTORY CONTROL

The process of determining the appropriate level of inventory to be manufactured, shipped, and stored at a reasonable cost is the task of inventory control. A balance must be achieved between carrying too little inventory, which leads to *stock-outs* and lost sales, and carrying an excess of inventory. Stocks outs are especially troublesome for international marketers, because reorders take additional time for shipment. Customers may become impatient and withdraw orders. On the other hand, holding excess inventory increases *carrying costs*, or the monies needed to finance the inventory and warehouse the product.

Stock Turnover

The number of times per year in which the average inventory on hand is sold is the stock turnover figure. A high stock turnover rate allows a company to be more efficient, unless it creates stock-outs and the lost sales that result. Stock turnover is calculated by dividing net sales by average inventory in retail currency, or by dividing the cost of goods sold by average inventory in a country's currency. Table 12.1 provides an example of stock turnover calculations.

Net Sales (*euros*)	3,200,000
Cost of Goods Sold (60%) (*euros*)	1,920,000
Average Inventory (retail *euros*)	800,000
Average Inventory Costs (*euros*)	480,000
Inventory Turnover	4 times
Net Sales -:- Average Inventory = 3,200,000 -:- 800,000	= 4 times
Cost of Goods Sold -:- Average Inventory = 1,920,000 -:- 480,000	= 4 times

Table 12.1: **Calculating Stock Turnover**

When managing stock turnover, the goal will be to identify the optimal turnover rate that allows for the timely delivery or products without creating excess carrying costs.

Inventory Management Systems

To achieve the objective of finding the correct amount of inventory to carry, a producer may use various inventory management system protocols. The traditional approach involves calculation of the *economic ordering quantity*, which identifies the point at which merchandise should be reordered along with the amount or volume to reorder. Unfortunately, the formula assumes zero *lead time*, which is the time from which merchandise is ordered until the time it is received. In international marketing, this assumption would almost always be false or inaccurate.

Instead, many marketers employ the *just-in-time* inventory control system. Just-in-time systems serve two purposes. The first is to order raw materials efficiently, but having them arrive at the precise time they are needed. The second goal is to reduce inventories of finished goods by anticipating future needs, which includes identifying times when sales will be low or at their peak. Just-in-time systems rely on dependable transportation systems, which can be problematic in many countries. The just-in-time method also counts on the marketing team's ability to accurately forecast future sales and future raw material needs, which may be harder to calculate in less stable international markets.

The retail equivalent of just-in-time systems is the *quick response* inventory system. It creates a flow that approximates consumer purchasing patterns. An electronic data

INTERNATIONAL INCIDENT //

A recent graduate of a Canadian university was thrilled to land a position as a sales representative with a major technology company. His first international sales call was to Britain. He studied the differences between British use of language as compared to American terminology, recognizing that a "lift" is an elevator, a "mate" was a term of endearment, and that a detour is called a "diversion." At his first meeting with a set of potential customers, the Canadian ordered a glass of red wine with dinner. Later, he ordered white wine with dessert. The British prospects seemed quite upset with his choice. What social *faux pas* had he committed?

interchange system will be required to link the supplier's inventory system with the retailer's system. Technological constraints may limit the use of such a system. Trust will be required to establish the link.

ORDER PROCESSING

Order processing involves completion of the paperwork associated with shipping orders as well as oversight of the physical movement of the goods. Bills of lading and other documents should be inspected to make certain an order contains all items. Then, payment for the shipment can be authorized by the importing company.

Air
Water
Railroad
Motor Carrier
Pipeline
Intermodal

Figure 12.8: Major Transportation Modes in International Distribution

METHODS OF TRANSPORTATION

Reducing shipping costs offers one method to make products more affordable in foreign markets.[15] Inbound transportation costs represent 6% to 12% of the gross sales of imported products.[16] The choice of transportation method also determines the speed with which goods will arrive at foreign destinations. The primary modes of transportation are displayed in Figure 12.8.

Air

Air transportation has grown in usage by international marketers. Air transportation is especially useful for products that require overnight shipping. Two important issues regarding air transportation in international distribution include cost considerations and size constraints. Air transportation can be relatively expensive for the marketer. Also, the size of product generally directly affects its distribution costs with air transportation. International air transportation relies on adequate airports in or near destination regions. Air transportation in mountainous countries such as Bhutan will be especially limited. For these reasons, some international marketers will look at other options.

Water

Water transportation remains the most extensively used method of distributing products internationally. Ocean transportation, in particular, can be quite cost effective. Ocean-going vessels, such as container ships, play key roles in international distribution. Barges also provide an important role in international distribution. The Mississippi River in the United States offers a major transportation route. *Containerization* allows

Water transportation remains the most extensively used method of distributing products internationally.

international marketers to save significant costs associated with overseas distribution. Water transportation is relatively slow when compared to air transportation, and shipping schedules constrain marketers from the availability of utilizing frequent shipping. Table 12.2 presents container port traffic for selected countries.

Railroad

Railroad transportation provides another useful transportation method in international marketing. Although railroad infrastructures vary greatly by country, this method is utilized widely in several industries and countries. Railroad transportation remains popular in developed countries and is the major form of inland transportation in countries such as China, Russia, and Poland. The total rail lines in kilometers in selected countries are shown in Table 12.3.

Motor Carrier

Trucks and other smaller vehicles offer another important component of international distribution. The utility of trucking as a mode of transportation depends directly on the availability of well-maintained highway systems worldwide. India, which remains an important emerging market for many international companies, is well known for its challenges with its highway and local street system. Motor carrier transportation is the primary method of domestic distribution in several developed countries, including France, Germany, and Spain.[17]

Argentina	1,997,000
Australia	6,143,000
Brazil	6,879,000
Chile	3,123,000
China	115,061,000
France	4,619,000
Germany	14,177,000
Italy	10,520,000
Japan	18,795,000
Mexico	3,161,000
United Kingdom	7,081,000
United States	40,645,000

Table 12.2: **Container Port Traffic 2010 (in twenty-foot equivalent units)**

Source: Adapted from "Container Port Traffic," World Bank, accessed at http://data.worldbank.org/indicator/IS.SHP.GOOD.TU/countries.

COUNTRY	2008
Argentina	35,753
Australia	9,661
Brazil	29,817
Chile	5,898
China	60,809
France	29,901
Germany	33,862
Italy	16,862
Japan	20,048
Mexico	26,677
Russia	84,158
United Kingdom	16,321
United States	227,058

Table 12.3: **Rail Line Availability in Selected Countries (in kilometers)**

Source: Adapted from "Rail Lines: Total Route Km," World Bank, accessed at http://data.worldbank.org/indicator/IS.RRS.TOTL.KM.

Pipeline

Pipelines work very well for liquid and gas-based products. Oil is transported through vast arrays of pipelines in many countries worldwide. Natural gas can also be transported by pipeline. Although this form can be inexpensive, it is generally slow. Pipelines are used extensively throughout the world, and are especially prevalent in the oil fields found in the Middle East.

Intermodal

Intermodal transportation combines various transportation modes. Containerization has enabled international marketing firms to reap the efficiencies that result from intermodal transportation. Products may be loaded into containers at the factory, shipped via rail transportation to a port, transported across an ocean, and then loaded onto trucks in the destination country. Other forms of intermodal transportation include *piggybacking*, the practice of loading flatbed trailers on rail cars for delivery on part of a distribution route, at which point they are transferred back to trucks for the balance of the delivery. Intermodal techniques also include *birdybacking* (combining motor carriers and air carriers in a delivery effort) and *fishbacking* (combining water carriers and motor carriers in a delivery effort). FedEx often combines both motor carrier and air carrier deliveries on international shipments.

The choice of transportation method affects the efficiency and cost of the delivery systems. Maps 12.1 and 12.2 display the global movements of beef and dairy products. Exporters would choose transportation systems that would avoid spoilage while keeping shipping costs as low as possible.

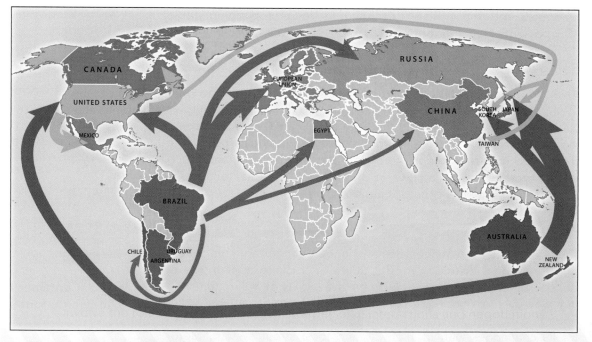

Map 12.1: **Beef Exports Globally**
Beef exports reflect both the importance of geographic proximity and the growth of emerging markets.

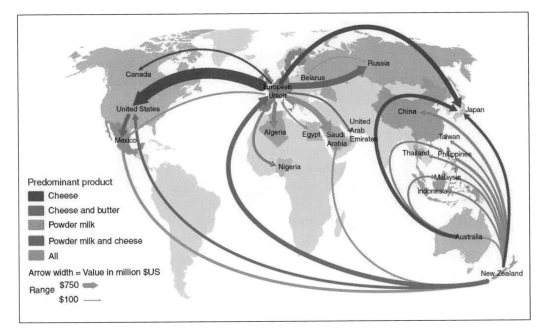

Map 12.2: **Dairy Exports Globally**
Cultural preferences for dairy products in Europe influence the methods of distribution used to reach consumers.

SUSTAINABILITY AND INTERNATIONAL DISTRIBUTION SYSTEMS

International marketing channels contribute significantly to problems associated with pollution, particularly in the area of international distribution. Airplane emissions, including carbon dioxide and nitrogen oxide, are significant contributors to global warming and climate change.

Shipping also poses environmental problems. Several studies have investigated the environmental impact of the shipping industry, and the results have varied widely. One recent study revealed that the world's fleet of ocean-going ships generates as much air pollution as half of the world's automobiles.[18]

Trains powered by diesel engines are also significant sources of environmental pollutants. International marketers consider the impact of these methods of transportation in the delivery of products worldwide. Though most marketers are limited in their ability to improve efforts, they can select carriers that focus on sustainability of transportation.

RADIO FREQUENCY IDENTIFICATION DEVELOPMENT AND INTERNATIONAL TRANSPORTATION

Technology plays an important role in international transportation. Radio frequency identification development (RFID) technology continues to grow in importance in the international transportation of products as well as in warehousing systems. RFID allows for real-time identification and tracking of products over long distances, which offers advantages to international marketers. Unfortunately, many challenges currently exist with the technology. A lack of international standards for RFID operation,

Trains powered by diesel engines are also significant sources of environmental pollutants.

environmental limitations pertaining to the distribution of liquids, information security, and RFID tag failures are problems associated with the global adoption and use of these technologies.[19] Some international marketers continue to adopt this technology regardless of these complications. Dutch-based SmartTrac Technology is a leader in RFID applications worldwide.

INTERNATIONAL DISTRIBUTION AND THE BOTTOM-OF-THE-PYRAMID

Reaching the millions of bottom-of-the-pyramid consumers worldwide can be challenging. Rural areas tend to have disproportionately high numbers of consumers living on meager incomes. Most of these consumers get by on the barest of essentials and shop only out of necessity. In many of these countries, agricultural products are not available in such quantity as to satisfy demand. In some cases, monopolization occurs because there is only one supplier for the most basic necessities, which can lead to artificially high prices.

Two challenges are associated with reaching bottom-of-the-pyramid customers: cost and access. With regard to cost, transportation can be difficult given the primitive infrastructures that exist, which adds to the expense associated with distributing products to the poor. International distribution channels are adjusted to account for these challenges.

In terms of access, international marketers focus on developing the simplest of product solutions for these consumers at the lowest prices possible. Distribution channels are often relatively primitive, with products having to be transported great distances through sometimes highly challenging conditions. Issues such as refrigeration create additional complexities. Firms that succeed in finding methods to reach such consumers often develop strong levels of loyalty.

TERRORISM AND INTERNATIONAL MARKETING CHANNELS

The increased occurrence of global terrorism has exhibited a significant impact on international distribution activities. Due to tighter security restrictions worldwide, delays in shipments of products to international destinations have become more common. Many international marketers now consider the impact of terrorist activities when formulating strategic plans.[20]

In general, terrorism is considered an external risk that directly impacts product flow. It can affect all of the forms of transportation. A recent concern for the transportation of products has been the increase in piracy, particularly in the Gulf of Aden, the Indian Ocean, and the Arabian Sea near Somalia. While piracy levels have dropped due to the global recession, pirates still are taking hostages. Many ship owners find it less expensive to pay the hostage demands than to pay for the delay in transporting the products to buyers.[21]

The United States Customs Service adopted the Container Security Initiative (CSI) as a response to the terrorist events of September 11, 2001. The initiative addresses the need for greater scrutiny of containers that are shipped into the United States and works to, among other things, identify high-risk containers, and to prescreen and evaluate containers before they are shipped to final destinations.[22] The U.S. Customs and Border Protection developed the Customs-Trade Partnership Against Terrorism (C-TPAT), which also focuses on securing supply chains from terrorist activity.[23]

VIDEO LINK 12.3: Piracy

International Marketing Channels and Utility

International marketing channels work to create various forms of utility for customers. *Utility* refers to the needs-satisfying ability of a product or service. In general, four types of utility are provided by international marketing channels, as shown in Figure 12.9.

Place utility:	making a product available at a place that is convenient for buyers
Time utility:	ensuring that a product is available when a consumer needs it
Possession utility:	transferring ownership of products to customers
Communication or information utility:	providing information to other channel members and customers

Figure 12.9: Types of Utility Associated With Distribution Channels

Cell phones may be used to illustrate utility as it applies to an international marketing channel. Mobile phones are manufactured in several countries. They are delivered through many types of distribution channels to a final destination, providing place utility.

Mobile phones are available in many different retail locations daily, providing time utility. They are also relatively easy to buy, assuming one has the resources, providing possession utility. Finally, marketing channel members share information up and down the distribution channel, providing communication or information utility to channel members. Retailers and manufacturers alike typically keep in contact with consumers about product upgrades and innovations, providing communication utility to the end users.

LEARNING
OBJECTIVE #5:

*What factors influence
the choice of retail
outlets in host
countries?*

International Retailing

The final destination for many distribution activities will be the retail store or retail outlet. Retailing activities occur worldwide. From the smallest villages to the largest cities, retail commerce plays a significant role in the everyday lives of consumers. International retailers Wal-Mart, Costco, Tesco, Carrefour, and Stockmann are well known in many areas. At the same time, thousands of small, independent retailers operate around the world. These retailers play an important part in international marketing.

Carrefour is a major international retailing chain.

International retailing refers to all of the retail activities that occur across national boundaries.

VIDEO LINK 12.4:
Small Businesses

The terminology associated with worldwide retailing may seem confusing. Retailing includes all marketing activities that are aimed at selling a product or service to a consumer, or end user. **International retailing** refers to all of the retail activities that occur across national boundaries. The definition focuses specifically on large, international retail firms that conduct operations in more than one country. Wal-Mart offers a simple example. Another way of considering retailing, however, is to approach it from the perspective of an international marketing channel that utilizes small retail firms located in targeted countries that are outside the producer's home country. Here, the foreign firm is simply a part of the international marketing channel and plays the key role of offering the product to the consumer.

International marketers use great care when selecting retail outlets. Issues such as store image play an important role in the selection process for high-end products. Boutique Dos Relógios Plus is an international retailer in Portugal for International Watch Company of Switzerland. Image is vital in this industry and the fit between retailer and manufacturer must be appropriate. The agreement between Mamas & Papas of the U.K. and the Al Tayer Group of the United Arab

Emirates for retail distribution provides an example of how local companies help international marketers through their knowledge of the local business climate. Local businesses represent great assets for companies considering international retailing arrangements.

Types of International Retail Outlets

Many forms of retailing are present worldwide. Many major international retailing firms operate across retail sectors. The Rewe Group, located in Germany, operates nearly 11,000 retail stores internationally that range from supermarkets to hypermarkets to specialty stores.[24] South African retailer Shoprite operates more than seventy supermarkets and hypermarkets throughout South Africa and in other African nations.[25] Many international retailers, such as Netherland's Ahold, use several different brand names internationally. Ahold operates under the names Peapod, Giant, and Martin's in the United States, and Gall & Gall, Etos, and Albert throughout Europe. The various types of international retail outlets are presented in Figure 12.10.

| Convenience Stores |
| Supermarkets |
| Hypermarkets |
| Open Air Markets |
| Department Stores |
| Discount Stores |
| Specialty Stores |
| Online Retailing |

Figure 12.10: Types of International Retail Outlets

CONVENIENCE STORES

Convenience stores offer widely available, intensively distributed products to consumers at convenient locations for a price premium. Prices at these stores are higher than at discount stores or supermarkets, but consumers are generally willing to pay slightly more in exchange for convenience. 7-11 is the largest convenience store chain in the world, with approximately 32,000 locations in countries such as Canada, Denmark, Indonesia, Japan, Malaysia, Mexico, and the United States.[26] Convenience outlets are usually smaller than their supermarket counterparts; the store size varies from country to country and from town to town. Japanese *conbinis* are found throughout the country and are especially prevalent in large cities such as Tokyo.

SUPERMARKETS

A variety of variations are present in supermarkets worldwide. Many international retailers operate grocery stores throughout the world. These stores are located in developed economies. The stores often carry more than food items. Utensils, paper products, cleaning supplies, and other items make the inventory more appealing to customers. Sainsbury's, headquartered in London, is the second-largest supermarket chain in the United Kingdom.

HYPERMARKETS

Hypermarkets, or *hypermarts,* are large retail outlets that combine elements of supermarkets and discount clubs in bringing a great deal of product variety to consumers. They can be as large as several hundred thousand square feet. Auchan Group, a major retailing company headquartered in France, operates numerous hypermarkets throughout Europe and Asia, including China, Dubai, France, Luxembourg, Poland, Spain, and Taiwan. Hyper Panda is the largest hypermarket chain in Saudi Arabia.[27] Hypermarkets offer consumers worldwide the advantages of convenient shopping, large product selection, and low prices.

Open air markets are common around the world.

OPEN AIR MARKETS AND BAZAARS

In many regions of the world, open air markets are common. Merchants in these markets often vend items such as fruit, vegetables, and grocery products, but may also include other products as well. *Tianguis* are open air markets in Mexico. Bazaars, which are not always open air, are also popular worldwide. These marketplaces bring consumers and retailers together for all types of products worldwide. The Grand Bazaar in Istanbul is an example. The market is one of the oldest in the world. It includes more than one thousand shops and attracts thousands of consumers every day.

DEPARTMENT STORES

Department stores present distinct product lines in numerous sections, or departments, throughout the retail establishment. Department stores have long been major players in the retail sector and several large companies operate locations worldwide. Shinsegae Centum City, located in Korea, is currently the largest department store in the world, surpassing U.S. giant Macy's. The Korean store occupies more than 500,000 square meters.[28] Department stores offer consumers the advantages of carrying a large number of products in carefully organized sections under one roof.

DISCOUNT STORES

Discount stores sell many different product lines at discounted prices. Wal-Mart, the world's largest retailer, is a well-known discount chain that operates more than eight thousand stores in fifteen countries worldwide.[29] Discount stores have grown in usage worldwide due in large part to the low prices combined with high product selection. *Outlet centers* or *outlet malls* are also popular in international retailing. The Barcelona Roca Village Outlet and Las Rozas Village Madrid are popular outlet centers in Spain.

SPECIALTY STORES

Specialty retailers focus on relatively narrow product lines. Many variations of specialty stores exist worldwide. United States–based Starbucks is a well-known international specialty store that focuses on premium coffee and related products. The chain currently operates stores in more than fifty countries.[30] Another example of a major international specialty store chain is Footlocker, which sells athletic footwear. Footlocker is based in the United States, and operates 3,500 retail stores throughout Australia, Europe, and North America.[31]

Specialty stores offer the consumers a limited selection of very specific products, and are popular in developed countries such as Japan, the United Kingdom, and the United States. One advantage for consumers is that retail employees in these outlets tend to be very knowledgeable about the limited lines. Quite often, prices in these stores are higher than in discount or hypermarkets, but the quality of the products carried tends to be higher as well.

ONLINE RETAILING

Many international marketers have turned to online retailing due to the continued proliferation of Internet technologies. This is true for both traditional online companies, such as Amazon, and other large companies attempting to increase their global marketing reach. The recent bankruptcy of United States–based Borders bookstore was largely attributed to a failure to move more quickly into online retailing, which has become a dominant force in the worldwide marketplace.[32]

 **International Marketing in Daily Life**

Online Purchasing

Purchases of many products have increasingly moved online. Consumers in more-developed countries increasingly use outlets such as Amazon.com and eBay.com and the trend has spread to emerging markets as well. Responding to these purchases represents a challenge for marketers entering or operating in these markets.

The Chinese online retailer Taobao.com is one of the companies that use local e-commerce websites to reach emerging market consumers. Taobao.com operates a consumer auction website similar to eBay.com, and the Taobao Mall retail portal, where merchants can set up online storefronts, which is similar to Amazon.com. The company's growth has been rapid. In 2010 Taobao experienced a 100% increase in gross merchandise volume, to nearly $60 billion, which surpassed eBay's $53 billion.[33] Taobao.com held 70% of China's online retail market in 2010 with sales of more than $60 billion. Payments on the site are run through Alipay, similar to Pay Pal, and the service processes around $382.7 million in sales daily.[34] Overall, Taobao has more than 800 million product listings, serves more than 370 million registered users, and is one of the top twenty most-visited websites in the world.[35]

Advertising drives much of the company's revenue, with the company being the second-largest drawer of online advertising revenue, behind Baidu.com but ahead of Google.com's Chinese earnings.[36] Facing competitors such as 360Buy.com, Dangdang.com, and Amazon's Joyo.com, Taobao.com must constantly innovate to keep consumers satisfied.[37]

Distribution represents a key component of an online retailer's success. With almost 70% of domestic mail in China being a Taobao shipment, the company faces a bottleneck. In response, Taobao.com has begun investing up to $4.5 billion to build a network of warehouses and distribution outlets to better distribute purchased products including building distribution centers in fifty-two Chinese cities. The company also has a Taobao supply-chain management platform, and provides value-added services to assist suppliers with logistics. The company's goal is to ship any product ordered online to the customer within eight hours.[38]

THE FUTURE

The future of retailing will be influenced by improvements in distribution systems and other technologies. As more roads are built and more companies become involved in middleman activities, product access will increase in many developing nations. Growth in all of the forms of retailing, including supermarkets, hypermarts, convenience stores, and specialty stores, can be expected, assisted by new technologies such as RFID and social networking.

At the same time, the engine of many economies continues to be small, independent companies. This holds true in retailing segments as well as other industries. In less-developed countries, the local bazaar remains the primary retail outlet for the majority of customers.

Chapter 12: Review and Resources

STRATEGIC IMPLICATIONS //

The decision to export constitutes a major strategic activity. Internal reasoning can guide such a strategic response include managerial urges, the development of unique product characteristics, motives to increase economies of scale in operations, the choice to extend sales or lower risk, or mere overcapacity. External factors that lead to exporting include the influence of change agents, unique features in foreign markets, changes in domestic markets, and unsolicited orders.

A second strategic choice involves use of a market concentration or market spreading approach to exporting. Market concentration focuses on expanding to a small number of markets. Market spreading involves exporting in several different markets simultaneously.

The third strategic decision involves selection of retail outlets. Top managers choose the types of retail stores to be contacted. Then, the same managers complete agreements with those retail outlets.

These strategic choices will be made following an analysis of the target country or countries. The marketing management teams examine the potential of the market to support profitable exporting arrangements. When the decision has been made, tactical plans are devised and implemented.

TACTICAL IMPLICATIONS //

Selection of export entry modes constitutes a tactical plan. Choices include home country–based activities, including utilizing the current marketing department, a separate exporting department, or an export sale subsidiary. In other instances, a foreign country–based approach will be deployed, taking advantage of the services provided by a foreign sales branch, a foreign sales subsidiary, or foreign-based distributor agents and representatives. When a company uses indirect exporting as the primary method, agents and merchants direct exporting activities on behalf of the company.

A second tactical plan involves price setting. The marketing team may decide to price items lower than domestic products, higher than domestic products, or on par with those products. The choice will be most influenced by the nature of the competition present.

The third area of tactical activity will be designing and carrying out the tasks associated with the physical distribution of products. These include materials handling, inventory location, inventory control, order processing, and choosing methods of transportation. Specialists in each of those areas guide decisions and choices.

OPERATIONAL IMPLICATIONS //

Operational managers carry out the daily activities associated with exporting. Most notably, this involves completing the exporting documentation. Marketers must make sure the proper documentation needed to satisfy the government accompanies shipments. Operational managers also finalize drafts, documents against acceptance, documents against payment, and letters of credit.

Operational managers complete the paperwork associated with the tasks of physical distribution. They look to make sure bills of lading are in order as shipments arrive. They manage actual warehouse and inventory location facilities and activities. Finally, operational managers retain and reimburse various carriers that physically deliver products.

The point has been made that a great deal of marketing involves spending money to make money. Advertising and promotional dollars are spent to increase sales and profits. Physical distribution is one area in which a company might be able to increase profits through efficient and effective management of the systems involved.

TERMS

market concentration	direct exporting	logistics
market spreading	indirect exporting	international retailing

REVIEW QUESTIONS

1. Define exporting and importing.
2. What internal reasons lead to exporting?
3. What external factors lead to exporting?
4. Define market concentration and market spreading.
5. What are the home country–based methods of direct exporting?
6. What are the foreign country–based methods of direct exporting?
7. What the major types of merchants and agents used in indirect exporting?
8. What three approaches can be used to price exported products?
9. What are the two main kinds of documents that accompany exports?
10. What are the five tasks of physical distribution?
11. What modes of transportation are used in international marketing?
12. What forms of utility are created by international distribution systems?
13. Define international retailing.
14. What are the major types of international retail outlets?

DISCUSSION QUESTIONS

1. Compare the internal and external reasons for exporting. Can you think of a situation in which one contradicts the other? In other words, are internal reasons compelling to export but external reasons not, or vice versa?

2. Explain which approach, market concentration or market spreading, should be the primary strategy used in the following situations:
   - a new type of sports energy drink
   - 3-D digital video players
   - wines made in Africa
   - tennis equipment by a manufacturer in Brazil

3. Discuss the transportation modes that would work best for the following products that are to be shipped overseas:
   - personal computers
   - industrial equipment
   - cell phones
   - petroleum products

4. Discuss how place, time, possession, and communication utilities can be created for each of the following:
   - motorcycles in Spain
   - video games in Japan
   - soft drinks in Portugal
   - cereal in Australia

5. Discuss how well you think online retailing would work for the following products:
   - groceries
   - appliances
   - fast food
   - business products

ANALYTICAL AND INTERNET EXERCISES

1. Visit the website of a major international marketer of fruit, such as United States–based Chiquita (www.chiquita.com). What can you learn about the worldwide distribution of fruit from these websites? What logistical activities are critical for the company's success? Search the Internet for information on open air markets and bazaars. In what countries are they popular? Why do you think this is so?

2. Go to the website for the U.S. Department of Commerce. See if you can find where government officials have recently made trade visits, either on the Commerce site or elsewhere. What was the purpose of the junket? Do you think it will succeed?

3. Using the Internet, identify three major export merchants that are from places other than the United States. What services do the companies offer? What regions do they serve?

4. For the following products and countries, identify the type of warehouse that should be used as well as the method of transportation that should deliver the product to end users. Using the Internet, identify a company that offers the type of warehouse you have chosen and the name of the transportation service.

   - tires manufactured in South Korea and sold in Indonesia
   - golf clubs manufactured in Japan and sold in Australia
   - fruit products grown in Australia and sold in New Zealand
   - high-end dresses and fashions sewn in France and sold in South Africa

▶ **ONLINE VIDEOS**

Visit **www.sagepub.com/baack** to view these chapter videos:

Video Link 12.1: Alibaba and Online Selling

Video Link 12.2: Exporting Chopsticks

Video Link 12.3: Piracy

Video Link 12.4: Small Businesses

🌐 **STUDENT STUDY SITE**

Visit **www.sagepub.com/baack** to access these additional learning tools:

- Web Quizzes
- eFlashcards
- SAGE Journal Articles
- Country Fact Sheets
- Chapter Outlines
- Interactive Maps

CASE 12 ///

Tesco Targets China

United Kingdom–based Tesco is no stranger to international marketing success. Tesco is the world's third largest retailer, trailing only United States–based Wal-Mart and the French giant Carrefour. In terms of profit, the company ranks second only to Wal-Mart. Founded in England in 1919 by Jack Cohen, the company has steadily grown to become a major power in England and in several other international markets. The company has been able to thrive over the years by offering high-quality products and services along with great value for consumers.

While the core of its business model is grocery retailing, the company offers much more. Tesco has gradually grown to become an international leader in hypermarkets. The company sells products ranging from grocery items to electronics to clothing. It is also involved with several other industries including banking, telecommunications, and even the recording industry. In addition to its traditional hypermarkets and supermarkets, the company also maintains a full line of smaller stores, including convenience stores. A key component of the success has been on focusing on its own brands, including the brands Tesco and Finest.

Tesco has been an international presence for many years. It operates store worldwide, including outlets in countries such as China, Ireland, Poland, South Korea, Thailand, the United Kingdom, and the United States. As of this writing, the company owns nearly five thousand outlets worldwide. Operating in diverse countries such as these signals the central role that international marketing plays in Tesco's success.

A recent focus of the company is China. Tesco has operated stores in China since 2004. The company first entered China as part of a joint venture with Ting Hsin International Group. China, with its immense population and hunger for international products, continues to grow, which presents opportunities for the future. One issue has been that competitors Wal-Mart and Carrefour were established in China for several years before Tesco entered the market.

Tesco has been successful in the United Kingdom for more than eighty years. Other markets including the United States have been challenging.

Tesco's Chinese strategy focuses on "tier two" cities in the country. One example is the city of Qinhuangdao, which is more isolated than the "tier one" cities of Shanghai and Beijing. Wal-Mart and Carrefour already have a strong presence in those cities. By focusing on locales such as Qinhuangdao, as well as Fushun and Qingdao, Tesco is able to market valuable products and services to millions of consumers who would otherwise not enjoy access to such international retailing variety.

A central component of the company's strategy is to offer large shopping centers, referred to as Lifestyle Malls, that will include Tesco–owned stores, along with other retail outlets. These centers are huge by retail standards, including as much as 400,000 square feet of space. The massive spaces reportedly will include outlets such as restaurants and cinemas. Tesco has been able to secure joint-venture support from local businesses that enable the firm to share part of the costs involved in the operations. Owning the store property enables the

United Kingdom–based Tesco is the world's third largest retailer.

company to enjoy several benefits, most notably control over building features and standards. Building such large retail outlets and establishing reliable distribution networks constitute two primary challenges. Very few distribution center alternatives currently exist for these regions.

Regardless of the challenges, Tesco plans to move quickly into China. Company reports indicate that as many as eight Lifestyle Malls, in addition to several hypermarkets, are in the works for the Chinese market. Given the company's achievements in other countries, it seems that Tesco is well poised to make China an integral part of the company's international marketing success.[39]

1. What types of products will be featured in Tesco stores: those with intensive, selective, or exclusive distribution strategies?

2. When choosing a distribution system in China, what factors should Tesco's marketing team consider?

3. What sources of channel power might Tesco hold in China?

4. While focusing on "tier two" cities, what type of utility is Tesco attempting to provide?

PART VI
International Promotion and Personal Selling

13 Globally Integrated Marketing Communications

After reading and studying this chapter, you should be able to answer the following questions:

1. How can the individual communications model be used to describe international marketing processes?

2. What steps are taken to develop an effective international advertising program?

3. What traditional and culturally based types of advertising appeals do marketing professionals use?

4. How are the traditional executional frameworks adapted to international advertising programs?

5. What types of alternative marketing programs are available to international firms?

IN THIS CHAPTER

Advertising Jewelry

Jewelry adorns citizens of countries around the world. It has a rich history dating back centuries. People wear jewelry as part of religious ceremonies, dating, engagements, marriages, anniversaries, making fashion statements and political statements, and in other contexts. Small items such as an earring or stud are worn by both men and women. One maritime tradition includes having an ear pierced after crossing the equator on a ship. Rings are exchanged in wedding ceremonies around the world. Necklaces are worn by men and women for a variety of reasons, including the expression of personal religion. Nose rings can be found in some countries. A recent global fad involved toe rings. Friendship bracelets are exchanged in many countries.

The marketing of jewelry requires adaptation to all of the elements that affect the international business environment. Culture dictates various aspects of jewelry wearing, including the designation of a "ring finger" to signify that one is married. The language of jewelry continues to evolve. Currently, the term "bling" has been assigned to gaudy displays of jewelry in some cultures. The term "junk jewelry" has been used to disparage other products. Legal restrictions include the taxation of jewelry exports and other limitations. Infrastructure dictates the distribution of jewelry in less-developed countries. Economic conditions have a major impact on the price and availability of jewelry. In 2011, with record-setting gold prices, the cost of an engagement or wedding ring rose dramatically.

Jewelry is sold in stores as small as a convenience mart and as large as a high-end specialized retail outlet. Jewelry may be bargain priced in big box retail outlets and marketed as a luxury item in other stores. In some countries, street vendors offer various types of jewelry. Religious jewelry items are sold in the Vatican and in many nearby shops.

Advertising for jewelry can be found in practically every venue, from traditional media such as television, radio, magazines, newspapers, and billboards to nontraditional locations, including trade shows, country fairs, religious festivals, and cultural events. Jewelry has been marketed on television infomercials, on the Internet, and by direct mail. The endless variety of jewelry uses dictates the large number of advertising programs.

Making commercials to sell jewelry can take the traditional format of selecting an advertising appeal and matching it with an executional framework. Marketers create advertising appeals based on sex, fantasy, rational information, and scarcity for rings, necklaces, or bracelets. Executions including slice-of-life, dramatization, demonstration, testimonial, and even animation are possible.

Marketing and advertising jewelry in international markets requires careful consideration by the foreign company. Culture, shopping habits including bargaining, and methods of payment should be considered first. Marketing messages and advertisements incorporate gender roles, religious constraints, popular culture, and other local considerations as the marketing team attempts to match these elements with the level of quality and price of various items.

As the global market continues to expand, the possibilities for making and selling jewelry rise. Turquoise jewelry made by Navajo and Zuni tribes can be found in worldwide markets. The blending of cultures and concepts of beauty and art will continue to create a rich world of personal ornamentation.

QUESTIONS FOR STUDENTS

1. How does culture affect the purchase and display of jewelry?

2. Which advertising media would be most effective for advertising low- and high-end jewelry?

3. Which advertising approaches best match selling jewelry for romantic purposes, religious purposes, and popular culture purposes?

Jewelry adorns citizens of countries around the world.

Overview

One of the key strategic activities performed by the marketing team and its leaders, coordinating a firm's **globally integrated marketing communications program**, consists of a carefully designed combination of all communications with the company's internal and external publics. Internal publics include the company's employees, board of directors, and affiliates. External publics include customers, suppliers, wholesale and retail intermediaries, members of the media, the public, and the government. An effective globally integrated marketing communications system speaks to these groups with a clear and consistent voice that represents the firm's image, positioning, brand status, and approach to business.

Part VI of this book considers all of the aspects of a globally integrated marketing communications program. This chapter examines advertising and alternative marketing methods of making contact with customers, potential customers, and others. Chapter 14 covers international sales promotions and public relations. Chapter 15 is devoted to personal selling. Figure 13.1 portrays promotions in relation to other activities associated with a firm's overall international marketing system.

Figure 13.1: The International Marketing Context

A globally integrated marketing communications program requires the strategic management of the firm's **promotions mix**, which is depicted in Figure 13.2. As shown, the mix consists of the traditional advertising, personal selling, sales promotion, and public relations efforts. Also, this newer conceptualization of the promotions mix includes social media due to its worldwide success and rapid adoption. These tools and activities serve the basic purpose of promoting a firm's products and services to end user customers and intermediaries such as wholesale distributors and retail outlets. The optimal promotional mix depends on customer and channel partner needs, as well as the company's marketing goals.

> A globally integrated marketing communications program requires the strategic management of the firm's promotions mix.

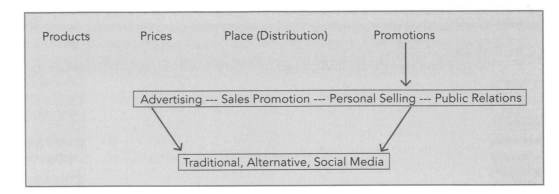

Figure 13.2: The Marketing Mix and the Promotions Mix

This chapter begins with a brief review of a communications model featuring the primary challenges related to language in interpersonal relationships. Next, advertising programs are presented, including the tasks involved as well as the complications that arise in international marketing programs. One of the strategic decisions to be made when creating an advertising program will be in regard to standardization or adaptation of the marketing messages that will be delivered to customers and potential customers.

Advertising appeals and executional frameworks are described next, including international differences and nuances that affect these programs. The chapter concludes with a presentation of nontraditional marketing programs that have become increasingly utilized in many international settings.

The Communication Process

LEARNING OBJECTIVE #1:

How can the individual communications model be used to describe international marketing processes?

International advertising and promotional activities are profoundly influenced by communication issues. **Communication** is the process of sending, receiving, and interpreting information. Two levels of communication exist in organizations. The first, *individual interpersonal communication*, involves the transmission of a message from one person to another, such as when a sales representative makes a presentation to a prospective client or customer. The individual model also applies to an individual speaking to a group of people, such as when an advertising manager begins a meeting with a short speech. Further, the individual communications model applies to marketing messages sent via various media, including advertising venues. The second level, *communication systems*, includes the transmission and movement of information throughout an organization. Organization-wide communication systems are described in the final chapter of this book.

INDIVIDUAL INTERPERSONAL COMMUNICATIONS

VIDEO LINK 13.2:
Nonverbal
Communication

Figure 13.3 models communication between individuals. As shown, the *sender* is the person signaling a message or idea. *Encoding* is the process of forming verbal and nonverbal cues. Verbal cues include anything than can be spoken as language, including print on a page or a text message. Nonverbal cues are the other methods by which messages are sent, including gestures, facial expression, posture, eye contact, and physical distance between the sender and the receiver.

The *transmission device* will be any medium that carries a message. Devices include a vast variety of modes, beginning with light and sound waves but extending to cell phone signals, radio waves, Internet transmissions, physical sensations of touch, paper with writing on it, and numerous others.

Decoding occurs as the receiver processes the message using his or her various senses. One can hear, see, feel, and sometimes taste or smell a transmission. Most of the time more than one sense is involved. A person engaged in a conversation both hears and sees the other individual, who may touch him on the arm or poke his ribs when making a joke. All of these signals are decoded. When a salesperson (the sender) speaks to a customer (the receiver), the customer decodes the information as he listens to the message and seeks to understand its meaning.

The *receiver* is the person or group of persons for whom the message was intended. In a one-on-one setting, there will be one sender and one receiver. During a speech at a meeting, one sender transmits the message to all of the receivers in the audience. An advertising message will be transmitted from the sender (the company) via a transmission device (television signal) to receivers, or members of the television audience.

Feedback consists of the perceived evaluation of the message. In essence, feedback is the response given by the receiver to the sender, verbally or nonverbally. A receiver may convey "I understand," "I disagree," or "That's funny" by how she reacts to the message, using laughter, eye contact, or a nod.[1]

As shown in Figure 13.3, noise can prevent the effective transmission of a message. *Noise* is the name given to all of the potential barriers to communication.

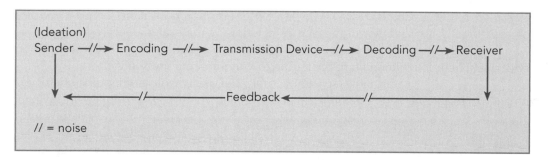

Figure 13.3: An Individual Communications Model

BARRIERS TO COMMUNICATION

Anything that can distort or disrupt a message constitutes noise or barriers to communication between individuals. As shown in Figure 13.4 numerous types of noise may be present in any conversation or presentation. For effective communication to take place, the individuals involved in the conversation must overcome the barriers. International marketing research can be designed to help reduce or eliminate the barriers that emerge during an interaction with a person from another country.

Individual Differences

Each category of barriers presents obstacles to effective communication. An older person may intimidate a young person when speaking to him. Gender differences in communication have been described in many formats, including use of Mars to

Individual Differences	Situational Factors	Mechanical Problems
age	emotions	language and slang
gender	context	technical terminology
level of education	distractions	physical disabilities
status		transmission device issues
personality		nonverbal contradiction of the verbal message

Figure 13.4: Barriers to Communication

represent males and Venus to represent females. Educational attainments introduce more complex thinking and a wider vocabulary, which can hinder communication between someone with a graduate degree and someone who is nearly illiterate. Differences in status appear when someone of high rank in an organization encounters a first-level employee or when a celebrity runs into a fan. Personality problems exist when either the sender or the receiver is bombastic and outgoing when the other person is shy and retiring. In an international context, differences between individuals may be due to different cultural backgrounds, traditions, and histories. Understanding how to respond to these differences increases the likelihood of successful communication.

Situational Factors

Two major emotions that disrupt communication include anger and depression. Careful listening becomes less likely when either emotion is present. Context consists of emotionally charged settings, such as a funeral or announcement of a death, or when management announces layoffs at a company meeting. After the initial shock, little quality communication transpires. Distractions include noisy settings or meetings

An interesting translation.

in which violent weather is taking place nearby. Senders and receivers become more involved with the distraction than with the conversation. Also, a lack of cultural understanding can lead to anger or frustration.

Mechanical Problems

Language and slang may interfere with communication even in domestic settings. A person who speaks two languages may be less fluent in one, causing difficulty when conversing in the second language. Slang varies by age, culture, and other variables. Technical terminology exists when someone who is well-versed in an area, such as information technology, uses words only those in the field would understand when nontechnical individuals are present. These mechanical issues become intensified in an international marketing context. A great deal of communication in this context includes at least one non-native speaker who must cope with both the technical terminology and the unfamiliar language.

Physical disabilities can be a problem for the sender when she has a speech impairment. A physical disability can cause difficulties for any receiver who is hard of hearing, deaf, or blind. Transmission device problems include poor cell phone signals, trying to shout over wind and rain from a distance, and any other problem with the medium carrying the message. Nonverbal contradictions occur when the sender's verbal cues do not match his gestures, facial expression, or posture.

International Barriers

Each of the individual barriers listed in Figure 13.4 may become more extreme in international settings and can greatly influence international marketing programs. For example, older persons may be highly respected in one culture and disrespected in another. Even asking questions about a person's age can make the receiver uncomfortable in some cultures. Gender equality and inequality strongly affects patterns of communication between males and females. Percentages of a population that are educated vary widely across countries, thereby affecting status levels. Personalities may be influenced by cultural surroundings as well. The most commonly cited barriers to communication in international marketing and promotions include

- language and slang
- directness of address
- eye contact
- ethnocentrism
- stereotyping
- differences in the meanings of nonverbal cues
- personal space issues
- use of symbols and cultural icons

Language and slang create initial barriers to communication. An individual who only speaks Mandarin will have difficulties when a business partner only speaks Spanish, even when a translator is present. Slang within both languages can further complicate communication. Mandarin is written using characters rather than letters, which adds further potential disruptions.

Directness of address is culturally based. In some countries, such as Japan, language and conversation are highly deferent. Disagreement would be expressed

This gesture means different things in various cultures.

in the most modest terms possible. Often, Japanese business people will go to extreme lengths to avoid telling a business partner "no." In other nations, such as the Netherlands, the opposite will be true. Unless strong, direct language is used, others may view the speaker as weak or not reliable.

Eye contact may be closely related to directness of address. In some cultures, such as Canada, the failure to make eye contact makes a person seem suspicious and untrustworthy. In others, such as South Korea, looking away displays deference and respect.

Ethnocentrism, the belief that one's culture is inherently superior, may cause either the sender or receiver to convey a sense of feeling superior. Not surprisingly, misunderstandings may result and conflicts or confrontation may emerge.

Stereotyping exists when a person assumes things about another based on that person's race or national heritage. Believing all Germans are rigid, structured, rational thinkers lumps them into a group that undoubtedly does not truly exist. Corresponding methods of speaking would be affected by such an assumption.

Nonverbal cues vary widely by culture. Nodding "yes" in one country is nodding "no" in others. In many Arab nations, the act of crossing one's legs is a sign of disrespect and males holding hands as part of a business relationship indicates trust. Gestures also vary widely. What may have a benign meaning in one country may be an obscene gesture in another. Examples include the "V for victory" with two fingers sign, and use of the middle finger to point.

Personal space is the distance between two persons in a conversation. Standing two to three feet away from another person may be the norm in one culture such as France, Spain, or the United States, where greater personal space exists. That same distance may indicate shiftiness or distrust in Central Africa and the Middle East. As an extension of personal distance, in the culture of Japan a business partner would find a pat on the back to be disconcerting, as the Japanese tend to not make physical contact in business relationships, other than a handshake with a Western trading partner.[2]

High- and Low-Context Cultures

A final communication barrier results from the methods used to communicate. Use of symbols and cultural icons also affects patterns of communication. Religious symbols are major components of many cultures. Failing to recognize them may place a person in an embarrassing situation. The terms *high-* and *low-context* have been applied to culture differences in language usage. Misunderstanding these elements may lead to poorly designed advertising and marketing programs.[3]

Low-context cultures are characterized by explicit verbal messages. **Low-context cultures** demonstrate high values toward and positive attitudes regarding words. The meaning of a message is mainly contained in the words used. Much of the

Western world is historically rich with rhetoric. This, in turn, continues to emphasize the importance of verbal messages. Germany, Switzerland, and the United States are examples of low-context cultures.

High-context cultures rely more on symbols and language with less-explicit or spelled-out codes. The meaning of the message is mainly contained in the nonverbal components of the message. This includes facial expressions, body language, the person presenting the message, and the context in which the message is transmitted. High-context communication moves quickly and efficiently. Unfortunately, often the verbal messages are less complete, and for those not familiar with the symbols in a given area, the information becomes difficult to accurately decipher. High-context societies are less accessible to outsiders. Many Asian cultures are high context. Figure 13.5 presents differences in high- and low-context cultures.

> High-context cultures rely more on symbols and language with less-explicit or spelled-out codes.

	High-Context	Low-Context
Meaning of Words	meaning derived largely by context	meaning derived from verbage
Nonverbal Communication	strong emphasis on nonverbals	smaller emphasis on nonverbals
Symbolism	important role in communication	smaller role in communication
Use of Data	smaller role in communication	important role in communication
Descriptions	often incomplete	fully explained
Status of Speaker	major role in communication	smaller role in communication

Figure 13.5: High- and Low-Context Cultures

In advertising and marketing, messages are more explicit, clear, and complete in low-context cultures. Selling points are articulated and spelled out. Consumers expect this precision in messages. In essence, numbers, figures, and concise language guide message development. Advertising will be more verbally oriented in many instances.

For high-context cultures, marketing messages and commercials rely more on symbolism and indirect verbal messages. The importance of logos combined with local cultural icons including colors rises. The color red symbolizes celebration in Asian culture. Its use in a commercial sends a widely understood signal in that region. Visual variables play important roles in high-context cultures.[4]

Complications arise when a company fails to recognize the cultural context. Unless the advertising team can explain why context matters, marketing messages may become misinterpreted or misunderstood. At the same time, a well-designed symbolic message can succeed in a low-context culture. Many persons in low-context countries are able to interpret the Nike swoosh, McDonald's arches, and other logos; religious symbols; and numerous jingles or musical taglines. Also, a well-written advertisement can succeed in a high-context culture, especially when accompanied by appropriate symbols. Focus groups and pretesting of advertisements can help the marketing team predict the effects of a marketing message.

Concepts of family resonate with high-context cultures.

Sender Duties	Receiver Duties
Awareness of Barriers	Active Listening
Empathy	Seeking Clarification of the Message
Careful Attention to Nonverbal Cues	
Confirmation of the Message	

Figure 13.6: Creating Quality Individual Communication

OVERCOMING BARRIERS TO COMMUNICATION

Quality communication results from careful preparation by a sender and receiver in any context, and plays a major role in designing quality international market research. Both senders and receivers have responsibilities that can overcome the barriers that are present. Figure 13.6 summarizes these duties.

Senders are charged with making sure they understand the barriers that might be present. In international settings, speakers should pay even greater care to these issues. Empathy means attempting to understand the receiver's background and point of view. Knowing about nonverbal cues and their usage in other cultures can help avoid many potential conflicts and misunderstandings in a research project. Confirmation of the message may be summarized by the phrase, "Do you understand?" At the same time, the use of such a "yes" or "no" question can be frustrating in high-context cultures, because consumers rarely are comfortable giving such direct answers. Consequently, extra attention is given to make sure the message was received as intended.

Receiver duties include listening carefully and not allowing distractions to interfere with a conversation or presentation. Multi-tasking during long distance phone calls overseas is a bad idea. Clarification of a message means saying, "I don't understand" at the appropriate times. Otherwise a receiver may overreact to what was meant to be a noncontroversial comment.

In international settings, translators and cultural assimilators are key individuals. *Translators* should speak the native language of the host country. Many times the best choice for a translator will be someone who lives in the host country, and uses its language as a first language. *Cultural assimilators* are employees who examine messages and prepare individuals for interactions with members of other countries. They can help a person avoid any uncomfortable lapses in manners as well as explain how to show friendliness and respect in that country. Both of these individuals play vital roles in preparing, interpreting, analyzing, and presenting the findings of an international marketing research effort.

COMMUNICATING MARKETING MESSAGES

The individual communications model can be adapted to advertising programs. Sender companies are advised to understand how media are used and perceived in various cultures. State-owned television stations may cause distrust or even disdain by the public. Commercials and other advertising messages should be translated and back translated to make sure they do not violate local cultural norms. Marketers should monitor the use of visual images and examine photos, especially of women, to make sure an image does not insult local patrons. Even the use of animals or animated characters as brand characters deserves attention. In the United States, a squirrel is viewed as a "thrifty saver." In Latin America, squirrels are in the same category as nasty rats. Feedback may be solicited in the form of focus groups or other methods of market research to make certain advertisements are understood in the manner that they were intended.

Noise and Clutter

In the individual communications model, noise represents all of the elements that can distort or disrupt a message. In advertising, noise would be all of the factors that prevent advertising messages from reaching the intended audience. Clutter presents the predominant form of advertising noise. **Clutter** describes the abundance of marketing messages that consumers routinely encounter. In a developed nation such as France or the United States, a typical citizen will be bombarded with six hundred commercial messages each day. The messages are delivered by a variety of traditional and nontraditional media. Those who ride the rapid-transit system in Paris, the Métro, view advertisements as they enter the station, on the walls of the waiting area, and inside the subway trains. The same is true of airports, bus terminals, and other locations. Radio, television, newspaper, magazine, and outdoor ads become a constant part of the day. Outdoor advertising is growing in usage in developing markets also. In 2010 outdoor advertising usage rates in Malaysia increased by 30% to 40%.[5]

> **Clutter** describes the abundance of marketing messages that consumers routinely encounter.

The typical consumer has become adept at tuning out clutter. DVR technology makes it possible to skip over television commercials. Satellite radio and iPods allow music to be enjoyed commercial free. Internet surfers have become increasing skilled at ignoring advertisements on various websites. Most people look past billboards and advertisements on buses or a taxi.

Finding ways to cut through clutter and reach the intended audience represents the marketing challenge for international advertisers. This effort has become increasing difficult as the number of media outlets expand in a wider set of countries. In each culture, what consumers will view and what they will ignore varies by country, age, gender, and other demographics.

The most traditional approach to overcoming clutter, the *three-exposure hypothesis*, suggests that it takes three encounters with a message before a viewer will notice and recall it. To make sure a message will be effective, advertising programs and campaigns must continue to send the message in a series of venues in order to reach potential customers.[6] A contrasting approach, the *recency theory*, argues that a message need only be viewed once, *if* the consumer or business is ready to buy.[7] Either way, continual messaging is required to overcome the barrage of commercials customers come across each day.[8]

International Advertising Management

Advertising management is the process of developing and overseeing a company's advertising program.[9] In an international context, the forces that shape the global marketing environment have a substantial impact on the entire advertising program. Political, legal, language, culture, economic, and infrastructure issues receive attention as a company and its marketing and advertising teams prepare messages for customers and potential customers. Figure 13.7 displays the steps involved in advertising management.[10]

LEARNING OBJECTIVE #2:

What steps are taken to develop an effective international advertising program?

1.	Establish international advertising objectives.
2.	Create an international advertising budget.
3.	Choose an advertising agency.
4.	Oversee the advertising program.
5.	Assess advertising effectiveness.

Figure 13.7: Steps of International Advertising Management Programs

Create brand and product awareness.
Build or improve a brand's image.
Increase sales/market share.
Persuade customers to try a product.
Provide information.
Support other marketing efforts.
Encourage action.

Figure 13.8: International Advertising Objectives

ESTABLISH INTERNATIONAL ADVERTISING OBJECTIVES

Above all other advertising objectives, presenting a clear and consistent message regarding a company's image and theme constitutes a key international marketing priority. In many parts of the world, advertisements bleed across national borders via television, the Internet, and other media, which means it would be nearly impossible to adapt completely to each individual nation. Even when language differences exist, the goal will be to create a somewhat universal image of the company. In Figure 13.8, standard international advertising objectives are presented.

Objectives are chosen based on multiple variables. Creating brand and product awareness becomes the primary goal when a company enters a new host country. Soon after, persuading customers to try a product and encouraging action become logical objectives. Both goals may be accompanied by the drive to provide information. Information may also be the primary objective when company circumstances change, through a disaster or hardship, a merger or acquisition, or when negative publicity arises. Increasing sales and market share serve as objectives during the growth and maturity stages of the product life cycle and later into a company's entry into a host country.

CREATE AN INTERNATIONAL ADVERTISING BUDGET

Achieving one or more of the advertising objectives noted in Figure 13.8 requires funding. Company leaders allocate funds to achieve marketing goals in various ways. The primary budgeting methods include

- percentage of sales,
- match the competition,
- arbitrary allocation, and
- objective and task.

In international advertising programs, the percentage of sales method can refer to overall company sales, sales in one market or country, or percentage of sales in a region. Should the overall company sales figure be used, funds may be distributed equally across all countries in which the company operates or divided according to various priorities. If Nestlé's marketing team decides to increase marketing efforts for Perrier bottled water products in South Korea, additional funds may be devoted to expanding product awareness.

When matching the competition is the method chosen, the advertising team seeks to identify the amount a key competitor spends in a given market. An arbitrary allocation allows the marketing team to set the budget at the level members believe will be best, or at the amount they believe the company can afford.

The most complicated method, objective and task, assigns a monetary amount to the advertising objective chosen. In the case of Nestlé and South Korea, the funds might be set in terms of Swiss *francs* or South Korean *won*. The objective of increasing product awareness would likely require a different amount than increasing market share and other goals.

CHOOSE AN ADVERTISING AGENCY

The first decision made by a company's marketing leaders will be between using members of the company's marketing department to create advertisements, the in-house method, or selecting an external advertising agency. The choice becomes more complex when designing commercials for other countries. One advantage to in-house advertising is that locals will be acquainted with host country circumstances and will be the most familiar with the company's products. Most of the time, the in-house option is less expensive. Companies can complete the entire advertising program or retain boutique agencies for certain activities, including

- purchasing media time or space (media buyers);
- conducting market research regarding media availability or target audience preferences;
- writing copy;
- filming or printing the commercial or advertisement;
- preparing additional marketing materials such as coupons, contests, sweepstakes, and premium programs; and
- assisting in designing company logos, letterhead, and signage.

Outside Advertising Agencies

When the company's marketing department concludes that an external agency would be most advisable, a local agency provides one option. A globally based advertising agency, such as Dentsu Worldwide or Euro RSCG, may have a subsidiary located in the target country. Major agencies often provide the full range of advertising services; other agencies offer some of the functions and outsource others to boutiques. When an outside agency will be chosen, the most common criteria for selection are shown in Figure 13.9.

| Familiarity with local circumstances |
| Familiarity with the company or industry |
| Size of the agency |
| Relevant experience |
| No conflicts of interest |
| Creative ability |
| Services provided |
| Chemistry with the client |

Figure 13.9: Selection Criteria for International Advertising Agencies

In international advertising programs, the first two criteria are primary considerations. Whether an advertising approach will be standardized or adapted, knowing local circumstances, including cultural constraints, legal restrictions, language, slang, and other nuances, makes it possible to develop the best possible set of messages. Familiarity with the company helps the advertising team match the message to the specific product as well as how it might be used in the local culture.

Matching the size of the agency to the size of the company involved helps make certain the account receives the proper attention. When the advertising agency is far bigger than the client, the account may become lost or ignored. When the advertising agency is too small, the account may overwhelm it.

Relevant experience means that an agency has been engaged in something similar. An agency that has represented a tire manufacturer has relevant experience in the automobile industry and could effectively serve a firm wishing to advertise windshield wipers or batteries. At the same time, the agency would have a conflict of interest if it tried to capture the account from a second tire manufacturer.

Creative abilities and a company's creative reputation may be assessed by the number of awards a firm has earned or by observing the agency's work with other clients. The company examining various agencies will seek out the types of services the agency provides that it desires. Finally, intangibles such as the chemistry between the agency and potential client may become the deciding factor.

Euro RSCG is an international advertising agency.

OVERSEE THE ADVERTISING PROGRAM

A creative brief normally serves as a template for an advertising program (see Figure 13.10). The advertising agency or in-house advertising director will use the components of the brief in making other decisions.

Advertising objective
Target audience
Advertising message
Message support (facts, research findings, endorsements)
Constraints (legal restrictions)

Figure 13.10: Elements of a Creative Brief

International advertising objectives should be carefully selected before the agency and client company move forward with any type of advertising program. Marketers identify the target audience from the list of methods used to define market segments, including demographics, psychographics, geographic area, geodemographics, product use, and product user variables. The advertising message should be clearly stated with a single sentence. Typically only one message will be delivered in an advertisement. The message generally focuses on the product's unique selling proposition. Trying to send a series of messages in the same commercial will create confusion. Message support will be used to convince potential buyers that the message claim is true and verifiable. Constraints include any local conditions, such as those imposed by theocratic law, along with any warnings or warranties that must be included in an advertisement. The creative brief serves as a guide for the selection of traditional and nontraditional media to be used in the advertising program.

Traditional Media Advertising

In international advertising programs, media selection may be more complicated than in some domestic settings. The agency or advertising manager will become familiar with local preferences and local availability. The most common choices of traditional advertising media include

- television,
- radio,
- magazines,
- newspapers,
- billboard/outdoor, and
- direct mail.

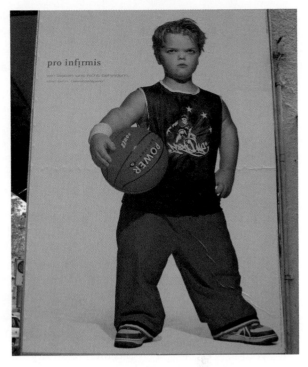

Outdoor advertising is a traditional medium.

It is commonplace for a nation's government to control some or all media. State-owned television, radio, and newspapers stations may restrict or bar various advertisements. An advertisement for Unilever's skincare brand, Pond's, was pulled from the air by Chinese authorities due to the use of an actress, Tang Wei, who was banned from all mainland Chinese media.[11] Other legal restrictions include the prohibition of billboards or the use of direct mail. Cultural nuances will also be considered. For example, in nations with low levels of literacy, the use of newspaper, magazine, and direct mail advertising would be unlikely.

Nontraditional Media

In the past decade, many new forms of advertising have arisen. These media may be used to accompany traditional media or as methods to reach customers in unique new ways. Nontraditional media include

- video game advertising,
- movie trailers,
- subway tunnels,
- in-flight airline magazines,
- carry-home and take-out bags,
- clothing bearing company names or logos,
- mall signs,
- kiosks, and
- posters.

The more developed the local economy has become, the greater the number of nontraditional media alternatives. Nontraditional media assist in overcoming clutter. Someone wearing a t-shirt with a Nike swoosh on it advertises to friends and acquaintances who may not even watch television. Many nations feature numerous kiosks dispersed to metropolitan areas. Consumers in those regions are accustomed to finding information on them. Video game advertising has shown great promise in reaching younger males who are not inclined to watch television or spend time searching the web.

Internet, Social Media, and Digital Marketing

The most rapidly growing method of reaching customers with advertising messages takes place via the Internet, social media websites, and digital marketing technologies. Internet advertising can be featured on the websites of other companies or news agencies, such as an advertisement on the BBC home page. Other Internet advertisements are posted on search engine sites including Google and Bing, normally as a side bar to items that emerge organically to the top of a search engine page. Also, marketers create advertisements on company websites.

Social media advertising has exploded over the past decade. Facebook and Twitter advertising occurs worldwide. Many traditional advertisements encourage viewers to visit the company's Facebook, Twitter, or Digg page for additional information. While Facebook and Twitter are leading social networking sites, international advertisers often utilize other sites that are found in various regions. Popular sites such as Bebo (especially in Europe), Orkut (in India and Brazil), Hyves (the Netherlands), Cyworld (Korea), and Renren (China) offer rich opportunities for international marketers. The use of these sites for international marketing campaigns will continue as they grow in popularity.

Digital marketing technologies encompass both Internet and social media websites. They include marketing messages sent via smart phones, personal data assistants (PDAs), and in-store point-of-purchase tools. Digital marketing has become a critical part of international marketing campaigns due to the rapid worldwide proliferation of technology. This is particularly the case in countries where the penetration rates for these technologies are high such as Japan and the United States, as well as several countries in Europe. Many international companies employ workers in positions such as director of digital sales, social media metrics specialist, or digital strategist. Obviously, these positions did not exist even a few years ago. The use of digital technologies in international marketing campaigns will continue to grow in the future.

MEDIA SELECTION FACTORS

In choosing from the vast variety of potential advertising venues, international marketers consider three main factors. The nature of the product, the size of the market, and its location are related to choices of advertising media. The primary elements marketers consider include costs, availability, and coverage.

Costs

Two phenomena have influenced media selection in major ways during the past decade. The first is the growing price tag for traditional media advertising time. In many markets worldwide, time on a television or radio station, space in a magazine or newspaper, and even billboard rental fees have risen dramatically. With the explosion of potential media outlets, including the vast number of television stations available worldwide, choosing those that fit in a budget becomes more problematic. This growth in spending is especially true for emerging or developing markets. Advertising spending in the United Arab Emirates was projected to grow by 78% in 2010.[12]

The second issue is an increasing demand by companies that advertise for evidence that an advertising campaign or program produces tangible results. The increasing emphasis on accountability places major pressure on advertising agencies to create messages that lead to more immediate responses.[13] A company's marketing team considers the cost of an advertising program and balances that cost with the potential to achieve the desired objective.

Availability

Oftentimes a company's marketing team would prefer to use an advertising medium only to find out that the medium is not available in a specific nation or region. The Internet is the most common example of a medium that cannot be used in certain countries. In 2010, Google experienced a significant challenge when the Chinese government threatened to ban its use due to content that the Chinese government wanted to censor. The company partially withdrew from the Chinese market, resulting in growth for the local Chinese search engine Baidu, a company that has been more cooperative with government censorship efforts.[14] State-owned media sites may not be available to some potential advertisers.

Coverage

Even when media are available, sufficient coverage of potential customers may not be possible, especially when those customers are geographically disbursed. Coverage can be affected by infrastructure, such as when television and radio signals do not reach all parts of a country. Magazines and newspapers may not be distributed throughout an entire area. Billboards may not be legal on certain roads, or it may be that so few people pass by them that the signs are not effective. The Australian government in 2010 considered banning many billboard advertisements as offensive and as an attempt to reclaim public spaces.[15]

The marketing team examines the available and viable media and seeks to purchase time and space in a manner that optimizes coverage to potential customers. To achieve this goal, marketers develop a clear understanding of the members of a target market, the media usage habits within that group, and the costs of using that media to run commercials.

ASSESS ADVERTISING EFFECTIVENESS

International advertisements may be presented in three formats. A *continuous* format means commercials will run consistently throughout the year. A *pulsating* format features advertisements throughout the year, with bursts during key seasons, such as New Year's Day or May Day. A *discontinuous* format includes periods where no advertisements are run and heavy amounts are run during key seasons, such as the period surrounding the Cannes Film Festival. Each of the three formats will be evaluated in two areas: attitudinal effects and behavioral effects. The criteria used to assess the effectiveness of international advertising programs include the items displayed in Figure 13.11.

Some attitudinal changes may take time to instill. An effective advertising program can quickly achieve recognition and recall, especially in the short term. Developing the desired perception of position, brand loyalty, and brand equity normally takes more time, especially when a company enters a new host country. During the 2010 World Cup in South Africa, the low-cost South African airline Kulula.com ran a series of ads that purposely walked the line regarding using World Cup images without permission. One advertisement included the copy "the Unofficial National Carrier of You-Know-What." The governing body of the World Cup, FIFA, responded by taking legal action seeking to remove the ads. The company enjoyed the free publicity and added to the already existing brand position as an irreverent, fun brand.[16]

Attitudinal	Behavioral
brand recognition	inquiries
brand recall	website visits
recall of the advertisement	store traffic
perceptions of position	direct marketing responses
brand loyalty	redemptions of marketing offers (coupons, premiums, contest entries)
brand equity	sales by unit changes in sales volume

Figure 13.11: Attitudinal and Behavioral Effects

Behavioral effects also experience varying results. Inquiries often occur quickly. Changes in other variables, such as sales of big-ticket items, may take longer. Also, competitive reactions and even the weather can delay responses to various promotions and offers. Shopping patterns vary widely. In countries where living spaces are small and storage of any kind is limited, it becomes more difficult to encourage customers to stock up on items. In countries where shopping, especially for convenience items, is a more daily occurrence, advertisements often stress the need for immediate or habitual purchase.

Standardization or Adaptation

A marketer seeking to advertise across national boundaries confronts several key decisions as part of the process. The first will be in regard to the standardization or adaptation of marketing messages. As has been noted in an earlier chapter, both products and messages are considered in this process.

Recently, the trend appears to be increasing standardization of messages as media usage becomes more widely available. When a product remains unchanged regardless of the country in which it is sold, messages are often consistent across borders, except for language translation when needed. The Bhalaria Metal Forming Company in India markets cutlery internationally. It would likely market basic knife, fork, and spoon sets, combined with more-specialized tableware, with a standardized marketing approach emphasizing quality and value.[17]

Standardized messages are also designed when products are adapted. Food products may be adapted to local tastes, yet marketing messages remain consistent, as is the case with Knorr soups and sauces. Knorr packages are standardized with the same brand name and logo, and the company promotes the same image, even though products are tailored to individual countries, including the company's goulash soup in Hungary and chicken noodle soup in Singapore.[18] The same would be true when appliances are adapted to meet local conditions, including differences in electrical current, or the amount of space devoted to a product such as a refrigerator. Larger products including automobiles will be adapted to meet local legal requirements and consumer needs, yet the basic message sent by a giant such as Audi remains consistent (www.audi.com).

When a company such as Proctor & Gamble creates individual brands for various nations or regions, P & G marketing messages are often adapted more significantly. The same will be true when a company expands in other ways. In 2011, PepsiCo acquired Russian juice maker Wimm-Bill-Dann, achieving access into the market for the two distinct types of products, which PepsiCo likely will continue to market separately.[19]

International Law and Globally Integrated Marketing Communications

The use of globally integrated marketing communications must also follow the various laws that pertain to advertising and promotion. Many differences pertaining to advertising and international promotion activities are present across country borders. The Unfair Commercial Practices Directive of the European Union (Directive 2005/29/EC), passed in 2005, outlines a number of marketing and promotional activities that are prohibited in the EU. India, a country of growing importance, has a number of laws that pertain to advertising. The Indecent Representation of Women Act of 1986 covers what were deemed to be inappropriate depictions of women in advertising, promotions, and product or labeling designs. The advertising or promotion of cigarettes, tobacco products, and liquor in India is covered under the Prohibition of Advertisement and Regulation of Trade and Commerce, Production, Supply and Distribution Act of 2003.

While laws are established and enforced internationally, most marketers prefer some degree of self-regulation over governmental intervention, and as a result, many self-regulatory bodies exist. The European Advertising Standards Alliance (EASA) is a self-regulatory association useful for learning about advertising and promotion standards throughout the European Union. Similar standards exist in India through the Advertising Standard Council of India. Self-regulation codes also were adopted recently for marketers in China. The China Association of National Advertisers, the China Advertising Association, and the China Advertising Association of Commerce adopted the code. As China continues to grow in importance in the world's economy, codes such as these assist international marketers to ensure that promotional practices are within established guidelines. International marketers that pay close attention to international advertising and promotions laws, as well as the codes established by self-regulatory entities, encounter fewer problems with governments over time.

Message Design: Types of Appeals

Traditional advertising theory suggests that products can be marketed using a method from a set of basic types of advertising appeals. The goal will be to match the message's objective to the medium selected and the appeal format. For many markets, the choice would be made from one or more of the following set of advertising appeals:

- fear
- humor
- sex/sensuality
- music
- rationality
- emotions
- scarcity

LEARNING OBJECTIVE #3:

What traditional and culturally based types of advertising appeals do marketing professionals use?

A fear appeal walks a fine line. When the amount of fear becomes too great, the viewer tends to turn away from the message. When the degree of fear is too low, the viewer might ignore the message or not take it seriously. Cultural adaption will be required when assessing the degree to which citizens in a region are sensitive to danger. In Western culture, bad breath and body odor can be made to seem catastrophic. In other nations, these issues may be less important. Fear may be generated by a number of sources, including being viewed as a social outcast, worries about financial issues, the desire to protect one's family, concerns about personal health, and other issues.

Humor appeals may be difficult to design due to cultural and legal problems. What people think is funny varies widely across and within each country. Various countries may restrict the use of humor with religion or other values. A cultural assimilator may be able to assist with some aspects of humor, but the assimilator's opinion will only represent one point of view regarding whether the commercial was actually funny.

Academic research investigating humor in advertising reveals that the foundation of humor is incongruity. An unexpected, implausible, or nonactual event forms the roots of humor, regardless of country. The following joke uses the unexpected: A doctor tells a man, "Your wife must have absolute rest. Here is a sleeping tablet." "When do I give it to her?" the man asks. "You don't," explains the doctor, "you take it yourself." The mild humor in this joke is due to the unexpected nature of the punch line. Some research suggests that this type of incongruity is funny globally. Research also indicates that cultures vary in terms of the roles of groups, equality, and other aspects of advertising humor based on the cultural background of the country. Basically, whereas the unexpected typically makes consumers laugh, what is considered unexpected differs from country to country.[20]

A sexy orange juice advertisement.

A perfume product may have the objective of increasing brand loyalty by suggesting the scent will make the user feel more feminine. The choice of advertising appeal would likely be a sensual sexual appeal coupled with a medium where romantic music could be played in a quiet, soft setting, and an attractive model would use the perfume. Careful thought will be given to what is legally and culturally acceptable when sexual messages are framed. In Chile, one advertising campaign featured nude celebrities drinking milk, and authorities allowed it to air. In many Middle Eastern countries, sex and gender-related issues are prohibited to the point that sexual appeals in any form are not used.[21]

The use of music occurs in several ways in advertising. It can serve as a background for some other type of appeal, such as dramatic music supporting a fear appeal or a light-hearted tune in a humorous ad. A musical appeal makes the tune the primary element in the advertisement. Music will be tailored to local tastes and the product being marketed.

Cultural matches dictate the most viable moments to feature rational appeals. Many business-to-business advertisements take advantage of a rational presentation of a product's benefits or the endorsement of a professional. The most expensive advertisement in Indian history, costing near *Rs* 4.5 *crore* (approximately $1 million) was a 2010 television commercial for the leading Indian soda Thums

Up. The commercial stars the popular Bollywood actor Akshay Kumar and features a rational appeal to attach the popularity and style of the actor to the soda.[22]

Emotional advertising is favored in some nations over others. Western Union recently ran emotional advertising in El Salvador. The message presented a mother talking about her son who had left the country to move to the United States and each month he sent her money using Western Union. Many Latin American citizens have relatives they have not seen for years. The emotional approach worked. Emotions used in advertising include friendships, trust, happiness, security, serenity, anger, family bonds, and passion.[23]

Scarcity appeals are effective when a product is offered only for a limited time. Often these advertisements focus on a specific event, such as the World Cup or the Olympics. They are used during holiday seasons, including red and green candy wrappers during the Christmas season. Scarcity approaches also fit with marketing to bottom-of-the-pyramid customers, who seek out special deals when they have money available to make purchases.

International Marketing in Daily Life

Culture, Gender, and Advertising

Advertising constitutes one of the most visual marketing elements in everyday life. Consumers worldwide are continually bombarded with thousands of advertising messages. The communications often reflect cultural variables. One important variable is gender roles. Gender roles are reflected in advertisements and differ greatly across cultures. In Western cultures, women have historically been portrayed as inferior to men and, quite often, as sex objects. In the United States in particular, women have historically been depicted in housewife roles or in sexually provocative ways. These depictions have evolved over time. Ironically, men are often portrayed in sexually suggestive ways in today's commercials.

Attitudes toward sex and gender roles in advertising tend to be much more liberal in Europe, especially in France where overtly sexual imagery in advertising is commonplace. The European Advertising Standards Alliance (EASA) acts as the main body for advertising self-regulation in the region and works to foster positive depictions of women in advertisements as well as high ethical standards in all advertising campaigns. The body passed guidance principles for the industry regarding sex role depictions in 2009.[24] The principles promote the belief that advertisements should respect human dignity and should not discriminate against either males or females.

In Eastern cultures, advertising practices are much more conservative. The depiction of women has traditionally been based on the stereotype that the place for the woman is in the home. The phrase *danson johi*, a Chinese term that means respect for men and contempt for women, has often emerged in advertising campaigns.[25] In Eastern cultures, women have often been associated with lower-priced products while men have been associated with higher-priced items. The difference originates from a stereotypical view that men are valued more highly than are women. Some of the tactics appear have begun to change, especially the case in China where recent advertisements have promoted more equality between men and women and portray more positive roles for women.[26] In India, women have also historically been portrayed in stereotypical ways, such as performing housework and caring for the husband or family. Such a viewpoint appears to be evolving as well, as women are increasingly being portrayed as being independent and career-oriented.[27]

Religious beliefs continue to play an important role in the depiction of women in advertising. In Muslim countries, sexually explicit or inappropriate advertisements are strongly rejected.[28] International marketers carefully consider religious beliefs when constructing advertisements in these regions. Core cultural beliefs vary greatly across countries, and advertisers have much to gain by observing these differences.

CULTURAL PARADOXES

Marketers trained in Western culture and settings would be tempted to rely on traditional appeals. In international marketing programs, however, cultural differences create differing environments. To meet the challenges, overcoming various paradoxes takes precedence. Three often receive the most attention: the equality paradox, the dependence and freedom paradox, and the success paradox.[29]

Equality Paradox

In much of Europe, equality conceptually suggests that income distribution should be relatively uniform. In contrast, those in New Zealand and Great Britain view equality in terms of opportunity rather than income distribution. The net result would be much more dramatic differences in what would be perceived as income disparity. Therefore, advertisers would need to account for host country perceptions of equality when designing commercials.

Dependence and Freedom Paradox

Dependence and independence are opposing values related to power distance and individualism/collectivism. In a collectivist culture such as Japan with greater power distance, children depend on their parents for much longer periods of time. Where power distance is lower and the culture is more independent, children are often encourage to become self-reliant and go out on their own at a much earlier age. Again, advertisers would need to be aware of these factors when creating messages.

Success Paradox

In masculine cultures, a male may be more likely to knowingly display personal success, or "show off." British culture, which tends to be more masculine, would feature advertisements containing terms such as "best" or "better." In contrast, more-feminine cultures, including those in Sweden and Denmark, would refrain from such claims. Instead more subtle messages are presented, such as "True refinement comes from within," the tagline for a recent Volvo commercial in Sweden.

INTERNATIONAL INCIDENT ///

A copywriter for an advertising company suggests an advertising campaign that appears to be very materialistic and masculine in a feminine culture. The writer insists that such an ad will stand out in the clutter and be noticed. The international marketing team disagrees with this assessment and believes that the ad does not appropriately match the culture. Should the team attempt such an appeal in a highly feminine culture in order to be noticed? Or, would this effort backfire?

INTERNATIONAL ADVERTISING APPEALS

Due to these paradoxes and other cultural differences, appeal formats are often based in other factors in international advertising. Advertisers account for cultural nuances when selecting the dimension to be used. The most common formats include advertisements that reflect the cultural values displayed in Figure 13.12.

Power distance
Individualism/collectivism
Masculinity/femininity
Uncertainty avoidance
Long- or short-term orientation

Figure 13.12: International Advertising Appeals and Values

Power Distance

Cultures with high degrees of power distance often experience advertising with verbal and direct power claims. Feeling of status and prestige may be associated with products. In Portugal, the Alfa 33 automobile has been advertised featuring a reference to feelings of royalty.[30]

Power distance will be displayed in relationships (young/old) between persons featured in advertisements and how those relationships are demonstrated. In a low power distance, advertisements may be designed with a mother and daughter sharing an experience as "friends," whereas in a high power distance culture the same two will be viewed with the elder advising, counseling, or teaching the younger person. High power distance cultures normally exhibit greater degrees of respect and deference to older persons.

Power distance is related to perceptions of independence. Advertisements featuring a child standing on his own would be more appreciated in a low power distance culture where independence is valued. A recent print ad in the Netherlands shows a young boy by himself and references Blue Band margarine, emphasizing his ability to make his own choices. At the opposite extreme, high power distance would lead to commercials featuring dependent relationships between children and parents.[31]

Individualism / Collectivism

When the advertising team knows that messages are being constructed for members of an individualistic culture, the language in the copy will be more direct and personalized, such as the "Treat yourself right" tagline for Crystal Light. Direct references to "I," "we," and "you" become more likely.[32] A recent Nike advertisement in Spain featured the headline, "The energy I get." The Nike tagline "Just do it" reflects the same direct, individualized message.

Visual elements of commercials focused on individualistic cultures tend to feature a person enjoying the product alone. In the individualistic German culture, a woman takes pleasure in a container of Magnum ice cream by herself, and the copy states, "I share many things, but not everything."

In collectivist cultures, sharing and being part of a group become important elements of the message strategy. The Portuguese product food sweetener Hermesetas is advertised with the comment, "It is so good, you want to share it with others." A person experiencing a product alone may be more pitied than envied. Any advertisement for a restaurant, automobile, or clothing item would need to find a way to be presented in a social setting, enjoyed by the purchaser and his or her friends. Restaurants would have an abundance of food to share with an unexpected guest. Automobiles would be driven with several passengers onboard. Clothing would be enjoyed and shared with others. One estimate suggests that 70% of the world's population is collectivist, which suggests that many individualistic commercials do not fit with the target audience.[33]

An example of an individualistic advertisement.

As an example of adaptation of the message for the same product in differing cultures, Jever beer was recently marketed in the individualistic climate of German with a photograph of a man standing alone on the beach holding a bottle of the product. In Spain, where the culture is more collectivist, a group party setting portrays the enjoyment of the beer in one advertisement and by a couple close together in another.

As marketing messages travel across international boundaries, it becomes more difficult to structure a message to one sole culture. Media selection can help. Local magazines and newspapers can be utilized for culture-specific messages; television and radio are more likely to bleed into other countries or be sent by Internet messages.[34]

Another new development may be found when global brands appear alongside local brands in the same market. In China, consumers often view global brands as being sophisticated and modern. Western-style individualistic advertising of those products would be expected. Local Chinese brands would continue to be advertised with messages and images that reflect local values, and would therefore contain more collectivist elements.[35]

Masculinity/Femininity

Masculinity often connects with individualism. The net result becomes an emphasis on aggression, competitiveness, and winning. An advertisement for the Japanese Nikon camera suggests, "More winners per second," which reflects this perspective. Beyond winning, size becomes an issue in masculine cultures, where bigger is better.[36]

Gender portrayals differ in masculine as opposed to feminine cultures. Often, men are depicted as being incompetent in domestic settings in masculine cultures; the kitchen is the woman's domain and she has the greater expertise. Also, however, women can be portrayed as stronger and more aggressive. A Japanese television commercial for Hitachi features a woman in battle with flies. Women may be shown winning and being successful in masculine cultures.

Feminine cultures are more caring, appreciate softness, and favor small over large. Sweden's Volvo tag line "True refinement comes from within" expresses the value that you do not have to show off, win, or make sure everyone knows your car is bigger and better. The company often advertises safety and protection over power and performance.

In a feminine culture, an advertisement for a pain reliever would likely carry the message that you can relieve the suffering of someone you love by using the product. The same medicine in a masculine culture would likely be marketed as, "The number one pain reliever," or "The medicine doctors recommend most."

Gender role portrayal will be different in feminine cultures. In Denmark, a product sold in Matas drugstore has been advertised with a male model wearing an apron. In Spain, a man may be shown shopping with his children and nurturing them. In Sweden, one advertisement for Ajax cleaner features a man swinging a mop as if it were a golf club.

Uncertainty Avoidance

Advertisements in countries with high levels of uncertainty avoidance tend to be highly structured and contain a great deal of information and detail. Strong uncertainty avoidance is connected to the desire for explanation, testing, proof, advice, and testimonials by experts. An advertisement for the Russian facial cream Purity Line contains a substantial amount of discussion of the company's laboratory methods, including scientific proof that the product will work. Demonstrating competence becomes important in strong uncertainty avoidance cultures. Automobiles manufactured in Germany can be portrayed as containing superior engineering. Facts and figures reinforce these claims. Using the standard fear appeal is an effective strategy in high uncertainty avoidance cultures.[37]

Where uncertainty avoidance is less of a driving force within a culture, advertisers are able to construct messages that are less precise, because they do not need to reduce anxiety or tension. At the extreme, advertisement for Jamaican tourism portray, "One love, one life" as the musical theme with the tagline "Welcome to Jamaica," which does not require proof.

Long- or Short-Term Orientation

Customers in countries with a short-term orientation may often view advertisements featuring a scarcity appeal. The approach matches the sense of urgency present in the culture, and leads to phrases such as "Buy now!" Short-term orientation is related to immediate gratification. In the United Kingdom, one advertising headline created by *Häagen-Dazs* ice cream entices the consumer to enjoy "instant pleasure." Investments in the long-term future, through saving or insurance policies, are hard to advertise in short-term orientation situations. Instead the advertiser would need to find a way to convince the individual to act immediately, such as through a teaser rate for savings or a gift or premium to accompany the purchase of an insurance policy.

Long-term orientation advertisements are associated with symbols and words regarding the future, stability, and future generations. Mountains, trees, and other long-lasting natural phenomena are displayed in advertisements aimed at long-term cultures, especially in high-context cultures. LG International has advertised in Korea with an elderly man surrounded by the harmony of nature, a message directed to long-term orientation.

Combinations

As is the case in traditional advertising, various combinations of appeals can be devised to match a product, target market, culture, or specific message objective. Traditional approaches are often developed, including humor with fear, humor with sex, rationality with scarcity, and music with practically any other approach. A wide variety of combinations are possible. Those same traditional appeal formats may also be connected to the international appeals. As noted, fear appeals effectively reach those with higher levels of uncertainty avoidance. Scarcity appeals match with short-term orientation. Creative advertisers can develop many combinations of traditional methodologies with these international formats.

Cultural experts also note combinations of the international approaches. Often, masculine cultures are also individualistic. Feminine cultures may be more collectivist. The advertising team can examine other combinations of cultural characteristics in order to construct the best possible advertising program.

Advertising Executional Frameworks

LEARNING OBJECTIVE #4:

How are the traditional executional frameworks adapted to international advertising programs?

When creating an advertising program, a key element to consider will be the campaign's message strategy. A **message strategy** is the primary tactic or approach used to deliver the key idea in an advertisement. International message strategies are carefully matched with the company, product, target market, local culture, and other conditions in the host country. Three major types of message strategies are cognitive, affective, and conative.[38]

Cognitive message strategies present rational arguments or pieces of information to consumers. The key idea will be in regard to a product's attributes and benefits. Consumers can enjoy these benefits by purchasing the product.[39] Cognitive message strategies fit with more rational cultures and those with higher levels of uncertainty avoidance. They also can spell out the extended benefits of a product in a culture with a long-term orientation. In a high power distance culture, a cognitive message strategy can be used showing a parent or teacher explaining a product's benefits to a child or student.

Affective message strategies invoke feelings or emotions and match those feelings with a product, service, or company. A resonance approach connects the product with the consumer's experiences to develop stronger ties between the product and the individual. Emotional advertising elicits emotions related to product recall and choice by developing positive feelings toward the brand. Affective advertising is more emotive and matches with feminine cultures and low power distance cultures. Collectivism also fits with the affective approach, appealing to family, friends, and social connectedness.

Conative message strategies are designed to lead directly to a consumer response, such as a store visit or purchase. Such an approach connects well with short-term orientation cultures. In more masculine cultures, where direct messages are delivered, the advertisement can encourage a "Take action now" response. Individualism can be emphasized with a "Do this for yourself" communication.

TRADITIONAL EXECUTIONAL FRAMEWORKS

In order to deliver cognitive, affective, or conative messages, a delivery system will be employed. The **executional framework** is the manner in which an advertising appeal and message strategy is delivered. Figure 13.13 lists the standard methods of sending messages to consumers.

The growing sophistication of computer graphics programs has led to greater use of animation to present commercials. Animation appears in television spots, on the Internet, and in print media when cartoon characters or other figures pitch products. Animation captures attention, especially when it portrays things that are physically impossible. Many countries are experiencing growth in Internet usage, leading to consumers viewing animation as a cutting-edge, modern method of advertising.

Animation
Slice-of-life
Dramatization
Testimonial
Authoritative
Demonstration
Fantasy
Informative

Figure 13.13: Traditional Executional Frameworks

Slice-of-life executions involve four stages: encounter, problem, interaction, and solution. Two or more people meet. They discover they experience a common dilemma, such as a dirty shirt. In the interaction, one explains to another how a product provides a solution. Using the good or service resolves the quandary, making everyone happy. Slice-of-life executions match with high-context cultures, where symbols and rituals supplant lengthy explanations. Collectivist and feminine cultures often feature slice-of-life executions. Japan's collectivism and Norway's feminism fit with this approach.

When a slice-of-life ad contains additional intensity, it becomes a dramatization. Expressive cultures in which more-extreme circumstances are needed to capture attention relate to dramatization. Dramatization meshes with high-context cultures, because less attention to in-depth explanation is given; instead, the problem is simply resolved by the product.

Satisfied customers provide testimonials. In collectivist cultures, the recommendation of friends or endorsement by a group of peers will be persuasive. Testimonials of family members or friends giving out advice work well in feminine cultures.

A billboard featuring animation.

Authoritative messages are delivered by experts, such as doctors, lawyers, and those who use a product in some technical manner. These individuals explain a product's benefits. Experts take on additional status in high power distance countries and those in which low-context communication prevails. For countries with greater degrees of uncertainty avoidance, expertise provides key purchase reassurance. Authoritative messages appear in business-to-business advertisements, where an expert gives a product greater credibility.

Demonstration executions gain value in high-context cultures, where visual images portray a product's benefits. Demonstration also reduces uncertainty for those who require such information. A demonstration in a masculine culture will be designed to show a product's superiority. In feminine cultures, the use of a product to help a loved one, such as a disinfectant being applied to a cut to make it hurt less and heal faster, creates a powerful image of caring.

For those with a short-term orientation, a *fantasy* offers a "get away from it all" option involving sex, love, romance, or self-indulgence. Fantasies are not as well accepted in logical, rational cultures, but a fantasy can be constructed to show someone gaining status and power by using a product in a high power distance culture. Another fantasy could show a high-status person being embarrassed or moved to a lower level in a low-power distance country, thereby emphasizing common humanity.

Informative executions deliver straightforward presentations. They work better in low-context cultures and with those seeking to avoid uncertainty. Many business-to-business advertisements are informative, regardless of cultural differences, due to the nature of the message and the audience, which expects more rational and clear-cut information.

INTERNATIONAL EXECUTIONAL FRAMEWORKS

The traditional executional frameworks can be adapted to local conditions for a variety of marketing messages. In a global marketing context, however, other forms of executions are popular. Seven basic forms of advertising in global markets are

- announcement,
- association transfer,
- lesson,
- drama,
- entertainment,
- imagination, and
- special effects.

Announcements

Announcements are presentations of facts without the use of people. Visuals portray the message. A *pure display* appears in a shop window. A *product message* transmits information about product attributes in a factual, logical manner. These messages are used in low-context cultures that desire fuller explanations. The *corporate presentation* form of announcement describes the overall corporation with a voice-over or a song. A voice-over presents facts, and a song provides additional context. Each announcement method achieves the goal of providing information to customers and potential customers regarding products, product improvements, releases and offers, and other basic information. Announcements often match the traditional informative executional framework.

> Announcements are presentations of facts without the use of people. Visuals portray the message.

Association Transfers

Association transfers offer a format in which a product is combined with another object, person, situation, or environment. One form of transfer, the *lifestyle* method, associates people with a culture or counterculture of a country. A standard lifestyle presentation connects a product to a youthful approach to life. Germany's Beck's beer often presents commercials depicting young people engaged in active hobbies or events. With the *metaphor* form of association transfer, the characteristics of an animal or idea are connected with the product. Visual metaphors, often found in high-context cultures, can be concrete or abstract images. Verbal metaphors will be placed in low-context cultures. The *metonymy* approach transfers the meaning of an original object into the brand, such as when a flower blossoms into a bottle of perfume. *Celebrity* *transfers* associate other persons with a celebrity, who does not demonstrate, endorse, or provide a direct testimonial about the product. Hong Kong actor Jackie Chan has appeared in celebrity transfer commercials.

Lessons, Demonstrations, and Comparative Advertising

The **lesson** form of presentation applies facts and arguments to the audience in the form of a lecture. In low-context cultures, straightforward presentations of facts are welcome. The viewer learns how a product solves a problem or improves her life. In one format, a *presenter* is the dominant present in the advertisement speaking directly and sending the main message. The presenter can use the demonstration format to explain the product's benefits. For collectivist cultures, a set of presenters may appear in the commercial. A second form of lesson takes the form of *endorsement and testimonial*, which is highly similar to the testimonial and authoritative executional frameworks. A third version, the *vignette*, uses a series of independent sketches or visual situations with no continuity in the action. The product is displayed as the focus of the vignette with a voice-over or song suggesting how it is connected to the story being portrayed. The fourth version of the lesson format, the *demonstration* is the same as that used in the traditional framework.

Product comparisons may be part of a demonstration presentation, where two items are shown in use side by side. The marketing team should be aware of cultural sensitivities to these types of advertisements as well as any legal restrictions. Argentina, China, El Salvador, Italy, and South Africa do not allow using competitors as part of **comparative advertising**. Other countries, such as the Philippines, have strong restrictions on how advertising can be conducted. Many cultures frown on such comparisons as well, including most of the Scandinavian countries.[40]

The lesson form of presentation applies facts and arguments to the audience in the form of a lecture.

VIDEO LINK 13.3: Marketing Beer

Entertainment

When theatrical drama, musicals, shows, comedies, slapstick, humor, horror, or satire provides the primary advertising format the mode is called **entertainment.** The use of *humor* as an advertising appeal has been presented previously, with the caution that humor is subjective and difficult to create. A *play or act around the product* presents a story that may or may not be connected to the product. A Japanese commercial for Nissin Noodle Cup featured people throwing rocks at a dinosaur, with the tag line, "Hungry? Noodle Cup." The concept was to attract attention in a unique way.

Imagination

The **imagination** format utilizes cartoon or other visual techniques to make unrealistic presentations of a make-believe world. Imagination essentially combines the traditional animation and fantasy executional frameworks. An animated bear has been used across national boundaries to promote the cleaning brand Cif, a French product. The bear's name is *Cajoline* in Greece, *Bamseline* in Denmark, *Coccoline* in Italy, and *Kuschelweich* in Germany.

VIDEO LINK 13.4: Marketing With Humor

Special Effects

The **special effects** format delivers a variety of messages by combining animation, cartoon, camera effects (camera motion), recording techniques, music, and other sounds in commercials. MTV takes advantage of special effects to promote the channel globally. Special effects can highlight a dramatization, fantasy, or animation executional framework.[41]

Combinations

These international advertising executional frameworks do not stand alone. Special effects can be part of an imagination or part of a demonstration. Imagination can be combined with entertainment. The international frameworks also are utilized in conjunction with traditional frameworks. Animation and fantasy can be part of imagination, entertainment, demonstration, and special effects. The role of the advertising agency or in-house marketer will be to discover the most important cultural characteristics and then combine that knowledge with the selection of the advertising appeal(s) and executional framework(s) that best match the product and brand image. The additional challenge is to make the commercial or advertising interesting enough to cut through clutter and be remembered by the target audience.

An advertisement connecting beer consumption with football (soccer).

Alternative Marketing Programs

LEARNING OBJECTIVE #5:

What types of alternative marketing programs are available to international firms?

In addition to the alternative media choices marketers employ to present advertisements, a series of new approaches to reaching consumers has evolved. Alternative marketing programs take advantage of the creativity and imagination of the company's marketing professionals. Effective alternative marketing programs overcome clutter and reach consumers in comfortable settings. They allow the company to present a message to an interested audience. Four of the alternative marketing programs that have achieved success are

- buzz marketing,
- guerrilla marketing,
- product placements and branded entertainment, and
- lifestyle marketing.

BUZZ MARKETING

One of the fastest growing areas in alternative media marketing is buzz marketing, which is also known as word-of-mouth marketing. The system emphasizes consumers passing along information about a product. Three approaches to buzz include

- consumers who like a brand and tell others,
- consumers who like a brand and are sponsored by a company to tell others, and
- company or agency employees telling others about the brand.

Consumers Who Tell Family and Friends

Consumers who like a brand can be encouraged to tell family and friends. The emergence of social media facilitates this type of buzz. A clever song or video can quickly go viral, leading to greater interest in a product. This type of buzz is the opposite of negative word of mouth, which can quickly damage a brand's image. Prior to the Internet, a disenchanted customer was likely to tell around eleven people about a negative experience but only five or six people about a positive encounter. Currently both numbers can quickly rise to dramatic figures. Many international companies monitor what is being said on Facebook and Twitter, seeking to take advantage of positive buzz and to combat any negative comments.

A common tactic for technology companies is to hire advertising agencies to help create buzz around a new product release. Typically, this includes a fake leak of the new product. The company acts as if the leak was unintentional, and sends cease-and-desist letters, but the actual goal is to get bloggers and technology writers to begin writing about the product pre-release. This creates buzz and increases initial sales.[42]

Sponsored Consumers

When a person enjoys a product and the company becomes aware of the individual, marketers can develop *brand advocate* or *brand ambassador* relationships. Recently, Sony employed brand advocates to help launch the GPS camera. One ambassador was paid to travel to Australia and send back photos of the trip, complete with a map showing where various beaches were located. Another variation of the sponsored consumer approach employs *customer evangelists* who are paid to spread the word about products in various social circles, including family, friends, reference groups, and work associates. These enthusiasts host parties and other events featuring the product. Red Bull has employed customer evangelists to host parties, especially on college campuses, in a variety of countries.

Creating buzz for Red Bull.

Company or Agency Employees

Two methods of using company employees to spread word of mouth are possible. The first occurs when the employee openly notes he or she works for the company but feels strongly about its products and brands. This type of positive endorsement occurs in organizations with satisfied and committed employees who are proud to work in the company. Individuals with strong bonds to a firm solicit use of the product, and encourage family and friends to seek employment in the company.

The second method of buzz marketing involves an employee passing along positive word of mouth but poses as a "regular person," not revealing her employment status. As an example, a female could stop tourists in front of the Colosseum in Rome, and ask them to take her picture. She can then demonstrate the camera, emphasizing the brand name and its features to the tourists, without ever saying that she works for the company that manufactures the camera. The Word of Mouth Marketing Association frowns on this type of activity, but others believe it is ethical and does not violate any laws.[43]

Buzz Marketing Stages

International word-of-mouth marketing has been compared to a virus going through three states: inoculation, incubation, and infection. *Inoculation* occurs when a product is introduced to a new host country. *Incubation* represents the point at which brand advocates can create the greatest amount of buzz. *Infection* represents a successful program in which brand awareness has been greatly enhanced by positive endorsements.

GUERRILLA MARKETING

Guerilla marketing offers an aggressive, grassroots approach to marketing. The program emphasizes one-on-one relationships with consumers through innovative alternative means. Typically, a successful guerrilla marketing approach takes advantage of a combination of media, advertising, public relations, and surprise tactics that create buzz.

In Shanghai, only 10% of the population is wealthy enough to ride in a taxi. Passengers are often between the ages of twenty-one and forty-nine. They tend to be white-collar workers. An advertising agency identified the group as a viable market and created contracts in which video-streaming screens were placed in taxis for customers to watch. Estée Lauder, Procter & Gamble, KFC, and Volkswagen took advantage of the opportunity. When Christina Aguilera agreed to perform in Shanghai, nearly 50% of tickets were reserved by persons calling the concert phone number displayed on the taxi screens.[44]

Effective guerilla marketing programs rely on the energy and imaginations of employees. Success is achieved through profits rather than sales, and by targeting individuals and small groups with marketing messages rather than with mass media advertising. Guerrilla marketers seek cooperative arrangements with other companies. The customer base grows through referrals and through return business.

In 2008, Skoda asked British Facebook users to prove just how "mean" or "lovely" they were. The winners at each personality extreme won a new car. Havas-agency-owned Archibald Ingall Stretton created the social-media campaign for Skoda. The first version was "made of lovely stuff" campaign that ran in 2007. The entrant deemed most lovely received the prize. Then, a "made of meaner stuff" TV and print campaign created by Fallon, London, followed. It was, in essence, a dark reworking of the made of lovely stuff campaign, in which the meanest participant won the car. Both contests created considerable buzz for Skoda.[45]

International guerilla marketing programs begin with the identification of *touch points*, where customers eat, drink, shop, socialize, and sleep. Connecting with consumers in logical places where the product can become part of their lives will be the goal. The marketing team then looks for creative and imaginative ways to enhance the connection.

PRODUCT PLACEMENTS AND BRANDED ENTERTAINMENT

Movie presentations and television programs offer quality venues to reach customers in ways other than traditional advertising. A *product placement* is the planned insertion of a brand or product into a movie or television show with the goal of influencing viewers. The international appeal of films makes it possible to influence consumers in a more subtle way.

James Bond films have featured a variety of automobiles. Each time, the impact on sales of that vehicle selected has been noticeable. Classic Bond cars include Aston Martin, Audi, BMW, and Lotus.[46]

Many international television programs include product placements. *Britain's Got Talent*, the British version of *America's Got Talent*, began featuring placements in 2011. The high-profile American program has a longstanding relationship with Coca-Cola. Television critics worried that placements in British programs would affect their credibility, calling them "stealth advertising," while others believed they would generate much needed revenues.[47]

Branded entertainment weaves a product or brand into the storyline of a movie or television show. In the CTC drama *The Eleventh Hour*, Nicorette gum was integrated into a story about a character trying to quit smoking. The George Clooney film *Up in the Air* prominently featured American Airlines as part of the storyline.

Program Success

To achieve success in product placements and branded entertainment programs, marketers follow some basic principles. First, the product or brand should plausibly fit with the program. A sports program logically matches with sports or energy drinks. Placements flow sensibly in those venues. In the case of Nicorette gum and American Airlines, the products wove seamlessly into the stories. Second, the brand must be prominently featured. In the U.S. version of *American Idol*, more than four thousand placements were made during the 2006–2007 season. Only a few will actually become noticed, such as the glass of Coca-Cola on the judges' table. For other products, payments to place products probably did not yield positive results. Third, the attempt should be made to create an emotional connection between the product and the audience. This feature will be the most difficult to achieve. Any time a product can be given as both a prize with a corresponding gift to a charity, the potential to increase an emotional attachment rises. If the product can in some way assist or comfort a character in a story, it also becomes more likely that viewers will see the brand in a more favorable light.

Product placements and branded entertainment are growing in use worldwide. The programs benefit advertising companies seeking to gain exposure in ways other than traditional media advertising. From the perspective of movie and television studios, charging money to use brands in shows generates much-needed revenues.

LIFESTYLE MARKETING

In many countries, lifestyle marketing practically occurs as a natural event. Lifestyle marketing involves making contact with customers in comfortable settings, including where they take part in hobbies, at entertainment venues, and at shopping locations. In many nations, the majority of shopping takes place in central locations where vendors meet to sell their goods on nearly a daily basis. Festivals featuring religious holidays or cultural events are common. A marketer can look for a logical tie to an event and set up a booth or table to take advantage of the connection.

Musical performances offer lifestyle marketing opportunities. An opera or symphony will attract one type of company, such as a high-end fashion designer. A rock concert or hip-hop event attracts other types of clothing companies, energy drinks, and other products. A country and western or bluegrass-type festival may be linked to farm equipment and products.

Effective lifestyle marketing goes beyond simply finding the right venue. The marketer looks for a special enticement that will attract attention, such as a giveaway or free sample. Those who make contacts with potential customers become key company representatives. They should be trained to be engaging, polite, and upbeat about the brand.

Bottom-of-the-Pyramid

Of all the alternative marketing and media programs available, lifestyle marketing best matches with reaching bottom-of-the-pyramid customers. These individuals have less access to traditional media. They may not even own television sets. They may encounter people wearing clothing with company endorsements, but they often cannot afford such clothing. Kiosks and outdoor/billboard advertisements may attract their attention, but these customers must view the product as being within their financial reach in order to achieve any effect.

Lifestyle marketing reaches bottom-of-the-pyramid customers in the most comfortable settings, such as where they shop. Products that have been adapted to smaller packages with lower prices can easily be presented in farmers' markets, local street markets, and in places such as outdoor markets in rural areas.

Ethical Issues in International Advertising

Advertising professions receive a great deal of criticism from social commentators. The complaints typically center on the role advertising plays in a country, with arguments suggesting that many advertising activities are, or can be, unethical. Some of the most common objections include these:

- Advertising overemphasizes materialism.
- Advertising increases prices.
- Advertising perpetuates stereotypes.
- Advertising unfairly focuses on children.
- Advertisements are often offensive.
- Advertising dangerous products is unethical.

The first criticism, that advertising overemphasizes materialism, takes on additional significance in the case of bottom-of-the-pyramid consumers. The argument is that these individuals, who may be less savvy with money, are encouraged to purchase items that they want but do not need. For example, soft drink products may be sold at a low cost ($0.025), but that price may represents one-fourth to one-eighth of a person's daily income. Should advertising target such individuals?

A longstanding complaint has been that advertising increases prices. The counter-argument is that advertising lowers prices by increasing competition and that, without advertising, fewer items are sold, thus raising the price. Both sides of the argument provide statistics favoring their point of view.

Some critics suggest that advertising perpetuates stereotypes. A narrow distinction may be made between stereotyping and market segmentation. At the same time, many protests center on the ways in which advertisers portray older people, minorities, and citizens of other countries. In the 2011 Super Bowl, an advertising attempt at humor using doddering senior citizens drew complaints, as did an effort at humor featuring citizens of Tibet. In international marketing, careful attention should be paid to unpopular stereotyping.

Many products consumed by children are advertised in ways that social critics deem unacceptable, arguing that advertising unfairly focuses on children. The use of cartoon characters and small premiums such as children's toys combined with food products advertising unfairly influences those who are unable to form mature judgments. Some governments restrict the amount of commercials that may be targeted at young people, or do not allow them at all.

Advertising can be offensive in a number of contexts. Beyond stereotyping, messages may offend the audience, which may perceive that they violate cultural norms or are mean-spirited toward a group of people. Negative reactions to ads have long-lasting effects. Advertisers are advised to carefully screen commercials before their release.

Some object that advertising dangerous products *is unethical*. Many unsafe products have been advertised for years, including smoking products, alcohol, and others. Governments in various nations create laws regarding what may be advertised and in which venues. International advertising accounts for these legal restrictions prior to beginning an advertising program.

Common wisdom suggests that advertising must be handled carefully in order to be both ethical and effective. The use of cultural assimilators, focus groups, and even local attorneys can help a marketing organization make sure that company messages will be well received and not violate any local customs, religious practices, or notions of fairness.

Chapter 13: Review and Resources

STRATEGIC IMPLICATIONS ///

Effective international advertising programs require the combination of three variables: the message, the media, and the audience. Many of the advertising elements described in this chapter represent strategic choices. Advertising management programs include the steps of establishing objectives, creating an advertising budget, choosing an advertising agency, overseeing the advertising program, and assessing advertising effectiveness. Advertising objectives are strategically selected, depending on the situation. A company entering a new market will seek different objectives as compared to one with a longstanding operation in another nation. Top managers choose which form of advertising budget to employ. Options include the percentage of sales, match the competition, arbitrary allocation, and objective and task methods. The choice between an in-house advertising program and a relationship with an advertising agency will be a strategic decision.

Further selection of a standardization or adaptation format for advertising will be made by top-level managers. The overall direction of the advertising program takes place under the guiding hand of the company's top marketers. The strategic direction of a company's advertising program carefully accounts for cultural factors, legal restrictions, infrastructure concerns, economic conditions, and communications issues. The advertising agency will present choices, including the use of fear, humor, sex/sensuality, music, rationality, emotions, and scarcity to the marketing management team, who will then make the decision as to which approach to feature. In international settings, additional choices will include considerations of power distance, individualism/collectivism, masculinity/femininity, uncertainty avoidance, and long- or short-term orientation.

Choices of nontraditional marketing programs, including buzz marketing, guerrilla marketing, product placements and branded entertainment, and lifestyle marketing, are also strategic in nature.

TACTICAL IMPLICATIONS ///

Media choices are normally tactical decisions made by the advertising agency in conjunction with marketing managers. The advertising team selects logical combinations of traditional media, including television, radio, magazines, newspapers, billboard/outdoor, and direct mail. These choices are supplemented by the use of nontraditional media such as video game advertising, movie trailers, subway tunnels, in-flight airline magazines, carry-home and take-out bags, clothing bearing company names or logos, mall signs, kiosks, and posters.

Tactical level marketers implement nontraditional marketing programs. They will select specific buzz marketing formats. They develop and implement guerilla marketing programs. They negotiate product placements and branded entertainment packages with movie and television studios. They select lifestyle marketing locations and establish operations in those locations.

OPERATIONAL IMPLICATIONS ///

First-line supervisors carry key responsibilities associated with effective advertising and nontraditional marketing programs. In the area of advertising, these managers should make certain that entry-level employees are aware of company advertisements, especially those making special offers. When extra merchandise will be required as part of a heavily advertised promotion or special offer, the first-line supervisor makes sure the merchandise is ordered, received, and then placed in attractive and convenient ways.

Entry-level employees and first-line supervisors will be on the front lines of lifestyle marketing, guerrilla marketing, and buzz marketing programs. They will be at the booths and will directly interact with customers. An advertising program cannot succeed unless the efforts of those in contact with the public implement all levels of an advertising program.

TERMS

globally integrated marketing communications program

promotions mix

communication

low-context cultures

high-context cultures

clutter

advertising management

message strategy

cognitive message strategies

affective message strategies

conative message strategies

executional framework

announcements

association transfers

lesson

comparative advertising

entertainment

imagination

special effects

REVIEW QUESTIONS

1. Define globally integrated marketing communications.
2. What elements make up the promotions mix?
3. Define communication.
4. What elements are included in a model of individual interpersonal communication?
5. What are the primary barriers to effective international communication and marketing programs?
6. Describe low- and high-context cultures.
7. Outline the sender and receiver duties in creating effective individual interpersonal communication.
8. What are the steps of an international advertising management program?
9. What four methods can be used to create international advertising budgets?
10. Name the traditional media advertising venues.
11. Name the nontraditional advertising media venues.
12. Name the most common attitudinal and behavioral measures of advertising effectiveness.
13. Briefly describe the traditional advertising appeal formats.
14. Explain the three cultural paradoxes that complicate international advertising.
15. Briefly describe the international advertising appeal formats.
16. Describe the three most common message strategies.
17. Briefly describe the traditional advertising executional frameworks.
18. Briefly describe the seven most common international executional frameworks.
19. What are the four most common alternative marketing programs?

DISCUSSION QUESTIONS

1. Make a list of the most common barriers to individual interpersonal communication. Explain how these factors become more complicated in international marketing. Explain how each of these variables also constitutes a barrier to communication throughout an organization.
2. For each of the international advertising objectives displayed in Figure 13.8, explain how each of the traditional advertising appeals could (or should not) be used to achieve the objective. For each of international advertising appeals and values noted in Figure 13.12, explain how each could (or should not) be used to achieve the objective.
3. Explain how each of the international advertising appeals and values noted in Figure 13.12 would influence the selection of a cognitive, affective, or conative message strategy.

4. Explain how each of the traditional executional frameworks noted in Figure 13.13 is or is not related to the international advertising executional frameworks.

5. Discuss how the four nontraditional marketing methods would fare in low-context cultures. Explain how the methods match or do not match such a culture. Explain how each would be different in high-context cultures.

ANALYTICAL AND INTERNET EXERCISES

1. Explain how the presence of a low- or high-context culture would affect the advertising program of the following products:

   - health and life insurance
   - professional soccer (football)
   - men's clothing
   - automobiles

2. Write down the selection criteria used when choosing international advertising agencies. Explain how each criterion would affect the selection of an agency for the following products and situations:

   - Perrier water sold in South Korea
   - Wrigley chewing gum sold in Australia
   - Kia automobiles sold in Brazil
   - Rawlings baseball products sold in Japan

3. Using an Internet search engine, look up five international advertising agencies. Write a report on how each conducts operations in global markets, including differences and similarities.

4. Develop a creative brief for the following companies. Make sure you match the advertising objectives with a message strategy, type of international advertising appeal, and type of international advertising executional framework to be used in advertising the following products:

   - Muenchen-Flughafen (Germany) fashion jewelry
   - Gottex (Israel) swimwear
   - Crédit Suisse Group (bank in Switzerland)
   - Pepsi Cola or Coca-Cola

5. Go to the website of the Word of Mouth Marketing Association (www.womma.org). Find its ethical statement regarding stealth marketing and company employees as brand advocates. Write a report about what the organization believes is and is not ethical.

▶ **ONLINE VIDEOS**

Visit **www.sagepub.com/baack** to view these chapter videos:

Video Link 13.1: Jewelry and Culture

Video Link 13.2: Nonverbal Communication

Video Link 13.3: Marketing Beer

Video Link 13.4: Marketing with Humor

STUDENT STUDY SITE

Visit **www.sagepub.com/baack** to access these additional learning tools:

- Web Quizzes
- eFlashcards
- SAGE Journal Articles

- Country Fact Sheets
- Chapter Outlines
- Interactive Maps

CASE 13 ///

Mobile Phone Marketing

International competition in the cell phone market can be described as intense. With the vast number of companies that manufacture mobile phones on the rise, and with increasing signal coverage, the number of potential individual and business customers continues to grow. Reaching this vast marketplace in a manner that cuts through clutter constitutes the primary challenge for many marketers.

Mobile phones are advertised in every medium. Television, radio, magazine, newspaper, outdoor, and direct mail commercials for various devices are abundant. Many nontraditional media also carry marketing messages. Social media rely on visits by those using the Internet and other mobile devices. Capturing the attention of the intended audience has become increasingly difficult.

One recent example of a successful advertising and marketing campaign in the mobile phone marketplace occurred in the Philippines. The Nokia N8 phone campaign began with a sixty-second teaser posted on Facebook and YouTube. It was followed by thirty-second spot ads on television. The primary character in the campaign was named Pier Roxas.

Pier is discovered in a Southeast Asian city. He has no memory of the past eight days, and has a bruised face, a lipstick smudge on his collar, a parking ticket, a key to something. In addition, his wallet is missing. He does have a Smart-branded SIM card and cell phone. There are no phone contacts in the phone's memory. The marketing messages ask viewers to help Pier reconstruct his memory.

The advertising and creative agency JWT Manila established a website. Viewers were invited to go to the site and post versions of the story that would explain Mr. Roxas' lost eight days. Nokia created a text hotline where "Pier" answered questions from those involved. A film-making contest was launched noting the video capabilities of the Nokia N8 phone camera.

In the first month, consumers sent 25,000 text messages to Pier. They entered nearly one thousand stories into the competition to explain his lost days. Eight finalist stories were chosen, with each entrant receiving Nokia N8 devices to shoot their stories. The eventual winner was chosen by a panel of three movie makers, and received a cash prize.

The combination of social media with traditional advertising and a traditional marketing contest received both local and international attention. The campaign was featured in a story in *Advertising Age*, one of the most-cited magazines covering the industry, before the contest had even reached its completion.[48]

1. Describe the target market, advertising objective, and type of international appeal used in the N8 campaign in the Philippines.

2. Describe the traditional and international executional frameworks that best match the N8 campaign.

3. Using Internet resources, identify the Philippines as a low- or high-context culture. Explain how the N8 advertising program fits with that type of culture. Would the campaign be as successful if the opposite type of culture were present? Why or why not?

4. Explain how the N8 campaign combines traditional advertising with nontraditional marketing. Which nontraditional marketing program does it contain?

5. Of the attitudinal and behavior outcomes listed in Figure 13.11, which effects did this advertising and marketing campaign achieve? Explain your answer.

Nokia created a unique alternative marketing program to capture consumer interest.

14 International Sales Promotions and Public Relations

LEARNING OBJECTIVES ///

After reading and studying this chapter, you should be able to answer the following questions:

1. What are the relationships between international consumer promotions, trade promotions, push strategies, and pull strategies?

2. How do international consumer promotions help a company achieve its marketing goals?

3. When are international trade promotions incentives used?

4. How does the public relations team or department handle negative publicity or image-damaging events?

5. How can the public relations function help build a positive image of a company and its brands?

IN THIS CHAPTER

Marketing Headaches

Headaches are a common denominator shared by people around the world. Remedies for headaches take a variety of forms. Headache and pain relievers offer a multitude of marketing opportunities at all levels of economic development.

In most-developed nations, millions of dollars are spent each year on advertising and promotions. Companies routinely offer coupons, price-off discounts, bonus packs, free samples, and other enticements for the vast variety of forms these products take, including gel tabs, capsules, powders, and tablets. The incentives are designed to pull products onto the shelves of drugstores, grocery stores, convenience marts, big box retailers, and even airport shopping portals by encouraging consumers to ask for them. Trade incentives are routinely offered to these retail outlets to help push the product from the manufacturer through to the retail shelf and on to consumers.

Pain reduction products experience all of the forces that affect international marketing. Concepts about how to deal with pain vary by culture; some individuals are naturally apprehensive about taking any kind of medication. The language of pain and medicine also varies. Even the word "aspirin" serves an early example of the generic problems for marketers. The original product produced for broad consumption was discovered by the German company Bayer AG and called "Aspirin." The pain reliever had the brand name so strongly associated with it that other companies adopted the term *aspirin* over other product descriptions. Generic or common usage affects other products, including "escalator," "Xerox" copies, and, more recently, "Googling" something.

Political and legal systems influence pain medicines through regulations regarding pricing, distribution, and advertising. Use of aspirin for children is carefully monitored due to links to Reye's syndrome. Labeling may be affected if a country insists on a warning about the potential side effects on children.

Economic systems affect the sale of aspirin, among other ways, through the size of the package. Pain medicines are more salable to those at the bottom-of-the-pyramid when they are offered in single-dosage packages. In developed countries, retailers can place generic versions of pain relievers alongside brand name products. Infrastructure affects the distribution and availability of a product that will normally be marketing intensively in most-developed economies, but in other formats in less- and least-developed nations.

In the most-developed countries, four headache medicines are widely used: aspirin, ibuprofen, naproxen sodium, and acetaminophen.[1] Aspirin-like substances have been used dating back to the ancient Greeks, who used willow bark as a fever fighter. The leaves and bark of the willow tree contain salicin, a naturally occurring compound similar to acetylsalicylic acid, the chemical name for aspirin. In 1899, the Bayer Company began to provide aspirin to physicians to give to patients.[2] Advil, Motrin, and other products contain ibuprofen, a nonsteroidal anti-inflammatory drug (NSAID). Naproxen sodium, the key ingredient in Aleve, is also an NSAID. Tylenol contains acetaminophen, which reduces pain reliever and fever, and is especially popular for treating cold symptoms. It is not an NSAID.[3]

Effective international marketing means that pain relievers can be made available to the vast number of individuals experiencing the inconvenience of the occasional headache. The products can be distributed to individual consumers, to health-care providers such as hospitals and walk-in clinics, as well as to doctors and nurses. Savvy marketers recognize the potential to vend these items to people and businesses around the world using sales promotion tactics coupled with advertising and other promotional efforts.

QUESTIONS FOR STUDENTS

1. How are coupons, price-off discounts, bonus packs, free samples, contests or sweepstakes, and premium prizes used to sell pain relievers in international markets?

2. What types of offers could pain reliever manufacturers offer to retailers to increase sales?

3. What should the relationship be between a pain reliever company's advertising program and its sales promotion program?

International marketing means that pain relievers can be made available to the vast number of individuals experiencing an occasional headache.

Overview

Promotional activities play an important role in international marketing, both during boom economic times and in periods of recession. As noted in the previous chapter, a firm's promotions mix consists of advertising, personal selling, sales promotion, and public relations. The promotions mix also includes the use of social media in today's global marketplace. This chapter continues the description of international promotions that began with globally integrated marketing communications in Chapter 13. Figure 14.1 serves as a reminder of the role of promotions in international marketing.

Sales promotions represent an additional method of reaching consumers and moving them toward purchases. Effective promotional programs are carefully integrated components of a firm's communications. In this chapter, the nature of sales promotions in the international context and the distinction between a push strategy and a pull strategy are described. The chapter continues with evaluations of the various types of consumer promotions offered to individual buyers. The international implications of each consumer promotional tactic influence the choice of those to be used. Consumers react to promotions in different ways, which means the international marketing team examines how they respond to promotions in various regions and countries.

Trade promotions are designed to push products onto retail shelves and create positive relationships between manufacturers and intermediaries. Some of the incentives are financial, and others involve cooperative efforts and manufacturer-generated training programs. Trade shows offer venues in which buyers and sellers can meet. The international differences in all of these programs are considered when seeking to market products in another country.

This chapter concludes with a brief description of public relations activities. The public relations team facilitates communications between the company and all internal and external publics. Public relations involve responding to negative events and publicity as well as highlighting a company's positive contributions to a local community or the larger society.

SALES PROMOTIONS AND THE COMMUNICATION PROCESS

The communication process plays an important part in all elements of marketing. Personal and impersonal forms of communication take place in sales promotions. Personal communication includes face-to-face visits between a salesperson and a customer. In these meetings, coupons are redeemed, discounts are given, and other promotional items change hands.

Impersonal communication takes place over various media, such as television, radio, and mobile phones. The media delivers whatever message is sent, including electronic coupons and other sales promotion offers. In international marketing, additional potential barriers to communication emerge, including differences in language, use of slang, forms of technical terminology, and cultural nuances. Effective communication facilitates the development and delivery of quality sales promotions.

LEARNING OBJECTIVE #1:

What are the relationships between international consumer promotions, trade promotions, push strategies, and pull strategies?

Figure 14.1: The International Marketing Context

International Sales Promotions

VIDEO LINK 14.1:
Language

Sales promotions are marketing activities designed to stimulate consumer and marketing channel demand for a product or service. Sales promotions take two major forms: consumer promotions and trade promotions. **Consumer promotions** are directed at retail customers. Consumer promotions include coupons, sweepstakes, refunds and rebates, premiums, bonus packs, price-off programs, and samples. **Trade promotions** are aimed at intermediates, most notably wholesalers and retail outlets. Trade promotions consist of trade allowances, trade contests, trade shows, and point-of-purchase materials. Social media can be aimed at both consumer and trade groups.

International sales promotion efforts focus on stimulating demand across national or cultural boundaries. Some of these efforts concentrate on short-term goals, especially when sales promotions are aimed at stimulating the immediate purchase of products or services. Effective strategic international sales promotions programs also work to achieve longer-term objectives, such as building brand loyalty and strengthening the company's image. Advertising campaigns can be designed in concert with sales promotions to boost sales in the short term as well as to increase consumer loyalty over time.

International marketers take cultural differences into account when designing sales promotions programs. Differences in motivation, consumer behaviors, and decision-making processes are considered as a company markets products across national boundaries.[4] Marketing research activities become part of developing quality international promotions. As a simple example, offering product samples in some cultures might be discouraged or even considered as inappropriate by some consumers. In other cultures the use of sampling is commonplace and widely accepted.

PUSH VS. PULL STRATEGIES

One key strategic decision facing international marketers in both distribution channels and the promotions mix is whether to feature a push or a pull promotional strategy.

International marketers take cultural differences into account when developing sales promotions programs.

A *push strategy* occurs when a marketer promotes a product to intermediaries. In general, these efforts are aimed at wholesalers first, who then promote the product to retailers. Retailers promote the product to consumers. Here, the product demand is pushed downward through the marketing channel.

Trade promotions represent push strategy techniques. They focus specifically on establishing intermediary demand and support. English brewing company SABMiller utilized a push strategy when it introduced Kozel, a Czech lager, to the United Kingdom in 2010.[5] SABMiller and other firms develop sales contests, training programs, and point-of-purchase materials specifically aimed at members of the marketing channel. These activities can play an important part in international marketing success because of the critical role that intermediary support plays.

A *pull strategy* focuses on stimulating product demand at the consumer level. When a consumer expresses interest in a product at the retail store, retailers are encouraged to carry the item. The product will be ordered from wholesalers who purchase the product from the manufacturer. Consequently, demand for the product is "pulled" through the marketing channel by the consumer from the intermediary and then the manufacturer. Consumer promotions support pull strategies, because the individual buyer receives the incentive.

International marketing giant McDonald's employed a pull strategy with the introduction of *kazasu* coupons in Japan. The mobile marketing pieces allowed consumers to redeem coupons, choose meals, and pay for purchases using mobile phones.[6] The promotion targets retail consumers. The demand pulls the products through the marketing channel.

International Consumer Promotions

Consumer promotions target consumers. The use of international consumer promotion tactics has grown dramatically in the past several years. Many explanations for the growth in popularity of these techniques exist. Decreasing mass media advertising budgets, the fragmentation of media audiences, difficulties with measuring mass media effectiveness, the increasing power of retailers, and advertising clutter have all contributed to this growth.

LEARNING OBJECTIVE #2:

How do international consumer promotions help a company achieve its marketing goals?

Many international consumers have either tuned out mass media advertising, or have cynical attitudes about advertising on television, radio, in newspapers, and other traditional media. For these consumers, making a more personal connection has become more important. Consumer promotion efforts facilitate these interactions. Most consumers enjoy direct personal contact. Consumer promotions enable companies to interact more intimately with consumers than mass media advertising.

Reaching consumers who do not have access to traditional media such as television or radio continues to present a significant challenge to international marketers. At the same time, media such as cellular technologies and the Internet have emerged. The adoption of these technologies varies dramatically from country to country. Table 14.1 lists the top twenty countries in terms of Internet usage.

COUNTRY	RANK	PERCENT OF POPULATION WITH INTERNET ACCESS
Iceland	1	100%
Norway	2	95%
Sweden	3	93%
Netherlands	4	89%
Bahrain	5	88%
Denmark	6	86%
Finland	7	85%
New Zealand	7	85%
Luxembourg	7	85%
United Kingdom	10	83%
South Korea	11	81%
Australia	12	80%
Brunei Darussalam	12	80%
Germany	14	79%
Japan	15	78%
Canada	15	78%
Singapore	15	78%
United States	18	77%
United Arab Emirates	19	76%
Switzerland	20	75%
Austria	20	75%
Estonia	20	75%

Table 14.1: **Top Twenty Major Countries for Internet Usage (population 300,000 or above)**

Source: Adopted from "Top 58 Countries With the Highest Internet Penetration Rate," *The Internet Coaching Library* (March 2011), accessed at www.internetworldstats.com/top25.htm.

International marketers often find that consumer promotion techniques that are ineffective in one market or country are highly effective in another market or country. Direct mail serves as an example. Although direct mail, which is used to deliver coupons and premium prizes, has waned in its effectiveness in the United States, the tactic continues to be effective in other parts of the world. International marketers monitor developments in direct mail marketing to ensure that it does not become inefficient or wasteful.

International marketers often use these consumer promotions with one or more of the following goals in mind:

- Obtaining initial trial usage of a product by consumers
- Increasing consumption of an existing brand
- Building brand loyalty
- Maintaining or building market share in mature markets
- Preempting competitive efforts, including competitor consumer promotions
- Supplementing advertising and personal selling activities

Many types of consumer promotions may be utilized in international sales promotions activities, as shown in Figure 14.2. In many countries, sales promotion decisions are dependent, at least in part, on social class. Premiums and couponing may work well for one social class but not another. Using coupons in some societies presents the impression that the buyer is poor and from a lower social class.

Coupons
Premiums
Bonus Packs
Contests and Sweepstakes
Refunds and Rebates
Price-Off Promotions
Sampling

Figure 14.2: International Consumer Promotions

COUPONS

Coupons are certificates that allow consumers to save on the cost of specific products or services. They are popular with many consumer groups and marketers have used them for many years. Coupons can help stimulate product trials, especially when a new product is being marketed. They are also offered for mature products. The types of coupons companies offer include the forms displayed in Figure 14.3.

Coupons have historically been placed in newspapers as inserts (print media) or mailed directly to consumers. In European nations, a central focus of many couponing strategies has been on direct mail delivery. European consumers tend to be receptive to couponing. Many European retailers rely more heavily on couponing and in-store promotions than on traditional sales or price-off promotions. In recent years, coupons have been placed on retail store shelves and are delivered at check-out counters with merchandise receipts by electronic scanner.

Coupons are also placed on popular social networking sites or sent via email. These electronic coupon distribution techniques have become quite common. A proliferation of mobile couponing has taken place worldwide. Mobile coupons are delivered through various mobile media, including cell phones and PDAs. The format has become especially popular in Japan and Korea. Consumers in these countries tend to be more receptive to mobile delivery of coupons than are consumers in other regions, because consumers in Asia are often more technologically advanced than those in other parts of the world.[7] The

Print media
Direct mail
In- or on-package
In-store (display)
In-store (scanner delivered at check-out)
Response offer
Internet delivered (electronic coupons)

Figure 14.3: Types of Coupons

Japanese market research firm Netasia estimates that 76% of Japanese consumers have scanned a QR coupon bar code using a mobile device.[8]

Mobile couponing continues to grow in use. In 2010, the United States–based marketer Groupon, which offers daily deals on products through the Internet, announced a move into the European market.[9] Groupon recently purchased international competitors including Germany's CityDeal as part of the effort to expand internationally.[10]

Mobile coupons are not popular everywhere. Reactions vary greatly by region and by culture and are strongly impacted by the availability and cost of these technologies. International marketing research should be conducted in order to gain an understanding of consumer reactions to electronic coupons.

Couponing can be tied to a firm's overall marketing strategy. Kellogg's Canada ran a "resolution" campaign during 2010 in which consumers received an on-package coupon on specially marked boxes of Special K cereal. The promotion granted consumers a price break on the cereal while it promoted healthier living and weight loss.[11] These types of promotions work to stimulate the immediate sale of product and can then become part of achieving a company's strategic marketing effort, including building brand loyalty. In this instance, Kellogg's was able to achieve the goal of promoting better living for its consumers while seeking a more immediate purchase response.

PREMIUMS

A premium is an item offered as a reward for purchasing another item. The reward item is usually given free of charge, but it can sometimes be priced modestly, sometimes under the guise of a shipping and handling fee. Premiums take the form of gifts or prizes. A premium represents an additional incentive for a consumer to buy a product.

Premiums may be used as part of an international marketing program. Consumer acceptance of premiums tends to vary by culture. A recent study of grocery shoppers in Hong Kong revealed that premium programs were more effective than either contests or sweepstakes.[12]

Consumers enjoy receiving extra products, and, as a result, premium-type promotions have become increasingly common. Kellogg's recently gave away free packets of cereal to consumers in the United Kingdom as part of its "Wake Up to Breakfast" campaign. To redeem the free product, consumers had to collect a coupon placed on various cereal boxes. After the consumer collected three coupons, they were entitled to a free box.[13]

Premiums incur the costs associated with developing the prize or reward. Often, a package will be altered to accommodate the prize. Gifts that are viewed as cheap trinkets may harm a firm's image in the marketplace. Consequently, marketers should give consideration to matching the nature and value of the premium to the product and its target audience.

BONUS PACKS

A bonus pack offers additional merchandise in a package for the same price, such as a "buy three, get one free" package of bar soap. A bonus pack may also take the form of a bottle that is larger than the product's standard size and is marked "25% more, free." By purchasing the pack, consumers receive additional merchandise at the standard price. Bonus packs are often used when the goal is to entice consumers to stock up on a given item. This decreases the chance that the consumer will switch to a competitor, and can be a proactive way to protect a product's market share. In response to losing market share to store brands, in 2010 Proctor & Gamble began offering a bonus packs for Duracell batteries with the goal of maintaining market share. The program's costs were offset by a reduction in traditional advertising spending.[14] Bonus packs can be a tool to help cope with the rapidly intensifying nature of international competition.

Bonus packs incur the additional expense of providing extra merchandise at the standard price. Also, shipping costs become greater when items are sent greater distances, and bonus packs will be bulkier and heavier. Such costs may be more dramatic when products are shipped long distances or across international borders. The expense of providing the free additional item(s) should be weighed against the benefits of maintaining customer loyalty and/or fending off competitive efforts. In many countries, living quarters are often substantially smaller than in the United States. Bonus packs that take up additional storage space may not be as attractive in those circumstances.

Contests may lead to immediate consumer responses but not have an impact on long-term sales results.

CONTESTS AND SWEEPSTAKES

Contests are promotions with game-like qualities that rely on a consumer's skill at some activity. The winner of the contest receives a prize in the form of a product or money. An example of a contest is when consumers compete to develop a new advertising slogan for a company or when consumers compete to predict the winners of a sports event, such as the World Cup. These activities require a degree of skill or knowledge.

VIDEO LINK 14.2:
Contests and Sweepstakes

Sweepstakes rely on chance drawings of consumer names in order to select the winner of a promotion. Sweepstakes take a form much like a lottery or random drawing. If a certain number or name is selected, the consumer wins a prize.

Both contests and sweepstakes are found in international marketing programs. A recent sweepstakes was held by Dubai's City Centre Mall. The Mall rewarded consumers who spent at least 300 United Arab Emirates *Dirhams* (*AED*) with lottery numbers that could be redeemed online for chances to win prizes of up to 100,000 *AED*.[15]

Contests are useful in many international markets. Walkers, a UK-based potato chip marketer, held a successful skill-based contest in which customers were invited to compete by developing a new flavor of potato chip. The winner won £ 50,000 in prize money and a percentage of product sales revenues. Contests and sweepstakes such as these often generate consumer interest and excitement.

Although these techniques often lead to immediate consumer responses, they may not have an impact on long-term sales. Consumers sometimes quickly lose interest in a product or brand after the contest or sweepstakes has ended. At that point, a new form of promotion should be designed to sustain consumer involvement.

Participation and interest in contests and sweepstakes are strongly influenced by cultural norms as well as by local political and legal systems. Therefore, preliminary research will be necessary to understand the type of contest or prize that the targeted segment of consumers will value, and it must be acceptable to the local community and government.

REBATES

Rebates require consumers to mail a form or certificate to a marketer along with a receipt or proof of purchase in order to receive money back from the manufacturer or retail outlet. This type of sales promotion tends to work well at generating consumer interest in an item as long as consumers value the amount of the rebate. It should generate sufficient desire to lead to the effort to take the steps necessary to receive the money.

Not every consumer will take the time or expend the effort necessary to receive a rebate. Estimates reveal that a large percentage of consumers, up to 40% in the United States, do not complete the steps necessary in order to receive rebates in the electronics industry. One side effect of unclaimed rebates is additional program profitability, because money is not paid out. Rebates tend to be effective methods for generating consumer attention and interest. They can also be useful tools for salespeople who attempt to sell products to end users, especially in international markets. Utilizing rebates can therefore be effective for gaining entry into new markets globally.

A recent study of Chinese consumers indicated that they highly value rebates. The study suggests that consumers often view rebates positively. The results also revealed that consumers with higher incomes were particularly pleased with these promotions.[16] Although this may seem like an unexpected result, it may be that higher-income consumers do not rely on rebates for cost savings but rather view them as pleasant surprises.

PRICE-OFF PROMOTIONS

Price-off promotions present the consumer with an immediate price break, expressed as a percentage of the price or an absolute amount, at the time of purchase. The manufacturer can push this type of promotion by printing the price on a product's package, or a retailer might offer the price on a shelf tag signage. Price-offs promotions are widely used in international marketing. Capcom Europe, a leading international developer and marketer of videogames with worldwide headquarters in Japan, utilized this approach as a means of promoting popular video game titles throughout Europe.[17]

Consumer responses to price-off promotions tend to be generally favorable. Marketers run the risk, however, of teaching consumers to wait for special pricing deals before buying the products if they use this technique too often. Price-off reductions also reduce revenues and can cut into bottom line profits. Only when sufficient additional volume offsets the price cut is the program cost effective. At the same time, many international marketers believe price-offs help to fend off competitive offers, thereby sacrificing short-term revenues for longer-range customer loyalty. The marketing team should first study any local laws pertaining to granting discounts as they relate to "standard" prices.

SAMPLING

A consumer is able to try a product free of charge in a sampling program. Sampling helps to stimulate consumer interest in a product as it reduces purchase risk. The consumer can take advantage of testing the product without paying any money. Samples are often mailed to consumers or are given out in retail outlets. Retailers throughout the world often offer free samples to consumers in order to entice them to make purchases.

One example of a new approach to sampling was designed by Japan's Sample Lab, Ltd. The company offers retail outlets that specialize in giving away product samples from dozens of companies. The firm also operates the Lcafe in Tokyo's Shibuya district, a well-known, popular destination for young consumers in Tokyo. When customers purchase food items or drinks at the café, they receive tokens they can exchange for sample products.[18] The sampled products become strong enticements for eventual purchase.

Consumers often exhibit positive attitudes toward sampling and these attitudes influence decisions to seek out samples, a finding that was confirmed by a study of Hong Kong consumers. The study revealed that the more positive that consumer attitudes were toward sampling, the greater the likelihood that consumers would seek out samples, especially when consumers stated they were the types of individuals who would engage in such behaviors.[19]

Sampling can be particularly effective at boosting short-term sales, because the vast majority of consumers who try a product will buy the product at least once. Sampling provides an effective method of enticing an immediate sale in the grocery industry, where it becomes relatively easy to persuade consumers to sample an item. Sampling can also be successful when the consumer requests the sample either in writing or via the Internet. Social networking sites also offer consumers an efficient method of requesting a product sample. Vaseline recently distributed free samples of products to consumers who requested them in the United Kingdom.[20] One notable disadvantage of sampling is that it can be expensive. International marketers should calculate trade-offs between the benefits and costs of sampling.

Sampling programs can be coupled with other consumer promotions. Once a free sample has been given, the consumer may be presented with a coupon redeemable at the first purchase. Samples are also passed out during sponsored events, such as an energy bar being given to spectators as they enter a stadium to see a soccer match.

INTERNATIONAL INCIDENT ///

In certain cultures, gift-giving and what may be considered bribery remains a standard way of conducting business. It is considered to be unethical in other cultures. Imagine that you are meeting with a prospective buyer who requests a "sample" of one of your products. The problem is that the sample she requests is not one of the ones that you are attempting to sell. Also, you are restricted by company policy from offering samples that may not result in an immediate sale. The buyer is adamant that you must give her a sample of the other product if you intend to do business with her. What do you do? How would you approach this subject with the prospective buyer? How might you communicate the problem to your boss?

SOCIAL MEDIA AND CONSUMER PROMOTIONS

Social media and social networking sites such as Facebook have become important components of marketing strategy. The majority of international Internet users visit social networking sites regularly. International marketers are therefore increasing the focus on these sites and including them in their consumer promotion campaigns. One estimate reveals that the international use of social media promotions will reach $3.3 billion in 2010.[21] Some international marketing firms are now hiring search engine optimization managers to assist in online international marketing campaigns. Japanese marketers have used social networking sites longer than firms in most other countries.

International marketers employ social networking sites for advertising and send promotional materials such as coupons and contest entries directly to consumers. Consumers are able to register for contests and to print coupons directly from these sites. Consumers can become fans of companies and brands by joining their social networking pages.

Facebook and Twitter are often targets of international marketing efforts, but firms also pay attention to foreign sites because the popularity of these media varies by country.[22] International marketers work to ensure that they are present on the appropriate sites. Renren is a popular social networking site in China, while Gree and Mixi are widely visited in Japan. One popular French site, Viadeo, has millions of users worldwide. The Google-owned site Orkut is especially well received in India and Brazil. Nasza Klasa is commonly used in Poland. One of the first decisions for the international marketer will be selecting the most effective social networking site for use in sales promotion campaigns.

While social media sites tend to appeal to younger segments, the use of the media cuts across demographics. In some countries, Internet access is limited to those with higher incomes. In other countries, social media and the Internet reach a much broader demographic. The rapid penetration of the technologies allows these sites access across segments.

To achieve success in social media programs, the marketing team matches messages with other content and consumer promotion offers as well as a country's language and culture. International marketers make sure that bloggers are either from the local country or, at the very least, are familiar with the language, dialect, and customs of that country.

One often-overlooked reason for including social media in international marketing campaigns is to reveal to consumers that a company and its products are adapting to the changing times. The Ford Motor Company has used social media internationally, at least in part for that specific purpose.[23] International customers tend to view brands as more relevant when they make connections through the Internet, which is why social media plays such an important role in consumer promotions campaigns.

LEGAL ISSUES IN CONSUMER PROMOTIONS

Several legal concerns must be addressed when offering sales promotions internationally. As noted, contests and sweepstakes face legal restrictions. In Canada, a contest cannot offer money solely as a prize and the contest must test some type of skill. The marketing team would wish to know if coupons can be copied and redeemed by retailers that do not actually receive them from customers. Counterfeiting coupons by retailers can create an unnecessary expense. Premium programs may have restrictions with regard to charging shipping fees in some countries.

Many countries regulate what is a standard price and how often prices can be reduced through techniques such as price-off programs. Germany, for example, did not allow sales discount prices until 2004. For several years, consumers were unaware of the concept unless the English word "sale" was included in marketing materials.

Similar laws regulate bonus packs. Offers, such as "three for the price of two," are illegal in some European countries. Consequently, the European Union has begun the process of trying to standardize regulations regarding sales promotions.[24]

Sampling programs can face legal restrictions as to where they can be distributed, or require a permit to give them in various parts of a city. The marketing team should first investigate the local legal system before using consumer promotions tactics.

TYPES OF CONSUMERS AND
INTERNATIONAL CONSUMER PROMOTIONS

Individual reactions to consumer promotions can be divided into four groups. *Promotion-prone consumers* take advantage of coupons, price-off programs, and premiums. They are not loyal to any given brand and look for the best deal. Consequently, targeting consumer promotions in this group does not lead to the best results, because they will simply move on after a deal ceases to be offered.

Price-sensitive consumers use price as the only purchase criterion. They take advantage of consumer promotions that reduce the price or increase a purchase value, such as a bonus pack offer. Once again, the consumer promotion being offered does not truly succeed with this group; it may increase sales in one instance, but these individuals will continue to look for the best price.

Brand-loyal consumers purchase only a favored brand and do not look for, nor do they often buy, substitutes. Promotions targeted at this group should work toward maintaining loyalty and increasing consumption. When loyal consumers perceive the promotion as a "reward," it has succeeded.

Consumer promotions can be highly useful in targeting *preferred-brand consumers*. These individuals select from a set of brands they favor most. The right consumer promotion can make the difference in a purchase decision, causing the consumer to select a brand due to the additional incentive offered.

Few customers consistently remain in one category. A person may be price sensitive for some items and brand loyal when it comes to others. The ideal promotions program targets individuals that respond to the promotion and may be moved toward greater loyalty over time. Should Coca-Cola wish to build loyalty in Argentina, coupons, bonus packs, and sweepstakes may be used over time with the shorter-term goal of building interest and immediate purchases, combined with the longer-term objective of increasing preference for Coke over Pepsi or a local competitor such as Chola de Oro.

International consumer promotions managers examine a country or region to discover the most prevalent types of consumer promotions. Consumer research can take the form of surveys and interviews or test markets. When people in a region are price sensitive, coupons and price-offs are likely to work most effectively. When consumers are brand loyal, premiums and contests that allow them to express loyalty in some way are most advisable. For areas with larger pockets of promotion-prone consumers, the marketing pieces should attempt to inspire loyalty in some way.

CONSUMER PROMOTIONS AND BOTTOM-OF-THE-PYRAMID CONSUMERS

Bottom-of-the-pyramid consumers may be targeted with consumer promotions that are based on price. Couponing and bonus packs, as well as special price-off promotions, can all be effective methods of promoting items to these consumers. Many bottom-of-the-pyramid consumers do not live close to any traditional retail outlets, so in many cases products are transported to remote areas or villages where many of these consumers live. This can be expensive for the international marketer, but the goodwill associated with the effort can outweigh the short-term monetary costs. The concern is that bottom-of-the-pyramid consumers may wait for the next promotion, instead of transitioning to buying the product at a higher price. Promotions that cause a loss may be ineffective to penetrate this market. Promotions that leave a small profit margin are an effective method for encouraging bottom-of-the-pyramid consumption.

International Trade Promotions

LEARNING OBJECTIVE #3:

When are international trade promotions incentives used?

Trade promotions are aimed at marketing channel intermediaries. They often play an important role in the success of products worldwide. Trade promotions have gained a great deal of international marketing attention and tend to be used extensively. The promotions are particularly useful for establishing initial support for new brands, for encouraging intermediaries to promote existing brands, and for building and maintaining strong working relationships with marketing channel members. Intermediary cooperation is essential to the success of international marketing campaigns. Trade-oriented promotions help ensure cooperation from channel members. Producers can use some techniques, such as sampling, as both consumer and trade promotions. Other international trade promotion techniques are summarized in Figure 14.4.

Trade Shows
Trade Allowances
Cooperative Advertising
Trade Contests
Training Programs
Point-of-Purchase Materials

Figure 14.4: International Trade Promotions

TRADE SHOWS

A trade show gathers industry representatives to examine products and services presented to prospective buyers. Trade shows generally focus on generating buyer interest. Shows are also useful for making contacts with industry representatives. When many companies and representatives attend trade shows, this method of trade promotion can be both effective and efficient.

One advantage of utilizing trade shows is that a product can be demonstrated. Trade shows are well attended in European nations. In general, a greater percentage of promotional expenditures are allocated to trade shows in Europe than in other regions of the world.[25]

Many examples of large worldwide trade shows can be found. Tecno Bebida is the largest beverage industry trade show in Latin America.[26] Exhibitors from food, drink, hotel, restaurant, and packaging companies attend the show held annually in Brazil. RetailTech, held in Tokyo, is Japan's largest trade show. It specializes in retail information technologies. Participants are able to make valuable contacts and learn about the latest developments in areas such as retail information systems, warehouse efficiencies, and digital marketing.[27] Events such as these can be effective when a firm tries to reach new prospects, learn about new technologies, or study industry developments.

Marketing teams examine the cultural context surrounding a trade show. In many parts of the world, the trade show attendees are corporate officers who are authorized to finalize purchases. In these circumstances, the manufacturer goes beyond demonstrating a product to trying to make the sale. In the United States, attendees are more likely to be information seekers who are not authorized to buy merchandise. Further, effective marketing efforts involve making certain those attending trade shows follow the cultural norms of the region. In Asian shows, giving of gifts to those who visit a booth common. Also, the use of female decorative models to adorn products may be routine in one country and inappropriate in another. The trade show strategy can often by combined with sponsorships in international markets.

Tecno Bebida is a large beverage industry trade show that is held in Brazil.

TRADE ALLOWANCES

A **trade allowance** is a price reduction or other consideration paid by a company to intermediaries as an incentive to purchase or promote a specific product. Many types of trade allowances are available to international marketers, including those presented in Figure 14.5.

> A trade allowance is a price reduction or other consideration paid by a company to intermediaries as an incentive to purchase or promote a specific product.

| Off-Invoice Allowances |
| Bill-Back Programs |
| Slotting Fees and Slotting Allowances |
| Display Allowances |

Figure 14.5: Trade Allowances

Off-Invoice Allowances

Invoice allowances, which are often referred to as "off-invoice" allowances, are price reductions taken off orders (literally off the invoice for the order) based on agreements between the manufacturer and the retailer. These invoices identify a predetermined purchase quantity that triggers the discount. They can also apply to other agreements. The price incentives directly increase the margins that retailers realize, and as such, are generally viewed quite favorably. An example of an off-invoice allowance occurs when an international marketer such as Samsung grants a price break to wholesalers who distribute a certain volume of Samsung products internationally.

Bill-Back Allowances

A bill-back allowance takes the form of a monetary allowance presented to the retailer or intermediary at the end of a promotional period. In order to qualify for the allowance, the intermediary must perform one or more promotional activities, such as putting up displays, providing free samples, redeeming consumer coupons, or offering price cuts.

Bill-back programs increase the manufacturer's reach by creating incentives for additional marketing activities. Merchandise sold as a result of those marketing activities will be at full price. Only the actual marketing activity creates additional costs. These programs often help create positive relationships between manufacturers and intermediaries, which will be crucial to the success of international marketing campaigns.

Coca-Cola utilizes trade allowances for retailers that perform important marketing functions.

Large international beverage marketers, including Pepsi and Coca-Cola, utilize these allowances for retailers who perform important marketing functions. The retailer initially pays for the activity, and then submits an invoice to the manufacturer for the cost, thus leading to the term "bill back."

Slotting Fees and Slotting Allowances

A slotting fee or slotting allowance is a payment made by a manufacturer to a retailer in order to secure shelf space in the store. Retailers set fees based on the amount of space allotted to a product, such as a twelve-inch space on an eye-level shelf, or an eighteen-inch space on a ground-level shelf. Retailers claim that, as the proliferation of brands in each category increases over time, competition for shelf space rises as well. Slotting fees help to spread the risk of new product introductions between the retailer and manufacturer. Consequently, manufacturers will be inclined to only pay slotting fees when they have a great deal of confidence about a new product's potential.

Slotting allowances are common in European countries, where they are generally referred to as *listing fees*.[28] They are also prevalent in the United States and in all parts of the world. The practice has recently drawn attention in China where major retailers such as Wal-Mart and Carrefour have utilized them.[29] International marketers seeking to conduct business in Europe may expect to pay slotting allowances at the retail level, especially in larger stores and big box chains.

Display Allowances

A display allowance promotion involves a retailer contracting with a manufacturer to place a product display in a prominent location in the retail outlet for a predetermined amount of time. When the retailer agrees to the terms of the allowance and performs the activities as agreed, the company earns an incentive in the form of a rebate at the end of the promotional period. The incentive can take many various forms. Display allowances are common in the grocery market where large manufacturers encourage retailers to help promote products. Proctor & Gamble pays Nucare, a British pharmacy, display allowances to receive key shelf locations and prominent displays.[30]

COOPERATIVE ADVERTISING

Cooperative advertising, or co-op advertising, results from an agreement between a manufacturer and an intermediary. Under a co-op advertising arrangement, a manufacturer agrees to pay for part of the advertising expenses of a retailer when the retailer promotes a product in a local market. Co-op advertising agreements are widely used. It is most common to see an advertisement that says something like, "Our products are found in finer stores, including ABC retailers." The expense of the promotion would be split based on an agreement between marketer and retailer. Co-op advertising continues to grow in popularity, much like slotting fees, when the risks and marketing costs of products are split between international marketer and retailer.

TRADE CONTESTS

Manufacturers develop trade contests to provide a reward or incentive for intermediaries that either reach certain sales goals or outsell other intermediaries. These contests have proven to be effective in some international markets. In general, the reward or incentive takes a monetary form. Other things of value, ranging from special event tickets to merchandise, can also be used as incentives in trade contests. From the retailer's perspective, it will be necessary to balance winning a given sales contest with providing information and service about other products not in the contest. When retail salespeople become overly focused on one marketer's contest, other products may be neglected. This can particularly be the case for electronics retailers who often focus efforts on a number of product categories.

TRAINING PROGRAMS

Manufacturers often offer training programs to marketing intermediaries as part of a trade promotions effort. Although training does not necessarily apply to every industry, it can be an important form of trade promotion for complex products. IBM Business Solutions offers a number of trade promotions and training opportunities for retail customers.[31] Training retail sales personnel can be valuable in an international context. Training programs have been positively correlated with increased sales and productivity.[32] General Electric has gained attention for its high-quality training program. The company has recently focused on training customers in the Southeast Asia region, a region that continues to grow in importance for international marketers.[33]

POINT-OF-PURCHASE MATERIALS

Point-of-purchase materials take a variety of forms, but the goal is the same: to encourage the immediate sale of the product by the end user. **Point-of-purchase** materials can be classified as trade promotions, because they assist intermediaries, most generally retailers, in promoting a product to the end user. These materials are effective because many items that are purchased in retail stores are chosen on impulse with little or no preplanning. Marketers understand that making contact with consumers at the point of purchase increases the probability a product being chosen.

Retailers and other intermediaries consider point-of-purchase support from manufacturers to be valuable. They do, however, often require an incentive for allowing point-of-purchase displays in an outlet. For this reason, trade allowances are frequently provided by manufacturers in exchange for the placement of point-of-purchase materials. Retailers recognize the value of display space on retail floors and often charge for the use of the space.

In many countries, few big box stores are present. When designing point-of-purchase displays to be sent to an international customer, the marketing team first examines the amount of retail space available for displays. The display's size can then be adapted to that space. Then, other factors, including the most popular and symbolic colors, proper language, and other local circumstances, are addressed as part of the design of the display.

CHALLENGES

The varying levels of access to new technologies continue to present a major challenge in the area of international sales promotions. In lesser-developed regions of the world, sales promotions, such as sampling, take on additional importance. Other challenges include varying consumer responses to the individual sales promotion techniques. Couponing and in-store promotions are particularly popular in Europe, as are direct mail campaigns. Direct mail has taken on a smaller role in the United States. Mobile couponing is especially popular in Japan and Korea. The international marketer should carefully consider differences such as these when entering a new country or market. International marketers also consider legal differences and restrictions that are placed on sales promotion activities worldwide. Language differences also pose a serious challenge for international marketers, as does the appropriate selection of social networking sites.

Large retailers, including chains such as Tesco (United Kingdom), Carrefour (France), and Wal-Mart (United States), as well as regionally based chains, hold increasing channel power, due to the number of choices available for each product line. Big box retailers carry thousands of products, presenting consumers with seemingly endless options. As a result, manufacturers are compelled to offer trade promotions to gain favor with retailers and achieve placements in stores. Many suppliers believe trade promotions are the only effective tool available to keep other companies from capturing space on retail shelves. This may be especially true for international companies attempting to gain shelf space in foreign countries in the face of rapidly growing global competition.

International Sales Promotions Campaign Management

One continuing issue in international sales promotion is how the programs are to be managed. Company leaders decide whether local offices, regional offices, or world headquarters will manage the promotions. Ultimately the decision may boil down to standardization versus adaptation. Although adaptation offers the advantage of catering to local market needs, it can dilute the image of a brand globally due to contradictory messages being delivered. Significant research will be required when considering this choice.

A complicating factor is that in many instances sales promotions *must* change country by country due to the wide variance in technological availability. Consumer promotions play an important role in countries where mass media advertising possibilities do not exist due either to technological limitations or consumer poverty. Some countries are geographically diverse. In many areas, rugged terrain makes access to traditional television or Internet connections difficult or impossible. International marketers are often creative when attempting to reach these consumers with sales promotions.

Regardless of whether a standardization or adaptation strategy is chosen, international marketers should ensure that sales promotions are managed strategically. To ensure continuity of communication and message, each promotion should fit within the overall strategic direction set by marketing managers, which constitutes a critical part of the success of a promotional campaign.[34]

Numerous international marketing opportunities accompany the manufacture, distribution, and sale of facial tissues.

International Marketing in Daily Life

VIDEO LINK 14.3: Communication

Marketing Facial Tissues

Sooner or later, everyone sneezes. It many parts of the world, the response will be to reach for a facial tissue. Numerous international marketing opportunities accompany the manufacture, distribution, and sale of facial tissues.

When marketing facial tissues products, all of the elements present in the international marketing context should be addressed. With regard to culture, facial tissue is used in a variety of ways, dependent on the country or region where it is sold. In Taiwan, paper towel products are not widely available. Spills are cleaned up with facial tissue. In other nations, facial tissue is used as toilet paper, even though technically the two are different. Toilet paper should be designed to decompose in a sewer system or septic tank, but some nations such as Iraq often do not have such systems. In Western culture, facial tissue may be for more than sniffles: women employ it to remove make-up. In less-developed countries, bottom-of-the-pyramid customers may not even be acquainted with the product.

The language of facial tissue also varies. The French call them *mouchoirs*. The Swedish version is *ansiksservetter*. At the same time, the term "Kleenex" remains the same in France or Sweden. A person in China might be confused by the concept of a facial tissue, even though the person has purchased an equivalent product, but for alternate uses.

Governments may regulate the ingredients used to create facial tissue. As greater environmental concerns emerge regarding deforestation, an impact on harvesting trees to produce facial tissues may occur. Some facial tissues carry ingredients such as lotions or perfumes, which might subject them to additional regulations, including those associated with medical and cosmetic products.

Economic conditions influence the patterns of the distribution of facial tissue. In developed and Western cultures, such products are widely distributed convenience items made available in a variety of packages. For bottom-of-the-pyramid markets or for least-developed economies, the same product may receive limited or no distribution support.

Infrastructure affects the delivery and price of facial tissue. The products are light, but packages do take up some space. Modes of transportation as well as the information technology that might be used to market facial tissue will be tailored to individual countries.

CONSUMER PROMOTIONS

All of the forms of consumer promotions could be utilized to distribute facial tissues in international markets. Developing the goal of the consumer promotions program constitutes the first concern marketers address. In some countries, the first goal would be to create consumer awareness. A new brand, Miracles of the Dead Sea, has been established in the nation of Jordan. Should the company expand product lines from bath salts and other beauty products to include facial tissues, awareness would become the goal. As time passes, the company might seek to establish or build market share. In others companies and countries, an established brand might have the goal of preempting competition or to build market share.

Following the development of marketing objectives for the consumer promotions program, individual choices would be made. *Coupons* may be chosen for a variety of reasons, including enticing initial purchases, matching competitive offers, generating brand switching, or seeking to create some stockpiling of the product by consumers.

Premium offers would be limited. A creative marketer might find a method to offer a premium based on a series of purchases, such as offering a facial tissue dispenser in exchange for five proofs of purchase pieces plus €8 to cover shipping and handling.

Bonus packs could be shipped to larger retail stores where more shelf space is available. The packs may be tied with a discount given to the retailer for purchasing and displaying the packs. Often the objective of a bonus pack offer is to have the consumer stock up and not buy a competing brand. At other times a bonus pack of tissues might encourage a customer to choose one brand over another based on the perceived bargain of more product for the same price.

Contests and/or sweepstakes might be featured in a number of ways. A simple drawing for a prize based on entries might entice some customers to select a particular brand while in the store. A contest associated with a product's use might also be possible. For example, a cold and flu season theme might be tied to creating a new tagline or commercial for a given brand. This might include social media as a method of inviting participation.

Rebates are probably the least likely alternatives for facial tissue products. The low price of the item would discourage this type of promotion.

Price-off programs are logical candidates for tissues, especially in developed economies where distribution is widespread. In these markets, facial tissues are in the maturity stage of the product life cycle. If it is not possible to create perceptions of differences in quality, then the primary method of competition will be based on price. Should a tissue company be able to create brand loyalty based on quality distinctions, then consumers might view a price-off program as potentially diminishing the difference and therefore would not use it.

Sampling programs entice people to try products they have never used. When entering a region in which facial tissues are not widely available, free samples offer a quick and convenient method to encourage initial purchases. In other markets, should a company try to establish quality differences in the minds of consumers, samples may be given to them in order to demonstrate the superiority of a brand in a direct comparison with the competition.

Creativity in marketing facial tissue products is possible. The Fine company recently announced the introduction of a new line of facial tissues in the Middle East. The products were developed in partnership with Walt Disney Company and targeted children, which makes a premium program possible using cartoon characters as prizes. A similar marketing approach between Kimberly-Clark and Walt Disney Company for facial and pocket tissues proved to be successful in Thailand. The Fine-Disney tissues come in an exclusive three-dimensional packaging set of five boxes with the popular Disney characters—Donald Duck, Daisy Duck, Mickey Mouse, Minnie Mouse, and Goofy. Each tissue box comes in a different color with innovative dispensing features.[35]

TRADE PROMOTIONS

Facial tissues may also be sold to retailers and through wholesalers using various trade promotions. Beginning with the key marketing goal, producers can establish programs to push products onto retail shelves in new countries.

> **VIDEO LINK 14.4:**
> Culture and Promotions

Trade show participation seems unlikely. Very few shows deal with these types of products, unless there is a logical tie-in, such as Disney characters marketed in conjunction with facial tissues. Most of the time, however, other trade promotion programs will be more effective.

Trade allowances offer a great deal of promise. Off-invoice allowances would be given for larger bulk purchases. Bill-back programs may be established for any large retailer that could perform a marketing function, such as housing a sweepstakes or putting up a display. Slotting fees may be paid to large retailers that require such funds to stock products. Display allowances provide a further incentive to place a facial tissue brand in a prominent part of a retail store.

Cooperative advertising programs may be constructed with drug stores, grocery stores, and other retail outlets. They may be held in conjunction with bonus pack offers or price-off programs. The goal would be to establish favorable relationships with retailers over time.

Trade contest options are limited. The type of product once again confines the marketing team. The same would be true for *training programs*. Product features do not require an explanation, and there would be few actual salespeople to target with such an effort.

Point-of-purchase materials might be developed either to display new product uses or to highlight the product during the cold and flu season. Tie-ins with cold medications, free samples, bonus packs, and coupons are all possibilities the marketing team could explore.

In summary, the marketing of products as small as facial tissues and as large as refrigerators can be improved using sales promotions programs. The goals of the program determine the types of sales promotions chosen and the linkages with other aspects of promotion, including advertising and personal selling. As shown in this example featuring facial tissues, creative marketing teams can design promotions that make even the most mundane product seem more exciting and desirable.

International Public Relations

LEARNING OBJECTIVE #4:

How does the public relations team or department handle negative publicity or image-damaging events?

The promotions mix contains other key elements and activities. Many of these are designed to tie together consumer and trade promotions with other marketing tactics. Public relations efforts can then combine with other promotional efforts to present a more fully integrated image to customers and others.

Public relations involves the management of communication with all organizational stakeholders. The public relations function is handled by the department or unit in a firm that manages publicity and other marketing communications programs. The public relations team may be part of the marketing department or a stand-alone unit in the organization. Public relations includes developing quality contacts with all publics and stakeholders. *Internal stakeholders* are the employees who work in a company. *External stakeholders* include all others who have contact with the organization. A list of external stakeholders is provided in Figure 14.6.

CHANNEL MEMBERS

These stakeholders will be informed about company activities and responses to events using various media and communication methods. The standard tools available to the public relations department include

Unions	Customers
Shareholders	Local Community
Government	Financial Community
Media	Special Interest Groups

Figure 14.6: External Stakeholders

- public relations releases,
- correspondence with shareholders,
- company newsletters,
- annual reports,
- the public relations section of the organization's website, and
- special messages and special events.

The two primary activities conducted by the public relations department include addressing negative publicity and events and promoting positive publicity and image-enhancing events.

ADDRESSING NEGATIVE PUBLICITY AND EVENTS

Damage control involves reacting to negative events caused by a company's mistake, consumer grievances, or unjustified or false claims made by the press or others seeking to injure a company. When the company is in the wrong, company executives ask the public relations team to repair the damage to whatever degree possible. Two of the more common methods used to address company-created problems are crisis management programs and apology strategies.

Crisis Management

Crisis management involves refuting a false claim in a forceful manner. Company leaders will make public statements explaining why the charges are not valid. They also can provide evidence proving that the negative publicity is unjustified. The next element of crisis management will be promoting the positive aspects of a company's operations that also refute the negative claim. A company that has been accused of using child labor in dangerous working conditions, when innocent, will dispute the basic premise, provide evidence that child labor has not been employed, and then may continue with employee endorsements of the company's safety and overall environment.

Apology Strategies

An apology strategy consists of four elements. First, the company's leader offers an expression of guilt, embarrassment, or regret. Second, a statement acknowledging the inappropriate activity and accepting any sanctions imposed should be provided. Third, the company's leader publicly rejects the inappropriate behavior and approves of the proper action. Finally, the company provides compensation or penance to correct the wrong.

In international circumstances, ceremonies and methods for offering apologies vary. In Asia, an apology would be finalized with a bow to an individual consumer or to a representative of an organization or consumer group. In other countries, a handshake might finalize the apology. In 2010, Toyota's chief executive officer promised a "fresh start" after a series of incidents involving vehicles that included rapid, unexplained acceleration and other defects. The move was made quickly to limit damage to the firm's reputation for building high-quality cars.[36]

Partial Guilt

When a company is connected to a negative event and is partially responsible, leaders may offer excuses, explanations, or justifications. An *excuse* will be a pronouncement that the firm and its leaders cannot be held fully responsible for the predicament because it could not be foreseen. An *explanation* may be created to explain that the negative publicity has been disproportionate to the act. In essence, the public relations response will be, "This was a singular incident and is not how we typically conduct business."

A *justification* involves using logic to diminish the degree of negativity associated with the event, such as, "It wasn't that bad," or "If we don't pollute, we will be out of business and people will lose jobs." Many of the oil companies have made this argument with regard to offshore drilling, in essence that the consequences of not drilling are greater than the problems (oil spills and accidents) that are part of the process.

POSITIVE PUBLICITY AND IMAGE-ENHANCING EVENTS

The other aspect of public relations programs includes all of the actions that support the generation of positive publicity along with programs that enhance an organization's image. Various public relations tools can be used to optimize these programs. An *entitling* involves the company taking credit for a positive outcome, such as when a pharmaceutical company takes credit for reducing illness and mortality rates by vending its products in a less-developed nation.

An *enhancement* emphasizes the value of an outcome. A firm dedicated to lessening carbon emissions will likely note that it is, at the same time, "helping to save the planet for the next generation." At times, entitlings and enhancements result from less-concrete linkages, such as when a sports drink takes credit for an athlete's success or a team's performance.

LEARNING OBJECTIVE #5:

How can the public relations function help build a positive image of a company and its brands?

Several marketing programs can be coupled to the goal of creating positive publicity and enhancing a firm's image. These include

- sponsorships,
- event marketing,
- cause-related marketing, and
- green marketing and sustainability.

Sponsorships

> A sponsorship creates an agreement between a marketing organization and an individual, team, or a landmark.

A **sponsorship** creates an agreement between a marketing organization and an individual, team, or a landmark. International car racing, such as the twenty-four hours of Le Mans (*24 heures du* Mans), in France, features sponsors for drivers and cars. Both the racer and the vehicle are covered with patches and decals endorsing a wide variety of products. The racetrack will be lined with additional sponsor advertisements. In the same country, bicycle-racing teams in the *Tour de France* receive compensation and support from sponsors.

A building or sports stadium may also be the basis for a sponsorship. Reebok Stadium houses the English Premier Football Club, the Bolton Wanderers. In Yorkshire, England, the former Huddersfield Stadium has been renamed McAlpine Stadium.

Sponsorships are designed to assist in brand recall and help build brand loyalty. Fan allegiance to a participant or team should transfer to the sponsor. Stadium sponsors believe naming rights grant an organization greater credibility and enhance brand recall. Sponsors are expected to invest a sum of money in exchange for some type of promotional consideration on the part of the person or team.

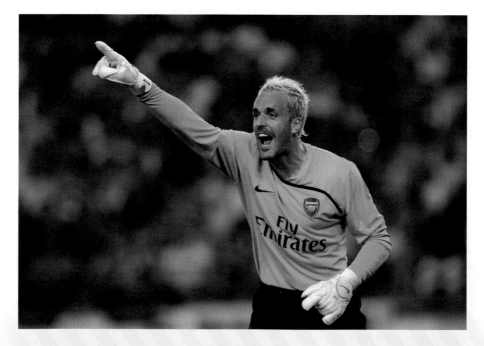

Stadium sponsors believe naming rights grant an organization greater credibility and enhance brand recall.

Event Marketing

A promotional tactic closely related to sponsorships is **event marketing**. Event marketing uses marketing techniques to connect with buyers through specific live events including concerts, performances, or festivals to promote a product or brand. Event marketers use these techniques for connecting with both consumers and trade channel members, making them a form of both consumer and trade oriented sales promotions. An example of event marketing includes the efforts by Chinese company Yingli Green Energy. In 2010, the company became the first renewable energy company to sponsor the FIFA World Cup.[37]

> Event marketing uses marketing techniques to connect with buyers through specific live events including concerts, performances, or festivals to promote a product or brand.

Sponsorships programs and event marketing have grown rapidly in international marketing over the past several years. The programs often accompany other consumer promotions efforts. At an event in which a sponsored participant is involved, a company can set up a booth, offer free samples and coupons, offer a contest or sweepstakes, and employ social media to make on-site connections as part of the program.

Cause-Related Marketing

Opportunities exist for firms to support social causes that are important to consumer values. Swedish giant Ericcson continues to support and sponsor the Swedish Paralympic Team. The sponsorship reflects the company's desire to break down walls of prejudice against persons with disabilities.[38] Sagami Rubber Industries of Japan sponsors music events, which not only helps promote the company's products but also heightens consumer awareness of contagious diseases such as AIDS. The company's sponsorship of the music event "Protected" promoted the safe sex message as well as condom products. The event also allowed Japanese hip-hop artists to advertise the products with free samples.[39]

Cause-related marketing can be an effective activity for a company seeking to promote and publicize its mission and core values. When the cause does not fit with the organization or its activities, consumers quickly become cynical and may develop negative attitudes toward the company. Consequently, care should be given to the selection of proper causes for a firm to engage with, noting that customers and the public often comment on such programs using various social media outlets.

Green Marketing and Sustainability

An increasing number of international companies have become engaged in sustainable marketing practices. For some, the opportunity to publicize these efforts creates more favorable consumer attitudes toward the company. Other firms undertake green programs but do not emphasize them in marketing or public relations activities. The reasoning is that consumers may not believe the claim that the company has become more environmentally friendly, instead concluding that only a token effort has been made. Other consumers think that green products and production methods have higher costs and will lead to price increases.

The public relations team faces the challenge of highlighting green efforts in a manner that does not overemphasize what has been done. Often the goal is to simply add a layer of positive thought about a company and its brands, and no more.

SOCIAL MEDIA AND PUBLIC RELATIONS

The international growth of social media usage presents an additional set of tasks for the public relations team. Large organizations in particular will monitor what bloggers

> **Internet interventions involve identifying false statements about a company and then responding to the allegations.**

and others engaged in social media connections are saying and writing about the company. A negative event can quickly go viral and cause the company embarrassment or create a bad impression of the company.

Internet interventions involve identifying false statements about a company and then responding to the allegations. A member of the public relations team will identify himself or herself and present the organization's perspective. At times, the public relations employee can correct false information or present alternative interpretations of an event that has transpired.

MARKETING IMPLICATIONS

In the international arena, public relations programs have become vital links between companies and various stakeholders. The public relations team remains vigilant to identify any negative publicity and to respond to it in a culturally appropriate fashion. Reactions may be sent out through traditional public relations tools such as press releases or via social media outlets.

Positive publicity and image-enhancing marketing programs receive support from the public relations team. The goals are to inform, persuade, and remind the public that the company seeks to do the right thing and contribute positively to the local community and all constituents.

Public relations efforts are influenced by the major factors affecting international business. Public relations releases must be tailored to an individual country's language, culture, legal and political systems, economic conditions, and infrastructure. The marketing team works to make sure the language is correct and does not offend, and that the cultural implications of both negative and positive events are clearly understood. In some countries, the media are owned or controlled by the government, which influences how messages are designed and delivered. Economic conditions and infrastructure influence media choices and method of delivering messages as well.

Chapter 14: Review and Resources

STRATEGIC IMPLICATIONS ///

Outlining the direction of the promotions mix and sales promotions programs generates a seriesof key strategic decisions. The promotional mix facilitates the direction of the overall marketingprogram. The promotions mix also supports the desired company image and product position globally. International marketing managers seek to identify the correct mix of consumer and trade promotions, with carefully chosen marketing objectives in mind. Normally, both forms of sales promotions are utilized.

As international marketers consider the brand's global position, they also select a standardization or adaptation strategy for sales promotions. Language and cultural differences greatly influence these decisions, as do legal restrictions. Questions will be asked regarding whether promotional efforts translate effectively across borders. International marketing managers then decide whether these promotional decisions should be made at the corporate or regional offices. The ultimate strategic objective remains to present a consistent message that accentuates the firm's image and position across all boundaries.

TACTICAL IMPLICATIONS ///

Middle level managers implement the various consumer and trade promotions chosen at the strategic level. Should a company's marketing team decide to use coupons, the methods of delivery are studied and those that are most likely to succeed are employed. Premium programs require understanding of the most efficient method for delivering prizes to customers. Contests and sweepstakes must meet any local legal requirements as well as cultural expectations. Price-off programs must account for regulations regarding what constitutes the standard price and how often a discount can be granted. Refund and rebate programs must comply with regulations and meet with cultural understanding of the promotions.

Trade promotions are adapted to meet standard business practices of a region or country. Company leaders carefully choose which trade shows to attend and how to conduct business at those shows. Trade allowances will be granted to companies with managers that understand and appreciate them. Cooperative advertising programs must fit with local laws and customers. The same will be true for trade contests and training programs. Point-of-purchase materials are distributed to retailers that will use them.

International marketing managers work to ensure that the tactics that are selected match the overall promotional strategy. By following the overall marketing strategy, continuity and consistency of communications will be the result.

OPERATIONAL IMPLICATIONS ///

At the operational level, marketing employees at the entry level are the ones who actually deliver consumer and trade promotion. Consumer promotions must be managed so that entry-level employees know how to redeem coupons, present premium prizes, and grant price-off discounts. Employees should be trained to understand the overall marketing goals of the consumer and trade promotions, and how these factors apply to the individual contest, sweepstakes, coupon, bonus pack, or free samples they will handle. Employees play a critical role in the success of international promotional campaigns, and their training is crucial. For trade-oriented promotions, supervisors monitor the activities of employees who interact with wholesalers and retailers to ensure that these channel members are carrying out their promotional duties by following up on offers that are accepted.

TERMS

sales promotions

consumer promotions

trade promotions

trade allowance

point-of-purchase materials

public relations

damage control

sponsorship

event marketing

Internet interventions

REVIEW QUESTIONS

1.   What elements comprise a firm's promotional mix?

2.   Define sales promotion and name its two primary activities.

3.   Describe a push strategy and a pull strategy in international marketing.

4.   Define consumer promotions and name the major types of consumer promotions.

5.   Name the forms of coupons and how they are offered in international markets.

6.   Describe a premium and a bonus pack.

7.   What is the difference between an international contest and an international sweepstakes?

8.   How can international marketers use social networking sites in marketing campaigns?

9.   What three types of consumer reactions are present when individuals encounter international consumer promotions?

10. Describe trade promotions and the forms they take.

11. What are the major forms of trade allowances?

12. What is cooperative advertising?

13. Define public relations and name the types of internal and external stakeholders reached by public relations programs.

14. What is damage control?

15. What methods can a company use for damage control?

16. Define entitling and enhancement.

17. What positive publicity and image-enhancement programs are used in international public relations efforts?

DISCUSSION QUESTIONS

1.   Which do you think is more important for an international marketer who is introducing a new product: a push strategy or a pull strategy? Why? What specific types of tactics do you think are most important in introducing new products?

2.   What consumer promotion technique or techniques would work best in a country that does not have wide-scale access to mass media technologies such as television or the Internet? Defend your answer.

3.   What role do social media play in international consumer promotions? How will the use of social networking grow in the future?

4.   How do trade promotions differ in developed versus developing nations? In what ways could an international marketer use this information when developing sales promotions in these countries?

5.   Explain how a public relations program would be different in a country in which the media are owned and operated by the government, as opposed to those that operate freely.

6.   Describe an incident that occurred in another country that caused a company negative publicity. How did the company respond? Was the response appropriate? Why or why not?

ANALYTICAL AND INTERNET EXERCISES

1. Visit the website of a major international marketer such as Coca-Cola. What do you learn about the company's worldwide sales promotions? What tactics do you like? Are you surprised by any of them? Compare them to the sales promotion tactics used by a direct competitor. Are they similar, or very different? Explain your answer.

2. Visit the website of the international promotions company DDB (www.ddb.com). What sales promotion techniques are highlighted? What clients does the company list? How many of these clients can be considered to be international marketers? Go to one of the DDB international subsidiaries. What differences are present on those sites?

3. Visit the website of the major European retailer Tesco (www.tesco.com). What consumer-oriented sales promotions are highlighted? If you were shopping at one of the stores, which promotion would interest you the most?

4. Visit Facebook.com. What international companies to you see using the site for sales promotion? What types of promotion do you see? Do you think that these are effective or ineffective? What could the company do better to improve its use of social networking?

5. Using Google or Bing, identify an international public relations firm. Write a report describing the organization's activities and programs.

▶ **ONLINE VIDEOS**

Visit **www.sagepub.com/baack** to view these chapter videos:

Video Link 14.1: Language

Video Link 14.2: Contests and Sweepstakes

Video Link 14.3: Communication

Video Link 14.4: Culture and Promotions

STUDENT STUDY SITE

Visit **www.sagepub.com/baack** to access these additional learning tools:

- Web Quizzes
- eFlashcards
- SAGE Journal Articles

- Country Fact Sheets
- Chapter Outlines
- Interactive Maps

CASE 14 ///

Nestlé, S.A.

Recently, international marketing giant Nestlé, S.A., offered a cross-category consumer promotion entitled "Get Set, Go Free." The promotion was greeted with a great deal of consumer interest and excitement.

Nestlé, a global marketing giant, has its home office in Switzerland. It offers approximately 10,000 different products, in 130 countries.[40] Popular brands such as Nestlé, Nestea, Dreyer's, Kit Kat, Nesquik, CoffeeMate, and Pure Life are marketed by the company internationally.

The "Get Set, Go Free" promotion was specifically aimed at consumers in the United Kingdom and Ireland.[41] The promotion allowed consumers to try a range of activities free of charge. "Get Set, Go Free" is part of a £3 million marketing campaign that runs across many of the company's products including confectionery singles and multipacks, cereals, chocolate cookies, Nesquik powders, and Pure Life water.[42] To participate, the consumer purchases select products and collects "activity points" that are included on the inside of packaging of these products. The consumer then saves the points and redeems them through a website in exchange for a voucher for the desired activity.[43] The activity is then offered free to the consumer courtesy of Nestlé.

Thirty-seven different activities were offered for consumers during the latest version of the promotion. Activities ranged from martial arts, to dancing, swimming, and even paintballing. The company reported that between 2006 and 2011 1.6 million activity sessions were given away free of charge through the promotion.

Obesity is a major problem for many consumers worldwide. Estimates reveal that as many as 17% of males and 21% of females in the United Kingdom are obese.[44] Obesity is also on the rise in Ireland. One Irish study noted that fully 41% of men over the age of fifty do not regularly exercise and that nearly 20% of men over the age of twenty-five watch between sixteen and twenty hours of television per week.[45] Health concerns also exist for children in the region. Estimates reveal that almost three quarters of children do not get at least sixty minutes of daily activity outside of school. Statistics also indicate that a large percentage of school-aged kids watch TV or play nonactive video games before school, and as little as 22% participate in exercise after their evening meal.

Many international food and beverage marketers have developed promotions aimed at improving consumer health and exercise routines, and Nestlé leads with these efforts. "Get Set, Go Free" promotion works well within Nestlé's overall focus on helping families become more active.[46]

The promotion was reportedly one of the largest on-pack promotions in the United Kingdom and Ireland. As such, it provides a good example of how promotions can be utilized to stimulate consumer interest while helping the firm achieve its core values and bring good food and good life to consumers.[47]

International marketers have much to gain by offering promotions such as these across national boundaries. The promotions help to generate consumer excitement and immediate sales and help firms to achieve other corporate mission elements. The success of the "Get Set, Go Free" promotion helps Nestlé maintain its position as a worldwide leader in health, nutrition, and fitness.

The Nestlé "Get Set, Go Free" promotion was specifically aimed at consumers in the United Kingdom and Ireland.

1. How does "Get Set, Go Free" use additional promotional tools such as coupons, premiums, or free samples to help create consumer interest in Nestlé products?

2. How does "Get Set, Go Free" help Nestlé promote its core value of nutrition, health, and fitness?

3. Will a promotion such as "Get Set, Go Free" generate long-term interest in the company's products?

4. How could Nestlé utilize social networking in this promotion? How could the marketing team improve its efforts in this area?

5. How could Nestlé take advantage of this program in its public relations efforts?

6. If you worked for an international competitor of Nestlé, what types of promotions would you develop that would be based on health, nutrition, and fitness? Or, would you run such a promotion? Why or why not?

15 International Personal Selling and Sales Management

LEARNING OBJECTIVES ///

After reading and studying this chapter, you should be able to answer the following questions:

1. How does culture influence international personal selling?

2. What tasks are completed in the business-to-business international personal selling process?

3. What are the alternatives available for international sales force composition?

4. What are the keys to effective international sales force management?

5. What are the methods available for international sales force compensation?

IN THIS CHAPTER

International Personal Selling and Real Estate:
Complications and Opportunities

Ownership of property constitutes a key economic activity in the global environment. Whether the property is an office building, a home, land, or rental property such as apartments or condominiums, buying and selling real estate presents a variety of opportunities and challenges. Transactions take place between individuals and between companies, with both represented by an owner seeking to make a sale by himself or herself, or with the assistance of a real estate agent. The forces that influence the global marketing environment play significant roles in real estate markets.

Politically, purchasing land may be a relatively straightforward process in some countries, such as Australia or the United States, and not possible in others, where communist governments do not allow private ownership of property. Further, governments may limit or prohibit the purchase of land or property by foreign investors. Singapore and Hong Kong enforce limits to property ownership. Constitutional restrictions on land ownership and public utilities in place since 1935 are the most formal barriers to foreign participation in the Philippine economy.[1] In the United States, Japanese ownership of property in Hawai`i recently became a source of contention, with many American citizens believing too many parcels were being held by foreign investors.

Communication barriers also affect real estate purchases. Methods of communication during negotiations can influence offers and acceptances and disrupt the sale and transfer of property. A phrase such as "as is" has specific meaning in the United States: someone from another country may not understand the implications of those words. In England, the terms "property" and "real estate" have different meanings.

Cultural influences also affect sales of real estate. From the moment a salesperson is introduced to a buyer or seller, differences in culture can affect the entire real estate sales process. Greetings, patterns of speech, eye contact, personal space, and gender may alter how the proposed sale and final transaction are enacted. Women in many countries do not have the right to own property. In Swaziland, women were granted the right to own property for the first time in January 2010.[2]

Property ownership can be strongly linked to individual economic freedom and personal power. In less- or least-developed economies, owning farmland or a home is often nearly impossible. Selling to low-income or bottom-of-the-pyramid customers will be problematic at best. Economic recessions are often strongly linked to real estate sales and foreclosures.

Infrastructure affects the ability to gain access to property. A piece of land with no road leading to it has far less value than one beside a highway. Land located at a key intersection is more valuable for a business owner wishing to capture access to traffic and potential customers. Information technology has shifted the ways in which property transactions take place. Many buyers are able to go online and scout potential properties prior to meeting with a real estate salesperson.

A person seeking a career in international real estate sales will encounter a series of challenges. The salesperson will need to know whether financing in the form of a mortgage or loan is available in a given country. Foreclosure laws and other specific real estate statutes must be understood. In a host country, the sales rep will need to adapt to the monetary system as well as differences in the ways in which property is registered to an owner. The agent then will study specific cultural differences that affect property sales in various countries. Methods of compensation of real estate agents may also vary, with some receiving commissions and others salaries or salary plus commission packages. In general, a successful real estate salesperson will likely have a strong level of cultural intelligence and cross-cultural competence, along with the ability to make both the buyer and seller comfortable during the transaction.

QUESTIONS FOR STUDENTS

1. What characteristics are the most valuable for a person wishing to sell real estate in international markets as a career?

2. What should a person know before buying property in a foreign country?

3. How would buying and selling real estate be the same or different, as compared to other international business-to-business sales processes?

The forces that influence the global marketing environment play significant roles in real estate markets.

Overview

International sales personnel play crucial roles in international marketing programs. Salespeople provide direct contact between the company and its global customers. International salespeople are motivated to inform and persuade potential buyers, to achieve both short- and long-term sales results, and to establish long-lasting customer relationships. The personal relationships between members of the international sales force and customers largely influence the success of an international marketing program. Successful international salespeople understand that culture influences business relationships, decision-making styles, and personal interactions between buyers and sellers.

In this chapter, strategic issues pertaining to international personal selling are presented. First, the natures of retail and business-to-business personal selling are described. Then attention is given to cultural variables and how they impact the personal selling process, including the importance of cultural adaptation. Figure 15.1 notes that culture is closely linked to the personal selling aspect of promotion.

International business-to-business sales processes are described in detail, because these types of transactions are most prevalent in global marketing programs. The forms of international sales force composition are outlined, followed by discussions of virtual selling, sales teams, and the importance of foreign language skills in international sales. Finally, the tasks associated with international sales force management, including compensation and performance evaluation programs, are detailed.

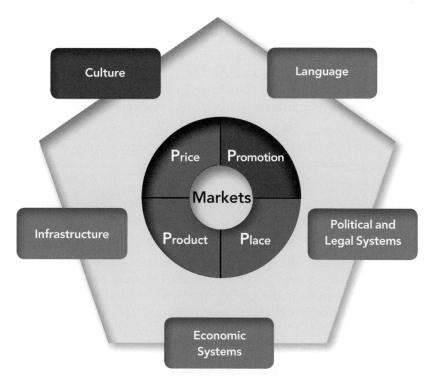

Figure 15.1: The International Marketing Context

The Nature of Personal Selling

Personal selling takes place on every populated continent and in every country. Much of the time, the salesperson represents the primary point of contact between the manufacturer or service provider and the end user. A bad experience with a salesperson can lead to a customer changing brands, to negative word of mouth, and to complaints to others in the company. A positive experience with a salesperson can lead to brand loyalty, return business, positive word of mouth, and other benefits. Effective strategic international marketing relies on quality personal selling programs.

Several forms of personal selling exist. A street vendor hawking fresh fruit and a high-powered business-to-business "heavy hitter" are both salespersons. Personal selling can be divided into two primary forms: retail selling and business-to-business selling. Both activities are part of international marketing systems.

RETAIL SELLING

The street vendor offering fruit engages in retail personal selling at its most basic level. In many corners of the world, a substantial amount of commerce takes place in local shops and stores as well as in street markets. Most of the purchases made by bottom-of-the-pyramid customers are made in these venues. Other forms of retail selling include

- order takers,
- commission sales, and
- service salespeople.

An order taker normally serves as both a salesperson and a cashier. In many shops and stores including big box retail outlets, order takers answer questions, restock shelves, process orders, and finalize sales. A retail order taker at the Grand Bazaar in Istanbul takes a purchase request and fills it. In many of these situations, little persuasion takes place. Rather, the salesperson simply records the customer's order and works to fulfill it. Sometimes fulfillment includes physically completing the order and/or carrying inventory to a delivery truck or from a retail store to the customer's vehicle.

Commission sales involve larger-ticket items, including appliances, automobiles, expensive clothing, real estate, and luxuries. The salesperson receives a percentage of the sales price as part of the compensation package.

Service salespeople offer a variety of services, including insurance, stocks, financial services, and personal services. In the case of personal services, such as hair care, the salesperson also renders the service.

Retail selling has been called the "last three feet of marketing." Any company that exports goods to be sold in retail outlets in other countries relies on the quality of the sales force to make profits. Many of the communication issues and cultural barriers described in this text can complicate retail selling in international markets.

BUSINESS-TO-BUSINESS PERSONAL SELLING

As companies expand into the international marketplace, a series of business-to-business personal selling positions will emerge. Some of these focus on making contact with wholesale intermediaries in the hopes of gaining distribution through the more traditional marketing channel. Others concentrate on retail outlets, thereby establishing local ties with companies in various countries. The nature of the product, the primary form of distribution, and company resources dictate the course that receives the most attention. Business-to-business selling can be conducted by three types of salespersons:

- field salespeople
- missionary salespeople
- telemarketers

Field salespeople call on intermediaries. Due to the expenses associated with travel and often with the commissions paid, field selling remains the most expensive form of personal selling, especially in the international marketplace.

Missionary salespeople make contacts with businesses to deliver samples, provide information, build relationships, and solve problems. Missionary selling takes place after relationships have been started with various intermediaries.

Telemarketers receive calls from customers as part of an inbound telemarketing program. These individuals take orders, answer questions, and attempt to resolve problems or conflicts. Outbound telemarketers make phone calls to potential clients. Outbound telemarketing is rarely used in international marketing programs.

Retail and business-to-business selling programs require attention to detail, constant training and retraining, and effective motivational and leadership systems. These programs help companies acquire and retain customers, the lifeblood of any domestic or international enterprise. Gaining customers can be expensive and difficult. Losing them is costly and time consuming. The challenge of personal selling becomes even more dramatic in international programs, where issues such as local language and culture become part of the scenario.

LEARNING OBJECTIVE #1:

How does culture influence international personal selling?

Culture and International Personal Selling

Culture plays a major role in the success of international promotions. While globalization of business has broken down many barriers to international marketing, consumers from many cultures continue to be unwilling to buy foreign-made products.[3] The salesperson can help to lessen customer reluctance.

International salespeople pay close attention to cultural variables and how they impact international sales. Faulty cultural assumptions can adversely affect sales presentations. Even in regions as seemingly homogeneous as the European Union, several different cultural influences may be at work.[4] One of the most important cultural variables that the international salesperson should understand is the business communication context.

Cultural context plays a key role in personal selling.

CULTURAL CONTEXT

Cultural context refers to how communication varies across cultures, which in turn affects promotional efforts. In low-context cultures, communication is expressed verbally and

Figure 15.2: High- and Low-Context Cultures

little emphasis is placed on nonverbal communication. Communication in low-context cultures tends to be more direct, yet informal. A salesperson operating in a low-context culture would want to make sure her language precisely conveyed a product's benefits as well as the advantage of choosing her firm. Western cultures, such as the United Kingdom and the United States, tend to be low-context regions. Figure 15.2 contains greater detail.

In high-context cultures, nonverbal communication is important and people tend to be heavily influenced by the backgrounds of the communicators, their positions in society, and their status.[5] Communication in high-context cultures is formal, yet indirect. In essence, many things are left "unsaid" in a high-context culture and word choice becomes crucial. Salespeople pay close attention to the meanings that are conveyed by their nonverbal communication in these regions. This would include how to dress, how to present a business card, whether to make eye contact, and how to sit properly. Customs and manners will matter greatly to members of high-context cultures.

TIME AND CULTURAL CONTEXT

Beyond the role nonverbal communication plays in high-context regions, buyers in these countries tend to be more lenient with issues such as the timeliness of meetings. In India or China, for example, it may not appear to be rude to be a few minutes late to a sales meeting. In England or the United States, tardiness will be frowned upon. A salesperson might lose a sale due to being late for a meeting in a low-context region. Being unaware of time presents an obvious problem for salespeople who are not accustomed to these differences. When a sales lead arrives late to a meeting, the salesperson might wonder if it means that the lead does not care about the meeting, or whether being late is normal in the home culture. The salesperson would want to know prior to the meeting.

INDIVIDUALISM/COLLECTIVISM

The distinction between individualistic and collectivist cultures also impacts international sales efforts. Customers in collectivist societies, as in high-context regions, are often more likely to repurchase from salespeople with whom they already have established relationships, because of the roles that friendship and trust play in business relationships.[6] The same will not necessarily be true for customers in individualistic societies. International salespeople learn the value of establishing relationships in collectivist societies even though the effort may take more time and effort.

International salespeople quickly discover that time can be perceived quite differently throughout the world. Decisions to make the purchase can also take longer in collectivist societies, such as Japan or Russia. Decisions in collectivist societies also often involve more individuals than in individualistic societies. Effective international salespeople understand the role of patience in personal selling in the global environment, especially in collectivist settings.

TRANSACTIONS VS. RELATIONSHIPS

Customers in individualistic cultures also tend to focus more on the transactional or functional elements than on the relational elements of sales negotiations.[7] Transactional elements such as price, delivery, and functionality of specifications become important to buyers in individualistic cultures. These customers are often less concerned with personal relationships. While transactional elements are important also in collectivist cultures, greater attention will be given to relational elements in collectivist cultures. Customers in Western cultures may believe that relationships form only after successful transactions, whereas buyers from Eastern cultures most often believe that relationships are forged well before agreements are reached.[8]

Guanxi

Relationship marketing has become a mainstay of the contemporary international marketing environment. Salespeople work to build close relationships with customers. For businesspeople in China, *guanxi* represents networks of relationships between business partners that lead to many advantages for its participants. Although connections are important in any culture, they are especially important in Eastern cultures.

Trust constitutes one of the key elements of *guanxi*. Businesspeople in China greatly value the concept of trust. Any Western businessperson seeking to conduct business in China must first work to establish relationships—not only between companies, but also between people. Sales reps must also understand that the relationships will be expected to begin before business deals are made and will continue well after any specific transaction takes place. The face-to-face interactions that are expected also take a special kind of person who is attuned to cultural differences. Not everyone feels comfortable in cross-cultural situations. One of the many differences the salesperson can seek to understand after accepting an assignment to China is the tradition of *guanxi*. [9]

BUSINESS ETIQUETTE

Other elements of business etiquette require the attention of international salespeople. Cultural differences play an important role in business etiquette. A number of these issues have been addressed in earlier chapters. The issues that pertain specifically to international selling revolve around[10]

VIDEO LINK 15.1:
Business Manners

- language, slang, and colloquialisms;
- eye contact and nonverbal communication;
- gift giving;
- shaking hands or bowing;
- physical distance;
- business card use;
- dining manners; and
- other business protocols.

Language, Slang, and Colloquialisms

International salespeople should be careful when making "small talk," especially with regard to the use of colloquialisms that may apply in one culture but not the other. Phrases such as "our business is red hot" may not hold meaning across cultures.[11] International salespeople are also cautioned to not rely on telling jokes, which is commonplace in many Western cultures. Jokes can be taken the wrong way in many cultures, and, depending on the content, can be insulting. Salespeople in international settings distinguish between being able to speak a language and understanding it completely within a given cultural context. A buyer may be familiar with the words that a salesperson uses, but not understand the context in which they are used.

The phrase "our business is red hot" serves as an example. Although it may seem strange, international buyers could misunderstand the meaning of this phrase and think that it literally means that doing business with this seller might burn them, particularly in a high-context culture. In these cultures, words may be taken much more literally than originally intended by the international salesperson. Consequently, care should be given to word choice. In the Philippines, referring to a woman as a "hostess" translates into calling her a prostitute.

Eye Contact and Nonverbal Communication

Maintaining eye contact and shaking hands are received differently across cultures. Keeping in constant eye contact may seem rude or being overly forward in high-context regions, but may be expected in others. In the Dominican Republic, losing eye contact will likely be interpreted as a sign that the person has lost interest in the conversation. Looking away in a deferent manner signals respect in low-context regions, such as Asia.

Salespeople moving into new countries carefully study the use of gestures before arriving. The symbol made by connecting the thumb and index finger in a circle means "OK" in the United States, something obscene in Germany and Brazil, "nothing" or "zero" in France, and "money" in Japan. Patting someone on the head violates a person's soul in the Buddhist tradition, which means patting a client's child in that manner would not bode well for the relationship.

Gift Giving

Gift giving may be considered to be appropriate in some cultures but not in others. In some Western nations, elaborate gifts are likely to be considered as bribery. In many Eastern cultures, gifts are considered to be common business practice. Businesspeople in China or Japan may view a gift as a part of forming a relationship. Businesspeople in Germany or Switzerland may be uncomfortable with the practice, and may conclude that it is either bribery or a method of manipulation based on a perceived obligation to reciprocate.[12] International salespeople pay close attention to cultural differences surrounding gift giving.

Shaking Hands or Bowing

Shaking hands is a common practice in Western cultures but is less prevalent or different in Eastern cultures. In Korea, a person will touch his elbow while shaking hands as a sign of respect. In Japan, a handshake is often accompanied by a 90-degree bow for the same reason. In many regions, Muslim men are forbidden to shake a woman's hand. Women do not shake hands with each other in Pakistan. Greeting a business contact with a kiss on the cheek is a common gesture in certain European countries. An international salesperson unfamiliar with these practices may become uncomfortable.[13]

Physical Distance

Culture exhibits a major impact on physical distance. Businesspeople in Latin America and in Middle Eastern cultures are used to standing more closely to one another than are salespeople from Western cultures.

International salespeople should learn to differentiate between social space, personal space, and intimate space. Sales presentations are generally given in *social space* where the persons involved share less of an interpersonal relationship. Face-to-face interactions occur in *personal space*, where the relationship moves beyond social interaction to some form of friendship or companionship. Only close family members or partners tend to enter *intimate space*. Perceptions of the three forms of space vary greatly across cultures. A buyer from a Middle Eastern country, such as Egypt, may think that he is in a salesperson's personal space whereas the salesperson feels uncomfortable because the interaction is taking place in his intimate space.

Business Card Use

International salespeople consider the ways in which business cards are handled. In Eastern cultures, for example, the business card is treated with much more respect than in Western cultures. In Japan, writing on someone's business card will be

Many business relationships include sharing meals and food.

considered disrespectful. The same is true of simply stuffing it into one's pocket, which discounts the importance of the business card. Business people in South Korea tend to use caution in handing out business cards, due to worries the card may be used in an inappropriate manner, especially if the business person does not know the other individual well.

Dining Manners

Many business relationships include sharing meals and food. Training and preparation in the cultural nuances should take place prior to any dining experience. In France, moving hands onto one's lap is a breach of etiquette, even though the same act is customary in the United Kingdom. In parts of Asia, a loud belch after a meal signifies enjoyment and appreciation of the food. In China people use chopsticks to eat rice. In Korea, diners leave the rice bowl on the table and often use a spoon. In most countries, refusing a delicacy will be considered as poor manners, because often the host went to extra expense to obtain the food item. In Spain, a person should always request a check when the meal is complete. It is considered rude to have the wait staff bring a check before the individual has asked for it.

Other Business Protocols

Other cultural nuances can affect long-term business relationships. Understanding the frame of reference of a prospective client can make or break a business deal. A Silicon Valley company recently booked a flight for a French guest to visit the country. The guest received a limousine ride to his hotel, but no one from the company met him upon arrival. The company's marketing team assumed the French prospect would prefer to rest up, because the plane arrived in the early evening. The French normally dine after 7:30 p.m., which meant the guest was left on his own to find a place to eat. It nearly ended the deal before it began.[14]

The left hand has meaning in many cultures. In Malaysia, the left hand will be considered as unclean. In India, the left hand is considered as less important, and should not be used for ceremonies such as ribbon cutting, even when the person is left-handed.

CULTURAL ADAPTATION

In order to successfully navigate cultural differences, international salespeople require cultural intelligence and cross-cultural competence. **Cultural intelligence** refers to a salesperson's ability to detect differences between cultures and how individual behavior is influenced by and distinguished from a home culture.[15] Developing cultural intelligence takes time and requires the support and training of international sales managers. Cultural intelligence helps an international salesperson distinguish individual behavior from cultural influences and to recognize how or why a particular product would be valued within a particular culture. Perceptions of product attributes and benefits can be greatly impacted by culture. A culturally intelligent salesperson recognizes these influences when meeting with prospects.[16]

Cross-cultural competence reflects a salesperson's effectiveness in utilizing knowledge, skills, and personal attributes in order to work successfully with buyers from other cultures.[17] Even if an international salesperson possesses a high degree of cultural intelligence, he or she still needs to be competent in utilizing knowledge and skills when working with international buyers.

Cultural intelligence and cross-cultural competence allow salespeople to succeed in international settings. These skills also help the international salesperson adapt to other countries, especially for **expatriate** salespeople who are stationed in foreign countries for extended periods. Expatriates who possess little cultural intelligence or cross-cultural competence may suffer from **culture shock**, or a disorientation that results from a person losing familiar cultural props while living abroad.[18] A third-country salesperson from Asia conducting business in New York City might experience instances of culture shock if he were not prepared for the drastic differences in culture.

In summary, culture influences personal selling in both retail and business-to-business relationships. In international marketing, the primary emphasis will be on business-to-business selling situations. International business-to-business selling will be complicated by numerous cultural nuances. These include differences in language, slang, nonverbal communication, religion, business etiquette, dining habits, and other variables. The salesperson who has already been charged with understanding a company's products and its methods of operations must also know about differences in financial systems including monetary systems, and the challenges associated with international travel, and then will need to adapt to something as simple as time change. Culture shock affects a vast number of international salespersons. Those adept at cultural adaptation become valuable members of a company's marketing team.

INTERNATIONAL INCIDENT //

When going to meet with a sales prospect in Japan, you notice that another salesperson, who is Japanese, arrives at the same building with a gift for his customer. You have not brought anything for your prospect and become worried that you will be leaving a negative impression on him. It is too late for you to find a gift for him because your meeting is only in a few minutes. What do you do? Would you attempt to explain your situation to the prospect or would you simply ignore the situation?

International Business-to-Business Selling

In most cases, the process of international business-to-business selling follows the procedures used in domestic settings. Differences arise, however, from time to time based on culture and buyer expectations. The international personal selling process is presented in Figure 15.3.

PROSPECTING

Identifying potential sales leads constitutes an important part of the business-to-business selling process in domestic and international markets. Some of the tactics used to generate leads may be available in some countries but not in others. The most common methods used by the sales staff to generate a list of possible new clients include

- customer referrals,
- vendor referrals,
- channel referrals,
- networking, and,
- using directories.

Customer referrals emerge from satisfied clients in nearby countries, or those with relationships to companies in other countries. A business that supplies low-cost medical equipment to a customer in Brazil may receive leads for companies in nearby countries such as Bolivia, Colombia, Peru, or Venezuela.

Vendor and *channel referrals* result from relationships with intermediaries. In the European Union, distribution systems are more sophisticated than in other parts of the world. An Italian distributor may conduct operations in nearby Austria or Switzerland and might provide leads to a manufacturer.

Networking and *using directories* become more problematic in international marketing. Many times, networks do not transfer across national boundaries, and many directories are dedicated to a single country.

The marketing team may be able to generate additional prospects. Some of the sources to be used include

- databases,
- inquiries, and
- trade shows.

LEARNING OBJECTIVE #2:

What tasks are completed in the business-to-business international personal selling process?

Prospecting
Preapproach
Approach
Presentation
Negotiation
Handling Objections
Closing
Follow-Up

Figure 15.3: International Business-to-Business Selling

An effective data warehouse contains three types of names: current customers, prospective customers, and former customers. The data warehouse will require expansion to include prospective customers from other countries. Normally a database takes time to develop for the purposes of international expansion. Databases are often also available through various entities such as trade association groups in various countries.

Inquiries are made in response to company advertising and, more importantly to international personal selling programs, to a company's website. A well-constructed website can become a key portal to entry into a new country, providing the sales team with quality leads.

International personal selling often involves attendance of trade shows. At these events, prospects are developed and, at times, sales are made on the spot. Quality marketing programs identify the most viable trade shows to attend and send the best possible sales team to those events.

In the process of business-to-business prospecting, a **market development** strategy focuses on increasing sales of existing products to new customers. A *market concentration* strategy focuses on increasing sales of existing products to existing customers. In practice, most international sales efforts focus on both strategies.

> A market development strategy focuses on increasing sales of existing products to new customers.

PREAPPROACH

The preapproach stage includes all of the efforts that the salesperson undertakes to prepare for the actual sales approach. As with other elements of international personal selling, salespeople work to develop a solid understand of the individuals who will be involved in the buying process, along with the buyer's culture.

The amount of time devoted to the preapproach should be viewed as an investment. Buying teams are increasingly the norm in international transactions. Consequently, the salesperson works to ensure that she understands the role of each person in the process. The status of each buyer is important in international selling, especially in high-context cultures that place a great deal of importance on position and rank.[19] In some situations, the most influential person in the room remains quiet. The status of the buyer may be more important than any words that she uses.[20]

Failing to respect the status of the buyer can be disastrous for the international salesperson. Businesspeople from Poland, for example, pay close attention to status in a company, and the most senior of businesspeople are expected to make most decisions.[21] Making eye contact with someone of greater status can also be a problem in countries in Asia or Africa. When a company already has an established relationship with the buyer, the roles may be well defined ahead of time. This will not be the case when the salesperson meets with a client for the first time.

Although culture constitutes a key part of the preapproach process, salespeople also must become familiar with company needs, competitive offerings, and specific industry information. Most companies face much more competition in the international environment than in home countries. The salesperson seeks out as much information about the competitive environment as possible. A strong brand name in the home marketplace will not be sufficient, especially when buyers are reluctant to purchase from foreign marketers.

Part of preapproach preparation involves understanding the type of purchase a prospect would make. Three situations are possible:

Purchases of automobile fleets such as police vehicles are often modified rebuys.

- a rebuy,
- a modified rebuy, and
- a new buy,

A *rebuy* resembles a reorder. The seller has established an ongoing relationship with the buyer and the details of purchases have been fined tuned, which means re-orders are routine. A difficult selling task involves trying to convince a prospect to end a rebuy relationship with one company to switch to another. Only when the salesperson can present a dramatic and tangible difference will a sale become possible. Even then, however, the sale may be difficult to close, because the customer may have formed a friendship with the current supplier, especially when both are from the same country and the new company is from another country.

A *modified rebuy* occurs when the customer considers the potential to switch vendors. Modified rebuys are more common for a product with longer-term use and the sale may be accompanied by a service contract, lease arrangement, or buy-back option. When a computer, copy machine, or fleet of delivery trucks reaches the end of one of these contracts, company procedures often dictate that the purchasing department should examine all options.

A *new buy* takes place when a company will buy a good or service for the first time. Part of the sales process may be assisting the buyer in establishing specifications for the product. A helpful salesperson can take advantage of this moment to help build a relationship with the prospect.

The preapproach stage is complete when the salesperson has a solid understanding of the prospective buyer's purchasing team as well as the type of purchase to be made. Other information the salesperson would seek includes the items shown in Figure 15.4.

Prospect's business
Prospect's customers
Local culture and language
Satisfaction with current vendors
Risk factors and switching costs to change vendors
Names of decision-makers and influencers
Special needs

Figure 15.4: Preapproach Information

APPROACH

Order getting consists of the activities involved with actively persuading customers, or sales leads, to purchase products from the company. In business-to-business marketing, field salespeople work closely with potential sales leads and customers. The way in which an international salesperson approaches a prospect depends heavily on cultural variables. The salesperson knows in advance when a handshake will be appropriate and whether eye contact should or should not be maintained. He may engage in a slight bow in China, Japan, Taiwan, or Vietnam. He may kiss the cheek of a prospect in Argentina or Uruguay. A careful examination of business cards exchange practices will have revealed that Turkish businesspeople expect visitors to pass the card with two hands.[22]

Introduction formalities may be brief in some countries and elaborate in others. In Finland, for example, a popular saying is *suoraan liiketoimintaa*, which means "straight to business." This type of direct language would not be useful in situations where the *guanxi* relationship building takes place prior to any business discussions. Robert Burns, who owns CC Bloom's Hotel in Phuket, Thailand, inadvertently upset his business partners by starting a meeting with a discussion of business. "That's a no-no," he said. "I quickly figured out that I was creating problems by talking business before eating lunch."[23]

VIDEO LINK 15.2:
Body Language

PRESENTATION

Making an effective sales presentation can create a major asset for the company.[24] Key sales elements are presented in Figure 15.5.

Careful study of the local language will dictate the types of words that are persuasive words without being misinterpreted. To say "You can't live without this" would cause a great deal of distress in Japan, where persuasion would more likely evolve from a statement such as "It is my humble opinion that your company might find the use of this product to be highly satisfactory."

Visual aids should match the context of the culture. The use of symbols, colors, models, and situations should be carefully examined prior to the presentation. A woman with her face revealed or head uncovered in a visual may be off-putting to purchasers in Saudi Arabia. Red is the color of mourning in South Africa but of good luck and celebration in Asia. Yellow is the color of mourning in Egypt. Green represents Islam in some countries and St. Patrick's Day in Ireland and the United States.

Evidence of claims depends on either scientific, factual proof or endorsements by professionals. Cultural context influences the status of an endorser with a client.

Audience participation would be expected in some cultures and nonexistent in others. For uninhibited employees in Italy, an exciting interaction would take place fairly easily. The same would not be true in Scandinavian countries such as Finland or Norway.

Persuasive words
Visual aids
Evidence of claims
Audience participation
Product demonstration

Figure 15.5: Elements of Effective International Sales Presentations

Product demonstrations can be used to provide evidence of claims and to engage the audience. Any product that can be displayed featuring a visual, observable advantage over the competition will be easier to sell in the international marketplace.

Canned, or preplanned, sales techniques rarely work in international markets. The number of cultural variables that differ around the global makes them difficult to create. Most international sales presentations must be catered to the specific customer and need, especially in most business-to-business selling situations.

NEGOTIATION

Negotiating is the process of determining an acceptable arrangement, or sale, from both the buyer's and the seller's perspectives. To be truly customer-oriented, international salespeople ensure that buyer needs are taken into account during the negotiation process. Culture exhibits a major influence during the negotiation process.

When both buyer and seller are from the same culture, negotiations can be fairly straightforward. In cross-cultural negotiations, difficulties become more likely. Buyers and sellers have different ways of thinking and behaving, and these differences directly influence sales negotiations.[25] High-context negotiators, as an example, are much less rigid than are low-context negotiators.[26] As a result, they are less likely to follow any predescribed negotiating script or routine. What is left unsaid may be as important as what is actually said.

A variety of techniques can be used in a sales negotiation (see Figure 15.6). Salespeople attempt to control the agenda of the sales meeting by ensuring that only relevant information that pertains to the potential sale is discussed. Buyers may attempt to control the agenda as well. Either party may attempt to *slice* a deal by tabling issues on which they cannot reach agreement and instead focusing on smaller slices of the deal. They may also attempt to split the difference when arriving at a final deal. Here, they would focus on meeting halfway on subjects such as price, delivery demands, and other issues pertaining to the final agreement.

Time perceptions affect negotiations. Some buyers take longer than others during the negotiation process. Buyers in Japan, for example, are usually much slower in making decisions than are buyers in the United States. Attempting to set a specific deadline, which is another popular negotiation tactic, may be met with much hesitation in Japan. Closely related to setting deadlines, bluffing involves threatening to walk away from negotiations when the other side will not move from a position or is not willing to concede as much as is needed to close the deal. Effective salespeople utilize cultural intelligence and cross-cultural competence to arrive at an agreement that is satisfactory to both their company and the purchasing organization.

| Control the Agenda |
| Slicing |
| Split the Difference |
| Setting Deadlines |
| Bluffing |

Figure 15.6: Negotiation Techniques

International Marketing in Daily Life

The Art of Haggling

Many consumers are familiar with the term "haggling," the process of bargaining for a better price when purchasing a product. The practice will be expected in some cultures but be seen as being rude and overly aggressive in others. Understanding when and where to haggle constitutes a valuable skill for a consumer traveling to a foreign country. It is also important for the international marketer who is trying to understand targeted consumers and markets. In many ways haggling resembles the negotiation process that takes place between business buyers and sellers.

Cultural variables such as Hofstede's dimensions play important roles in determining whether haggling will be appropriate. In Mexico, as an example, it is commonplace for a consumer to haggle (or *regatear* in Spanish) with a salesperson over the purchase of a good. The practice routinely occurs with street vendors, but also in other contexts including automobile sales. Haggling in Mexico is nearly always expected. In many ways the *regatear* process becomes like a game, which can be exhausting for the consumer.

In other cultures such as in Japan, haggling would be perceived as being rude. In Japan's high-context culture, communication tends to be formal. Customs and manners play major roles in business interactions. Maintaining "face," or a sense of personal dignity, is highly important to citizens in these cultures. Aggressive bargaining would violate cultural norms. In many situations, the price stated on an item is exactly that—the final price. Haggling cannot only lead to an unsuccessful attempt to buy a product, but also can damage the relationship between the salesperson and the customer. Ironically, haggling continues to be used in other Eastern cultures. Korea provides an example. In Korea, a consumer may ask for a discount on a product (by asking *kaka juseyo*) and the seller will respond. In general, a consumer can arrive at a good deal by engaging in haggling. Haggling may also be found in Europe, especially in France, where a consumer would *marchandage*.

As with other international marketing concepts, consumers and businesses should consider their own cultures as well as the culture of the salesperson with whom they are interacting. Carefully considering cultural similarities, differences, and expectations can go a long way toward arriving at an acceptable final price while not offending the other party in the negotiation.

HANDLING OBJECTIONS

Handling objections should be a skill that all salespeople, whether domestic or international, seek to master. Several methods of overcoming objections in sales calls are possible (see Figure 15.7). The culture of the buyer often affects the method to be employed. Direct confrontation, or the head-on method, rarely provides the answer. It will be effective only in low-context regions such as the United States, where buyers tend to be quite vocal about objections.

Head-on
Indirect denial
Compensation
"Feel, felt, found"
Boomerang

Figure 15.7: Methods for Overcoming Objections in Sales Calls

Buyers in high-context regions may be uncomfortable with directly instigating an argument and may go to great lengths to avoid such confrontations. An indirect denial allows the salesperson to avoid telling the customer he is wrong and instead sympathizes with the person's point of view and then gently suggests an alternative. Also, the compensation method takes the approach of not answering the objection but instead showing product features that might solve the problem.

The "feel, felt, found" approach is often valuable in more feminine cultures. The salesperson empathizes with the customer's fears and worries and then uses a demonstration or testimony to allay those fears.

A boomerang approach turns the customer's objection into the reason why the product should be purchased. A salesperson hearing that the customer believes locals will not adapt to the product can ask what will happen if a competitor buys the item and successfully sells it.

When overcoming objections, international salespeople should also be careful not to confuse silence with rejection. Whereas silence is often considered to be awkward in many cultures, it is much more commonly accepted in others. Buyers in Sweden, for example, tend to be comfortable with silence.[27] Salespeople need not take the silence as a barrier. Patience will be required to finalize the sale.

Assumptive close
Choice close
Continual-yes close
Balance-sheet close
Contingent close
Act-fast close

Figure 15.8: Types of International Sales Closing Techniques

CLOSING

The process of ensuring that the buyer makes the purchase decision is the closing. Final agreements, determined during the negotiation phase, are completed and an exchange takes place.

Fear of rejection, lack of confidence, and poor training are all commonly cited reasons for closing failures. Many sales professionals attempt to "trail close" a sale by subtly asking a customer for a sale during the sales presentation. Other techniques, such as those listed in Figure 15.8, are also useful.[28]

Assumptive Close

The assumptive close, as its name implies, assumes that a customer will decide to purchase the product. The salesperson says, "How many units will you be ordering today?" Buyers in many cultures might perceive this technique to be overly forward or aggressive.

Choice Close

The choice close works under the assumption that product will be purchased and the only decision to be made would be the choice of delivery terms or product type.

The salesperson would use a line such as, "Would you prefer our standard delivery or express delivery?"

Continual-Yes Close

The continual-yes close works on the psychological principle of self-perception. The idea is that if a customer continues to say "yes" to a series of questions, she can be motivated to continue to say "yes" to other inquiries. The salesperson would ask questions such as "You appreciate high-quality products, don't you?" and "Keeping up with the competition is very important, isn't it?" The next question would be the final close question, which would be something along the lines of, "You see how vital our product is to your success, don't you?"

Balance-Sheet Close

The balance-sheet close technique allows the salesperson to list the pros and cons associated with either acting today or failing to act at all. The advantages are associated with buying the product being offered and the disadvantages are associated with failing to make the purchase. By presenting the customer with a visual record of both pros and cons, the salesperson can emphasize that the advantages of buying play into the customer's best interests.

Contingent Close

The contingent close method involves the salesperson suggesting that if he can solve a particular problem with his product, then the buyer should agree to buy the product. As an example, the salesperson would say, "If I can show you how you can increase your bottom line by 5%, could I get your order today?"

Act-Fast Close

This is when the salesperson warns the customer about a product's high demand and hints that if she does not act quickly delivery may be delayed or unattainable. The salesperson would use a line such as, "We have taken many orders for this product, and I don't want your delivery to be delayed, so maybe you should buy the product today."

Cultural Influences on the Close

Cultural context influences how final agreements are made and also how lasting relationships are viewed. A salesperson from a low-context culture might believe that she has secured a long-term relationship with a buyer simply because she has secured a signature on a contract. When the buyer comes from a high-context culture, this may not be the case. In high-context cultures, relationships are valued more highly than the terms of a sale.[29] Some customers in Eastern cultures may be offended by too much pressure to sign a contract.[30]

The meaning of the word "yes" should also be carefully considered. In many Asian countries such as China, for example, the use of this word can meaning anything from "I understand you," to "I am listening," to "no."[31] This obviously impacts the effectiveness of the continual-yes close. Navigating these differences takes a good deal of time, experience, and cross-cultural competence.

Unfortunately, some international salespeople are so uncomfortable with closing that they attempt to skip the step entirely, especially when the seller comes from a cultural context that is different from the buyer's. It also happens between salespeople and customers from the same culture. One recent study of retail sales in India, for example, revealed that fewer than half of salespeople studied even attempted to close a sale.[32] Rather, they simply allowed customers to walk away from potential sales. Failing to recognize the importance of closing can be costly.

Cross-Selling

The close may present the opportunity to persuade existing customers to upgrade recent purchases or purchase quantities, or to cross-sell additional products to the buyers. **Cross-selling**, or selling additional items from the same company, can be an important part of the international personal selling process. It increases the "ticket total" on the sale without the expense of making an additional sales call or finding an additional customer. Cross-selling becomes easier when a relationship has been built with a client over time. The customer develops a degree of trust with the salesperson and confidence in the products.

THE FOLLOW-UP

Providing after-sale service represents another important component of the international personal selling process. In high-context regions, close personal relationships with the account management are expected. Buyers from these regions may expect direct contact with the salesperson. In low-context regions, a buyer expects after-sale service but may have lower expectations for personal contact. Managing these accounts through customer service representatives may be acceptable.

After-sale service also provides value in low-context regions. It remains an important component in almost all international personal selling situations, although face-to-face meetings and relationships take on additional importance in high-context regions. Simply referring the customer to a call center or website address will rarely be enough to provide adequate attention and service.

International Sales Force Composition

LEARNING OBJECTIVE #3:

What are the alternatives available for international sales force composition?

International marketers face a number of issues when they consider the composition of the international sales force. The extent to which expatriates will be employed constitutes the first issue. An *expatriate salesperson* works in a country that is not his home country. Expatriates are used extensively in international personal selling. Three types of expatriates are listed in Figure 15.9.

A **home-country national salesperson** is a native from the home country of the company and has been assigned to a foreign market. An example would be a salesperson for an English manufacturing company who is assigned to and lives in Germany.

Perhaps the most truly international expatriate salesperson is one from a third country, known as a **third-country salesperson**. An example would be an Italian native who is hired by a English firm to live and work in a German sales territory. As a part of the overall sales training process, many international marketers have begun to regularly assign domestic salespeople and managers alike to foreign markets in an attempt to increase international knowledge and perspective.[33]

In most instances, third-country salespeople have proven themselves to be successful in the firm's home country, in the targeted sales territory, or in their own home country. Being assigned to a third-country can be difficult for these salespeople. Sales managers

| Home-country national salesperson |
| Third-country salesperson |
| Host-country national salesperson |

Figure 15.9: International Personal Selling Expatriates

monitor the level of comfort and confidence that third-country salespeople possess or run the risk of high turnover. Fortunately, many third-country expatriates are quite experienced and comfortable with adapting to new cultures and situations.

Moving an expatriate into a new sales territory will often be expensive. Companies face many costs, including moving allowances, cost-of-living adjustments, legal fees associated with work permits, and in some cases housing allowances.

A host-country national salesperson will be someone from the targeted country who knows the host country's business climate and culture well. The knowledge and familiarity of these salespeople to the local business environment make them attractive in many situations. Significant training is generally required to ensure that they are well-versed in the technicalities of the products that they will sell. Sales managers should consider cultural differences between these salespeople and the home company. As an illustration, with regard to time perceptions, the home company may find that a host-country national is seemingly late for sales appointments when in the reality of the host country she is not.

> A host-country national salesperson will be someone from the targeted country who knows the host country's business climate and culture well.

Many international personal selling situations require expatriates. Management orientation often influences the selection of the type of salesperson. Ethnocentric managers may be biased toward using home-country expatriates, where polycentric managers may favor host-country nationals.[34] When a need for close contact between the international office and the home office exists, home-country nationals become useful, especially when marketing highly sophisticated products.[35] Home-country nationals may also be used to train both international customers and other international salespeople, including third- and host-country nationals.

INTERNATIONAL INCIDENT ///

Recently, a female sales executive for a major pharmaceutical company went on a trip to finalize a deal with a major Japanese retail medical company accompanied by a male assistant. Upon arrival, the Japanese company's management team immediately assumed that the male was the salesperson and the female was the assistant. She allowed them to continue with the error for several minutes. When her assistant finally spoke up and clarified who was in charge, the Japanese team was highly embarrassed and continued to apologize throughout the negotiation. She accepted their apology and knew she had a major bargaining advantage from that point forward. What was the primary failure on the part of the Japanese management team? Did both sides handle the situation appropriately? What could have been done to avoid the misunderstanding at the beginning of the meeting?

TECHNOLOGY AND INTERNATIONAL SALES FORCE COMPOSITION

As with other aspects of international marketing, advances in technology have offered new alternatives for international sales force composition decisions. **Virtual selling**, or selling via the Internet, has increased. Telecommunications continue to play a major part in many international selling programs. A variety of software packages that enable online sales meetings to occur are currently available. These alternatives provide efficient methods for making contact with international buyers and can potentially dramatically lower the costs associated with the international sales effort.[36] With these

Virtual selling, or selling via the Internet, has increased.

technologies, international salespeople have a variety of options for staying in contact with customers and the home office. Companies that rely more heavily on the newer technologies can potentially operate with smaller sales forces.[37]

Most sales professionals tend to agree that technology can be useful, but it rarely substitutes for the personal touch.[38] Relationship marketing requires at least some degree of face-to-face contact. Customers in high-context regions expect direct, in-person contact. In some cases, virtual meetings may be appropriate, but only after initial face-to-face meetings.[39] Sales managers also consider the amount and type of information that must be relayed in sales meetings. In general, face-to-face meetings work best when a large amount of information must be relayed, when customers have unique needs that require some degree of product adaptation, and when the company faces heavy competition from well-established competitors.[40]

While virtual selling technologies assist in making a business productive, their use may appear to be rude or overly impersonal in some cultures.[41] As an example, customers in high-context regions may find a salesperson overly distracted by a smartphone. to be acting inappropriately. An international salesperson who intends to use a smartphone as part of a sales presentation should consider this possibility.

SALES TEAMS

It is becoming increasingly common for international salespeople to work in sales teams. Sales teams bring together individuals from different parts of the organization, including sales, customer service, and production, to handle and service global accounts. The complex nature of the international selling task and the increased demand for high-quality customer service has led to this development. Sales teams can be organized around specific customers, countries, or even regions. The knowledge that accumulates from combining many different experts from the organization can greatly enhance the customer service a company provides. Sales teams, while helpful to the individual salesperson, increase the coordination responsibilities of salespeople because they often have to deal with several different people within both the buying and the selling organizations. International customers often demand that the salesperson act as the primary contact person for their needs.

Foreign Language Skills and International Sales

An international salesperson will have an advantage when she is able to speak the language of the host country. Although interpreters are employed in certain circumstances, their use can seem impersonal to many potential buyers. Even when they are accepted, conversations take longer with awkward pauses as the recipient waits for the translation. Many international prospects respect the time and effort required for a salesperson to learn elements of their native language.

Bilingual salespeople are in great demand from international marketers. Multilingual salespeople are even in greater demand. While companies frequently provide at least some developmental seminars in a foreign language, it is becoming the norm for incoming job applicants to be, at least, bilingual. Many business schools now require at least some training in foreign languages for marketing and international business majors. Figure 15.10 presents the most commonly spoken languages in the world.

1. Mandarin Chinese: 882 million
2. Spanish: 325 million
3. English: 312–380 million
4. Arabic: 206–422 million
5. Hindi: 181 million
6. Portuguese: 178 million
7. Bengali: 173 million
8. Russian: 146 million
9. Japanese: 128 million
10. German: 96 million

Figure 15.10: Top Ten Most Common Languages Worldwide

Source: Adapted from Photius Coutsoukis, "The 50 Most Widely Spoken Languages (1996)," accessed at www.photius.com/rankings/languages2.html.

International Sales Force Management

Cultural norms and behaviors influence the decisions made by international sales managers.[42] Managers keep in mind the culture of the targeted country or region when they hire, train, motivate, evaluate, and compensate salespeople. These essential tasks of international sales management are presented in Figure 15.11. The complex nature of international marketing makes managing the sales force challenging.

RECRUITING AND SELECTION

Finding the right international salesperson constitutes a key activity in international sales force management. Selling internationally can be both difficult and tiring. International salespeople need to become accustomed with cultural differences, deal with new languages, and travel significant distances when meeting with prospects or customers. The physical demands of traveling internationally can be exhausting to some. Finding candidates who are comfortable with international travel and possible relocation may be challenging. Selecting the international salesperson who can physically and mentally deal with these demands should be the goal.

LEARNING OBJECTIVE #4:

What are the keys to effective international sales force management?

The selection process involves establishing the target characteristics a candidate will possess. The primary methods used to identify the best potential new employee include examination of

- level of education,
- degree of experience,
- personality and personal characteristics,
- aptitudes, and
- skill level.

Typically, the human resource department gathers educational achievements and the degree of experience from application forms and resumes. Personality and personal characteristics may include features such as being a self-starter, having high levels of energy, being able to cope with rejection, and other traits. Aptitudes include a persona's natural abilities, including verbal abilities, cognitive thinking skills, and problem-solving expertise. Skill level includes a person's learned proficiencies, such as product knowledge, interpersonal communication skills, and presentation skills. A number of tools are used by managers as they review international sales job candidates. These include personal interviews, personality tests, intelligence exams, and physical examinations. Smaller companies and many entrepreneurial organizations often have difficulties using some of these techniques. Nevertheless, the instruments can play an important role in sales force recruitment.

Personal Interviews

International sales force candidates are usually required to undergo a series of personal interviews before any hiring decision will be made. Structured and unstructured interviews work effectively for these purposes. In a **structured interview**, all applicants are asked the same questions. The advantage of using this interview technique is that applicants can easily be compared on the same types of questions and the interviewer can ensure that all relevant questions are asked, including questions pertaining to attitudes toward expatriation.

> In a structured interview, all applicants are asked the same questions.

In an **unstructured interview**, the interviewer and interviewee talk freely without using a predetermined list of questions. The information obtained from unstructured interviews often presents deeper information than that obtained from structured interviews. The responses cannot as easily be compared across applicants when unstructured interviews are used. Managers should therefore use care when relying on these techniques to ensure that any local discrimination laws are not broken.

Personality Tests

| Recruiting and Selection |
| Training |
| Motivation |
| Evaluation |
| Compensation |

Figure 15.11: Tasks of International Sales Management

Personality variables are frequently considered when hiring international sales personnel as well. Traits such as emotional stability, maturity, creativity, and conscientiousness have been shown to be relevant factors in personnel selection.[43] One popular instrument is the *NEO Personality Inventory*.[44] Recently, the use of personality tests has come under fire in the United States due to various legal considerations. In general, managers must be sure that the traits identified actually pertain to the specific requirements of the sales job.[45]

Intelligence Exams

Some companies use intelligence or aptitude tests during the selection process. The Wonderlic Personnel Test is available in many different languages.[46] Simply locating the most intelligent prospect or the prospect with the "right" education will rarely be sufficient.[47] Managers also assess the candidate's level of cultural intelligence and cross-cultural competence for international sales job openings. These tests can be effective when the abilities measured are tied directly to the requirements of the international sales job.

Physical Exams

Physical examinations are also used in some international sales hiring situations. The demands of international travel internationally and living abroad can necessitate a physical. The human resources department must ensure that the exam corresponds to the requirements of the job, that all applicants are subjected to the same examination, and that the results are held in strict confidence.[48] When such is not the case, an applicant could have grounds for a lawsuit based on discrimination.

TRAINING

International sales training can be expensive. In some cases, training international salespeople may cost as much as three times the amount required when hiring and training solely domestic salespeople.[49] For this reason, international sales managers pay close attention to international sales training programs.

Effective international sales training can lead to improved sales productivity and efficiency. Additional benefits of sales training include improving morale, lowering sales force turnover, and improving customer relations.[50] Relationship development will be an important component of successful international personal selling. Global giant IBM offers a well-known Graduate Sales School program aimed at equipping their salespeople with the skills needed to succeed both domestically and internationally.

Sales training can help to educate the new hire about cultural differences. Sales training can be the means by which new salespeople acquire the tools necessary to more effectively carry out cross-cultural negotiations while minimizing conflicts and deadlocks.[51] Companies often use *on-the-job* training to help new international salespeople to learn by joining established salespeople on international sales trips. Role-playing, though popular in many sales training efforts, will be less effective when preparing for foreign assignments.

The type of sales training required depends heavily on whether the company utilizes expatriate, home-country nationals, or third-country nationals. Expatriates may be well-versed and comfortable with the company and its products, but they may be less comfortable with the specifics of their international assignments. On-the-job training can be especially useful for expatriate sales personnel. Host-country nationals would likely understand the target market very well, but may need additional training with regard to the home company and its products. Host-country nationals can also benefit from on-the-job training by accompanying home-country salespeople during domestic sales calls. Third-country nationals would likely require training about both the company and the country, especially when a third-country national does not have previous experience in the targeted country or region.

Additional training takes place *off the job*, in meetings and classrooms, assisted by computer websites and reading materials. In classrooms, most international sales training programs focus more on company needs. In the process, the trainer should be realistic and careful when setting sales force expectations about what it will be like to operate in a foreign country. The sales training process can be a good time to cover these expectations, which will be particularly important when assigning home-country expatriates to foreign countries for the first time. Setting unrealistic expectations for these salespeople can lead directly to increased turnover and higher costs.[52] Voluntary turnover, or quitting, creates additional expenses in terms of lost training and relocation costs. Turnover also leads to lower sales, reduced market share, and intangible losses such as damage to a company's image.[53]

MOTIVATION

Motivating international sales personnel constitutes another vital important task for sales managers. Sales managers consider both intrinsic and extrinsic factors when attempting to motivate the sales force.

Intrinsic motivators are those internal factors within the salesperson that guide behavior, such as feeling valued by the company or enjoying the feeling associated with "winning" a new client or a sales contest. Personal needs play a big role as intrinsic motivators. International sales managers realize the important role that intrinsic factors play in international selling success and they attempt to assess these factors when making hiring decisions. When motivating international sales force members, the company should consider differences in intrinsic motives.

A sales contest offers intrinsic and extrinsic motives.

In other cases, *extrinsic motivators* including monetary compensation, awards, and companywide recognition can help to influence behavior. Some salespeople value these items more than others. Many successful salespersons find such tangible rewards to be motivating.

Motivational Needs Theory

One approach to understanding personal needs is David McClelland's motivational needs theory. The theory suggests three needs that can drive behavior:

- need for achievement,
- need for affiliation, and
- need for power.

The need for achievement will be expressed as the desire to excel at work and enjoy specific work-related achievements. This need applies well to the sales setting, which is often a competitive environment in which "winning" can be fulfilling. Oftentimes, the achievements that occur in selling are intrinsically gratifying, as would be the case when a salesperson realizes that she has outperformed others.

The need for affiliation results in the drive to develop meaningful interpersonal relationships, such as those found in collectivist societies. Matching someone with this type of social need can lead to positive outcomes in many international sales positions.

The need for power can be detrimental to international selling. Someone with the desire to dominate others becomes unlikely to succeed in relationship building. A salesperson with a strong need for power may fit in a high power distance setting, because, ironically, such a person understands where he does not hold power and should act in a more deferent manner.

Expectancy Theory

Another theory of motivation that applies to personal selling situations is expectancy theory, originally proposed by Victor Vroom. Expectancy theory suggests that the level of effort devoted by a salesperson will lead to performance, and performance can be improved by expectancies, instrumentalities, and the valence of a reward. *Expectancies* represent the perceived linkage between effort and performance, *instrumentalities* represent the perceived link between improved performance and the attainment of a reward, and the *valence* of the reward represents the perceived attractiveness of the reward being offered.

In order for a reward to be effective, the salesperson should believe that effort lead to success, that success will lead to a reward, and that the reward is worth the effort necessary for attainment. Rewards can be both intrinsic and extrinsic. A salesperson may be motivated by winning a sales contest (an intrinsic motive) along with the prize awarded for winning (the extrinsic motive).[54]

Financial Incentives

The most common financial incentives for international salespeople are pay raises, bonuses, and sales contest prizes.[55] Pay raises are common financial incentives in business. To achieve the highest level of motivational power, raises should be structured so that the highest performances receive the largest pay increases. Across-the-board pay raises do not obtain the same results, because they do not tie performance with a pay increase. Bonuses that attach a monetary reward to performance above a standard or quota can motivate an international sales team.

Sales contests and the prizes awarded may be part of a motivation program. Sales contests offer a monetary incentive or a prize for making the most sales or bringing in the most new customers in a certain period. Contests also allow managers the opportunity to motivate salespeople to concentrate on one specific product or product line. New products can also be emphasized by utilizing some type of sales contest.

Nonfinancial Incentives

Nonfinancial incentives include awards and public recognition. Public recognition includes certificates of achievement or "salesperson of the year" awards. In order for this type of incentive to be effective, the importance of the award should be stressed throughout the company and winning it should be challenging. Awards can be supplemented with additional incentives, including flight upgrades for international travelers, certificates for meals in other countries, and other creative incentives that combine the intrinsic value of the nonfinancial incentive with an extrinsic reward.

Combined Incentives

A company's promote-from-within policy features the financial incentive of receiving a pay raise associated with the promotion and the nonfinancial incentive of higher rank and status. Internal promotions may often be an overlooked part of motivating an international sales force. A promote-from-within policy can increase employee loyalty. It also enables the company to tap the expertise of its international sales force while reducing turnover and improving morale.[56]

Managerial Style and Leadership

The role of the sales manager himself or herself should be considered. Leadership styles greatly influence the motivation levels of workers throughout the company. Sales managers can motivate sales personnel through day-to-day activities, by how they treat their subordinates, and by their leadership styles. Leader-member exchange theory stresses the importance of close ties between sales manager and salespeople. The theory suggests that close ties foster trust and improved communication and, ultimately, improved sales performance.

Path-goal theory also applies to international personal selling situations and leadership styles. The theory posits that leaders can succeed in motivating subordinates when they consider the employee's personal characteristics and the characteristics of the sales situation. Sales managers can use a directive style, a supportive style, a participative style, or an achievement-oriented style.[57] A sales manager using a directive style sets clear instructions, deadlines, and schedules. A supportive sales manager exhibits friendliness and concern for her salespeople. A participative manager includes the opinions and ideas of his salespeople when making decisions. An achievement-oriented sales manager focuses on goal-setting and rewarding salespeople who reach their sales goals. Effective sales managers are able to ensure members of the international sales force that their efforts will be noticed and that the rewards that they seek are indeed within reach.

EVALUATION

Evaluating international sales personnel can be difficult, especially when a company operates in multiple countries and has a mix of expatriates, home-country nationals, and third-country nationals in the international sales force. Sales force control systems are involved with monitoring, evaluating, and compensating salespeople.[58] Control systems should also take into account the differences in cultures within the sales force.

Consider the differences in the daily routine of an Italian salesperson who is assigned to a region in China to work on behalf of a Mexican company. Decision-making styles, presentation styles, and time perceptions will differ. Salespeople from individualistic cultures are more likely to value their own personal goals and motivations over group needs. The opposite might be true for salespeople from collectivist cultures. International sales managers therefore consider these differences when developing control systems for international salespeople. Control systems are established that tend to focus either on specific behaviors or on various outcomes.

Behavioral Measures

Behaviors are the activities that management can readily identify and quantify. Company leaders consider preselling behaviors, selling behaviors, and postselling behaviors.[59] *Preselling behaviors* are measured through variables such as

- the amount of time the salesperson spent in presale activities,
- the number of sales proposals prepared, and
- the number of sales prospects reviewed.

Preselling behaviors constitute a major evaluation measure in international sales. The goal of building relationships can only be reached when members of the sales force are willing to take the time to carefully select and evaluate target clients and then spend sufficient time with those clients.[60] Measures of *selling behaviors* include the number of

- sales calls,
- presentations,
- prospects contacted, and
- conversions of new leads into customers.

The sales manager considers the additional time needed to make international sales calls and balances the cost of making calls with potential revenues. *Postselling activities* include the number of

- follow-up contacts made and
- service calls made per day or month.

Maintaining relationships will be a key criterion. It takes far more time and money to develop a new account than it does to retain an existing account. A salesperson should be held accountable for service after the sale in order to keep quality customers.

Outcome Measures

Outcome measures can often be easier to use for the international sales manager because international sales personnel are often thousands of miles away from the home office. Obtaining quality measures of specific behaviors are difficult in these settings, especially when infrequent contact occurs between the salesperson and the home office. Outcomes measures include

- gross sales,
- profitability of sales, and
- customer satisfaction ratings.

Financial Measures

Financial measures focus on the profit, revenue, and expenses that result from selling internationally. International sales managers most frequently consider sales volume and the profitability of each sales account. The profitability of each account is directly influenced by the salesperson's efforts to control expenses and to negotiate the most attractive sales price per transaction.

In many international sales situations, salespeople are given considerable latitude in negotiating a final sales price. They often make final price offers based on the competitive environment that exists in the specific country or region. International salespeople often have at least some control over expenses. Taken together, the revenue and expenses devoted to each account directly impact both the company's overall profitability and the individual salesperson's effectiveness.

Customer Satisfaction Ratings

Customer satisfaction ratings are taking on increased importance in international personal selling due to the emphasis on relationship marketing at the international level. The accurate measurement of customer satisfaction can be difficult in international markets due to differences in how customers respond to customer satisfaction surveys or questions. International sales managers pay attention to the wording of questions and how individuals in other cultures tend to respond. Some will be unwilling to register complaints due to the culture in which the client lives. Managers work to ensure that differences in cultural expectations are accounted for in customer satisfaction ratings.

Sales Manager Orientation and Evaluation

Sales managers can be biased in the ways in which they evaluate international salespeople. This can occur even when the firm has predetermined criteria on which to evaluate salespeople. Sales managers can be predisposed toward the end-results, the activities, or the capabilities of sales personnel.[61]

A sales manager who favors end results will first consider sales and market share figures and other forms of objective measures. A sales manager who is focused on activities pays closer attention to statistics such as the number of sales calls made per week or how well international salespeople manage their budgets. A sales manager who concentrates on capabilities considers the quality of sales presentations to be most important. As with other elements of evaluating international salespeople, assessing many of these efforts can be difficult due to the distance between the home office and the sales territory along with cultural differences.

Compensation

LEARNING OBJECTIVE #5:

What are the methods available for international sales force compensation?

Developing compensation programs for an international sales force can be challenging for the international sales manager. Cost of living, tax codes, and exchange rates complicate compensation program designs. The problems become acute when the company uses a mix of expatriate and host-country salespeople, and when salespeople tend to compare their compensation packages across the company.[62] Some compensation packages made lead to less teamwork and increased unethical behaviors when they overemphasize certain factors, such as sales only outcomes.[63] Figure 15.12 presents the major forms of compensation that are available to the international salesperson.

SALARY

Straight salary arrangements designate a specific level of pay for the salesperson that does not vary with sales. In general, this type of compensation package will be appropriate when the salesperson focuses on long-term relationships rather than short-term sales results. A salary pay structure system works well when servicing accounts constitutes a major part of the salesperson's job and when incentives for salaried salespeople to generate additional sales or to find new customers are not needed. Salespersons earning salaries face less day-to-day pressure to increase sales, which may translate into more relaxed interactions with international customers. Service expectations that often accompany straight salary compensation can be affected by culture. In high-context cultures, additional face-to-face service time may be expected on the part of the buyer.

Straight salary compensation programs will be complicated by the tax codes in which salespeople operate. Salespeople who work in countries with high taxes on income may not prefer these arrangements. In these countries, nonsalary benefits are often valuable.

Salary
Commission
Salary plus commission
Bonuses
Benefits and allowances

Figure 15.12: Compensation Methods for International Salespersons

COMMISSIONS

Commission-based compensation packages determine the amount paid to the international salesperson as a percentage of the prices of products that have been sold. Companies can offer commissions based on actual sales value, the profitability of these sales, or a combination of the two. Commission programs focus the attention of the salesperson more on making sales and less on other aspects of the job, such as after-sale follow up, record-keeping, answering consumer inquiries, or resolving problems such as incomplete shipments or goods damaged in transport.

Commission-based compensation tends to provide motivation for the international salesperson but it can also create unwarranted stress. When income directly ties to sales, it becomes tempting to take any action necessary in order to make a sale. The customer can believe she is being unduly pressured to make a purchase. A commission-only system makes it more difficult for the company to manage the day-to-day actions of its sales force. Companies run the risk of losing their customer focus when compensation packages are based solely on commissions.

While commission-only arrangements are used in international marketing, they tend to be in the minority of most compensation packages. In many situations, international sales are affected by forces outside of the control of the salesperson, which only adds to the stress of the commission-only based system.

SALARY PLUS COMMISSION

A combination of salary and commission can form an effective compensation plan. Salary plus commission arrangements are useful in many international personal selling settings. The compensation program offers a set amount of the salary plus a certain percentage, which is a commission based on sales or profitability. Salary plus commission programs offer some stability and regularity in pay, plus help motivate salespeople beyond to generate additional sales. International salespeople often prefer this type of compensation package.

Whereas salespeople often appreciate the motivating influence of the commission, managers value the control element of the salary portion. Maximizing both control and motivation can be difficult, and the salary plus commission package can help to achieve both company sales and company service goals.[64]

BONUSES

A bonus is an amount above a salary or commission that is paid when the salesperson exceeds a target sales level. The bonus can provide an additional incentive to members of an international sales force and has experienced frequent use in international sales programs. Many international salespeople appreciate the opportunity to earn the extra pay that bonus packages offer.

BENEFITS AND ALLOWANCES

Many international companies offer benefit packages and allowances for international salespeople, especially for expatriates. Benefits include health insurance, purchase discounts for company-produced items, paid vacations, holiday pay, and pension plans. These benefits are especially valued in countries that have high income tax rates.

Benefits play important roles in two key areas: recruiting and employee retention. In the area of recruiting, a strong benefit package may be the deciding factor when an applicant receives job offers from two companies. The individual might choose a firm because it offers a health insurance plan and the other does not.

In terms of employee retention, pension plans are referred to as the "golden fetters" that hold onto valuable employees. When a pension builds up to high value, the individual has a strong incentive to remain in the company. The same will be true when the amount of time given as paid vacation increases with seniority. Someone who has reached the level of three or four weeks of annual paid vacation rather than one or two has a major enticement to stay with a given company.

Allowances include expense accounts, company cars, housing payments, cost-of-living allowances, moving allowances, and home-leave allowances. These payments help adjust the expatriate to the financial costs associated with relocating to foreign countries. Allowances are often highly valued by sales force members who face the challenge of relocating.

Repatriation

In addition to the other tasks associated with international sales management, sales managers also face the responsibility of recalling expatriates from foreign assignments. **Repatriation** is the process of adjustment that a salesperson goes through upon returning to his or her home country. The process can be emotional and mentally draining, especially when the salesperson has to relocate his or her family back to a home country. Family members can feel the same types of stressors that the salesperson feels after re-entering the home country.

Many expatriates who are returned to home countries face a number of difficulties when adjusting to former lifestyles. Expatriates might encounter financial difficulties, particularly if there are significant differences in cost of living or tax codes. In most cases, the allowances enjoyed while stationed abroad are forfeited upon returning to the home country. Sales managers work to ensure that compensation packages are fair upon repatriation and that services are made available to the salesperson and their families if problems do arise.

REPATRIATION KNOWLEDGE ACQUISITION

One benefit of sending salespeople on international assignments is increasing their international knowledge and perspective. Harnessing this knowledge can be a direct benefit of the repatriation process.[65] Knowledge and experience acquired during repatriation can be as valuable as information obtained from international marketing research. Seeing how a salesperson adjusts to repatriation assists the manager in future relocation decisions for other salespeople. The organization should make every effort to learn as much as possible about the culture of the foreign setting so that future expatriates more easily assimilate.

MANAGEMENT ISSUES

When an organization commences international operations, one department that undergoes the most radical reorganization is often human resources. These individuals will be required to adjust recruiting and selection practices that identify potential employees who will succeed in other countries. Training programs will be adapted to more fully account for cultural issues. The programs target the specific countries the company intends to enter.

Company leaders need to make sure financial and nonfinancial incentives are suited to the types of salespeople and other employees that will serve in the host country. Performance evaluation systems should account for new tasks, including a greater emphasis on finding new accounts and customers, particularly in early stages of international expansion. At the same time, the system should note that trusting relationships often must be built

The repatriation process can be emotional and mentally draining.

before any sale will be made. Compensation programs require fine-tuning to account for strategic sales objectives and host country conditions. Commission-only systems may be modified to account for the longer time it takes to generate new customers and sales and to stress relationship building as much as pure selling.

In essence, the mindset of the human resource department, sales department, and other areas will change to accommodate operations in new host countries. The company's leaders cannot expect to continue with business-as-usual practices; doing so will likely lead to a failed international expansion effort.

Chapter 15: Review and Resources

STRATEGIC IMPLICATIONS //

As with other elements of successful international marketing management, international personal selling and sales force management efforts must fit within the overall global direction of the firm. The first strategic choice for marketing managers will be in the type of sales force to send to a host country: field salespeople, missionary salespeople, or a telemarketing team.

The chief marketer will be responsible for making certain that the sales force will be able to succeed in new host countries. The term *strategic human resource management* suggests that every aspect of the human resource program should be adapted to the new situational context in which recruiting, training, and managing the sales force will take on additional dimensions. This includes designation of home-country, host-country, or third-country expatriate salespeople.

International sales managers work to identify specific market segments, including individual companies, regions, or countries and to target sales programs at those areas. They also work to ensure that the marketing efforts within the regions fit the overall marketing mix program. Strategic decisions pertaining to market development or market concentration guide sales manager decisions at this level. The competitive advantages of the company and the overall brand position should appeal to the culture that is being targeted.

TACTICAL IMPLICATIONS //

At the tactical level, sales programs approaches are selected and sales managers choose methods of prospecting, along with formats for sales preapproach, approach, and presentation. Additional training will likely be required to assist expatriate salespeople in matters of negotiation, handling objections, closing, and following up on sales calls. The importance of relationship building constitutes a key tactical element in international personal selling.

Cultural training and foreign language education can assist the expatriate in adapting to a host country. Cultural assimilators are retained to explain how business will take place in the host country. The training combines the essence of the company's offerings with the characteristics of the culture in which the salesperson will operate.

Compensation packages are determined at the tactical level. Straight salary structures may be used when the primary emphasis is on relationship-building and service to the client. Commissions are added to emphasize selling activities. A salary plus commission program balances sales and service goals.

Evaluation systems are prescribed by tactical marketing managers. Preselling, selling, and postselling activities may be considered. Some companies will favor one aspect over others. Financial and nonfinancial indicators of performance are often evaluated as part of the process.

The final tactical activity will be establishing effective repatriation programs. Someone returning home may require adaptation similar to what was needed when the person moved to the host country. The international sales program will be enriched by retaining salespersons who have adapted to both leaving and returning.

OPERATIONAL IMPLICATIONS //

The operational component of international personal selling and sales force management focuses on the day-to-day activities of both salespeople and sales managers. Selling in international markets can be difficult and tiring, and sales managers work daily to keep their salespeople motivated and well compensated. Sales people spend their days meeting with prospects and customers, selling new accounts and servicing existing accounts. Sales managers monitor sales force production and sales reports, and work to ensure that the sales goals of the company are being realized.

Salespeople should be reminded that, in the eyes of customers, they are the face of the company. The company can combine extrinsic incentives such as bonuses and prizes in sales contests with intrinsic rewards to make certain the sales team feels appreciated, motivated, and remain attentive to the daily grind of selling in a foreign country.

TERMS

cultural intelligence	order getting	host-country national salesperson
cross-cultural competence	cross-selling	virtual selling
expatriate	expatriate salesperson	structured interview
culture shock	home-country national salesperson	unstructured interview
market development	third-country salesperson	repatriation

REVIEW QUESTIONS

1. What types of retail sales are parts of international marketing programs?
2. What are the three primary types of business-to-business selling positions?
3. What are the differences in selling in low-context and high-context cultures?
4. How does the concept of time affect international personal selling?
5. Name some of the business etiquette issues that can affect international personal selling.
6. Describe cultural adaptation, cultural intelligence, and cross-cultural competence.
7. What tasks are involved in international business-to-business selling?
8. What methods are used to overcome objections in international personal selling?
9. What are the primary international sales closing techniques?
10. What is cross-selling?
11. Explain the three types of expatriate salespersons.
12. What are the main tasks involved in international sales management?
13. Describe the behavioral measures that are used to evaluate international salespeople.
14. Describe the primary forms of compensation used in international personal selling.
15. What does the term *repatriation* mean?

DISCUSSION QUESTIONS

1. Discuss the different ways in which international salespeople should communicate with potential buyers in low-context cultures, then discuss how they should communicate with buyers in high-context cultures. What differences do you see?
2. Compare and contrast how the gift-giving ritual is perceived in different cultures. How is it different in China or Japan as compared to the United States? What difficulties do you think an international salesperson would encounter if she were not familiar with these differences?
3. Is a motivator such as "salesperson of the month" award appropriate in a collectivist culture? Why or why not? How would this compare to the way in which such an award would motivate an international salesperson from an individualistic culture?

4. What difficulties do you think would arise for an international salesperson who is repatriating from a low-context culture back to a high-context culture? As an example, consider a Japanese salesperson who is returning to Japan after a lengthy assignment in London or New York City.

ANALYTICAL AND INTERNET EXERCISES

1. By using online sources, research the international sales force activities of major *Fortune* 500 companies, such as those listed below. In what international markets do they operate? How would you describe the cultural context of these markets? Are they high-context or low-context markets? What can you learn about the size of the sales force in these markets?

   - General Electric
   - Proctor & Gamble
   - Boeing
   - Lockheed Martin
   - General Dynamics
   - Raytheon

2. Visit the website for the popular marketing magazine *Sales and Marketing Management* (www.salesandmarketing.com). What do you learn about international personal selling and sales management from this site? What are the current hot topics in international personal selling and sales management? What trends does the magazine identify?

3. Research a large international company, such as Royal Dutch Shell (www.shell.com). How does the company utilize an international sales force? In what ways is the sales force effective? Do you see any weaknesses in their approach that you think could be improved? Compare what you have learned to a company from your own home country. How do the personal selling efforts from the two companies compare? A list of companies could include the following:

   - Royal Dutch Shell
   - Siemens
   - Axa
   - Nestlé
   - Unilever
   - Hitachi

4. Conduct an Internet search on popular employee selection instruments, such as personality or intelligence test. An example would be the Wonderlic exam or the NEO Personality Inventory. What elements of these tests do you think most closely relate to the international personal selling career? Do you think that these tests would be useful to a sales manager looking to deploy a salesperson in an overseas market?

▶ ONLINE VIDEOS

Visit **www.sagepub.com/baack** to view these chapter videos:

Video Link 15.1: Business Manners

Video Link 15.2: Body Language

🌐 STUDENT STUDY SITE

Visit **www.sagepub.com/baack** to access these additional learning tools:

- Web Quizzes
- eFlashcards
- SAGE Journal Articles

- Country Fact Sheets
- Chapter Outlines
- Interactive Maps

CASE 15 ///

Oriflame and the Indian Marketplace

The marketing team at European cosmetic giant Oriflame understands the importance of the Indian cosmetics market. The Swedish company has focused on India for several years and has successfully positioned itself as a leading cosmetics marketer throughout the region. Currently, the company markets products in over 1,300 cities throughout the country, with the efforts managed from twelve centralized offices. Operating under a direct-selling strategy, Oriflame has become one of the fasting-growing beauty companies in all of Europe.

The vastness of the Indian marketplace presents challenges for direct marketers. Oriflame has adapted its strategic marketing model to address these challenges. Oriflame marketers made the decision to emphasize online retailing as a response to these challenges. Online retailing offers the advantage of tremendous market reach in countries that have reliable Internet infrastructure. Although the Internet is not available in all areas of India, millions of consumers have access. The platform has met with some success. The Internet-based sales platform offers twenty-four/seven access to consumers worldwide, a level of contact that is simply not possible with a direct sales force.

The potential for success in India due to the country's size and scope is enticing to numerous international marketers. The country has a large population and strong consumer demand that continues to grow. This is particularly true for the cosmetics industry, which may be expected to expand by more than $1 billion in the coming years.

Online retailing can help to reduce some of the marketing challenges present in large marketplaces such as India. The selling platform helps marketers with strong brand identities to capitalize on brand equity, as is the case for Oriflame. The move to online retailing allowed the marketing team to build on a strong brand identity and to establish what will essentially become "virtual offices."

With sales approaching 1.3 billion *euro*, Oriflame has developed the capacity and market power to continue its strong business growth. The company sells its products in over sixty countries, and is the market leader in more than half of those countries. Oriflame products include natural ingredients that provide solutions to many common skin problems that many consumers experience.

Based on the Oriflame success story, it is likely that other international marketers of cosmetics products use this approach when attempting to tap the market potential of India.[66]

1. What factors allow Oriflame's online retailing program to succeed in India?

2. What cultural variables would impact cosmetic marketing in India? How does online retailing pertain to these variables?

3. Should Oriflame abandon face-to-face selling in India? If not, how should the direct sales force be selected? How should the salespersons be compensated?

4. What are some of the biggest threats to the success of online retailing of cosmetics in a country such as India?

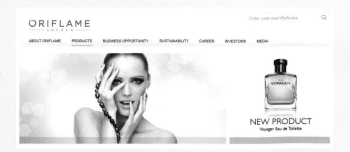

Oriflame marketers made the decision to emphasize online retailing.

16 International Marketing Planning, Organization, and Control

LEARNING OBJECTIVES ///

After reading and studying this chapter, you should be able to answer the following questions:

1. How do planning, organizing, and controlling activities influence international marketing programs?

2. What activities are involved in international strategic planning?

3. What forms of organizational structures do international companies use?

4. What are the basic components of an international marketing plan?

5. How does internal communication affect international planning, organizing, and control?

6. What emerging trends might affect international marketing in the future?

IN THIS CHAPTER

Nintendo: Marketing Strategies in a Turbulent Environment

Nintendo has a unique history in the computer game market. Founded in Kyoto in 1889 as a playing card manufacturer, the company has experienced high and low points in its more than 120 years of existence. Nintendo's reputation began as a toymaker providing games that consumers want to play. The company's original game machine, which consumers hooked up to television monitors, was introduced in 1983.

Nintendo viewed its product as a gaming machine rather than a small computer that played games. The company focused on producing games for simple, cheaper-to-manufacture machines that could be priced at around $100, far less than competitors.[1] The approach was initially successful. Then the gaming industry changed. Early competitors Atari and Sega were replaced by multinational firms. Sony introduced the PlayStation, and Microsoft produced the Xbox. Both companies invested substantial funds in new products.

By the mid-2000s, Nintendo faced problems. Faster, most powerful machines, such as Sony's PlayStation 2, dominated the market. The Nintendo 64 was a disappointment. The Gamecube, introduced in 2001, appeared to target children rather than serious gamers.[2] Nintendo began to concentrate on hand-held gaming devices, including the Gameboy and DS, and became the market leader with little presence in any other type of gaming system.[3]

By the mid-2000s, the video game industry was experiencing a significant decline in demand.[4] Nintendo's marketing team began listening more closely to consumers.[5] Company leaders discovered that some consumers walked away because games were becoming too complex.[6] The success of simple trivia games for the DS, such as Brain Age, provided evidence that a different approach might succeed.[7] The marketing team concluded that the biggest competitor was not Sony or Microsoft, but instead ignorance of gaming.[8]

Soon after, the revolutionary Wii was introduced to a target market consisting of people over twenty-five years old, particularly nonplayers. The Wii is easy to play, meeting the needs of nonplayers and the whole family. The strategy was to attract a new audience to gaming with the goal of breaking the wall between players and nonplayers.[9] The console was a stark contrast to the Sony PlayStation 3. Instead of focusing on high-tech issues, Wii made games simple to enjoy, using a wand instead of a traditional controller. The console game with five sports, including bowling and tennis, appealed to a broader audience. The price was half that of the PlayStation 3.

Nintendo promoted the Wii by hosting parties for families. Wii demonstrations were made to tastemakers, including DefJam records, Phat Farm clothing, and *Vice* magazine.[10] The advertising campaign featured the facial expressions of users playing video games for the first time as well as older persons playing.[11] Targeting casual users was a success. Nintendo had sold more than 50 million Wii consoles and more than 100 million DS portable players by 2009. The 2008 recession presented some challenges, but the low price helped Nintendo weather the storm. Also, many consumers turned to at-home entertainment, helping the Wii.[12]

Currently, Nintendo faces new challenges. The Apple iPhone can be used as a portable game player and the iPad also threatens to move into the gaming market.[13] Online games through Facebook have captured consumers' attention.[14] Sony and Microsoft have developed motion-based controllers that both companies initially dismissed as a "novelty."[15] Nintendo introduced Wii U, a Wii that includes a touch-screen controller, and DS 3D, a 3D portable game player that does not need 3D glasses in response to these new competitors.[16]

The successes of Nintendo resulted from the use of marketing controls to track company effectiveness and effective marketing strategies designed to respond to changing external forces. The company's future will likely be determined by its effectiveness in adapting to an ever-changing marketplace.

QUESTIONS FOR STUDENTS

1. What role has technology played in the hand-held and console game industries?
2. How have demographic trends influenced mobile game playing?
3. What forces will shape the next generation of these types of games?

Nintendo's future will likely be determined by its effectiveness in adapting to an ever-changing marketplace.

Overview

The cornerstone of successful international marketing programs includes the strategic planning, organizing, and control processes. The overall strategic plan directs every element of a marketing program. This chapter begins with a discussion of the strategic planning process as it relates to international marketing. Organizational structure is then described, including numerous alternatives for devising an effective and efficient organizational design.

International marketing plans follow. These plans are prepared at the tactical level based on overall corporate, or strategic-level, plans. International marketing plans guide the international marketing program for specific products and markets. As such, they apply to specific strategic business units within the overall international organization.

The role of internal communication is then examined, followed by a discussion of various control mechanisms that apply to international strategic marketing. The chapter concludes with an analysis of trends that might impact international marketing management and influence marketing programs in the future.

Figure 16.1 presents the overall international marketing context within which all of these strategic, operational, and tactical decisions are made. All of the components of the international marketing context influence these processes. The emerging trends in international marketing presented at the end of this chapter will also affect the overall international marketing context.

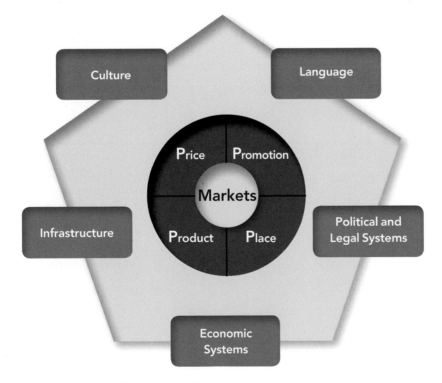

Figure 16.1: The International Marketing Context

International Marketing and Strategic Planning

Planning, organizing, and controlling international marketing operations are critical elements of successful international marketing. The **planning** process involves managers developing the goals, strategies, and activities that will best position the

LEARNING OBJECTIVE #1:

How do planning, organizing, and controlling activities influence international marketing programs?

firm for success in the international marketplace. **Organizing** is the process through which management designs the structure of the organization, assigns responsibilities, and ensures effective communication flows throughout the company. **Control** in an international marketing environment focuses on measuring progress against what was planned, taking corrective actions when they are needed, and rewarding success.

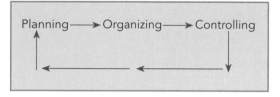

Figure 16.2: Planning, Organizing, and Controlling

Planning, organizing, and control are interrelated concepts in international marketing, as well as in all aspects of strategic marketing, as displayed in Figure 16.2. Organizational communication plays an important role in the entire process. When dealing with multiple countries, employees, and cultures, communication plays a vital role in overall success. Communication barriers between cultures, countries, and employees present significant challenges for international marketing management.

INTERNATIONAL MARKETING EFFICIENCY AND EFFECTIVENESS

Two important themes in strategic planning, organizing, and controlling include organizational efficiency and effectiveness. *Efficiency* means conducting international marketing activities without wasting time and resources. *Effectiveness* focuses on conducting international operations in ways that enable the firm to reach its international marketing goals.[17] Management writers describe efficiency and "doing things right" and effectiveness as "doing the right things." Successful international marketing requires both. Strategic planning, organizing, and controlling enable managers to maximize the efficiency and effectiveness of international marketing operations.

PLANNING LEVELS

The international marketing planning process occurs at three levels: strategic, tactical, and operational. **Strategic planning** focuses on the overall direction of the firm, the development of goals, and the allocation of resources in the pursuit of those goals. Top managers develop strategic plans, which identify the long-term direction of a company.

Tactical planning focuses on specific marketing activities and programs that support the overall direction set at the strategic level. Middle-level managers normally concentrate on specific marketing functions, such as product design, advertising, or distribution, and prepare tactical plans.

Operational plans dictate the day-to-day entry-level activities that are crucial parts of successful international marketing programs. Operational plans guide the efforts of first-level managers.

Effective planning utilizes the competitive advantages and opportunities of the firm as a springboard for international marketing programs. A complete planning program begins with managers emphasizing the purpose and overall direction of the firm. The process includes scanning the organization's external and internal environments, forecasting future events, and making decisions about which plans to undertake. Managers can then specify marketing goals, and allocate the resources needed to implement and complete the plan.

INTERNATIONAL STRATEGIC PLANNING

All aspects of the international marketing program relate to and are influenced by the planning process. The plan dictates markets to be targeted, products to be sold, pricing methods, distribution channels, and promotional activities. The plan specifies an organizational design, communication systems, and strategic goals to be achieved.

LEARNING
OBJECTIVE #2:

*What activities
are involved in
international strategic
planning?*

International strategic planning focuses on the overall direction of the firm. The key elements in the process are summarized in Figure 16.3. Each of these components has direct applications for an international marketing program. An international strategic plan provides the basis for all international marketing activities.

In July of 2011, HSBC France presented the company's strategic plan. The document listed a series of objectives and activities for the company including, "(1) focusing on wealth management for personal customers, (2) bolstering international connectivity for business customers, (3) further developing the Global Banking and Markets platform in Paris as a strategic hub for the HSBC Group, and (4) strengthening synergies between customer groups." To carry out these initiatives, the company established various steps. The activities included increased training for wealth management staff, establishing twenty-five new branches by 2015, hiring more relationship managers focused on business customers, and opening three new regional offices within France.[18]

Mission Statements

The overall corporate, or strategic, plan of the organization sets the direction of the firm, states its mission, and sets goals for the business. The **mission statement** delineates why the organization exists and guides the overall direction of the firm. Recently, many mission statements have undergone revisions to incorporate the concept of seeking to serve a global marketplace. Ford Motor Company's mission statement reads, "We are a global family with a proud heritage passionately committed to providing personal mobility for people around

Mission Statement Formulation
Environmental Assessment
Forecast of Future Events
Determination of Goals
Allocation of Resources in Pursuit of the Plan

Figure 16.3: Elements of Strategic Planning

the world." Anadarka, a global petroleum company, states in the company's mission statement that the company intends to create "a competitive and sustainable rate of return by developing, acquiring, and exploring for oil and gas resources vital to the world's health and welfare." Other mission statements pay attention to additional visible issues. The global beauty product company Avon states that its mission is "continually improving our profitability, (as) a socially responsible, ethical company that is watched and emulated as a model of success."

Mission statements guide major company decisions. The company Google referenced its mission "to organize the world's information and make it universally accessible and useful" when leaving the Chinese market. Facing censorship from the Chinese government, Google's management team believed that it was no longer able to achieve the company's mission.[19]

Corporate-level planning also determines the division of the firm into *strategic business units*, or parts of the overall business. A strategic business unit operates in a specified market area and has specific goals, objectives, and control mechanisms. A strategic business unit for a firm engaging in international marketing may be a division or office in a foreign country.

International strategic planning focuses on the overall direction of a firm such as Rolex.

The Volkswagen Group (Germany) consists of two main divisions including the Automotive Group and the Volkswagen Financial Services Group. The Automotive Group contains seven brands worldwide, including Audi, Bentley, Bugatti, Lamborghini, SEAT, Škoda, Scania, Volkswagen, and Volkswagen Commercial Vehicles.[20] As international operations expand, the division of an international company into strategic business units grows in importance.

Environmental Assessment

The mission of the firm combined with an assessment of potential market areas, countries to be served, and marketing responsibilities determines how the firm will be divided into strategic business units. These assessments include an analysis of various internal and external factors present in the marketing environment. External factors have been described throughout this text, including culture, language, political and legal systems, economic systems, and infrastructure. Internal factors include factors also described throughout the text, such as human and financial capital, competitive advantage, market knowledge, and responsiveness to market changes and demands.

As noted in Chapter 1, the company's internal environment consists of organizational strengths and weaknesses. The external environment poses threats and presents opportunities. These elements combine to form a SWOT analysis (strengths, weaknesses, opportunities, threats) and suggest various strategic responses, as depicted in Figure 16.4.

In the first situation, an opportunity has presented itself in an area where the company is strong. This will likely lead to a plan designed to take advantage of the situation. In the second box, an opportunity exists in an area where the company is weak. Managers in that circumstance will decide whether to commit resources to strengthen the company and pursue the opportunity, or instead let some other firm

		Environment	
		Opportunity	Threat
Company	Strength	Plan to Pursue	Monitor
	Weakness	Decide to Pursue or Not	Plan to fend off threat

Figure 16.4: SWOT Analysis

that is better suited to the situation move forward. In the third circumstance, a threat occurs where the company is strong. Managers will monitor this situation and take action as needed. In the fourth box, a threat exists in an area where the company is weak. Failure to respond may lead to the downfall of the company.

As an example, in many emerging markets, particularly China and India, consumers prefer cell phones with multiple SIM or identification card slots, which allow one phone to be used for multiple phone numbers, a circumstance that creates a threat to mobile phone manufacturers without such features. Facing dropping market share in these markets, in 2011 Nokia introduced three separate phones, all of which contained multiple SIM card slots.[21] The change represents an example of a company responding to an external factor; the differences in features consumers prefer in a phone.

Forecast Future Events

Strategic managers forecast in three main areas: economic conditions, sales projections, and changes in technology. Economic conditions set the framework for the strategic planning process. For example, the turbulence in Greece in 2011 regarding governmental cuts in spending and tax increases could have a profound impact on the economic status of the European Union in the coming years. Forecasters account for issues including global economic growth and periods of recession when making strategic decisions.

VIDEO LINK 16.1:
The Future of
YouTube

Sales forecasts indicate levels of revenue a company expects to receive during the coming year. These projections shape planning processes in terms of expenditures on strategic activities. When sales revenues are projected to increase, companies allocate additional funds for raw materials, inventory levels, sales force activities, and other more general projects such as research and development. When sales revenues are expected to decline, company leaders often cut back on some activities.

Changes in technology impact the overall marketplace. As noted in the opening vignette, Nintendo responded to changes in technology by designing a different type of product—one that was easier to use and less dependent on complex technological designs.

Some events are impossible to predict. International managers could not have predicted the massive earthquake and resultant tsunami that devastated Japan in early 2011. Nevertheless, the event drastically affected international business. Car makers in particular were hit hard. The tsunami heavily damaged a semiconductor plant in Ibaraki owned by Renesas Electronics Corporation. The plant manufactured chips for the major Japanese automakers, and Toyota and Honda both faced inventory shortages. Honda had just begun using a new type of chip and faced the sharpest shortage as a result. The shortages particularly affected business in China, with Toyota sales declining by 35% and Honda dropping by 32%.[22]

Determination of Goals

At the strategic level, goals are often set in financial terms, such as return on investment, sales figures, market share attained, and overall market penetration. Strategic goals can also be nonfinancial, such as increased brand recognition, awareness, or improved company image worldwide. These company-wide standards provide the basis for the strategic control process. They guide the general direction of the company and alert managers when the organization has begun to drift off course from its stated mission.

Allocation of Resources in Pursuit of the Plan

Strategic planners allocate the resources needed to achieve strategic goals. Allocating resources coincides with the development of an overall organizational structure. Determining the most efficient and most effective organizational structure is a major component of the organizing element of international strategic marketing planning. The organizational structure also impacts and is impacted by organizational communication.

The American pharmaceutical company Pharmacopeia updated the company strategic plan in early 2008. As a result, the company shifted its focus to late-stage, closer-to-market research and development efforts. The new strategy led to a reduction of the company's workforce by 15%. Employees engaged in early-stage research were laid off. Other staff resources were moved to different positions to add human resources to help achieve the company's new strategic focus.[23]

The five components of the strategic planning process set the tone for marketing tactics and activities. The mission statement guides the direction of the organization, including its approach to the marketplace. An environmental assessment provides valuable information to the marketing team regarding potential opportunities and threats that arise in conjunction with company strengths and weaknesses. These, in turn, shape marketing efforts to take advantage of opportunities and fend off threats by employing both strategic and tactical responses. Company leaders forecast future events in the areas of economic conditions, sales projections, and changes in technology. Marketing teams can then respond with tactics designed to adapt to changes in the environment. Organizational leaders determine strategic and tactical goals in order to spell out what would constitute successful efforts. These goals form the basis of the strategic control process. Finally, managers allocate resources to implement strategic plans and achieve strategic goals. Resources granted to the marketing department should be used efficiently and effectively, as part of the overall international marketing program.

International Marketing Organization

LEARNING
OBJECTIVE #3:

*What forms of
organizational
structures do
international
companies use?*

A well-defined organizational structure is usually already in place for many international companies. Changes in the internal or external environment, the decision to expand operations globally, or changes in existing strategies often create the need for either a new structure or at least an adaptation of the existing structure. Regardless of the events that lead to the organizational structure decision, all decisions should be based on designing the most effective and efficient international organization possible.

ORGANIZATIONAL STRUCTURES

Numerous forms of organizational structure can be employed by international businesses. Company executives base choices on the strategy of the company and the intensity of international marketing activities. A company that engages solely in international exporting will have a different structure than that of a truly multinational corporation. The important task for managers is to select and install the organizational structure that most effectively and efficiently enables the firm to reach its international marketing goals. Alternative forms of structure are presented in this section. No one form of organizational structure can be identified as the correct way in which to conduct marketing activities internationally. Any of the alternatives discussed below, or a combination of approaches, may be suitable in certain international situations.

Direct Exporting Structure

A simple structure often used by businesses new to international marketing supports direct exporting. In this form of structure, international orders are shipped to customers from the company either directly or through an intermediary. Direct exporting was described previously in the mode of entry and marketing channel chapters of this text in Chapter 12.

The decision to engage in either direct (home-based or foreign-based) exporting or indirect exporting through agent or merchant middlemen will be based on operational efficiencies and synergies with existing strategies. The responsibility for the exporting function, along with responsibility for international sales, falls within the marketing function. Marketing efforts are largely undifferentiated between domestic and international efforts. All sales, in effect, are treated in the same way and little attention is paid to international differences in customer wants, needs, or requirements.

It will be difficult for a firm to continue with a direct exporting form of structure when international sales begin to account for a relatively large portion of revenue. The company tends to reorganize around international marketing activities. Nevertheless, a simple direct exporting structure, such as the one displayed in Figure 16.5, can work well for a company just beginning to engage in international marketing or just beginning to introduce a product internationally.

The Indian company Tata has begun to sell the company's low-cost car, the Nano, to consumers in Indonesia, Thailand, Sri Lanka, and potentially parts of Africa through direct exporting. While only approximately five hundred units had been exported by May of 2011, the company plans to use exporting to build demand for the product before moving to more expensive methods of getting the Nano to consumers.[24]

International Division Structure

As international activities begin to intensify, company leaders might choose to develop an international department, office, or division to oversee international sales. Depending on the size and complexity of the organization, the division may

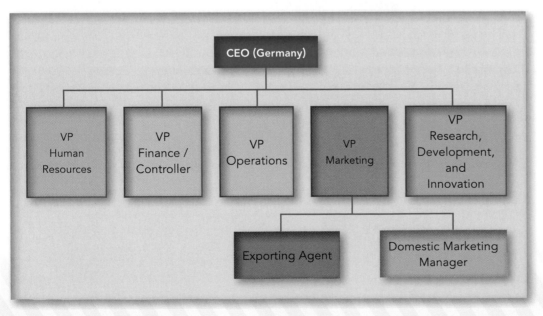

Figure 16.5: Direct Exporting

manage several international offices or salespeople. For smaller organizations, however, all international sales may be managed domestically by the international office or department. This structure is similar to the direct exporting structure; the main difference is that one central control department is responsible for international marketing and sales activities and this division is held distinct from domestic marketing activities (see Figure 16.6). Delegating responsibility and authority for international sales can be both efficient and effective for international marketers.

When international offices are developed, managers decide whether to hire home, host, or third-country national employees. Establishing international offices allows the company the advantage of gaining a local presence and creating better access to market-relevant information. Governmental forces may require a local office in order to conduct business in some countries. The international division structure can help meet these requirements and gain favor with foreign governments and is widely used in international marketing.

South Korean automaker Kia Motors uses this organizational approach. [25] The company has an international business division, headed by Senior Vice President Thomas Oh; Kia Motors has sales subsidiaries in Australia, Belgium, Canada, China, France, Germany, New Zealand, Russia, Spain, Sweden, the United Kingdom, the United States, and part of Eastern and Central Europe.[26]

Direct Functional Reporting

A compromise between the direct exporting and international division structures is a functional structure with direct reporting duties to a home-based marketing manager or vice president (see Figure 16.7). This method allows for the presence of foreign offices, but streamlines the reporting duties directly to the domestic marketing manager. The approach may be useful in limited situations, but many global companies prefer to develop international divisions or offices.

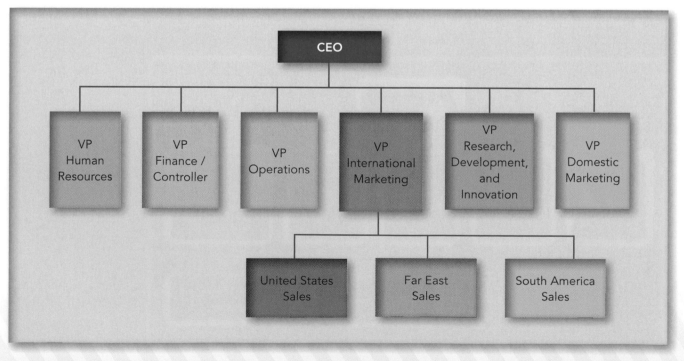

Figure 16.6: International Division

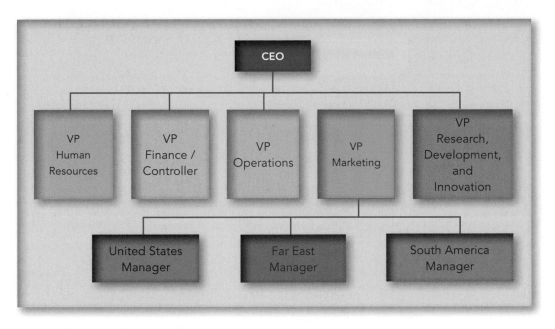

Figure 16.7: Direct Functional Reporting

Strategic Alliance Organization

Many market entries involve partnering with local companies. Based on common goals between the companies, strategic alliances may be organized in a variety of ways. The type of control creates one key concern. Under the first control option, the strategic alliance has its own independent management. The alliance becomes an entity with separate goals and decision-making from the partner companies. This may lead the strategic alliance to make choices contrary to the interests of the companies that started the alliance. Collective control represents the other organizational option. Under this approach, the partners work together to manage the alliance, with the goal of generating optimal mutual benefits for the partner companies, even at the expense of the alliance.[27]

Trust will be one of the key factors influencing the type of organization used and the degree of linkage between alliance partners. In cases of high trust, companies share highly sensitive or important knowledge with partners.[28] Trust may be especially important in instances of partner asymmetry, which occurs when one alliance partner is an unequal member of the alliance. Asymmetry results from differences in market position, proprietary knowledge, overall company size, or a variety of other factors. Overall, the asymmetry is rooted in unequal contributions to or benefits from the alliance.[29] Organizational structure, particularly control and structured contributions, can help mitigate the negative effects of asymmetry.

Region-Based Organization

A truly global organization may choose to have distinct office locations, and strategic business units in each specific region served (see Figure 16.8). This form of structure is a region-based organization. It offers the advantage of allowing the company to be responsive to local market differences while presenting a relatively simple organizational structure with clear lines of authority and responsibility.

As each region grows in importance to the organization's international strategy, the region-based organizational structure may become the most viable. As with the

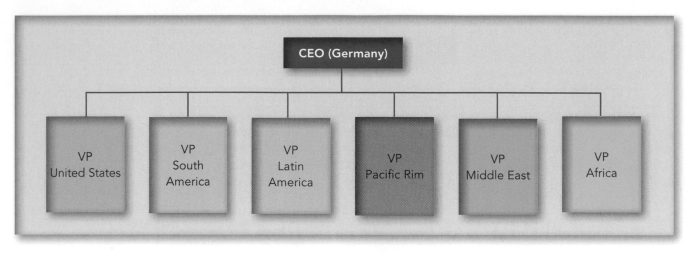

Figure 16.8: Region-Based Organization

international division or direct functional reporting structure, the company may choose from home, host, or third-country nationals for staffing purposes.

As trade areas (such as the European Union or NAFTA) continue to grow in importance for international marketers, the region-based approach grows in usage. Each region's division employs a marketing staff devoted specifically to the region. The regional structure will be viable as long as trade barriers remain minimal within the targeted regions. When barriers become significant, a different form of structure may become more attractive for international marketing purposes.

The Sage Group, a United Kingdom based provider of business software, services, and support that targets small and medium-sized business, employs a regional structure. Focused on providing local-based service, the company serves seven broad regions: Europe, Africa, the Middle East, Asia, Oceania, Latin America, and North America. Within those broad regional markets, the company maintains offices in many countries.[30]

Matrix Organization

Some successful international marketing firms choose an organizational design that is not limited to geographic responsibilities, but instead groups some employees based on skills or product focus. These groups of employees then report to various broader regional or national managers. The matrix form of structure allows flexibility as a group of engineers or financing experts can provide services to various regions. The main concern with a matrix organization is that it can lead to conflicts when different regions have different needs or goals. The engineering team, for example, might find itself being pulled in different directions by the various regional operations that have authority over the team's activities.

Honda employs a region-based matrix organization, as presented in Figure 16.9. The company conducts regional operations in North America; Latin America; Europe, the Middle and Near East, Africa; Asia and Oceania; and China. The company then has separate functional operations that serve across each region, such as separate motorcycle operations or purchasing operations. Employees in automobile operations report to the various regions and are responsible for effective automobile production and sales across the regions.[31]

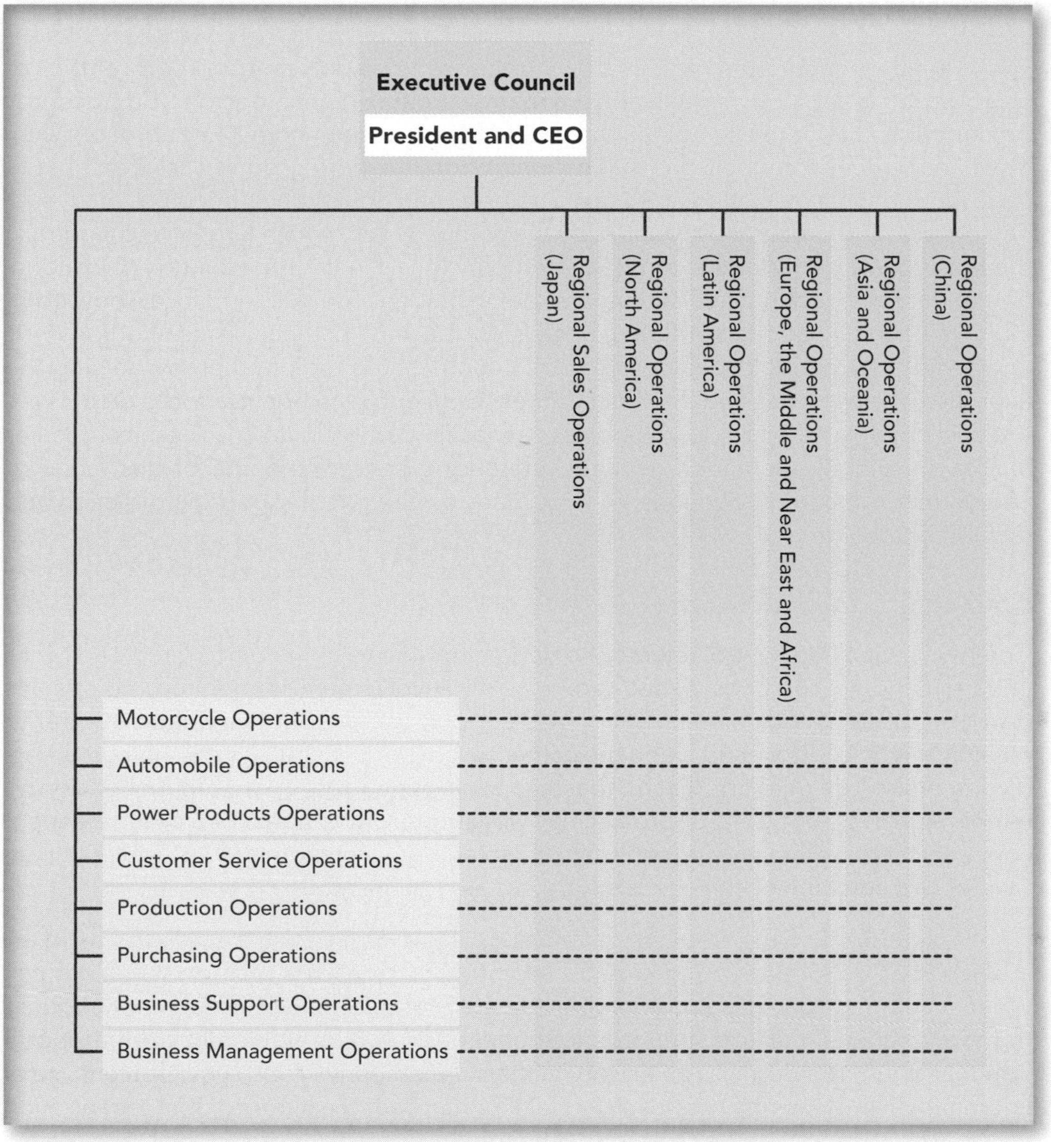

The chart shows an organizational structure with "Executive Council / President and CEO" at the top, branching to regional divisions: Regional Sales Operations (Japan), Regional Operations (North America), Regional Operations (Latin America), Regional Operations (Europe, the Middle and Near East and Africa), Regional Operations (Asia and Oceania), Regional Operations (China). The functional operations listed are: Motorcycle Operations, Automobile Operations, Power Products Operations, Customer Service Operations, Production Operations, Purchasing Operations, Business Support Operations, Business Management Operations.

Figure 16.9

Source: "Organization Structure," Honda, accessed at http://world.honda.com/profile/organization/.

Each of these forms of structure facilitates international marketing programs in different ways. Various factors lead to the selection of one organizational design over another.

INTERNAL FACTORS AND ORGANIZATIONAL DESIGN

Internal and external factors influence the design of organizational design in a way similar to how they impact overall strategic planning. Some of the most compelling factors include the company's international orientation, communication and control issues, the intensity of international marketing efforts, a company's existing organizational design, and the degree of technology development. An executive makes an important strategic choice involving the form of structure to utilize after considering these and other factors.

Company Orientation

The company orientation, whether it is ethnocentric, polycentric, regiocentric, or geocentric orientation, significantly impacts organizational design. Ethnocentric organizations prefer to use home market employees at both home and abroad. When the management team believes that nationals from the home country are best able to drive international marketing activities, a home country orientation becomes the result. The policies and procedures enacted by the company will remain largely unchanged in the host country. Polycentric companies employ locals in the host country to conduct operations, and each market is treated as being unique. The skills and local knowledge of host country nationals influence decision making in these firms. Regiocentric companies utilize employees from several countries in a region, thereby pooling the expertise of employees in different countries. Geocentric companies focus on utilizing the best employees available, regardless of specific country location. These companies maintain a global orientation, without referencing a specific home or host country. The correct orientation depends, in large part, on the overall strategic direction and mission of the firm.

Communication and Control

Communication and control refer to the degree to which a home office directs activities in various home countries. When strong, daily involvement is required, companies develop sophisticated communication and control systems. Some managers prefer to maintain tight controls and frequent contact with overseas markets, whereas others favor a much less rigid approach. These approaches impact organizational design. A direct-reporting, functional approach may work better when tight control and frequent communication is desired; a national or regional approach may work better when control and communication concerns are not as significant.

Intensity of International Marketing Efforts

When a company devotes considerable resources to and derives substantial business from international markets, the organizational design will be different from that of a firm that does little business in foreign markets. A company with a small percentage of international business may prefer a simple export approach. A truly global organization requires organizational designs such as the regional or matrix form of structure. These differences may also be at the product level. Tata Motors started reaching the foreign markets for the Nano through exporting. As demand grows, the company may shift organizational structure. A company such as Honda, with millions of automobiles sold globally, already uses a matrix approach to effectively respond to the needs of those markets.

Existing Organizational Design

In the event that a firm is relatively new in the international marketplace, the existing organizational design often affects its international structure. The new structure tends to develop slowly and deliberately. A new entry to international marketing may begin its operations with a simple exporting strategy and eventually move to one of the other designs. Maruchan, the best-selling ramen noodle brand in the United States, started out as a frozen fish distributor in Japan. The company began to produce ramen noodles in 1961 and in 1972 began exporting the noodles to neighboring countries. In 1977 the company entered the American market with the opening of a ramen noodle manufacturing plant in California. At first the company kept a simple organizational structure while exporting, but, as international business grew, the company shifted organizational structure. The unit is now headquartered in Richmond, Virginia.[32]

Technological Investment

Technology increasingly plays an important role in international marketing. The level of technological sophistication and commitment of a company often influences organizational design. While technology remains important in all aspects of international marketing, it becomes especially important when establishing international communication and control systems. Communicating with offices in international markets requires efficient and effective technology. For simpler designs, such as direct exporting, relatively modest technological investments are required. Synchronizing operations with locations around the globe often requires significant investments.

VIDEO LINK 16.2:
Technology

EXTERNAL FACTORS AND ORGANIZATIONAL DESIGN

External factors also influence organizational design decisions. These factors include levels of international competition, distances from international customers, customer profiles, and governmental forces. These external factors require responses, including how the company will be structured in order to cope with them.

International Competition

Organizational structure decisions are affected by the level and intensity of international competition. When few international competitors are present, or if the level of competition stays low, companies may choose to engage largely in exporting and maintain a functional, direct exporting structure. For more intense levels of competition, a national or regional presence may be more effective. Maintaining a close contact with the marketplace enables the firm to more closely monitor competitive actions.

Distance to International Customers

Companies desiring to stay close to international customers often choose the region-based approaches to organizational design. The local presence afforded by these alternatives can be an important part of maintaining close relationships with international customers. Close relationships are more readily maintained when there are a number of customers clustered in regions that are far from a firm's world headquarters.

Customer Profiles

Regardless of distance to international customers, some customers simply demand a local presence, such as a local sales office. The international division alternative can work well in these situations. Establishing a presence in a country will be more important when frequent contacts are made between buyer and seller, as when rebuy or modified rebuy situations are the norm. In many industrial buying situations, a matrix organizational design specific to regions grants an effective level of coordination and control.

Governmental Forces

Governmental forces can dictate organizational structure when tariffs or other barriers to trade make exporting to the market too expensive. In those cases, companies may instead choose to set up subsidiaries within the country. These subsidiaries may lead to a different organizational form. Governments may also require that companies use a local partner when setting up a subsidiary. In some cases, the local partner may be required to have a majority stake in the local business. These requirements may also lead to a different organizational form.

Analysis

A combination of internal and external factors leads to the eventual development of organizational structure. External factors such as the level of international competition influences managerial decisions regarding the nature of an organization chart and the designation of responsibilities for managers and employees. Also the distances from international customers, customer profiles, and governmental forces affect the choice of an organizational design.

A combination of internal and external factors leads to the eventual development of organizational structure.

LEARNING
OBJECTIVE #4:

*What are the basic
components of the
international marketing
plan?*

International Marketing Tactics and the Marketing Plan

Tactical planning concentrates on specific international marketing activities, guided by the overall strategic level planning process. Tactical level planning involves management of the segmentation, targeting, and positioning of the firm's products or services in specific international markets combined with the other elements of the marketing mix—pricing, promotion, and distribution.

THE INTERNATIONAL MARKETING PLAN

Developing an international marketing plan constitutes an essential ingredient of successful international marketing management. Different businesses develop different marketing plan structures; the typical parts of the international marketing plan are presented in Figure 16.10.

The executive summary provides a brief overview of the overall marketing plan, including goals and objectives, recommendations, and tactics. It supplies a snapshot of the international marketing program. Normally the summary will be the last component of the marketing plan to be written, in order to accurately portray the remainder of the document. The summary should clearly link the international marketing plan to the company's broader strategic goals.

| Executive Summary |
| Situational Analysis |
| Analysis of the Internal Environment |
| Analysis of the External Environment |
| Target Market Description |
| International Marketing Goals and Objectives |
| Evaluation, Measurement, and Control |

Figure 16.10: Components of the International Marketing Plan

A situational analysis considers an analysis of the internal, external, and customer environments, along with the development of a SWOT (strengths, weaknesses, opportunities, and threats) analysis. The information leads to the development of specific marketing goals, objectives, and programs for a targeted international market.

The analysis of the internal environment assesses the factors that are relevant to the marketing program for a given international market. The analysis includes market knowledge, the success of current marketing programs, and the firm's competitive advantage. The firm's competitive advantage, based on market-relevant capabilities, enables the marketing team to address customer needs more effectively than the competition.

The analysis of the external environment contains the factors that are relevant to the marketing campaign for a given market. An assessment of economic conditions, political and regulatory forces, language, culture, and other external factors offers insights into any challenges present in a market.

Effective marketing plans contain an in-depth description of the target market for the product or service in the to-be-entered country. The target market discussion confirms whether sufficient demand for the product exists, and whether the product can be effectively positioned to attract that demand.

The marketing plan confirms that the target market will be large enough to support market entry and will lead to the selection of an entry mode. Much of the information for this analysis will be obtained from international marketing research. Issues such as consumer wants and needs, and preferences, cultural influences, and brand loyalty play an important role in the analysis of customers. Most of this information comes from primary research. The target market description and entry mode selections steps of the marketing plan present crucial information used in identifying viable international market segmentation strategies.

Based on the analyses of the previous items, company leaders set international marketing goals and objectives for the program. An international marketing goal might be to increase brand awareness and penetration in a particular market over the next five years. Part of that objective would be, for example, to increase sales in the marketplace by 2% annually.

The actual marketing program represents one of the most critical elements in an international strategic marketing program. Product decisions, pricing methods, promotional approaches, and distribution systems are designated. The international marketing program details the appropriate product positioning for the market and the product's unique selling proposition.

Middle and first level managers devise specific action plans that enable the firm to pursue the overall marketing strategy. The implementation portion of the international marketing plan includes duties such as job assignments, responsibilities, and support for the various marketing activities. Action plans outline the "on the ground" elements of a marketing program.

Evaluation, measurement, and control efforts at the tactical level pertain to the specific goals and objectives identified by the marketing plan. Evaluation, measurement, and control of an international marketing plan indicate what has gone right and what has gone wrong in a specific marketing program. Middle managers may perform a marketing audit with the aim of assessing the overall international marketing program. They then can consider corrective actions when goals and objectives have not been met.

PLANNING TACTICS AND STRATEGIC PLANS

Many of the efforts listed in the international marketing plan are similar to those conducted as part of the strategic planning process. International marketing plans are generally constructed for specific programs, products, or services, in specific international markets. In most cases, these plans are devised for specific SBUs. Strategic plans outline the direction of the overall organization, specifically its structure, direction, and goals. Marketing plans are more narrowly focused, centering on individual marketing activities, such as a pricing system or method of distribution.

Internal Marketing Communications

LEARNING OBJECTIVE #5:

How does internal communication affect international planning, organizing, and control?

Organizational communication plays a vital role in international marketing success. The flow and clarity of international communication within the company impacts planning, organizing, and control activities as well as the success of international marketing plans. The quality and quantity of international communications directly impact strategic and tactical plans. Many challenges exist in international communication. Effective communication systems overcome these problems and provide the basis of high-quality international marketing programs.

INTERNATIONAL INTERNAL COMMUNICATIONS

Language and interpersonal communication received in-depth attention in an earlier chapter. An individual communications model was presented to explain how messages pass from one person to another or from a single sender to multiple receivers. The model suggests the process includes encoding by the sender, a transmission device to carry the message, and decoding by the receiver. The receiver then provides feedback to the sender, in the form of acknowledgment, disagreement, confusion, or other messages. Noise, or barriers to communication, can distort or disrupt a message transmitted. Many of the principles and concepts that apply to individual communications also apply to communication systems in international organizations.

FORMAL COMMUNICATION IN GLOBAL COMPANIES

A number of analogies have been applied to the role that internal communication plays in global organizations. It has been compared to the "glue" that holds things together, to electrical current that gives a company its energy, and to gasoline that provides the firm with fuel to get things done. No matter the comparison chosen, what becomes clear is that effective organizational communication represents one of the keys to effective strategic international marketing.

Organizational communication takes two primary forms. **Formal communication** travels through channels that are designated or chosen by organizational leaders. Figure 16.11 lists some of the more common traditional and emerging formal communication channels. **Informal communication** takes place in the form of rumors or gossip, and messages that travel through the organizational grapevine.

> Formal communication travels through channels that are designated or chosen by organizational leaders.

Traditional Formal Communication Channels	Emerging Formal Communication Channels
Direct messages	Websites
Meetings	Intranet
Memos	Teleconferencing
Letters	Mobile phones
Company manuals/handbooks	Satellite transmissions
Bulletin boards	
Company magazine/newsletter	

Figure 16.11: Formal Internal Communication Channels

Traditional Formal Communication Channels

Many internal communications continue to rely on traditional channels. A supervisor speaking to an employee (a direct address) takes place on a daily basis. Meetings are held both in person and through the use of newer electronic technologies. Memos and letters, while increasingly rare, do carry pertinent information at times. Most company manuals, handbooks, magazines, and newsletters are now sent via electronic format. Actual bulletin boards are less likely to be used by international firms, because there is no central location in which they can be placed.

In international companies, these traditional channels remain useful tools. A direct address may take place on the phone or through a visual format such as Skype. Direct communications assist both employees and managers in asking and answering questions, making and fulfilling requests, receiving and clarifying assignments and directions, and in creating relationships with coworkers. International sales meetings may not often take place in person, but still serve to make sure the home office keeps in contact with employees operating in host countries. In essence, while international marketing programs require adjustment and alterations to standard operating procedures, many of the traditional marketing management tasks are still completed using traditional formal communication channels.

Emerging Formal Communication Channels

Global trade has been vastly improved through the use of emerging formal communication channels, and these communication channels work within the overall corporate structure. Company websites connect employees with customers and with each other. An Intranet system serves a variety of purposes, including those displayed in Figure 16.12. Teleconferencing, mobile phones, and satellite transmissions connect employees with each other and with managers at higher ranks.

State corporate policies and vision
Provide information to the sales force while making contacts with clients
Maintain human resource records
Facilitate payroll
Pass along employee recognition
Provide information about company events and altruistic causes

Figure 16.12: Intranet Uses

BARRIERS TO INTERNATIONAL FORMAL COMMUNICATION

A series of barriers can distort or disrupt messages in formal communication systems (see Figure 16.13). In individual communications, language and slang create significant barriers, especially in international marketing operations. The same holds true for formal organizational communication systems. Multinationals feature employees that speak a variety of languages, have different dialects of the same language, and experience variations in the meaning and use of slang terms.

Language and Slang
Cultural and Subcultural Differences
Time Differences
Ethnocentrism

Figure 16.13: Barriers to International Formal Communication

Language-related formal communication barriers interrupt interpersonal conversations and company business meetings, especially in terms of gestures and nonverbal methods of communication. In the Balkan region, the up and down nod means "no," and the sideways nod means "yes." A company posting a website with a "V" for victory signal with the palm out might be surprised to find out the gesture is practically an invitation to fight in Great Britain when the palm is turned in. The same is true for the "hook 'em horns" signal, which is also widely used at heavy metal concerts and by Hawai`ian locals. Similar unanticipated outcomes may result from use of the "thumbs up" gesture.

All of the cultural and subcultural differences that can harm interpersonal communications can damage formal communication systems as well. The use of colors, symbols, religious references, portrayals of women, certain numbers, and a variety of additional cultural nuances, when misinterpreted, can damage a firm's international marketing efforts by offending members of the company that are from other countries.

Time differences can disrupt international commerce. When the home country is many time zones away from the host country, communication schedules that are not carefully designed can lead to phone calls or other contacts in the middle of the night as well as the failure to send important information to company members in other countries in a timely fashion. Noon Thursday in Tokyo is 2:00 a.m. Friday in Mexico City.

Ethnocentrism interferes with internal operations when a supervisor's attitude shows through to employees or coworkers, which may occur in companies with an ethnocentric orientation. Anything from making belittling jokes to caustic comments about the culture of a host country may create friction within the firm. In 2011, following the earthquake and tsunami in Japan, Aflac quickly fired comedian Gilbert Gottfried, the voice of the duck in the United States, for insensitive comments about the crisis. A great deal of Aflac's business revenues are generated in Japan. Ethnocentrism damages all forms of managerial styles, but most notably regiocentric, polycentric, and geocentric formats. Employees working for ethnocentric management-style companies may be the most prone to ethnocentrism problems, especially when dealing with publics in host countries.

Aflac recently changed the voice actor for its duck due to cultural sensitivity concerns.

OVERCOMING BARRIERS TO FORMAL COMMUNICATIONS

When managing strategic marketing operations in foreign countries, communication processes are challenging but also vital to effective functioning, planning, organizing, and control. To successfully navigate the pitfalls that can disrupt formal communication in such organizations, the following concepts are helpful:

- Cultural training for employees
- Careful selection of media when transmitting messages
- Use of multiple channels for important messages
- Establishing effective management information systems
- Monitoring informal communication

Cultural training will be used to complement and supplement other forms of employee instruction. Individuals who will be transferred to host nations receive information about the company and how it operates in conjunction with messages regarding how operations differ in various nations. The training of expatriate employees creates a vital link between the company's home office and its marketing activities in other countries.

When sending messages to and from the home office and foreign subsidiaries, media selection plays a vital role. In the current landscape, many expatriates are likely to prefer newer technologies, such as smart phones, tablets, and the Internet. Messages can be transmitted more quickly through these formats than through traditional channels. Users should give care to the using of too many shortcuts, such as the abbreviations that are part of the language of Twitter and other electronic messaging. Someone who has moved to a foreign country may be less aware of culturally-driven abbreviations.

Oftentimes, key messages are sent at odd times and require a rapid response. Employees in both the host and home countries are advised to use multiple channels for important information. A text message should be accompanied by a phone call or email. The use of a second channel makes it more likely that a message will be received on time and that the message will be deemed important by the recipient.

INTERNATIONAL INCIDENT ///

Not all employees are equally comfortable with communicating via electronic media. In fact, some can be nearly hostile toward the use of the media, while others embrace it completely. A complication occurs when an employee who is comfortable with electronic media is stationed in a country with an underdeveloped technological infrastructure. The employee can suffer from loss of work morale and feelings of isolation. Such an outcome may not be surprising, considering that many consumers have become addicted to media like the Internet. What could be done to improve communications with the employee and improve his or her morale?

In summary, formal communication travels through channels that organizational leaders designate or choose. Systems include traditional and emerging formal communication media. In international companies, these traditional channels remain useful. Global trade has become more efficient through the use of emerging formal communication channels. The barriers to formal communication include language and slang, cultural and subcultural differences, time differences, and ethnocentrism. To overcome the barriers to formal communication, company leaders can provide cultural training for employees, carefully select media when transmitting messages, use multiple channels for important messages, establish effective management information systems, and monitor informal communication.

International Marketing Control

International marketing control includes assessments of all marketing activities individually and collectively within international markets. The assessment may be at the regional, national, or other appropriate levels. Regardless of level, marketing controls are based on the standards set in the planning process. Control is more than examining numbers: It represents carefully analyzing all of the factors that lead to organization success.

Control in an international marketing environment focuses on measuring progress against what was planned, taking corrective actions when they are needed, and rewarding success. In general, international control consists of four steps.[33]

1. Restate the standard.

2. Measure performance as it relates to the standard.

3. Compare performance to the standard.

4. Make a decision (make corrections or reward success).

The first step is to restate the standard that was set as part of the planning function. In current terminology, many standards are known as **metrics**, which is another term for performance measures.

> In current terminology, many standards are known as metrics, which is another term for performance measures.

CONTROL MEASURES

Strategic controls are those that apply to the CEO and any other manager involved in directing the portfolios of businesses or activities held by a single company or corporation. These standards are more encompassing than goals set by a marketing department. They include corporate profitability figures measured by return on investments, the value of a share of common stock, overall company growth in assets, and similar measures.

The highest-ranking member of the marketing department is likely to hold a title such as "vice president of marketing and sales" or "director of marketing." This individual has the ultimate responsibility for the strategic direction of the marketing department, as well as for establishing and evaluating strategic marketing standards. The size of the company and the marketing department dictate the types of controls that will be put in place. In a smaller company, sales, marketing, and public relations may all be contained in a single unit. In larger organizations, the three may each be deemed a separate department with its own manager. In any case, at the strategic level, the typical objectives and goals established for the marketing department's planning and control systems are found in the areas of

- market share,

- sales,

- profitability,

- customer satisfaction, and

- corporate and brand image.

Figure 16.14 lists various specific methods to measure success for each of the above factors.

CORRECTIONS

When the first three steps of the control process have been completed, the standards have been set, performance has been measured, and a comparison has been made between the established standard and actual performance. The final step of control is to either reward success or make corrections. Corrections take place at the strategic, tactical, and operational levels.

Strategic Indicators	Tactical Standards	Operational Standards
Profitability (Return on Investment)	New Markets Served	Sales Figures: Individual Salespersons
Market Share Home country Host countries	New Product Introductions Home country Host countries	Advertising Reach/ Effectiveness
Corporate/Brand Image Brand Awareness Brand Loyalty Brand Equity	Distribution Costs Domestic International	Delivery Efficiency on time percentage damaged goods cost per unit
Overall Sales Home country Host countries	Distribution Effectiveness Domestic International	Public Relations positive stories negative press
	Product Lines/Brands	

Figure 16.14: Marketing Controls

Strategic Corrections

> The resource-based approach focuses on the organization's core competence, which is the most proficiently performed internal activity that is central to the firm's strategy and competitiveness.

Strategic management at the top level of the company will focus on either a resource-based approach to strategic direction or a competitive approach. The resource-based approach focuses on the organization's **core competence**, which is the most proficiently performed internal activity that is central to the firm's strategy and competitiveness. Core competencies are based in knowledge and people, not capital and assets. In this approach to strategic management, the goal becomes to develop a **distinctive competence**, in which a company performs an activity such as production or sales more efficiently and effectively than all rivals. In marketing terms, this equates to *brand equity* because it creates competitive superiority.[34]

Tactical Corrections

Strategic responses are the most dramatic and sweeping types of corrections made in control systems. They are normally accompanied by various tactical responses. Tactical corrections may be developed by brand, by product, and by function. At the product level, corrections may involve introducing new products, cutting existing products, or repositioning. Corrections may also focus at finding new users or uses, or encouraging more frequent usage. Tactical corrections may also be functional. These include changing promotional methods and approaches, such as starting a new advertising campaign, or changing the channel used to distribute products.

Operational Corrections

At the entry level, first-line supervisors work with employees to ensure that they correctly carry out the company's marketing directives. Performance appraisal systems and reward systems help ensure that those who make face-to-face contact with the public present the company in a positive fashion. Additional operational corrections include changing methods for conducting daily activities, such as when a cash-based economy begins to shift to the use of debit and credit cards.

Analysis

International marketing control includes assessments of all marketing activities individually and collectively within international markets at the regional, national, or other appropriate levels. *Metrics* is the term used to describe performance measures. Metrics are applied at the strategic, tactical, and operational levels. Strategic management at the top level of the company will focus on either a resource-based approach to strategic direction or a competitive approach. The resource-based approach focuses on a core competence. The competitive approach seeks to achieve distinctive competence. The goal is to create competitive superiority. In marketing, tactical corrections involve alterations or adjustments to the basic functions of products, prices, distribution, or promotional programs. At the operational level, performance appraisals and the reward system are used to guide employee activities.

Emerging Trends in International Marketing

Many trends affect international marketing practices. Although it is difficult to predict unforeseen events, it is likely that the following issues will affect international marketing into the foreseeable future. Major changes center on technological, cultural, and economic issues.

LEARNING OBJECTIVE #6:

What emerging trends might affect international marketing in the future?

TECHNOLOGICAL ISSUES

The proliferation of cell phones and smartphones worldwide has had a major impact on international marketing. The impact of smartphone technology influences many international businesses, but especially international service providers. Increased usage of smartphones directly affects cellular phone companies dependent on sales of lower-end, more traditional phones. Nokia and LG Electronics, the number one and number three sellers of cell phones, have both recently faced declining sales. The CEO of LG, Nam Yong, resigned in 2010 due to a failure to aggressively move into the smartphone market.[35]

In emerging or less-developed markets, counterfeit smartphones constitute a growing market. Forty-percent of the smartphones manufactured in China are counterfeits. Beyond being less expensive, in many cases new product features are offered. Some fake iPhones in China allow the user to install two SIM cards, which makes it possible to maintain two different phone numbers. As was noted earlier, these models are popular with consumers in many countries. Chinese counterfeits in Ghana can receive television broadcasts. In Kenya, the phones feature quotes from President Obama.[36]

Citizens of developing countries also typically exhibit higher usage rates of new mobile and digital technologies than many individuals in mature markets. India already has approximately 765 million phones, with 95% of the phones being mobile.[37] Table 16.1 ranks the top fifteen countries in terms of number of cell phones used. A recent survey revealed that only 27% of Canadians who were online had written a blog post or posted on an online forum. In comparison, 51% of online Brazilians and 88% of online Chinese had done so. Also, 92% of online Thais and 88% of online Malaysians had shared personal photographs while using the Internet, compared to only 60% of Canadians. For all of these activities, emerging market consumers are more likely to use a cell phone whereas Canadians are more likely to use a personal computer. The dependency on the older technology of computers may prevent developed-market consumers from taking complete advantage of the mobile revolution.[38]

COUNTRY	NUMBER OF USERS
1. China	747 million
2. India	670 million
3. United States	286 million
4. Russia	230.5 million
5. Brazil	174 million
6. Indonesia	159 million
7. Japan	115 million
8. Germany	105 million
9. Pakistan	103 million
10. Vietnam	98 million
11. Philippines	92 million
12. Italy	90 million
13. Mexico	83.5 million
14. Thailand	83 million
15. United Kingdom	80 million

Table 16.1: **The Top Fifteen Countries Cellular Phone Users**

Source: The World Factbook, Central Intelligence Agency, accessed at https://www.cia.gov/library/publications/the-world-factbook/rankorder/2150rank.html?countryName=China&countryCode=ch&regionCode=eas&rank=1#ch.

CULTURAL ISSUES

Differences in culture continue to be a major cause of international marketing misunderstandings. International marketers that correctly adjust to cultural differences and the interaction between culture and technology will generate substantial advantages over competitors. Culture's pervasive influence, particularly on consumption, presents a challenge for marketers globally. The future of international marketing will likely be influenced by two forces: cultural convergence and cultural trends.

Increased standardization may be the result of *cultural convergence,* or the growing similarities between consumers globally. These similarities take place in many aspects of life. Part of this textbook has been focused on consumption at a basic, daily life level. International Marketing in Daily Life segments are interspersed throughout the chapters. Also, the opening vignettes to each chapter have discussed products that are consumed or used on a daily basis. While these excerpts explore cultural differences as they relate to international marketing and product use, it is clear that cultures are in many ways converging.

Technological similarities and adoption of those technologies may help drive increased convergence globally. The practical and societal benefits of many technologies, such as headache medicines or social media, create demand. Consumers then transition to using these new technologies, regardless of the underlying cultural preferences.

Convergence may also be accelerated by political and economic changes. The transition to a more capitalist economy and open, democratic political structure often leads to more similar consumption patterns by consumers across those growing economies. Some of these consumers seek to mimic and, to at least some degree, also idealize Western, developed-country consumption patterns. Increased wealth and financial stability create additional discretionary income that can be used by consumers to purchase goods.

Businesses also influence this process. The economic development of various countries coupled with more efficient methods to sell goods to all markets leads to global brands. As these businesses move into countries, the employment of local sales people and distributors, and eventually the establishment of local subsidiaries also result in increased cultural convergence.

Consider the case of Levi Strauss jeans. Founded in 1873, the company created the first blue jeans. At first denim jeans were for the working class only. During the 1950s the famous singer Bing Crosby was once turned away at a luxury hotel for wearing denim jeans instead of more formal slacks. During the 1960s the company began to enter Europe (the region of origin for denim) and Japan.[39] By 2011, consumers were wearing Levi jeans in 110 countries, and more than half of the company's earnings were generated outside the United States.[40]

Consumption exists within the context of a local culture. Product preferences rooted in a culture may cause some people to resist outside goods and new patterns of behavior. The persistence of specific values due to sociocultural influences, particularly in the face of outside alternatives, is **cultural divergence**.

David Ralston has studied convergence, divergence, and a third term: crossvergence. **Cultural crossvergence** refers to the emergence of a new, global value system as countries become more interconnected. It represents a melting-pot approach.[41] Consumers take the best from various locations and a global culture starts to emerge. The ubiquity of soy sauce, the increasing popularity of fruits from all over the world, and the leadership of an Indian company in the global steel market are all arguments for crossvergence. Increasing evidence suggests that instead of consumers all morphing into "Americans," many consumers increasingly enjoy the benefits of the best goods from a variety of countries.

> Cultural crossvergence refers to the emergence of a new, global value system as countries become more interconnected.

The 2008 recession had an unequal impact globally.

ECONOMIC ISSUES

Over the past several decades, an increasing global consensus had emerged with regard to lowering barriers to trade, reducing governmental intervention, eliminating business regulations, and adopting the Western model of economic development in which the market is trusted to best serve the interests of citizens. After the fall of the former Soviet Union and the transition toward a more capitalist system for the People's Republic of China, Eastern Europe, and much of Latin America, many nations became increasingly "American" in their approaches to business.

The economic recession that started in December 2007 in the United States and the following year for many Western countries was contrary to this trend. The underlying financial crisis at the root of the economic downturn increased skepticism of the traditional, Anglo-Saxon model. In the United States, more than 8 million jobs were lost in late December 2007 and early 2008, which raised the unemployment rate from 4.4% to above 10%. The recession lasted eighteen months, longer than any downturn since the Great Depression. In response, unprecedented steps were taken by the Federal Reserve and the Treasury Department.[42]

The Great Recession had an unequal impact globally. Developed economies, particularly Western Europe, faced steep downturns. While France, Germany, and Japan avoided sharp drops, the United Kingdom and much of the remaining developed countries did not. The recession hit Portugal, Ireland, Greece, and Spain (known as the PIGS, although this acronym is offensive to some) particularly hard. Greece and Ireland received assistance from the European Central Bank to prevent the countries from defaulting on loans. Spain and Portugal faced similar problems.[43] The crisis put pressure on maintaining both the *euro* and the connection between countries, but also, to some degree, drew the members of the European Union closer together.[44]

VIDEO LINK 16.3:
The EU and the
Sovereign Debt Crisis

With the recession attacking the assumption, as Alan Greenspan, former Federal Reserve chair described it, "that the self-interest of organizations, specifically banks and others, was such that they were best capable of protecting their own shareholders," countries have begun to look for new models. Out of Western countries, the Nordic countries, with a combination of higher regulation and a larger social safety net, arguably weathered the economic storm better than any other European nation. The countries provided generous support to citizens during the downturn, which meant the countries faced less unrest and a quicker ability to bounce back. Nicolas Sarkozy claimed that the global recession marked a turning of the page on the traditional, Anglo-Saxon, British, and American economic model.[45] Table 16.2 lists the gross domestic product growth (GDP) or reduction for various key economies in 2008, 2009, and 2010.

COUNTRY	2008	2009	2010
Denmark	7.2%	4.6%	5.3%
France	0.1%	–2.5%	1.6%
Germany	1%	–4.7%	3.6%
Greece	2%	–2%	–4.8%
Ireland	–3.5%	–7.6%	–1.6%
Japan	–1.2%	–5.2%	3%
Norway	1.8%	–1.4%	1.5%
Portugal	0%	–2.6%	1%
Spain	0.9%	–3.7%	–0.2%
Sweden	–0.6%	–5.1%	4.1%
United Kingdom	–0.1%	–5%	1.6%
United States	0%	–2.6%	2.7%

Table 16.2: **Gross Domestic Product Growth for Key Developed Economies, 2008–2010**

Source: Adapted from *The World Factbook*, Central Intelligence Agency, accessed at https://www.cia.gov/library/publications/the-world-factbook/index.html.

Responses to Financial Crises

Companies exhibit differing responses to financial crises. For many, the collapse in consumer confidence and spending may lead to retrenchment and divestment. *Retrenchment* refers to a reduction in spending and investment, with the focus on weathering the downturn. *Divestment* involves selling low-performing assets. Together, these tactics may result in companies leaving the most difficult markets. During the global recession, strong indicators of global retrenchment emerged, especially as evidenced by the flow of money between countries.[46] In the United Kingdom, dropping consumer confidence led retailers to retrench and divest, with the potential for more than 250 storefronts being closed in response to the downturn.[47] The closures have implications for companies selling products through those retailers.

For other companies, financial crises can represent an opportunity. One typical response to a crisis is extreme movement in lending rates. A company may be able to react to these high or low rates by increasing its amount of lending or borrowing. High rates can lead to increased lending, which results in higher profits, whereas low rates can lead to a less expensive cost of debt. International companies may then use borrowing to expand into new markets or more aggressively pursue new product development.

Many company leaders believe that marketing investments during a recession will result in an improved company position when the economy recovers.[48] Academic research has revealed some support for this approach, particularly when investments in research and development or advertising are thoughtful and targeted.[49]

Company position before the recession affects the company's ability to respond to the financial crises. Diversified companies, both in terms of the countries or markets in which the company conducts business and in terms of the breadth of products offered, weather financial downturns more effectively than companies offering a limited number of products or single product. The global recession negatively affected General Motors in various ways, leading to the company selling off many brands, closing plants, and laying off employees. The company's struggles led to American government intervention and financial support. One of the few bright spots for the company is market-leading positions in Brazil and China, two of the fastest growing international markets for sales. Without diversifying into these markets, the company may not have been able to survive the recession.[50]

EMERGING MARKETS ASCENDING

The decreased dominance of the traditional Western powers due to the recession shifted the focus to the rising powers in Asia and Latin America. During the downturn, China continued to grow, with GDP expansion of 8.3% in 2009 after 9% in 2008. The growth pattern was partially due to aggressive government action, including a large amount of spending. India's economy continued to grow, as did Brazil's.[51]

The Shanghai skyline reflects the country's rapid growth.

As a result, these emerging market countries have experienced greater political and economic influence. China has been a prime investor in Africa and helped to support the Euro zone during the bailout of Greece and Ireland.[52] India continued to increase its role in software offshoring, and Brazil leveraged advantages in terms of natural resources, including offshore oil. The iPhone, a smart phone discussed earlier, helps illuminate the role of non-Western countries in the global economy. While designed in California, the product is assembled in China. The parts are made in Taiwan, Japan, South Korea, and six other countries.[53] The growing importance of these emerging markets will exert a strong influence on international marketers in the coming decade.

As the developing world continues to make economic progress, prognosticators have begun to introduce new groupings of countries that move beyond Goldman Sach's BRIC designation (Brazil, Russia, India, and China). One grouping proposed by the magazine *The Economist* is CIVETS (Colombia, Indonesia, Vietnam, Egypt, Turkey, and South Africa). Another grouping, introduced by the Spanish bank BBVA, is EAGLES (Emerging and Growth-Leading Economies). These include the BRIC countries plus South Korea, Indonesia, Mexico, Turkey, Egypt, and Taiwan.[54] Analysts at Goldman Sachs have also introduced the MIST countries (Mexico, Indonesia, South Korea, and Turkey).[55] While it remains to be seen which countries or group of countries successfully develop, the new nicknames highlight the broadening influence of emerging economies globally. Table 16.3 notes the gross domestic product growth rates of these countries.

COUNTRY	2008	2009	2010
Brazil	5.1%	–0.2%	7.5%
China	9%	9.1%	10.3%
Colombia	2.7%	0.8%	4.4%
Egypt	7.2%	4.6%	5.3%
India	7.4%	7.4%	8.3%
Indonesia	6%	4.5%	6%
Mexico	1.5%	–6.5%	5%
South Africa	3.7%	–1.8%	3%
South Korea	2.3%	0.2%	6.1%
Taiwan	0.7%	–1.9%	10.5%
Turkey	0.7%	–4.7%	7.3%
Vietnam	6.3%	5.3%	6.8%

Table 16.3: **Gross Domestic Product Growth for Key High-Growth Economy Countries, 2008–2010**

Source: Adapted from *The World Factbook*, Central Intelligence Agency, accessed at https://www.cia.gov/library/publications/the-world-factbook/index.html.

BOTTOM-OF-THE-PYRAMID

The global recession hurt many bottom-of-the-pyramid consumers. The World Bank estimated that 90 million more people globally moved to earning less than $1.25 a day during the downturn.[56] Even with this setback, many believe international marketing firms will increasingly focus on bottom-of-the-pyramid consumers.

The continent of Africa is home to a billion people, many of which are bottom-of-the-pyramid consumers. Africa has the potential to emerge in the coming decades much as China and India have in the past twenty years. The growth of middle-class Africans, as estimated by the World Bank, is projected to be from 13 million in 2000 to 43 million by 2030.[57] Many local African firms realize this potential and have taken aggressive steps to meet the needs of the local market. Zambeef, an African meat and produce company, has spent millions of dollars expanding throughout the continent.[58]

Whether in Africa or in other emerging markets, successful targeting of bottom-of-the-pyramid consumers presents a major challenge for many developing-country firms. Those firms that meet this challenge will build a solid foundation with these consumers. As least- and less-developed countries then begin to grow economically, the relationship and brand loyalty with these consumers will help drive profit and long-term success for these companies.[59]

Chapter 16: Review and Resources

STRATEGIC IMPLICATIONS ///

Strategic marketing managers continually assess effectiveness of the overall marketing program. Figure 16.14 identifies some of the strategic criteria that are used to analyze the well-being of an international marketing system. In each instance, the marketing leader examines success at the domestic and global level.

The five forces that affect the international marketing environment will continue to exhibit dramatic effects on strategic choices regarding markets, products, pricing tactics, distribution systems, and promotional programs. Top managers consider the influence of infrastructure, economic conditions, political and legal environments, and cultural trends as plans and decisions are made. Effective communication of the strategic direction of the company assists in building a quality marketing program. At the international level, barriers to communication must be overcome in order to maintain an efficient and effective marketing system.

TACTICAL IMPLICATIONS ///

Tactical managers often oversee product lines, brands, or more-specific marketing activities such as distribution. The standards used to evaluate success at the tactical level are noted in Figure 16.14. These managers consider larger trends in the international marketing environment but focus on more-tangible, shorter-term considerations. Launching a new product or entering a new market in a host country requires understanding of the current conditions within that nation. The brand leader will consult with the firm's cultural assimilator to make sure that a product's name, package, label, price, and promotions all fit with local conditions.

OPERATIONAL IMPLICATIONS ///

Individual department managers review outcomes at the day-to-day, operational level. Figure 16.14 suggests some of the more common standards that first-line supervisors seek to achieve. Sales figures are likely to be examined on a monthly basis for each salesperson. Advertising and promotional programs will be assessed within the time frame in which they take place. Operational managers are most likely to hear customer complaints about various activities, from late arrivals of goods to a salesperson's poor service. Local culture dictates how these criticisms will be raised. An expatriate manager adjusts to a new culture in dealing with host-country employees as well as with customers and others in the area.

TERMS

planning	international strategic planning	strategic controls
organizing		core competence
control	mission statement	
strategic planning	formal communication	distinctive competence
tactical planning	informal communication	cultural divergence
operational plans	metrics	cultural crossvergence

REVIEW QUESTIONS

1. Define planning, organizing, and controlling.

2. Describe the concepts of efficiency and effectiveness.

3. Define strategic planning, tactical planning, and operational planning.

4. What are the main elements of international strategic planning?

5. Describe the four elements in a SWOT analysis.

6. Describe a direct exporting structure.

7. Describe an international division structure and a direct functional reporting structure.

8. Describe a region-based organization and a matrix organization structure.

9. Name the internal and external factors that affect the choice of organizational structure.

10. Identify the components of an international marketing plan.

11. Identify the most common traditional and emerging formal communication channels.

12. What are the barriers to international formal communication?

13. What steps can company leaders take to overcome the barriers to international formal communication?

14. What are the four steps of the control process?

15. Name the strategic, operational, and tactical standards companies use.

16. Describe core competence and distinctive competence.

17. Describe cultural convergence, cultural divergence, and cultural crossvergence.

18. What emerging trends might have an impact on international marketing in the coming years?

DISCUSSION QUESTIONS

1. Relate the elements of the strategic planning process to the concepts of efficiency and effectiveness. Explain how the elements are carried out at the tactical and operational levels.

2. Explain which form of international organizational structure would best match each of the following companies. Explain your reasoning for each choice.

    • Nike
    • Tommy Hilfiger
    • Bank of India
    • Southern African Diamonds
    • A Chinese company that manufacturers chopsticks

3. Create a complete international marking plan for one of the following companies:

    • Japanese company seeking to export rice to other Asian countries
    • Italian automobile company seeking to sell fuel-efficient cars in Africa
    • Information technology software company in India seeking to expand to Australia
    • Spanish winery seeking to open markets in Central America

4. When a company experiences a crisis, external and internal audiences seek information about the situation. Using Figure 16.11, discuss how formal internal communication channels could be used to communicate with employees. Which would be more valuable: traditional channels or emerging channels? Why? What if the company employs individuals from vastly different cultural backgrounds? Would that influence the channels or messages that should be used?

5. The first draft of this textbook was written in 2011. Make a list of the emerging trends in international marketing identified in this chapter. Explain how they have appeared, or become less relevant in the time since July 2011. What new trends to you believe will affect international marketing? Explain your answer.

ANALYTICAL AND INTERNET EXERCISES

1. Visit coca-cola.com. The website gives the viewer the option to switch to the websites for various countries. This option is typically a tab at the top right. Using the tab, explore websites for various countries. Look at least-developed country websites, websites for countries on each continent, and websites for emerging markets. Based on an in-depth review of at least five websites, discuss how Coca-Cola changes the website content to reflect local technological and cultural preferences.

2. Youtube.com contains videos from throughout the world. Search for consumer-generated videos from various countries. Vary the countries based on factors of your choosing, but be certain to include countries that are different. Examining the videos, do you find evidence of cultural convergence, divergence, and/or crossvergence? Use specific examples to support your claims. After finishing, consider how the target market for youtube.com across these markets may or may not explain finding convergence.

3. Tables 16.2 and 16.3 list the gross domestic product growth rates for key developed and key high-growth countries for 2008–2010. Calculate an average level of growth for both groups and then interpret these averages. Also scan the various country specific numbers. Which countries jump out as exceptions? Looking at the high-growth countries, do you find any evidence that CEVITS, EAGLES, or MIST are a better grouping of potential high-growth countries?

4. Examine the websites of five companies that are not based in the United States. Find the organizations' mission statements. Compare the statements in terms of an emphasis on being a global company, a sustainable company, or an ethical company.

▶ ONLINE VIDEOS

Visit **www.sagepub.com/baack** to view these chapter videos:

Video Link 16.1: The Future of YouTube

Video Link 16.2: Technology

Video Link 16.3: The EU and the Sovereign Debt Crisis

🌐 STUDENT STUDY SITE

Visit **www.sagepub.com/baack** to access these additional learning tools:

- Web Quizzes
- eFlashcards
- SAGE Journal Articles
- Country Fact Sheets
- Chapter Outlines
- Interactive Maps

CASE 16 ///

Virgin Galactic and Space Travel

Many of the promises of science fiction have not yet come true. Magical transporters do not allow individuals to travel long distance in the blink of a fuzzy light. Light sabers remain a special effect, as do practical jet packs for personal travel. While consumers will have to wait for many of these advances, the dream of private businesses offering trips to space may become reality in the near future.

Virgin Galactic, under the broader Virgin Group, offers consumers the opportunity to fly into space. The Virgin Group traces its roots to 1970 when Richard Branson, the company founder and current chair, began a small magazine. Moving into mail order records, a recording company, and a retailer (Virgin Records and Virgin Megastores), the group is now truly an international organization with many diversified strategic business units. In forty years, the company has expanded to include more than three hundred different branded companies employing around 50,000 people and operating in thirty countries. Company revenues in 2009 approached $18 billion.[60] Now the Virgin Group is selling tickets to the first space tourists.

Space tourism technology will be complicated. The company proposes the use of two ships to get to space. The first, *WhiteKnightTwo*, launches far into the atmosphere. The second, the *VSS Enterprise*, then disengages from *WhiteKnightTwo* at an altitude around 40,000 feet and glides back to the earth. Currently, the *VSS Enterprise* does not reach space, but an engine is in development to allow for propulsion out of the atmosphere. The rocket, called RocketMotorTwo, marks the final advance needed before commercial flights. Burt Rutan, one of the seminal aeronautical engineers in history, designed the ships. The original versions of the ships, *SpaceShipOne* and *WhiteKnightOne*, won the Ansari X Prize of $10 million to the first ship that entered space twice in a two-week time period.[61]

As of this writing, the company has completed almost fifty test flights since inception in 2004. Almost $250 million has been invested in the project and $150 million more will be spent prior to the first flight.

The average risk for typical space flight is a crash on one out of fifty flights; the company is working hard to improve those numbers before launching the first commercial flight. The hope is for the business to begin sometime in the fall or winter of 2012.

Costing $200,000 per flight, the price, while high, undercuts competitors. The Russian Federal Space Agency charges $30 million plus six months of training for consumers wanting to enter space. For Virgin Galactic tourists, training will take only two days. Consumers would then travel 120 kilometers above the Earth's surface and experience weightlessness for almost six minutes. The ship has been designed with large windows to facilitate viewing.

While less expensive than the only real competitor, buying a $200,000 ticket to travel to space clearly represents a luxury purchase. The high price has limited demand to the global elite. While the majority of purchases have been made by American consumers, Indian, European, Russian, and Middle Eastern consumers have also made purchases. The Abu Dhabi company AABAR Investments owns 30% of Virgin Galactic, and the company is considering building a second spaceport there to take advantage of the extreme levels of wealth in the region.[62]

Book your place in space

and join over 430 Virgin Galactic astronauts who will venture into space

Virgin Galactic may benefit from the United States' withdrawal from space exploration.

To build on this cultural cachet, the company has allied with an online company, introNetworks, to leverage what a company spokesperson called an "exclusive rich community." An online social network website is being designed for exclusive use by ticket purchasers. Options will include sharing videos, personal information, and eventually photos of the trip to space. In prepration for the future launch date, space tourists have enjoyed parties together in various luxurious locales, including islands in the Caribbean. [63]

Demand for the product has been strong. Virgin Galactic has allied with Virtuoso, a luxury travel network, to reach its target market. By March of 2011, more than $10 million worth of tickets had been sold. Consumers are willing to put down a deposit for just the potential to enter space.[64] Time will tell whether these tickets will ever be used for those seeking the excitement of traveling in space.

1. What factors in the international marketing environment, as described in this chapter, might influence the Virgin Galactic company? How will the impact be felt?

2. Visit www.virgin.com/company to see a list of the various companies owned by the Virgin Group. How does Virgin Galactic fit with the overall company? How does the broader Virgin brand help sell Virgin Galactic?

3. Create a marketing plan for Virgin's plan to expand into space travel.

4. Using Figure 16.14, identify strategic and operational standards for the Virgin Group and Virgin Galactic.

Appendix A

Comprehensive Cases

CASE 1   ALPEN BANK

Launching the Credit Card in Romania

V. Kasturi Rangan

Sunru Yong

Introduction

In September 2006, Gregory Carle sat pensively at his desk at Alpen Bank's corporate headquarters in Zurich. The previous evening he and the senior management team had enjoyed themselves dining late above the picturesque Limmat Valley, but now it was time to focus his attention on the task at hand. As Alpen's country manager for Romania, Carle was contemplating a credit card launch in the Romania market, which he would pursue if he could be confident that it would add €5 million of annual profit to the Consumer Bank segment within two years (see **Exhibit 1** for a summary of the financial performance of the Consumer Bank segment of Alpen Bank in Romania).

Carle had been with Alpen since 1992, when he joined the bank's global marketing group. His appointment in 2000 to country manager for Romania coincided with the bank's opening its first branch in the capital city of Bucharest. Since then, Carle had overseen the opening of 14 additional branches in Romania, with Alpen Bank developing a reputation for excellence in serving affluent clientele. In addition to basic deposit, checking, and personal loan services, customers had access to a wealth management program composed of financial planning and investment products.

The idea of a credit card for Romanian consumers was not new. Historically, Alpen management had balked at launching a card business due to low per-capita income levels, a poorly developed infrastructure of point-of-sale terminals, and the population's inexperience with consumer credit. The country's imminent entry into the European Union had led to a reassessment of this decision. However, Richard Tschumperlin, head of the bank's International Consumer Businesses and Carle's boss, remained skeptical that it was time for Alpen to introduce a card business:

> I'm not sure there is enough of a market there. Are there enough households with

HBS Professor V. Kasturi Rangan and writer Sunru Yong prepared this case solely as a basis for class discussion and not as an endorsement, a source of primary data, or an illustration of effective or ineffective management. The authors thank Judy Bei of Citibank (HBS MBA 2001) and Rob Chen of Visa (HBS MBA 1999) for their valuable contributions to the development of this case. This case, though based on real events, is fictionalized, and any resemblance to actual persons or entities is coincidental. There are occasional references to actual companies in the narration.

	2003	2004	2005
Net revenue	66.0	82.0	87.5
Fees/commissions/insurance	4.0	6.9	13.1
Customer net revenue	70.0	88.9	100.6
Net credit losses	9.8	11.5	14.4
Credit collection	3.3	3.9	4.9
Total credit cycle	13.2	15.5	19.3
Delivery expense	47.0	54.5	57.9
Other revenue/(expense)	(4.9)	(5.5)	(6.7)
Earnings before tax	4.9	13.4	16.7
Customer liabilities (€M)	2,343	2,745	3,000
Customer assets (€M)	1,640	1,922	2,400
Average total assets (€M)	1,875	2,232	2,573
Full-time equivalent employees	564	611	705
Number of accounts (000)	209	256	297
Number of customers (000)	157	179	201
Number of branches	12	13	15

Exhibit 1: Alpen Bank Romanian Consumer Segment Performance (€ millions)

enough money? How much would it cost us to build a customer base? We have been very successful building a profitable banking business for the wealthy—over 200,000 customers in a country with just 7.7 million households, which is great penetration. I worry that pursuing this credit card idea would be a risky distraction."

Unlike Tschumperlin, Carle believed a credit card business would be an important growth vehicle, but he was aware of the skepticism within the Zurich headquarters. Certainly, he had to consider the financial and reputational costs of any missteps. He would need convincing analysis to win support from the Zurich team. If he recommended a "go" for the decision, he had to articulate a compelling business strategy with clear product positioning and a strong economic case.

Credit Card Industry Background

The credit card industry comprises four key parties that work together to provide card transaction services: networks or card associations, merchant acquirers, merchants, and card issuers:

Networks/card associations are the backbone of the payment system and enable transactions to be cleared by connecting merchants, merchant acquirers, and card issuers. Visa and MasterCard are the two most extensive networks and set the operating rules by which all parties in the system abide.

Merchant acquirers are the distribution and sales arm of the payments industry and are frequently affiliated with banks. They sign up **merchants** for card acceptance and provide the support that merchants require to process card transactions: point-of-sale terminals, data transmission, payment authorization, and payment settlement.

Merchants are the restaurants, retailers, gas stations, etc., that accept cards.

Card issuers are typically banks, and they own the relationship with the cardholders themselves. Issuers authorize payments and bill cardholders. As members of the Visa/MasterCard associations, banks must abide by card-logo design standards, but it is left to their discretion to decide on branding, positioning, pricing, and loyalty programs.

Revenue in the card payments industry is determined by transaction volume. A percentage of every transaction, called the "merchant discount," is taken and split among the merchant acquirer, network association, and card issuer. Hence merchant acquirers seek to sign up attractive merchants with frequent transactions and high "per-ticket" spending, while Visa and MasterCard encourage customers to use their cards for every purchase.[1] Similarly, card issuers benefit from the amount spent by the cardholder, receiving a portion of the merchant discount known as "interchange." Merchants, on the other hand, tend to prefer cash except when card acceptance will encourage their customers to spend more (see **Exhibit 2** for a representation of a typical transaction cycle).

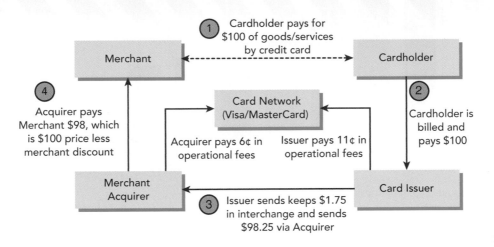

Exhibit 2: Typical Credit Card Transaction Cycle

In addition to interchange revenue, card issuers—the role under consideration by Alpen Bank—also generate revenue by charging annual fees, penalty fees, and interest income. Interest income is charged to cardholders who do not pay off their full balance each month, but instead use their credit cards for "revolving" financing. Card issuers profit from having such "revolver" customers and may attract customers by offering temporary low-interest financing. However, the potential profit of "revolvers" must be managed against the risk of default, which can be significant and costly, particularly during economic downturns.[2]

Romanian Credit Card Market

In the early 2000s, the executive team in Zurich felt that Romania lacked credit-card growth potential relative to other emerging markets. Consumer spending was largely cash-based, and merchant acceptance of card payments was low. Furthermore, the Romanian consumer lacked experience in managing credit. This made it difficult to determine credit limits and set interest rates that would attract customers, yet fully protect Alpen Bank from default risk. Carle described the conditions the bank faced:

In 2000, Romania was just emerging from a very tough three-year recession. Average per-capita income was just 3,500 RON [approximately €1,700]. It was true that the middle class was growing, but it was very small, and less than half of the population was urban. We discussed it with the Zurich team, but decided our efforts were better spent developing the branch banking business and building an upscale customer base than in building a credit card business.

However, the macroeconomic trends during the first half of the decade were encouraging. Rapid economic growth and rising incomes, particularly among the emerging middle- and upper-middle class, had dramatically increased total disposable income. An independent consumer behavior study indicated that over one-third of Romanian households were likely to purchase branded imports from the EU rather than lower-priced domestic products, and in Bucharest there was growing interest in luxury goods.

Consumers were also increasingly likely to use cards instead of cash. In 2006, total financial cards, including both debit and credit cards, grew by 35% over the prior year, and there were an estimated 9.5 million cards in circulation in Romania. In addition, the infrastructure required for a payments system was rapidly developing, and by 2006 Romania had approximately 8,000 ATMs and 150,000 point-of-sale terminals for card transactions. Even with such growth, the market remained underpenetrated relative to other central and eastern European countries (see **Exhibit 3** for cards-per-household data).

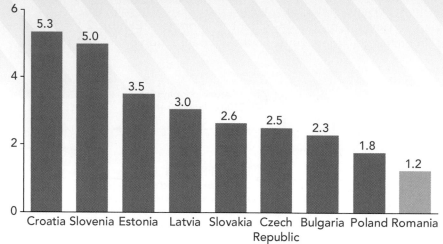

Financial cards per household (Debit + Credit)

Exhibit 3: Cards per household in Central and Eastern Europe

The vast majority of cards in circulation were debit cards, and many cardholders used their cards exclusively for cash withdrawals, rather than the purchases needed to drive up revenue for card issuers. However, Carle and his team believed the Romanian market was poised for further growth in financial cards overall, and in credit cards specifically. Indeed, competing Romanian banks had been marketing credit cards for several years already. Actual usage rates of the cards remained quite low, since many merchants still required cash only, but it was evident that other banks were bullish on the prospects of a Romanian credit card business (see **Exhibit 4** for data on card issuances from competing banks).

	Credit Cards	Credit Card Utilization
Romanian Commercial Bank (BCR)	180,000	10%
Raifeissen Bank	200,000	70%
Bancpost	29,000	6%
Romanian Bank for Development (BRD)	606,000	27%
Estimated total credit cards, Romania	1,710,000	20%

Exhibit 4: Credit Card Issuances, Romania (2006)

Credit Card Positioning and Economics

In addition to determining whether to enter the credit card market at all, Carle had to make a recommendation on the positioning of Alpen Bank's credit card. Clearly, only a subset of the 18.6 million adults in Romania would actually want and qualify for a credit card. Alpen Bank's existing customer base was affluent and was likely an easier segment to target, but Carle was unsure whether a credit card business could be viable without marketing to the broader middle class (see **Exhibit 5** for income distribution data). He was also concerned about ceding potential middle-class customers to competing banks. The other leading banks in Romania had tiered offerings, with both standard and premium cards. Carle commented:

Today's middle class may become the affluent customers of tomorrow. We have seen in other emerging markets that credit cards tend to be "stickier" than in developed countries—consumers are less likely to switch from one credit card to another. Do we need to build a credit card business that also targets the middle class? Does that fit with Alpen Bank's premium image?

Income inequality was increasing in Romania, and the top 10% of households by income had nearly 24% of the wealth. These potential customers had net incomes of at least €500 per month and were typically active, career-oriented professionals who were increasingly conscious of their image and sought goods and services that matched their status. These customers were the most attractive for credit card issuers. They were less price-sensitive about annual fees and more likely to be experienced with low levels of consumer debt. They were also likely to use their cards with greater frequency and for higher-average tickets, and premium cards carried by the affluent could command higher interchange rates.[3]

Middle-class households that were potential credit card customers earned over €200 monthly. They were a mix of young professionals and families that valued quality, but were more willing to compromise and make price-driven decisions. While many were interested in having credit cards, Alpen Bank's experience in other emerging markets showed that actual card utilization was significantly lower for middle-class customers than for the affluent. Carle suspected that the relatively low utilization rate of credit cards in circulation in Romania was due to middle-class customers.

Annual Income (€)	% of Population
<1,500	23.2%
1,500 – 2,000	11.9%
2,000 – 3,000	18.8%
3,000 – 4,500	18.2%
4,500 – 6,000	15.0%
6,000 – 7,000	6.6%
7,000 – 10,000	3.8%
10,000 – 15,000	1.2%
>15,000	1.3%

Exhibit 5: Distribution of Annual Income, Romania (2005)

Serving them could mean lower interest income and interchange for the banks.

Credit card revenue would be derived from several streams: joining/annual fees, penalty fees for late payments, interest payments, and interchange. Several country managers in the Asia-Pacific region had chosen to waive the joining fee entirely when launching their credit card business, but Carle believed that the premium image of Alpen Bank in Romania would allow for joining and annual fees without significantly hurting customer acquisition and retention. Using Alpen Bank's experience in Poland, Bulgaria, and the Czech Republic as a guide, Carle's team modeled the net revenue impact of the potential credit card business (see **Table A** for estimated revenue by cardholder).

SEGMENT	ANNUAL INCOME (€)	REVENUE PER CARDHOLDER		
		INTEREST REVENUE (€)	OTHER REVENUE (€)	ANNUAL REVENUE (€)
Middle Class	3,000–4,500	37.13	23.50	60.63
Affluent	4,500–6,000	86.63	36.75	123.38
Most Affluent	6,000+	148.50	61.25	209.75

Table A: **A Net Revenue Impact Estimates, 2007**

Note: "Other revenue" includes fees and interchange.

Market Entry Costs

The costs for Alpen Bank to enter the market included investments in direct marketing, advertising, and support infrastructure. Carle knew that building a customer base would require a direct marketing plan with a multi-prong effort, each with its advantages and drawbacks:

Direct mail could target credit card applications to the intended audience, resulting in a higher yield, but it tended to be more expensive than other methods.

"Take-ones" were brochures offered via countertop displays at various retailers and offered a very broad reach. However, because this was made available to the general public, many applicants would not qualify for bank credit.

Free-standing inserts (FSIs) were newspaper and magazine inserts or bind-ins that were inexpensive to circulate, but tended to have a very low response rate.

Direct sales efforts through telemarketing enabled Alpen Bank to target both existing customers and high-potential new customers, but required considerable investment in each salesperson. Carle estimated he needed a team of 10 sales representatives, each making 25 calls per day.

Branch cross-selling was a targeted sale to existing customers who entered a bank branch. This leveraged Alpen Bank's fixed costs and because it was a more personal sale, Carle expected the response rate to be much higher.

Carle hired a market research agency to estimate the rate at which prospects would respond to, and qualify for, a credit card given the marketing channel through which they were reached (see **Table B** for customer acquisition estimates).

SEGMENT	UNIT COST (€)	REVENUE PER CARDHOLDER		
		PROSPECTS REACHED	RESPONSE RATE	QUALIFICATION RATE
Direct Mail	0.50	2,500,000	3.0%	60.0%
Take One	0.10	2,000,000	2.5%	30.0%
FSIs	0.05	3,500,000	1.5%	30.0%
Direct Sales	€3000/rep	60,000	25.0%	60.0%
Branch Cross-Sell	1.00	50,000	50.0%	90.0%

Table B: **Customer Acquisition Estimates, Year 1 (All Customers)**

Targeting affluent customers only would reduce the available direct-mail prospects by half and reduce the take-one and FSI qualification rate by half. Based on conversion rates in other central and eastern European markets, the agency estimated that 85% of prospects who qualified for the credit card would convert into customers. Alpen Bank's experience in other central and eastern European markets was that using several direct marketing channels was necessary to build a customer base. Carle wondered whether it made sense to be aggressive and use all five avenues, or whether there were meaningful savings in being more selective. Direct mail, in particular, appeared to be quite expensive.

To complement the direct marketing program, Alpen would also need to invest in advertising. A €2 million budget could support targeted magazine advertisements and 30-second television spots on the major channels during the holidays— Christmas, Great Union Day (celebrating the union of Transylvania with Romania), and National Anthem Day. The magazine and television advertising would not only generate interest among prospective card applicants but also help convert prospects already in the sales pipeline.

Beyond the customer acquisition and advertising costs, Alpen Bank needed to invest in an in-country infrastructure support, and incremental fixed overhead costs were substantial. Costs associated with new staff, computer systems, customer support, and other overhead costs were estimated at €5 million annually to support the first 50,000 customers. For every additional 50,000 customers, Carle would need to spend €750,000 per year for overhead. The direct variable costs associated with each cardholder included billing, loyalty program administration, collections, fraud, and loan default and were estimated at €20 per customer. With every additional 50,000 customers, economies of scale would reduce the direct costs by €2.50 per card.

The Decision

Carle had one week to prepare his presentation to Richard Tschumperlin on whether Alpen should launch a new credit card in the Romanian market. It was clear that the heart of the presentation would rest on his analysis of the economic opportunity. In order to win approval, he would need to demonstrate that generating €5 million in profit within two years was a realistic objective. What level of customer acquisition would be required to break-even, and how quickly would the business generate profit beyond break-even? How should the new card be positioned, particularly given its current upscale customer base? How would the credit card opportunity compare to focusing on the core business of banking services for the affluent? A compelling business case would need to address these issues for Alpen Bank to proceed with confidence.

NOTES

1. In the payments industry, the term "ticket" refers to the actual amount spent in a transaction. For example, electronics stores have high average tickets, whereas dry cleaners typically have low tickets.

2. Cardholders fall into two generic categories: "transactors" and "revolvers." Transactors use their cards for cashless transactions and perhaps to earn loyalty rewards (e.g., airline miles, cash rebates), but pay off their full balance each month. With transactors, banks must profit from interchange and fees alone.

3. Merchants pay a "merchant discount fee," calculated as a percentage of the transaction spend, which includes the interchange rate that is paid to the card issuer. Premium cards carried by affluent cardholders (e.g., American Express or Diner's Club, historically) are more attractive customers to merchants, and thus issuers can command a higher interchange rate.

CASE QUESTIONS

1. How do demand conditions in Romania impact the decision to enter the market with credit cards?

2. How does Romania's infrastructure impact Alpen's decision regarding expanding credit cards?

3. What kind of product/market growth strategy is Alpen considering with the entry into the credit card market in Romania? Do you think that this is a good approach to pursue?

4. What are the bases for segmentation that are relevant to Alpen's decision in this case?

5. Do you think that the direct marketing strategies presented in this case would work well for Alpen entering the Romanian market? Why or why not? What techniques would you recommend and why?

CASE 2   UNITED CEREAL

Lora Brill's Eurobrand Challenge

Christopher A. Bartlett

Carole Carlson

Lora Brill, United Cereal's European vice president, was alone in her office early on a cold March morning in 2010. "I've given approval to a dozen big product launches in my career," she thought. "But the implications that this one has for our European strategy and organization make it by far the most difficult I've had to make."

The decision related to Healthy Berry Crunch, a new breakfast cereal that the French subsidiary wanted to launch. But Europe's changing market and competitive conditions had led Brill to consider making this the company's first coordinated multimarket Eurobrand launch. It was a possibility that had surfaced some equally challenging organizational questions. "Well it's only 7 AM," Brill thought to herself, smiling. "I have until my lunch appointment to decide!"

United Cereal: Breakfast Cereal Pioneer

In 2010, United Cereal celebrated its 100th birthday. Established in 1910 by Jed Thomas, an immigrant grocer from England, the company's first product was a packaged mix of cracked wheat, rolled oats, and malt flakes that Thomas sold in his Kalamazoo, Michigan, grocery store. UC, as it was known in the industry, eventually diversified into snack foods, dairy products, drinks and beverages, frozen foods, and baked goods. By 2010 UC was a $9 billion business, but breakfast cereals still accounted for one-third of its revenues and even more of its profits.

UC'S CORPORATE VALUES, POLICIES, AND PRACTICES

Thomas grew the company with strong set of values that endured through its history, and "commitment, diligence, and loyalty" were watchwords in UC. As a result, it attracted people who wanted to make a career with the company, and it promoted managers from within.

Among its managers United Cereal instilled a strong commitment to "The UC Way," a set of time-tested policies, processes, and practices embedded in iconic company phrases. For example, "Listen to the customer" was a deeply rooted belief that led UC to become a pioneer in the use of consumer research and focus groups. "Spot the trend, make the market" was another iconic phrase reflecting the high value placed on extensive market testing prior to launching new products. Finally, the value of "Honoring the past while embracing the future" led UC to reject the conventional wisdom that processed food brands had fixed life cycles. Through continuous innovation in marketing and product development, many of its products remained market leaders despite being more than half a century old.

United Cereal had a well-earned reputation as an innovator. During its 100-year history, its R&D labs had secured more product and process patents than any other competitor. The company had also pioneered the "brand management" system in the food industry, giving brand managers leadership of cross-functional teams that included manufacturing, marketing, and other functions. Each brand was managed as a profit center and was constantly measured against other brands. Brand managers also competed for R&D and product development resources.

Although this system reduced lateral communication, vertical communication was strong, and top managers were very involved in seemingly mundane brand decisions. For example, advertising copy and label changes could require up to a dozen sign-offs before obtaining final approval at the corporate VP level. "It's due to the high value we attach to our brands and our image," explained a senior executive. "But it's also because we give our brand managers responsibility at a very young age." While the company took few risks (a failed launch could cost millions even in small markets), it balanced deliberate cautiousness with a willingness to invest in products it decided to support. "The competitors can see us coming months ahead and miles away," the senior executives said. "But they know that when we get there, we'll bet the farm."

THE BREAKFAST CEREAL MARKET

Breakfast cereal was in its infancy when UC was founded, but it soon grew to be one of the great food commercialization successes of the 20th century. From the 1890s when Keith Kellogg created corn flakes in his attempt to improve the diet of hospital patients, the industry had grown to achieve worldwide revenues exceeding $21 billion in 2009. The U.S. industry included more than 30 companies with combined annual revenues of $12 billion. But just five players accounted for 80% of sales.

The industry recognized two categories of cereals—hot and ready-to-eat. The latter accounted for 90% of sales in both the United States and Europe. In this highly competitive industry, more than 10% of revenues was spent on advertising and marketing. Profitability also depended on operating efficiently, managing materials costs, and maximizing retail shelf space. Larger companies had significant advantages in purchasing, distribution, and marketing.

In the fight for share, several new-product introductions typically occurred each year. Developing a new brand was time-intensive and expensive, typically taking two to four years. Brand extensions—for example, General Mills's creation of Honey Nut Cheerios—were generally less expensive and less risky due to scale economies that could be leveraged in both production and marketing. But for most U.S. cereal companies, growth was increasingly coming from expansion into new offshore markets, and UC was no exception.

UC's European Operations

United Cereal entered European markets in 1952 by acquiring an English baked goods company. (Its European offices were still in London.) Over the next 30 years, UC expanded its European presence, typically by acquiring an established company with local market distribution, and then growing it by introducing products from the U.S. line. By 2009, Europe accounted for 20% of United Cereal's worldwide sales.

EUROPEAN INDUSTRY AND COMPETITIVE STRUCTURE

Europe's $7 billion breakfast cereal market in 2010 had been overlaid on a variety of national tastes and breakfast traditions—cold meats and cheese in the Netherlands, pastries in Greece, bacon and eggs in Britain, and croissants in France. As a result, per capita consumption of cereals varied significantly across markets from 8 kg. a year in the United Kingdom to 0.5 kg. a year in Italy. Channels also varied widely by country, with supermarkets and hypermarkets accounting for more than 80% of grocery sales in Germany, 37% in France, and only 17% in Italy.

U.S.-based companies Kellogg and United Cereal were the largest two competitors in the European market with 26% and 20% share, respectively. Cereal Partners, a joint venture between General Mills and Nestlé, ranked third with 17%, and UK-based Weetabix trailed these leaders with 7%. Numerous smaller manufacturers divided the remaining 30% of the market.

United Cereal regarded Kellogg as its toughest competitor. Operating through strong national subsidiaries, Kellogg used its volume to lower operating costs and to establish and maintain shelf space. Cereal Partners sold brands that included Cheerios and Shredded Wheat, and leveraged

Nestlé's technical expertise and its European retailer relationships to compete. Although Weetabix was a smaller private company, like the bigger competitors, it also relied on strong branding and promotions to gain market share. Smaller competitors tended to hold niche market positions, but often challenged larger players with targeted price promotions.

UC'S EUROPE STRATEGY AND ORGANIZATION

Major differences across European markets had led United Cereal to establish national subsidiaries, each led by a country manager (CM) who operated with wide latitude to make product and marketing decisions that would maximize the subsidiary's local profit. Based on their market understanding, these CMs usually selected from United Cereal's stable of more than 100 branded products, adapting them to the local situation.

Expecting its CMs to conform to its embedded values, policies, and procedures, United Cereal built its subsidiaries as "mini UCs"—exact replicas of the parent organization staffed by managers well-versed in UC's corporate values and practices. So while CMs were able to customize products, adjust manufacturing processes, and adapt advertising and promotions, they had to do so while respecting the "UC Way."

This approach unleashed CMs' entrepreneurial instincts and led to strong penetration in most national markets. While many products flourished through such local customization, over time, wide differences in product profiles and market strategies became problematic. For example, in the U.K., the Wake Up! instant coffee brand was formulated as a mild to medium roast beverage promoted as "the perfect milk coffee." But in France and Italy it was sold as a dark roast product and advertised as "the instant espresso." And differences in the positioning of Mother Hubbard's Pies resulted in it being offered as a high-end dessert in Germany, while in the U.K. it was priced aggressively and positioned as "a convenient everyday treat."

INCREASING PRICE AND PROFIT PRESSURE

Over the preceding decade, the cereal market in Europe had become increasingly competitive. While total grocery sales had remained remarkably stable through the 2008-09 global recession, all manufacturers had seen their product mix shift toward their lower-priced offerings. Market growth slowed to less than 1% annually, and UC experienced growing price and promotion pressure from Kellogg and Cereal Partners in virtually every country in which it operated. As margins came under pressure, achieving lower costs and implementing more efficient processes became vital. (See **Exhibits 1** and **2** for financial performance.)

	2007	2008	2009
Sales	8,993,204	9,069,242	9,254,329
COGS	4,226,806	4,271,613	4,445,671
SG&A	2,787,893	2,856,811	2,868,842
Depreciation and amortization	362,500	375,000	370,173
Operating Income	1,616,005	1,565,818	1,569,643
Interest expense	44,120	45,667	46,271
Other income	19,653	22,500	18,508
Income before taxes	1,679,778	1,633,985	1,634,422
Income taxes	410,232	415,450	420,000
Net income	1,269,546	1,218,535	1,214,422
Total Assets	6,313,000	6,215,890	6,300,000
Long-term debt	1,021,300	998,100	1,050,000
Shareholder's equity	1,722,900	1,786,200	1,751,400

Exhibit 1: United Cereal Selected Financial Results (USD in 000s)

2009 Sales and SG&A Expense

	United Cereal	Europe	France
Sales	9,254,329	1,850,866	388,682
SG&A			
Advertising and Other Marketing	1,526,964	378,687	75,737
Product Development	188,815	54,701	5,553
Other SG&A	1,153,063	216,263	46,071
SG&A subtotal	2,868,842	649,651	127,361
SG&A as a % of Sales	31.00%	35.10%	32.77%

Exhibit 2: United Cereal SG&A by Market (dollars in 000s)

In this changing landscape, some of UC's historical policies came under the microscope. The company's focus on local products and markets, with its need for significant marketing and product development teams in each country, had led to a situation where sales, general and administrative (SG&A) expenses were 25% higher than in the U.S. operations. Furthermore, due to the high costs of developing and launching new products for single country markets, the pace of major new product introductions had slowed considerably in recent years. Lacking the resources for either large-scale market testing or new product launches, most CMs now favored product extensions over new product introductions, and many increasingly relied on cost reductions in their existing portfolios to maintain profits. It was a situation that raised concerns.

UNITED CEREAL RESPONSE

The earliest response to these problems had been initiated by Arne Olsen, a Norwegian appointed as UC's European VP in 2002 with a mandate to invigorate the product portfolio and reverse declining profitability. Olsen quickly reorganized R&D, reinforcing the European research facility near UC Europe's headquarters in London. To link these food scientists working on basic issues with the subsidiary-based technologists refining and testing products in local markets, Olsen created a European Technical Team (ETT) for each major product group. Each ETT was composed of the strongest local product development technologists teamed with central R&D scientists to provide overall direction

on European product development. To facilitate collaboration, Olsen encouraged transfers between the London team and the country offices, and also strengthened relationships with the R&D labs in Kalamazoo.

In 2004, Olsen expanded this technical program into what he called the "Europeanization Initiative," aimed squarely at product market strategies. His first test was UC's frozen fruit juice line, which had languished for years. He was convinced that there was little difference in tastes for fruit juice across markets, and that there were significant benefits in standardizing the products as well as their marketing, promotion, and advertising. He transferred a senior manager from Germany to the European headquarters and gave him responsibility to standardize products, develop a coordinated Europewide strategy, and oversee implementation across subsidiaries.

The experiment was a disaster. Local CMs perceived the initiative as a direct challenge to their local autonomy—a belief made worse by the domineering personality of the individual they called the "European Juice Nazi." While they reluctantly implemented his imposed product positioning and advertising directives, they provided minimal support from the local sales forces that remained under their control. Unsurprisingly, the frozen juice category stagnated, and eventually responsibility for juice products was returned to the countries.

In 2006, Olsen was transferred to Kalamazoo in a senior marketing role, and Lora Brill, former UK country manager, became the new European vice president. In the aftermath of the 2008/2009 recession, with continuing pressure on margins, Brill needed to leverage marketing resources—the largest controllable expense in subsidiary budgets. Eventually, she too became convinced that the coordinated European approach that had succeeded in product development could be adapted for product marketing. It was in this context that she began to pursue an idea she referred to as the "Eurobrand" concept. And in 2010, a proposal by the French subsidiary to launch Healthy Berry Crunch offered the possibility of a first test case.

The Healthy Berry Crunch Project

In the late 1990s, aging baby boomers took an increased interest in natural, healthy foods in both the United States and Europe. This created a challenge for cereal companies whose highly processed products were typically high in sugar. In response, some felt that the addition of fruit could provide "a halo of health." The main technical problem was that fruit's moisture content made it difficult to maintain the crispness and shelf life of cereal. But a solution was found in the use of freeze-dried fruits, which also retained their color and shape in a cereal mix.

THE FRENCH OPPORTUNITY

In 2003, Kellogg introduced Special K with freeze-dried strawberries in the U.K., and in 2007 Cereal Partners launched Berry Burst Cheerios. Seeing interest in healthy breakfast foods growing in France, UC's French country manager Jean-Luc Michel felt there could be a market for an organic fruit-based cereal in his market. Although Kellogg's Special K with Strawberries had been launched in France in 2006, to date it was alone in this new segment.

In 2008, Michel started initial product development and testing in France, later involving the ETT to develop detailed specifications. He recommended an organic blueberry-based cereal as a product extension of Healthy Crunch—a UC cereal already positioned in the health-conscious adult segment but experiencing no growth in recent years. He felt the use of blueberries, with their well-known antioxidant qualities, would reinforce the positioning.

In keeping with UC policy, as soon as the product was ready, Michel implemented a full-scale test market in Lyon. (See **Exhibit 3** for test market results.) Results were mixed, with some consumers finding the berries too tart. With the "intention to repurchase" rate below UC's 60% minimum target, an alternate raspberry-based product was developed but proved too expensive to manufacture. So a sweeter blueberry version was taste-tested with focus groups in six French cities. While lacking the validated full test-market data UC policy required, Michel felt focus group data indicating a 64% intention to repurchase was very promising. He was ready to launch:

> It's clearly a big improvement on our initial test market data. But this is a new product concept, so any test only provides a general indication. In a fast-growing category like this, we need to launch now before competitors preempt us. . . . We've been in development and testing for more than a year. We can't wait three months more to mount another full-scale test market. Besides, my budget won't support the $2 million it would cost.

THE EUROPEAN DEBATE

Even before Michel set about obtaining launch approval, Brill was aware of his intention and had begun exploring the idea of launching Healthy Berry Crunch Europewide to test her nascent Eurobrand concept. Her director of finance had estimated that implementing coordinated European product market strategies could result in staff reductions and other savings that would cut product development and marketing costs by 10% to 15% over three years. Since these costs were running above 23% of sales in Europe, the savings could be very significant.

Brill next met with Kurt Jaeger, her Division VP responsible for Northern Europe and the person she regarded as Europe's most knowledgeable about breakfast cereal strategy. He was strongly in favor of a coordinated European rollout:

> Our strategy of responding to local market differences was right for its time, but not necessarily today. Consumer tastes are converging, old cultural habits are disappearing, and EU regulation of labeling, advertising, and general marketing practices is eroding market differences . . . I've had my CMs in Germany and Benelux conduct consumer panels on Healthy

Lyon Test Market: September – November 2009

Month	Shipments in Stock Taking Units (000s) (volume index)	
	Actual	Target
September	4.6	1.9
October	4.0	2.5
November	3.1	4.0

Share %	
Actual	Target
1.5	0.6
1.3	0.8
1.0	1.3

Use and Awareness (After 3 months, 188 responses)	
Ever consumed	14
Consumed in past 4 weeks	4
Ever purchased[a]	3
Purchased past 4 weeks	2
Advertising awareness	19
Brand awareness	28

Attitude Data (After 3 months, 126 responses: Free sample and purchase users)	
Taste: cereal	65/11[b]
Taste: fruit	49/19
Health aspect	37/4
Form, consistency	13/6

Intent to Repurchase (After 3 months: 126 responses from free and sample purchase users)	%
"I plan to repurchase the product in the next three months"	56/26/18[c]

Exhibit 3: Test Market and Consumer Panel Results

[a] Difference between consumed and purchased data due to free sampling

[b] Number of unsolicited and unduplicated comments Favorable/Unfavorable in user interviews (e.g., among 126 consumers interviewed, 65 commented favorably on the cereal taste and 11 commented negatively)

[c] Percentage split Yes/No/Unsure

Berry Crunch. The samples are small, but it's encouraging that their results are similar to the French panel findings . . . Our biggest risk is the competition. The PodCafé debacle shows that they are way ahead of us in coordinating European strategy.

The "PodCafé debacle" to which Jaeger referred had occurred following UC's introduction of its innovative PodCafé single-serve coffee pods for home espresso machines in Germany in 2003. But by the time the French subsidiary decided to launch its version in 2006, and Italy the following year, the coffee pod market had become crowded with copycat products, and United Cereal's product was relegated to a third-place share in both of those key markets.

But Jorge Sanchez, the Division VP for Southern Europe to whom Jean-Luc Michel reported, was less enthusiastic about the Eurobrand idea. He told Brill:

Although Jean-Luc has only been in his CM role for 18 months, I think his enthusiasm for Healthy Berry Crunch is just the kind of entrepreneurial initiative we want from our CMs. But a launch like this will cost at least $20 million in France—10 times my approval level, and twice yours. Frankly, I have real concerns about whether his budget can support it . . . . Even if France goes ahead, my Italian CM tells me he doesn't think he could get shelf space for a specialty cereal. And our struggling Spanish subsidiary is still in recovery from the recession. There's no way they have a budget for a new launch now.

Brill also heard from her old boss, Arne Olsen, who told her that word of the proposed French launch had already reached to Kalamazoo. Olsen thought she should know about a conversation he recently had with the company's executive vice president:

> Lou's an old traditionalist who has spent his whole career here in corporate headquarters, and sees himself as a guardian of the company's values. He told me over lunch that he's worried that Europe is rushing into this launch, shortcutting the product, consumer, and market research that has ensured UC's past successes. His is one of the signatures you'll need to authorize the launch, so I thought you should know his views.

THE ORGANIZATIONAL CHALLENGE

As she listened to this different advice, Brill was also aware that her decision would be based on organizational as well as strategic considerations. Having witnessed the disastrous European fruit juice strategy years earlier, she was determined to learn from its failure. In meetings with her HR director, she began to develop some alternative organizational proposals.

For some time, she had been planning to expand the responsibilities of her three regional vice presidents. In addition to their current roles supervising subsidiaries by region, she proposed giving each of them Europewide coordinating responsibility for several products. For example, Kurt Jaeger, who was responsible for UC's subsidiaries in Germany, Austria, Switzerland, and Benelux, would also oversee the cross-market coordination of

strategy for cereals, snacks, and baked goods. For the first time, the structure would introduce a European perspective to product strategy. But Brill was conscious that she did not want to dilute the responsibility of CMs and clearly described the VPs' new-product roles as advisory. She hoped that the status, position, and experience of these senior managers would ensure that their input would be carefully considered. (**Exhibit 4** shows the proposed organization.)

Conscious that these changes would not be sufficient to implement her Eurobrand concept, Brill begin to explore the idea of creating Eurobrand Teams modeled on the European Technical Teams that had proved so effective. The proposed teams would be composed of brand managers from each country subsidiary that sold the product, representatives of the European central functional departments including manufacturing, R&D, purchasing and logistics, and a representative from the appropriate regional division VP's office. They would be chaired by the brand manager of an assigned "lead country," selected based on the individual's experience and the subsidiary's resources, expertise, and strong market position in the brand.

Brill envisioned that European brand strategies would be developed by the relevant Eurobrand Teams rather than by someone at European headquarters. This meant that these teams would decide product formulation, market positioning, packaging, advertising, pricing, and promotions. In her vision, the teams would also be responsible for finding ways to reduce costs and increase brand profitability.

As she tested these ideas with her HR director and others in the London office, the European VP received some positive feedback but also heard some criticisms and concerns. Some wondered whether the CMs might still see this as a challenge to their local authority; others raised the question of whether the allocation of "lead country" roles might not concentrate power in a few large subsidiaries like Germany; and still others questioned whether teams with a dozen or more members would function effectively.

But the strongest pushback Brill received was from James Miller, the Division VP responsible for U.K. and Scandinavian countries. "This all sounds far too complex for me," he told her. "If we're serious about competing as one company in Europe, let's forget about all these teams and just move to a

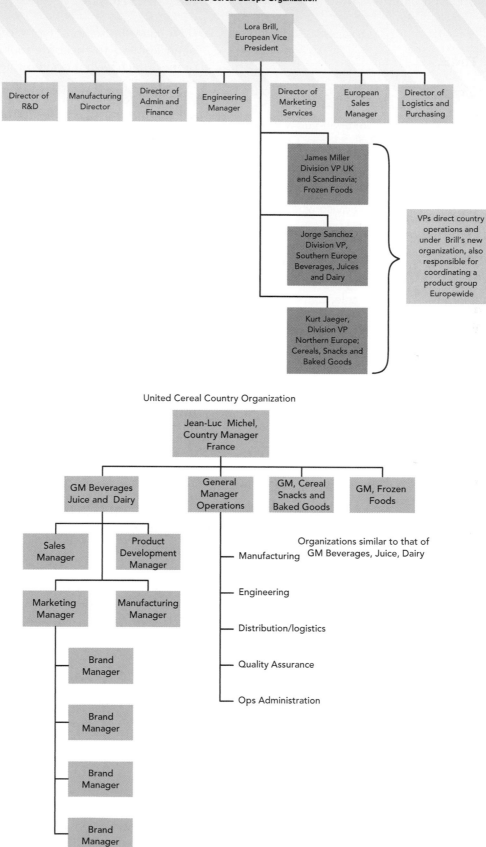

Exhibit 4: Organization Chart

European product structure with someone clearly in charge."

DECISION TIME

On a cold March morning, Brill arrived in her office at 7 AM and began checking her e-mail. At the top of the inbox was a message from Jean-Luc Michel to Jorge Sanchez with a copy to Brill: "Jorge: One of my sales reps just heard a rumor that Cereal Partners is planning to launch Berry Burst Cheerios in France. It's now two weeks since I submitted my Healthy Berry Crunch launch request. Can you advise when I might expect a decision? Regards, Jean-Luc."

Brill nodded silently as she checked her appointment schedule for the day and saw that Kurt Jaeger had set up a lunch meeting with her for noon. Her assistant had noted on the calendar entry: "Re. Eurobrand launch decision."

It was clear that both men quite reasonably would be looking for answers today. Should she authorize the launch in France? Should Healthy Berry Crunch become UC's first Eurobrand? And if so, what kind of organization did she need to put in place to ensure its effective implementation? These were big questions, and the stakes were high for both United Cereal and for her career. But Brill realized she had all the information. Now it was decision time.

CASE QUESTIONS

1. How have the various types of market research been applied to the potential launch of Health Berry Crunch? What do you think has been done correctly? Incorrectly? What suggestions would you have for an improved international market research program?

2. What cultural issues are relevant as they apply to cereal purchasing behavior?

3. What type of international brand management pertains to the launch of Health Berry Crunch? Do you agree that the strategy selected is most appropriate?

4. How could the Product and Communication Adaptation Model be applied to this case? Do you agree that standardization is the best method available for the launch of Health Berry Crunch?

5. How do market channels differ for breakfast cereal throughout Europe? How should UC use this information?

6. Do you agree with Brill's decision to institute a new organizational structure for this launch? Why or why not?

7. Should Health Berry Crunch become UC's first "Eurobrand"?

CASE 3   CLAYTON INDUSTRIES

Peter Arnell, Country Manager for Italy

Christopher A. Bartlett

Benjamin H. Barlow

In late September 2009, Peter Arnell, country manager of Clayton SpA, the Italian subsidiary of U.S.-based Clayton Industries, faced some daunting challenges as the global recession took its toll. Sales were down 19%, and after decades of solid returns, Clayton SpA was in its third year of losses, now accumulating at more than $1 million a month.

Arnell's attention was sharpened by the imminent visit of Dan Briggs, Clayton's recently appointed CEO, and Simonne Buis, Arnell's direct boss and President of Clayton Europe. Both expected him to turn around Clayton SpA and position it for future growth. And although he had only been in Italy for just over two months, Arnell knew that Briggs and Buis would want to know exactly what action he intended to take.

The Parent Company: Clayton Industries

Founded in Milwaukee in 1938, Clayton Industries Inc. had built a successful business around window-mounted room air conditioners, which it sold for residential and light-commercial applications. In the early 1980s, management perceived two important growth opportunities—one in the North American commercial sector, and the other in residential and commercial markets in Europe—and took steps to exploit both.

As it expanded abroad, Clayton established its position in Europe by acquiring four companies:

- Corliss, a U.K.-based manufacturer of home heating, ventilation, and air conditioning (HVAC) systems.

- Fontaire, a Brussels-based manufacturer of fans and ventilating equipment.

- Control del Clima, a Barcelona-based manufacturer of climate control products for industrial and commercial applications.

- AeroPuro, a Brescia, Italy-based manufacturer of compression chillers for large commercial, public, and institutional installations. (Chillers are the units at the core of most industrial air conditioners.)

To manage international expansion, Clayton restructured its organization in 1988. All operations in the United States and Canada were placed under Clayton North America, while the European acquisitions reported to a newly created Clayton Europe. Each of these entities was headed by a regional company president. (See **Exhibit 1** for the organizational chart.)

Clayton Europe

In 1989, Clayton Europe adopted the Brussels offices formerly occupied by Fontaire as its headquarters. Recognizing the need for strong management in each country where it had a presence, the new president of Clayton Europe appointed four country managers. They were given responsibility for sales of the full line of Clayton products in their home country and their allocated export markets in Europe.

HBS Professor Christopher A. Bartlett and writer Benjamin H. Barlow prepared this case solely as a basis for class discussion and not as an endorsement, a source of primary data, or an illustration of effective or ineffective management. The authors thank Sisto Merolla (HBS MBA 2002) of Merloni Termosanitari Spa of Fabriano, Italy, for his helpful contributions to the development of this case. This case, though based on real events, is fictionalized, and any resemblance to actual persons or entities is coincidental. There are occasional references to actual companies in the narration.

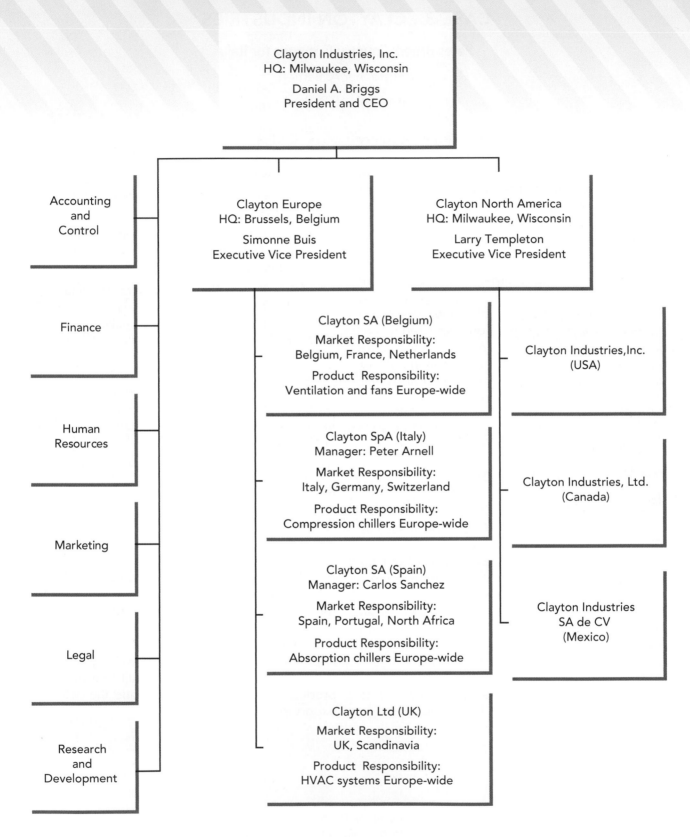

Exhibit 1: Clayton Industries: Organization of Operations, August 2009

Early progress was slow. While the European market for air conditioning began to grow in the 1990s, it was from a low base. Even in 1998, air-conditioning was in only 7% of homes in Italy, and 11% in Spain, compared with U.S. penetration of 71%. Many Europeans saw air conditioning as an expensive American luxury that harmed the environment.

Clayton's slow market penetration also reflected Europeans' different needs and national brand preferences. For example, Clayton's window units (assembled in Belgium from components shipped from the United States) did not sell as well as familiar local brands that Europeans seemed to prefer. And its central AC units also struggled in Europe where few buildings had duct work required for such systems. But a couple of Asian producers had been able to gain penetration in Europe, largely on the basis of price.

As a result of Europeans' strong national brand preferences, the Corliss-sourced HVAC systems and the Fontaire line of fans both sold much better in their home markets than elsewhere in Europe. But no product represented this geographic concentration more strongly than the chiller line built in Italy. A decade after it had been offered to all Clayton's European companies, sales outside Italy accounted for only 12% of the total.

In 2001, Simonne Buis, previously the hard-driving head of the Belgian company, was named president of Clayton Europe. Determined to create a more integrated European organization, her first priority was to increase the operational efficiency of Clayton's diverse portfolio of inherited plants. She set tough targets that required them to slash costs, build scale, or both. Then, to encourage Europe-wide penetration of the entire product line, she informed country managers that in addition to their national sales responsibility, they would now be held responsible for Europe-wide profitability of products produced in their plants. She encouraged them to emerge from their country subsidiary silos and collaborate. The simple geographic-based structure was evolving toward a product-overlaid matrix.

Millions of USD (except where indicated)	2004	2005	2006	2007	2008	2009
Revenues						
Clayton N. America (USA/Canada/Mexico)	565.7	577.1	590.0	598.1	557.7	216.6
% Change		2.0%	2.2%	1.4%	(6.8%)	(22.3%)
% Contribution	63.2%	61.8%	60.7%	59.6%	58.0%	54.7%
Clayton SA (Belgium/France/Netherlands)	107.5	118.6	129.7	142.3	148.7	68.0
% Change		10.3%	9.3%	9.8%	4.4%	(8.5%)
% Contribution	12.0%	12.7%	13.3%	14.2%	15.5%	17.2%
Clayton SpA (Italy/Germany/Switzerland)	125.0	132.5	138.0	141.8	134.3	54.1
% Change		6.0%	4.2%	2.7%	(5.3%)	(19.4%)
% Contribution	14.0%	14.2%	14.2%	14.1%	14.0%	13.7%
Clayton SA (Spain/Portugal/N. Africa)	58.1	62.9	68.1	72.3	72.2	36.0
% Change		8.1%	8.4%	6.2%	(0.1%)	(0.3%)
% Contribution	6.5%	6.7%	7.0%	7.2%	7.5%	9.1%

Clayton Ltd (UK/Scandinavia)	39.3	42.8	45.9	48.3	48.6	21.6
% Change		8.9%	7.2%	5.2%	0.6%	(11.1%)
% Contribution	4.4%	4.6%	4.7%	4.8%	5.1%	5.5%
Total	895.7	933.8	971.7	1,002.8	961.4	396.3
% Change		4.3%	4.1%	3.2%	(4.1%)	(17.6%)
EBITDA						
Clayton N. America (USA/Canada/Mexico)	70.7	69.2	53.1	47.8	27.9	6.5
% Margin	12.5%	12.0%	9.0%	8.0%	5.0%	3.0%
Clayton SA (Belgium/France/Netherlands)	20.2	21.3	17.5	17.1	11.1	3.1
% Margin	18.8%	18.0%	13.5%	12.0%	7.5%	4.5%
Clayton SpA (Italy/Germany/Switzerland)	25.1	24.5	18.1	5.2	(12.8)	(7.6)
% Margin	20.1%	18.5%	13.1%	3.7%	(9.5%)	(14.1%)
Clayton SA (Spain/Portugal/N. Africa)	10.0	10.4	8.4	6.9	6.6	3.2
% Margin	17.2%	16.5%	12.4%	9.5%	9.1%	8.9%
Clayton Ltd (UK/Scandinavia)	7.0	7.3	5.9	4.8	2.9	0.7
% Margin	17.9%	17.2%	12.9%	9.9%	6.0%	3.4%
Total	133.0	132.8	103.0	81.8	35.8	5.9
% Margin	14.8%	14.2%	10.6%	8.2%	3.7%	1.5%
Net income (loss)						
Clayton N. America (USA/Canada/Mexico)	31.1	28.9	11.8	(6.0)	(22.3)	(17.3)
% Margin	5.5%	5.0%	2.0%	(1.0%)	(4.0%)	(8.0%)
Clayton SA (Belgium/France/Netherlands)	8.9	9.5	10.1	10.2	5.9	0.7
% Margin	8.3%	8.0%	7.8%	7.2%	4.0%	1.0%
Clayton SpA (Italy/Germany/Switzerland)	10.8	10.5	6.0	(1.1)	(11.9)	(6.7)
% Margin	8.7%	7.9%	4.4%	(0.8%)	(8.8%)	(12.3%)
Clayton SA (Spain/Portugal/N. Africa)	4.1	4.1	3.7	1.9	0.2	0.0
% Margin	7.1%	6.5%	5.4%	2.6%	0.3%	0.1%
Clayton Ltd (UK/Scandinavia)	2.9	2.9	2.6	1.3	(0.3)	(0.9)
% Margin	7.4%	6.8%	5.6%	2.7%	(0.5%)	(4.2%)
Total	57.9	55.8	34.2	6.4	(28.3)	(24.2)
% Margin	6.5%	6.0%	3.5%	0.6%	(2.9)%	(6.1)%

Exhibit 2: Clayton Industries: Income Statement—Summary, 2004–2009

Over the next seven years, Europe became a major growth engine for Clayton, increasing its share of the company's global revenue from 33% in 2000 to 45% by 2009. During this period, Belgium/France overtook Italy as Clayton Europe's lead market, its 38% of 2009 revenues ahead of Italy's 30%. Spain accounted for 20%, and the U.K. for 12%.

But the European growth engine stalled when the global recession of 2008-09 hit. (**Exhibit 2** summarizes Clayton's financial statements.) It was a crisis that triggered strategic adjustments and management changes in both the U.S. and European operations.

Crisis Response in the United States and Europe

As the economic crisis deepened in 2009, the Clayton Industries board convinced its 63-year-old, long-time CEO to step aside in favor of Dan Briggs, a 16-year company veteran who, along with Buis, had been groomed as a potential CEO successor. Briggs was a no-nonsense manager who was previously EVP of Clayton North America.

On assuming his new role in March 2009, Briggs quickly established two priorities. Facing a cash crisis, he underlined the urgency of reducing capital use and bringing costs under control. But he also emphasized that "great opportunities always reside inside crisis," and urged managers to use the downturn to rationalize the company's portfolio and focus on products that could position it for post-recession profitable growth.

As he discussed these priorities with Buis, Briggs told her that he saw Europe as a continued source of growth. But he questioned whether the company should continue its attempts to penetrate the commercial air conditioning sector. In Briggs's view, it was a business in which only the top three or four competitors in any market could make money, and he was skeptical that Clayton could get there from its current situation.

Buis argued that several record-breaking hot European summers were changing consumer attitudes and that the market was on the cusp of embracing air-conditioning. She felt that the company should be positioning for a post-recession expansion. Recognizing Buis's successes in Europe, Briggs asked her to prepare a growth plan to review with him.

To translate Briggs's corporate priorities into European actions, Buis met with her country managers and told them she wanted all country operations to achieve a 10/10/10 plan to cut both receivables and inventories by 10 days, and reduce headcount by 10%. She also announced the "Top Four in Four" initiative, and asked each manager to prepare plans showing how the product for which he had Europe-wide responsibility would be in the top four in European market share within four years.

Problems at Clayton SpA

While these new targets would be difficult for all of Clayton's European companies, in Italy they would be a real challenge. Lagging other countries in revenue growth since 2004, Clayton SpA actually recorded a 5.3% sales decline in 2008, followed by a 19.4%

Millions of USD	2004	2005	2006	2007	2008	2009
Current assets	**$ 277.0**	**$ 291.6**	**$ 303.8**	**$ 308.8**	**$ 284.2**	**$ 254.4**
Clayton SpA	*$ 9.0*	*$ 54.1*	*$ 58.7*	*$ 62.6*	*$ 61.6*	*$ 59.6*
Other Europe	*$ 60.6*	*$ 66.5*	*$ 71.7*	*$ 75.2*	*$ 72.5*	*$ 71.5*
North America	*$ 167.4*	*$ 171.0*	*$ 173.5*	*$ 171.0*	*$ 150.1*	*$ 123.3*
Facilities	**$ 417.6**	**$ 400.4**	**$ 385.5**	**$ 371.1**	**$ 354.4**	**$ 336.6**
Clayton SpA	*$ 50.4*	*$ 54.6*	*$ 48.9*	*$ 44.7*	*$ 40.7*	*$ 38.0*
Other Europe	*$ 139.4*	*$ 129.4*	*$ 124.9*	*$ 118.7*	*$ 112.6*	*$ 109.6*
North America	*$ 227.9*	*$ 216.4*	*$ 211.6*	*$ 207.8*	*$ 201.1*	*$ 189.1*

Other assets	**$ 88.0**	**$ 118.7**	**$ 124.1**	**$ 141.3**	**$ 125.2**	**$ 140.2**
Clayton SpA	*$ 12.3*	*$ 16.8*	*$ 17.6*	*$ 20.0*	*$ 17.5*	*$ 19.1*
Other Europe	*$ 20.1*	*$ 28.5*	*$ 31.1*	*$ 37.0*	*$ 35.1*	*$ 44.4*
North America	*$ 55.6*	*$ 73.4*	*$ 75.4*	*$ 84.3*	*$ 72.6*	*$ 76.6*
Total assets	**$ 782.7**	**$ 810.7**	**$ 813.4**	**$ 821.2**	**$ 763.8**	**$ 731.2**
Clayton SpA	*$ 111.6*	*$ 125.5*	*$ 125.2*	*$ 127.2*	*$ 119.7*	*$ 116.7*
Other Europe	*$ 220.2*	*$ 224.4*	*$ 227.7*	*$ 230.9*	*$ 220.2*	*$ 225.5*
North America	*$ 450.9*	*$ 460.8*	*$ 460.5*	*$ 463.1*	*$ 423.8*	*$ 389.0*
Current liabilities	**$ 204.3**	**$ 224.3**	**$ 238.6**	**$ 255.3**	**$ 251.7**	**$ 255.4**
Clayton SpA	*$ 28.5*	*$ 32.9*	*$ 36.7*	*$ 41.2*	*$ 42.7*	*$ 45.5*
Other Europe	*$ 46.7*	*$ 51.3*	*$ 54.6*	*$ 58.4*	*$ 57.6*	*$ 58.4*
North America	*$ 129.0*	*$ 140.1*	*$ 147.3*	*$ 155.6*	*$ 151.4*	*$ 151.5*
Long-term debt	**$ 310.5**	**$ 340.9**	**$ 362.6**	**$ 388.0**	**$ 382.5**	**$ 388.2**
Clayton SpA	*$ 43.3*	*$ 50.0*	*$ 55.8*	*$ 62.7*	*$ 64.9*	*$ 69.1*
Other Europe	*$ 71.1*	*$ 81.9*	*$ 91.5*	*$ 102.8*	*$ 106.4*	*$ 113.4*
North America	*$ 196.1*	*$ 209.0*	*$ 215.3*	*$ 222.5*	*$ 211.3*	*$ 205.7*
Stockholders' equity	**$ 267.9**	**$ 245.5**	**$ 212.3**	**$ 177.9**	**$ 129.6**	**$ 87.6**
Clayton SpA	*$ 37.4*	*$ 32.2*	*$ 23.1*	*$ 12.2*	*$ (0.9)*	*$ (14.8)*
Other Europe	*$ 61.3*	*$ 61.5*	*$ 57.9*	*$ 54.1*	*$ 50.1*	*$ 59.9*
North America	*$ 169.2*	*$ 151.8*	*$ 131.3*	*$ 111.6*	*$ 80.4*	*$ 42.5*
Total liabilities and equity	**$ 782.7**	**$ 810.7**	**$ 813.4**	**$ 821.2**	**$ 763.8**	**$ 731.2**
Clayton SpA	*$ 109.2*	*$ 115.0*	*$ 115.6*	*$ 116.1*	*$ 106.7*	*$ 99.8*
Other Europe	*$ 179.1*	*$ 194.7*	*$ 204.0*	*$ 215.3*	*$ 214.1*	*$ 231.7*
North America	*$ 494.4*	*$ 501.0*	*$ 493.9*	*$ 489.8*	*$ 443.0*	*$ 399.6*

Exhibit 3: Clayton Industries: Balance Sheet—Summary, 2004–2009

Millions of USD (except where indicated)	2003	2004	2005	2006	2007	2008
Units ('000)						
United States	61,263.4	64,104.4	67,137.1	70,380.4	71,142.0	71,410.2
% Change		4.6%	4.7%	4.8%	1.1%	0.4%
Europe	15,315.9	16,667.1	18,127.0	19,706.5	20,986.9	22,137.2
% Change		8.8%	8.8%	8.7%	6.5%	5.5%

(Continued)

(Continued)

Italy	2,718.9	2,832.2	2,940.5	3,074.6	3,273.6	3,482.5
% Change		4.2%	3.8%	4.6%	6.5%	6.4%
Millions of USD—current prices						
United States	5,794.7	6,012.4	6,386.9	6,862.9	6,886.9	6,921.7
% Change		3.8%	6.2%	7.5%	0.3%	0.5%
Europe[a]	1,997.4	2,386.8	2,519.8	2,683.3	3,502.2	4,274.1
% Change		19.5%	5.6%	6.5%	30.5%	22.0%
Italy[a]	755.7	861.0	887.8	934.5	1,149.3	1,336.4
% Change		13.9%	3.1%	5.3%	23.0%	16.3%
Millions of USD—constant prices						
United States	5,794.7	5,855.6	6,016.2	6,262.6	6,107.3	5,959.4
% Change		1.1%	2.7%	4.1%	(2.5%)	(2.4%)
Europe[a]	1,945.4	2,335.5	2,499.8	2,691.4	3,540.2	NA
% Change		20.0%	7.0%	7.7%	31.5%	
Italy[a]	736.1	820.5	829.7	855.3	1,030.2	NA
% Change		11.5%	1.1%	3.1%	20.5%	
[a] Converted annually at following exchange rates:						
EUR / US$	0.8854	0.8051	0.8045	0.7970	0.7308	0.6834

Exhibit 4: Industry Sales of Air Treatment Products (including Chillers) 2003–2008

Source: Euromonitor International and casewriter estimates.

drop in the first half of 2009. As a result, receivables and inventories were both above 120 days sales. In addition, headcount reduction faced tough local laws and a tense union relationship. In short, achieving the 10/10/10 plan would be very difficult.

The "Top Four in Four" requirement would also be a challenge for the Italian unit's Europe-wide responsibility for chillers. While this line accounted for 55% of 2009 Italian revenues, it generated only 12% of sales for the rest of Europe. (See **Exhibits 3** and **4** for industry sales and projections.) Of the seven companies in the European chiller market, Clayton was in a distant fifth place with a 7% overall market share.

As performance declined, Paolo Lazzaro, president of Clayton SpA since 1998, claimed that the problems were due to the commodity cycle, and suggested that Clayton should "weather the storm." Frustrated by this attitude, Buis terminated Lazzaro in June 2009. As she began thinking about who could take over, her mind turned to Peter Arnell.

PETER ARNELL

Peter Arnell was the 42-year-old head of the British subsidiary, Clayton Ltd. Raised in a working-class family on the outskirts of London, Arnell served seven years in the Royal Marines where he rose to the rank of Captain before attending business school in London. A brief stint in management consulting left him missing the sense of impact he had experienced in the Royal Marines. So in 1998 he joined Clayton's Birmingham office in a sales and marketing job that he thought would let him test himself again on the front lines.

An avid weekend footballer, Arnell was a born competitor, quick with both a handshake and a smile. He drove himself hard and expected the same from others. While very outgoing, he expressed opinions bluntly and had alienated a few colleagues during his time at Clayton. Quickly promoted to marketing manager, Arnell had expanded Clayton's distribution network from four distributors in central England to 14 throughout the U.K. and Ireland, positioning Clayton's product line to capitalize on the U.K. real estate boom. In 2002, when the head of Clayton Ltd. retired, Buis promoted Arnell to fill the role.

Within weeks, Arnell took the tough decision of closing the old Corliss boiler plant—a move that was in line with the cost cutting program that Buis had initiated a few months earlier. After enduring months of labor pressure and personal threats over the closure, he set about revitalizing the UK business by replacing the lost revenue. He solicited support from product managers of other Clayton lines to help them understand the UK market.

Buis was impressed by Arnell's military discipline and propensity for bold action and felt he could be the change agent Italy needed. She was also aware that years of summers spent in Italy with his maternal grandparents had given him a good command of Italian. When she asked him to consider taking on Clayton SpA, Arnell saw it as a career advancing opportunity to turn around a larger operation that was key to Clayton's European strategy.

A NEW SUBSIDIARY MANAGER ARRIVES

Arnell arrived in Brescia alone on July 20, 2009, having asked his wife and two children to follow in October so he could focus his energies on work. Buis met him and took him around the offices, personally introducing him to Brescia's 10 senior managers. At a group lunch, she told them that the future of Clayton SpA was in their hands. Reflecting her commitment to empowering country managers and encouraging them to take initiative, she said she would "get out of their way," and returned to Brussels.

That afternoon, Arnell called a management meeting to share his early assessment of Brescia's grave situation and to ask for their support. Emphasizing that this was a time for immediate action, he requested all of them to postpone vacation plans until further notice. August being the Italian vacation month, three managers expressed misgivings—the plant manager, the QC manager, and the company controller. Arnell asked them to meet with him individually before the end of the day. In those meetings, after each manager reiterated an unwillingness to change plans, Arnell dismissed them on the spot.

The following day, after a meeting with his HR director to identify strong successors, he announced internal replacements for all three positions. He then met individually with his top team, asking each to help him use his first 60 days to understand the situation and develop a strategy for the company. He then scheduled follow-up meetings with each of them to share their perspectives on the operations, and also to review their individual work plans for the next 60 days.

But events at Clayton SpA did not wait for Arnell to complete his 60-day analysis. On his second day, he arrived at work to find four union officials from Federazione dei Lavoratori della Manifatture (FILM) outside his office with a local TV news crew. These officials suggested he was a hatchet man sent to close the Brescia plant and implement a mass layoff. Arnell assured them he had no such directive, that his mind was open, and that all options were on the table. He told them he would keep them informed, and promised to meet with union representatives the following week.

On August 4, Arnell met seven FILM representatives to show them how much money the operations were losing. He explained that in the current economic environment, Clayton's U.S. parent could not subsidize these losses. (It was a presentation he had made earlier that day to Brescia's Mayor who expressed concern about a plant closure and had arrived for his appointment with press photographers in tow.) After hours of acrimonious discussion, FILM agreed to recommend shortened shifts to its Brescia members. But Arnell knew that the concessions were far less than the company needed to break even.

The following week, Arnell made an appointment to meet with Clayton's bank to renegotiate terms on the company's credit line. As a gesture of goodwill, and because he thought it would help his case, he invited a politically connected union representative to accompany him and his finance manager. The three men secured the bank's agreement to postpone large payments due over the coming quarter. Arnell knew that while these few changes would not return the plant to profitability, they might buy the company some time as he completed his assessment of the situation.

ASSESSING CLAYTON SPA'S SITUATION

Over the next few weeks, in meetings with his management team, Arnell learned a great deal about the company's current situation as well as the history that brought it there. He learned that despite being given Europe-wide responsibility for compression chiller sales, Lazzaro had continued to focus on building political relationships to support large projects in Italy. As a result, chillers accounted for 55% of Italy's revenues, and its strong position in the public and institutional segments ensured its "top three" competitive position at home. However, it lagged among commercial customers who increasingly favored Asian products that promised lower lifecycle costs through more efficient design.

He also learned that Clayton's other product lines were struggling in Italy. Its central air-conditioning system fit poorly with Italian buildings, many of which lacked the duct work an integrated system required. In room air conditioners and ventilators, the market was split between low-priced foreign imports and familiar Italian brands. Offering neither low-price nor name familiarity, the Clayton and Fontaire brands struggled in Italy's residential climate-control market. And by focusing resources on the chiller line, the company had failed to develop a broader marketing capability needed to sell these other products.

On the production side, Arnell discovered that the unionized work force (which had tried to block Clayton's 1985 acquisition of AeroPuro) still enjoyed very generous benefits. For many years, the plant's high cost position was masked by political relationships that gave it an inside track on government contracts. It was because of these relationships that Lazzaro refused to consider permanent layoffs, which were permitted in Italy only for "good cause" in firms with more than 15 employees. He even rejected using the Cassa Ingrazione Guardagni (CIG), a temporary layoff provision that exempted workers coming to work in exchange for a significant pay cut, with costs shared between the companies and the state.

This vulnerable cost position had put Brescia under threat in 2004 when Buis announced the second phase of her plant efficiency drive. Focusing on efficient sourcing, she had insisted that all plants become cost-effective European-scale operations. An early focus of the program was to decide whether Brescia or Barcelona should become Clayton's European source of commercial air-conditioning chillers.

In conversations with Carlos Sanchez who headed the Spanish company, Arnell learned that after much political maneuvering, Lazzaro had convinced Buis to make Brescia the European source. Barcelona was smaller and older than the Italian plant, and was able to build only 300 to 1000 kW units compared to the 500 to 2000 kW units Brescia could make. So despite Barcelona's 20% lower labor costs and its more flexible work force, Buis felt that only the Italian operation had the capacity to meet European demand. She committed $18 million to upgrade and expand its operation, which eventually employed 203 people. But Sanchez told Arnell that he felt Brescia's staffing levels were still 20% to 30% too high.

Nonetheless, as Sanchez explained, with the support of labor, he had kept the Barcelona plant open by licensing technology to manufacture specialized absorption chillers suitable for Spain's growing thermal industry.[1] Sanchez was proud that with growing exports, this line contributed $35 million to his company's revenues in 2008, and with a 10% EBITDA, was already far more profitable than compression chillers had ever been.

Arnell also wanted to understand why Brescia's chiller penetration outside Italy was poor. Its 7% European market share (well below the 21% Italy boasted) made Clayton a distant number five behind competitors with shares of 36%, 23%, 16%, and 12%, respectively. He spoke with country manager colleagues in other major European markets as well as several major customers who told him that the product was too expensive and also behind competitors in innovative features such as variable speed technology. Furthermore, the Clayton chillers lagged the operating efficiencies of market-leading units by 15%.

Customers in some markets—particularly Scandinavia and Germany—told Arnell of a trend toward "district energy systems" which produced steam, hot water, or chilled water at a central plant and then piped it to buildings in the district for space heating, hot water, and air conditioning. Such systems favored absorption technology over the compression chillers Brescia produced. While

Millions of USD (except where indicated)	2009	2010	2011	2012	2013
Units ('000)					
United States	72,391.6	73,911.5	75,532.5	77,253.8	79,130.0
% Change	1.4%	2.1%	2.2%	2.3%	2.4%
Europe	22,441.4	23,651.7	24,925.7	26,266.3	27,695.5
% Change		5.4%	5.4%	5.4%	5.4%
Italy	3,692.2	3,910.4	4,128.6	4,347.9	NA
% Change	6.0%	5.9%	5.6%	5.3%	
Millions of USD—current prices					
United States	7,013.6	7,139.2	7,287.8	7,462.0	7,632.0
% Change	1.3%	1.8%	2.1%	2.4%	2.3%
Europe	4,249.4	4,687.6	5,106.9	5,486.5	NA
% Change		10.3%	8.9%	7.4%	
Italy[a]	1,328.1	1,414.9	1,493.2	1,558.7	NA
% Change	(0.6%)	6.5%	5.5%	4.4%	
[a]Converted annually at following exchange rates:					
EUR / US$	0.7389	0.7389	0.7389	0.7389	0.7389

Exhibit 5: Forecast Sales of Air Treatment Products (including Chillers), 2009–2013

Source: Euromonitor International and casewriter estimates.

Millions of USD (except where indicated)		2004	2005	2006	2007	2008	2009
Units		348.0	372.0	382.0	386.0	375.0	155.0
Revenue	Italy	67.1	73.2	76.7	79.0	76.0	29.9
	Contribution to Clayton SpA	53.7%	55.3%	55.6%	55.7%	56.6%	55.2%
	Other	10.9	11.3	11.1	11.3	11.5	4.1
	Total	75.2	82.4	86.7	89.6	86.7	34.0
Operating Expense							
	Direct materials	19.7	23.7	29.2	37.5	50.1	18.5
	Labor	16.1	16.6	16.9	15.3	15.7	7.2
	Overhead—Fixed	29.0	31.3	32.2	34.9	33.6	15.7
	Total	64.8	71.5	78.3	87.6	99.4	41.3

(Continued)

(Continued)

EBITDA	10.4	10.9	8.4	2.0	(12.8)	(7.3)
EBITDA Margin	13.8%	13.2%	9.7%	2.3%	(14.7%)	(21.5%)
Capital Expenditures	10.8	11.2	2.3	2.8	3.0	0.8
Capex Margin	14.4%	13.6%	2.7%	3.1%	3.5%	2.3%
Headcount	190	196	204	208	204	203
[a]Converted annually at following exchange rates:						
EUR / US$	0.8051	0.8045	0.7970	0.7308	0.6834	0.7389

Exhibit 6: Brescia Plant Economics

compression chillers still had 85% of the market, environmentalists emphasized that absorption chillers were less carbon-intensive and used water instead of the ozone-depleting refrigerants that compression systems required.

Finally, Arnell's financial director reviewed current results showing that the company was currently losing more than $1 million a month. He felt the losses were primarily due to a 27% increase in steel prices in the past two years—a cost that could not be recouped due to foreign competitors' aggressive pricing. And rather than recognizing the problem, FILM, wielding great influence during a time of high unemployment, had increased its demands.

Decision Options

In early September, to help his senior team develop their plans, Arnell organized two internal conferences to expose them to outside input. At a manufacturing conference, production, engineering, and QC managers from Brescia described their situation and tested their emerging ideas with respected counterparts from the Spanish, Belgian, and UK plants. And in the marketing conference, the sales, marketing, and product development managers exchanged views with colleagues invited from other Clayton country organizations.

Not surprisingly, the Italian managers' presentations focused on restoring Brescia's profitability and ensuring its long-term viability. Their emerging plan involved programs to boost plant efficiency, product development initiatives to revitalize the compression chiller line, and a sales and marketing plan to expand market share outside Italy. Early cost estimates were about $5 million, with most of that investment in the first 12 months.

Meanwhile, Arnell had been in ongoing discussions with Sanchez who had raised an alternative option. He explained to Arnell that he had approached Buis several times to fund a major new plant in Spain, but she had told him she was not convinced that absorption chillers would ever be more than a niche market. She had also told them that she had placed her investment bet on Brescia, and wanted to give Italy a chance to prove itself.

"But the absorption chiller is the market of the future, and we have the license for a first-class technology," Sanchez said. "We still can't produce large-scale chillers in Barcelona, and we're site-constrained to grow the plant. Why don't you phase out your compression chiller line and convert capacity to absorption chillers to meet the growing market? Together, we could make Clayton a dominant force in this segment."

It was an intriguing idea, but one that would involve significant costs in layoffs and restructuring, even with the gradual phased changeover process. Arnell estimated the investment would be about $15 million over five years, with most costs starting in the phase-out and restructuring stages two to three years out.

A third option was proposed by Arnell's finance director who felt that it was too early to make major strategic commitments in an economy that was still unstable. He was skeptical of the government's July draft budget, which projected a 2009 contraction of 4.8% in the Italian economy, before a rebound to 0.7% growth in 2010. He argued for a tight focus on efficiency measures to restore profitability while studying the various strategic options for at least another six months or until things became clearer.

In considering these alternatives, Arnell knew that while he did not have all the answers, what he did know was that Briggs and Buis were booked at the Hotel Ambasciatori for two nights the following week. They would expect to hear his analysis, his vision for a healthy Clayton SpA, his plans for a turnaround, and the results he expected to achieve.

NOTE

1. While compression chillers such as those made in Brescia rely on electricity, absorption chillers are driven by heat, often from waste hot water, and are increasingly solar-powered.

CASE QUESTIONS

1. How do international positioning challenges affect the difficulties faced by Clayton SpA?

2. How does the Market/Product Matrix apply to this case? How has Clayton SpA utilized market penetration, market development, product development, or diversification strategies?

3. How have consumer attitudes toward air conditioning in Italy changed in recent years? What types of market research could be used to discover these changes? How can international marketers use information such as this?

4. How would you assess Clayton Industries' organizational structure? Do you believe that this structure lends itself to international marketing success?

5. How can Clayton utilize IMC to better promote its products throughout Italy?

CASE 4   BEST BUY INC.

Dual Branding in China

R. Chandrasekhar

In June 2006, John Noble, senior vice president at Best Buy International, a division of Best Buy Inc. (Best Buy), the largest retailer of consumer electronics (CE) in the United States, faced a major strategic branding decision. Earlier that month, the company had acquired a majority stake in Jiangsu Five Star Appliances (Five Star), the third-largest retailer of appliances and consumer electronics in China. Noble had been assigned to the international division just a month earlier from the company's Canadian operations, where he had held a similar position since 2002. In his new role, Noble was tasked to decide and plan how Best Buy should implement a dual-brand strategy in China. The dual-brand strategy adopted in Canada four years earlier seemed to have worked well. "Will the dual-brand strategy work in China?" he wondered. "How should I make it work?"

While negotiating for a majority stake in Five Star, which had 135 stores in China, Best Buy announced plans to open its first Best Buy store in China in December 2006, to be followed by two more stores in the next 12 to 18 months. Five Star also announced its own agenda of opening 25 additional stores in China, under the Five Star banner, during approximately the same period.

Context

When Best Buy decided to go beyond the domestic market in the United States in December 2000, the company had found neighboring Canada to be a logical first step. The Canadian CE market was fragmented, with only one dominant player, Future Shop. Best Buy's original objective was to set up its own stores in various Canadian cities to compete directly with Future Shop stores. It had planned to open the first of several stores in the Toronto area in 2003, and then embark on a three-year expansion program that would see the launch of 15 stores in major Canadian cities. Best Buy had a target of setting up 60 to 65 stores across Canada, competing with the 95 stores of Future Shop, which itself was planning to increase its stores to 120 over four years. As part of a defense strategy, Future Shop was also finalizing plans to relocate or renovate at least half of its existing stores by 2005.

In August 2001, the founders of the two companies met and decided, over the course of three weeks, that "together we could accomplish infinitely more than if we were to go our own ways and compete with each other."[1] By January 2002, Best Buy had acquired 100 percent ownership in Future Shop. Then, when the time came to finalize integration, the management of Best Buy took a surprising decision: to retain the Future Shop brand and let it compete with Best Buy as an independent brand, a strategy that had no precedent within the company. The dual-brand strategy—wherein two brands, both part of a common corporate entity, vied for market share—was an initiative being tested for the first time at Best Buy (see Exhibit 1).

In reference to whether the dual brand strategy could be implemented, Richard Schulze, the founder

R. Chandrasekhar wrote this case under the supervision of Professor Niraj Dawar solely to provide material for class discussion. The authors do not intend to illustrate either effective or ineffective handling of a managerial situation. The authors may have disguised certain names and other identifying information to protect confidentiality.

	Best Buy	Future Shop
Typical store size	35,000 square feet	26,000 square feet
Store associates	Blue Shirts	Product Experts
Staff mandate	Technology is fun. We make it easy for the customer	Providing Trusted Personalized Service
Customers	Tech enthusiasts who enjoy the interactive shopping experience and grab-and-go convenience	Tech savvy; a notch higher than the Best Buy customer; at the cutting edge of developments in technology
Aisles	Wide aisles to provide for grab-and-go shopping	Highlights key technologies first
Service	Upon request	Attentive
Sales	Customer led No high-pressure salespersonship	Sales-person led Commission-based sales
Target group	Higher success rate with female customers	Male-oriented
Customer profile	15 to 39 years	25 to 44 years
Brand identity	"Turn on the fun"	"The place to get it first"
In-store experience	Relaxed	Guided
Product mix	Although by category the two store brands were very similar, each was able to offer a unique selection of products and brands. Product brands and depth of selection differed within product categories. On average, 45 percent overlap of the product assortment (excluding entertainment software) between the two store brands.	
Areas of distinction	Higher propensity toward self-service; non-commissioned sales staff; greater assortment of ready-made electronics packages; wider aisles and more interactive displays; higher ratio of female customers, seeking to integrate products into their lifestyles; customers with higher incomes and higher levels of education	Commissioned sales staff guiding the customer by providing customized, trusted and personalized approach; tech savvy, early adopters looking for the best deal; customer base more diverse

Exhibit 1: Best Buy And Future Shop In 2002
Source: Company files

of Best Buy, was famously quoted for saying, at the time of the acquisition, "I'm not saying it can't be done, I'm saying it's never been done before. . . ."

Best Buy

Headquartered in Minneapolis in the United States, Best Buy was driven by a vision of "meeting consumers at the intersection of technology and life."[2] The company saw its core strategy as "bringing technology and consumers together in a retail environment that focuses on educating consumers on the features and benefits of technology and entertainment while maximizing overall profitability."[3] Best Buy was positioned to deliver new technologies at the retail level in the three segments of devices, connections, and content, enabling the company to capitalize on the progressive digitization of analog products and the accelerating digital product cycles to mobilize consumer demand. The company was selling its products at moderate to upper moderate price points.

Growing at a rate of between 15 percent and 20 percent every year, Best Buy had attained sales revenues of US$30.9 billion for the year ending March 2006 (see Exhibit 2). The company had more than 20 percent share of the retail American consumer electronics market, which was valued at US$152 billion in 2006.[4] Globally, the CE market was averaging a growth rate of 10 percent and was expected, according to CEA/GfK Worldwide Consumer Electronics Sales & Forecast, to reach revenues of US$700 billion by 2009.[5] In planning

to maintain a double-digit growth rate year after year, Best Buy saw, in its international expansion, a window of opportunity.

HISTORY

Best Buy was founded in 1966, by Richard Schulze, an American entrepreneur from the midwest. The chain, which was known at the time as Sound of Music, was retailing audio components sourced from vendors. The company struggled through the recession years of the 1970s, and with the arrival of the video cassette

Year ending March (in US$million)	2006	2005	2004	2003	2002	2001	2000	1999
Revenue								
Domestic	27,380	24,616	22,225	20,946	17,711	15,326	12,494	10,064
International	3,468	2,817	2,323	–	–	–	–	–
Total	30,848	27,433	24,548	20,946	17,711	15,326	12,494	10,064
Less: Cost of goods sold	23,122	20,938	18,677	15,710	13,941	12,267	10,100	8,250
Gross profit	7,726	6,495	5,871	5,236	3,770	3,059	2,394	1,814
Less: S&G expenses	6,082	5,053	4,567	4,226	2,862	2,455	1,854	1,463
Operating income	1,644	1,442	1,304	1,010	908	604	539	351
Net interest income	77	1	(8)	4	18	37	23	1
Earnings before tax	1,721	1,443	1,296	1,014	926	641	562	352
Income tax	581	509	496	392	356	245	215	136
Other (Loss)/Gain	–	50	(95)	(523)	–	–	–	–
Net earnings	1,140	984	705	99	570	396	347	216
Category wise revenue Domestic								
- Home Office	8,762	8,380	7,556	–	–			
-Video & Audio	11,773	9,609	8,445	–	–			
- Ent. Software	5,202	5,169	4,889	–	–			
- Appliances	1,643	1,476	1,335	–	–			
International								
- Home Office	1,526	1,127	929	–	–			
- Video & Audio	1,318	1,155	930	–	–			
- Ent. Software	487	422	348	–	–			
- Appliances	139	113	116	–	–			
Number of employees (in 000s)	128							
Cash and equivalents (in US$million)	681	354	245					

Exhibit 2: Best Buy Inc.—Income Statement

Source: Best Buy annual report.

recorder in the early 1980s, the music chain expanded into retailing video components. In 1983, Sound of Music moved into mass merchandising by switching to a superstore format (characterized by a wide range of products and boxes of merchandise in a warehouse atmosphere) under the new, distinctive yellow Best Buy banner. Six years later, Best Buy refined its retailing techniques in three ways: the introduction of self-service, the placement of its salespersons (referred to as "Blue Shirts") on fixed pay instead of on commission, and reconfiguration of stores' formats to a discount style. The changes were made in recognition of both a trend in customers of being knowledgeable enough to choose products on their own and their preference of shopping in a consumer-friendly environment.

INNOVATIONS

The company's decision to stop paying commissions to salespersons and put them on salary did not go well initially with vendors such as Toshiba and Hitachi. These manufacturers had long felt that a high-pressure, incentives-oriented and results-driven approach at the store was necessary to move products. But Best Buy soon realized that its customers were comfortable in the new, informal ambience at its stores.

After entering new domestic markets, such as Chicago, Philadelphia, and Boston, Best Buy became the biggest seller of home personal computers (PCs) in 1995, in time for the Internet boom. In 1996, Best Buy surpassed Circuit City to become the top CE retailer in the United States, a position that Best Buy had since held.

Best Buy had spotted another trend. Digital devices and home networks were growing in complexity, opening up a prospect for marketing the necessary technical services to homes and small businesses. This opportunity was pegged at being worth more than US$20 billion a year in the United States. Best Buy had acquired, in October 2002, a Minneapolis-based startup specializing in repairing and installing PCs, called Geek Squad. Within a year, Best Buy had Geek Squad precincts, staffed by newly recruited techies, in more than 20 stores. By 2005, the geeks had set up shop in all Best Buy stores. The move was an advantage over competitors, such as Wal-Mart, which did not provide service back-up for their CE sales.

CENTRICITY

Best Buy had identified the technology enthusiast as its core customer. This target group was characterized by the following attributes: aged 15 to 39, male, highly educated, above-average income, and eager for products and services that would render personal time both productive and enjoyable and resonate with being fun, honest, young, and techno-savvy. Best Buy was building its brand promise on those very lines: "being fun, honest, young and techno-savvy."

In the late 1990s, Best Buy established a standard operating platform (SOP) for replication across the chain, which included procedures for inventory management, transaction processing, customer relations, store administration, products sales, and merchandising. SOP had a harmonizing effect on the company, helping ensure consistency and enforcing discipline across the network of stores. Best Buy was now a process-driven organization with systems and procedures firmly in place. By early 2000, however, Best Buy was evolving from being an organization thriving on standardization to one offering, within a standard format, different value propositions appealing to different groups of customers. Thus, the company began in 2001 to test and implement a concept it called centricity.

The concept was based on four elements:

1. Identifying customers generating the most revenue

2. Segmenting these customers

3. Realigning the stores to meet the needs of these customers

4. Empowering the store sales staff, known as Blue Shirts, to steer these customers toward products and services that would encourage them to visit more often and spend more on each visit

The company's market researchers combed through reams of sales and demographic data to determine whether a particular location should be tailored to, say, empty nesters or small business owners. A store located in a geographical area characterized by a higher density of homemakers would, for example, include features such as personal shopping assistants (PSAs) who were chosen from among Blue Shirts to help a shopper with such tasks as selecting the right digital camera for her family. Blue Shirts were schooled in financial metrics, such as return on capital, so that they could ascertain for themselves the effectiveness of merchandising.

Centricity was a big investment in terms of enhancing end user experience. The company examined, in detail, everything from store fixtures and layout to the product-employee mix and staff training. Recasting a store toward affluent tech enthusiasts would cost approximately US$600,000 alone for lighting and fixtures. The concept of centricity, which was built essentially on customer insights, was also meant to encourage employee innovations in support of a better customer experience, not just at a single moment in time but on a continuous basis. The goal was to drive customer engagement and foster repeat visits.

STORE OPERATIONS

At headquarters in Minneapolis, Best Buy store operations were organized into three divisions. Each division was divided into regions under the supervision of a senior vice president overseeing store performance through regional managers with responsibility for a number of districts within the region. The district managers monitored store operations closely. Each district also had a loss prevention manager, and product security personnel employed at each store controlled inventory shrinkage. Best Buy controlled advertising, pricing, and inventory policies from corporate headquarters.

COMPETITORS

The CE retail market in the United States was competitive at four levels. The major competitors were mass merchandisers (e.g., Wal-Mart and Costco). These competitors were regularly increasing their portfolio of CE products, particularly of those products less complex to sell, install, and operate. Contemporary channels of distribution (such as Internet shopping, facilitated by e-commerce platforms set up by some manufacturers themselves) were the second source of competition. Also competing in the CE market and gaining market share were factory-direct shopping services (e.g., Dell Computers). Finally, home improvement retailers (e.g., Home Depot and Lowe's) were also entering into the consumer electronic product market. Lines were blurring as retailers of all kinds were widening their product assortments in pursuit of revenues and margins.

Dual Branding in Canada

Best Buy paid Cdn$560.71 million (US$363.95 million) to acquire Future Shop, based on the offering price of Cdn$17 per share, a 47.8 per cent premium over the market price of Cdn$11.50 per share. However, a little over a year after deciding to expand internationally, Best Buy experimented with a concept that was novel in the CE market worldwide. Said Noble:

There were four reasons why Best Buy veered toward a dual-branding strategy in Canada. First, the Canadian CE market was fragmented with the leader, Future Shop, having only about 15 per cent share. We felt there was room for a second brand. Given that most retail sectors in the US had at least two major players—for example, Home Depot/Lowe's and Staples/Office Depot—we felt that a second major retailer in CE in Canada would be in order. Second, Best Buy had already signed, before perceiving Future Shop as a potential target for acquisition, about eight real estate leases as part of its original greenfield approach. Some of these leased spaces (as in the Heartland location at Mississauga, a suburb of Toronto) were situated right next to Future Shop stores for planned head-to-head competition. We were committed to those locations. Third, there were operational factors. Conversion of Future Shop stores into Best Buy stores would take a while, particularly in terms of store redesigns and staff transition. Not all the elements of Best Buy's SOP could simply be set up "as is" in Canada. There would be a period of time when the two brands had to be managed independently. As it turned out, it gave us a window through which to look at issues differently. But, the most important reason was the recognition that Future Shop was a well established brand, with over 95 per cent unaided brand awareness among Canadians. Replacing such a hugely successful brand with Best Buy, which was unknown in Canada, seemed counter-intuitive.

Best Buy also had other reasons for pursuing a dual-brand strategy. If the senior staff at Future Shop were focused on setting up the Best Buy operation, their activities risked affecting negatively the existing sales of Future Shop stores. Putting together a separate team at Best Buy fully dedicated to opening the greenfield stores of Best Buy, as originally planned, would speed up the process of the company's market entry.

But the dual-brand strategy also had some downsides. Said Noble:

We had four concerns about the dual-branding strategy. Cannibalization was, of course, a major issue. It was likely that each Best Buy store would eat into the earnings of a Future Shop store and vice versa, particularly when the two were in close proximity. Since the company would have to manage two different brands, the marketing dollars in Canada would be split in half, minimizing the impact of ad-spend. Also imminent was the possibility of a blurring of brand identity in the eyes of the consumer. Finally, there would be duplication of roles at the corporate headquarters at Minneapolis, with the two brands requiring separate staff inputs.

The two brands were each headed by a vice president based in Vancouver, the location of Best Buy Canada Ltd. (BBYC), the newly formed subsidiary that maintained the two brands. BBYC took several steps to reinforce the operations of both brands at ground level: opening an automated 450,000-square-foot distribution center in Ontario and, eventually, another 500,000-square-foot distribution center in British Columbia, to support store growth for both brands; outsourcing a call center to provide 24-hour service, seven days a week; and retaining a premier insurance company to underwrite product warranties. Stores of both brands were open 60 to 75 hours per week, seven days a week. All stores used the parent company's SOP.

An average Future Shop store was staffed by a general manager, an operations manager, one to four department managers and 48 to 95 sales associates, as well as part-time sales associates. An average Canada Best Buy store was staffed by a general manager; assistant managers for operations, merchandising, inventory, and sales; and 80 to 110 sales associates, including full-time and part-time sales associates.

Although Best Buy and Future Shop effectively competed for market share, the positioning for each company was different. Best Buy, with its yellow-price-tag logo, continued to offer the "grab and go" option by providing an open floor plan that allowed customers to shop on their own or with the help of a no-pressure (i.e., non-commissioned) Blue Shirt product specialist if desired. Future Shop focused on offering the trusted, personalized customer service for which it was already well known in Canadian cities.

By the end of the first year of operations, there were indications that the dual-branding strategy was working in Canada. For example, the Future Shop store at Mississauga had sales revenues of $40 million in 2001/02. In 2002/03, post-acquisition, revenues were $38 million. Cannibalization was minimal because the Best Buy store, located across the street, had delivered an additional $30 million in sales for the same period. Overall, Best Buy had achieved a combined market share in Canada of 34 percent. In some places, the proximity of the two banners had created a shopping destination. The company's research also pointed out that the customer bases of Best Buy and Future Shop were different. Canadian customers viewed the two brands as distinct, not interchangeable. One indication was that only 18 percent of customers applying for a Best Buy credit card in fiscal 2004 already held a Future Shop credit card (see Exhibit 3).

The board of Best Buy was now willing to support the dual-brand strategy in Canada as long as Best Buy entered new markets in Canada and delivered on sales targets, while Future Shop continued to deliver on its own sales targets. In negotiating with Five Star in China, the board was willing to support a similar strategy on similar expectations (see Exhibit 4).

ENTERING CHINA

A country of 1.3 billion consumers, China had been attracting the attention of overseas investors since it began liberalizing the economy in 1985. Over the next two decades, its manufacturing side boomed, with the growth in gross domestic product (GDP) averaging 10 percent per annum. The consumption side, however, was growing at a pace slower than output and not catching up. Consumption as a percentage of GDP had in fact dropped from 47 percent in 1995 to 37 percent in 2005.[6] A process of adjustment was under way, and because the Chinese economy was moving from the historical investment-led growth model to a consumption-led growth model, many multinational marketers were beginning to see an opportunity. McKinsey Global Institute had predicted that China would become the third-largest consumer market in the world by 2025 (see Exhibit 5).

Best Buy's original interest in China had been flagged by China's manufacturing base. Since the 1990s, China had become a major hub in the Asian region for the manufacture of CE components. In

Metric	2000		2006	
	Best Buy (in US)	Future Shop	Best Buy (in Canada)	Future Shop
Sales growth	21.4%	17.0%	34.3%	14.2%
Gross margin	20.2%	22.7%	24.2%	24.8%
SG&A expense ratio	16.2%	20.1%	17.8%	16.7%
Operating margin	4.0%	2.6%	6.4%	8.1%
Sales per square foot	$870	$746	$1,010	$1,069
Inventory turn	7.5	7.4	6.4	6.4
Operating ROA	18.7%	12.77%	n/a	n/a

Exhibit 3: Best Buy and Future Shop — Performance Metrics 2000 and 2006

Note: SG&A = selling, general and administrative; ROA = return on assets; n/a = not applicable

Source: Deutsche Banc Alex. Brown estimates for 2000 data, Company records for 2006 data.

Province/State	Canada		China	
	Best Buy stores	Future Shop stores	Best Buy stores	Five Star stores
Alberta	7	15		
British Columbia	7	21		
Manitoba	2	5		
New Brunswick	–	3		
Newfoundland	–	1		
Nova Scotia	1	3		
Ontario	25	55		
Prince Edward	–	1		
Quebec	8	24		
Saskatchewan	1	3		
Anhui			–	12
Henan			–	9
Jiangsu			–	99
Shandong			–	9
Shanghai			1	–
Sichuan			–	6
Yunnan			–	4
Zhejiang			–	21
Total	51	131	1	160

Exhibit 4: Best Buy —Number of International Stores 2006

Source: Best Buy 2008 annual report.

	Unit	2005	2004	2003
Gross National Income	100 million Yuan	183,956.1	159,586.7	135,174.0
Gross Domestic Product	100 million Yuan	183,084.8	159,878.3	135,822.8
Per capita Gross Domestic Product	Yuan per person	14,040.0	12,336.0	10,542.0
Population	Million	1,307.56	1,299.88	1,292.27
- Male		673.75	669.76	665.56
- Female		633.81	630.12	626.71
- Urban		562.12	542.83	523.76
- Rural		745.54	757.05	768.51
Economically active persons	Million	778.77	768.23	767.05
Number of employed persons	Million	758.25	752.00	744.32
Annual Per Capita Income	Yuan	10,493	9,422	5,160
- Urban households		3,255	2,936	2,090
- Rural households				
Annual Per Capita Consumption Expenditure-Urban households	Yuan	7,943	7,182	4,186
- Rural households		2,955	2,185	1,617

Exhibit 5: China's Economy, 2003–2005

Source: National Bureau of Statistics of China, Chinese Statistical Yearbook, 2006, www.stats.gov.cn/tjsj/ndsj/2006/indexeh.htm, accessed December 10, 2008.

a little more than a decade, China was playing host to a number of manufacturers from the United States and Europe. Attracted by the country's low labor costs, these manufacturers had started relocating their domestic manufacturing operations to China. A fast-growing home market was also spurring China's CE manufacturing industry. According to Instat, an American high-tech market research firm with an office in China, the manufacturing end of the CE industry in China, which was estimated at $71.5 billion in 2006, was expected to more than double by 2010.[7]

In September 2003, Best Buy opened a 25-person sourcing office in Shanghai, China. This move complemented the company's plans to expand its existing 450 stores in the United States and 127 stores in Canada to at least 1,200 stores in North America over the long haul. The Shanghai office was seen as a means of both lowering the cost of goods sold and driving gross profit rates on individual products. This office was also meant to fill the gaps in the company's product assortment with private labels from the Asian region. Said Noble:

China was chosen as the second international expansion market primarily due to the overall market opportunity, consumer fundamentals

and macro-economic factors. We did look at other markets such as Europe, especially France and Germany, but, they were mature, competitive and offered less quality retail real estate at a high cost.[8]

The Chinese CE retail market was fragmented. The top five players together held less than 20 percent of the market share. However, the Chinese market was expected to account for 25 percent of the global CE market by 2010. Taking a slice of the new growth opportunity ranked high on the agendas of multinational corporations. Best Buy was the first, and so far the only, multinational to have entered the retail end of the Chinese CE market.

China's CE retail market was, however, a complex terrain to navigate for a new entrant. Price wars were rampant. In categories such as TVs and white goods, excess capacity had squeezed profit margins to less than three percent, the lowest in the world. Although consolidation among electronics retailers had been ongoing, a new wave of mergers and acquisitions (M&As) was evident within a space of a few months in early 2006. Gome Electrical Appliances Holdings Ltd. (Gome), China's leading electronics specialty chain, had already mounted a bid on China Paradise

Electronics Retail Ltd. (China Paradise), which itself had struck—and then put on hold—an alliance with the privately owned Dazhong Electrical Appliance Co. Ltd., the fifth-largest CE retailer in China. The formalities pertaining to acquisition of China Paradise by Gome were to reach closure in late July 2006. Best Buy had already acquired Jiangsu Five Star in April 2006.

The Chinese CE market had some unique characteristics. For example, approximately two-thirds of the sales staff in a retail store were on the payroll of suppliers. Also, the rate of growth of "other income" was often higher than the rate of growth in sales. The gross margin of Chinese retailers was understated without taking into account "other income," which included rebates and listing fees, often the equivalent of a retailer's gross profit. Instead of a mark-up on the cost of goods sold, the retailers received rebates.[9]

BUYER BEHAVIOR

In 2004, approximately 36 million urban Chinese households had a disposable income of at least RMB25,000 (approximately US$3,000) a year, which was considered, by local standards, a reasonable threshold for entering the consumer class. By 2009, the number was expected to almost triple, to 105 million urban households. A massive influx of new consumers was now reaching the retail cash registers. Every year, approximately 20 million Chinese (the population of Australia) turned 18 years of age. Prosperity was lifting the incomes of tens of millions more.[10]

Chinese consumers were not prone to opening their wallets freely. The savings rate in China in 2006 was 28 percent of monthly household income, compared with three percent in the United Kingdom and two percent in Canada. Chinese consumers were also not accustomed to the concept of credit. The credit card penetration rate in urban households was less than four percent, compared with 75 percent in the United States, 78 percent in Japan, and 91 percent in Germany. Less than six percent of credit card holders in China carried forward their ongoing balances.[11]

Observers had found that Chinese consumers responded better to messages focusing on functional features than those focusing on brand imagery. At one level, Chinese consumers were attracted to brand names but, on another level, they were wary of premium prices. Brand preferences of customers did not always translate into revenues in the form of increased market share for companies. Salespersons held sway over the buying decisions of consumers, who were also influenced by point-of-sale promotions to make last-minute switches. Because Chinese consumers had a sense of national pride, a multinational corporation, by seeming foreign, could lose potential customer segments.[12]

GROWTH CENTERS

In markets such as the United States and Canada, consumers exhibited few differences between regions, which required companies to make choices only between products and segments. In China, the trade-offs had an additional dimension, requiring product-segment-region choices. Marketers had to factor in regional differences because as one moved across tiers of cities in China, a steep drop-off was experienced in infrastructure, channels, and disposable income. When a mass merchandiser entered China, it evaluated the country's cities, giving each locale a tier designation on the basis of size, sophistication, purchasing habits, attitudes, and disposable income of its population and its own product offerings.[13] A typical classification is shown in Exhibit 6.

A massive increase in retail space was evidence of increasing competition in China's tier-one cities in particular. Major players were eyeing growth opportunities in tier-two and tier-three cities. The attendant risk was the longer break-even point because, given the much lower income levels in those cities, sales would be slower. However, the costs of retail space would be lower, and given less competition, margins were likely to be higher.

China also had other limitations. Land acquisition in cities was often difficult; procedural delays meant that a new entrant would take at least six months to open a store; relationships between vendors and retailers were so close and guarded by local customs and preferences that an outsider did not have an easy time getting a foot in the door. Manufacturers of CE were not likely to cut a new entrant such as Best Buy much slack on pricing, particularly because personal relationships (referred to as "guanxi" in local terminology) influenced the conduct of business among Chinese, who were more comfortable dealing with people they knew.

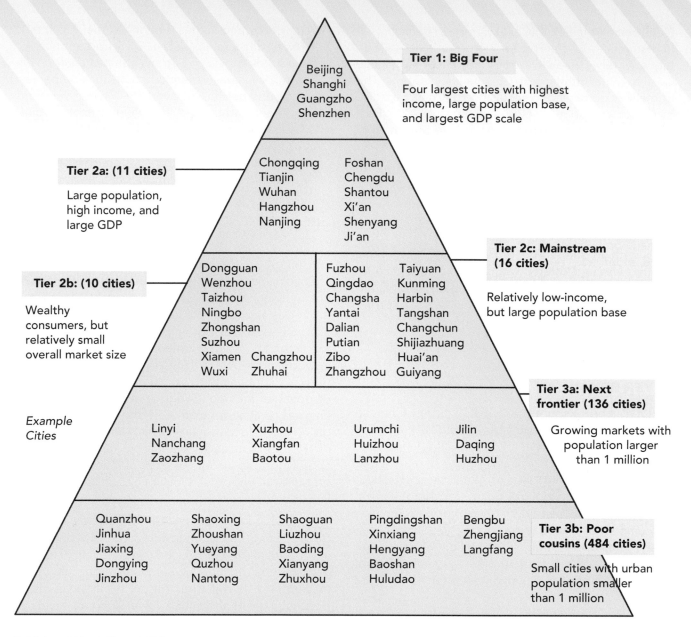

Tier 1: Big Four

Four largest cities with highest income, large population base, and largest GDP scale

Beijing
Shanghi
Guangzho
Shenzhen

Tier 2a: (11 cities)

Large population, high income, and large GDP

Chongqing
Tianjin
Wuhan
Hangzhou
Nanjing

Foshan
Chengdu
Shantou
Xi'an
Shenyang
Ji'an

Tier 2c: Mainstream (16 cities)

Relatively low-income, but large population base

Tier 2b: (10 cities)

Wealthy consumers, but relatively small overall market size

Dongguan
Wenzhou
Taizhou
Ningbo
Zhongshan
Suzhou
Xiamen   Changzhou
Wuxi   Zhuhai

Fuzhou   Taiyuan
Qingdao   Kunming
Changsha   Harbin
Yantai   Tangshan
Dalian   Changchun
Putian   Shijiazhuang
Zibo   Huai'an
Zhangzhou   Guiyang

Tier 3a: Next frontier (136 cities)

Growing markets with population larger than 1 million

Example Cities

Linyi   Xuzhou   Urumchi   Jilin
Nanchang   Xiangfan   Huizhou   Daqing
Zaozhang   Baotou   Lanzhou   Huzhou

Quanzhou   Shaoxing   Shaoguan   Pingdingshan   Bengbu
Jinhua   Zhoushan   Liuzhou   Xinxiang   Zhengjiang
Jiaxing   Yueyang   Baoding   Hengyang   Langfang
Dongying   Quzhou   Xianyang   Baoshan
Jinzhou   Nantong   Zhuxhou   Huludao

Tier 3b: Poor cousins (484 cities)

Small cities with urban population smaller than 1 million

Exhibit 6: China's Tiered Cities

Source: Diana Farrell et al., From "Made in China" to "Sold in China": The Rise of the Chinese Urban Consumer, McKinsey Global Institute, November 2006.

China was also experiencing a crunch of quality human resources because retailing, as an industry, had not yet developed in the country.

Major Competitors

Before being acquired by Best Buy, Five Star had two major competitors, Gome Electrical Appliances Holdings Ltd. (Gome) and Suning, both publicly held (see Exhibit 7). Together, the two companies had saturated many of the country's largest cities over the past few years. Although the total market shares in 2005 of the top five in 2005 (comprising Gome, Suning, Five Star, and two others) accounted for less than 20 percent of market share, Gome and Suning held a combined market share of 70 percent in some appliance product categories, such as air conditioners.

Financials (in RMB million)	Gome		Suning	
	2004	2005	2004	2005
Revenue	12,647	17,959	9,107	15,936
Net profit	486	496		
Revenue by geography (%)				
- Northeast China		5		3
- North China		33		15
- East China		9		59
- West China		23		5
- South China		26		15
- Central China		4		3
Sales per square meter	25,940		32,141	23,929
Number of stores	442		94	224
Revenue by category (%)				
- Air conditioners		16		
- Audiovisual		28		
- Refrigerators/Washing machines		18		
- Telecom		16		
- Small electrical appliances		10		
- Digital/IT products		12		
- Service		–		
Mission	"Competitive pricing from high volume"		"Service is the sole product of Suning"	
Store formats, positioning	a. Traditional (3,500 square meters): price-conscious mass market b. Digital (260 square meters): high-end customer in downtown c. Eagle (15,000 square meters): service-conscious, mid to high-end customers		Flagship: in large cities Central: the most common	

Exhibit 7: Major Competitors in China

Sources: Gome Electrical Appliances Holdings Limited website, www.gome.com.hk/eng, accessed December 5, 2008; Suning website, www.cnsuning.com/include/english, accessed December 5, 2008; Jean Zhou, Deutsche Bank equity research Report, dated April 7, 2006; Sandy Chen, Citigroup equity research report on Gome, dated October 12, 2005.

GOME GROUP

The Gome Group had two companies: Gome Electrical Appliances Holdings Ltd. and Beijing Gome (an unlisted company). In 1993, Gome opened its first store in Beijing, and soon expanded into other major cities in China, gaining widespread consumer acceptance. By mid-2005, the group had 437 stores (of which 263 belonged to the listed company) in 132 cities in China, with the most extensive distribution network of all the home appliance retailers in China. It was leading in all regional markets (Northeast China, North China, Northwest China, Southwest China and South China) with the exception of East China, the home market of Suning, where Gome was ranked number three.[14] Gome was the largest CE retailer in China, with six per cent market share, prior to its acquisition of China Paradise. The company was mounting a bid on China Paradise, likely to come through in a few weeks, for a record sum of $677 million.[15]

At the beginning of 2005, Gome had announced its four-year growth initiative aimed at enlarging its geographical coverage and raising its national market share to 10 to 15 percent by the end of 2008. Although Gome had set itself apart, to start with, on a super-store format offering the lowest prices, the differentiation had been subsequently commoditized in by its competitors. Gome had then cracked the traditional business model (of selling through intermediaries to various retail formats) by dealing directly with mega brands. In introducing category killers, the company had set a new trend in CE retailing in China. The company had also begun to focus on pre-sales service, as opposed to the industry practice of after-sales service, by advising customers on which brands to choose. Because this service was not easy to implement at the store level, where brands had their own commission-based sales staff, Gome was examining a new store format it called Eagle (Gome had been known earlier as China Eagle). Gome opened its first Eagle store in December 2005, in Shenyang. This mega-store, which occupied 15,000 square meters, differed in two ways: all sales staff at Eagle were on the payroll of Gome; and the display format was based on categories, not brands. The company was planning to open six to nine Eagle stores in the next three years, depending upon the performance of the first two.

The group was planning to expand rapidly into tier-two cities in particular, not only because of improvements in economies of scale and customer acquisition but also because, as a first mover, it could secure preferential tax treatments from local governments welcoming job-creation opportunities. It was unlikely that the second or third movers would be entitled to the benefits offered to the first mover.[16]

SUNING

Suning had grown from a regional air-conditioning retailer to a leading CE retail chain in China in less than a decade. It was in the process of converting its stores into a customer-oriented format it called "3C" (computers, communications, and consumer electronics). The company was on an expansion spree, increasing its stores fivefold in the last three years to 224, with more than half of them opening in 2005 alone, covering 61 cities. It was now planning to double the number of stores in two years. By the end of 2006, only 25 percent of Suning's retail space would have been open for two years or more. In common with Gome, which also had a high proportion of new retail space, rapid store expansion and entry into less affluent tier-two cities had led to lower productivity of retail space at Suning.[17]

Suning operated three types of stores that shared the same format: flagship, central, and community. The stores differed in size and product assortment. Flagship stores were found in large cities or regional headquarters. These stores were the largest in size and sold a wide variety of products. The central stores were most common. All the stores were CE retail stores targeting the mass market.

Suning sought differentiation in two ways. It was aligning its product assortment to address the needs of what it called "3C" customer groups (computers, communications, and consumer electronics). It was also using service as its key competitive advantage. The company had set up 15 regional distribution centers, 30 customer service centers, and 500 service stations of its own to reinforce the message that service was its main product.

Five Star

Five Star was China's third-largest electronics and appliances chain. It had 135 stores located mostly in the fast-growing, second-tier cities, in eight of China's 34 provinces. Founded in 1998 and headquartered in Nanjing in Jiangsu province, it had revenues of US$700 million in 2005, a 50 percent increase over 2004. The company's founder Wang Jianguo wanted to expand internationally but was constrained by delays in official permissions for listing his company abroad. "Our scale was becoming a bottleneck to development," he said.[18] When Best Buy sounded the idea of making an investment in the company, he decided to cash out and offload 75 percent stake in the company to Best Buy for $180 million. Five Star employed more than 12,000 of its own employees (see Exhibit 8).

ISSUES IN JUNE 2006

In examining the prospects of dual-branding strategy in China, Noble had to make a call on whether it would serve as well in China as it did in Canada. He had to define the road map for implementing the strategy in China. In a broader context, he also had to explore the possibility of developing dual branding into Best Buy's main competence over time.

Metric	Best Buy*	Five Star
Store size	86,000 square feet	35,000 square feet
Customers	Middle- to upper-income young singles and couples	Middle-income families Somewhat price sensitive
Service	Mixed-brand packaged solutions displayed by lifestyle requirements	Personal shopping assistants guiding customers through vendor booths; Attentive
Sales	Led by non-commissioned staff on Best Buy's payroll	Led by staff on the payroll of manufacturer
Customer profile	18–42 years old	20–50 years old
Brand identity	Premium full service	Good price with good services
In-store experience	Grab and go	Guided
Product mix (%)		White goods: 16% Air conditioning: 23% Home entertainment: 25% Digital products: 7% Cell phones: 13% Kitchen utensils: 9% Small appliances: 5%
Store associates	100% employed by Best Buy and non-commissioned	30% employed by Five Star on non-commission; 70% employed by vendors on commission
Sales growth Gross margin SG&A expense ratio Operating margin Sales per square foot Inventory turn Operating ROA		44% 13.5% 11.5% 2.0% $230 7 5%

Exhibit 8: Best Buy and Five Star – July 2006

Note: SG&A = selling, general and administrative; ROA = return on assets

Source: Company files

*Best Buy was yet to open its store in China as of June 2006.

Best Buy was now at a stage at which the learning it had gained from international expansion, initiated in 2002, could be used to accelerate the company's transformation in the U.S. domestic market, which it considered its core market. In his new role at Best Buy International, Noble was regularly tracking and evaluating global opportunities, looking for growing economies with buoyant consumer demand. Turkey and Mexico were potential targets for international expansion.

Customer centricity was a home-grown competence that Best Buy had deployed in Canada, and that seemed to have a universal appeal, applicable to any new market. SOP, which the company owned, was another. Geek Squad, a company innovation, seemed to be equally pervasive. Noble wondered whether a dual-branding strategy, which had been executed in Canada, could be as readily implemented in the international markets of the future. Was there a template of dual-branding that could be deployed, with a minor tweaking where necessary, to any new market, he wondered. What would that template be?

NOTES

1. "Best Buy Snaps up Future Shop for $580 Million," CBCNews.ca, August 14, 2001, www.cbc.ca/money/story/2001/08/14/futureshop140801.html, accessed September 12, 2008.

2. Best Buy 10-K filings 2001, p 5.

3. Ibid.

4. www.ce.org/research/US.CE industry growth 2004–2009(e), referenced March 31, 2009.

5. Consumer Electronics Association, "Global Consumer Electronics Industry Will Grow to $700 Million by 2009, CEA/GfK Study Finds," press release, July 9, 2008, www.ce.org/Press/CurrentNews/press_release_detail.asp?id=11535, accessed March 31, 2009.

6. Diana Farrell et al., From "Made in China" to "Sold in China": *The Rise of the Chinese Urban Consumer,* McKinsey Global Institute, November 2006.

7. Instat, "China's Consumer Electronics Manufacturing Will More Than Double by 2010," press release, October 11, 2006, www.instat.com/press.asp?ID=1768&sku=IN0602785CSM, accessed November 28, 2008.

8. In May 2008, Best Buy and Carphone Warehouse announced the creation a new joint venture company, in which Best Buy acquired 50% of The Carphone Warehouse's European and U.S. retail interests for a cash consideration of £1.1 billion, or US$2.1 billion.

9. Jean Zhou, Deutsche Bank equity research report on Suning Appliances, dated April 7, 2006.

10. Andrew Grant, "The New Chinese Consumer," *The McKinsey Quarterly*, Special Edition, June 2006, p. 1.

11. Claudia Suessmeth-Dykerhoff et al., "Marketing to China's New Traditionalists," *Far Eastern Economic Review,* April 2008, p. 29.

12. Kevin P. Lane et al., "Building Brands in China," *The McKinsey Quarterly*, Special Edition, June 2006, p. 39.

13. Normandy Madden, "Tier Tale: How Marketers Classify Cities in China," *Advertising Age,* March 19, 2007, p. 21.

14. Sandy Chen, Citigroup equity research report on Gome, dated October 12, 2005.

15. Russell Flannery, "Best Buy's Art of War," Forbes.com .www.forbes.com/services/forbes/2007/1015/066.html, accessed November 27, 2008.

16. Sandy Chen, Citigroup equity research report on Gome, dated October 12, 2005.

17. Jean Zhou, "Suning Appliance," Deutsche Bank Equity Research Report dated April 7, 2006.

18. Russell Flannery, "Best Buy's Art of War," Forbes .com, www.forbes.com/services/forbes/2007/1015/066.html, accessed November 28, 2008.

CASE QUESTIONS

1. Do you believe that the dual-branding option would work well for Best Buy in China? Why or why not?

2. What do you see as advantages for Best Buy acquiring Five Star?

3. Discuss the industry-level competitive advantage forces that exist in the CE market in China.

4. What types of research could Best Buy undertake in order to better address the dual-branding question?

5. How does buyer behavior toward electronics differ from behavior in the United States and Canada as it pertains to consumer acceptance and perception of consumer electronics? Discuss how this market may, or may not, be much different from the Canadian market.

CASE 5   LA HACIENDA DEL SOL

Neeta Khera

It was the morning of January 7, 2004, and Juanita Garcia, vice-president of administration of La Hacienda del Sol, a resort hotel in San Felipe, Mexico, was reviewing the fiscal 2003 financial records. The hotel catered primarily to American tourists during the country's hot summer months, but it had experienced another winter of low sales levels. Garcia had this problem each winter season and wondered how to better promote the hotel. Garcia considered targeting the Mexican market to improve sales levels in the off-season.[1]

San Felipe

La Hacienda del Sol (Hacienda) was located in San Felipe, Baja California. San Felipe was approximately 230 miles[2] from the United States/Mexican border. See Exhibit 1 for a map of Baja California. Due to its location in the northern part of the California Gulf, San Felipe attracted tourists who sought and enjoyed a beach vacation of two to four days in length. The city was known for its green-blue waters, clean beaches and comfortable climate and, as a result, was the most popular tourism spot, offering 1,600 hotel rooms, in Baja California. With a population of 25,000, the city attracted approximately 250,000 tourists each year.[3] See Exhibit 2 for a breakdown of the resort accommodations available in San Felipe.

La Hacienda del Sol

ACTIVITIES AND EVENTS

Hacienda offered a wide range of activities to tourists of all ages including swimming, surfing, jet-skiing, parasailing, jogging, and whale-watching. On the beach itself, there were many independent vendors who sold hair braiding services, horseback rides, ATV[4] rentals, and souvenirs. The hotel's premises included two outdoor swimming pools, children's playgrounds, pool tables, table tennis, racquetball courts, gardens, and shopping facilities. Additional activities during the summer months included bingo games, contests, and arts and crafts, to name a few.

DINING FACILITIES

There were two restaurants and three dining halls located on-site. One of the restaurants offered both American and Mexican food, with the focus mainly on traditional Mexican meals. This restaurant served food in two locations: a full-service sit-down room and a buffet-style room, with both rooms providing a wide variety of foods. The sit-down location had a casual atmosphere, and customers could come in and out of the restaurant at their convenience. The buffet-style location had specified hours for breakfast, lunch, and dinner. During the summer months, there were often regular performances on a stage during dinner (e.g., traditional Mexican dances) and, on some nights of the week, the room served as a nightclub after dinner. Consequently, it characteristically exhibited a fun and energetic atmosphere.

The second restaurant, adjacent to the hotel's main building, focused on a fine-dining experience and served French and Continental cuisine for lunch and dinner only. The restaurant was located in the founder's original mansion, with most of the mansion's original drapery, carpets, floors, lighting, and

Neeta Khera prepared this case under the supervision of Elizabeth M.A. Grasby solely to provide material for class discussion. The authors do not intend to illustrate either effective or ineffective handling of a managerial situation. The authors may have disguised certain names and other identifying information to protect confidentiality.

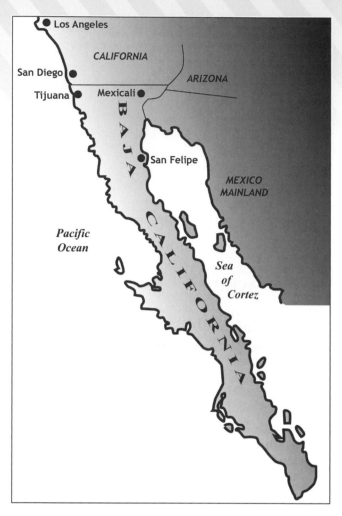

Exhibit 1: Map of Baja California

Type of Accommodation	Number of Facilities
Resorts	4
Hotels/motels	8
Condominiums and apartments	15
Bed and breakfasts	1
RV and campgrounds	2
Total	30

Exhibit 2: Accommodations Available in San Felipe
Source: Company files.

background added to the spa's relaxing atmosphere and sophisticated ambiance.

Many wedding packages were made available by the hotel to suit customers' needs. For example, a package that included a three-course meal for 50 guests, champagne, a reception site by the garden or ocean, soft drinks, linens and seat covers, waiters, and flower arrangements for the reception tables cost $1,260.[6] Between the months of July and October, the hotel held, on average, one wedding per week. Many brides and their bridal parties took advantage of the spa before their wedding ceremony at the hotel.

HOTEL ROOMS

The price of the rooms changed each season depending on the expected demand. See Exhibits 3 and 4 for a breakdown and prices of the rooms. Each room included a full bath, telephone, cable television, and bottled water. The price of the room also included one margarita per person and dinner for two from the hotel's Special Getaways menu. For families with up to two children, the children were given free accommodations and three meals each day from the children's menu. Rates were also lowered for seniors. Parking was available on-site to customers at $3 per car per night.

The hotel operated at a 90 percent to 100 percent occupancy rate from the last week of June to the first week of September. The weekends were generally fully booked, while some rooms were available during the weekdays. Due to the seasonality of the business, the hotel depended on its success in July and August to carry it through the rest of the year. After Labor Day weekend,[7]

furniture originating from the 1920s. Occasionally, a pianist would play on a grand piano to create a mellow ambiance.

In addition to the two restaurants, the hotel had three bars. The bars were the second largest source of income, representing 25 percent of revenue.[5]

THE SPA

The hotel's European-style spa offered a variety of services, which were growing in popularity even though many customers were unaware of the hotel's spa prior to arrival. Garcia recently introduced a promotional offering that included a room and spa deal, which helped encourage the growth in spa sales. The spa, located in the second half of the founder's mansion, offered hairstyling, waxing, over 10 different types of body treatments, reflexology, manicures, pedicures, and facials. The pleasant service, pastel-colored walls and furniture, and soft music playing in the

Type of Room	Number of Rooms Available	Number of People/Room
Garden view rooms	40	2
Ocean front rooms	134	2
Junior suites	26	2
One bedroom suites	42	2
Apartments	4	4
Two bedroom suites	11	4
Master suite	18	4
Presidential suite	1	4
Total	**276**	

Exhibit 3: Breakdown of Hotel Rooms

Source: Company files.

Type of Room	Summer Rates	
	Sunday to Thursday	Friday and Saturday
Garden view rooms	$ 97.30	$ 125.30
Ocean front rooms	$ 111.30	$ 160.30
Junior suites	$ 125.30	$ 174.30
One bedroom suites	$ 132.30	$ 188.30
Apartments	$ 139.30	$ 209.30
Two bedroom suites	$ 160.30	$ 237.30
Master suite	$ 174.30	$ 244.30
Presidential suite	$ 300.30	$ 370.30

Type of Room	Autumn, Winter, Spring Rates (off-season)	
	Sunday to Thursday	Friday and Saturday
Garden view rooms	$ 69.30	$ 118.30
Ocean front rooms	$ 90.30	$ 139.30
Junior suites	$ 111.30	$ 153.30
One bedroom suites	$ 125.30	$ 174.30
Apartments	$ 139.30	$ 195.30
Two bedroom suites	$ 160.30	$ 209.30
Master suite	$ 174.30	$ 230.30
Presidential suite	$ 307.30	$ 349.30

Exhibit 4: 2003 Hotel Rates[*]

Source: Company files.

All prices are in U.S. dollars per night (regardless of occupancy).

occupancy levels dropped dramatically, reaching 30 percent on weekdays and between 60 percent to 80 percent on some weekends. From November to March, occupancy averaged 20 percent all week. The hotel would reach 90 percent occupancy only during the weeks that college students had their spring break holiday (typically in late February); the hotel continued to average an occupancy rate of 20 percent between the end of spring break and the last week of June. U.S. holidays typically put the resort at full capacity regardless of the time of year.

Juanita Garcia

The hotel had been a private, family-run business for over 75 years. Juanita Garcia was the third generation family member to operate the business, with her father holding the position of chief executive officer (CEO) for over 20 years. Garcia's father, his two daughters, and his three sons were the only shareholders of the business.

Garcia and her siblings were approached by their father to take over the family business in the summer of 1999. Juanita Garcia was the only one interested, since the other children knew how difficult the task would be from witnessing the number of hours worked by their father. She stepped into the role of vice-president of administration and was initially responsible for promoting the hotel, creating new marketing strategies, and managing communications between the company and its shareholders. Juanita knew that if she was going to take over the business one day, she needed to understand the company and what would make it successful.

Los Angeles	
Total Population (2003)	3,819,951
Average Personal Income per Capita	$26,773
Unemployment Rate	6.8%
% of Family Households	16.4%
% of Families with children under the age of 18	53.5%
% of People 65 years and older	9.7%
Distance from San Felipe	6.5 driving hours

Source: City of Los Angeles: www.ci.la.ca.us, February 7, 2005, and U.S. Census Bureau: www.census.gov/statab/www, February 7, 2005.

San Diego	
Total Population (2003)	1,266,753
Average Personal Income per Capita	$27,657
Unemployment Rate	3.0%
% of Family Households	16.4%
% of Families with children under the age of 18	53.4%
% of People 65 years and older	10.5%
Distance from San Felipe	4.5 driving hours

Exhibit 5: Los Angeles and San Diego demographics

Source: City of San Diego: www.sandiego.gov, February 7, 2005, and U.S. Census Bureau: www.census.gov/statab/www, February 7, 2005.

Running a family business provided the flexibility needed to make quick operational decisions; however, all recommendations had to be approved by Garcia's father. If her father was not convinced initially or was remotely skeptical, he completely dismissed any recommendations. All proposed recommendations had to be well supported.

HOTEL GUESTS

From late June to early September, Hacienda targeted families who spent, on average, $500 during their stay at the hotel (typically three days and two nights). During the off-season, the hotel attracted seniors and couples who were looking for a peaceful getaway. The highest-spending consumers were between the ages of 28 and 49, primarily due to their liquor purchases.

At one time, the hotel attracted a large number of college students during the spring break season. Garcia wondered if this market was suitable given the hotel's reputation.

Ninety-five percent of the hotel's customers were from the United States, half from Los Angeles and the other half from San Diego. See Exhibit 5 for selected information on the two cities. Of the remaining five percent, two percent were from the state of Baja California with the remaining three percent from the other parts of the United States.

The Mexican Market

Garcia was hopeful that targeting the Mexican market during the off-season would help boost sales. Hotel management had never considered entering this market since it was believed that Hacienda's rates would be too high. Furthermore, it was well known that Hacienda catered to the American market, leaving Mexicans with the perception that they were not welcome. Garcia knew that if the company were to enter this market, she would have to address this perception.

MEXICALI

Mexicali, the capital of Baja California, was 124 miles from Hacienda and was well known for its agriculture and Maquiladoras;[8] however, half the working population was employed in the tourism industry with 44 percent employed by hotels and restaurants.

Of Mexicali's 813,853 population, 14 percent lived in rural areas. See Exhibits 6 and 7 for additional information on the Mexicali population.

Mexicali was also known for its extreme climate. See Exhibit 8 for typical annual temperatures. Residents were always looking to get away during the hot months. Those who could afford it generally owned a second home where the climate was not as uncomfortable.

HOTEL RATES

Mexicans viewed the hotel as overpriced, so Garcia knew that she needed to come up with a package

Age Bracket	Percent of Population
0 to 14	32
15 to 24	20
25 to 54	38
55 and over	10

Exhibit 6: Age Distribution of Mexicali Residents

Source: California Center for Border and Regional Economic Studies: www.ccbres.sdsu.edu, July 19, 2004.

Annual Household Income	Percent of Population
Less than $1,174	1.4
$1,174 to $1,388	2.3
$1,389 to $2,669	7.1
$2,670 to $3,949	7.7
$3,950 to $5,337	14.8
$5,338 to $10,674	25.1
$10,675 to $16,011	22.5
$16,012 to $21,349	9.7
More than $21,350	9.4

Exhibit 7: Annual Household Income of Mexicali Families

Note: Converted from pesos to U.S. dollars on December 31, 2002, at a rate of $0.08895/peso.

Source: California Center for Border and Regional Economic Studies: www.ccbres.sdsu.edu, July 19, 2004.

Month	Temperature
January	75°F
February	73°F
March	84°F
April	80°F
May	93°F
June	105°F
July	116°F
August	96°F
September	105°F
October	98°F
November	69°F
December	64°F

Exhibit 8: Annual Weather in Mexicali 2003

Note: The maximum temperature on the 15th of each month.

deal to attract these customers to the hotel; nevertheless, she was uncertain whether a lower rate should be offered just to Mexicali residents. A marketing manager who used a similar strategy in another hotel suggested advertising at a rate equal to half the season's average monthly temperature (in Fahrenheit) for a garden view room. The rates of all other rooms would have to be priced accordingly. Garcia wanted to consider this pricing strategy due to the hotel's vacancy rates. She did not want to limit her analysis to this pricing strategy and was open to any alternatives.

PROMOTION TIMING

Garcia also needed to decide when to offer such a promotion. She wanted to focus only on one of the seasons initially: summer (June to August), autumn (September to November), winter (December to February), or spring (March to May). Consideration would need to be given to the $20 daily cost to maintain each room, regardless of size, which included employee wages, linens, electricity, water, sewage costs, and any other amenities. These costs were only incurred while the room was occupied.

Promotion

The hotel spent, on average, $150,000 to $200,000 on advertising during its off-season each year. Currently, Hacienda promoted through newspaper, press releases, radio, and on its website. The hotel could not afford the expensive television advertising in the United States.

The hotel's website was the first of its kind to be listed on the Internet in Mexico. Although the site was not aesthetically appealing, it was known as being user-friendly and received approximately 1,000 hits per day. It had been the most up-to-date hotel website in Mexico until December 2003 when one of its competitors had upgraded its site. Garcia suggested to her father on numerous occasions that the website should be upgraded, but he remained unconvinced. He thought that since the hotel reached 100 percent capacity during the summer months, the website upgrade could not be justified from a financial perspective.

Approximately five percent of the Mexicali population had access to a computer. Garcia estimated that only one percent of the population in Mexicali had access both to a computer and to the Internet and, of those who had access to the Internet, 0.5 percent of targeted consumers would visit the hotel by viewing the hotel's website, per season.

Television was very common in Mexicali, regardless of the income level of the household. Garcia estimated that 85 percent of Mexicali residents had access to a television and watched regularly. She predicted that 15 percent of targeted television viewers would visit the hotel in the summer months and 2.5 percent would visit during the off-season. There were two local television stations in Mexicali. If Hacienda were to advertise on television, Garcia thought it would be best to pay for airtime during the peak times of the day: 7 a.m. to 8 a.m. and 7 p.m. to 9 p.m. During these time periods, the cost was at its highest: $41.25[9] for each 30-second advertisement.

There were also two popular radio stations to consider. Each 30-second ad cost $10.50. Statistics indicated that 45 percent of the population listened to the radio. Garcia predicted six percent to 8.5 percent of targeted listeners would visit the hotel in the summer, and one percent would visit the hotel in the off-season.

Although newspaper was a popular form of advertising to Americans, Garcia believed distributing flyers in a local mall would be a more viable option. Since there was only one air-conditioned mall in Mexicali, a large portion of the population shopped at this mall during the hot months. The cost to produce 1,000 flyers would be $2.30. For every 1,000 flyers, there was an additional distribution cost of $27.50. A response rate between two percent and three percent of the target market was expected per season.

Garcia needed to estimate a reasonable budget in order to promote to this market segment, and she wanted to initially use one type of promotional medium for one season to test the new market. She knew that her father would not agree to spend more than $50,000 per season on additional promotions. She had to assess how best to spend the budget—all on radio ads, all on television ads, or $10,000 per season on flyers.

Decision

Garcia knew that the hotel needed a solution to its low sales in the off-season. She wondered whether it was viable to target the Mexicali market and whether it was a good fit with the company's marketing strategy. If so, she needed to decide on the room rates, the type of promotional media to use and when to start advertising. She knew she had to give some incentives to the Mexicans to entice them to come to the hotel in addition to heavily promoting specific services that would cater to this new market. She had to have a convincing argument to give to her father if some positive changes were to be made to the company's current financial position.

NOTES

1. The months when travel activity was at its lowest.

2. One mile is equivalent to 1.609 kilometers.

3. State Government of Baja California: www.bajacalifornia.gob.mx/english/home.htm, July 19, 2004.

4. All-terrain vehicles.

5. Rooms represented 60 percent of revenue with remaining revenues derived from restaurant and spa sales.

6. All prices in the case are in U.S. dollars.

7. The weekend prior to the first Monday in September of each year.

8. Maquiladoras are assembly plants in Mexico that import raw materials from a foreign country, namely the United States, and export the finished goods to the same foreign country.

9. All costs converted to U.S. dollars as at January 7, 2004.

CASE QUESTIONS

1. What types of market segmentation appear to work well for La Hacienda del Sol?

2. What types of sales promotion techniques would work well for La Hacienda del Sol?

3. What pricing strategies would work well for La Hacienda del Sol?

4. How can La Hacienda del Sol work to change Mexican consumer perceptions of the resort?

5. What cultural issues are relevant as they apply to hotel purchasing behavior?

CASE 6   DABUR INDIA[1]

Manish Khandelwal

I don't want to be seen as just an Indian company. I want to be seen as a company which does business in various parts of the world.

—Sunil Duggal, chief executive officer, Dabur India

In the autumn of 2010, Sunil Duggal was deep in thought as his flight was announced for departure from Chicago to Delhi. O'Hare International Airport was bustling with activity, but Duggal had hardly taken any notice of his surroundings. As he headed toward the departure gate, he pondered the challenges that lay ahead. He was returning to India after signing a deal to acquire a U.S.-based natural hair care company, Namaste Laboratory, for $100 million, a deal that would determine the future of his bold global strategy for the personal care company he headed, Dabur India.

History of Dabur[2]

Dr. S. K. Burman established Dabur in 1884 to produce and dispense ayurvedic medicine. Ayurveda originated in India approximately 3,000 years ago. It is a system for living in harmony with nature and oneself in order to remain healthy. This is achieved through an equilibrium among biochemical processes, balance of fluids in the body, and the principle of movement. Dr. Burman's mission was to provide effective and affordable care for ordinary people in far-flung villages. With missionary zeal and fervor, he undertook the task of preparing natural cures for killer diseases such as cholera, malaria, and plague.

Soon the news of his medicines traveled, and he came to be known as the trusted Daktar (doctor) who came up with effective cures. That is how Dabur got its name: it is derived from the Devanagri rendition of Daktar Burman.

Dr. Burman's commitment and ceaseless efforts resulted in the company going from a fledgling medicine manufacturer in a small Calcutta house to become a household name that evoked trust and reliability (**Exhibit 1**). Dabur had grown from a market capitalization of Rs.17 billion to 170 billion ($1 = Rs.45[3]) from 2001 to 2010 and had declared strong financial results in 2010 (**Exhibits 2–4**). By the end of the twentieth century, Dabur had become the fourth-largest Fast Moving Consumer Good (FMCG) company in India, next only to Hindustan Unilever, Indian Tobacco Company, and Nestlé India (**Exhibit 5**). The Burman family, who still controlled the firm, had forged ahead within the founding concepts of Dr. Burman, while also evolving and progressing in line with the changing demands of a growing business. In particular, the company had transitioned from being purely ayurvedic to becoming the "herbal specialist," and while herbal businesses accounted for 85 percent of revenues, the company's growth ambitions were not limited by it but extended to natural products more generally.

The company operated through three business units: consumer care (72 percent of 2010 revenues), consumer health (8 percent), and international (18 percent). [4]

The consumer care division (CCD) catered to seven distinct segments: hair care, oral care, health supplements, digestives and candies, home care, baby oil and skin care, and foods. The hair care segment products included hair oils, widely used in India, and shampoos. These products were marketed in India under the brands Dabur Amla, Vatika, and Anmol. In the oral care segment the company offered products including toothpastes, tooth powder, and toothbrushes under the brands Dabur, Babool, Meswak, and Promise. The health supplement products included chyawanprash (an immunity

Manish Khandelwal, Sloan Fellow 2011, and John Roberts, the John H. Scully Professor of Economics, Strategic Management and International Business, prepared this case as the basis for class discussion rather than to illustrate either effective or ineffective handling of an administrative situation.

Dabur India: Key Highlights

✓ Established in 1884 - more than 125 Years of Trust & Excellence

✓ Among top 4 FMCG companies in India

✓ World's largest in Ayurveda and natural healthcare

✓ Revenue of Rs. 34 billion and profits of Rs. 5 billion in FY2009-10

✓ Strong brand equity

  ❖ Dabur is a household brand

  ❖ Vatika and Real are Superbrands

  ❖ Hajmola , Real & Dabur ranked among India's Most Admired Brands

✓ 10 Brands with sales of over Rs. 1 billion each

✓ Wide distribution network covering 2.8 million retailers across the country

✓ 17 world class manufacturing plants catering to needs of diverse markets

✓ Strong overseas presence with 20% contribution to consolidated sales

Ten Billion Rupee Brands

Dabur ranked 200 in the Fortune India 500 list

SUPER

Dabur moves up to take the 78th spot in the Super-100 list, released by Business India

INDIA'S MOST TRUSTED BRANDS

Dabur ranked 45 among Most Trusted Brands in India, according to Brand Trust Report, India Study, 2011

Exhibit 1: Dabur India: Key Highlights

Source: Dabur India.

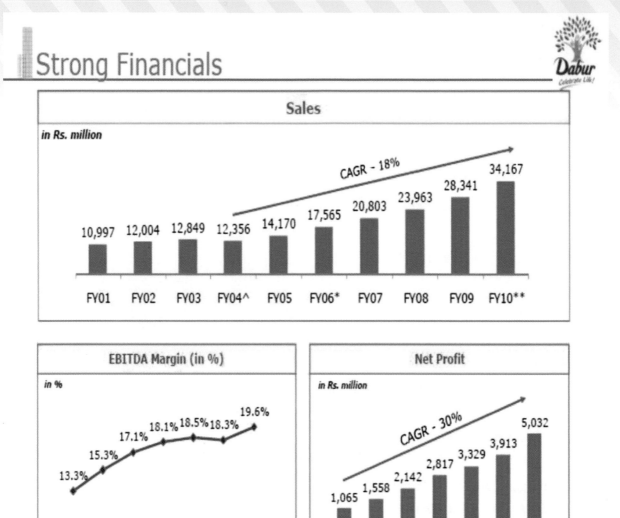

^Sales show a decline in FY04 on account of de-merger of Pharma business
*Balsara acquisition added 10% to topline in FY06
** Fem acquisition added 3.5% to topline in FY10

Exhibit 2: Dabur Financial Summary

Source: Dabur India.

PROFIT & LOSS ACCOUNT for the year ended March 31, 2010

(All amounts in Indian Rupees in lacs, except share data)

	Schedule	For the year ended March 31, 2010	For the year ended March 31, 2009
INCOME :	J		
Sales Less Returns		288045	242368
Less: Excise Duty		2358	2752
Net Sales		**285687**	**239616**
Other Income		3284	4306
Total Income		**288971**	**243922**
EXPENDITURE :			
Cost of Materials	K	137393	122243
Manufacturing Expenses	L	7618	7076
Payments to and provisions for Employees	M	21234	16732
Selling and Administrative expenses	N	65706	50901
Financial Expenses	O	560	1334
Miscellaneous Expenditure Written off	IB	566	394
Depreciation		3191	2742
Total Expenditure		**236268**	**201422**
Balance being Operating Net Profit before Taxation		**52703**	**42500**
Provision for Taxation Current		8966	4748
Deferred		404	-255
Fringe Benefit		0	651
Net Profit After Taxation		**43333**	**37356**
Balance Brought Forward		42894	32323
Provision for Taxation of earlier years written back		(2)	0
Provision for Taxation of earlier years		21	72
		86208	69607
APPROPRIATIONS			
Interim Dividend		6498	6488
Proposed Final Dividend		10862	8651
Corporate Tax on Interim Dividend		1104	1103
Corporate Tax on Proposed Dividend		1846	1470
Transferred to Capital Reserve		207	1
Transferred to General Reserve		13000	9000
Balance carried over to Balance sheet		**52691**	**42894**
		86208	69607
EARNING PER SHARE (in Rs.) after consideration of extraordinary item (Re 1/- Per Share)			
Basic		4.99	4.31
Diluted		4.97	4.29
EARNING PER SHARE (in Rs.) without consideration of extraordinary item (Re 1/- Per Share)			
Basic		4.98	4.31
Diluted		4.96	4.29
NOTES TO ACCOUNTS	P		

Exhibit 3: Dabur 2010 Income Statement

Source: Dabur India.

BALANCE SHEET as at March 31, 2010

(All amounts in Indian Rupees in lacs, except share data)

	Schedule	As at March 31, 2010		As at March 31, 2009	
SOURCES OF FUNDS :					
Shareholders' Funds :					
Capital	A	8,690		8,651	
Reserves & Surplus	B	66,248	74,938	65,169	73,820
Loan Funds:					
Secured Loans	C	2,427		1,065	
Unsecured Loans	D	8,570		13,072	
			10,997		14,137
Deferred Tax Liability (Net)	EB		1,195		695
Total			**87,130**		**88,652**
APPLICATION OF FUNDS :					
Fixed Assets :					
Gross Block	F	68,723		51,877	
Less : Depreciation		23,628		21,045	
Net Block		45,095		30,832	
Capital work in Progess (including capital advances)		2,331	47,426	5,171	36,003
Investments	G		34,851		43,690
Current Assets, Loans and Advances:	H				
Inventories		29,844		26,172	
Sundry Debtors		13,048		11,236	
Cash & Bank Balances		16,391		14,369	
Loans & Advances		32,512		22,728	
		91,795		74,505	
Less: Current Liabilities and Provisions	EA				
Liabilities		43,206		33,121	
Provisions		44,010		33,289	
		87,216		66,410	
Net Current Assets			4,579		8,095
Miscellaneous Expenditure (To the extent not written off or adjusted)	IA		274		864
Notes to Accounts	P				
Total			**87,130**		**88,652**

Exhibit 4: Dabur 2010 Balance Sheet

Source: Dabur India.

Key Players: FMCG

USD Million

Company	Key Categories	Sales	Profit	Market Cap
Hindustan Unilever Ltd	Soaps, Detergents, Personal Care, Foods	4,479	538	12,897
Nestle India Ltd*	Food, Beverages, Infant nutrition	1,101	141	6,867
Dabur India Ltd	**Personal, Health & Homecare, Foods**	733	108	3,475
Britannia Industries Ltd*	Biscuits	734	33	918
Colgate Palmolive (I) Ltd*	Oral Care & Toiletries	364	62	2,381
Marico Ltd.	Hair care, Food, Skincare	571	49	1,513
Glaxo Smithkline Consumer*	Consumer Health Care	412	50	1,881
Godrej Consumer	Hair Care, Soaps	438	72	2,315
Procter & Gamble^	Feminine Hygiene, personal care	166	39	1,033

Source: Published results for year ending 31.03.10

*Year ending 31.12.09

^Year ending 30.06.09

Note: Market Cap. as of 06.02.11

Exhibit 5: Fast Moving Consumer Goods: Key Players

Source: Dabur India.

builder), glucose D, and honey. The digestives segment sold herbal products to aid digestion under numerous brands such as Hajmola, Pudin Hara, Sat Isabgol, and Hingoli. The baby and skin care products included Lal Tail, Dabur Gulabri, honey saffron soap, and Dabur ayurvedic baby care products. The company's home care products segment was comprised of Odomos (mosquito repellant), Odonil, and Sani Fresh, a toilet cleaner. The company's food segment focused on providing juices, nectars, and drinks under the Real, Activ, Homemade, and Coolers brands. It also supplied food additives such as garlic pastes, peach halves, pear halves, snack dressing, and tomato puree.

The consumer health division (CHD) dealt in products based on the ayurvedic medicinal platform. The range of offerings, which were based on traditional medicinal formulations, was classified into over-the-counter products (OTCs), branded ethical, and generic products.

The international business division offered health and personal care products across different markets including the Middle East, North and West Africa, the European Union, and the United States.

Dabur India's success was based on dedication to natural products, hygiene, dynamic leadership, and commitment to partners and stakeholders.

In 2011, Dabur had three subsidiary group companies—Dabur International, Fem Care Pharma, and New U, as well as step-down local subsidiaries in Nepal, Egypt, Bangladesh, Pakistan, Nigeria, the United Arab Emirates, and the United States. There were 17 ultra-modern manufacturing units spread around the globe, and the company's products were marketed in over 60 countries. Dabur had a strong focus on innovation, although it used an unusual model for product development. New product ideas were collected from local operations and then outside labs were commissioned to develop the products to Dabur's specifications, with Dabur owning the intellectual property.

Over the years, the Burman family had recognized the need for professional management to launch Dabur onto a high-growth path. The company was listed on the Bombay Stock Exchange in 1994 and the family hired professional management to oversee day-to-day operations in 1998. Since 2000, family members had withdrawn from all management positions and participated only as directors on a board with an equal number of independent non-executive directors.

The company had problems in transitioning from family management to professionals. A team of senior managers from multinationals was recruited in 2000, but it failed, forcing a further change after a year. Duggal, who had been with the company for seven years at that time, took over as CEO in 2001 and brought the company back on track through operational efficiencies and smart marketing.

The International Division

The international division was set up in the early 1990s and was more the result of an accident than a strategy.

Duggal explained: "Dabur globalization followed a certain evolutionary path, and it was not something which was decided on the template and then executed." The genesis of the overseas business lay in the demands of the Indian diaspora in the Middle East. This emigration began in the mid-twentieth century and resulted in a substantial concentration of ethnic Indians in the Middle East, specifically in Dubai and Saudi Arabia. They wanted the Dabur products they knew from home. Their demand was met through underground or gray channels. Most of the products were bought by individuals in India, carried in their luggage to the Middle East, and sold at a hefty premium. Driving this business was Amla hair oil, which took its name from an Indian medicinal fruit used in its preparation.

While this expatriate market was attractive, the company soon realized that Dabur's beauty care and hair care products also had value for many Arab women. For centuries, Indians and Arabs had interacted. More recently, Bollywood had had a large influence, and Indian beauty care products were associated with Indian film stars.

Dabur decided to pursue the local business actively. To build on the opportunity this market offered it set up a distribution system in Dubai. Dabur began to gain a foothold in the GCC (Gulf Cooperation Council, a free trade area of the United Arab Emirates, Bahrain, Saudi Arabia, Oman, Qatar, and Kuwait), as well as in Egypt. The business soon became profitable, since margins in the region were significantly higher than in India. Arab consumers had a significantly higher income and propensity to spend, which opened up new opportunities to expand the product portfolio.

This was a critical step and, as Duggal explained:

> Once we decided to pursue this international opportunity, we started slowly building up global supply chains. I think that was really something which nobody else had even thought of. We set up our first overseas plant in Jebel Ali in the UAE in the early 1990s, which enabled savings of 5 percent duties as per the GCC Trade agreement. Dabur could sell its hair oil all across the Middle East and parts of North Africa with zero duties. And then we took a big leap of faith and created the international business division in 2004.

Dabur decided to build a new premium brand, Vatika, substantially for Arab women. It invested upfront in building a consumer franchise through electronic media. This was facilitated by the fact that the media environment was comparatively un-fragmented. There were a couple of very powerful and popular pan-Arabic channels. Advertisements on those channels, which were reasonably priced despite the market concentration, gave huge visibility across the Arab world, including in the GCC, Yemen, North Africa, Jordan, Syria, and Iraq.

Meanwhile, in the domestic market, Dabur acquired two companies, Balsara Hygiene and Fem India. The Balsara acquisition was driven by a peculiar tactical problem. The company's only oral care product was a tooth powder, a rapidly declining category. So Dabur launched a line extension via a herbal toothpaste called Red Toothpaste. Being an ayurvedic product, it had a limited reach, and Dabur needed to create a portfolio for toothpaste brands quickly. Balsara filled the gap through its oral care brands such as Promise, Babool, and Meswak toothpastes. It also brought mosquito repellants like Odomos and household products like Odonil bug repellant. The acquisition marked Dabur's entry into the $400 million household care business in India.

Fem Care Pharma Ltd. had a leadership position in the fairness bleach (skin lightening) category and a strong market position in hair removal and liquid soap, and was best known for its brand "FEM." The other brands in its portfolio included Oxybleach cream, Botanica anti-aging cream, Stratum color-protecting hair conditioners, and Bambi fabric softeners. Fem Care had a sizeable international presence in markets such as Yemen, Maldives, Mauritius, Malaysia, UAE, and Oman.

Dabur then introduced its new oral care products to international markets, again mainly in the Middle East. It aggressively promoted Meswak toothpaste and gained substantial market share through aggressive brand building and effective supply chain management. However, this growth was not without its own set of challenges.

The Middle East had a different distribution model than the one that prevailed in India. India's retail sector had been growing at over 7 percent annually. A large proportion was unorganized, in the form of scattered mom-and-pop stores that required a very resource-intensive distribution process in terms of manpower and logistics. In the traditional Indian distribution system, there were three layers of middlemen between manufacturer and consumers: the distributor (carrying and forwarding agent), the wholesaler (who would make investments in stocks and sell in smaller quantities), and the retailer (owners of small grocery shops spread across the country). In contrast, the trade that prevailed in the Middle East was more "cash and carry," in which very large retailers would buy directly from the manufacturer and sell to consumers. This meant that manufacturers had to be much more proactive in sales and distribution and could not depend on an army of distributors or wholesalers to push their products. Indian managers in the international division were quick to learn the new trade model, and they were successful.

Encouraged by its success in the region, Dabur decided to expand its production capability to new countries. Egypt was first. The initial outcome was quite adverse, as Duggal recalled:

> So we then put up [a] plant in Egypt, which I think was ahead of its time, because the market was too tiny to sustain all the costs and infrastructure of a plant. That business struggled for many years. I think the plant was set up in the early '90s, and for around 10 years we didn't see any money. In fact, the losses were pretty substantial. The whole overseas play became a matter of deep concern, whether this was something which we should pursue, or . . . just something which we got a little bit lucky in and we could not extend beyond the GCC area.

But Dabur persisted, and patience was rewarded as sales started picking up slowly and then gained momentum between 2001 and 2003. Dabur was lucky with its next big break, in 2004, which came in the field of oral care products in Nigeria. Dabur was exporting its Dabur herbal toothpaste brand to Nigeria and was third in market share after Close-Up and Colgate. However, the government of Nigeria suddenly decided to ban imports of toothpastes, and Colgate decided to exit the market, leaving a large gap. Dabur was quick to take advantage of the opportunity and set up a manufacturing facility in Nigeria. Once a supply chain was established in Nigeria, Dabur started selling to nearby markets and ramped up considerable growth.

CHANGING COMPETITIVE LANDSCAPE IN INDIAN MARKETS

Meanwhile India was already achieving almost 8 percent growth, and there was a huge middle class willing to spend money on the best global brands. Hindustan Unilever and ITC were market leaders in home and personal care products, followed by Colgate and Dabur. Market attractiveness, along with increasing pressure for growth, drew the increasing attention of big and small multinational corporations to Indian markets (**Exhibit 6**). Seeking quick entry into these markets led to intense M&A activity. Most Indian companies were valued at rich premium as measured by valuations to sales. As an example, Paras Pharmaceuticals, another home care product company, was acquired by Reckitt at nearly seven times sales, making it one of the most expensive deals in the FMCG sector worldwide in 2010.[5] Duggal explained the implications for Dabur: "People are signing blank checks to get a foothold and presence and scale in the Indian market. And I am worried that 80 per cent of my business is in India. There is vulnerability, because at the end of the day, I am competing with MNCs, the big boys, in every category."

This opinion was echoed by a report from the Confederation of Indian Industry:[6]

There are numerous instances of foreign FMCG attention to India: Kraft Foods acquired Cadbury in 2009 to establish a foothold in developing countries such as India. Ferrero Roche is planning to expand presence in India in the confectionary segment. French cosmetics major L'Oreal is planning to enter the deodorant segment, which is growing at 30 per cent annually. GSK Consumer has recently expanded into the noodles and biscuits market in India through its flagship brand Horlicks. We can expect the foreign FMCG MNCs already operating in India to focus on the Indian business even more strongly and develop their Indian subsidiaries as a significant contributor to global business by increasing penetration of existing products, while introducing greater variety, broadening category portfolios and developing new brands and innovations. The multinationals not present in India can be expected to look for entry opportunities in terms of organic or inorganic expansion in the future.

International Acquisitions

Dabur was quick to realize the possible consequences of increased competition in its Indian markets. It had to choose between local inorganic growth and international acquisitions if it were to grow (**Exhibit 7**). In 2009 the board decided to grow the international business, increasing its share of revenue from 25 percent to 50 percent over the next two years. Mohit Malhotra, CEO of the international division, had built a strong case for international focus through robust growth in the preceding few years, and he was confident of future prospects for Dabur outside India (**Exhibit 8**).

Dabur did, however, pass on one potential international acquisition opportunity that another Indian firm bought, and it was beaten to the punch by an Indian rival on another. In Egypt it had the opportunity to buy Fiancee and Hair Code, which manufactured hair cream and hair gels. After due diligence and negotiations, the deal did not come through, as Dabur felt the multiples being asked for were much higher than the estimated brand valuation. Marico (an Indian company) finally bought these brands. Similarly, in Malaysia, there was an acquisition opportunity of a company called Unza. This was a personal care and toiletries company with business primarily in Southeast Asia and some equity in the Middle East through brands like Enchanteur. This company was taken over by Wipro.[7] These lost opportunities made Duggal reassess his valuation parameters and served as good lessons for subsequent acquisitions.

Per Capita Consumption: Room for Growth

India has low per capita consumption as compared to other emerging economies

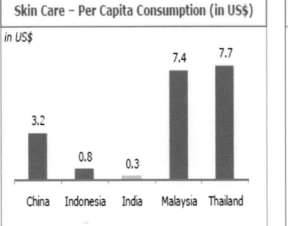

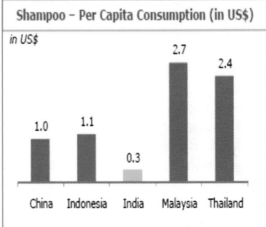

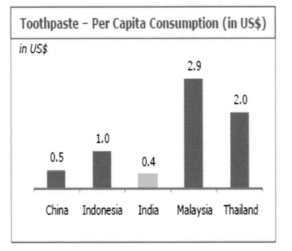

Source: MOSL

Exhibit 6: India: Personal Care Products Per Capita Consumption

Source: Dabur India.

Expansion Strategy

Strengthening new categories
- ✓ **Skin Care:** Ayurvedic skin care range under a new brand launched; Acquisition of Fem
- ✓ **OTC Healthcare:** Leveraging Ayurveda knowledge for a range of OTC herbal products
- ✓ **Fruit Drinks and Culinary:** Entry into the fast growing fruit drinks category leveraging the Real franchise

Targeting inorganic opportunities
- ✓ **Market Entry:** Acquisitions critical for building scale in existing categories & markets
- ✓ **Synergies:** Should be synergistic and make a good strategic fit
- ✓ **Geographies:** Opportunities in focus markets

Strong innovation programme
- ✓ **Contribution:** New products to contribute 5-6% of revenues
- ✓ **Focus Categories:** New product activations planned up in all categories
- ✓ **Renovation:** Periodic brand renovations to keep older products salient

Expanding across geographies
- ✓ **Overseas markets:** 20% of overall company; target to sustain higher growth rates
- ✓ **South India:** Increased contribution from 7% to 12%; Continued focus on the relevant portfolio to grow contribution

Exhibit 7: Dabur Expansion Strategy

Source: Dabur India.

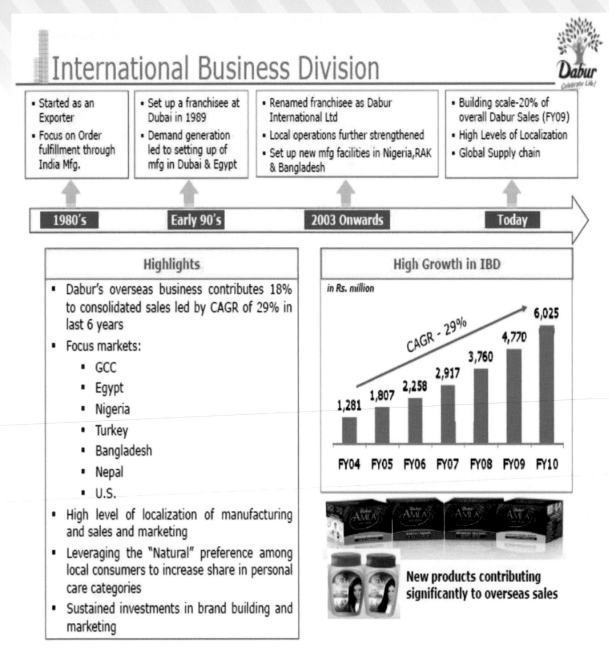

International Business Division

1980's	Early 90's	2003 Onwards	Today
• Started as an Exporter • Focus on Order fulfillment through India Mfg.	• Set up a franchisee at Dubai in 1989 • Demand generation led to setting up of mfg in Dubai & Egypt	• Renamed franchisee as Dabur International Ltd • Local operations further strengthened • Set up new mfg facilities in Nigeria,RAK & Bangladesh	• Building scale-20% of overall Dabur Sales (FY09) • High Levels of Localization • Global Supply chain

Highlights

- Dabur's overseas business contributes 18% to consolidated sales led by CAGR of 29% in last 6 years
- Focus markets:
  - GCC
  - Egypt
  - Nigeria
  - Turkey
  - Bangladesh
  - Nepal
  - U.S.
- High level of localization of manufacturing and sales and marketing
- Leveraging the "Natural" preference among local consumers to increase share in personal care categories
- Sustained investments in brand building and marketing

High Growth in IBD

in Rs. million

CAGR - 29%

FY04	FY05	FY06	FY07	FY08	FY09	FY10
1,281	1,807	2,258	2,917	3,760	4,770	6,025

New products contributing significantly to overseas sales

Exhibit 8: Dabur: History of International Business Division

Source: Dabur India.

With an existing robust business in North Africa, the company decided to focus on expansion into the sub-Saharan region of the continent. Malhotra was extremely bullish on the region and felt it was imperative for Dabur to pursue these opportunities aggressively. He said, "Sub-Saharan Africa has a huge potential in terms of business expansion. McKinsey estimated that by 2015, 221 million additional basic-needs consumers [income of $1,000 to $5,000] will enter the African market. We cannot afford to miss out on this huge potential and future growth engine." This strong growth potential, along with the fact that the company already had a supply chain infrastructure in the region, were two key reasons to pursue opportunities in this part Africa.

Sub-Saharan markets were quite different from those in North African and Arab countries, both in terms of consumer attributes as well as tastes and habits. Hair oils and creams that were prized in countries where people mostly had straight hair were not attractive in sub-Saharan Africa. Thus, Dabur was initially restricted to its oral care products. As Malhotra explained, "Sub- Saharan people mostly have tight curly hair, and obviously our hair oils, you know, can't sell there. Shampoos don't sell there either. We didn't have any hair care products, so we made a beginning with oral care, and became very successful. Now we needed to expand our portfolio, especially in hair care products."

While on a market study trip in the region, a Dabur team came across a hair curl relaxant, Organic Root Stimulator (ORS), that seemed popular in wealthy pockets of sub-Saharan markets. ORS was a natural product used to straighten curly hair without any of the harsh side effects commonly associated with chemical-based products. The team recommended buying the product as an entree to the sub-Saharan hair care market. Duggal put his M&A team into action to pursue the U.S.-based owner of the ORS brand, Namaste Lab.

NAMASTE LAB

Namaste Lab specialized in hair care products for women of African descent. It was headquartered in Chicago, and three-quarters of its $100 million in sales were in the United States. It also had some international distribution in Africa, the Caribbean, and parts of Latin America. The company was doing reasonably well, but it was small and had limited resources. It was run by its founder, Gary Gardner, who was very passionate about his company and products but was never much motivated by the thought of making money. Instead, he was focused on creating value for his customers. Duggal explained the acquisition issues:

I want management along with the company acquisition. It also adds to my bandwidth. I think it also adds to my stature as a transnational company, that I have people from different cultures, from different backgrounds, all working for the same organization.

I think in the case of Namaste, the promoter was the founder who was pretty keen to continue running the show, because that's his passion. So he was very comfortable with the thought of selling to Dabur, as he probably preferred us to a transnational, which would have told him, "OK, Mr. Gardner, thank you very much, we've got our own management. Please move away." We said, "Gary, we are interested in buying your company only if you continue to lead it, and we are willing to have you share in the wealth creation opportunity if you lead it well." And that was very compelling.

He gets $100 million cash in the bank and a hefty bonus linked with performance. After three years he gets an opportunity to get $40 million more. More important to him is he continues to do the thing he loves doing.

Namaste Labs was founded in 1996 to address the needs of the health-conscious, African American consumer market. Namaste had developed a portfolio of natural therapeutic hair care and relaxant products under the brand Organic Root Stimulator and had a strong presence in the hair care market for women of color. Gardner relished the opportunity to extend the products to Africa. He said, "The passion that I have is that every woman of color should be able to get a reasonably priced set of hair products that can give her the [crowning glory] that she expects. For the largest population of women of color not to have that is just a travesty." But Gardner realized Namaste itself could not build the markets internationally that would meet his ambition. So he was open to being acquired.

Gardner's father had developed one of the first businesses specializing in hair care products aimed at women of African descent, but he had sold it to a renowned multinational company that failed to further the brand values and promise. This experience weighed heavily in Gardner's mind and was one of the reasons for his inclination toward Dabur over other, bigger bidders. Commenting on the acquisition by Dabur, Gardner said:

> In the course of looking for a potential buyer, Dabur flushed up. We quickly saw all the synergies because we knew that the real prize is getting affordable, natural hair care to Africa, which has the largest population for our technologies and one that is completely underserved. Everything is exported from America in bits and pieces, from inconsistent containers to suitcases. It's just such a large opportunity that no one was taking advantage of and I knew I couldn't do it by myself because the ultimate answer is that you manufacture on the continent, and we don't have manufacturing expertise. Also, I didn't really have the stomach or the expertise to handle the debt that would be required or the necessary management skill sets. So this acquisition was actually a perfect marriage.

With presence and infrastructure in Africa, Dabur provided Namaste an opportunity to offer high quality, natural-based products to consumers on that continent. "Due to the increasingly global nature of the marketplace, Namaste recognizes that to become a global brand today required expertise and resources in regions outside North America," Gardner said. He was also conscious of the need to re-engineer Namaste's products so they would be affordable for Africans.

Namaste's existing management team, led by Gardner, as well as the sales team would continue to run the operations even after the acquisition. Specific targets for growth were set mutually by Duggal and Gardner for the next three years, followed by an attractive incentive package. Duggal was hopeful that the arrangement would allow a smooth transition and at the same time motivate the incumbent team to deliver strong results.

CHALLENGES

Duggal had many challenges ahead, and he tried to list each one of them on his flight back home:

1. Namaste was the first major acquisition by Dabur outside of India. Was the organization ready for such a big step forward? After all, they had very little experience dealing with U.S. business and culture. And they would be completely dependent on Namaste to undertake product re-engineering, on which the future of Dabur's plans for sub-Saharan markets rested. Duggal also had to figure out the new reporting and monitoring structure required for efficient management to drive Gardner and his team toward new commercial goals.

While financially, the Namaste acquisition made a lot of sense, Duggal knew that cultural or soft issues were far trickier than they sounded. His filtering criteria for any acquisition target included seeking good, strong, local management with whom Dabur management was comfortable. Unlike large multinationals, Dabur did not have the management depth to pull people from Dabur India to manage newly acquired assets. Duggal believed he had acquired a strong local management at Namaste that seemed aligned with Dabur and would operate their home base in an effective manner. He expected Namaste management to help Dabur take the business forward in the geographies where Namaste did not have considerable play.

2. What should be the future structure of global operations? While Dubai had been an ideal base for the international division until now, this would need to be reconsidered, given the new geographic expanse. Sub-Saharan markets, along with a substantial investment in the United States, might need new hubs for effective management. He said:

> I wonder whether we would have to now set up three hubs. Should they be large hubs, or should they be smaller, fairly spread out, with all the controls coming out of India? But with a lot of local independence and autonomy given to the CEOs? So we might have India as the sort of repository for ayurvedic and hair care products aimed at people in Asia and the Middle East, and, you know, Turkey for skin care (Dabur had recently acquired a small cosmetic company in Turkey), Namaste for all products aimed at black people. So we may have four hubs: Chicago, Istanbul, Dubai and Delhi.

Duggal still did not have any firm decision on this but he had figured out one piece of the puzzle in his mind regarding functional distribution across geographies. He said, "Purchasing and finance have to be centralized. Dabur followed a global sourcing platform, so purchasing needed to have common goals and policies and finance required consolidation. The architecture of these functions will be a little bit different in the future. On the other hand, operations, marketing and sales would be largely decentralized."

3. How would Dabur identify and recruit good talent in sub-Saharan countries? There would not be many Indians willing to relocate to Africa (unlike Dubai), making the resource pool largely local. "We can only look to send young, unmarried staff members from India, or else they would be unable to sustain the challenges of being so far away from families."

4. How would Dabur deal with the turbulent geopolitical situation in Dabur's many markets? Within weeks of the formal acquisition of Namaste in the spring of 2010, Egypt, one of the biggest African markets for Dabur, experienced a revolution that brought the country to a standstill for several days. Two months later the Egyptian economy was still contracting at a substantial rate and instances of violent religious conflict had been seen. In fact, Duggal had to personally supervise safety operations for Dabur India staff in Egypt during the turbulence. Across the Arab world, demonstrations and rebellions broke out, disrupting business. Further, tensions in Nigeria between the Muslim north and the largely Christian south were increasing. This was just on the heels of Dabur coming out of another crisis in Nepal, where their local CEO almost got arrested for alleged breach of regulations at a fruit juice plant. The Nepal situation appeared to be a political conspiracy, but nevertheless it triggered adverse publicity for Dabur India.

It was a long flight home, and Duggal was wondering if he was expecting too much from his organization and whether his management team had the capability to overcome the recognized challenges as well as unexpected ones that were surely waiting around the corner. Duggal had tremendous faith in his team and his strategy, although it remained to be seen if his confidence was justified.

NOTES

1. All information in this case is based on interviews or data provided by Dabur India unless otherwise noted.

2. Section based on information from Dabur India website, www.dabur.com (March 2011).

3. "American Dollar," X-rates.com, www.x-rates.com/d/USD/table.html (April 26, 2011).

4. "Dabur India Limited—Company Profile Snapshot," Wright Reports, http://wrightreports.ecnext.com/coms2/reportdesc_COMPANY_C356G5800 (April 26, 2011).

5. U.S. FMCG companies at the time were being valued at about 1x sales.

6. Confederation of Indian Industry report, "FMCG road map 2020."

7. Wipro had a large consumer care business besides its better-known information technology business.

CASE QUESTIONS

1. Dabur India has followed an aggressive approach to growth that is marked by both market development and product development. Do you think that the entry into the U.S. market was appropriate? What alternatives could the marketer have pursued?

2. Discuss the competitive landscape of the Indian market and how this relates to international marketing decisions.

3. What international organizational structure would be best for Dabur India with the latest expansion initiatives?

4. Discuss the various marketing channels that must be established for consumer care and health products. How do these differences affect the international marketing efforts of Dabur India?

Appendix B
Notes

CHAPTER 1

1. Statistics obtained from Facebook.com, accessed at www.facebook.com/press/info.php?statistics.

2. "Person of the Year 2010," *Time,* accessed at www.time.com/time/specials/packages/0,28757,2036683,00.html.

3. Information obtained from Socialbakers.com website, accessed at www.socialbakers.com/facebook-statistics/.

4. Information obtained from MediaStory.net website, accessed at wwwmediastory.net/2011/07/top-most-popular-brands-on-facebook/.

5. Vicki Passmore, "Wow, You Really 'Like' These Global Brands," accessed at www.dailyfinance.com/2010/12/15/10-most-popular-brand-pages-on-facebook/.

6. B. M. Oviatt and P. P. McDougall, "Toward a Theory of International New Ventures," *Journal of International Business Studies* 25 no. 1 (1994): 45–64.

7. Shameen Prashantham and Julian Birkinshaw, "Dancing with Gorillas: How Small Companies Can Partner Effectively with MNCs," *California Management Review* 51 no. 1 (2008): 6–23.

8. Proven Models, "Howard V. Perlmutter," accessed at www.provenmodels.com/578/ep%5Br%5Dg/howard-v.-perlmutter/.

9. Donald Baack, *International Business* (Los Angeles: Glencoe-McGraw-Hill, 2008).

10. Kenneth D. Clow and Donald Baack, *Marketing Management: A Customer Oriented Approach* (Los Angeles: SAGE Publications, 2010).

11. Fred Palumbo and Paul A. Herbig, "Trade Shows and Fairs: An Important Part of the International Marketing Mix," *Journal of Promotion Management* 8 no. 1 (2002): 93–108.

12. Jacci Howard Bear, "Red" (2010), accessed at http://desktoppub.about.com/cs/colorselection/p/red.htm.

13. Amanda J. Broderick, Gordon E. Greenlet, and Rene Dentiste Mueller, "The Behavioural Homogeneity Evaluation Frameowork: Multi-Level Evaluations ofConsumer Involvement in International Segmentation," *Journal of International Business Studies* 38 no. 5 (2007): 746–763.

14. Demetris Vrontis, Alkis Thrassou, and Iasonas Lamprianou, "International Marketing Adaptation Versus Standardisation of Multinational Companies," *International Marketing Review* 26 no. 4/5 (2009): 477–500.

15. May Gregory, "Globalisation: How China and India are Changing the Debate," *Teaching Business & Economics* 10 no. 2 (2006): 8–12.

16. Ibid.

17. Theo Notteboom and Jean-Paul Rodrigue, "The Future of Containerization: Perspectives from Maritime and Inland Freight Distribution," *GeoJournal* 74 no. 1 (2009): 7–22.

18. David Hummels, "Transportation Costs and International Trade in the Second Era of Globalization," *The Journal of Economic Perspectives* 21 no. 3 (2007): 131–154.

19. Susan F. Martin, "Heavy Traffics: International Migration in an Era of Globalization," *Brookings Review* Fall (2001): 41–44.

20. James Nelson, "What's Driving Globalisation?" *New Zealand Management* (June 23, 2006), accessed at http://findarticles.com/p/articles/mi_qn5305/is_20060623/ai_n24915192/.

21. Attila Yaprak, "Culture Study in International Marketing: A Critical Review and Suggestions for Future Research," *International Marketing Review* 25 no. 2 (2008):215–229.

22. Shu-Chuan Chu and Szu-Chi Huang, "College-Educated Youths' Attitudes Toward Global Brands: Implications for Global Marketing Strategies," *Journal of International Consumer Marketing* 22 no. 2 (2010): 129–145.

23. Steve Hamm and Nandini Laksman, "The Trouble With India," *Business Week,* April 26, 2007.

24. Diane Brady, "Pepsi: Repairing a Poisoned Reputation in India," *Business Week,* June 11, 2007.

25. Andrew Downie, "7 Cool Ideas. A Sweet Ride in Brazil (The Future of Energy)," *Time* (Canadian Edition), 166 no. 18 (2005): 40.

26. Ram Nidumolu, C. K. Prahalad, and M. R. Rangaswami, "Why Sustainability Is Now the Key Driver of Innovation," *Harvard Business Review* 87 no. 9 (2009): 56–64.

27. C. K. Prahalad, *The Fortune at the Bottom-of-the-Pyramid: Eradicating Poverty Through Profits* (Upper Saddle River, NJ: Pearson Education Inc., Wharton School Publishing, 2006).

28. Ibid.

29. Phatak Arvind and Mohammed Habib, "How Should Managers Treat Ethics in International Business?," *Thunderbird International Business Review* 40 no. 2 (1998): 101–118.

30. Larry R. Smeltzer and Marianne M. Jennings, "Why an International Code of Business Ethics Would be Good for Business," *Journal of Business Ethics* 17 no. 1 (1998): 57–67.

31. "All Carrefour Outlets in Japan to Be Renamed Aeon Wed," *Jiji Press English News Service* (Tokyo), March 8, 2010; Stanley Pignal, "Carrefour Cuts 1,700 Jobs," FT.com (London), February 23, 2010.

32. Pitsinee Jitpleecheep, "Carrefour Launches Mini Format: Reflects Commitment to Thai Market," *McClatchy–Tribune Business News* (Washington), October 13, 2009.

33. "Carrefour UAE Donates Food Supplies Worth AED 625,000 to People in Need," *Al Bawaba* (London), October 12, 2009.

34. "Business: Exit the Dragon?; Carrefour in Emerging Markets," *The Economist*, 393 no. 8652 (2009, October 10): 68.

35. Elena Berton, "Carrefour Seeks to Overturn Antitrust Ruling in Indonesia," *WWD* 198 no. 95 (2009, November 5): 15.

36. Vivek Sinha, "Carrefour Plans to Open Stores in 7 Cities," *McClatchy–Tribune Business News* (Washington), December 11, 2009.

37. Kala Vijayraghavan, Chaitali Chakravarty, "Carrefour Sees Future in India, May Ink JV Soon," *McClatchy–Tribune Business News* (Washington), January 19, 2010.

CHAPTER 2

1. Mark Kleinman, "The High Price of Levi's Victory," *Marketing*, November 29, 2001.

2. "Daily Bread Caracas," *Economist.com / Global Agenda* (London), March 17, 2008.

3. Marc Frank, "Cuba Bows to Pressure to Reform Its Economy," *FT.com* (London), December 13, 2010.

4. W. W. Rostow, *The Stages of Economic Growth: A Non-Communist Manifesto* (Cambridge: Cambridge University Press, 1991).

5. Ying Fan, "The Rise of Emerging Market Multinationals and the Impact on Marketing," *Marketing Planning & Intelligence* 26 no. 4 (2008): 353–358.

6. Peter Enderwick, "Large Emerging Markets (LEMs) and International Strategy," *International Marketing Review* 26 no. 1 (2009): 7–16.

7. Guogun Fu, John Saunders, and Riliang Qu, "Brand Extensions in Emerging Markets: Theory Development and Testing in China," *Journal of Global Marketing* 22 no. 3 (2009): 217–228.

8. David Oakley, "Gloom Hits Russia and Brazil," *Financial Times*, October 17, 2008.

9. Robert Issak, "Making 'Economic Miracles': Explaining Extraordinary National Economic Achievement," *American Economist* (Spring, 1997): 59.

10. "The Official Travel Guide by Slovenian Tourist Board," Slovenian Tourist Board (2010), accessed at www.slovenia.info/en/zgodovina-in-kultura .htm?zgodovina_in_kultura=0&lng=2.

11. Erdener Kaynak, Ali Riza Apil, and Serkan Yalcin, "Marketing and Advertising Practices of Turkish Entrepreneurs in Transition Economies: Evidence From Georgia," *Journal of International Entrepreneurship* 7 no. 3 (2009): 190–214.

12. Simon Johnson and Gary Lovman, "Starting Over: Poland After Communism," *Harvard Business Review* (March–April, 1995): 44–56.

13. Donald Baack, *International Business* (New York: Glencoe McGraw-Hill, 2008).

14. Duane Stanford, "Africa: Coke's Last Frontier," *Bloomberg Business Week*, October 28, 2010.

15. Ronald Paul Hill, "A Naturological Approach to Marketing Exchanges: Implications for Bottom-of-the-Pyramid," *Journal of Business Research* 63 no. 6 (2010): 602–607.

16. "What Is Couture?," *Wisegeek.com* (2011), accessed at www.wisegeek.com/ what-is-couture.htm.

17. Scott Duke Harris, "Nokia Finds Research Edge in Silicon Valley," *McClatchy–Tribune Business News* (Washington), November 25, 2007.

18. M. E. Porter, "The Competitive Advantage of Nations," *Harvard Business Review* (March–April, 1990): 78.

19. Ibid.

20. James Callan and Jody Shenn, "Cameron's 'Avatar' Near Global Movie Sales After 6 Weeks," *Bloomberg Business Week* (January 25, 2010), accessed at www .businessweek.com/news/2010–01–25/cameron-s-avatar-near-global-movie-sales-record-after-6-weeks.html.

21. Jocelyn Ford, "Chinese Windmills Blowing Your Way Posted," *Science Friday*, December 10, 2009, accessed at www.sciencefriday.com/blog/2009/12/ chinese-windmills-blowing-your-way/.

22. Matthew Dalton, "World News: Europe Raises Cry Over Chinese Technology," *Wall Street Journal*, October 6, 2010; Ben Hunt, "Juggernaut Has Arrived: Chinese Telecoms: New Entrant Tours Europe," *Financial Times*, July 27, 2005.

23. Nachum Lilach and Cliff Wymbs, "Product Differentiation, External Economies, and MNE Location Choices: M&As in Global Cities," *Journal of International Business Studies* 36 no. 4 (2005): 415–434.

24. "Cott Says Wal-Mart Will End Supply Pact," *Wall Street Journal*, January 28, 2009.

25. Jeffrey S. Podoshen, Lu Li, and Junfeng Zhang, "Materialism and Conspicuous Consumption in China: A Cross-Cultural Examination," *International Journal of Consumer Studies* 35 no. 1 (2011): 17–25.

26. Mario Toneguzzi, "Walmart Opens Sustainable Hub; $115M Distribution Centre Near Calgary Boasts Green Innovations," *Edmonton Journal* (Alberta), November 11, 2010.

27. Peter Bosshard, "Dam Nation," *Foreign Policy* (March 8, 2011), accessed at www .foreignpolicy.com/articles/2011/03/08/dam_nation.

28. A.K. Chapagain and A.Y. Hoekstra, "Water Footprints of Nations," *UNESCO-IHE: Institute for Water Education* 16 no. 1 (November 2004), accessed at www .waterfootprint.org/Reports/Report16Vo11.pdf.

29. Veronica Baena, "Modeling Global Franchising in Emerging Markets: An Entry Mode Analysis," *Journal of East–West Business* 15 no. 3/4 (2009): 164–188.

30. Diane H. B. Welsh, Ilan Alon, and Cecilia M. Falbe, "An Examination of International Retail Franchising in Emerging Markets," *Journal of Small Business Management* 44 no. 1 (2006): 130–149.

31. Peter Hessler, *Country Driving: A Journey Through China From Farm to Factory* (New York: HarperCollins, 2010).

32. J. Johanson and F. Wiedersheim-Paul, "The Internationalization of the Firm—Four Swedish Cases," *Journal of Management Studies* 12 no. 3 (1975): 305–323.

33. J. Johanson and J.-E. Vahlne, "The Internationalization Process of the Firm: A Model of Knowledge Development and Increasing Foreign Market Commitments," *Journal of International Business Studies* 8 no. 1 (1977): 23–32.

34. P. Magnusson, D. W. Baack, S. Zdradkovic, K. Staub, and L. S. Amine, "Meta-Analysis of Cultural Differences: Another Slice at the Apple," *International Business Review* 17 no. 5 (2008): 520–532.

35. P. J. Buckley and M. Casson, *The Future of the Multinational Enterprise* (New York: Holmes and Meier, 1976).

36. J. H. Dunning, "The Eclectic Paradigm of International Production: A Restatement and Some Possible Extensions," *Journal of International Business Studies* 19 no. 1 (1988): 1–31.

37. *The World Factbook,* Central Intelligence Agency, Washington, DC, updated September 30, 2011, accessed at https://www.cia.gov/library/publications/the-world-factbook/.

38. "Data Visualizations for a Changing World," *Google Public Data Explorer* (2011), accessed at www.google.com/publicdata/home.

39. "The Telecommunications Sector," *African Business* (London) no. 349 (January 2009): 27–30.

40. "Mobile Phone Growth Biggest in Africa," *African Business* (London) no. 352 (April 2009): 8.

41. Anver Versi, "How Do You Rebrand an Icon?," *African Business* (London) no. 346 (October 2008): 42–43.

42. Ibid.

43. Neil Ford, "Jumping the Technology Gap," *African Business* (London) no. 347 (November 2008): 62–63.

44. M. J. Morgan, "North Africa Leads Growth," *African Business* (London), no. 353 (May 2009): 54–55.

45. Jack Ewing, "Upwardly Mobile in Africa: How Basic Cell Phones Are Sparking Economic Hope and Growth in Emerging—and Even Non-Emerging—Nations," *Business Week*, September 24, 2007.

46. Dominique Magada, "Esoko: The New Market Info System for African Farmers," *African Business* (London) no. 353 (May 2009): 46–47.

47. "A Doctor in Your Pocket," *The Economist* 391, no. 8627, April 18, 2009.

48. Christina Kennedy, "Cheap and Cheerful: Economy Handsets Enter the Market," *African Business* (London) no. 353 (May 2009): 52–53.

49. "Mobile Phone Growth Biggest in Africa," *African Business* (London) no. 352 (April 2009): 8.

50. Jonathan Hujsak, "The Transformative Effect of Cellular Communications on Emerging Economies," *Cost Management* 24, no. 4 (July/August 2010): 5–20.

51. Ibid.

52. M. J. Morgan, "North Africa Leads Growth," *African Business* (London) no. 353 (May 2009): 54–55.

53. "The Telecommunications Sector," *African Business* (London) no. 349 (January 2009): 27.

CHAPTER 3

1. Norio Tanaka, "Shoyu: The Flavor of Japan," *The Japan Foundation Newsletter* 27 no. 2 (2000): 1–7.

2. "Asia: Democracy in Action: China's National People's Congress," *The Economist* 394 no. 8671 (2010): 51.

3. *The World Factbook,* Central Intelligence Agency, Washington, DC, accessed at https://www.cia.gov/library/publications/the-world-factbook/index.html.

4. "Background Note: North Korea," U. S. Department of State, accessed at www.state.gov/r/pa/ei/bgn/2792.htm.

5. Matthew J. Slaughter, "Let's Have a Real Debate on Globalization," *Wall Street Journal*, September 26, 2007.

6. "Gulf News: RAK Free Zone Registers 1,740 New Companies," *Gulf News*, February 8, 2011.

7. "Mission," Export-Import Bank of the United States, accessed at www.exim.gov/about/mission.cfm.

8. James T. Areddy, Yoshio Takahashi, Christopher Rhoads, "China and Japan Take New Jabs at Each Other," *Wall Street Journal*, September 28, 2010.

9. "BPO India Chronology," *Businessworld*, accessed at www.bpoindia.org/knowledgeBase/india-bpo-chronology.shtml.

10. "India Retains Global Top Slot in BPO Race," *Mail Today* (New Delhi), February 8, 2011.

11. Julie Jargon, "KFC Intends to Double Its Restaurants in Africa," *Wall Street Journal* (Hong Kong), December 9, 2010.

12. All of the WTO discussion, except where noted, is adapted from "What Is the World Trade Organization?," World Trade Organization, accessed at www.wto.org/english/thewto_e/whatis_e/tif_e/fact1_e.htm.

13. Tracy Watkins and Jon Morgan, "'Comprehensive' Win for NZ in 89-Year Apple Stoush," *Dominion Post* (Wellington, New Zealand), August 10, 2010.

14. "US Say India, China and Brazil to Decide Fate of Doha Round," *The Pak Banker* (Lahore), June 18, 2010.

15. Juliane von Reppert-Bismarck, "Activists Take the Fight Inside; Some Former Protesters Soften Tactics, See Trade Helping the Poor," *Wall Street Journal* (Eastern edition), December 13, 2005.

16. "North America: United States," *The World Factbook*, Central Intelligence Agency, Washington, DC, accessed at https://www.cia.gov/library/publications/the-world-factbook/geos/us.html.

17. The EU history information is drawn from "The History of the European Union," *Europa: Gateway to the European Union,* accessed at http://europa.eu/abc/history/index_en.htm.

18. "Europe: European Union," *The World Factbook,* Central Intelligence Agency, accessed at https://www.cia.gov/library/publications/the-world-factbook/geos/ee.html.

19. "The Council Is an Essential EU Decision Maker," *Consilium,* accessed at www.consilium.europa.eu/council.aspx?lang=en.

20. "European Parliament," *Europa: Gateway to the European Union,* accessed at http://europa.eu/institutions/inst/parliament/index_en.htm.

21. "EU Institutions and Other Bodies," *Europa: Gateway to the European Union,* accessed at http://europa.eu/institutions/inst/comm/index_en.htm.

22. "The Court of Justice and the European Union," *Europa: Gateway to the European Union,* accessed at http://europa.eu/institutions/inst/justice/index_en.htm.

23. "Structure of the ECA," European Court of Auditors (Luxembourg), accessed at http://eca.europa.eu/portal/page/portal/Organisation/Structure.

24. "Home Page," CVCE (Luxembourg), accessed at www.ena.lu/.

25. Neil King Jr., "Europe to Enshrine Beef Ban and Ask U.S. to Lift Tariffs," *Wall Street Journal* (Eastern edition), October 15, 2003.

26. "The European Free Trade Association," EFTA (Geneva, Switzerland), accessed at www.efta.int/about-efta/the-european-free-trade-association .aspx.

27. "About Commonwealth of Independent States," Statistical Committee of the CIS, accessed at www.cisstat.com/eng/cis.htm.

28. "Russia, Belarus, and Kazakhstan Agree on Customs Union," *Journal of Turkish Weekly,* December 5, 2009.

29. Central European Free Trade Agreement (Brussels, Belgium), accessed at www .cefta2006.com/.

30. "North American Free Trade Agreement (NAFTA)," Office of the United States Trade Representative (Washington, DC), accessed at www.ustr.gov/trade-agreements/free-trade-agreements/north-american-free-trade-agreement-nafta.

31. "Overview," NAFTA Secretariat, accessed at www.nafta-sec-alena.org/en/view .aspx?x=202.

32. "International Dairy Foods Association; IDFA Commends U.S. Administration's Plan to Resolve NAFTA Trucking Dispute," *Economics Week* (Atlanta), January 28, 2011.

33. Shida Rastegari Henneberry, Joao E. Mutondo, "Agricultural Trade Among NAFTA Countries: A Case Study of U.S. Meat Exports," *Review of Agricultural Economics* 31 no. 3 (2009): 424–445.

34. Ibid.

35. Ibid.

36. "The Americas: A Turning Point?; Mercosur," *The Economist* 384 no. 8536 (2007): 52.

37. Kristin Bushby, "To Make Mercosur Legitimate Brazil and Neighbors Need to Define Goals," *Brazzil* (Los Angeles), July 2, 2008.

38. "Chemical Business NewsBase: Oils and Fats International: In Brief: Egypt, Mercosur Sign Free-Trade Pact," *Chemical Business Newsbase* (Cambridge), November 1, 2010.

39. Tobias Buck, "Palestinians Open Trade Talks With Mercosur," *FT.com* (London), September 24, 2010.

40. Jonathan Riley, "EU Ministers See Mercosur Trade Deal as Threat to Farmers," *Farmers Weekly* (Sutton) 152 no. 20 (2010): 8.

41. Kristin Bushby, "To Make Mercosur Legitimate Brazil and Neighbors Need to Define Goals," *Brazzil* (Los Angeles), July 2, 2008.

42. Jude Webber, "Argentina's Rivals Bite Into Global Beef Export Market," *Financial Times* (London), October 6, 2010.

43. "Uruguay: Terry Johnson Wants Quality Beef," *El Observador Económico (SABI English Language Abstracts)* (Montevideo), October 15, 2006.

44. "Brief History," Comunidad Andina, accessed at www.comunidadandina.org/ ingles/quienes/brief.htm.

45. "Trade Among the CAN Countries Shows 36% Growth in the First Half of 2010," Comunidad Andina (Lima), Aug 20, 2010, accessed at www.comunidadandina .org/ingles/press/press/np20–9-10.htm.

46. "UNASUR: Union of South American Nations," Comunidad Andina, accessed at www.comunidadandina.org/ingles/sudamerican.htm.

47. "Colombia, Peru Lift Bans, Open Markets to U.S. Beef," *Western Farm Press* (Clarksdale), 28 no. 27 (2006): 14.

48. "Pushing for Peru Beef," *Minneapolis* 44 no. 4 (2007): 54.

49. Oana Dan, "Peru's National Day Celebrated With Spicy Cuisine and Potent Drinks," *Knight Ridder Tribune Business News* (Washington), July 31, 2006.

50. "CAFTA-DR (Dominican Republic- Central America FTA," Office of the United States Trade Representative (Washington, DC), accessed at www.ustr.gov/trade-agreements/free-trade-agreements/cafta-dr-dominican-republic-central-america-fta.

51. "Caribbean Single Market and Economy," *csmett.com,* accessed at www.csmett .com/content2/csme/history/caricom_organisation.shtml.

52. "About Us," Eastern Caribbean Central Bank, accessed at www.eccb-centralbank .org/About/who-we-are.asp.

53. "Overview," Association of Southeast Asian Nations, accessed at www.aseansec .org/about_ASEAN.html.

54. "ASEAN Economic Community," Association of the Southeast Asian Nations, accessed at www.aseansec.org/18757.htm.

55. "ASEAN Free Trade Area (AFTA Council)," Association of Southeat Nations, accessed at www.aseansec.org/19585.htm.

56. James Hookway, "Currency Discussion to Dominate Asia Summit," *Wall Street Journal* (Eastern edition), October 29, 2010.

57. "What Is Asia-Pacific Economic Cooperation?," Asia-Pacific Economic Cooperation, accessed at www.apec.org/About-Us/About-APEC.aspx; "Member Economies," Asia-Pacific Economic Cooperation, accessed at www.apec.org/About-Us/ About-APEC/Member-Economies.aspx.

58. "History," Asia-Pacific Economic Cooperation, accessed at www.apec.org/ About-Us/About-APEC/History.aspx.

59. "Trans-Pacific Partnership (TPP) Negotiations," New Zealand Ministry of Foreign Affairs & Trade, accessed at www.mfat.govt.nz/Trade-and-Economic-Relations/2-Trade-Relationships-and-Agreements/Trans-Pacific/index.php.

60. "Home Page," South Asian Association for Regional Cooperation (SAARC), accessed at www.saarc-sec.org/#.

61. "India Implements FTA on Goods With Lao," *The Pak Banker* (Lahore), January 29, 2011.

62. "Taiwan to Boost Screening of US, Canadian Beef Over Banned Drug," *McClatchy–Tribune Business News* (Washington), January 20, 2011.

63. "U.S. to Push for Wider Access to Beef Market in S. Korea," *Asia in Focus* (Rhodes), December 8, 2010.

64. "Supreme Council Urges Setting up of GCC Customs Union," *Arabianbusiness.com* (London), December 11, 2010.

65. "Home Page," The Cooperation Council for the Arab States of the Gulf: Secretariat General, accessed at www.gcc-sg.org/eng/index.html.

66. "Continued Economic Reforms Would Attract More Foreign Investment," World Trade Organization (April 23, 2003), accessed at www.wto.org/English/ tratop_e/tpr_e/tp213_e.htm.

67. "IMF Survey: Supplement on the Fund," International Monetary Fund, 31 (Sept 2002), accessed at www.imf.org/external/pubs/ft/survey/sup2002/index.htm.

68. "About EAC," East African Community, accessed at www.eac.int/about-eac .html.

69. "Africa Rising; Catering to New Tastes as Incomes Climb; Zambian Beef Processor Expands to Nigeria With Aim of Spreading Out Across the Continent," *Wall Street Journal* (Online), February 10, 2011.

70. Gwynne Dyer, "African Union: Limits of the Possible," *Belleville EMC* (Ontario), January 6, 2011.

71. "World Tariff Wars; U.S. Protectionism Is Hurting American Exports," *Wall Street Journal* (Online), April 9, 2010.

72. John W. Miller, "China Complains to WTO About EU Tariffs; Petition Against Antidumping Duties on Shoes Extends Fight Against What Beijing Says Is Unfair Protectionism," *Wall Street Journal* (Online), February 5, 2010.

73. "Say It Ain't So, Fidel," *Financial Times* (London), September 11, 2010.

74. Isabel Gorst, "Traders Rush to Beat Grain Export Ban," *Financial Times* (London), August 14, 2010.

75. "China's Rare-Earth Exports Slide, Still Bust Quota," *Wall Street Journal* (Online), January 19, 2011.

76. "Budget to Have Subsidies for Food Grain-Based Distilleries," *Hindustan Times* (New Delhi), February 2, 2011.

77. "Government Revokes 1,104 Import Licenses," *The Jakarta Post* (Jakarta), February 10, 2010.

78. Ibid.

79. Richard Katz, "Japanese Farmers Sow Protectionism," *Wall Street Journal Asia* (Hong Kong) December 13, 2010.

80. David Pilling, "China Has Every Right to Cheat, But Shouldn't," *Financial Times* (London), October 28, 2010.

81. Julie Jargon, "Corporate News: KFC Intends to Double Its Restaurants in Africa," *Wall Street Journal Asia* (Hong Kong), December 9, 2010.

82. Steve Cahalan, "Labor Leader, Workers Criticize Trade Policies," *La Crosse Tribune* (Wisconsin), October 27, 2010.

83. Tom Miller, "National Security Checks Raise Fears of Protectionism," *South China Morning Post* (Hong Kong), June 26, 2007.

84. "EU Says China Making 'Considerable Progress' in Product Safety," *BBC Monitoring Asia Pacific* (London), November 23, 2007.

85. Charita L. Castro and Jialin Wang, "Don't Be Tricked By Treats; Halloween; Say 'Boo' to Chocolate Companies That Use Cocoa Made From Exploiting Child Labor," *St. Louis Post—Dispatch* (Missouri), October 28, 2010.

86. Jane Spencer, "China Shifts Pollution Fight; New Rules Target Export Industry With Stiff Penalties," *Wall Street Journal* (Eastern edition), November 1, 2007.

87. Bruce Stanley, "Danger at Sea: Ships Draw Fire for Rising Role in Air Pollution; As Global Trade Grows, So Does the Spewing of Noxious Emissions," *Wall Street Journal* (Eastern edition), November 27, 2007.

88. Dave Rogers, "Bed Store Signs a Nightmare for French Advocate," *The Ottawa Citizen* (Ontario), February 4, 2010.

89. "Foreign Corrupt Practices Act: An Overview," The United States Department of Justice (Washington, DC), accessed at www.justice.gov/criminal/fraud/fcpa/.

90. "Shearman & Sterling; Shearman & Sterling's FCPA Digest, Web Site Report More Than $1.7 Billion in Fines," *Marketing Weekly News* (Atlanta), February 12, 2011.

91. "SEC Charges Tyson Foods With FCPA Violations; Tyson Foods to Pay Disgorgement Plus Pre-judgment Interest of More Than $1.2 Million; Tyson Foods to Pay Criminal Penalty of $4 Million," U.S. Securities and Exchange Commission (February 10, 2011), accessed at www.sec.gov/litigation/litreleases/2011/lr21851.htm.

92. Michael Freund, "US Company Fined for Complying With Arab Boycott of Israel," *Jerusalem Post* (Jerusalem), January 1, 2008.

93. P. R. Venkat, "Temasek Says It Will Pay Indonesia Fine," *Wall Street Journal Asia* (Hong Kong), January 19, 2011.

94. "Google in Talks With U.S. to Save ITA Deal," *Wall Street Journal* (Online), January 28, 2011.

95. Christopher Drew, "New Spy Game: Firms' Secrets Sold Overseas," *New York Times* (East Coast), October 18, 2010.

96. Allen R. Myerson, "In Principle, a Case for More 'Sweatshops,'" *New York Times,* June 22, 1997.

97. "Our History: From Humble Beginnings to Global Market Leader," DHL, accessed at www.dhl.com/en/about_us/company_portrait.html#history.

98. "DHL Launches International Trade Initiative for Small and Medium-Sized Enterprises," *Insurance Business Weekly* (Atlanta), August 8, 2010.

99. "DHL Launches Next Generation Shipping Software Designed for Small Businesses," *Computer Business Week* (Atlanta), July 21, 2008.

100. "DHL Provides Express Delivery for Stretchy Shapes," *Manufacturing Close—Up* (Jacksonville), September 3, 2010.

CHAPTER 4

1. Annie Lowrey, "Concerted Effort: The Dave Matthews Band Shows How to Make Money in the Music Industry," accessed at www.slate.com/articles/business/moneybox/2011/01/concerted_effort.html.

2. Jan-Benedict E. M. Steenkamp and Frenkel Ter Hofstede, "International Market Segmentation: Issues and Perspectives," *International Journal of Research in Marketing* 19 (2002): 185–213.

3. "Astral to Offer French-language Playhouse Disney Channel for Bell TV Subscribers," *Health & Beauty Close Up* (Jacksonville), June 6, 2010.

4. Charles Stone, "The Dialects That Daunt Switzerland's Ad Men," *Campaign Europe* May (1980): 43.

5. Liz Creel, "Ripple Effects: Population and Coastal Regions," *Population Reference Bureau* (September 2003): 1–8.

6. Jeffrey D. Sachs, Wing Thye Woo Performance, Columbia University—Columbia Earth Institute; National Bureau of Economic Research (NBER). NBER Working Paper No. W5935, University of California, Davis—Department of Economics 1997–02–01.

7. Noah Richler, "The Inuit Watch and Remember," *New Statesman* (London), 136 no. 4875–4877 (December 17, 2007–January 3, 2008): 52–54.

8. "Surfing 1: Tahitian Origins," *Hickok Sports* accessed at www.hickoksports.com/history/surfing01.shtml.

9. "An Imported Sport," Santa Cruz Surfing Museum.org (Santa Cruz, CA), accessed at www.santacruzsurfingmuseum.org/legends/index.html.

10. "The Buddha His Life and Teaching," *buddhanet,* accessed at http://www.buddhanet.net/buddha.htm.

11. H. Thurston, "Shrovetide," *The Catholic Encyclopedia* (New York), 13 (1912), accessed at www.newadvent.org/cathen/13763a.htm.

12. "Isis Rising," *Carnaval.com,* accessed at www.carnaval.com/isis/rising/.

13. Anne Shapiro Devreux, "Masked Revels of a Belgian Mardi Gras," *New York Times,* January 22, 1989.

14. Paulo Whitaker, "Brazil Carnival Begins (PHOTOS)," *International Business Times* (March 5, 2011), accessed at http://hken.ibtimes.com/articles_slideshows/119153/20110305/brazil-carnival-begins-photos_5.htm#article_header.

15. Richard Duckett, "Sight and Sounds of Carnival, Local Groups Bring Music of Uruguay to Latin Fest," *Telegram &* Gazette, August 18, 2011.

16. "Carnival in Venezuela," Caribbean Choice, accessed at www.caribbeanchoice.com/venezuela/carnival.asp.

17. "Carnivals of the World: Top 10 of 2011," Carnival Pig, accessed at www.festivalpig.com/Carnivals-of-the-World-Top-10.html.

18. S. H. Schwartz and W. Bilsky, "Toward a Universal Psychological Structure of Human Values," *Journal of Personality and Social Psychology* 53 (1987): 550–562.

19. Jenny A. Rapp, Richard A. Bernardi, and Susan M. Bosco, "Examining the Use of Hofstede's Uncertainty Avoidance Construct in International Research: A 25-Year Review," *International Business Research* 4 no. 1 (2011): 3–15.

20. Robert J. House, Narda R. Quigley, and Mary Sully de Luque, "Insights From Project GLOBE: Extending Global Advertising Research Through a Contemporary Framework," *International Journal of Advertising* 29 no. 1 (2010): 111–139.

21. Vas Taras, Bradley L Kirkman, and Piers Steel, "Examining the Impact of Culture's Consequences: A Three-Decade, Multilevel, Meta-Analytic Review of Hofstede's Cultural Value Dimensions," *Journal of Applied Psychology* 95 no. 3 (2010, May): 405–439.

22. Rodney L. Stump, Wen Gong, Cristian Chelariu, "National Culture and National Adoption and Use of Mobile Telephony," *International Journal of Electronic Business* 8 no. 4/5 (2010): 433–455.

23. Rajiv Mehta, Rolph E. Anderson, Alan J. Dubinsky, Pia Polsa, and Jolanta Mazur, "Managing International Distribution Channel Partners: A Cross-Cultural Approach," *Journal of Marketing Channels* (Binghamton) 17 no. 2 (2010, April): 89–117.

24. Jana Möller and Martin Eisend, "A Global Investigation Into the Cultural and Individual Antecedents of Banner Advertising Effectiveness," *Journal of International Marketing* (Chicago) 18 no. 2 (2010, June): 80–98; D. W. Baack and N. Singh, "Culture and Symbol Systems: An Investigation of the Link Between Culture and Web Communications," *Journal of Business Research* 60 no. 3 (2007): 181–188; Young Sook Moon and Kara Chan, "Advertising Appeals and Cultural Values in Television Commercials: A Comparison of Hong Kong and Korea," *International Marketing Review* (London) 22 no. 1 (2005): 48–67.

25. Leonidas Hatzithomas, Yorgos Zotos, and Christina Boutsouki, "Humor and Cultural Values in Print Advertising: A Cross-Cultural Study," *International Marketing Review* (London) 28 no. 1 (2011): 57–80.

26. Marieke de Mooij and Geert Hofstede, "The Hofstede Model: Applications to Global Branding and Advertising Strategy and Research," *International Journal of Advertising* (Eastbourne) 29 no. 1 (2010): 85–110.

27. Schwartz and Bilsky, "Toward a Universal Psychological Structure of Human Values."

28. S. H. Schwartz, "Universals in the Content and Structure of Values: Theoretical Advance and Empirical Tests in 20 Countries," in *Advances in Experimental Social Psychology,* edited by M. P. Zanna (1–65) (Orlando, FL: Academic Press, 1992).

29. Stanley C. Plog and Michael C. Sturman, "The Problems and Challenges of Working in International Settings," *Cornell Hotel and Restaurant Administration Quarterly* 46 no. 2 (2005): 116–124.

30. Andrew Morse, "Seaweed Booms for Dieters in Japan: 'Kanten' Plan Uses Gelatin to Give Feeling of Fullness, but Exercise Is Still Needed," *Wall Street Journal* (Eastern edition), January 3, 2006.

31. "Marketing to Muslims: Case Study: Chicken Cottage," *Marketing Week* (London), June 24, 2010.

32. Olivia Putnal, "11 Global McDonald's Menu Items," *Women's Day* (March 24, 2010), accessed at www.womansday.com/Articles/Food/11-Global-McDonald-s-Menu-Items.html.

33. Craig J. Thompson and Maura Troester, "Consumer Value Systems in the Age of Postmodern Fragmentation: The Case of Natural Health Microculture," *Journal of Consumer Research* 28 no. 4 (2002): 550–571.

34. "About Us: UBL at a Glance," United Breweries Limited, accessed at www.kingfisherworld.com/corporate/ubl_glance.aspx.

35. "Home Page," Pizza Hut, accessed at www.pizzahut.com.cn.

36. Philip Kotler and Gary Armstrong, *Principles of Marketing,* 12th ed. (Upper Saddle River, NJ: Prentice-Hall, 2007).

37. Nina Rosandic, "Dr. Martens Sets Sights on Fashion Positioning," *Marketing* (London), March 16, 2011.

38. Kenneth D. Clow and Donald Baack, *Integrated Advertising, Promotion, and Marketing Communications,* 4th ed. (Upper Saddle River, NJ: Pearson Prentice Hall, 2010).

39. Steenkamp and Hofstede, "International Market Segmentation."

40. Melissa Wilkinson, "Marketing Plays Critical Role," *Charter* (Sydney) 81 no. 3 (2010, April): 24–27.

41. Jimmy Yeow, "Ganad Unipoles Alter Cambodia's Ad Scene," *Business Times* (Kuala Lumpur), June 19, 1996.

42. Kutay Erdem and Ruth A. Schmidt, "Ethnic Marketing for Turks in Germany," *International Journal of Retail & Distribution Management* 36 no. 3 (2008): 212–223.

43. Lynn R. Kahle, Gregory Rose, and Aviv Shoham "Findings of LOV Throughout the World, and Other Evidence of Cross-National Consumer Psychographics," *Journal of Euromarketing* 8 no. 1/2 (1999): 1–14.

44. Esri, "About Esri," accessed at www.esri.com/about-esri/index.html.

45. Ulf Hannerz, "Cosmopolitans and Locals in World Culture," *Theory, Culture, and Society* 7 no. 2–3 (199): 237–251.

46. Kineta H. Hung, Stella Yiyan Li, and Russell W. Belk, "Glocal Understandings: Female Readers' Perceptions of the New Woman in Chinese Advertising," *Journal of International Business Studies* 38 no. 6 (2007): 1034–1052.

47. Mahesh N. Shankarmahesh, "Consumer Ethnocentrism: An Integrative Review of Its Antecedents and Consequences," *International Marketing Review* 23 no. 2 (2006): 146–172.

48. Alex Duval Smith, "How Africa's Party Animals Drank Themselves to Death," *The Independent* (London), September 25, 2009.

49. "Finance and Economics: Roll Up, Roll Up; Spain's Savings Banks," *The Economist* (London) 398 no. 8719 (2011, February 5): 87.

50. Tony Kontzer, "Wide-Angle View of Customers," *InformationWeek* (Manhasset) June 6, 2005.

51. "Worldwide Activities," General Electric, accessed at www.ge.com/company/worldwide_activities/index.html.

52. Clow and Baack, Marketing Management.

53. Judy Bayer, "Customer Segmentation in the Telecommunications Industry," *Journal of Database Marketing & Customer Strategy Management* 17 no. 3/4 (2010): 247–256.

54. *Marketing Dictionary. Dictionary of Marketing Terms* (Barron's Educational Series: Hauppauge, NY, 2000).

55. Jackie Crosby, "A Glimpse of Health Care in India; An Edina Doctor Says a Trip to India Showed Her the Need to Improve Health Care in Other Parts of the World," *Star Tribune* (Minneapolis), May 8, 2011.

56. Dick Ahlstrom, "Language Complexity Declined in Move Out of Africa," *Irish Times* (Dublin), April 21, 2011.

57. "South Africa," *The World Factbook,* Central Intelligence Agency (Washington, DC), accessed at https://www.cia.gov/library/publications/the-world-factbook/geos/sf.html.

58. Simcha Ronen and Oded Shenkar, "Clustering Countries on Attitudinal Dimensions: A Review and Synthesis," *Academy of Management Review* 10 no. 3 (1985): 435–454, accessed at www.grovewell.com/pub-GLOBE-intro.html.

59. Prahalad, *The Fortune at the Bottom-of-the-Pyramid.*

60. "Sustainability for Sound Business," *Industrial Management* 49 no. 4 (2007): 11.

61. Nicole Boyer, "The Base of the Pyramid: Reperceiving Business from the Bottom Up," *Global Business Network* (May 2003), accessed at www.visionspring.org/downloads/docs/GBN_BOP_Paper.pdf.

62. Jenny Dawkins, "Corporate Responsibility: The Communication Challenge," *Journal of Communication Management* 9, no. 2 (November 2004): 106–117.

63. "SC Johnson Grows Sustainability Around the World; New Ad Stems From a Flower," *PR Newswire* (New York), April 2, 2010.

64. "Pre-empting the Competition," *Strategyonline* (Canada), accessed at www.strategyonline.ca/articles/magazine/20031006/handb.html?page=3.

65. "History Time Line," Electrolux, accessed at http://group.electrolux.com/en/category/about-electrolux/history/history-time-line/.

CHAPTER 5

1. Julie Edgar, "Health Benefits of Green Tea," WebMD, (2010), accessed at www.webmd.com/food-recipes/features/health-benefits-of-green-tea.

2. "Middle East and Africa Accounts for Nearly 14 Per Cent of Global Tea Consumption," *Al Bawaba* (London), March 10, 2010.

3. Nick Woodsworth, "Heaven-Sent Moroccan Scents: The Bitter, the Sweet and the Fragrantly Aromatic Await Nicholas Woodsworth," *Financial Times* (London), December 22, 2001.

4. Ganesh Jaishankar and Gillian Oakenfull, "International Product Positioning: An Illustration Using Perceptual Mapping Techniques," *Journal of Global Marketing,* 13 no. 2 (1999): 85–111.

5. "Australia's Virgin Blue Casts Net to Catch More Biz-Class Flyers," *Asia Pulse* (Rhodes), February 23, 2011.

6. "Sony to Close Symbol of TV Business," *Knight Ridder Tribune Business News* (Washington), February 1, 2007.

7. Veronica Chufo, "Chinese Drywall: Judge Awards $2.6 M to 7 Local Homeowners," *McClatchy–Tribune Business News* (Washington), April 8, 2010.

8. Bill Britt, "Chevy Chase Does Turkish Cola Ads Aimed at Coke and Pepsi: Spots Air as Anti-American Feeling in Turkey Runs High," *Adage.com* (London), August 1, 2003, accessed at www.cenktolunay.com/articles/cola_turka.htm.

9. Richard McComb, "Put Some Fizz Into the New Year: We Road Test the Champagnes on Offer . . . So You Don't Have To," *Sunday Mercury* (Birmingham), December 26, 2010.

10. Johnny Diaz, "Buick Shifts to the Young; With New Lines and a New Marketing Campaign, a Brand Known for Decades as Your Grandparents' Car Hits the Streets," *Boston Globe* (Boston), October 8, 2010.

11. Elizabeth Weise, "Maker of Artisanal Tofu Aims to Bring Sexy to Soybean Curd; Think of Another Funny, Creamy Foreign Food That's Now Popular—Yogurt," *USA Today* (McLean, VA), December 29, 2010.

12. William Grimes, "How Curry, Stirred in India, Became a World Conqueror," *New York Times* (Eastern edition), February 1, 2006.

13. Miriam Jordan, "Down Market: A Retailer in Brazil Has Become Rich by Courting Poor—Payments of $14 a Month Add Up for Samuel Klein, Sao Paulo's Sam Walton—Self-Esteem for the Masses," *Wall Street Journal,* June 11, 2002.

14. Reeba Zachariah and Partha Sinhg, "Marlboro Man Rides Into Indian Terrain," *The Times of India* (New Delhi), September 9, 2009.

15. "Automotive; ADAC-Automarx: Mercedes-Benz Is Germanys Strongest Brand," *Journal of Transportation* (Atlanta), December 18, 2010.

16. Alison Smith, "The Conundrum of Maintaining Image: Marketing Consolidating Brands," *Financial Times,* May 11, 1998.

17. "Of Internet Cafes and Power Cuts: Technology in Emerging Economies," *The Economist* 386 no. 8566 (2008): 90.

18. "Analyse the Oral Care Market in India Where Low Penetration Offers Growth Opportunities," *Business Wire* (New York), May 1, 2008.

19. Israel D. Nebenzahl, Jaffe D. Eugene, and Shlomo L. Lampert, "Towards a Theory of Country Image Effect on Product Evaluation," *Management International Review* 37 no. 1 (1997): 27–49.

20. Hsin-Tien Han, "The Investigation of Country-of-Origin Effect-Using Taiwanese Consumers' Perceptions of Luxury Handbags as Example," *Journal of American Academy of Business* (Cambridge) 15 no. 2 (2010): 66–73.

21. Katharina P. Roth and Adamantios Diamantopoulos, "Advancing the Country Image Construct," *Journal of Business Research* 62 no. 7 (2009): 726–740.

22. "Business: Three-Point Turn; Hyundai in America," *The Economist* 383 no. 8534 (2007): 79.

23. Jeff Green, "We Got You Covered. Kia, Isuzu Add Warranties as Hyundai Learns," *Brandweek* 41 no. 29 (2000): 11.

24. Paul Ingrassia, "Why Hyundai Is an American Hit: What GM and Chrysler Can Learn From Its Success," *Wall Street Journal* (Online), accessed at http://online.wsj.com/article/SB10001424052970203917304574410692912072328.html.

25. Mahesh N. Shankarmahesh, "Consumer Ethnocentrism: An Integrative Review of Its Antecedents and Consequences," *International Marketing Review* 23 no. 2 (2006): 146–172.

26. "The Decline and Decline of Brand America," *BusinessLine* (Chennai), Febuary 4, 2005.

27. Petra Riefler and Adamantious Diamantopoulos, "Consumer Animosity: A Literature Review and a Reconsideration of Its Measurement," *International Marketing Review* 24 no. 1 (2007): 87–119.

28. Mohammed Y. A. Rawwas, K.N. Rajendran, and Gerhard A. Wuehrer, "The Influence of Worldmindedness and Nationalism on Consumer Evaluation of Domestic and Foreign Products," *International Marketing Review* 13 no. 2 (1996): 20–38.

29. "Indonesian Farmers Threatens to Boycott Nestlé Products," *Indonesia Government News* (New Delhi), March 24, 2010.

30. Youngtae Choi, Rahul Kale, and Jongkuk Shin, "Religiosity and Consumers' Use Of Product Information Sources Among Korean Consumers: An Exploratory Study," *International Journal of Consumer Studies* 34 (2010): 61–68.

31. Daniel Rathwell, "The Qibla Cola Path of Least Resistance," thinking-east. net, accessed at www.thinking-east.net/indexa2ec.html?option=com_ content&task=view&id=143.

32. George H. Condon, "Why Can't Canadians Buy Red Bull and Pro-Activ?," *Canadian Grocer* 117 no. 2 (2003):82.

33. "Made in the USA? The Truth Behind the Labels," *Consumer Reports* 73 no. 3 (2008): 12–14.

34. Mariko Sanchanta, "Tokyo's Luxury Market Matures," *Financial Times,* January 7, 2005.

35. "The Nation's Favourite Dish: Fish and Chips," Historic-UK.com, accessed at www .historic-uk.com/CultureUK/FishandChips.htm.

36. Laurel Wentz and Rebecca A. Fannin, "Crest, Colgate Bare Teeth in Competition for China," *Advertising Age* (Chicago), November 1996.

37. Tarun Khanna and Krishna Palepu, "Emerging Giants: Building World-Class Companies in Developing Countries," *Harvard Business Review* (October 1, 2006): 60–69.

38. Tarun Khanna and Krishna Palepu, "Emerging Giants: Building World-Class Companies in Developing Countries," *Harvard Business Review* (October 1, 2006): 60–69.

39. Jaishankar and Oakenfull, "International Product Positioning."

40. Linda Stradley, "Vegemite," What's Cooking America, accessed at http:// whatscookingamerica.net/History/VegemiteHistory.htm, accessed March 19, 2010.

41. "Modified Nano Meets EU Crash Regulations," *Automative Engineer* 34 no. 7 (2009): 6.

42. "Philips to Enhance Position as a Top-Notch Brand in Kitchen Appliances," *Bernama* (Kuala Lumpur), August 6, 2003.

43. Amy Kazmin, "India Exchanges Pools for Price; A Market Is Growing for Budget Hotels Aimed at Travellers Who Cannot Afford Luxury But Will Not Settle for Dilapidated, Socialist-Era State Tourist Bungalows," *Financial Times* (London), August 25, 2009.

44. Debanhan Mittra and Peter N. Golder, "How Does Objective Quality Affect Perceived Quality?," *IMarketing Science* 25 no. 3 (2006): 230–247.

45. "Italy: Findomestic Launches Brand Repositioning Campaign Based on 'Co-Responsibility,'" *The Pak Banker* (Lahore): June 19, 2010.

46. Mark Spaulding, "Greenwashing: Seven Deadly Sins," *Converting* 27 no. 6 (2009): 10.

47. Jamey Boiter, "Can Brands Launch Sustainable Campaigns Without Being Accused of Greenwashing?," *Fast Company,* February 25, 2010.

48. Daniel W. Baack and David J. Boggs, "The Difficulties in Using a Cost Leadership Strategy in Emerging Markets," *International Journal of Emerging Markets* 3 no. 2 (2008): 125–139.

49. Wichit Chantanusornsiri, "Bowled Over: TOTO of Japan Elevates Mundane Bathroom Fixtures," *Knight Ridder Tribune Business News* (Washington), May 27, 2005.

50. Ibid.

51. Pat Lenius, "TOTO Adds Aquia Toilet to Its Green Products Line," *Supply House Times,* 48 no. 8 (2005).

52. Chantanusornsiri, "Bowled Over."

53. Ibid.

54. Ibid.

55. Ibid.

56. Nanchanok Wongsamuth, "TOTO Flush With Sales Amid Industry Slump," *McClatchy–Tribune Business News* (Washington), October 21, 2009; Alexandra Clough, "Luxury Toilet Maker TOTO USA Opens in Wellington Mall," *Knight Ridder Tribune Business News* (Washington), March 14, 2005; David Rilling, "TOTO Flushes Old Ways Down the Pan: Toilet Maker Sells to Remodellers and China's Super Rich," *Financial Times*, March 2, 2004.

57. Shinichi Terada, "TOTO Ads Take Aim at America's Great Unwashed," *McClatchy–Tribune Business News* (Washington), November 15, 2007.

CHAPTER 6

1. Al Arabia News. "Iran Bans Make-Up for Women on TV," accessed at www .alarabiya.net/articles/2009/12/02/92966.html.

2. "African Beauty With Long False Lashed and Golden Natural Makeup Wearing a Turquoise Necklace," EvaStory, accessed at www.shutterstock.com/ pic-16647949/stock-photo-african-beauty-with-long-false-lashes-and-golden-natural-make-up-wearing-a-turquoise-necklace.html.

3. This definition is based on the American Marketing Association's definition of the concept found at www.marketingpower.com.

4. Naresh K. Malhotra, James Agarwal, and Mark Peterson, "Methodological Issues in Cross-Cultural Marketing Research: A State-of-the-Art Review," *International Marketing Review* (London) 13 no. 5 (1996): 7–45.

5. Anonymous, "MARKETING TO WOMEN: Femininity, Roles and Pigeonholes," Brand Strategy. (London), September 14, 2007. pg. 40–41.

6. R. L. Tung, "Managing in Asia: Cross-Cultural Dimensions," in *Managing Across Cultures: Issues and Perspectives,* edited by P. Joyn and M. Warner, 233–245 (Albany, NY: International Thomson Business Press, 1996).

7. Jane Sigal, "In Paris, Burgers Turn Chic," *New York Times* (Online edition), July 16, 2008.

8. Jemima Bokaie, "Coca-Cola Plans 'Chinese' Drinks," *Marketing,* October 17, 2001.

9. Norihiko Shirouzu, "Toyota Tries to Shift Gears in China—Car Maker Sees Growth Slowing to 14%, Bets on Models With Smaller Engines," *Wall Street Journal,* November 27, 2009.

10. Marguerite Moore, Karen McGowan Kennedy, and Ann Fairhurst, "Cross-Cultural Equivalence of Price Perceptions Between U.S. and Polish Consumers," *International Journal of Retailing & Distribution Management* 31 no. 4/5 (2003): 268–280.

11. James Murphy, "Giving Pizza Hut a Real Bit in Hong Kong," *Media,* January 13, 2006.

12. G. Prendergast, B. Ho, and I. Phau, "A Hong Kong View of Offensive Advertising," *Journal of Marketing Communications* 8 no. 3 (2002): 165–177.

13. Kara Chan, Lyann Li, Sandra Diehl, and Ralf Terluttee, "Consumers Response to Offensive Advertising: A Cross Cultural Study," *International Marketing Review* 24 no. 5 (2007): 606–628.

14. Carlos Pestana Barros and Ricardo Sellers-Rubio, "Analysing Cost Efficiency in Spanish Retailers With a Random Frontier Model," *International Journal of Retail & Distribution Management* 36 no. 11 (2008): 883–900.

15. Li-Wei Mai and Hui Zhao, "The Characteristics of Supermarket Shoppers in Beijing," *International Journal of Retailing & Distribution* 32 no. 1 (2004): 56–62.

16. Manjeet Kripalani, "A Profitable Passage to India: Armed With Market Research, Korean Companies Succeed," *Business Week,* May 12, 2003, pg. 50.

17. Jennifer Hodson, "Apparel Chief Buying," *Wall Street Journal* (Eastern edition), December 8, 2010.

18. Joseph F. Hair, Jr., Robert P. Bush, and David J. Ortinau, *Marketing Research Within a Changing Environment,* 2nd ed. (New York: McGraw-Hill, 2003).

19. "China's Statistics Are Private Property," *Wall Street Journal* (Online), February 17, 2011.

20. "Growing Terrorism to Hamper Economic Growth: Acting President ICCI," *The Balochistan Times* (Quetta), July 5, 2010.

21. "Indonesia Objects US Move to Include Country on Copyright Watch List," *BBC Monitoring Asia Pacific* (London), March 19, 2010.

22. Matt Steinglass, "Vietnam Motorbike Company in Trouble Over Vespa Lookalike," *McClatchy–Tribune Business News* (Washington), September 27, 2010.

23. Lim R. Macnamara, "The Crucial Role of Research in Multicultural and Cross-Cultural Communication," *Journal of Communication Management* 8 no. 3 (2004): 322–334.

24. Peter Hessler, "China's Boomtowns," *National Geographic Magazine* 211 no. 6 (2007, June): 88–111.

25. Pablo Sanchez, Joan Enric Ricart, Miguel Angel Rodriguez, "Influential Factors in Becoming Socially Embedded in Low-Income Markets," *Greener Management International* no. 51 (2006): 19–38.

26. N. K. Maholtra, J. Agarwal, and M. Peterson, "Methodological Issues in Cross-Cultural Marketing Research," *International Marketing Review* 13 no. 5 (1996): 7–43.

27. Lorraine Watkins-Mathys, "Focus Group Interviewing in China: Language, Culture, and Sensemaking," *Journal of International Entrepreneurship* 4 no.4 (2006): 209–226; G. Eckhardt, "The Role of Culture in Conducting Trustworthy and Credible Qualitative Business Research in China," in *Handbook of Qualitative Methods for International Business Research,* edited by R. Marschan-Piekkari and C. Welch, 402–420 (Cheltenham, UK: Edward Elgar, 2004).

28. Watkins-Mathys, "Focus Group Interviewing in China."

29. Kevin Watkins, et al., "EFA Global Monitoring Report 2010: Reaching the Marginalized," United Nations Educational, Scientific, and Cultural Organization, Paris (2010).

30. Susan P. Douglas and C. Samuel Craig, *International Marketing Research* (Prentice Hall: Englewood Cliffs, NJ, 1983).

31. "Market Research: Digging Deep to Find the Right Insight," *Marketing Week* (London), September 23, 2010.

32. "Internet World Stats," Internet World Statistics: Usage and Population Statistics, accessed at www.internetworldstats.com.

33. Ibid.

34. William G. Zikmund and Barry J. Babin, *Exploring Marketing Research,* 10th ed., (Eagan, MN: Southwestern / Cengage Publishing, 2010).

35. S. T. Cavusgil and A. Das, "Methodological Issues in Empirical Cross-Cultural Research: A Survey of the Management Literature and a Framework," *Management International Review* 37 no. 1 (1997): 71–96.

36. N. L. Reynolds, A.C. Simintiras, and A. Diamantopoulos, "Theoretical Justification of Sampling Choices in International Marketing Research: Key Issues and Guidelines for Researchers," *Journal of International Business Studies* 34 no. 1 (2003): 80–89.

37. Zikmund and Babin, *Exploring Marketing Research.*

38. Kallol K. Bagchi, Adriano O. Solis, and Leopoldo A. Gemoets, "An Empirical Study on Telecommunication Product Adoption in Latin America and the Caribbean," *The Electronic Journal on Information Systems in Developing Countries* 15 no. 3 (2003): 1–17.

39. "Kenya," CIA World Factbook, accessed at https://www.cia.gov/library/publications/the-world-factbook/geos/ke.html.

40. Jack Ewing, "Upwardly Mobile in Africa," *Business Week,* September 24, 2007.

41. "Latin American Internet Usage Statistics," Internet World Stats: Usage and Population Statistics, accessed at www.internetworldstats.com/stats10.htm.

42. "Latin American Internet Usage Statistics," Internet World Stats: Usage and Population Statistics, accessed at www.internetworldstats.com/stats10.htm.

43. "Liberia at a Glance," *Development Economic LDB* (February 25, 2011), accessed at http://devdata.worldbank.org/AAG/lbr_aag.pdf.

44. "How Does the Japanese Addressing System Work?," accessed at www.sljfaq.org/afaq/addresses.html.

45. Shintaro Okazaki and Barbara Mueller, "Cross-Cultural Advertising Research: Where We Have Been and Where We Need to Go," *International Marketing Review* 24 no. 5 (2007): 499–515.

46. Michael R. Mullen, "Diagnosing Measurement Equivalence in Cross-National Research," *Journal of International Business Studies* 26 no. 3 (1995): 573–596.

47. V. Kumar, *International Marketing Research* (Prentice Hall: Upper Saddle River, NJ, 2000).

48. Chol Lee and Robert T. Green, "Cross-Cultural Examination of the Fishbein Behavioral Intentions Model," *Journal of International Business Studies* 22 no. 2 (1991): 289–305.

49. Martijn G. De Jong, Jan-Benedict E M Steenkamp, Jean-Paul Fox, Hans Baumgartner, "Using Item Response Theory to Measure Extreme Response Style

in Marketing Research: A Global Investigation," *Journal of Marketing Research* 45 no. 1 (2008): 104–115.

50. Gerald Albaum, Edwin Duerr, and Jesper Strandskov, *International Marketing and Export Management* (Harlow, UK: Prentice Hall Financial Times, 2005).

51. Jamie Anderson and Costas Markides, "Strategic Innovation at the Base of the Pyramid," *MIT Sloan Management Review* 49 no. 1 (2007): 83–88.

52. Douglas and Craig, *International Marketing Research.*

53. The product and company used in this case are fictitious.

54. "The Highs and Lows of Germany's Drinking Culture," *DW-World,* November 18, 2006, accessed at www.dw-world.de.

55. "EU Urged to DO More to Protect Young People From Alcohol," *DW-World,* October 24, 2006, accessed at www.dw-world.de.

56. "How to Germany," accessed at www.howtogermany.com; "Why Is a Drink and Driving Program Necessary?,"World Health Organization, accessed at www.who.int/roadsafety/projects/manuals/alcohol/1-Why.pdf.

57. "DUI & DWI Penalties Hefty With Revised Traffic Law," *Japan Update* (2007), accessed at www.japanupdate.com.

CHAPTER 7

1. "Sleep Habits Vary by Race," *Discovery News* (March 8, 2010), accessed at http://news.discovery.com/human/sleep-habits-race.html.

2. "Staple Foods: What Do People Eat?," FAO Corporate Document Repository, accessed at www.fao.org/docrep/u8480e/u8480e07.htm.

3. Barry J. Babin and Eric G. Harris, *CB–Consumer Behavior* (Mason, OH: Cengage, 2009).

4. "Home Page," Europa Park (Rust, Germany), accessed at www.europapark.de/lang-en/Home/c51.html.

5. Robert L. Underwood, "The Communicative Power of Product Packaging: Creating Brand Identity Via Lived and Mediated Experience," *Journal of Marketing Theory and Practice* 11 no. 1 (2003): 62–76.

6. Pinya Silayoi and Mark Speece, "The Importance of Packaging Attributes: A Conjoint Analysis Approach," *European Journal of Marketing* 41 no. 11/12 (2007): 1495–1517.

7. Michael Fridjhon, "Wine," *Business Day* (South *Africa*), April 8, 2011.

8. Ibid.

9. "Packaging and Packaging Waste," Europa, accessed at http://europa.eu/legislation_summaries/environment/waste_management/121207_en.htm.

10. "Towards a 'Green' Ramadan," *Gulf News* (Dubai), August 28, 2009.

11. Efthalia Dimara and Dimitris Skuras, "Consumer Demand for Informative Labeling of Quality Food and Drink Products: A European Union Case Study," *Journal of Consumer Marketing* 22 no. 2/3 (2005): 90–100.

12. "CE Marking-Home," International Trade Administration, accessed at www.export.gov/cemark/index.asp.

13. Neil Katz, "Cigarette Warning Label Pictures," *Cbsnews.com Health Blog* (November 11, 2010), accessed at www.cbsnews.com/8301-504763_162-20022483-10391704.html.

14. "A Global Language for Packaging and Sustainability," Consumer Goods Forum (July 8, 2010), accessed at www.ciesnet.com/pfiles/programmes/gpp/2010-07-01-GPP-Report.pdf.

15. "Towards Sustainable Packaging," Packaging Council of Australia (2007), accessed at www.pca.org.au/site/index.php/page/sustainability.

16. "Home Page," Sustainable Packaging Coalition (n.d.), accessed at www.sustainablepackaging.org/.

17. "Home Page," Ecology Coatings (n.d.), accessed at www.ecologycoatings.com/profiles/investor/fullpage.asp?f=1&BzID=1672&to=cp&Nav=0&LangID=1&s=0&ID=8935.

18. "KFC Bags Go Green," *Townsville Bulletin* (Townsville, Qld.), February 2, 2010.

19. "Introducing the Green Bottle That's Made From Paper," *Sunday Times* (London), July 5, 2009.

20. "Study: Consumers' Demand for Sustainable Products Remains Strong," Dupont Tate and Lyle BioProducts (May 21, 2009), accessed at www.duponttateandlyle.com/news_052109.php.

21. "Home Page,"Mercatto Group (n.d.), accessed at http://www.mercattogroup.com/.

22. "About Us," Comstar Corporate (n.d.), accessed at http://comstarauto.com/comstar_company_history.html.

23. "Home Page," Industrial Resin Sdn Bhd (n.d.), accessed at www.irmb.com.my/resins/irm.htm.

24. "Our Company," Advanced Machinery and Automation (n.d.), accessed at http://adv-mach.com/our-company.php.

25. "About Us," Agrium, Inc. (n.d.), accessed at www.agrium.com/about_us/who_we_are.jsp.

26. This section based on Mohsin Habib and Leon Zurawicki, "The Bottom-of-the-Pyramid: Key Roles for Businesses," *Journal of Business & Economics Research* 8 no. 5 (2010): 23–32.

27. Van R. Wood, Dennis A. Pitta, and Frank J. Franzak, "Successful Marketing by Multinational Firms to the Bottom-of-the-Pyramid: Connecting Share of Heart, Global 'Umbrella Brands,' and Responsible Marketing," *Journal of Consumer Marketing* 25 no. 7 (2008): 419–429.

28. Rajagopal, "Brand Paradigm for the Bottom-of-the-Pyramid Markets,"*Measuring Business Excellence* 13 no. 4 (2009): 58–68.

29. C. K. Pralahad and A. Hammond, "Serving the World's Poor, Profitably," *Harvard Business Review* (2002, Sept.): 4–11.

30. J. Dubey and R. P. Patel, "Small Wonders of the Indian Market," *Journal of Consumer Behaviour* 4 no. 2 (2004): 145–151.

31. M. Sehrawet and S. C. Kundu, "Buying Behavior of Rural and Urban Consumers in India: The Impact of Packaging," *International Journal of Consumer Studies* 31 no. 6 (2007): 630–638.

32. D. E. Bowen and R. Hallowell,"Suppose We Took Services Seriously? An Introduction to the Special Issue,"*Academy of Management Executive* 16 no. 4 (2002): 1–5.

33. Arindam Banerjee and Scott A. Williams, "International Service Outsourcing: Using Offshore Analytics to Identify Determinants of Value-Added Outsourcing," *Strategic Outsourcing: An International Journal* 2 no. 1 (2009): 68–79.

34. "Key Development Data and Statistics," The World Bank (2011), accessed at http://web.worldbank.org/WBSITE/EXTERNAL/DATASTATISTIC/0, contentMDK:20535285~menuPK:64909264~pagePK:64909151~piPK:64909148~theSitePK:6950074~isCURL:Y,00.html.

35. "Services, etc., Value Added (% of GDP)," The World Bank, (2011), accessed at http://data.worldbank.org/indicator/NV.SRV.TETC.ZS.

36. "Economic Data Search Tool," World Trade and Tourism Council (n.d.), accessed at www.wttc.org/eng/Tourism_Research/Economic_Data_Search_Tool/.

37. "Copenhagen in New Drive for Tourists," The Copenhagen Post Online (May 17, 2010), accessed at www.cphpost.dk/business/business/119-business/48989-copenhagen-in-new-drive-for-tourists.html.

38. Thomas W. Lin, "Haier Is Higher," Strategic Finance (2009, December): 41–49.

39. "The World's Most Innovative Companies," Bloomberg Businessweek (Online) accessed at www.businessweek.com/magazine/content/06_17/b3981401.htm (July 27, 2010).

40. Danny King, "Tablets and Smartphones Slow Laptop Sales," Dailyfinance.com (2011), accessed at www.dailyfinance.com/2011/03/03/tablets-and-smartphones-slow-laptop-sales-growth/.

41. "Laptop Sales Exceed Desktop Sales Globally," Laptop Logic.com, (2008, December 26).

42. "Over Five Billion Mobile Phone Connections Worldwide," European Journalism Centre, (2010), accessed at www.ejc.net/media_news/over_5_billion_mobile_phone_connections_worldwide/.

43. Philip Kotler and Kevin Lane Keller, A Framework for Marketing Management, 4th Edition (Upper Saddle River, NJ, Prentice Hall, 2009).

44. James Bander, "Ending Era, Kodak Will Stop Selling Most Film Cameras," Wall Street Journal, January 14, 2004.

45. This section is based on Dennis R. Appleyard, Alfred J. Field, Jr., and Steven L. Cobb, International Economics (Boston: McGraw-Hill, 2008).

46. B. M. Oviatt and P. P. McDougall, "Toward a Theory of International New Ventures," Journal of International Business Studies 25 no. 1 (1994): 45–64.

47. "SA's Joule Car Aims to Electrify Car Market," BusinessDay.co.za (July 27, 2010), accessed at www.businessday.co.za/Articles/Content.aspx?id=116064.

48. Devin Banerjee, "Expanding Banking in India," Wall Street Journal (Online edition), July 28, 2010, accessed at http://online.wsj.com/article/SB10001424052748703700904575391460677186520.html?mod=WSJ_latest headlines.

49. "Taiwan's High-Tech Firms Diversify to Survive," Taipei Times (2010, February 11), accessed at www.taipeitimes.com/News/biz/archives/2010/02/11/2003465735.

50. "About TeaGschwender," TeaGschwender (2010), accessed at www.teagschwendner.com/US/en/About_us.TG.

51. "Starbucks Reports Strong First Quarter Results as Via, International Sales Take Off," The Seattle Times (Online), (2010, January 21), accessed at http://seattletimes.nwsource.com/html/businesstechnology/2010846852_starbucks21.html.

52. "Harley Davidson Reports First Quarter 2010 Results," Harley Davidson (April 20, 2010), accessed at www.harley-davidson.com/wcm/Content/Pages/HD_News/Company/newsarticle.jsp?locale=en_US&articleLink=News/0685_press_release.hdnews&newsYear=&history.

53. Holger Elfes, "Adidas Leaps From Hot Sneakers to Warm Jackets," Bloomberg BusinessWeek (Online), December 9, 2009, accessed at www.businessweek.com/innovate/content/dec2009/id2009129_588770.htm.

54. July 28, 2010.

55. "Welcome to Kevlar," Kevlar (2011), accessed at http://www2.dupont.com/Kevlar/en_US/index.html.

56. These assertions are based on David Aaker, Building Strong Brands (New York: Free Press, 1996).

57. Gina Chon, "Audi Pursues Brand Recognition in U.S.," Wall Street Journal (Online), May 8, 2007.

58. Information in this section is based on David Aaker, Managing Brand Equity: Capitalizing on the Value of a Brand Name (New York: Free Press, 1991); also Aaker, Building Strong Brands.

59. This definition based on the conceptualization by the American Society for Quality, www.asq.or.

60. Johan Anselmsson, Ulf Johansson, and Niklas Persson, "The Battle of Brands in the Swedish Market for Consumer Packaged Food: A Cross-Category Examination of Brand Preference and Liking," Journal of Brand Management 16 no. 1/2 (2008): 63–79.

61. John Dawes, "Brand Loyalty in the U.K. Sportswear Market," International Journal of Market Research 51 no. 4 (2009): 449–463.

62. Philip Kotler, Marketing Management, 11th ed. (Upper Saddle River, NJ: Prentice Hall, 2003).

63. "A New ISO Standard on Brand Valuation?," Business Review Europe (Online), accessed at www.businessrevieweurope.eu/blogs/economics/new-iso-standard-brand-valuation, on May 31, 2010.

64. Arwa Damon, "Mom of Toddler Smoker in Indonesia Seeks Help for Him," CNN World (May 31, 2010), accessed at www.cnn.com/2010/WORLD/asiapcf/05/31/indonesia.smoking.baby/index.html.

65. "Indonesia: Overview," International Resource Center (March 2011), accessed at http://tobaccofreecenter.org/resources_country/indonesia.

66. "Home Page," Interface (2008), accessed at www.interfaceglobal.com/default.aspx, on August 30.

67. "Companies and Governments Lag NGOs in Driving Sustainability but New Corporate Leaders Emerging, According to Experts," The Sustainability Survey 2009 (Online) (2009), accessed at www.globescan.com/news_archives/tss_release01/.

68. "Toward a More Sustainable Way of Business," Interface (Online), (2008), accessed at http://interfaceglobal.com/Sustainability.aspx.

69. Ibid.

70. Craig Reiss, "Why You Need to Know TED," Entrepreneur (Online) (2010), accessed at www.entrepreneur.com/article/217243.

CHAPTER 8

1. "11 Global McDonald's Menu Items," Woman's Day (Online) (2010, March 24), accessed at www.womansday.com/Articles/Food/11-Global-McDonald-s-Menu-Items.html.

2. "McDonald's Global Sales Drive Second Quarter Earnings up 15%," PR Newswire (July 23, 2010), accessed at www.prnewswire.com/news-releases/mcdonalds-global-sales-drive-second-quarter-earnings-up-15-99094629.html.

3. Raj Aggarwal, "Business Strategies for Multinational Intellectual Property Protection," Thunderbird International Business Review 52 no. 6 (2010): 541–551.

4. "Madrid Facts," United States Patent and Trademark Office (n.d.), accessed at www.uspto.gov/trademarks/law/madrid/madridfaqs.jsp#q1.

5. "Corporate Spying Costs $45 Billion," *Information Management Journal* 42 no. 3 (2008):16.

6. Ed Lee, "Global Issues: Fighting Back Against Economic Espionage," *Sales & Marketing Management* 161 no. 6 (2009):5.

7. "New 3-D Scanners Speed Reverse-Engineering," *Manufacturing Engineering* (Dearborn) 141 no. 5 (2008): 28–31.

8. Kenji Hall, "Zeebo Takes Wireless Gaming to Emerging Markets," *Business Week* (Online), May 29, 2009.

9. John Cronin, Jed Cahill, and Mike McLean,"Prep Patents With Reverse Engineering in Mind," *Electronic Engineering Times*, June 8, 2009: 3–32.1

10. Elias Dinopoulos and Paul Segerstrom, "Intellectual Property Rights, Multinational Firms and Economic Growth," *Journal of Development Economics* 92 no. 1 (2010): 13–27; Titus O. Awokuse and Hong Yin, "Intellectual Property Rights Protection and the Surge in FDI in China," *Journal of Comparative Economics* 38 no. 2 (2010): 217–224.

11. Scott Foster, "Reverse Engineering Firm Ready for Asian Expansion," *Ottawa Business Journal* 9 no. 44 (2004): 9.

12. Robert S. Boynton, "The Tyranny of Copyright," *New York Times,* January 25, 2004.

13. Bambina Wise, "South African Textiles Strike Ends, But Problems Remain," *WWD* (New York) 198 no. 73 (2009): 19.

14. Sundeep Tucker and Amy Yee, "Ambani War Enters New Phase," *Financial Times* (London), July 18, 2008.

15. "Who Gets How Much in Reliance Split" (June 18, 2005). Accessed at www.rediff.com/money/2005/jun/18ri115.htm.

16. Irem Eren Erdogmus, Muzaffer Bodur, and Cengiz Yilmaz, "International Strategies of Emerging Market Firms: Standardization in Brand Management Revisited," *European Journal of Marketing* 44 no. 9/10 (2010): 1410–1436.

17. Robert D. Buzzell, "Can You Standardize Multinational Marketing?," *Harvard Business Review* 46 no. 6 (1968): 102–113.

18. Theodore Levitt, "The Globalization of Markets," *Harvard Business Review* 61 no. 3 (1983): 92–102.

19. "Time for Indonesia to Accelerate Use of Renewable Energy," *Bernama.com* (Malaysian National News Agency) (2010, July 27), accessed at www.bernama.com/bernama/v5/newsworld.php?id=516637.

20. "Citibank No. 1 Credit Card Issuer in the UAE, First in Retail Spending," *Al Bawaba* (London), October 5, 2005.

21. Boryana Dimitrova and Bert Rosenbloom, "Standardization Versus Adaptation in Global Markets: Is Channel Strategy Different?," *Journal of Marketing Channels* 17 no. 2 (2010): 157–176.

22. Marvin Harris, *The Sacred Cow and the Abominable Pig. Riddles of Food and Culture* (New York: Simon and Schuster, 1985).

23. "Foodstuffs, Cosmetics and Disinfectants Act, 1972 (Act 54 of 1972): Regulations Relating to the Labeling and Advertising of Foodstuffs," *Department of Health Government Gazette* no. 30075 (July 20, 2007), accessed at www.doh.gov.za/docs/regulations/2007/reg0642.pdf.

24. Roberto Iglesias, Prabhat Jha, Márcia Pinto, Vera Luiza da Costa e Silva, and Joana Godinho, "Tobacco Control in Brazil," Discussion Paper, Human Development Department Latin America and the Caribbean Region, The World Bank, and Health, Nutrition, and Population Department Human Development Network The World Bank (2007, August), accessed at http://siteresources.worldbank.org/BRAZILEXTN/Resources/TobaccoControlinBrazilenglishFinal.pdf?resourceurlname=TobaccoControlinBrazilenglishFinal.pdf.

25. Gregg Keizer, "EU Rejects Intel's Example of Apple in Antitrust Dispute," Computerworld (September 22, 2009), accessed at www.computerworld.com/s/article/9138374/EU_rejects_Intel_s_example_of_Apple_in_antitrust_dispute.

26. "Apple Adds the European Union to Its Antitrust Woes," 9TO5Mac (July 6, 2010), accessed at http://9to5mac.com/2010/07/06/apple-adds-the-european-union-to-its-antitrust-woes/.

27. "S. Africa: On High-Risk Products, Retailers Have New Obligations," *The Pak Banker* (Lahore), April 13, 2010.

28. John Crenshaw, "EU Consumer Law Sets Warranty Standard," *Bicycle Retailer & Industry News* 11 no. 6 (2002): 32.

29. Updated information for American companies can be found at www.business.gov/manage/green-business/green-marketing/regulations.html.

30. "Home Page," Promotion Marketing Awards of Asia (n.d.), accessed at www.pmaa-awards.net/documents/11.%20Best%20Effective%20Long%20Term%20Mkt%20Campaign.pdf.

31. "Ocean Park Embraces Interactive Marketing," New Media Power (2009, June 7), accessed at www.newmediapower.com/blog/ocean-park-embraces-interactive-marketing/.

32. "Home Page,"Flightstats.com (n.d.), accessed at http://opsawards.flightstats.com/.

33. Juliet Cox and Colin Mason, "Standardisation Versus Adaptation: Geographical Pressure to Deviate From Franchise Formats," *The Services Industries Journal* 27 no. 8 (2007): 1053–1072.

34. This definition based on C. Gronroos, "A Service Quality Model and Its Marketing Implications," *European Journal of Marketing* 18 no. 4 (1982): 35–42.

35. A. Parasuraman, V. Zeithaml, and L. Berry,"A Conceptual Model of Service Quality and Its Implications for Future Research," *Journal of Marketing* 49 no. 4 (1985): 41–50.

36. Linda C. Ueltschy, Michel Laroche, Axel Eggert, and Uta Bindl, "Service Quality and Satisfaction: An International Comparison of Professional Services Perceptions," *Journal of Services Marketing* 21 no. 6 (2007): 410–423.

37. K. F. Winsted, "The Service Experience in Two Cultures: A Behavioral Perspective," *Journal of Retailing* 73 no. 3 (1997): 337–360.

38. Olivier Furrer, B. Shaw-Ching Liu, and D. Sudharshan, "The Relationships Between Culture and Service Quality Perceptions: Basis for Cross-Cultural Market Segmentation and Resource Allocation," *Journal of Service Research* 2 no. 4 (2000): 355–371.

39. Linda Ueltschy, Michel LaRoche, Axel Eggert, and Uta Bindl, "Service Quality and Satisfaction: An International Comparison of Professional Services Perceptions," *Journal of Services Marketing* 21 no. 6 (2007): 410–423.

40. B. Imrie, J. W. Cadogan, and R. McNaughton, "The Service Quality Construct on a Global Stage," *Managing Service Quality* 12 no. 1 (2002): 10–18.

41. "China Bans Western Relibious Music," *The Telegraph,* April 28, 2011, accessed at www.telegraph.co.uk/news/worldnews/asia/china/3108810/China-bans-Western-religious-music.html.

42. "Organiser of Music Concerts Executed," *Freemuse* (August 21, 2008), accessed at www.freemuse.org/sw29564.asp.

43. John Borland, "Canada Deems P2P Downloading Legal," *CtNet News* (2003, December 12), accessed at http://news.cnet.com/2100–1025_3–5121479.html.

44. Crore is a unit of measure in South Asia equal to 10 million. E. Kumar Sharma, "License to Download," *Business Today,* June 14, 2009.

45. Eric Pfanner, "Music Industry Counts the Cost of Piracy," *New York Times* (Online edition), January 22, 2010, accessed at www.nytimes.com/2010/01/22/business/global/22music.html.

46. Paul Sonne and Max Colchester, "France, the U.K. Take Aim at Digital Pirates: New Weapons Include Laws That Put Pressure on Internet-Service Providers to Assist in Crackdown on Illegal Downloads," *Wall Street Journal* (Eastern edition), April 15, 2010.

47. S. C. Jain, "Standardization of International Marketing Strategy: Some Research Hypotheses," *Journal of Marketing* vo1.53(1989): 70–79.

48. Marieke de Global De Mooij, *Marketing and Advertising: Understanding Cultural Paradoxes* (Thousand Oaks, CA: Sage Publications, 2010), pg. 283.

49. "Huntkey Launches 'Universal' Power Strips; Compatibility, Safety, Functionality—Three is One 'Housekeeper,'" *PR Newswire* (New York), March 19, 2010.

50. Normandy Madden, "Unilever's Lipton Hirameki," *Advertising Age* 78 no. 29 (2007).

51. Sheridan Prasso, "Battle for the Face of China," *Fortune* 152 no. 12 (2005): 156–178.

52. Kenji Hall, "Zeebo Takes Wireless Gaming to Emerging Markets," *Business Week* (Online), May 29, 2009.

53. "Samsung Introduces Two New Mobile Sets in Bangladesh," *Bangladesh Business News* Thursday, July 29, 2010, accessed at www.businessnews-bd.com/index.php?option=com_content&view=article&id=1809:samsung-introduces-two-new-mobile-sets-in-bangladesh-&catid=36:business&Itemid=27

54. Reena Jana, "Inspiration From Emerging Economies," *Business Week* (New York), March 23, 2009.

55. Brian Palmer, "Why do Foreigners Like Fanta So Much?," *The Slate Group, a Division of the Washington Post Company* (August 5, 2010), accessed at www.slate.com/id/2262956/.

56. "History of Hybrid Vehicles," Hybrid Cars (June 13, 2011), accessed at www.hybridcars.com/history/history-of-hybrid-vehicles.html.

57. Annalyn Censky, "Porsche to Produce Plug-In Sports Car," cnnmoney.com (2010, July 28), accessed at http://money.cnn.com/2010/07/28/autos/porsche_hybrid/index.htm?hpt=T2.

58. Reena Jana, "Inspiration From Emerging Economies," *Business Week* March 23, 2009.

59. *Andrew Leckey*, "With InBev at Helm, Perhaps This Bud's For You," *Chicago Tribune* July 11, 2010.

60. Adam Thomson, "Modelo Loses Case Against AB InBev," *Financial Times* (London), July 13, 2010.

61. Hamish Champ, "AB InBevto roll-out Stella Artois Black," *The Publican* (June 29, 2010), accessed at www.thepublican.com/story.asp?storyCode=67361.

62. "The Belgian Beer Café concept was awarded in Australia. The concept of Creneau International and Interbrew is very popular in Australia and New Zealand," AB InBev:Global Press Releases (October 4, 2002), accessed at www.ab-inbev.com/go/media/global_press_releases/press_release.cfm?theID=193&theLang=EN.

63. "Anheuser-Busch InBev Is Reportedly Selling Its CEE Operations, Including Its Prominent Croatian Zagrebacka Pivovara (ZAPI) Arm," *M2 Presswire* (Coventry), January 31, 2010; "AB InBev Is to Offload Bass at Bargain Price," *Evening Standard* (London), May 26, 2010.

64. "INBEV Romania Changes Name," *Info–Prod Research* (Middle East), March 2, 2010.

65. Greg Farrell, "AB-Inbev Seeking to Revive Flat Bud Brand," *Financial Times* (London), June 14, 2010.

66. Matthew Dalton, "Earnings: Financing Charge Hurts AB InBev; Brazilian Sales Surge," *Wall Street Journal*. (Eastern edition), May 6, 2010.

67. Greg Keller, "A-B Inbev Profit Takes 34 Pct. Hit Global Beer Sales Are Lower, Marketing Expenses Higher Than Expected," *St. Louis Post–Dispatch* (Missouri), May 6, 2010.

68. Ben Cooper, "The Alcohol Market in the Enlarged EU," *Just—Drinks: Management Briefing* (November 2004).

69. Bill McClellan, "St. Louis Post-Dispatch, Bill Mcclellan Column: Lawyers Still Arguing Over A-B Sale," *McClatchy–Tribune Business News* (Washington), April 18, 2010.

70. "Vintage Law Ties Trade in Its Web WINE: Michael Chugani in Seattle," *South China Morning Post* (Hong Kong), August 1, 2000.

71. K. S. Jacob, "Alcohol Politics, Policies and Public Health," *The Hindu* (Chennai), November 3, 2009.

72. Benedict Mander, "The Dry Humour of Venezuela's Effort to Cut Drink-Driving Hugo Chavez's Ban on Alcohol Has Caused an Argumentative Easter," *Financial Times* (London), April 10, 2007.

73. Michael Steen, "Brazil Beer Sales Boost for AB InBev," *FT.com* (London), May 5, 2010.

74. John W. Miller, "Corporate News: Emotion Flows Over Beer in Belgium—Brewing Giant Anheuser-Busch Inbev Stirs Mixture of Pride Over Its Fame and Anger Over Its Efforts to Downsize," *Wall Street Journal* (Hong Kong), February 24, 2010.

CHAPTER 9

1. "Finland," *The World Factbook,* Central Intelligence Agency (2011), accessed at https://www.cia.gov/library/publications/the-world-factbook/geos/fi.html; "Small Wind Turbine Businesses in Finland." Momentum Technologies, LLC, accessed at http://energy.sourceguides.com/businesses/byP/wRP/swindturbine/byGeo/byC/Finland/Finland.shtml#29417; www.Tuulivoimala.com.

2. Otavio de Toledo Nobrega, Andre Ricardo Marques, Ana Cleire Gomes de Aruajo, Margo Gomes de Oliveira Karnikowski, Janeth de Oliveira Silva Naves, and Lynn Dee Silver, "Retail Prices of Essential Drugs in Brazil: And International Comparison," Rev Panam Salud Publica 22 no.2(2007), accessed at http://journal.paho.org/uploads/1192040443.pdf.

3. Craig Richardson, "China's New Landed Gentry: Foreigners," *Barron's,* October 27, 2008.

4. Ron Lieber, "BP Boycott Won't Do Much," *The Ledger* (Lakeland, FL), June 14, 2010.

5. Brendan ONeill, "Can the Lada Make a British Comeback?," *BBC News Magazine* (May 10, 2010), accessed at http://news.bbc.co.uk/2/hi/uk_news/magazine/8672464.stm; Brian McIver, "Up the Lada; Soviet 'Skip' Back on Road: To Celebrate Its Unlikely Return, We Toast World's Best 'Worst Car,'" *Daily Record* (Glasgow), May 13, 2010.

6. Clow and Baack, *Marketing Management,* 137–161.

7. "Mind Tools: Essential Skills for an Excellent Career," accessed at www.mindtools.com/pages/article/newSTR_69.htm; Kenneth E. Clow and Donald Baack, *Integrated Advertising, Promotion, and Marketing Communications,* 6th ed. (Upper Saddle River, NJ: Prentice-Hall, 2012).

8. Sujintana Hemtasilpa, "Thinking Small Pays Off for Unilever: Cambodia and Laos Strategy Fits Market," *Knight Ridder Tribune Business News* (Washington), January 29, 2005.

9. Aaron O. Patrick, "Unilever's Earnings Fall as Price Rises Hurt Sales," *Wall Street Journal* (Brussels), August 1, 2008.

10. "Indonesia Sweats High Chili Prices," *Global Post* (Chatham), August 5, 2010.

11. Karen Braun, Wendy M. Tietz, and Walter T. Harrison, *Managerial Accounting,* 2nd ed. (Upper Saddle River, NJ: Prentice Hall, 2010).

12. Sarah McBride, "Beer-Drinking Trends in Emerging Markets Bode Well for Big Brewers," NPR Planet Money blog, accessed at www.npr.org/blogs/money/2010/08/18/129275835/beer-drinking-trends-in-emerging-markets-bode-well-for-big-brewers on August 18, 2010.

13. Phillip Inman, "Food Inflation: Snack Attack: Price Increases About to Take a Big Bite Out of Your Office Sandwich: Speculation and Rumour Could Be the Driving Force Behind Sudden Market Rise," *The Guardian* (London), August 7, 2010.

14. Kana Inagaki, "Alcohol-Free Beer Makes Smashing Debut in Japan's Shrinking Market," *McClatchy–Tribune Business News* (Washington), July 12, 2009.

15. Jim Motavalli, "Transportation Inside the Think City Electric Car," Forbes.com, March 30, 2010.

16. Philip G. King and Sharmila Kumari King, *International Economics: Globalization and Policy* (New York: McGraw-Hill, 2010).

17. Brendan O'Neill, "The Oreo Invades Britain," *Christian Science Monitor* (Boston), May 13, 2008.

18. Hongju Liu, "Dynamics of Pricing in the Video Game Console Market: Skimming or Penetration?," *Journal of Marketing Research* 47 no. 3 (2010): 428.

19. Kenji Hall, "Zeebo Takes Wireless Gaming to Emerging Markets," *Business Week* (Online), May 29, 2009.

20. Shelley Emling, "That Ticket Cost How Much?," *The Atlanta Journal–Constitution* (Atlanta, GA), July 11, 2007.

21. Ming-jer Chen, *Inside Chinese Business: A Guide for Managers Worldwide* (Cambridge: Harvard Business School Press, 2001).

22. Alison Comish, "Capacity to Consume," *The American Economic Review* 26 no.2 (1936), accessed at www.jstor.org/pss/1803009.

23. C. K. Prahalad, *The Market at the Bottom-of-the-Pyramid* (Upper Saddle River, NJ: Wharton School Publishing, 2006), accessed at www.whartonsp.com/articles/article.aspx?p=389714&seqNum=4.

24. "Pepsi Plans Low-Cost Beverages, Snacks to Fight Anaemia," Businessline (Chennai), June 30, 2009.

25. Jamie Anderson and Costas Markides, "Strategic Innovation at the Base of the Pyramid," *MIT Sloan Management Review* 49 no. 1 (2007): 82–88.

26. Mimosa Spencer, "Carrefour, in Shift, to Exit Russia as It Reports 2.9% Drop in Sales," *Wall Street Journal* (Eastern edition), October 16, 2009.

27. Mike Karim, "Most Subcompacts Are Loss Leaders for Dealers," *Toronto Star* (Toronto), August 4, 2007.

28. "US for £ 7 Is a Loss Leader," *Travel Weekly* (UK), May 4, 2007.

29. "A Quarter of Firms Offer an Early Payment Discount," *Credit Control* (Hutton) 26 no. 8 (2005): 36–38.

30. "Telstra Profits Decline," *Lateline Business* (Ultimo), February 11, 2010.

31. Malcolm Gunn, "Volkswagen Beetle: Fine Lines Six Decades of Beetle: Originally Scoffed at and Called Cheap, More Than 21 Million Cars Later, The Beetle Truly Is the 'People's Car,'" *Prince George Citizen* (British Columbia), December 29, 2006.

32. Jen C. Brynildsen, "The International Pricing of CS3 Is Insane," *FlashMagazine .com,* accessed at www.flashmagazine.com/news/detail/the_international_pricing_of_cs3_is_insane/1421.htm.

33. Siseko Njobeni, "State Fury Over Mittal's Latest Price Increase," *Business Day* (Johannesburg), October 4, 2006.

34. Timothy Sexton, "Weber's Law and Why Big Businesses Believe You Won't Notice a Price Increase Under 10%," Associated Content, accessed at www.associatedcontent.com/pop_print-shtml.

35. "Mongolian Firms Fined for 'Collusion' on Flour Prices," BBC Monitoring Newsfile (London), August 17, 2010.

36. "Lawsuit Claims British Airways Guilty of Illegal, Deliberately Deceptive Pricing," Canada NewsWire (Ottawa), May 14, 2010.

37. Donald Baack and Daniel Baack, *Ethics and Marketing* (Pearson Custom Publishing, 2008).

38. "Mofcom Released the Final Ruling for Anti-Dumping Investigation Into Imported Purified Terephathalic Acid," Info: Prod Research (Middle East) Ramat-Gan, August 16, 2010.

CHAPTER 10

1. Based on information taken from "Home Page," ArcelorMittal, accessed at www.arcelormittal.com.

2. Roy Davies, "From Thalers to Dollars," University of Exeter (2008), accessed at http://projects.exeter.ac.uk/RDavies/arian/dollar.html.

3. Caitlin Kenny, "What Is a Direct Quote?," Conjecture Corporation, accessed at www.wisegeek.com/what-is-a-direct-quote.htm.

4. "Market Price in Japan," Rice Databank co., Ltd (July 27, 2011), accessed at www.japan-rice.com/Market-Price.htm.

5. Triennial Central Bank Survey (December 2007), Bank for International Settlements.

6. Saudi Arabia tops in flood aid to Pakistan, *McClatchy–Tribune Business News* (Washington) September 2, 2010.

7. "15.4 UK Trade: Rising Deficit With the EU, Surplus With the Rest of the World," Global Vision(2007), accessed at www.global-vision.net/facts/fact15_4.asp.

8. Kartik Goyal, "It's India's Year of Inflation," *Business Week,* July 26, 2010.

9. "Toys & Games; RC2 Reports Results for Second Quarter 2010; Increases Lower-end of Expected 2010 Earnings Range," *Economics Week* (Atlanta), August 6, 2010.

10. Suk H. Kim and H. Kim Seung, *Global Corporate Finance,* 6th ed. (Hoboken, NJ: Blackwell Publishing, 2006).

11. Peter Garnham, "Ireland Points Finger at UK Over Pound," *Financial Times* (London), January 13, 2009.

12. Liam Halligan, "The Real Lesson We Can Learn From Japan's Dramatic Currency Sell-Off," *The Telegraph* (September 18, 2010), accessed at www.telegraph.co.uk/finance/comment/liamhalligan/8010951/The-real-lesson-we-can-learn-from-Japans-dramatic-currency-sell-off.html.

13. Matt Steinglass, "Vietnam Devaluation Fails to Stem Dong's Fall," *FT.com* (London), August 18, 2010.

14. Glenn Whitney, "A Year Later, Britain Reaps Dividends From Its Decision to Pull Out of the ERM," *Wall Street Journal* (Eastern edition), September 13, 1993.

15. Pam Woodall, "Who's in the Driving Seat?," *The Economist* (London) 337 no. 7935 (1995): SS3–SS5.

16. Stephen Gordon, "Time to Stop Fretting Over the Canadian Dollar," *Canadian Business* (Toronto) 83 no. 2 (2010): 9.

17. Howard Fineman, "Is There a Doctor in the House?: Ron Paul, the GOP's Unlikely Savior," *Newsweek* (New York) 154 no. 24 (2009).

18. "IMF Would Consider Extending Greece More Aid," *Wall Street Journal* (Online), September 16, 2010.

19. "Greek Tourism Outlook Less Grim, China to Be Wooed," *Financial Mirror* (Nicosia), June 22, 2010.

20. Daekeun Park and Changyong Rhee, "Measuring the Degree of Currency Misalignment Using Offshore Forward Exchange Rates: The Case of the Korean Financial Crisis," *Journal of Asset Management* (London) 2 no. 1 (2001): 84–96.

21. Kim and Kim, *Global Corporate Finance.*

22. "Counterrade," *American Heritage Dictionary,* accessed at www.answers.com/topic/countertrade-1.

23. Michelle Wallin and Matt Moffett, "Argentina Says It Is Devaluing Its Peso by 29%," *Wall Street Journal* (Eastern edition), January 7, 2002.

24. Jeanne Whalen and Andrew Osborn, "Corporate News: Glaxo at Loggerheads With Russia Over HIV Drugs—Pharmaceutial Giant Rejects 15% Price Cut Sought by Government, Saying It Would Allow for Too Little Profit," *Wall Street Journal* (Eastern edition), June 12, 2009.

25. David Woodward, "The View From Here: Muhammad Yunus, Grameen Bank." *Director Magazine* (London) 62 no. 7 (2009): 12.

26. "Finance and Economics: Poor People, Rich Returns; Microfinance," *The Economist* (London) 387 no. 8580 (2008): 98.

27. Woodward, "The View From Here," 12.

28. Saumya Bhattacharya, "Want a Job, Go Rural; At a Time When Urban Jobs Are Dwindling, Microfinance Is Creating Jobs in Rural India Provided You Have the Right Skills and Aptitude," *Business Today* (New Delhi), March 8, 2009.

29. Woodward, "The View From Here," 12.

30. Rana Foroohar, "It's Payback Time; How a Bangladeshi Bank Is Growing in the U.S. by Making Tiny Loans to Groups of Poor Women With Entrepreneurial Dreams," *Newsweek* (New York) 156 no. 4 (2010).

31. Bhattacharya, "Want a Job, Go Rural."

32. E. Kumar Sharma, "Microfinance Players Must Innovate, Recall Social Goals: The Sector's Rapid Growth Has Not Meant That the Financially Excluded Are Better Off," *Business Today* (New Delhi), August 8, 2010.

33. Bhattacharya, "Want a Job, Go Rural."

34. Meredith May, "Microfinance's Next Frontier," *Stanford Social Innovation Review* (Stanford) 8 no. 4 (2010): 63–65.

35. Gary Gardner, "Microfinance Surging," *World Watch* (Washington) 21 no. 6 (2008): 30.

36. "Doing Good by Doing Very Nicely Indeed; Microfinance," *The Economist* (London) 387 no. 8586 (2008).

37. Dean Karlan, "Measuring Microfinance," *Stanford Social Innovation Review* (Stanford) 6 no. 3 (2008): 53.

CHAPTER 11

1. Richard Gibson, "Chiquita Sees an End to Storm," *Wall Street Journal* (Online edition), July 18, 2007.

2. "Remedent, Inc. Announces Exclusive Marketing and Distribution Agreement for Glamsmile(TM) Veneers Into Saudi Arabia," *Business Wire* (New York), April 24, 2008.

3. "Germany: Selling U.S. Products and Services," U.S. Commercial Service, United States Department of Commerce, accessed at www.buyusa.gov/germany/en/marketing_us.html.

4. "China Agri-Business's New Direct Sales Channel Continues to Grow," PR Newswire (August 13, 2010), accessed at www.prnewswire.com/news-releases/china-agri-businesss-new-direct-sales-channel-continues-to-grow-100610479.html.

5. C. J. Coppla, "Direct Marketing Sales Boom With the Proliferation of Wine Clubs," *Wine Business Monthly* 7 no. 6 (2000): 20–23.

6. Calin Gurau and Franck Duquesnois, "Direct Marketing Channels in the French Wine Industry," *International Journal of Wine Business Research* 20 no. 1 (2008): 38–52.

7. "The Airlines Discover 'Content'; They Want to Bypass Electronic Middlemen and Have a More Direct Relationship With Ticket Buyers," *Wall Street Journal* (Online), January 20, 2011.

8. Vanessa O'Connell, "Diamond Industry Makeover Sends Fifth Avenue to Africa," *Wall Street Journal* (Eastern edition), October 26, 2009.

9. "Japanese Trading Companies: The Giants That Refused to Die," *The Economist* 319 no. 7709 (1991): 72–73.

10. "Brazil: Classy Brands to Distribute Gisele Bündchen Cosmetics Sejaa," *Brasil Econômico* (SABI English Language Abstracts) (São Paulo), January 17, 2011.

11. Sean Poulter, "Victory for the Superstores Spells Doom to Small Shops," *Daily Mail* (London), February 16, 2008.

12. Armin Schmutz, "Breakthrough in the World's Longest Tunnel," *Trains* (Milwaukee) 71 no. 3 (2011): 36–38.

13. Harri Lorentz, Chew Yew Wong, and Olli-Pekka Hilmola, "Emerging Distribution Systems in Central and Eastern Europe," *International Journal of Physical Distribution & Logistics Management* 37 no. 8 (2007): 670–697.

14. Robert A. Guth, "New Child-Friendly Malaria Drug Presents Distribution Challenge," *Wall Street Journal* (Eastern edition), January 27, 2009.

15. "DOH Bans Junk Food Ads on Children's Television," *China Post* (Online edition) (January, 29, 2010), accessed at www.chinapost.com.tw/taiwan/national/national-news/2010/01/29/242772/DOH-bans.htm.

16. Paul Ziobro, "Ruling Lets Starbucks Take Over Packaged-Coffee Distribution," *Wall Street Journal* (Online edition), January 28, 2011.

17. "Business Floating on Air," *The Economist* 359, no. 8222 (2001): 8.

18. Kenneth D. Clow and Donald Baack, *Cases in Marketing Management* (Los Angeles: Sage Publications, 2011).

19. A. Parkhe, "Interfirm Diversity, Organizational Learning, and Longevity in Global Strategic Alliances," *Journal of International Business Studies* 22 (1991): 579–601.

20. J. K. Johansson, *Global Marketing: Foreign Entry, Local Marketing, and Global Management* (New York: McGraw Hill, 2003).

21. Rajiv Mehta, Pia Polsa, Jolanta Mazur, Fan Xiucheng, and Alan J. Dubinsky, "Strategic Alliances in International Distribution Channels," *Journal of Business Research* 59 (2006): 1094–1104.

22. This definition based on D. Duhan and M. Sheffet, "Gray Markets and the Legal Status of Parallel Importation," *Journal of Marketing* 52 no. 3 (1988): 75–83.

23. J. E. Inman, "Gray Marketing of Imported Trademarked Goods: Tariffs and Trademark Issues," *American Business Law Journal* 31 (1993): 18–23.

24. Tony Smith, "Sony Wins Nuplayer PSP Sales Ban," The Register (July 21, 2005), accessed at www.theregister.co.uk/2005/07/21/sony_vs_nuplayer/.

25. "Distribution Agreement," RealDealDocs, accessed at http://agreements.realdealdocs.com/Distribution-Agreement/DISTRIBUTION-AGREEMENT-2835241/.

26. Definition based on Adel I. El-Ansary and Louis W. Stern, "Power Measurement in the Distribution Channel," *Journal of Marketing Research* 9 (February 1972): 47–52.

27. "M4 Sciences Signs International Distribution Agreement With Fukuda Corp.," *MFRTech.com,* accessed at www.mfrtech.com/articles/3649.html.

28. "Mamas and Papas Launches Eighth International Store in the Kingdom of Bahrain," *Franchiseek.com,* accessed at www.franchiseek.com/Greece/NewsDetail.asp?NewsID=303.

29. Louis W. Stern, Adel I. El-Ansary, and Anne T. Coughlan, *Marketing Channels,* 5th ed. (Upper Saddle River, NJ: Prentice Hall, 1996).

30. Abdulaziz Abdulaziz, "Nigeria: Cleplas Rewards Distributors in Kano," accessed at http://allafrica.com/stories/201001290662.html.

31. "Wal-Mart Altering Culture of Mexico / Retailer's Power Similar to That in U.S.," *Houston Chronicle* (Texas), December 6, 2003.

32. A. I. Rokkan and S. A. Haugland, "Developing Relational Exchange: Effectiveness and Power," *European Journal of Marketing* 36 no. 1/2 (2002): 211–230.

33. Robert M. Morgan and Shelby D. Hunt, "The Commitment-Trust Theory of Relationship Marketing," *Journal of Marketing* 58 no. 3 (1994): 20–38.

34. Arvind V. Phatak and Mohammed M. Habib, "The Dynamics of International Business Negotiations," *Business Horizons* (May–June 1996): 30–38.

35. Hernandex William Requejo and John L. Graham, *Global Negotiation: The New Rules* (New York: Palgrave Macmillan, 2008).

36. These stages based on Leonard Greenhalgh, *Managing Strategic Relationships: The Key to Business Success* (New York: The Free Press/Simon & Schuster, 2001).

37. Roy J. Lewicki, Bruce Barry, and David M. Saunders, *Essentials of Negotiation* (New York: McGraw-Hill/Irwin, 2010).

38. Jeanne M. Brett, *Negotiating Globally: How to Negotiate Deals, Resolve Disputes, and Make Decisions Across Cultural Boundaries,* 2nd ed. (San Francisco: Jossey-Bass, 2007).

39. Edward T. Hall, "The Silent Language in Overseas Business," *Harvard Business Review* (May–June 1960): 87–96.

40. Phatak and Habib, "The Dynamics of International Business Negotiations."

41. These assertions based on the work of Lieh-Ching Chang, "An Examination of Cross-Cultural Negotiation: Using Hofstede Fraemwork," *Journal of American Academy of Business* (2003): 567–570.

42. Richard E. Nisbett, *The Geography of Thought: How Asians and Westerners Think Differently . . . and Why* (New York: The Free Press, 2003).

43. Requejo and Graham, *Global Negotiation.*

44. Ibid.

45. "Home Page," Oral-B, accessed at www.oralb.com/international/.

46. Gera A. Welker and Jacob Wijngaard, "The Role of the Operational Network in Responsive Order Processing," *International Journal of Manufacturing Technology and Management* 16 no. 3 (2009): 181–194.

47. This section based on Stern, El-Ansary, and Coughlan, *Marketing Channels.*

48. James Stock and Douglas Lambert, *Strategic Logistics Management* (Homewood, IL: Irwin, 2000).

49. N. Kumar, "The Power of Trust in Manufacturer-Retailer Relationships," *Harvard Business Review* 74 (November–December, 1996): 92–106.

50. Scott Bicheno, "Sony Consolidates Distribution Network to Ensure Highest Levels of Service and Expertise," *Hexus.channel* (2008), accessed at http://channel.hexus.net/content/item.php?item=16029.

51. JDA Software, "About JDA," found at www.jda.com/company/company-index/.

52. "MEBC, Inc. Expands Partnership With *JDA* Software," *The Pak Banker* (Lahore): May 11, 2011.

53. Editors of Supply & Demand Chain Executive, "2010 Green Supply Chain Awards 'Sustainability Becomes Strategic,'" Supply & Demand Chain Executive, accessed at www.sdcexec.com/print/Supply-and-Demand-Chain-Executive/2010-Green-Supply-Chain-Awards/1$13111.

54. Andrew K. Reese, "Green Is Global: Is Your Supply Chain Ready?," *Supply & Demand Chain Executive,* June 9, 2011.

55. "JDA Software Announces First Quarter 2011 Results," *The Pak Banker* (Lahore), May 4, 2011.

56. JDA Software, "About JDA," found at www.jda.com/company/company-index/.

CHAPTER 12

1. "Alipay Spat Leaves Alibaba Group, Yahoo Relationship Fraying," *Interfax: China Business Newswire* (Hong Kong), June 8, 2011; "Alibaba Overtakes Google in Mainland Ad Sales," *China Economic Review Daily Briefings* (Shanghai), December 10, 2010.

2. "Alibaba; China's Sourcing Trailblazer Reaches a Turning Point," *China Economic Review* (Shanghai), April 6, 2011.

3. "Alibaba Makes It Easier for U.S. Retailers to Acquire Top-Quality Chinese-Designed Products," *Business Wire* (New York), April 26, 2011.

4. "Alibaba; China's Sourcing Trailblazer Reaches a Turning Point."

5. "Alibaba Has New Express Delivery System," *China Economic Review Daily Briefings* (Shanghai), January 19, 2011.

6. "Alibaba and the 2,236 Thieves; An Online Scandal in China," *The Economist* (London) 398 no. 8722 (2011): 73.

7. "World," CIA World Factbook, accessed at https://www.cia.gov/library/publications/the-world-factbook/geos/xx.html.

8. "Our Locations," Winget Limited, accessed at www.winget.co.uk/ourLocations.aspx?Continent=Middle%20East.

9. "Red Bull's Good Buzz," *Newsweek*, May 14, 2001.

10. "Economic Recession? Diamond Jewelry Demand in India Is on the Rise," *Diamondpriceguide.com* (2010), accessed at www.diamondpriceguide.com/news/nc206_Investment/n87616_Economic-Recession-Diamond-Jewelry-demand-in-India-is-on-the-rise.

11. "DFA: Bangladeshi Trade Delegation to Visit PHL Late January," *gmanews.tv* (January 14, 2011), accessed at www.gmanews.tv/story/210592/nation/dfa-bangladeshi-trade-delegation-to-visit-phl-late-january.

12. "Export Broker Services," Export Trade Broker, accessed at www.exporttradebrokers.com/exportbrokerservices.html.

13. Satya S. Chakravorty, "Improving Distribution Operations: Implementation of Material Handling Systems," *International Journal of Production Economics* 122 no. 1 (2009): 89–103.

14. Online information obtained at Van Bon Stores corporate website, "H&S Group," accessed at www.vanbon.nl/.

15. Curt Barry, "Keeping DC Costs at Bay," *Multichannel Merchant* 4 no. 4 (2008): 1, 45.

16. "Transportation Services Overview," *U.S. Industry Quarterly Review: Transportation & Logistics,* 2nd Quarter, (2006): 135–137.

17. Ibid.

18. Robert Nolin, "Study Warns of Pollution From Ships," *Physorg.com* (Online), March 31, 2009, accessed at www.physorg.com/news157744326.html.

19. E. W. T. Ngai and Angappa Gunasekaran, "RFID Adoption: Issues and Challenges," *International Journal of Enterprise Information Systems* 5 no. 1 (2009): 1–8.

20. G. S. Suder, (ed.), *Corporate Strategies Under International Terrorism and Adversity* (Northampton, MA: Edward Elgar, 2006).

21. Arthur Herman, "Modern-Day Blackbeards: There Is Nothing New About Menace on the High Seas—or About the Solutions That Would Make It Disappear," *Wall Street Journal* (Online), April 9, 2010.

22. "CSI in Brief," U.S. Department of Homeland Security, accessed at www.cbp.gov/xp/cgov/trade/cargo_security/csi/csi_in_brief.xml.

23. "C-TPAT Overview," U.S. Department of Homeland Security, accessed at www.cbp.gov/xp/cgov/trade/cargo_security/ctpat/what_ctpat/ctpat_overview.xml.

24. "About Us," Rewe Group, accessed at www.rewe-group.com/en/company/about-us/.

25. "About Us," Shoprite, accessed at www.shoprite.co.za/pages/127416071/About.asp.

26. "International Licensing," 7–11, accessed at http://corp.7-eleven.com/AboutUs/InternationalLicensing/tabid/115/Default.aspx.

27. "Home Page," HyperPanda, accessed at www.panda.com.sa/english/index.php/about-us.html.

28. "Shinsegae Centum City: World's Largest Department Store," Bukisa.com, accessed at www.bukisa.com/articles/289228_shinsegae-centum-city-world-largest-departement-store.

29. "About Us," Wal-Mart, accessed at http://walmartstores.com/AboutUs/.

30. "Starbucks Coffee International," Starbucks, accessed at www.starbucks.com/business/international-stores.

31. "Annual Report 2010," Footlocker, accessed at www.footlocker-inc.com/investors.cfm?page=annual-reports.

32. Julie Bosman and Michael J. De La Merced, "Borders Files for Bankruptcy," *Dealbook.com* (2011), accessed at http://dealbook.nytimes.com/2011/02/16/borders-files-for-bankruptcy/.

33. Tom Orlik, "Alibaba's Jewel Still Hidden," *Wall Street Journal* (Eastern edition), March 18, 2011.

34. "Alipay Spat Leaves Alibaba Group, Yahoo Relationship Fraying," *Interfax: China Business Newswire* (Hong Kong), June 8, 2011.

35. "Alibaba Group to Drive Major Investment in Logistics in China to Allow Merchants to Meet Growing Domestic Consumption," *Business Wire* (New York), January 19, 2011.

36. "Alibaba Growth Echoes China Trend," *Wall Street Journal* (Online), November 2, 2010.

37. "Alibaba; China's Sourcing Trailblazer Reaches a Turning Point," *China Economic Review* (Shanghai), April 6, 2011.

38. "Alibaba Group to Drive Major Investment in Logistics in China to Allow Merchants to Meet Growing Domestic Consumption," *Business Wire* (New York), January 19, 2011; Kathrin Hille, "Alibaba Plans China Delivery Network," *FT.com* (London), October 20, 2010.

39. "Tesco Annual Report, 2010," online edition, accessed at http://ar2010.tescoplc.com/business-review/international.aspx; Richard Fletcher, "Ambitious Tesco Ready to Risk Expansion When Others Fear to Trade," *Telegraph.co.uk* (Online), September 15, 2010, accessed at www.telegraph.co.uk/finance/newsbysector/retailandconsumer/8003175/Ambitious-Tesco-ready-to-risk-expansion-where-others-fear-to-trade.html; "Tesco's Far Eastern Promise," *Retail Week* (online), September 17, 2010, accessed at www.retail-week.com/sectors/food/tescos-far-eastern-promise/5017133.article; Sarah Shannon, "Tesco's Clarke Says China Will Be Profitable Under His Tenure," *Bloomberg Businessweek* (Online), September 12, 2010, accessed at www.bloomberg.com/news/2010-09-12/tesco-s-ceo-designate-says-china-will-become-profitable-during-his-tenure.html.

CHAPTER 13

1. Adapted from Marieke de Mooij, *Global Marketing and Advertising: Understanding Cultural Paradoxes,* 3rd ed. (Thousand Oaks, CA: SAGE Publications, 2010), 164.

2. David A. Victor, "Cross-Cultural/International Communication" accessed at www.referenceforbusiness.com/encyclopedia/Cos-Des/Cross-Cultural-International-Communication.html.

3. E. Hall, *Beyond Culture* (New York: Doubleday, 1984); E. Hall, *The Dance of Life* (New York: Doubleday, 1994), 85–128.

4. Kyunghee Bu, Donghoon Kim, Seung-yon Lee, "Determinants of Visual Forms Used in Print Advertising: A Cross-Cultural Comparison," *International Journal of Advertising* (Eastbourne) 28 no. 1 (2009): 13–47; Gordon E. Miracle, Kyu Yeol Chang, and Charles R. Taylor, "Culture and Advertising Executions: A Comparison of Selected Characteristics of Korean and US Television Commercials," *International Marketing Review* (London) 9 no. 4 (1992): 5–18.

5. Ee Ann Nee, "Everybody 'Reads' the Bus: Study Shows Strong Advertising Awareness Among Commuters," *Malay Mail* (Kuala Lumpur), November 24, 2010.

6. Herbert E. Krugman, "Why Three Exposures May Be Enough," *Journal of Advertising Research* 1 no. 6 (1972): 11–14.

7. Laurie Freeman, "Added Theories Drive Need for Client Solutions," *Advertising Age* no. 31 (2003): 18.

8. Erwin Ephron and Colin McDonald, "Media Scheduling and Carry-Over Effects: Is Adstock a Useful Planning Tool?," *Journal of Advertising Research* 42 no. 4 (July–August, 2002): 66–70.

9. Kenneth Clow and Donald Baack, *Integrated Advertising Promotion and Marketing Communications,* 5th ed. (Upper Saddle River, NJ: Prentice Hall, 2012).

10. Clow and Baack, *Marketing Management,* 167.

11. Ella Fitzsimmons, "Ban Exposes China's Ad Censorship Anomalies," *Campaign* (Teddington), May 16, 2008.

12. "MMS 2010 Discusses Growth of TV Advertising Spend in UAE & Pan-Arab Forecasted at 78 Percent for 2010," *Al Bawaba* (London), May 27, 2010.

13. Clow and Baack, *Integrated Advertising Promotion and Marketing Communications,* 5th ed., p. 5.

14. Kathrin Hille, "Baidu Revenues Jump 94% in Wake of Google's Retreat in China," *Financial Times* (London), February 2, 2011.

15. "Aust Parliamentary Committee to Review Billboard Advertisements," *Asia Pulse* (Rhodes), December 14, 2010.

16. Colleen Dardagan, "Airline Flies Again With a New Advertising Campaign," *The Mercury* (Durban), March 22, 2010.

17. "About Us," Bhalaria, accessed at www.bhalariametal.net/profile.html.

18. de Mooij, *Global Marketing and Advertising,* 3rd ed., 30.

19. Hibah Yousuf, "Emerging Markets Are Hot: Place Your Bets," *CNN Money* (February 1, 2001), accessed at http://money.cnn.com/2011/02/01/markets/emerging_markets_us_companies/index.htm?hpt=T2.

20. Alden, Wayne D. Chol Lee, "Identifying Global and Culture-Specific Dimensions of Humor," *Journal of Marketing* (Chicago), 57 no. 2 (April 1993): 64–76.

21. Daniel A. Joelson, "Rebel Sell," *Latin Trade* 12 no. 8 (August 2004): 16; Clow and Baack, *Integrated Advertising Promotion and Marketing Communications,* 5th ed., 161.

22. "India: New Thums Up Ad Most Expensive," *The Pak Banker* (Lahore), January 8, 2010.

23. Joy Dietrich, "Western Union Retraces Roots: The Emotions of Money Transfers," *Advertising Age International* (October 1999): 24–25.

24. "Issue Brief Portrayal of Gender," EASA, accessed at www.easa-alliance.org/page.aspx/100.

25. John B. Ford, Patricia Kramer Voli, Earl D. Honeycutt, Jr., and Susan L. Casey, "Gender Role Portrayals in Japanese Advertising: A Magazine Content Analysis," *Journal of Advertising* 27 no. 1 (1998): 113–124.

26. "Women in Chinese Media," accessed at http://byip19-finalproject.blogspot.com/.

27. Shoma Chatterji, "Changing Sex Roles in Indian Advertisements," India Together (July 2006), accessed at www.indiatogether.org/2006/jul/med-roles.htm.

28. Clow and Baack, *Integrated Advertising Promotion and Marketing Communications,* 5th ed.

29. de Mooij, *Global Marketing and Advertising,* 3rd ed., 218–220.

30. Ibid.

31. R. Mitchell and M. Oneal, "Managing by Values," *Business Week,* September 12, 1994.

32. S. P. Han and S. Shavitt, "Persuasion and Culture: Advertising Appeals in Individualistic and Collectivistic Societies," *Journal of Experimental and Social Psychology* 30 (1994): 326–350.

33. de Mooij, *Global Marketing and Advertising,* 3rd ed., 226.

34. Y. Zhang and B. D. Gelb, "Matching Advertising Appeals to Culture: The Influence of Products' Use Condition," *Journal of Advertising* 25 (1996): 29–46.

35. J. Bowman, "Commercials Rise in the East," in *M&M Europe: Pocket Guide to Asian TV* (London: Emap Media, 2002), 8.

36. "Land of the Big," *The Economist,* December 21, 1996.

37. J. Reardon, C. Miller, B. Foubert, I. Vida, and L. Rybina, "Antismoking Messages for the International Teenage Segment: The Effectiveness of Message Valence and Intensity Across Different Cultures," *Journal of International Marketing* 14 no. 3 (2006): 115–138.

38. Henry A. Laskey, Ellen Day, and Melvin R. Crask, "Typology of Main Message Strategies for Television Commercials," *Journal of Advertising* 18 no. 1 (1989): 36–41.

39. David Asker and Donald Norris, "Characteristics of TV Commercials Perceived as Informative," *Journal of Advertising Research* 22 no. 2 (1982): 61–70.

40. Stephen P. Durschlag, "Comparative Advertising Doesn't Always Work Overseas," Promo (January 1, 1999), accessed at http://promomagazine.com/mag/marketing_comparative_advertising_doesnt/#.

41. For a more complete description of these formats, see de Mooij, *Global Marketing and Advertising,* 3rd ed., chapter 10.

42. Roberto Rocha, "Tech Companies Use Fake Leaks to Create Buzz," *The Vancouver Sun* (Vancouver), September 1, 2006.

43. Angelo Fernando, "Transparency Under Attack," *Communication World* 24 no. 2 (March–April, 2007): 9–11.

44. Noarmandy Madden, "Upstart's Taxi Play Helps Brands Flag Down Rich Chinese," *Advertising Age* 78 no. 43 (2006): 46.

45. Emma Hall, "Skoda Offers Cars to Nicest and Meanest Brits on Facebook," *AdAge Global* (November 17, 2010), accessed at http://adage.com/globalnews/article?article_id=147156.

46. "James Bond 007—The Films and the Vehicles," The Car Enthusiast, accessed at www.carenthusiast.co.uk/news0910/bond_4.htm.

47. This Is Money Staff, "How Product Placement Will Transform British TV," ThisIsMoney.co.uk, accessed at www.thisismoney.co.uk/news/article.html?in_article_id=521679&in_page_id=2.

48. Normandy Madden, "Nokia Invents Characters With Amnesia so Phone Can Fill in Lost Memories" (November 23, 2010), accessed at http://adage.com/globalnews/article?article_id=147223.

CHAPTER 14

1. Laura Dugger, "Best Selling Over-the-Counter Pain Relievers," Revolution Health Group (February 13, 2008), accessed at www.revolutionhealth.com/conditions/pain-management/treatment-medication/top-pain-relievers.

2. "The History of Aspirin: Who Invented Aspirin and What Is Its History?," Bayer Aspirin, accessed at www.wonderdrug.com/pain/asp_history.htm.

3. www.webmd.com

4. E. Foxman, P. Tansuhaj, and J. Wong, "Evaluating Cross-National Sales Promotion Strategy: An Audit Approach," *International Marketing Review* 5 no. 4 (1988): 7–15.

5. Gemma Charles, "SABMiller Introduces Kozel Beer to UK," Brand Republic (September 20, 2010), accessed at www.brandrepublic.com/news/1029404/sabmiller-introduces-kozel-beer-uk/.

6. Michael Keferl, "McDonalds Testing IC Card 'Kazau Coupon,'" Japan Trends (May 21, 2008), accessed at www.japantrends.com/mcdonalds-testing-ic-card-kazasu-coupon/.

7. Chris Brassington, "Mobile Coupons Are Failing to Catch On, Why?," *The Huffington Post* (2010), accessed at www.huffingtonpost.com/chris-brassington/mobile-coupons-are-failin_b_654714.html?ref=twitter.

8. Robin Harding, "Japan Leads Way With Coupons," *Financial Times* (London), May 18, 2010.

9. "Coupon Site Groupon Expands to Europe," Boston.com (May 17, 2010), accessed at www.boston.com/business/technology/articles/2010/05/17/coupon_site_groupon_expands_to_europe/.

10. Samuel Axon, "Going Global: Groupon Buys European Clone CityDeal," *Mashable.com* (2010), accessed at http://mashable.com/2010/05/16/groupon-citydeal-europe/.

11. Kellogg's Canada, accessed at http://www2.kelloggs.ca/Promotion/PromotionDetail.aspx?PID=21157.

12. Yi-Zheng Shi, Ka-Man Cheung, and Gerard Prendergast, "Behavioral Response to Sales Promotion Tools: A Hong Kong Study," *International Journal of Advertising* 24 no. 4 (2005): 467–486.

13. James Quilter, "Kellogg's Gives Away Free Cereal in £3 Million Campaign," Brand Republic (April 1, 2009), accessed at www.brandrepublic.com/news/895368/Kelloggs-gives-away-free-cereal-3m-coupon-push/.

14. Anjali Cordeiro, "Battery Makers Recharge War: Procter & Gamble to Continue to Offer Bonus Packs of Its Duracell Brand," *Wall Street Journal* (Eastern edition), January 27, 2010.

15. "Dubai's Cite Centre Mall Takes Its Sales Promotion Online," *Menafm.com*, accessed at www.menafn.com/qn_news_story_s.asp?StoryId=1093279166.

16. L. McNeill, K. Fam, and K. Chung, "Chinese Consumer Preference for Price-Based Sales Promotion Techniques—the Impact of Gender, Income and Product Type," *ANZMAC* (Sydney) (2008), 1–7.

17. Kev J, "Capcom Reveal Playstation Network Price Promotion," *Electronic Theatre* (February 8, 2010), accessed at http://electronictheatre.co.uk/playstation3/playstation3-news/4105/capcom-reveal-playstation-network-price-promotion.

18. Sarah Noorbakhsh, "Product Paradise in Tokyo's Consumer Hot Spot," Japan Inc (October 3, 2008), accessed at www.japaninc.com/mgz_october_2008_sample-lab.

19. Gerard Prendergast, Alex S. L. Tsang, and Chit Yu Lo, "Antecedents of the Intention to Seek Samples," *European Journal of Marketing* 42 no. 11/12 (2008): 1162–1169.

20. Vaseline, accessed at www.vaseline.co.uk/samples/Form.aspx?Path=Consumer/OurProducts/IntensiveRescueRange/FreeSamples&locale=en-GB.

21. Seshan Balasubramanyam, "Is Future of Social Media Global?," *International Business Times* (Online edition), accessed at www.ibtimes.com/articles/44646/20100823/emarketer-united-states-facebook-nielsen-brazil-italy-new-zealand-hong-kong-canada-singapore-experia.htm.

22. David Ward, "Social Media Goes Global," *Direct Marketing News* (Online), accessed at www.dmnews.com/social-media-goes-global/article/118726/2/.

23. Ibid.

24. Jean Eaglesham and Paul Solman, "EU Standard for Sales Promotions," *Financial Times* (London), December 10, 2001.

25. Srinath Gopalakrishna, Gary L. Lilien, Jerome D. Williams, and Ian K. Sequeria, "Do Trade Shows Pay Off?," *Journal of Marketing* 59 no.3 (July 1995): 75–83.

26. "Tecno Bediba," biztradeshows.com, accessed at www.biztradeshows.com/trade-events/tecno-bediba.html.

27. "Overview," *Shopbiz.com*, accessed at www.shopbiz.jp/en/rt/.

28. John L. Stanton and Kenneth C. Herbst, "Slotting Allowances: Short-term Gains and Long-term Negative Effects on Retailers and Consumers," *International Journal of Retail & Distribution Management* 43 no. 3 (2006): 187–197.

29. "Walmart Follows Carrefour on Raising Fees," *Global Times* (January 26, 2011), accessed at http://business.globaltimes.cn/industries/2011–04/617197.html.

30. "Nucare Encourages Pharmacies to Build Haircare Category," *Chemist & Druggist* (London), October 13, 2001.

31. "Digital media for retail solution from IBM and Cisco," IBM Business Solutions, accessed at www.ibm.com/solutions/cisco/us/en/solution/H186213N23135Z95.html.

32. M. F. Barcala, M. J. S. Perez, and J. A. T. Gutierrez, "Training in Small Business Retailing: Testing Human Capital Theory," *Journal of European Industrial Training* 23 no. 7 (1999).

33. Scott Malone, "GE Uses Training to Appeal to its Customers," *New York Times* (Online edition), accessed at www.nytimes.com/2007/11/26/business/worldbusiness/26iht-ge.1.8478485.html.

34. Rodney Mullin and Julian Cummins, *Sales Promotion: How to Create, Implement and Integrate Campaigns That Really Work,* 4th ed. (London: Kogan Page Publishers, 2008).

35. "Progress Bestrides the Jordan River," accessed at www.tissueworldmagazine.com/08AprMay/features4.php.

36. John Reed, "Toyota Chief Vows 'Fresh Start' for Carmaker," *Financial Times* (London), March 24, 2010.

37. "Yingli Green Energy Announces Global Sponsorship of 2010 FIFA World Cup," Yingli Solar corporate (February 3, 2010), accessed at http://ir.yinglisolar.com/phoenix.zhtml?c=213018&p=irol-newsArticle&ID=1382290&highlight=.

38. "Company Facts: Sponsorships," Ericsson, accessed at www.ericsson.com/thecompany/company_facts/sponsorships.

39. "Welcome to Sagami's Website," Sagami Rubber Industries, accessed at www.sagami-gomu.co.jp/en/index.html.

40. "Home Page," Nestlé, accessed at www.nestle.com/Pages/Nestle.aspx.

41. "Terms and Conditions," Get Set, Go Free, accessed at www.getsetgofree.com/2011/Public/Terms.aspx.

42. "Nestle UK Launches 'Cross-Category' Promotion," Ingredients Network (May 13, 2010), accessed at www.ingredientsnetwork.com/story/full/nestle-uk-launches-cross-category-promotion.

43. "Home Page," Get Set Go Free, accessed at www.getsetgofree.com/2011/.

44. "UK Obesity Statistics," Statistics of Obesity in UK, Trends in Obesity and Excess Weight, Childhood Weight, accessed at www.annecollins.com/obesity/uk-obesity-statistics.htm.

45. "Obesity in Ireland," IrishHealth.com, accessed at www.irishhealth.com/article.html?id=9499.

46. "Sporting Champions Launch Summer Sporting Campaign to Get Families Fit for Free," Nestlé (July 13, 2010), accessed at www.nestle.co.uk/media/pressreleases/Pages/GetSetGoFree.aspx.

47. "About Us: Nestle is . . . ," Nestlé, accessed at www.nestle.com/AboutUs/Pages/AboutUs.aspx.

CHAPTER 15

1. "Arangkada Phillipines 2010: A Business Perspective," *Joint Foreign Chambers Advocacy Paper,* accessed at www.investphilippines.info/wp-content/uploads/2010/12/21.-Part-4-General-Business-Environment-Foreign-Equity-and-Professionals1.pdf

2. James Hall, "Swaziland Women Secure Right of Land Ownership," *News From Africa* (March 2002), accessed at www.newsfromafrica.org/newsfromafrica/articles/art_7884.html.

3. T. Suh and I. W. Kwon, "Globalization and Reluctant Buyers," *International Marketing Review* 19 no. 6 (2002): 663–680.

4. Heather Skinner, Krzysztof Kubacki, Gloria Moss, and David Chelly, "International Marketing in an Enlarged European Union: Some Insights Into Cultural Heterogeneity in Central Europe," *Journal for East European Management Studies* 13 no. 3 (2008): 193–215.

5. A. Simintiras and A. Thomas, "Cross Cultural Sales Negotiations: A Literature Review and Research Propositions," *European Journal of Marketing* 15 no. 1 (1998): 10–28.

6. Kelly R. Hewett, Bruce Money, and Subhash Sharma, "National Culture and Industrial Buyer-Seller Relationships in the United States and Latin America," *Journal of the Academy of Marketing Science* 34 no. 3 (2006): 386–402.

7. C. Nakata and K. Sivakumar, "National Culture and New Product Development: An Integrative Review," *Journal of Marketing* 60 (1996): 61–72.

8. R. C. Smith, "Consulting Across East-West Boundaries," *Journal of Management Consulting,* 8 no. 4 (1995): 3–5.

9. Information from this opening vignette based on Shawn Ye Yuxan, "China Business Culture: What Part Should Guanxi Play in Importing From China" (March 4, 2008), accessed at www.smartchinasourcing.com/cultural-considerations/china-business-culture-what-part-should-guanxi-play-in-importing-from-china.html ; "Chinese Business Culture," Los Angeles Chinese Learning Center, accessed at http://chinese-school.netfirms.com/guanxi.html.

10. Clow and Baack, *Marketing Management.*

11. Michele Marchetti, "Mastering the Cross-Cultural Presentation," *Sales and Marketing Management* 147 no. 11 (1995): 40.

12. Clare D'Souza, "An Inference of Gift-Giving Within Asian Business Culture," *Asia Pacific Journal of Marketing and Logistics* 15 no. 1/2 (2003): 27–38.

13. Seiga Ohtani, "Shaking Hands Across Borders," *Ethos* (March 31, 2010), accessed at http://ethosmagazine.com/archives/2338.

14. Gary Stoller, "Doing Business Abroad? Simple Faux Pas Can Sink You," *USA Today,* August 24, 2007.

15. This definition is based on P. Christopher Earley and Elaine Mosakowski, "Cultural Intelligence," *Harvard Business Review* (October 2004): 139–146.

16. Saikat Banerjee, "Dimensions of Indian Culture, Core Cultural Values and Marketing Implications," *Cross Cultural Management: An International Journal* 15 no. 4 (2008): 367–378.

17. This definition based on James P. Johnson, Tomasz Lenartowicz, and Salvador Apud, "Cross-Cultural Competence in International Business: Toward a Definition and a Model," *Journal of International Business Studies* 37 (2006): 525–543.

18. This definition based on K. Oberg, "Culture Shock: Adjustment to New Cultural Environments," *Practical Anthropology* 7 (July/August 1960): 177–182.

19. P. A. Herbig and H. E. Kramer, "Do's and Don'ts of Cross-Cultural Negotiations," *Industrial Marketing Management* 21 (1992): 287–298.

20. Antonis C. Simintiras and Andrew H. Thomas, "Cross-Cultural Sales Negotiations: A Literature Review and Research Propositions," *International Marketing Review* 15 no. 1 (1998): 10–19.

21. "Polish Business Etiquette Tips," www.foreignrelations.com, accessed at www.foreigntranslations.com/languages/polish-translation/polish-business-etiquette/.

22. "Turkish Business Etiquette Tips," www.foreignrelations.com, accessed at www.foreigntranslations.com/languages/turkish-translation/turkish-business-etiquette/.

23. Stoller, "Doing Business Abroad?"

24. Based, in part, on Charles M. Futrell, *ABC's of Relationship Selling,* 7th edition (New York: McGraw-Hill, 2003).

25. C. Hamner, "The Influences of Structural, Individual, and Strategic Differences," in D. Harnett and L. Cummings (Eds.), *Bargaining Behaviour: An International Study* (Houston: Dame Publications, 1980).

26. Robert Gulbro and Paul Herbig, "Negotiating Successfully in Cross-Cultural Situations," *Industrial Marketing Management* 25 (1996): 235–241.

27. "Swedish Business Etiquette Tips," *www.foreignrelations.com*, accessed at www.foreigntranslations.com/languages/swedish-translation/swedish-business-etiquette/.

28. These techniques based on Futrell, *ABC's of Relationship Selling;* and Rolph E. Anderson and Alan J. Dubinsky, 1st ed. *Personal Selling: Building Customer Relationships and Partnerships,* (Boston: Houghton Press, 2004).

29. Gulbro and Herbig, "Negotiating Successfully in Cross-Cultural Situations."

30. H. Davies, T. K. P. Leung, S. T. K. Luck, and Y. H. Wong, "The Benefits of Guanxi: The Value of Relationships in Developing the Chinese Market," *Industrial Marketing Management* 24 (1995): 207–214.

31. Mia Doucet, "What Part of Yes Don't You Understand?," *Mechanical Engineering* (Online edition), accessed at http://memagazine.asme.org/articles/2008/november/Part_Yes_Dont_Understand.cfm.

32. Janani Krishaswamy, "Lapses on the Front Line," *The Hindu Business Line*, accessed at www.thehindubusinessline.in/catalyst/2010/01/14/stories/2010011450080300.htm.

33. M. Stanek, "The Need for Global Managers: A Business Necessity," *Management Decision* 38 no. 3/4 (2000): 232–242.

34. Earl D. Honeycutt and John B. Ford, "Guidelines for Managing an International Sales Force," *Industrial Marketing Management* 24 (March 1995): 139–144.

35. Nakiye Boyacigiller, "The Role of Expatriates in the Management of Interdependence, Complexity and Risk in Multinational Corporations," *Journal of International Business Studies* 22 no. 3 (1991): 357–381.

36. David G. Collings, Hugh Scullion, and Michael J. Morley, "Changing Patterns of Global Staffing in the Multinational Enterprise: Challenges to the Conventional Expatriate Assignment and Emerging Enterprises," *Journal of World Studies* 42 no. 2 (2007): 198–208.

37. Susan DelVecchio and Elaine Seeman, "Discriminant Analysis of Field Sales Force Adoption of Wireless Technologies," *International Journal of Mobile Communications* 5 no. 1 (2007): 32–47.

38. Michael Ahearne and Adam Rapp, "The Role of Technology at the Interface Between Salespeople and Consumers," *Journal of Personal Selling & Sales Management* 30 no. 2 (2010): 111–124.

39. Mitchell Beer, "Meetings Deliver," white paper published by The Conference Publishers (2010), accessed at www.mpiweb.org/Libraries/NTA-Reports/Meetings_Deliver.pdf.

40. Mark W. Johnston and Greg W. Marshall, *Churchill/Ford/Walker's Sales Force Management,* 9th ed. (Boston: McGraw-Hill, 2009).

41. Robert C. Nickerson, Henri Isaac, and Brenda Mak, "A Multi-National Study of Attitudes About Mobile Phone Use in Social Settings," *International Journal of Mobile Communications* 6 no. 5 (2008): 541–563.

42. D.K.Tse, K.Lee, I.Vertinsky, and D.A. Wehrung, "Does Culture Matter? A Cross-Cultural Study of Executives' Choice, Decisiveness, and Risk Adjustment in International Marketing," *Journal of Marketing* 52 (1988): 81–95.

43. Seymour Adler, "Personality Tests for Salesforce Selection: Worth a Fresh Look," *Review of Business* 16 no.1 (1994): 27–31; William Verbeke and Richard P. Bagozzi, "Exploring the Role of Self- and Customer-Provoked Embarrassment in Personal Selling," *International Journal of Research in Marketing* 3 (2003): 233–258.

44. P. T. Costa and R. R. McCrae, *The NEO Personality Manual* (Odessa, FL: Psychological Assessment Resources, 1992).

45. R. Hogan, J. Hogan, and B. Roberts, "Personality Measurement and Employment Decisions," *American Psychologist* 51 no. 5 (1996): 469–477.

46. J. Patrick Leverett, T. Darin Matthews, Kerry S. Lassiter, and Nancy L. Bell, "Validity Comparison of the General Ability Measure for Adults With the Wonderlic Personnel Test," *North American Journal of Psychology* 3 no. 1 (2001): 173–182.

47. Ramez Naguib, "Going International: Ideas for Entering Markets Around the Globe," *Sales and Marketing Management* (Online edition) (October 10, 2010), accessed at www.salesandmarketing.com/article/going-international-ideas-entering-markets-around-globe.

48. C. David Shepherd and James C. Heartfield, "Discrimination Issues in the Selection of Salespeople: A Review and Managerial Suggestions," *Journal of Personal Selling & Sales Management* (Fall, 1991): 67–75.

49. Stewart J. Black and Hal B. Gregersen, "The Right Way to Manage Expats," *Harvard Business Review,* 77 no. 2 (1999): 52–62.

50. Johnston and Marshall, *Churchill/Ford/Walker's Sales Force Management.*

51. Sergio Roman and Salvador Ruiz, "A Comparative Analysis of Sales Training in Europe: Implications for International Sales Negotiations," *International Marketing Review,* 20 no. 3 (2003): 304–327.

52. Earl Naumann, Scott M. Widmier, and Donald W. Jackson, Jr., "Examining the Relationship Between Work Attitudes and Propensity to Leave Among Expatriate Salespeople," *Journal of Personal Selling & Sales Management* 29 no. 4 (2000): 227–241.

53. Earl Naumann, "A Conceptual Model of Expatriate Turnover," *Journal of International Business Studies* 23 no. 3 (1992): 499–531.

54. Victor H. Vroom, *Work and Motivation* (New York: Wiley, 1964); Lyman Porter and Edward E. Lawler, *Managerial Attitudes and Performance* (Homewood, IL: Irwin, 1968).

55. Clow and Baack, *Marketing Management.*

56. Dominique Rouzies and Anne Macquin, "An Exploratory Investigation of the Impact of Culture on Sales Force Management Control Systems in Europe," *Journal of Personal Selling and Sales Management* 23 no. 1 (2003): 61–72.

57. Robert House, "A Path-Goal Theory of Leadership Effectiveness," *Administrative Science Quarterly* 16 (1971): 321–329.

58. Erin Anderson and Richard L. Oliver, "Perspectives on Behavior-Based Versus Outcome-Based Sales Force Control Systems" *Journal of Marketing* 51 (October 1987): 76–88.

59. Clow and Baack, *Marketing Management.*

60. Rouzies and Macquin, "An Exploratory Investigation of the Impact of Culture."

61. Ajay K. Kohli, Tasadduq A. Shervani, and Goutam C. Challagalla, "Learning and Performance Orientation of Salespeople: The Role of Supervisors," *Journal of Marketing Research* 35 no. 2 (1998): 263–274.

62. Michael Harvey, "Empirical Evidence of Recurring International Compensation Problems, *Journal of International Business Studies* (4th qtr., 1993): 785–799.

63. C. W. Von Bergen, B. Soper, and P. W. Pool, "Competition and Goal-Based Reward Systems," *Journal of Selling and Major Account Management* 4 no. 2 (2002): 33–43.

64. Ernest F. Cooke, "Control and Motivation in Sales Management Through the Compensation Plan," *Journal of Marketing Theory and Practice* 7 no. 1 (1999): 80–83.

65. Gary Oddou, Joyce S. Osland, and Roger N. Blakeney, "Repatriating Knowledge: Variables Influencing the 'Transfer' Process," *Journal of International Business Studies* 40 (2009): 181–199.

66. "India's Cosmetics Market Set to Grow," *The Times of India* (Online), January 6, 2008, accessed at http://articles.timesofindia.indiatimes.com/2008–01–06/india-business/27764868_1_cosmetics-brands-capita-consumption-industry-body; Oriflame, accessed at www.oriflame.com; "Oriflame Turns to Online Sales in India to Cut Costs," *Business Standard* (Online) (2010), accessed at www.business-standard.com/india/news/oriflame-turns-to-online-sales-in-india-to-cut-costs/92340/on; "Oriflame India to Launch 350 Products this Year" (February 10, 2011), accessed at http://indiareport.com/India-usa-uk-news/latest-news/994452/NCR/4/26/4. http://www.business-standard.com/india/news/oriflame-turns-to-online-sales-in-india-to-cut-costs/92340/on.

CHAPTER 16

1. Kathryn Graven, "Just Like in the Computer Games It Sells, Nintendo Defies Persistent Challengers," *Wall Street Journal* (Eastern edition), June 27, 1989.

2. Yukari Iwatani Kane and Nick Wingfield, "Outside the Box: Amid Videogame Speed Race, Nintendo Slows Things Down; Simpler Console Invites Adults to Get Off Couch and Play While Rivals Go for Power; Bowling by Remote Control," *Wall Street Journal* (Eastern edition), November 2, 2006.

3. Chris Nuttall, "Nintendo Plans a Revolution," *Financial Times* (London), May 18, 2005.

4. Kane and Wingfield, "Outside the Box."

5. Ibid.

6. Ibid.

7. Ibid.

8. "Nintendo Gambles on Converting the Entire Family," *Financial Times Asia Edition* (London), December 8, 2006.

9. Chris Nuttall, "Nintendo to Aim Low-Cost Console at Non-Gamers," *Financial Times* (London), September 15, 2006.

10. Kane and Wingfield, "Outside the Box."

11. "Nintendo Gambles on Converting the Entire Family."

12. Robin Harding, "Nintendo Resilient in Face of Downturn," *Financial Times* (London), October 31, 2008.

13. Robin Harding, "Nintendo Looks to Change Its Game Plan," *Financial Times* (London), April 14, 2009.

14. Pascal-Emmanuel Gobry and Nicholas Carlson, "Is Zynga the Most Profitable Company Ever?," *Business Insider* (February 23, 2011), accessed at www.businessinsider.com/how-stupid-facebook-games-made-zynga-the-most-profitable-company-ever-2011-2.

15. Kane and Wingfield, "Outside the Box."

16. Juro Osawa and Daisuke Wakabayashi, "Digital Media: New Wii Is Investor Fizzle—Despite Videogame Industry Buzz, Questions Linger Over Nintendo's Strategy," *Wall Street Journal* (Eastern edition), June 10, 2011.

17. Clow and Baack, *Marketing Management*.

18. "HSBC France Unveils Strategic Plan," *The Pak Banker* (Lahore), July 8, 2011.

19. "Google Stands Up to China's Censors; Search Engine Bravely Fulfils Its Mission Statement," *Financial Times* (London), January 14, 2010.

20. "The Volkswagon Group in Summary," Volkswagon Group, accessed at www.volkswagen.com/vwcms/master_public/virtualmaster/en2/unternehmen/konzern.html.

21. Christopher Lawton and Chun Han Wong, "Nokia Shows Off New Phones; Cellphone Maker Unveils Devices as It Prepares for Microsoft Software Transition," *Wall Street Journal* (Online), June 22, 2011.

22. "Nissan Sees Less Impact From Disaster Than Toyota, Honda," *Asia Pulse* (Rhodes), June 24, 2011.

23. "Pharmacopeia Advances Strategic Plan to Focus Resources on Development and Later-Stage Discovery Programs," PR *Newswire* (New York), May 30, 2008.

24. "Tata Exporting Nano," *Wall Street Journal* (Online), May 9, 2011.

25. "Kia Expects to Increase Market Share," *Wall Street Journal* (Online), May 6, 2011.

26. "Home Page," Kia, accessed at www.kmcir.com/.

27. Yadong Luo, Oded Shenkar, Haresh Gurnani, "Control-Cooperation Interfaces in Global Strategic Alliances: A Situational Typology and Strategic Responses," *Journal of International Business Studies* (Washington), 39 no. 3 (2008): 428–454.

28. Janet Y. Murray, "Strategic Alliance-Based Global Sourcing Strategy for Competitive Advantage: A Conceptual Framework and Research Propositions," *Journal of International Marketing* (Chicago) 9 no. 4 (2001): 30–59.

29. Pierre Dussauge and Bernard Garrette, "Determinants of Success in International Strategic Alliances: Evidence From the Global Aerospace Industry," *Journal of International Business Studies* (Washington) 26 no. 3 (1995): 505–531.

30. "About Us," Sage, accessed at http://sage.com/ourbusiness.

31. "Organization Structure," Honda, accessed at http://world.honda.com/profile/organization/.

32. "A Rich History of Product Innovation," Maruchan, accessed at www.maruchan.com/about_maruchan.html.

33. Ibid.

34. Birger Wernerfelt, "A Resource-Based View of the Firm," Strategic Management Journal (September–October, 1984): 171–180, accessed at http://onlinelibrary.wiley.com/doi/10.1002/smj.4250050207/abstract.

35. "LG's Woes; Smartphones in South Korea," *The Economist* (London), 396 no. 8701 (2010): 76.

36. "Talk Is Cheap; Counterfeit Handsets Proliferate in China," *The Economist* (London) 393 no. 8658 (2009): 68.

37. "Conference on Mobile Revolution in South Asia," *The Business Times* (Singapore), February 17, 2011.

38. "Canada Trailing Developing World in 'Mobile Revolution,'" *Dawson Creek Daily News* (British Columbia), October 13, 2010.

39. Lynn Downey, "A Short History of Denim," Levi Strauss & Co., accessed at www .levistrauss.com/sites/default/files/librarydocument/2010/4/History-Denim .pdf.

40. "Global Workplaces," Levi Strauss & Co. accessed at www.levistrauss.com/about/ global-workplaces.

41. David A. Ralston, David H. Holt, Robert H. Terpstra, and Yu Kai-Cheng, "The Impact of National Culture and Economic Ideology on Managerial Work Values: A Study of the United States, Russia, Japan, and China," *Journal of International Business Studies* (Washington) 39 no. 1 (2008): 8–27.

42. Mortimer Zuckerman, "The Great Recession Continues," *Wall Street Journal* (Eastern edition), January 22, 2010; David Wessel, "Did 'Great Recession' Live Up to the Name?," *Wall Street Journal* (Online), April 7, 2010.

43. Peter Garnham, "Sovereign Debt Fears Hit euro," *Financial Times* (London), February 11, 2011.

44. "Euroland Moves From Tragedy to Farce," *Wall Street Journal* (Online), December 28, 2010.

45. Alex Barker, Chris Bryant, Ben Hall, "Sarkozy Claims Credit for Regulation Plans," *Financial Times* (London), April 3, 2009.

46. Gian-Maria Milesi-Ferretti, and Cédric Tille, "The Great Retrenchment: International Capital Flows During the Global Financial Crisis," *Economic Policy* (Cambridge) 26 no. 66 (2011): 285–342.

47. John Hughman, "Retail Retrenchment Continues," *Investors Chronicle* (London), June 29, 2011.

48. "Finance Heads Believe Marketing Investment Is Needed in Recession," *Marketing Week* (London), March 19, 2009.

49. John A Quelch and Katherine E Jocz, "How to Market in a Downturn," *Harvard Business Review* (Boston) 87 no. 4 (2009); Raji Srinivasan, Gary L. Lilien, and Shrihari Sridhar, "Should Firms Spend More on Research and Development and Advertising During Recessions?," *Journal of Marketing* (Chicago) 75 no. 3 (2011): 49–65.

50. "Kicking GM's New-Stock Tires," *Wall Street Journal* (Online), November 12, 2010.

51. Ralph Atkins, "Global Strengths and Weaknesses Are Exposed," *Financial Times* (London), October 6, 2009.

52. "Euroland Moves From Tragedy to Farce," *Wall Street Journal* (Online), December 28, 2010.

53. Clyde Prestowitz, "Why Isn't the iPhone Made in America?," *Foreign Policy* (March 8, 2011), accessed at http://prestowitz.foreignpolicy.com/posts/2011/03/08/ why_isnt_the_iphone_made_in_america.

54. Betinna Wassener, "New Terms for Emerging Economies is Suggested," *The New York Times Online* (November 15, 2010), accessed at www.nytimes .com/2010/11/16/business/global/16eagles.html.

55. Udayan Gupta, "MIST: The Next Tier of Large Emerging Economies," Institutional Investor (February 7, 2011), accessed at www.institutionalinvestor.com/ banking_and_capital_markets/Articles/2762464/MIST-The-Next-Tier-of-Large-Emerging-Economies.html.

56. Atkins, "Global Strengths and Weaknesses Are Exposed."

57. Will Connors, "Africa Rising; In Nigeria, Used Cars Are a Road to Status; Growing Middle Class Makes Bumpy Transition From Perilous Buses; Taking 'Baby Boy' Home," *Wall Street Journal* (Online), January 18, 2011.

58. "Africa Rising; Catering to New Tastes as Incomes Climb; Zambian Beef Processor Expands to Nigeria With Aim of Spreading Out Across the Continent," *Wall Street Journal* (Online), February 10, 2011.

59. Wessel, "Did 'Great Recession' Live Up to the Name?"

60. "Virgin Group, Ltd.," Google Finance, accessed at www.google.com/ finance?cid=6444452.

61. "First Commercial Spaceliner Makes History and Launches New National Geographic Channel Series Virgin Galactic," *PR Newswire* (New York), October 10, 2010; "Virgin Galactic & Virtuoso(R) Travel Network Soar Into the Future With Space Tourism; Virtuoso Accredited Space Agents Surpass $10 Million in Space Sales," *PR Newswire* (New York), March 11, 2011.

62. P. K. Jayadevan and Harsimran Julka, "Virgin Galactic Is Offering Low-Cost Space Flights," *The Economic Times* (New Delhi), February 12, 2011.

63. "From Cyberspace to Outer Space: introNetworks Creates First Social Network to Connect Growing Base of Future Astronauts for Virgin Galactic; Company Also Announces Customer Roster Additions," *PR Newswire* (New York), June 24, 2008.

64. "Virgin Galactic & Virtuoso(R) Travel Network Soar Into the Future With Space Tourism."

Appendix C
Glossary

absolute advantage theory: a theory that states that a country has the ability to produce a greater amount of a good or service using the same amount of resources used by another country

adaptation: changing a component of the marketing mix to better meet the needs of a local market

advertising management: the process of developing and overseeing a company's advertising program

aesthetics: concepts about what constitutes beauty

affective message strategies: advertising messages that invoke feelings or emotions and match those feelings with a product, service, or company

agent middlemen: marketing channel members that do not take title or ownership of the products that they market

animosity: anger toward a country that is rooted in political, economic, or military conflict between countries

announcements: advertising presentations of facts without the use of people

arbitration: a formal conflict resolution process in which both parties agree to abide by the decision of a third-party arbitrator

association transfers: an advertising format in which a product is combined with another object, person, situation, or environment

back translation: a process in which a survey is translated from an original language into a targeted language and then back into the original language in order to check for accuracy and meaning

BATNA: best alternative to a negotiated agreement

bill of exchange: an agreement between parties in which one party, a drawer, directs a second party, the drawee, to issue a payment to another party, the payee

born-global firms: businesses that operate in two or more different countries from inception

bottom-of-the-pyramid: the approximately 4 billion people globally living on less than $2 per day

brand: a name, sign, symbol, or design, or some combination of these that identifies the products of a firm and distinguishes them from competition

brand awareness: the strength of a brand's presence in the consumer's mind

brand equity: the unique outcomes a product enjoys due solely to its brand name

brand extension: a strategy utilized when a brand name is extended from one product to another

brand image: consumer perceptions of a brand

brand loyalty: a consumer's commitment to a product based on positive attitudes that leads to consistent purchase of the brand

brand parity: when brands within one product category are viewed as similar or undifferentiated

brand valuation: the process of estimating the financial value of a brand

break-even analysis: a common method employed to discover the relationships between costs and price

capacity to consume: the power to use goods and services in the satisfaction of human wants

capital market: any location, online or physical, where businesses or individuals can raise funds

capitalist economic system: a marketplace in which transactions take place with limited government regulation or interference

civil law: a legal system in which law is based on written words or a legal code

clutter: the abundance of marketing messages that consumers routinely encounter

cobranding: placing two or more brand names on the same product

cognitive message strategies: advertising messages that present rational arguments or pieces of information to consumers

collusion: a pricing system in oligopolistic markets in which a set of major competitors sets prices at uniform levels either, overtly or covertly

command economy: an economy in which a central authority, normally the government, makes all key economic decisions

common law: a legal system where legal precedent and usage traditions are the basis of law

common market: a group of countries that have entered into an agreement to remove barriers to the movement of goods and services, to have a common tariff for nonmembers, and to allow the free movement of capital and labor within the market

communication: the process of sending, receiving, and interpreting information

communism: an extreme form of socialism where private ownership of property is outlawed

comparative advantage theory: a theory that states that a country has an ability to produce a good or service at lower levels of opportunity cost than that in other countries

comparative advertising: product comparisons where two items are shown in use side by side

conative message strategies: advertising messages designed to lead directly to a consumer response, such as a store visit or purchase

conciliation: the various forms of mediation or conflict resolution that companies can pursue before beginning the more formal arbitration process

consumer promotions: sales promotions directed at retail customers

contingency approach: marketers doing what is appropriate for individual markets, which typically leads to a combination of both standardized and adapted components

control: the process of comparing performance to standards, making corrections when needed, and rewarding success

core competence: the most proficiently performed internal activity that is central to the firm's strategy and competitiveness

cosmopolitanism: the view that a person is a member of a larger global community rather than merely maintaining an allegiance to a local culture and close-by circumstances

cost-based pricing: pricing based on a careful assessment of all costs associated with producing and selling an item

cost-plus pricing: setting a product's price based on fixed costs, variable costs, plus the desired profit margin for each item

countercultures: groups whose values set their members in opposition to the dominant culture

countertrade: when goods are traded or exchanged without the use of hard currency

country image: the attitudes and knowledge consumers have about a country

country-of-origin effect: the response a consumer has to a product due to the country that is the source, in the consumer's mind, for the product

cross-cultural competence: a salesperson's effectiveness in utilizing knowledge, skills, and personal attributes in order to work successfully with buyers from other cultures

cross-selling: selling additional items from the same company as part of a transaction

cultural convergence: the increasing similarities between global consumers

cultural crossvergence: the emergence of a new, global value system as countries become more interconnected

cultural divergence: persistence of specific values due to sociocultural influences

cultural intelligence: the ability to detect differences between cultures, and to understand how individual behavior is influenced by, and distinguished from, a national culture

culture shock: a disorientation that results from a person losing familiar cultural props while living abroad

culture: the beliefs, customs, and attitudes of a distinct group of people

currency: the form of money used by a specific country or region

customs union: a group of countries that have entered into an agreement to remove barriers to the movement of goods and services and to have a uniform tariff policy toward nonmember countries

damage control: reacting to negative events caused by a company's mistake, consumer grievances, or unjustified or false claims made by the press or others seeking to injure a company

deceptive pricing: a pricing system in which the marketer promotes one price, yet charges more using hidden charges, add-ons, or higher prices for products with more than the minimum of features

demand: the amount of a good or service that consumers will buy at various price levels

differentiation: emphasis of a unique benefit or component of a product that separates that product from competitors

diffusion: the process by which an innovation slowly spreads through a culture or group

direct exporting: also called *export marketing*, a system in which the producer or supplier is responsible for marketing to foreign buyers

distinctive competence: a production activity a company performs at a level that is better than all competitive rivals

distribution intensity: the extent to which products are distributed throughout a country and the number of intermediaries that are utilized to carry the product

dual channel marketing: selling virtually the same goods or services to both consumers and businesses

dumping: the practice of selling goods below costs in another country in order to capture a market

economic system: the means by which countries allocate resources, goods, and services to citizens

economic union: a group of countries seeking to harmonize economic policies among members, and attempting to follow the same economic policy

economies of scale: the reduction in per unit costs as the total volume produced increases

economies of scope: efficiencies that emerge from producing a variety of similar products

emerging markets: economies in countries that have moved through the transformation from developing to developed

entertainment: when theatrical drama, musicals, shows, comedies, slapstick, humor, horror, or satire provide the primary advertising format

ethnocentrism: the strongly held belief that one's culture is superior to others

event marketing: using marketing techniques to connect with buyers through specific live events including concerts, performances, or festivals to promote a product or brand

exchange rate: the rate at which one country's currency can be traded for another country's currency

exchange systems: the methods of facilitating payment for a product or service

exclusive distribution: an international marketing strategy that focuses on offering products at only one wholesaler or retailer in a particular market area

executional framework: the manner in which an advertising appeal and message strategy is delivered

expatriate: an employee who works in a country that is not his or her home country

experiments: research techniques that allow researchers to uncover cause-and-effect relationships by manipulating certain variables and controlling others

exporting: a mode of entry in which the product is shipped in one manner or another into a foreign market

external validity: when cause-and-effect relationships are expected to be found in other situations or settings

family branding: a strategy wherein a number of products in a line or mix share the same brand name worldwide

flexible or floating exchange rate: the rate when the value of the currency is allowed to respond freely to market forces

focus groups: semi-structured or unstructured group discussions that generally take place in groups of eight to twelve

formal communication: information that travels through channels that are designated or chosen by organizational leaders

forward rates: the exchange rates for the delivery of the currency at a specific time in the future

franchising: the contractual agreement to implement a business model

free trade: an economic situation in which goods travel across boundaries with little interference by individual governments

free trade area: a group of countries that have entered into an agreement to reduce tariffs, quotas, and other barriers to the movement of goods and services

free trade zones: specially designated areas within a country that have separate laws designed to encourage trade

futures contracts: contracts that allow the company to sell or buy a certain amount of a foreign currency at a set exchange rate on a specific date

global brand: identifies a company that uses the same brand name, image, and brand mark globally

globalization: the increased interconnectedness of consumers and businesses globally

globally integrated marketing communications program: a program that consists of a carefully designed combination of all communications with the company's internal and external publics

good: a physical product sold to and used by an individual, household, or business

gray market: the practice of distributing products through distribution channels that are not authorized by the marketer of the product

greenwashing: a practice in which a company exaggerates or even fabricates the degree of its sustainable or green activities

hard currency: currency that can be exchanged for other currencies at worldwide

hedging: any financial process that lessens financial risk

high-context cultures: cultures that rely more on symbols and language with less explicit or spelled-out codes

home country: the nation in which the business is located or the one that houses the company's main headquarters

home-country national salesperson: a native from the home country of the company that is assigned to a foreign market

horizontal channel conflict: conflict that occurs between members of a marketing channel at the same level

horizontal integration: a marketing strategy in which a company acquires or merges with another company

host country: the nation being targeted for expansion by a company

host-country national salesperson: an international salesperson who is from the country in which he or she sells

imagination: an advertising format that utilizes cartoon or other visual techniques to make unrealistic presentations of a make-believe world

importing: the transfer or shipping of goods into a country

indirect exporting: also called *export selling,* a system in which the manufacturer sells the product to intermediaries who then handle the foreign selling of the product

individual branding: a strategy in which distinct brand names are used for products

inflation: a situation in which the price of goods and services increase in a country or region

informal communication: communication in the form of rumors or gossip

infrastructure: the organizational and physical structures present in a country, such as roads, technology, and information systems.

intangible product benefits: the value drawn from the social, emotional, and nonphysical aspects of consumption

integration: the process of using agreements between countries to lower limits on the movements of products, capital, or labor

intellectual property piracy: the unauthorized use or reproduction of intellectual property that has been legally protected

intellectual property: creations of the mind or the intangible property that results from thought

intensive distribution: an international marketing strategy in which a product is distributed through several wholesalers or retailers in a particular market

interest rates: the percentage rate charged or paid for the use of money

intermediaries: organizations that move products from producers to consumers and end users

internal validity: when accurate cause-and-effect relationships are identified in a research finding

international distribution: the process by which products and services flow between producers, intermediaries, and consumers, including the transfer of ownership

international finance: the study of currency exchange, investments, and how these processes influence business activities

international logistics: the management of the flow of products and services among marketing channel members

international marketing channel: a marketing system that promotes the physical flow and ownership of products and services from producer to consumer, including producers, wholesalers, and retailers

international marketing: using the marketing mix to meet the needs and wants of consumers in foreign markets

international retailing: the retail activities that occur across and inside national boundaries

international strategic planning: the plan for the overall direction of the firm

Internet interventions: identifying false statements about a company and then responding to the allegations in the same communication channel

joint venture: a legal partnership that involves an investment, a division of ownership, and the creation of a new legal entity, or when two companies combine to create a product

jurisdiction: the power to apply law

language: the system used to communicate between peoples, including verbal and nonverbal cues

legal systems: the methods for applying and implementing the laws of a country

lesson: a form of advertising presentation that applies facts and arguments to the audience

letter of credit: a document issued by a bank to signal the creditworthiness of a buyer to a seller

licensing: a contract that grants a company the legal right to use another company's brand, image, and other marketing components

litigation: a legal proceeding through a judicial system

logistics: the activities that manage the physical movement and storage of goods from the producer to the consumer

loss leader: pricing certain items at or below cost in order to build store traffic

low-context cultures: cultures that demonstrate high values toward and positive attitudes regarding words

market: people with wants and needs, money to spend, and the willingness to spend money on those wants and needs

market concentration: the strategy a company uses when it exports a small number of markets or just one key market and then slowly expands to export to new countries

market development: a strategy that focuses on increasing sales of existing products to new customers

market economy: an economy in which most economic decisions are made in the marketplace

market research: the systematic gathering, storing, and analyzing of marketplace information for use in managerial decision-making

market segment: a set of businesses or a group of individual consumers with distinct characteristics

market segmentation: a process that involves identifying specific groups based on their needs, attitudes, and interests; the grouping of consumers based on their needs, attitudes, and interests

market spreading: a marketing strategy of growing exports in many different markets simultaneously and rapidly expanding to new markets

marketing: discovering consumer needs and wants, creating the products that meet those needs, and then pricing, promoting, and delivering those products and services

marketing channel power: the ability of one channel member to control or influence the marketing decisions of another channel member

marketing mix: the major activities used to develop and sell goods and services, including products, prices, distribution systems, and promotional programs

markup pricing: a pricing method that simply adds a standard markup to the costs assigned to a product

merchant middlemen: marketing channel members that take title and ownership of the products being marketed

message strategy: the primary tactic or approach used to deliver the key idea to be delivered in an advertisement

metrics: performance measures that serve as standards set during the planning process and that are used in the control process

mission statement: a document that delineates why an organization exists and guides the overall direction of the firm

mixed economy: an economic system in which part is guided by the marketplace and part is run by the government

multinational corporations: organizations conducting business activities in at least one other country that differs from the home country in which the organization is headquartered

national competitive advantage: a circumstance in which a country has built a reputation with regard to an aspect of producing a product, such as technological superiority or lower labor costs

nationalism: the strong pride and devotion consumers have in their country or nation

needs: the necessities of life that all humans require for their survival and well-being

newly industrialized countries: nations that have experienced rapid economic expansion and industrialization that are neither less- nor most-developed countries

nonprobability sample: a sample in which the probability of an element of the population being included in a sample is unknown

offshoring: the movement of a business activity to another country

operational plans: plans that dictate the day-to-day entry level activities that are crucial parts of successful international marketing programs

order getting: the activities involved with actively persuading customers, or sales leads, to purchase products from a company

organizing: the process through which management designs the structure of the organization, assigns responsibilities, and ensures effective communication flows throughout the company

outsourcing: relinquishing organizational control of a business process and instead hiring a third party external to the company to operate the process

parallel translation: a process in which two translators are used for the back translation process with the results being discussed and one translation selected

pegged or fixed regime: the value of a currency when it is set to a predetermined band or par value

penetration pricing: setting the product's initial price as low as a company can afford, to discourage entry by competition

personal interviews: one-on-one discussions between a researcher and a respondent

pioneering advantage: the advantage that results from being the first mover in a market

planning: the process whereby managers develop goals, strategies, and activities that will best position the firm for success in the international marketplace

point-of-purchase materials: displays and materials that take a variety of forms, with the goal of encouraging the immediate sale of a product by the end user

political risk: the chance that political forces, such as government activities, will hamper and harm business activities within a country

political systems: the people with an organization, typically governments, who possess the power and how that power is structured

political union: the complete integration of political and economic policy by a group of countries

positioning maps: tools used to study a company and its competitors in terms of consumer attitudes or perceptions

positioning statement: a one- or two-sentence summary of the company's positioning strategy

positioning: creating a perception in a consumer's mind regarding the nature of a company and its products relative to competitors

predatory pricing: the direct attempt by a major competitor to drive other companies out of business by setting prices unrealistically low

price: the amount a person, company, or government charges for a good or service

price elasticity of demand: a measure of the impact of price differences on demand and sales

price perceptual map: a map that depicts various companies or products along two dimensions, typically price and quality

primary data: data that are gathered by the researcher or research team for a specific project

probability sample: a sample in which each element in the population has a known, nonzero probability of being selected for a study

product: bundle of attributes, including tangible, intangible, and symbolic elements that provide value for exchange partners

product line: groups of similar products within a particular category

product line extension: a strategy that is utilized when new products are introduced that are in the related product category and that respond to specific opportunities in the marketplace

product mix: the total number of products that a firm carries

product position: what summarizes consumer opinions regarding the specific features of the product

product positioning: creating a perception in the consumer's mind regarding the nature of a company and its products relative to competitors

profit-based pricing: examining pricing from the perspective of what consumers are willing to pay rather than from the cost of the item

promotions mix: a company's combination of advertising, personal selling, sales promotion, and public relations efforts

protectionism: the desire to protect domestic businesses from the exports of foreign firms through governmental policy

public relations: the management of communication with all organizational stakeholders

qualitative research design: a research method that focuses on obtaining information without a reliance on numerical expression or measurement

quantitative research design: a research design that relies on numerical measurement and analysis

reliability: the internal consistency of a measure and its ability to be replicated over time

religiosity: the degree to which consumers within a country or region are religious

repatriation: the process of adjustment that a salesperson goes through upon returning to his or her home country

repositioning: the process of changing consumer perceptions of a brand relative to competitors on key attributes

sales promotions: marketing activities that are designed to stimulate consumer and marketing channel demand for a product or service

sampling: a process wherein only certain members of a population are included in a research study

scientific method: the use of observations, empirical evidence, and knowledge in order to make objective statements about certain phenomena

secondary data: data that have already been collected by an agency and are made available either free of charge or for a fee

selective distribution: an international marketing strategy of using only a limited number of channel intermediaries to sell products

self-reference criterion: when someone applies his or her own cultural values and background to the assessment of behaviors of others

service: an intangible product that generally centers on an act or performance that delivers value to individuals, households, and businesses

skimming: setting a product's initial price as high as the market will bear to allow the manufacturer or exporter to attain as much revenue as possible in a short period of time

socialism: an economic system in which the state owns at least some parts of industry

soft currency: currency that cannot be traded at major financial centers

sovereignty: governmental authority or control within its state

sovereignty debt ratings: a rating that represents the chance that a country will default on governmental debt

special effects: an advertising format used to deliver a wide variety of commercials by combining animation, cartoon, camera effects (camera motion), recording techniques, music, and other sounds

spin-off sales: sales that occur when individuals who buy a particular brand at work have positive experiences and, as a result, purchase the same brand for personal use

sponsorship: an agreement between a marketing organization and an individual, team, or a landmark

standardization: using the same marketing mix in all markets

STP approach: segmentation, targeting, and product positioning processes

strategic alliance: a formal agreement between companies to work together to achieve a common goal

strategic controls: performance measures that apply to the CEO and top-level management team that direct the portfolios of businesses or activities held by a single company or corporation

strategic planning: plans for the overall direction of the firm, the development of goals, and the allocation of resources in the pursuit of those goals, as prepared by top management

structured interview: interview situation in which all applicants are asked the same list of questions

subcultures: groups whose values and related behaviors are distinct and set members off from the general or dominant culture

surveys: research instruments that can be administered to large numbers of consumers with relative ease

sustainability: meeting the needs of the current generation in a way that leaves future generations with the ability to also meet their needs

tactical planning: plans for specific activities and programs that support the overall direction set at the strategic level

tangible product benefits: the value drawn from the physical components of a product

target market: a specific, identifiable market segment that a company seeks to reach

target ROI pricing: a cost-based pricing technique that specifies a desired return on investment (ROI) for a particular product

terms of payment: the agreed-upon payment in return for the goods or services

test market: a type of experiment that is constructed within realistic marketplace conditions

theocratic law: a legal system based on religious writings

third-country salesperson: an international expatriate salesperson who sells in a country other than his or her home or the home base of the company

trade allowance: a price reduction or other consideration paid by a company to intermediaries as an incentive to purchase or promote a specific product

trade deficit: the balance of trade that occurs when a country imports more than it exports

trade promotions: sales promotions targeted at intermediaries, most notably wholesalers and retail outlets

trade surplus: the balance of trade that occurs when a country exports more than it imports

transition economies: rapidly developing economies that occur in what were formally communist countries with centrally planned economies

unstructured interview: an interview in which the interviewer and interviewee talk freely without answering a predetermined list of questions

validity: the degree to which a concept is accurately measured by survey or research items

values: strongly held concepts that are pervasive within a culture

vertical channel conflict: conflict that occurs when there are disputes between channel members at different levels in the system

vertical integration: a marketing strategy in which one member of the market channel merges with or acquires another intermediary

vertical marketing system: a distribution arrangement in which the producer, wholesaler, and retailer performs marketing activities as a unified system

virtual selling: sales efforts that take place mediated by Internet technologies

wants: the specific expression of needs through the desire for specific objects

wholly owned subsidiary: a company enters a country by establishing a 100% ownership stake in a business in that country

Credits

Photo 12.3, page 420. Photo courtesy of Chih-Kuo, Kuo clearspace.tw.

Photo 12.4, page 423. Photo courtesy of Chih-Kuo, Kuo clearspace.tw.

Map 12.1, page 424. U.S. International Trade Commission. *Global Beef Trade: Effects of Animal Health, Sanitary, Food Safety and Other Measures on U.S. Beef Exports,*" pg. 34. Investigation No. 332–488, USITC Publication 4033, September 2008. http://www.usitc.gov/publications/332/pub4033.pdf

Map 12.2, page 425. Don P. Blayney, Mark J. Gehlar, U.S. Dairy at a New Crossroads in a Global Setting, Economic Research Service, USDA, November 2005.

Photo 12.5, page 426. Kenneth Sponsler/iStockphoto.

Photo 12.6, page 428. Photo courtesy of Chih-Kuo, Kuo clearspace.tw.

Photo 12.7, page 430. Peter Barritt/Alamy.

Photo 12.8, page 436. http://www.tesco.com/

Part 6 Opening Photo, page 438. Goodshoot/ Goodshoot/ Thinkstock.

CHAPTER 13

Photo 13.1, page 442. Photo courtesy of Chih-Kuo, Kuo clearspace.tw.

Photo 13.2, page 446. Photo courtesy of Chih-Kuo, Kuo clearspace.tw.

Photo 13.3, page 448. Photo courtesy of Chih-Kuo, Kuo clearspace.tw.

Photo 13.4, page 450. Center for Disease Control.

Photo 13.5, page 454. http://www.eurorscg.com/flash/index.html#/Our-Work/Our-Client%20Partners?id=3.1

Photo 13.6, page 455. Photo courtesy of Chih-Kuo, Kuo clearspace.tw.

Photo 13.7, page 460. *People Magazine*, 2008.

Photo 13.8, page 464. www.gm.com

Photo 13.9, page 467. Photo courtesy of Chih-Kuo, Kuo clearspace.tw.

Photo 13.10, page 470. http://millerlite.com/

Photo 13.11, page 471. Photo courtesy of Chih-Kuo, Kuo clearspace.tw.

Photo 13.12, page 479. http://mea.nokia.com/arabic

CHAPTER 14

Chapter Opening Photo, page 480. Jupiterimages/Photos.com/Thinkstock.

Photo 14.1, page 482. http://www.wonderdrug.com/

Photo 14.2, page 485. ton koene/Alamy.

Photo 14.3, page 489. Fabrice Bettex/Alamy.

Photo 14.4, page 495. Photo courtesy of Chih-Kuo, Kuo clearspace.tw.

Photo 14.5, page 496. Photo courtesy of Chih-Kuo, Kuo clearspace.tw.

Photo 14.6, page 499. Tom LeGoff/Photodisc/Thinkstock.

Photo 14.7, page 504. imagebroker/Alamy.

Photo 14.8, page 510. Larry Herfindal/iStockPhoto.

CHAPTER 15

Chapter Opening Photo, page 512. Brittak/iStockPhoto.

Photo 15.1, page 514. Photo courtesy of Chih-Kuo, Kuo clear space.tw.

Photo 15.2, page 517. Catherine Yeulet/iStockphoto.

Photo 15.3, page 521. Ryan McVay/Thinkstock.

Photo 15.4, page 524. Photo courtesy of Chih-Kuo, Kuo clearspace.tw.

Photo 15.5, page 532. Marcela Barsse/iStockphoto.

Photo 15.6, page 536. Gerenme/iStockphoto.

Photo 15.7, page 541. Pat Behnke/Alamy.

Photo 15.8, page 547. http://www.oriflame.com/

CHAPTER 16

Chapter Opening Photo, page 548. Kirza/iStockPhoto.

Photo 16.1, page 550. http://www.nintendo.com/3ds

Photo 16.2, page 554. John Henshall/Alamy.

Photo 16.3, page 564. John Henshall/Alamy.

Photo 16.4, page 569. Comstock/Thinkstock.

Photo 16.5, page 575. Photo courtesy of Chih-Kuo, Kuo clearspace.tw.

Photo 16.6, page 577. http://www.virgingalactic.com/

Name Index

Subject Index

Country Index

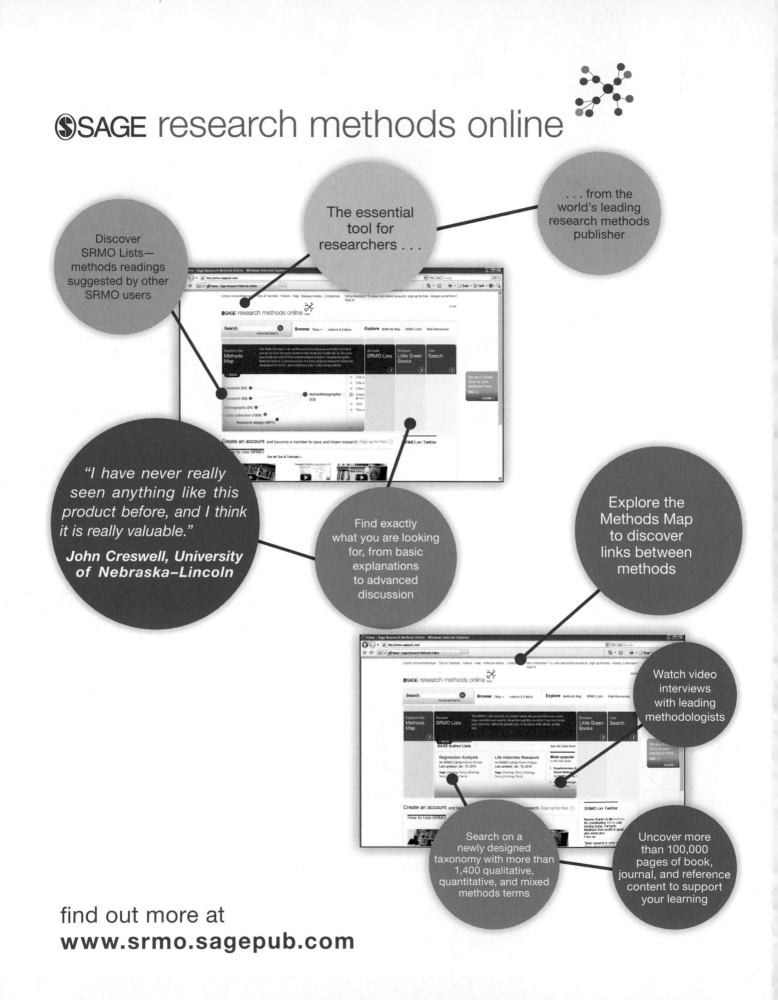

SAGE research methods online

The essential tool for researchers . . .

. . . from the world's leading research methods publisher

Discover SRMO Lists—methods readings suggested by other SRMO users

"I have never really seen anything like this product before, and I think it is really valuable."

John Creswell, University of Nebraska–Lincoln

Find exactly what you are looking for, from basic explanations to advanced discussion

Explore the Methods Map to discover links between methods

Watch video interviews with leading methodologists

Search on a newly designed taxonomy with more than 1,400 qualitative, quantitative, and mixed methods terms

Uncover more than 100,000 pages of book, journal, and reference content to support your learning

find out more at
www.srmo.sagepub.com